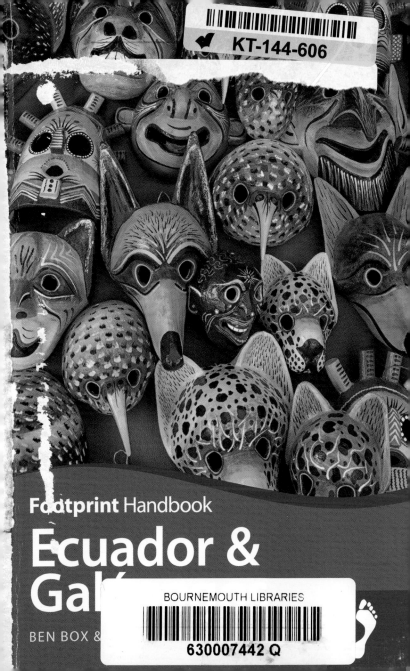

Footprint Handbook

Ecuador &
Galá

BEN BOX &

This is
Ecuador &
Galápagos

Footprint Handbook
Chile
CHRIS WALLACE

Footprint Handbook
Cuzco, Machu Picchu
& the Inca Heartland
ROBERT & DAISY KUNSTAETTER

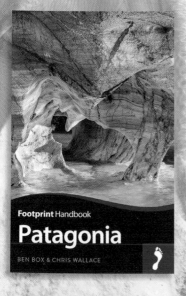

Footprint Handbook
Patagonia
BEN BOX & CHRIS WALLACE

Footprint Handbook
Western Brazil
IGUAÇU • AMAZON • PANTANAL
ALEX & GARDÉNIA ROBINSON

www.footprinttravelguides.com

Best of
Ecuador &
Galápagos

top things to do and see

❶ Colonial Quito and around

The capital's treasure trove of religious art and architecture is the heart of a vibrant city, offering many urban delights. It also provides access to outstanding natural areas nearby, such as Mindo and the cloudforests of Pichincha volcano, a nature lover's paradise. Pages 41, 84 and 87.

❷ Otavalo

Best known for the largest craft market in South America, this town is also home to a proud and prosperous indigenous people. They have made their name not only as successful weavers and traders, but also as symbols of cultural fortitude. Page 100.

❸ Parque Nacional Cotopaxi

Cotopaxi (5897 m) is one of the world's highest active volcanoes and it resumed activity in 2015. The surrounding national park is closed to visitors until volcanic activity subsides but the mountain's perfect snow-covered cone and impressive plume of ash can be admired from Quito and surrounding areas. Page 129.

Ecuador is compact by South American standards, compact enough for you to have breakfast as you watch dawn break over the Amazon jungle canopy, lunch at the foot of a smoking snow-capped volcano and dinner amid the last rays of sunset over the Pacific Ocean. Within this small area, it boasts extraordinary diversity: geographical diversity ranging from an avenue of volcanoes straddling the equator, to rainforest, beaches and tropical islands; biological diversity, among the highest in the world, protected by 50 national parks and reserves; and cultural diversity, with 17 ethnically distinct indigenous groups.

With so much variety, Ecuador has something for everyone. Birdwatching, trekking, mountaineering, mountain biking, whitewater rafting, paragliding and surfing are among the country's many privileged outdoor activities. Yet the draw is not only about hiking boots and adrenalin. Archaeology, art and local culture are also abundant and varied. The capital, Quito, and the southern highland city of Cuenca, have two of the finest colonial districts in South America, an excellent selection of museums and a lively tourist scene.

The smaller towns and villages of Ecuador offer the most authentic experience as well as the opportunity to share their traditions at fiestas and through community tourism. Indulge your senses at one of their many markets, with dizzying arrays of textiles, ceramics, carvings and other crafts, not to mention the plethora of domestic animals and cornucopia of fresh produce. They are all there for the local people but tourists are very welcome.

Either side of the country's Andean spine, the land falls away rapidly: east to Amazonian lowlands, with some fine lodges which are ideal bases for exploring, and west to the Pacific coast, with mangroves, dry forests, fishing communities and holiday spots large and small. Either is an enriching contrast to the mountains and a visit to one or both adds to an appreciation of the Ecuadorean spirit.

The Galápagos Islands, cradle and showcase of Darwin's theory of evolution, are the rich icing on the Ecuadorean cake. Fragile and expensive, the Galápagos are not for everyone, but if you are passionate about nature, they offer a once-in-a-lifetime experience worth saving for.

Ben Box and Sarah Cameron

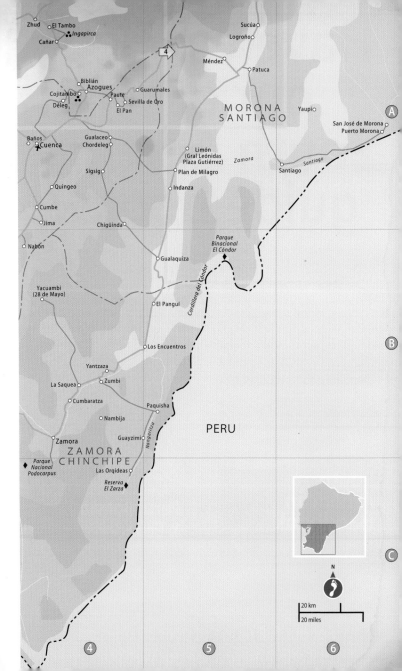

Have you seen our other South America guide books?

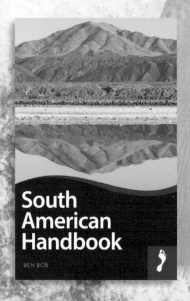

South American Handbook

BEN BOX

Footprint Handbook

Peru, Bolivia & Ecuador

ROBERT & DAISY KUNSTAETTER
AND BEN BOX

❺ Baños

A traditional Ecuadorean highland resort known for its thermal baths, Baños offers adventure and relaxation at the foot of active Volcán Tungurahua. It is a good base for trekking, horse riding, mountain biking, waterfall watching and watching the world go by. Page 148.

❻ Cuenca

A UNESCO World Heritage Site and the most congenial city in Ecuador, Cuenca's cobblestone streets, flowering plazas and pastel-coloured buildings make it a pleasure to explore. Its many charms have attracted the largest expat community in the country. Page 175.

❹ Quilotoa Circuit

This 200-km loop includes an emerald-green crater lake and many indigenous villages known for their authentic markets and distinctive crafts. Depending on your time and stamina, the circuit can be done by bus, bike, horse or on foot. Page 136.

❼ Vilcabamba

Once a fabled fountain of youth, this small town is the rainbow at the south end of Ecuador's gringo trail. It offers access to the hinterlands of Parque Nacional Podocarpus and everything from great horse riding to a colourful café scene. Page 197.

❽ Montañita

Famed for its surf scene, this seaside-village-turned-resort attracts many Ecuadoreans and foreigners. Easily reached from Guayaquil, it is packed with hotels, restaurants, surf shops, tattoo parlours and craft and jewellery vendors. There are also more tranquil beaches nearby. Page 233.

❾ Puerto López

A very popular base for whale watching from June to September, this seaside town provides year-round access to the gorgeous Los Frailes beach and Parque Nacional Machalilla, which protects tropical forests, a marine ecosystem and Isla de la Plata. Page 234.

⑩ Reserva Faunística Cuyabeno

This 603,000-ha wildlife reserve is filled with jungle rivers, lagoons and an extraordinary variety of Amazon wildlife. Paddle your canoe beneath the canopy to take in one of the finest protected natural areas in the country. Page 271.

⑪ Tena

Relaxed and friendly, Tena is Ecuador's most important centre for whitewater rafting. It offers ethno-tourism, with visits to indigenous communities, as well as jungle tours. It also makes a good stop when travelling overland between the highlands and Oriente jungle. Page 281.

⑫ Galápagos Islands

Here, in one of the world's foremost wildlife sanctuaries, you can snorkel with penguins and sea lions, watch 200-kg tortoises lumbering through giant cactus forest, and enjoy the courtship display of the blue-footed booby and frigate bird, all in startling close-up. Page 294.

COLOMBIA

Río Putumayo

SUCUMBÍOS

Reserva
Faunística
Cuyabeno

10

Río Aguarico

Parque
Nacional
Yasuní

Río Napo

Nuevo
Rocafuerte ○

PERU

Route
planner

Ecuador is small enough to make travelling around easy, and varied enough to make almost any itinerary worthwhile. The following are but a few suggestions and you are heartily encouraged to venture further afield.

One week

explore sights around Quito and the central highlands

Seven days is a bit rushed but feasible. You could fly to any one of the following regions – southern highlands, Pacific coast, Oriente jungle or Galápagos – and make visiting that one area your entire trip. Or stay close to Quito and visit places within easy reach of the capital. Acclimatize to the altitude while you get to know Colonial Quito, play tourist at Mitad del Mundo or visit a museum; then ride the TelefériQo high above the city. Head north to Otavalo, perhaps for the Saturday market. From Otavalo visit Lago San Pablo or Cuicocha crater lake, and one of the nearby craft towns. You could also visit Cotopaxi National Park, or the town of Mindo surrounded by cloudforest and birdwatching opportunities, followed by a visit to Papallacta thermal baths.

Below: TelefériQo cable car
Opposite page: King vulture

experience the highlands, jungle and coast

For most people, this is the ideal length of a visit to Ecuador. The following are all overland routes but you can take shortcuts by flying one way, such as travelling by bus as far as Cuenca and returning to Quito by plane. A two- to three-week trip often includes a visit to the Galápagos, or a three- to four-day stay in a jungle lodge, so any of the options below can be shortened accordingly.

Highlands and Oriente jungle Head south by road from Quito to Latacunga, then to Quilotoa's emerald-green crater lake. Spend a night in the traditional villages along the Quilotoa Circuit before continuing to Baños, where nearby 'Mama' Tungurahua, an active volcano, might welcome you with a bang. Trekking, biking and horse riding, thermal baths, cafés and nightlife are the main draws in Baños. Tear yourself away to continue along the spectacular Río Pastaza valley with its plethora of waterfalls, to Puyo, then north to Misahuallí or Tena. Although not primary, nearby rainforest is easy to visit.

Right: Waterfall, Baños
Below: Basílica del Voto Nacional, Quito
Opposite page: Humpback whale in Machalilla National Park

Tena also has whitewater rafting and kayaking, as does Quijos valley along the road back toward Quito. Don't miss Papallacta hot springs before returning to the capital.

Highlands and Pacific coast From Quito travel to Baños as above, then continue south to Riobamba. The city and its surroundings have the famous Devil's Nose train ride, as well as excellent climbing, trekking, mountain biking and highland indigenous culture. From Riobamba take a bus down to the city of Guayaquil. Spend a day here and stroll the riverside promenade, or just change buses and continue north to Montañita, a lively party/surfing beach, or the more tranquil Olón or Ayampe nearby. Continue north to Puerto López, where whale watching is a must from June to September, and a visit to Isla de la Plata and the Parque Nacional Machalilla is worthwhile year round. Further north is the friendly resort of Bahía de Caráquez and the popular beach at Canoa. Return to Quito from Bahía or continue beachcombing your way north, stopping at another great surfing beach at Mompiche.

El Austro The attractive city of Cuenca is easy to reach by road or air, and is worth visiting for a few days. It's also the ideal base for exploring this geographically and culturally distinct region of Ecuador. Not far away is Ingapirca, Ecuador's premiere archaeological site, and *páramo*-clad Parque Nacional Cajas, both good for either a day trip or over-nighter. Take the bus south from Cuenca to Loja and on to Vilcabamba, next to the Parque Nacional Podocarpus with good trekking. On one side of Podocarpus is high jungle accessed from the city of Zamora, a short bus ride from Loja. On the other side is a delightful backwater: the colonial gold mining town of Zaruma. You can loop back to Cuenca from either Zaruma or Zamora, the latter route taking you along back roads through Gualaquiza in the seldom-visited southern Oriente.

One month or more

head deeper into the jungle for wildlife and activities

Given sufficient time, any of the above can be combined into longer routes and circuits. You can also widen the scope by heading downriver to the Amazon. Start by riding from Quito to Lago Agrio via Baeza, visiting the active Reventador volcano and Cascada San Rafael, Ecuador's highest waterfall, along the way. From Lago Agrio visit the Cuyabeno Wildlife Reserve, with some of the best jungle wildlife in Ecuador. Head south to Coca on the lower Río Napo, the jumping-off point for several world-class jungle lodges and community-based jungle tours in Parque Nacional Yasuní. The truly adventurous can sail down the Río Napo from Coca to the frontier at Nuevo Rocafuerte, then to Iquitos (Peru) and beyond.

Best
markets
& crafts

Otavalo market

Home to what may be the largest and most-visited indigenous craft market in all South America, Otavalo on a Saturday morning is an unforgettable experience. The cornucopia of crafts fills the streets: paintings, jewellery, weavings, baskets, leather goods, hats, wood carvings, ceramics, antiques and almost anything else you can think of. Market traders come from all over Ecuador, and beyond. It's worth arriving early, so consider staying in Otavalo on Friday night. Page 100.

Saquisilí market

Fewer visitors make it to Saquisilí than to Otavalo, and the Thursday market here is primarily for the indigenous locals. The streets throng with colourfully dressed highlanders from surrounding communities, with their red ponchos and felt hats. In addition to produce, most goods for sale here are utilitarian but you can also find *shigras* (crocheted shoulder bags), shawls, blankets and other textiles and ornamental crafts. Page 139.

Left: Saquisilí market
Above: Otavalo market
Opposite top left: Guamote market
Opposite top right: Tagua jewellery
Opposite bottom left: Panama hats
Opposite bottom right: Bread babies

Guamote market
The Thursday market in the central highlands town of Guamote is even further off the beaten path and sees few outside visitors. Animals and local produce, including an impressive selection of local potatoes, are the main items here. The indigenous highland atmosphere is thoroughly authentic. Page 160.

Sombreros de paja toquilla
These most typical of Ecuadorean crafts are ironically known around the world as *Panama* hats. Montecristi, near Manta, is famous for the outstanding quality of its hats. They are also woven in the highlands, especially the provinces of Azuay and Cañar, near Cuenca, which is the main site of factories producing the hats and home to numerous shops selling them. Pages 183 and 358.

Tagua
The tagua or ivory nut is a palm which grows below 1200 m on both the eastern and western slopes of the Andes. During the late 1800s, its very hard creamy-white seeds, known as vegetable ivory, were used to make buttons and toys. Toward the end of the 20th century, the tagua tradition was revived and today Ecuador produces a wonderful variety of tagua crafts. Pages 232.

Bread figurines
Calderón, just north of Quito, is the place where figurines are made of bread dough. The original edible *guaguas de pan* ('bread babies') were placed in cemeteries on *Finados* (Day of the Dead) as offerings to hungry souls of the departed. Today they include a variety of themes, the Nativity collection is especially popular and attractive. Page 360.

Kichwa woman dancing in colorful traditional dress

When to go

...and when not to

Climate

Ecuador is a year-round destination and the climate is unpredictable. As a general rule, however, in the **Sierra**, there is little variation by day or by season in the temperature, this depends on altitude. The range of shade temperature is from 6°C to 10°C in the morning, to 19°C to 23°C in the afternoon, though it can get considerably hotter in the lower basins. The day length (sunrise to sunset) is almost constant throughout the year.

Rainfall patterns depend on whether a particular area is closer to the eastern or western slopes of the Andes. To the west, June to September are dry and October to May are wet (but there are usually a few dry weeks, El Veranillo del Niño, some time between end November and early January). To the east, October to February are dry and March to September are wet. There is also variation in annual rainfall from north to south, with the southern highlands being drier.

Along the **Pacific coast**, rainfall also decreases from north to south, so that it can rain throughout the year in northern Esmeraldas and seldom at all near the Peruvian border. The coast, however, can also be enjoyed year-round, although it may be a bit cool from June to November, when mornings are often grey with the *garúa* mists. Rains may start in November, even late October, but January to May is the hottest and rainiest time of the year. Like the coast the **Galápagos** may receive *garúa* from May to December; from January to April the islands are hottest and brief but heavy showers can fall. In the **Oriente**, heavy rain can fall at any time, but it is usually wettest from March to September.

Ecuador's **high season** is from June to early September, which is also the best time for climbing and trekking. There is also a shorter tourist season in December and January. At major fiestas (see below), especially **Carnival**, **Semana Santa** (Easter), **Finados** (2 November) and over **New Year**, accommodation can be hard to find. Hotels will be full in individual towns during their particular festivals and resorts may be busy at weekends year-round.

Festivals

Festivals are an intrinsic part of Ecuadorean life. In prehispanic times they were organized around the solar cycle and agricultural calendar. After the conquest, the church integrated the indigenous festivals with their own feast days and so today's festivals are a complex mixture of Roman Catholicism and indigenous traditions. Every community in every part of the country celebrates their own particular festival in honour of their patron saint and there are many more that are celebrated in common up and down the country, particularly in the Sierra. The exact dates of many fiestas vary from year to year, either with the ecclesiastic calendar or for other reasons; enquire locally to confirm current dates.

Outsiders are usually welcome at all but the most intimate and spiritual of celebrations and, as a gringo, you might even be a guest of honour. Ecuadoreans can be very sensitive, however, and you should make every effort not to offend (for example, by not taking a ceremony seriously or by refusing food, drink or an invitation to dance).

January One of the least-known and least-understood fiestas in Ecuador is the **Diablada** or dance of the devils which takes place in Píllaro, in the province of Tungurahua, during the first six days of the year. Thousands of people from the town and nearby indigenous communities parade dressed as devils wearing elaborate masks. The event is unique in Ecuador and apparently unrelated to the larger and more famous *diablada* held each year for Carnaval in Oruro, Bolivia.

February-March **Carnaval** The four days before Ash Wednesday is when Ecuador runs riot. Children begin to play with water pistols and throw water-filled balloons soon after New Year, but the fun begins in earnest a week or two before the holiday. In a few places, flour and ink add to the mayhem and the mess. Loud music and free-flowing alcohol are also the rule in most places, and Guaranda is known for its especially wild carnival. One island of sanity is Ambato, where water-throwing is banned and flour is replaced by flowers at the city's **Fiesta de las Frutas y Flores**. Here colourful parades featuring elaborate floats are the main attraction.

March-April **Semana Santa** (Holy Week) is held the week before Easter and begins on **Palm Sunday** (Domingo de Ramos). This is celebrated throughout the country, but is especially dramatic in Quito, with a spectacularly solemn procession through the streets on **Good Friday**; also in Riobamba on Tue.

A particularly important part of Holy Week is the tradition of eating *fanesca* with family and friends. *Fanesca* is a soup made with salt fish and many different grains, and a good example of the syncretism of Catholic and earlier beliefs. In this case the Catholic component is the lack of meat, which was not consumed during Lent, while the many grains came from native traditions to celebrate the beginning of the harvest at this time of year. The original native version might have been made with *cuy* (guinea pig).

May-June Corpus Cristi is celebrated on the Thursday and weekend after Trinity Sunday. This festival is especially impressive in the towns of Pujilí, Saquisilí and Píllaro, as well as surrounding indigenous villages in the highlands of Cotopaxi and Tungurahua. Most notable are the *danzantes*, masked dancers with elaborate and very tall headdresses who parade through the streets. In Pujilí the festival includes *castillos*, 20-m-high poles which people climb to get prizes suspended from the top, including sacks of potatoes and live sheep. Different, but equally colourful, Corpus Cristi celebrations take place in Cuenca.

21-24 June Inti Raymi The solstice has been celebrated throughout the Andes since time immemorial. It overlapped and blended with Catholic festivals following the Spanish conquest and, in recent years, has experienced a revival in the highlands of Ecuador. In Otavalo the solstice *per se* and the **San Juan** festival (21 and 24 June, respectively) merge to create a week-long celebration. This usually begins with a ritual bath in a stream or pond and is followed by house to house dancing to the tune of native

instruments. In Cayambe, **San Pedro y San Pablo** (29 June) is the preferred fiesta, when bonfires are lit and people jump over them. San Pedro is also celebrated in southern Chimborazo (Alausí and Achupallas) and among fishermen along the coast, where an image of St Peter is traditionally taken out in a boat.

23-25 September Mama Negra Held in Latacunga, once in September and again on the weekend before 11 November, Mama Negra is as unusual as festivals get in Ecuador. There is a tumultuous parade in which a man dressed as a black woman, the *Mama Negra*, is the focus of the celebrations. He/she rides a horse, carries a doll and changes kerchiefs at every corner. Another prominent character is the *Shanga*, also painted black and carrying a pig. The symbolism behind all this confusing choreography, which combines homage to the Virgen de las Mercedes with traditions of black slaves of colonial times, is all but inscrutable. Market vendors and other humble tradespeople are among the most enthusiastic participants in the September event, which is reputed to be the more authentic of the two.

2 November Día de los Difuntos or **Finados** (Day of the Dead) is a hugely significant holiday nationwide. In the Incaic calendar, November was the eighth month and represented *Ayamarca*, or land of the dead. *Colada morada*, a sweet drink made from various fruits and purple corn is prepared, as are *guaguas de pan* (bread dolls). In a few places, native families may build a special altar in their homes or take their departed relatives' favourite food and drink to the cemetery. Most Ecuadoreans commemorate *Día de los Difuntos* in more prosaic fashion, by placing flowers at the graveside of their deceased relatives.

December Navidad (Christmas) is an intimate family celebration, starting with *Misa del Gallo* (Midnight Mass) followed by a festive meal. *Pases del Niño* (processions of the Christ child), take place through the country on various dates around Christmas time. Families who possess a statue of the baby Jesus carry them in procession to the local church, where they are blessed during a special Mass. The most famous *Pase del Niño* is in Cuenca on the morning of 24 December.

Other notable celebrations take place in Saraguro, in Loja province, in Pujilí and Tanicuchí in Cotopaxi province and throughout the province of Cañar.

31 December Año Viejo (New Year's Eve) Life-size puppets or effigies are built and displayed throughout the country, depicting important events of the year gone by. Children dressed in black are the old year's widows, and beg for alms in the form of sweets or coins. Just before midnight the will of the *Año Viejo* is read, full of bawdy humour and satire, and at the stroke of midnight the effigies are doused with gasoline and burned, thus wiping out the old year and all that it had brought with it. In addition to sawdust, the puppets usually contain a few firecrackers making for an exciting finale.

What to do

tanagers, tandem jumps, tropical fish and trails

Birdwatching and nature tourism

With over 1600 known species, Ecuador is one of the richest places in the world for birds (see www.avesecuador.com and www.birdsinecuador.com). Some of the planet's most beautiful birds can be found here and birdwatching has gained recognition as an important tourist activity. The lowlands excel in cotingas, manakins, toucans, antbirds and spectacular birds of prey, while the cloudforests are noted for their abundance of hummingbirds, tanagers, mountain toucans and cock-of-the-rock.

Ecuador has an excellent network of lodges and reserves specializing in this wonderful avian diversity. These are a great asset not only for birdwatchers, but also for hikers, as well as orchid, bromeliad, frog, beetle and butterfly enthusiasts; indeed, for anyone who enjoys nature. See also page 368 for more on Ecuador's wildlife.

There is great pleasure in coming to grips with tropical birds on your own, but a good professional bird guide can show you many more species than you will find by yourself. There are some highly regarded Ecuadorean companies which specialize in bird tours, see page 70. Price is usually a good indicator of quality.

Sadly, natural habitat is quickly being destroyed in Ecuador and many birds are threatened with extinction. Responsible ecotourism is one way to fight this trend; by visiting the lodges you are making it economically feasible for the owners to protect their land instead of farming or logging it. Another way you can help protect important Ecuadorean forest tracts is by donating to foundations that buy land for nature reserves; among these are the **Jocotoco Foundation** (www.fjocotoco.org) and the **Ecominga Foundation** (www.ecominga.com). You can also help by observing the guidelines outlined in www.responsibletravel.org.

For a comprehensive list and map of national parks and reserves, see pages 372 and 374.

Climbing

Ecuador's mountains are one of its special attractions and there are 10 summits over 5000 m, of which six have glaciers. Many of the sub-5000-m mountains are enjoyable walk-ups and some of the big 10 are suitable for beginners, while others are only for experienced mountaineers.

Along with the exotic beauty of its mountains, outrageously easy access makes Ecuador a fantastic place to get some high-altitude climbing experience. From Quito, using public transport, you could theoretically arrive at the base of seven of the country's big 10 mountains the same day and summit the next day, after you have acclimatized to the altitude. Acclimatization is very important in Ecuador, as is preventing sunburn and snowblindness.

There are two climbing seasons in Ecuador: June to August and November to January, but the weather can be good or bad on any day of the year. More important than the time of year is the time of day. You should aim to reach the summit of any of the snow capped peaks at 0700 so that descent is completed well before midday. As the equatorial sun warms the snow it makes for difficult going and there is a risk of avalanches. Nights and early mornings are generally clear but cloud can roll in after sunrise, often reducing visibility to zero.

Due to deglaciation, conditions and routes are constantly changing. Neither the general descriptions provided in this book nor those in specialized climbing guides can be assumed to remain correct. Government regulations state that no one may climb in Ecuador without a licensed guide from an authorized agency. Independent climbers and guides may be refused entry to national parks but exceptions might be made for internationally (UIAA) certified guides and members of Ecuadorian climbing clubs.

The situation continues to evolve, so confirm current details locally.

There are mountain shelters on Cotopaxi, Chimborazo, Cayambe, Guagua Pichincha and the Ilinizas. Prices and access information are given in the main text. Equipment can be bought or rented from Quito's climbing and outdoor shops, but selection may be limited. Always check the condition of rented equipment before you take it out. Mountain rescue facilities in Ecuador are rudimentary but gradually improving. Report all emergencies first to T911. The most up-to-date climbing guide to Ecuador is *Bergführer Ecuador* by Günther Schmudlach (Panico Alpinverlag, 2009, in German). Climbing agencies are listed in the relevant chapters throughout this book. Rock climbing information and equipment is available from the **Mono Dedo** shop, see page 68.

Diving and snorkelling

The coast of Ecuador is a paradise for divers, combining both cool- and warm-water dive sites in one of the most biologically diverse marine environments on Earth. The Galápagos Islands are undoubtedly the most popular destination, but diving in lesser-known waters such as those off the central coast of Ecuador is also worthwhile. The secluded coves of Isla de la Plata, 24 km offshore and part of Parque Nacional Machalilla, contain an abundance of multicoloured tropical fish which make diving and snorkelling a great experience. Access is from Puerto López, see page 234.

The Galápagos Islands are well known for their distinctive marine environments and offer more than 20 dive sites including opportunities for night diving. Each island contains its own unique environment and many are home to underwater life forms endemic to this part of the world. For a detailed description of diving in Galápagos, see page 340. Dive operators in other parts of Ecuador are given in the main text.

The cost of doing a PADI course in Ecuador is relatively low by international standards. Equipment can be hired, but it is advisable to check everything thoroughly. The larger bookshops stock diving books and identification guides for fish and other marine life. There is only one decompression chamber on the Galápagos Islands, and possibly another operated by the navy in Guayaquil.

Horse riding

The horse was only introduced to South America during the Spanish conquest but it has become an important part of rural life throughout Ecuador. Horse riding, whether for a brief excursion or a multi-day trek, is an excellent way to get to know the countryside, its people and local equestrian traditions. Haciendas throughout the country (see page 30) generally offer horse riding. There are good riding opportunities in Otavalo, Machachi, Parque Nacional Cotopaxi, Baños and Vilcabamba; for details, see What to do in the listings of the corresponding towns.

Mountain biking

Ecuador offers excellent biking opportunities through spectacular mountain scenery or along rugged back roads throughout the country. You can rent bikes or sign up for day tours in many places; the most popular are Quito, Baños and Riobamba (see What to do in the listings for these cities). The tours are mostly downhill; you are driven up to a high point and ride down accompanied by a support vehicle. It's exhilarating and good fun.

Those seeking a longer cycling experience can either bring their own bike or purchase one locally, although the price, selection and quality of locally available models may not be as good as in other parts of the world.

What many people don't take into account is the frequently extreme conditions in which they find themselves cycling. Dehydration can be a very real issue when cycling at high altitudes or in the hot tropical lowlands. Always carry water; a water pump or other means of purification are useful away from towns. Sunscreen is essential at high altitudes even on cloudy days. Wraparound sunglasses help to restrict the amount of dust which gets into the eyes.

When planning routes you can use IGM 1:50,000 topographical maps (see page 389). You should in addition seek local knowledge, as the road network has changed substantially since these maps were made. In general, for biking as for hiking, the further from the main tourist trail, the safer you are. See advice about camping on page 32.

Paragliding and hang-gliding

These are pretty specialized and special activities, be it amid the high mountains or along the Pacific shoreline. They have a following in Ecuador and devotees can sometimes be seen in the rays of the afternoon sun drifting off toward a valley or the beach. The air sports are especially popular in the oceanside town of Crucita and to a lesser extent in Canoa, as well as highland locations including Ibarra and Ambato. Tandem flights and courses are available for beginners. See www.parapentecrucita.com and www.flyecuador.com.ec.

Rafting and kayaking

In Ecuador, the perfect storm of geological accidents and climatic conditions has resulted in high rainfall and year-round mostly warm whitewater. These factors combined with dozens of accessible rivers – ranging from easy to challenging – make the country an exceptional destination for rafters and kayakers, from beginner to expert.

Commercial river running, particularly rafting, has blossomed in recent years. About two dozen operators based out of Quito, Tena, Baños and the Quijos valley offer all-inclusive day trips. Multi-day trips involve either remote riverside camping or are based at lodges in more accessible areas. No previous rafting experience is needed to join most trips although participants should have a spirit of adventure and be able to swim.

Although more specialized than rafting, kayaking is becoming increasingly popular in Ecuador. Several operators offer guided trips for kayakers and rental kayaks are available for those with the experience and confidence to go it alone. Kayaking courses are likewise available (November-February are good months).

There are various grades of rivers in Ecuador. Plunging off the Andes are very steep creeks offering, if they're runnable at all, serious technical grade V, suitable for expert kayakers only. As the creeks join on the lower slopes they form rivers navigable by both raft and kayak. Some of these rivers offer up to 100 km of continuous grade III-IV whitewater before flattening out in the jungle or coastal alluvial plain.

The most popular rivers for commercial rafting include: the Jatunyacu and the Lower Jondachi (an incredible raft run), both accessed from Tena; the Quijos and its tributaries, accessed from Baeza; and the Toachi/Blanco, usually reached from Quito. Rafting is also offered in Baños. Operators are listed in the What to do sections for these places.

Although guiding and safety standards are generally improving, it is wise to ask a few questions before booking a trip. The most important things to look for are experienced guides and top-notch equipment. Ask about guides' licenses; their rafting, river rescue and first aid training; whether they carry first aid, raft repair and river rescue kits; whether they use safety kayakers and have emergency communications. Since some of Ecuador's rivers are badly polluted, also ask about water quality before signing up for a trip.

A useful book is *The Kayakers' Guide to Ecuador*, www.kayakersguideto ecuador. wordpress.com (2014).

Surfing

Ecuador has a few select surfing spots which are popular for both their waves and scene. On the mainland, from north to south, are: Mompiche, south of Muisne; San Mateo, south of Manta; Montañita, between Olón and Manglaralto; and Playas near Guayaquil. In Galápagos, there is surfing at Playa Punta Carola, outside Puerto Baquerizo Moreno on San Cristóbal Island. Details are given in the relevant chapter. Waves are best from December to March, except at Playas where the surfing season is from June to September. For more information contact the **Federación Ecuatorian de Surf**, http://fesurf.website.

Trekking

Ecuador's varied landscape, diverse ecological environment and friendly villagers make travelling on foot a delight. Although the most commonly travelled routes are in the Sierra, there are also a few good trekking opportunities that take you from the highlands to the coast or Oriente. You can descend east or west from the windswept *páramo* through cloudforest to tropical rainforest on either side of the Andes, and observe many of the ecosystems of Ecuador during a single excursion. Many hikes pass through protected natural areas (see box, page 374) but it is ruggedness and isolation, more than legislation, that protects most of these and makes them so appealing to wilderness travellers. There are not nearly as many well-marked

trails and facilities as you might find in national parks in other parts of the world. In some places routes have been used for hundreds of years and are relatively easy to follow. In other areas you may have to make your own trail.

Reasonable fitness, strong navigation skills (using a map, compass and GPS) and a basic knowledge of Spanish are the most important prerequisites for independent trekking.

It is also possible to join a group or hire guides from tour operators. Many Quito companies offer trekking tours; see page 70. Guides and gear can also be hired through agencies in Otavalo, Latacunga, Baños, Riobamba and Cuenca.

It is best to bring trekking equipment from home, but some gear can be purchased or hired at outfitters in Quito and elsewhere. Check rented gear carefully. Topographic maps can only be purchased at the IGM in Quito (see page 389). The 1:50,000 scale maps are most useful, but their coverage of roads and trails is dated. The standard hiking shoe for Ecuador is the calf- to knee-high rubber boot, which is worn by most *campesinos* (rural dwellers) and costs about US$10. When combined with a good pair of wool socks, they keep feet warm and dry on the often-muddy terrain. Note, however, that very large sizes may be hard to find.

On the trail and elsewhere, all water must be boiled or otherwise purified before drinking. The most common stove fuel available in Ecuador is the screw-on *camping gaz* canister; white gas is not available. Although dirty, all gasoline in

Ecuador is unleaded and may be burnt by some stoves.

Ecuador's climate is inherently unpredictable and, as a trekker, you must be prepared for all conditions at any time of the year. Acclimatization to altitude and preventing sunburn are both important precautions. It is worth carrying a mobile phone on the trail (report all emergencies on T911) but self-sufficiency is very important, in the event of an accident self-evacuation may be your only option. In terms of public safety, the further off the tourist track you go the safer you are. See advice about camping on page 32. Enquire locally about safety before starting any trek.

For further information, see www.trekkinginecuador.com. For trekking guidebooks, see page 380.

Shopping tips

Almost everyone who visits Ecuador will end up buying a souvenir of some sort from the vast array of arts and crafts (*artesanías*) on offer. The most colourful places to shop for souvenirs, and pretty much anything else in Ecuador, are the many markets which can be found everywhere. The country also has more than its share of shiny, modern shopping centres, but remember that the high overheads are reflected in the prices.

Otavalo's massive market is the best-known place for buying wall-hangings and sweaters. Another market, at **Saquisilí**, south of Quito, is renowned for shawls, blankets and embroidered garments. Fewer handicrafts can be found on the coast, but this is where you can buy an authentic Panama hat at a fraction of the international price. The best, called *superfinos*, are reputed to be made in the little town of **Montecristi** near Manta, but the villages around Cuenca claim to produce superior models. **Cuenca** is a good place to buy Panama hats, and other types of hats can be bought throughout the highlands. Ecuador also produces fine silver jewellery, ceramics and brightly painted carvings. Particularly good buys are the many beautiful items fashioned from tagua, or vegetable ivory. By purchasing these you are promoting valuable conservation of the rainforests where the tagua palm grows.

All manner of *artesanías* can be bought in **Quito**, either at the Mercado Artesanal La Mariscal (see page 69) or in any of the many craft shops. An advantage of buying your souvenirs in a shop is that they'll usually package your gifts well enough to prevent damage on the flight home. Craft cooperatives are also a good place to shop, since there is a better chance that a fair share of the price will go to the artisan.

Stall holders in markets expect you to bargain, so don't disappoint them. Many tourists enjoy the satisfaction of beating down the seller's original price and finding a real 'bargain', but don't take it too far. Always remain good natured, even if things are not going your way (remember that you're on holiday and they're working). And don't make a fool of yourself by arguing for hours over a few cents. See also Best markets and crafts (page 14), and Arts and crafts (page 358). For local markets and shops see the Shopping listings of the relevant town, city or village.

Yachting

Several hundred private yachts call on the Galápagos Islands every year, mainly en route from Panama to the Marquesas Islands and Tahiti. All yachts calling on Galápagos must use an agent and regulations are strictly enforced; see www.gos.ec and www.naugala.com.

The Pacific coast ports of mainland Ecuador also have their following. There are yacht clubs in Salinas (the most traditional), La Libertad/Puerto Lucía and Punta Blanca, all in Santa Elena; and Casa Blanca in Esmeraldas. All these are playgrounds of the Ecuadorean elite. Bahía de Caráquez, in Manabí, is the most low-key option for international boaters but due to silting of the Río Chone estuary it can't easily admit vessels with a draught greater than 2 m. A pilot is available.

You may also be able to arrange a secure berthing in commercial ports like Esmeraldas and Manta. If your vessel needs repairs or maintenance, or you just want some time to go travelling ashore, then the mainland may have more facilities and lower prices than Galápagos.

Where to stay

from haciendas to homestays

There are a great many hotels in Ecuador, with something to suit every taste and budget. The greatest selection and most upscale establishments are found in the largest cities and more popular resorts. In less visited places the choice of better-class hotels may be limited, but friendly and functional family-run lodgings can be had almost everywhere.

The following terms are loosely applied. *Hotel* is generic, much as it is in English. A *hostal* or *posada* (inn) may be an elegant expensive place, while the terms *pensión, residencial, hospedaje* and *alojamiento* often refer to more modest, economical establishments. *Hosterías* and *haciendas* (see page 30) usually offer upmarket rural lodgings. *Turismo comunitario* is another option, community tourism whereby visitors are offered accommodation as well as meals and activities by a local family (see www.turismocomunitario.ec). A *motel* is not a 'motor hotel' as it is in North America, rather it is a place where couples go for a few hours of privacy.

'Boutique hotel' as used in Ecuador is a buzz-word which does not necessarily mean anything except that a place is expensive. There is nonetheless a handful of very special lodgings in Ecuador which genuinely deserve distinction: exquisitely renovated old homes with a few beautifully appointed rooms or suites and personalized service from the owners or manager; all at the top end of the price range.

Price codes

Where to stay	Restaurants
$$$$ over US$150	$$$ over US$12
$$$ US$66-150	$$ US$7-12
$$ US$30-65	$ under US$7 and under
$ under US$30	

Price of a double room in high season, including taxes.

Price of a two-course meal for one person, excluding drinks or service charge.

During major holidays accommodation is hard to find and prices rise. It is advisable to book in advance at these times, as well as during school holidays and local festivals, and even on ordinary weekends in popular areas.

Hotel owners may try to let their less attractive rooms first, but they are not insulted if you ask for a bigger room, better beds or a quieter area. In cities, remember that rooms away from the street will usually be less noisy. Likewise, if you feel a place is overpriced then do not hesitate to bargain politely. Always take a look at the rooms and facilities before you check in; there are usually several nearby hotels to choose from and a few minutes spent selecting among them can make the difference between a pleasant stay and miserable one.

In cheaper places, do not merely ask about hot water; open the tap and check for yourself. Tall travellers (above 180 cm) should note that many cheaper hotels, especially in the highlands, are built with the modest stature of local residents in mind. Make sure you fit in the bed and remember to duck for doorways.

Air conditioning is only of interest in the lowlands of the coast and Oriente. If you want an air-conditioned room expect to pay around 30% extra, otherwise look for a place with a good fan or sea breeze, and mosquito net. Conversely, hot water is only necessary in the highlands, where almost all places have it. A cool shower feels refreshing in the steamy climate of the coast and jungle. The electric showers sometimes used in cheaper hotels should be treated with respect. If you do not know how to use them, then ask someone to show you, and always wear rubber sandals or flip-flops.

Most of the better hotels have their own restaurants serving all meals. Few budget places have this facility, though some may serve a simple breakfast. Better hotels will often have their own secure parking but even more modest ones can usually recommend a nearby public car park. Most places have sufficient room to park a bicycle or motorcycle safely.

Some hotels charge per person or per bed, while others have a set rate per room regardless of the number of occupants. If travelling alone, it is usually cheaper to share with others in a room with three or four beds, or in a larger dormitory.

Even cheaper hotels may charge 12% *IVA* (VAT or sales tax), but enquire beforehand if this is included in their price. At the higher end of the scale 22% (12% tax + 10% service) is usually added to the bill.

The cheapest (and often nastiest) hotels can be found around markets and bus stations. If you're just passing through and need a bed for the night, they may be OK. In small towns, better accommodation may be found around the main plaza.

Many hotels in Ecuador can be booked online, either through their own websites or one of the many e-businesses which offer this service. Remember that the latter charge a commission which inflates the price and that you will generally pay more online than if you show up in person and bargain politely, although there are exceptions. Some cheaper hotels may offer online booking but do not always take such bookings seriously. You might turn up with your neatly printed reservation sheet only to be greeted with a puzzled stare. Also keep in mind that all hotels look good on their websites.

When booking a hotel from an airport or bus station by phone, try to talk to the hotel yourself rather than having someone do it for you. You may be told the hotel of your choice is full and be directed to one which pays a higher commission. Likewise, make sure that taxi drivers take you to the hotel you want, rather the one they say is best; they may be touting for a commission.

Almost without exception used toilet paper should not be flushed, but placed in the receptacle provided. This is also the case in most Ecuadorean homes and may apply even in some upmarket places; when in doubt ask. Tampons and sanitary towels should likewise be disposed of in the rubbish bin. See also Choosing a hotel in Quito (page 57).

Haciendas

The great haciendas of Ecuador were founded shortly after the Spanish conquest, either as Jesuit *obrajes* (slave workshops) or land grants to the conquistadors. When the Jesuits fell from favour and were expelled from South America, these huge land holdings passed to important families close to the Spanish royalty. They were enormous properties covering entire watersheds; most of the owners never even laid eyes on all their land. The early European scientists who explored Ecuador, people like La Condamine and Humboldt, were guests at these haciendas.

The hacienda system lasted until agrarian reform in the 1960s. The much-reduced land holdings which remained in the hands of wealthy families, frequently surrounding beautiful historic homes, were then gradually converted to receive paying guests. Among the first to take in tourists were **Chorlaví**, near Ibarra; **Cusín**, by Lago San Pablo; **La Ciénega**, near Lasso; **La Andaluza**, outside Riobamba; and **Uzhupud**, between Gualaceo and Paute. They have since become successful, premium *hosterías* and are listed under the corresponding geographic locations in the text. Encouraged by the success of these first tourist haciendas, more and more have opened to the public since the 1990s. Some are no longer working haciendas, but offer comfortable accommodation in historic surroundings, often with first-class restaurants. Others are attached to working farms and feature activities like horse riding and cattle roundups. At the same time they are promoting themselves as bases for activities and excursions outside their own confines. This is especially true around Quito, where easy access to the airport without having to enter the city makes these places a convenient first or last port-of-call.

With unlimited funds, you could travel almost the length of Ecuador, from the Colombian border to Cuenca, moving from one hacienda to the next. None is remote, but private transport would make the journey easier. Just as a trip to a lodge in the Oriente can be taken as a special treat, so a couple of nights in an hacienda can provide a luxurious change of scene and, in many cases, a chance to ride to parts of the country to which no bus or pick-up will go. These are truly ancestral homes and a gateway to the country's past.

As the fashion for hacienda tourism grows, some modern hotels and lodges are entering the lists, not for their historic associations, but for their brand of higher-end, rural tourism with close links to nearby communities. A couple of hotel groups that feature both the old and the new are **Ecuador Boutique Hotels**, www.ecuadorboutiquehotels.com; and **Exclusive Hotels and Haciendas of Ecuador**, www.ehhec.com. Prices are generally in our $$$$ range, but some have $$$ rooms or are in that category throughout.

Some of the best-known haciendas open to visitors include: **Pimán**, northeast of Ibarra, www.haciendapiman.com; **Pinsaquí**, north of Otavalo, www.hacienda pinsaqui.com; **Zuleta**, between Ibarra and Cayambe, www.zuleta.com; **Chillo-Jijón**, outside Quito, www.hacienda-ecuador.com; **La Carriona**, outside Quito, www.lacarriona.com; **La Alegría**, near Machachi, www.haciendalaalegria.com; **San Agustín de Callo**, near Parque Nacional Cotopaxi, www.incahacienda.com; **Hato Verde**, near Lasso, www.haciendahatoverde.com; **Yanahurco**, near the Parque Nacional Cotopaxi, http://cotopaxihaciendayanahurco.com; **Haciendas Leito**, www.haciendaleito.com, and **Manteles**, www.haciendamanteles.com, both near Patate; **Abraspungo**, near Riobamba, http://haciendaabraspungo.com. These and others are described in the relevant chapters of this book.

Homestays

Homestays are especially popular with travellers attending Spanish schools in Quito and Cuenca. The schools can make these arrangements as part of your programme. You can live with a local family for weeks or months, which is a good way to practise your Spanish and learn about the local culture. Do not be shy to change families, however, if you feel uncomfortable with the one you have been assigned. Look for people who are genuinely interested in sharing (as you should also be), rather than merely providing room and board. Try a new place for a week or so, before signing up for an extended period.

Camping

Camping in protected natural areas can be one of the most satisfying experiences during a visit to Ecuador – see Trekking, page 25. Organized campsites, car or trailer camping on the other hand are very rare. The most frugal travellers may want to camp to keep costs down and long-distance cyclists will sometimes need to camp between towns. In this case the best strategy is to ask permission to camp on someone's private land, preferably within sight of their home for safety. It is not safe to pitch your tent at random near villages and even less so on beaches. Those travelling with their own trailer or campervan can also ask permission to park overnight on private property, in a guarded car park or at a 24-hour petrol station (although this will be noisy). It is unsafe to sleep in your vehicle on the street or roadside.

Food
& drink

Ecuadoreans take their meals pretty seriously, not only for nutrition but also as a social experience. In smaller towns, most families still gather around the lunch table at home to eat and discuss the day's events. Sharing food is also a very important part of traditional celebrations and hospitality. A poor family, who generally must get by on a very basic diet, might prepare a feast for a baptism, wedding or high school graduation.

In many Ecuadorean homes, *desayuno* (breakfast) is fresh fruit juice, coffee, bread, margarine, and perhaps a little jam or white cheese. On the coast, a mid-morning *ceviche* may be enjoyed with a cold drink. *Almuerzo* (lunch) is by far the most important meal of the day. It may begin with a small appetizer, such as an *empanada*, followed by soup – compulsory and often the most filling course. Then comes a large serving of white rice, accompanied by modest quantities of meat, chicken or fish and some cooked vegetables or salad. Dessert, if served at all, might be a small portion of fruit or sweets. Lunch is also accompanied by fruit juice or a soft drink. *Merienda* or *cena* (supper) is either a smaller repetition of lunch or a warm drink with bread, cheese, perhaps cold cuts, *humitas* or *quimbolitos*.

Typical dishes
The details of the above vary extensively with each region based on custom and traditionally available ingredients. The following are some typical dishes worth trying. A recommended cookbook is *Comidas del Ecuador* by Michelle O Fried (see her website, too: www.michelleofried.com).

In the highlands *Locro de papas* is a potato and cheese soup. *Mote* (white hominy) is a staple in the region around Cuenca, but used in a variety of dishes throughout the Sierra. *Caldo de patas* is cow heel soup with *mote*. *Llapingachos* (fried potato and cheese patties) and *empanadas de morocho* (a ground corn shell filled with meat) are popular side dishes and snacks. *Morocho*, on the other hand, is a thick drink or porridge made from the same white corn, milk, sugar and cinnamon. *Sancocho de yuca* is a meat and vegetable soup with manioc root. The more adventurous may want to try the delicious roast *cuy* (guinea pig), most

FOOD

Fruit salad

Treat your palate to some of Ecuador's exquisite and exotic fruits. They are great on their own, as *ensalada de frutas*, or make delicious juices (*jugos*), smoothies (*batidos*) and ice creams (*helados*). Always make sure these are prepared with purified water and pasteurized milk.

Babaco, highland papaya. Great for juice.

Chirimoya, custard apple. A very special treat, soft when ripe but check for tiny holes in the skin which usually mean worms inside.

Granadilla, golden passion fruit. Slurp it from the shell without chewing the seeds.

Guanábana, soursop. Makes excellent juice and ice cream.

Guava, ice cream bean. Large pod with sweet white pulp around hard black seeds. Not to be confused with *guayaba*, below.

Guayaba, guava (in English). Good plain or in syrup, also makes nice jam and juice.

Mango, the season is short: December and January. Try the little *mangos de chupar*, for sucking rather than slicing.

Maracuyá, yellow passion fruit. Makes a very refreshing juice and ice cream.

Mora, raspberry or blackberry. Not all that exotic but makes an excellent and popular juice and ice cream.

Naranjilla, very popular juice, often cooked with a dash of oatmeal to make it less tart.

Orito, baby banana. Thumb-sized banana, thin-skinned and very sweet.

Papaya, great plain or as juice.

Piña, pineapple. A popular juice.

Taxo, banana passion fruit. Peel open the thin skin and slurp the fruit without chewing the seeds.

Tomate de arbol, tamarillo or tree tomato. Popular as juice but also good plain or in syrup. The secret ingredient of Ecuadorean *ají*.

Tuna, prickly pear. Sweet and tasty but never pick them yourself. Tiny blond spines hurt your hands and mouth unless they are carefully removed first.

Zapote or sapote. Fleshy and sweet, get some dental floss for the fibres that get stuck between your teeth.

typical of highland dishes. Also good is *fritada* (fried pork) and *hornado* (roast pork). Vegetarians can try such typically Andean specialities as *chochos* (lupins) and *quinua* (quinoa). *Humitas* are made of tender ground corn steamed in corn leaves, and similar are *quimbolitos*, which are sweet and prepared with white cornflour and steamed in achira leaves.

On the coast Seafood is excellent and popular everywhere. *Ceviche* is marinated fish or seafood which is usually served with popcorn, *tostado* (roasted maize) or *chifles* (plantain chips). There are several varieties of *ceviche*: *camarón* (shrimp/prawn) and *langostino* (jumbo shrimp/king prawn) are cooked before being marinated, while *pescado* (fish) and *concha* (clam) use ingredients that are not cooked before marinating (bear this in mind if concerned about food hygiene). *Langosta* (lobster) is an increasingly endangered species but continues to be illegally fished; so please be conscientious. Other coastal dishes include *empanadas de verde* which are fried snacks: a ground plantain shell filled with cheese, meat or shrimp. *Sopa de bola de verde* is plantain dumpling soup. *Encebollado* is a tasty fish and *yuca* chowder served with pickled onions, especially popular in Guayaquil. *Encocadas* are dishes prepared with coconut milk and fish or seafood, which are very popular in the province of Esmeraldas. *Cocadas*, on the other hand, are sweets made with coconut. *Viche* is fish or seafood soup made with ground peanuts, while *corviche* is fish or seafood deep fried in a plantain dumpling. *Patacones* are thick fried plantain slices served as a ubiquitous side dish.

In the Oriente Many dishes are prepared with *yuca* (manioc or cassava root) and a wide variety of river fish. *Maitos* (in northern Oriente) and *ayampacos* (in the south) are spiced meat, chicken, fish or palm hearts wrapped in special leaves and roasted over the coals. A traditional treat for jungle natives which has become increasingly popular with the population at large, is *chontacuro*, the larva of a large beetle roasted on a skewer; it makes *cuy* seem tame.

Special foods
Fanesca is a fish soup with beans, many grains, ground peanuts and more, sold during Easter Week throughout the country. *Colada morada* (a thick dark purple fruit drink) and *guaguas de pan* (bread dolls) are made around the time of Finados, the Day of the Dead, at the beginning of November. Special *tamales* and sweet and sticky *pristiños* are Christmas specialities.

Ecuadorean food is not particularly spicy. In most homes and restaurants, however, the meal is accompanied by a small bowl of *ají* (hot pepper sauce) which may vary greatly in potency. *Colada* is a generic name which can refer to cream soups or sweet beverages. In addition to the prepared foods mentioned above, Ecuador offers a huge variety of delicious temperate and tropical fruits, some of which are unique to South America (see box, opposite).

Drink

The usual soft drinks, known as *colas*, are widely available. Much better and more interesting is the bewildering array of freshly made fruit juices. Bottled water (*agua mineral*) is available everywhere, either still or carbonated.

The main beers include Pilsener and Club, both of which are reasonable. Many places have good microbrews and throughout the country you will come across craft beers only found in a particular town or district. Upmarket bars offer a wide selection of local and foreign beers. Quality imported wines are available but are not cheap, whilst imported liquor is even more expensive. *Aguardiente* ('fire-water') is the local potent sugar cane liquor, also known as *paico* and *trago de caña*, or just *trago*. *Chicha*, a native beverage fermented from corn in the highlands (*chicha de jora*) and from *yuca* (manioc root) or *chonta* (palm fruit) in Oriente, is not for those with a delicate stomach. Alcoholic beverages may not be sold or served on Sunday or the final day of a holiday (for example, on the Tuesday of carnival).

Dining out

The simplest and most common eateries found throughout Ecuador are small family-run *comedores* or *salones* serving only set meals: *almuerzos* and *meriendas* of the type described above. These cost US$2.50-5 and are easiest to find at midday. As long as the establishment is clean, you are unlikely to go wrong at one of these places, but you are unlikely to discover a hidden gastronomic treasure either. One step up, and available in provincial capitals, are restaurants which serve both set meals (perhaps an *almuerzo ejecutivo* for lunch) and à la carte at night. They may feature Ecuadorean or international food, more swanky surroundings, and can be good for around US$10-12. Outside main cities and resorts, the above are seldom supplemented by more than *chifas* (Chinese restaurants, some quite good, others terrible) and Italian or pizza places, which are usually a safe bet. Vegetarians must be adaptable in small towns, but can count on the goodwill and ingenuity of local cooks.

In Quito, Guayaquil, Cuenca and the more popular tourist resorts, the sky is the limit for variety, quality, elegance and price of restaurant dining. You can find anything from gourmet French cuisine to sushi or tapas, very upscale Ecuadorean *comida típica*, plush cafés, and neon-on-plastic fast food chains. On the periphery of cities are many *paradores*, places where Ecuadorean families go at weekends to enjoy traditional fare or grilled meat. Some are very good.

At the lowest end of the price range, every market in Ecuador has a section set aside for prepared foods. You always take a chance eating in a market, but if a place is clean then you might still find a tasty nourishing meal for about US$2. Food vendors in the street, however, who have no way to wash their hands or utensils properly, should be avoided.

Menu reader

Aguado de pollo Chicken broth with rice.

Ají Hot pepper sauce, found on every table. It can be very tasty but also very strong.

Bolón de verde Fried plantain dumpling served for breakfast in the lowlands.

Caldo de gallina con presa Chicken soup with a large piece of chicken.

Caldo de patas Cow-heel soup with mote. A popular hangover remedy.

Ceviche or **cebiche** Marinated fish or seafood which is usually served mid-morning with *canguil* (popcorn), *tostado* (roasted maize) or *chifles* (plantain chips).

Chaulafán Rice mixed with vegetables and bits of chicken or meat, served mostly in *chifas* (Chinese restaurants).

Choclo Fresh young corn, often served on the cob.

Chupé Fish soup.

Cocada Coconut macaroon, typical of the province of Esmeraldas.

Cola Any soft drink.

Colada Can refer to cream soups or sweet warm or cold beverages.

Colada morada Thick purple spicy fruit drink, served warm or cold around the time of Finados, the Day of the Dead (2 Nov).

Cuy Guinea pig roast on the spit, served with potatoes and a peanut sauce. The most typical and prized of all highland dishes.

Dulce de leche Spreadable soft toffee.

Empanada Sweet or savoury, fried or baked, snacks in a pastry shell.

Encebollado Fish or seafood served with its broth on boiled *yuca* (manioc root) and pickled onions. Typical of the coast.

Encocado Savoury fish, seafood or chicken prepared in coconut milk, typical of the province of Esmeraldas.

Estofado Stew, may be de *res* (beef), *pollo* (chicken) or *pescado* (fish).

Fanesca Special soup made with salt fish, many different grains, beans, ground peanuts and more. Served during Easter Week throughout the country.

Fritada Deep-fried pork. Very popular with Ecuadoreans, especially in the highlands.

Guatita Tripe prepared with ground peanuts and potatoes.

Hornado Baked pork, the whole hog with a tomato in its mouth.

Humitas Sweet or savoury tender ground corn steamed in corn leaves.

Llapingachos or **tortillas** Fried potato and cheese patties.

Locro de papas A warming potato and cheese soup, served with slices of avocado.

Menestra Bean or lentil stew served as a side dish.

Mote White hominy. Soft corn kernels burst with alkali, common in Cuenca and the southern highlands.

Patacones Thick fried plantain chips.

Quimbolitos A sweet made with wheat or other flour steamed in achira leaves.

Sancocho Hearty meat and vegetable soup containing *yuca* (manioc root) and corn.

Seco Generic for second or main course, usually served with rice.

Sopa de bola de verde Hearty soup with plantain dumplings, typical of the coast.

Viche Hearty fish or seafood soup, with peanuts, typical of the province of Manabí.

Quito
& around

Few cities have a setting to match that of Quito, the second highest capital in Latin America. It sits in a narrow valley at the foot of the volcano Pichincha. From El Panecillo hill there are fine views of the city and the encircling volcano cones.

Quito is a city of many faces. The first UNESCO World Heritage Site city in the world, Quito's charm lies in its colonial centre, the Centro Histórico. Here, pastel-coloured houses and ornate churches line a warren of steep and narrow streets. Modern Quito is an altogether different place, with busy avenues lined with office towers, shopping malls, restaurants and bars, and a huge variety of hotels.

Quito is surrounded by scenic countryside which is well worth visiting. Within easy reach of the city are nature reserves, wonderful thermal baths, mountains to climb, quaint villages and the monument to the equator. The western slopes of Pichincha, also nearby, are covered in beautiful cloudforest where nature lovers can indulge their taste for adventure.

Best for
Churches ▪ Mountains ▪ Museums ▪ Nightlife

Footprint
picks

★ La Compañía, page 45

Among Quito's 86 churches, La Compañía has the most ornate and richly sculptured façade and interior.

★ Museo Nacional, page 49

This is the most comprehensive of Quito's many excellent museums.

★ El TelefériQo, page 51

This cable car climbs to 4050 m on the flanks of Pichincha, with gorgeous views along the way.

★ Mitad del Mundo, page 82

Every tourist knows that this is the place to straddle the equator. The ethnographic museum and Museo Inti-Ñan here are worth visiting.

★ Papallacta, page 82

There is nowhere to soak like Papallacta, the best developed thermal baths in Ecuador.

★ Mindo, page 87

Not far from Quito, Mindo and the cloudforests of the western slopes of Pichincha are a nature lover's paradise.

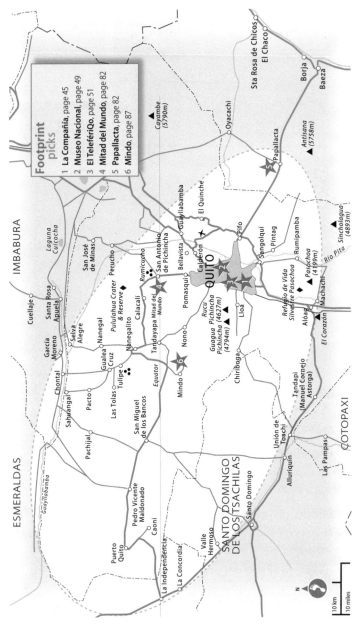

Quito

The city's main attraction is its colonial centre, where cobbled streets are steep and narrow, dipping to deep ravines. Modern Quito has broad avenues lined with contemporary office buildings, fine private residences, parks, embassies and villas. Here you'll find Quito's main tourist area in the district known as La Mariscal, bordered by Avenidas Amazonas, Patria, 12 de Octubre and Orellana. Beyond lie Quito's upmarket residential areas.

Colonial Quito

a pleasant place to stroll and admire the architecture, monuments and art

The revitalized colonial district of Quito has a lot of movement in the streets and plazas and is particularly lively on Sunday, when it is closed to vehicles. At night, the illuminated plazas and churches are very beautiful.

Plaza de la Independencia (Plaza Grande)

The heart of the old city is Plaza de la Independencia or Plaza Grande, whose pink-flowered arupo trees bloom in September. It is dominated by a somewhat grim **cathedral** ① *entry through museum, Venezuela N3-117 or off Plaza Grande, T02-257 0371, www.catedraldequito.org, no visits during Mass 0600-0900, US$3 for the museum, Mon-Sat 0900-1500, US$6 including cupolas with guide, night visits to church on request,* built 1550-1562, with grey stone porticos and green tile cupolas. On its outer walls are plaques

> **Tip...**
> The Municipal Band plays in Plaza de la Independencia every Wednesday at 1100.

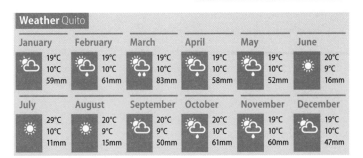

Weather Quito

January 19°C 10°C 59mm	**February** 19°C 10°C 61mm	**March** 19°C 10°C 83mm	**April** 19°C 10°C 58mm	**May** 19°C 10°C 52mm	**June** 20°C 9°C 16mm
July 29°C 10°C 11mm	**August** 20°C 9°C 15mm	**September** 20°C 9°C 50mm	**October** 20°C 10°C 61mm	**November** 19°C 10°C 60mm	**December** 19°C 10°C 47mm

Essential Quito

Finding your feet

Mariscal Sucre airport is about 30 km northeast of the city. Long-distance bus services arrive at terminals at the extreme edges of the city: Quitumbe in the south and Carcelén in the north.

Quito is a long, narrow city stretching from north to south, with Pichincha rising to the west. Its main arteries run the length of the city and traffic congestion along them is a serious problem. Avenida Occidental or Mariscal Sucre is a less congested road to the west of the city. The Corredor Periférico Oriental or Simón Bolívar is a bypass to the east of the city running 44 km between Santa Rosa in the south and Calderón in the north. Roads through the eastern suburbs in the Valle de los Chillos and Tumbaco can be taken to avoid the city proper. Most places of historical interest are in colonial Quito, while the majority of the hotels, restaurants, tour operators and facilities for visitors are in the modern city to the north.

The street numbering system is based on N (Norte), E (Este), S (Sur) and Oe (Oeste), plus a number for each street and a number for each building; however, an older system of street numbers is also still in use.

Getting around

Both colonial Quito and La Mariscal in modern Quito can be explored on foot, but getting between the two requires some form of public transport; taxis are the best option. There is plenty of public transport but it's not safe when crowded. See also Safety, page 396, and Transport, page 76.

When to go

Quito is within 25 km of the equator, but its altitude makes its climate similar to spring in England, with pleasantly warm days and cool nights. The rainy season is October to

Tip...
Take it easy for the first 48 hours because of the altitude, which may make you feel some discomfort. The city has a serious air pollution problem.

May with a lull in December and the heaviest rainfall in April. Rain usually falls in the afternoon.

Time required

Allow two to three days to acclimatize to the altitude and see the city's highlights, and one week or more for day trips.

Safety

For all emergencies T911. Safety in Quito appears to have improved in recent years, but it is still not a safe city. In colonial Quito, Plaza de la Independencia and La Ronda are patrolled by officers from the Policía Metropolitana who speak some English and are very helpful. El Panecillo is patrolled by neighbourhood brigades but walking up the stairs is not recommended. In modern Quito increased police presence has brought some improvement, but La Carolina and La Mariscal districts still call for vigilance at all hours. Plaza Foch (Calle Foch y Reina Victoria) in La Mariscal is also patrolled, but do not stray outside its perimeter at night. Also take care around the TeléfériQo. There have been occasional reports of 'express kidnappings', so choose your taxi judiciously (see page 79). Do not walk through any city parks in the evening or even in daylight at quiet times. There have been persistent reports of scams on long-distance buses leaving Quito, especially to Baños. Do not give your hand luggage to anyone and always keep your things on your lap, not in the overhead storage rack or on the floor. The Servicio de Seguridad Turística (Tourist Police), offers information and is the place to obtain a police report in case of theft (for details, see page 55.)

Flying into Quito at night

Several flights from North America, Central America, Colombia and Guayaquil arrive at night. Quito airport operates 24 hours, including the information desk at arrivals, restaurants, cafés, cyber café, phone office, currency exchange and pharmacy. If you have an early morning connection and want to stay at the airport, you can do so. The VIP lounges are open to the public for a fee (US$34 at International departures, US$19 at domestic departures), but only available after you have checked in for your next flight. There are several hotels 10-20 minutes away by taxi.

If your destination is Quito and you have not booked a hotel, ask for assistance at the information desk before leaving the airport. Taxis are available 24 hours and Aero Servicios express buses run to the old airport from 0430-0040 on weekdays, from 0500 at weekends. They offer transport from their terminus to any hotel. Use this transfer service or a taxi to your hotel. Taking a city bus is not safe.

If your destination is outside Quito, wait until the morning, then take a taxi to Pifo and take a bus which bypasses Quito going north or south, or catch a bus heading east. Another alternative in daylight is to take a city bus from the airport to one of the long-distance bus terminals: Quitumbe for the south and Carcelén for points north.

listing the names of the founding fathers of Quito and inside are the tomb of Sucre and a famous *Descent from the Cross* by the indigenous painter Caspicara. There are many other 17th- and 18th-century paintings; the interior decoration shows Moorish influence. The Capilla de las Almas, the oldest chapel, has a 16th-century *retablo* said to the earliest Escuela Quiteña work, attributed to Padre Carlos. In the Sala del Tesoro is a collection of golden vestments and mitres while the Sala Capitular has paintings of all the archbishops and cardinals of the archbishopric of Quito. The organ is the largest in working order in Ecuador. The crypts were due to be open to the public in 2018.

Facing the cathedral is the **Palacio Arzobispal**, part of which now houses a small shopping mall. Next to it, in the northwest corner, is the **Hotel Plaza Grande** (1930), with a baroque façade, the first building in the old city with more than two storeys. On the northeast side is the concrete **Municipio**, which fits in quite well. The low colonial Palacio de Gobierno or **Palacio de Carondelet** ① *T02-382 7700, www.presidencia.gob.ec*, silhouetted against the flank of Pichincha, is on the northwest side of the plaza. On the first floor is a gigantic mosaic mural of Orellana navigating the Amazon. The ironwork on the balconies looking over the main plaza is from the Tuilleries in Paris. To visit, go to the information booth next to the entrance, show your passport or ID and you will be given a time at which you can take a tour.

South to El Panecillo

From Plaza de la Independencia two main streets, Venezuela and García Moreno, lead straight towards El Panecillo. Parallel with Venezuela is Calle Guayaquil, the main shopping street. These streets all run south from the main plaza to meet Calle Morales, better known as **La Ronda**, one of the oldest streets in the city. This narrow, cobbled pedestrian way and its colonial homes with wrought-iron balconies have been refurbished and house hotels, restaurants, bars, cultural centres, artisans' workshops, galleries and shops (see Shopping,

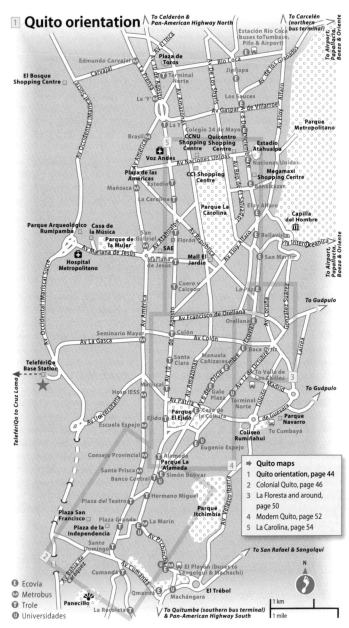

Quito orientation

To Calderón &
Pan-American Highway North

To Carcelén
(northern
bus terminal)

To Airport,
Papallacta,
Baeza & Oriente

Estación Río Coca
(buses to Tumbaco,
Pifo & Airport)

Río Coca

Plaza de
Toros

Edmundo Carvajal

El Bosque
Shopping Centre

Carvajal

Terminal
Norte

Jipijapa

Los Sauces

Av Gaspar de Villarroel

La 'Y'

Colegio 24 de Mayo

Brasil

CCNU
Shopping
Centre

Quicentro
Shopping
Centre

Estadio
Atahualpa

Parque
Metropolitano

Voz Andes

Av Naciones Unidas

Naciones Unidas

Plaza de las
Américas

CCI Shopping
Centre

Megamaxi
Shopping Centre

Mañosca

Estadio

La Carolina

Parque La
Carolina

Eloy Alfaro

Benalcázar

Parque Arqueológico
Rumipamba

Casa de
la Música

San
Gabriel

Capilla
del Hombre

Parque de
la Mujer

El Florón

Bellavista

Hospital
Metropolitano

SAE

Mall El
Jardín

San Martín

Mariana
de Jesús

Via Interoceánica

To Airport,
Papallacta,
Baeza & Oriente

Cuero y
Caicedo

La Paz

To Guápulo

Av Francisco de Orellana

Seminario Mayor

Colón

Orellana

Av La Gasca

Av Colón

Baca Ortiz

To Guápulo

Santa
Clara

Manuela
Cañizares

TelefériQe
Base Station

Mariscal

To Valle de
Los Chillos

Hosp IESS

Galo
Plaza

Madrid

To Guápulo

Av Patria

Terminal
Norte

TelefériQe to Cruz Loma

Casa de
la Cultura

Parque
El Ejido

Ejido

Av Universitaria

Parque
Navarro

Escuela Espejo

Coliseo
Rumiñahui

To Cumbayá

Consejo Provincial

Alameda

Parque La
Alameda

Eugenio Espejo

Santa Prisca

Banco Central

Simón Bolívar

Quito maps

Plaza del Teatro

Hermano Miguel

Parque
Itchimbía

	Quito orientation, page 44
1	Colonial Quito, page 46
2	La Floresta and around, page 50
3	Modern Quito, page 52
4	La Carolina, page 54
5	

Plaza San
Francisco

Plaza Grande

La Marín

Plaza de la
Independencia

Santo
Domingo

Cumandá

El Playón (buses to
Sangolquí & Machachi)

To San Rafael & Sangolquí

Panecillo

Qmandá

El Trébol

Machángara

La Recoleta

To Quitumbe (southern bus terminal)
& Pan-American Highway South

N

E Ecovía
M Metrobus
T Trole
U Universidades

1 km
1 mile

ON THE ROAD

El chulla quiteño

Quito's spectacular location and its beautifully restored colonial centre are matched only by the complex charm of the capital's people, the *'chullas quiteños'* as they call themselves; the term defies translation but is akin to 'real Quitonians'. These are not the colourfully dressed inhabitants of highland villages, tending crops and haggling with tourists to sell their crafts. They are young professionals, office workers and government bureaucrats, conservatively attired and courteous to a fault, and they form the backbone of a very urban society. You will see them going out for lunch with colleagues during the week, making even a cheap *almuerzo* seem like a formal occasion. You will also find them in the city's bars and clubs at weekends, letting their hair down with such gusto that they seem like entirely different people. When you hear them singing: "yo soy el chullita quiteño...", you will know what it is all about.

below). On García Moreno N3-94 is the beautiful church of **El Sagrario** ⓘ *Mon-Fri, 0800-1800, Sat and Sun 1000-1400, no entry during Mass, free*, with a gilded door. The **Centro Cultural Metropolitano** is at the corner of Espejo, housing the municipal library, a museum for the visually impaired, four exhibition rooms for temporary shows,

> **Tip...**
> La Ronda is a quaint corner of the city and is good for an afternoon stroll; at night the atmosphere changes completely with the bars packed, street food for sale and entertainers (best Wednesday to Sunday).

a small concert hall, a café and the **Museo Alberto Mena Caamaño** ⓘ *entry on C Espejo, T02-395 2300, Tue-Sun 0900-1700, US$1.50*. This wax museum depicts scenes of Ecuadorean colonial history. The scene of the execution of the revolutionaries of 1809 in the original cell is particularly vivid. The fine Jesuit church of ★ **La Compañía** ⓘ *García Moreno N3-117 y Sucre, T02-258 1895, Mon-Thu 0930-1830, Fri 0930-1730, Sat and holidays 0930-1600, Sun 1200-1600, Mass 0900, 1030, 1700, US$4, students US$2, visits including cupolas and night-time visits US$6, photography not permitted*, has an ornate and richly sculptured façade and interior. In the Sacristy are paintings by Hernando de la Cruz (1592-1646), a renowned painter of the *Quiteña* school. Diagonally opposite is the **Casa Museo María Augusta Urrutia** ⓘ *García Moreno N2-60 y Sucre, T02-258 0103, Tue-Sat 1000-1800, Sun 0900-1730, US$2*, the home of a Quiteña who devoted her life to charity, showing the lifestyle of 20th-century aristocracy.

Housed in the fine restored, 16th-century Hospital San Juan de Dios is the **Museo de la Ciudad** ⓘ *García Moreno S1-47 y Rocafuerte, entrance on Blv 24 de Mayo (between García Moreno and Venezuela), T02-228 3883, www.museociudadquito.gob.ec, Tue-Sun 0930-1730 (last group 1630), US$3, free entry on the last Sat of each month, non-Spanish guide service US$4 per group (request ahead)*. A very good museum which takes you through Quito's history from prehispanic times to the 19th century, with imaginative displays; there's a café by the entrance overlooking La Ronda. Almost opposite on García Moreno are the convent and museum of **El Carmen Alto** ⓘ *T02-295 5817, Facebook: MuseoCarmenAlto, Wed-Sun 0930-1730, last entry 1630, US$3, request ahead for guiding in English, small shop sells sweets and wine made in the convent*. In 2013, this beautifully refurbished cloister opened its doors to the public for the first time since 1652.

2 Colonial Quito

200 metres
200 yards

Quito maps
1 Quito orientation, page 44
2 Colonial Quito, page 46
3 La Floresta and around, page 50
4 Modern Quito, page 52
5 La Carolina, page 54

PANECILLO

Where to stay
Casa El Edén 1 *B3*
Casa Gangotena 2 *C2*
Casa Gardenia 3 *B2*
Community Hostel 5 *B3*
Guayunga 6 *A3*
Huasi Continental 7 *C3*
La Casona de La Ronda 8 *C3*

Mama Cuchara 9 *C3*
Patio Andaluz 10 *B2*
Plaza Grande 11 *B2*
Quito Cultural 12 *B3*
San Francisco
de Quito13 *C2*
Secret Garden 14 *A3*

Restaurants
El Palomar 1 *B2*
El Ventanal 2 *A1*
Govindas 3 *B2*
Hasta la vuelta, Señor 4 *B2*
Heladería San Agustín 5 *B2*
La Casa de
los Geranios 6 *C3*

Octava de Corpus 7 *C3*
San Ignacio 9 *C2*
Theatrum 8 *B3*
Vista Hermosa 10 *B2*

E Ecovía
M Metrobus
T Trole
U Universidades

BACKGROUND

Quito

Archaeological finds suggest that the valley of Quito and surrounding areas have been occupied for some 10,000 years. The city gets its name from the Quitus, who lived here during the period AD 500-1500. By the end of the 15th century, the northern highlands of Ecuador were conquered by the Incas and Quito became the capital of the northern half of their empire under the rule of Huayna Capac and later his son Atahualpa. As the Spanish conquest approached, Rumiñahui, Atahualpa's general, razed the city, to prevent it from falling into the invaders' hands.

The colonial city of Quito was founded by Sebastián de Benalcázar, Pizarro's lieutenant, on 6 December 1534. It was built at the foot of El Panecillo on the ruins of the ancient city, using the rubble as construction material. Examples of Inca stonework can be seen in the façades and floors of some colonial buildings such as the Cathedral and the church of San Francisco. Following the conquest, Quito became the seat of government of the Real Audiencia de Quito, the crown colony, which governed current day Ecuador as well as parts of southern Colombia and northern Peru. Beautifully refurbished, colonial Quito is today the city's most attractive district. In 1978, Quito was the first city to be declared a UNESCO World Heritage Site.

The 20th century saw the expansion of the city to the north and south, and later to the valleys to the east. The commercial, banking and government centres moved north of the colonial centre and residential and industrial neighbourhoods sprawled in the periphery. These make up the Distrito Metropolitano, which stretches for almost 50 km from north to south. The current population of Quito is estimated at 2,644,145.

Cerro Panecillo ⓘ *Mon-Thu 0900-1700, Fri-Sun 0900-2100, US$1 per vehicle or US$0.25 pp if walking (not recommended), for the neighbourhood brigade; entry to the interior of the monument US$2.* From the observation platform at the top of the hill there is a statue of the Virgen de Quito and a good view. Although the neighbourhood patrols the area, it is safer to take a tour or taxi (US$8 return from the colonial city, US$10 from La Mariscal, wait not permitted); the 'Mitad del Mundo' bus goes up from the foot of the hill at Bahía de Caráquez y Marañón (US$0.25), but this is not a safe place to wait. There is a **Museo del Monasterio de San Diego** ⓘ *Calicuchima 117 y Farfán, entrance to the right of the church, T02-317 3185, Mon-Sat 0900-1330, 1430-1700, US$2* (by the cemetery of the same name, just west of El Panecillo). Guided tours (Spanish only) take you to the cupolas and around four colonial patios where sculpture and painting are shown. Of special interest are the gilded pulpit by Juan Bautista Menacho and the Last Supper painting in the refectory, in which a *cuy* and *humitas* have taken the place of the paschal lamb.

Southeast of El Panecillo is the **Museo Interactivo de Ciencia** ⓘ *Sincholagua y Maldonado, Chimbacalle, T02-266 6061, www.museo-ciencia.gob.ec, Wed-Sun 0900-1730 (last entry 1600), US$3, children US$1.*

West of Plaza de la Independencia

Plaza de San Francisco (or Bolívar) is west of Plaza de la Independencia; here are the great church and monastery of

Tip...
A number of museums are closed on Monday.

the patron saint of Quito, **San Francisco** ① *Cuenca 477 y Sucre, T02-228 1124, daily 0800-1200, 1500-1800*. The church was constructed by the Spanish in 1553 and is rich in art treasures. A modest statue of the founder, Fray Jodoco Ricke, the Flemish Franciscan who sowed the first wheat in Ecuador, stands nearby. See the fine wood carvings in the choir, a high altar of gold and an exquisite carved ceiling. There are some paintings in the aisles by Miguel de Santiago, the colonial mestizo painter. The **Museo Franciscano Fray Pedro Gocial** ① *in the church cloisters to the right of the main entrance, T02-295 2911, www.museofraypedrogocial. com, Mon-Sat 0900-1730, Sun 0900-1300, US$2*, has a collection of religious art. Under the portico of the church is a popular craft shop and café, **Tianguez** ① *T02-257 0233, see Facebook, open daily from 0730*. Also adjoining San Francisco is the **Cantuña Chapel** ① *Cuenca y Bolívar, T02-295 2911, Tue and Thu 0800-0900, Sun 0900-1000, free*, with sculptures.

Not far to the south along Calle Cuenca is the excellent archaeological museum, **Museo Casa del Alabado** ① *Cuenca N1-41 y Bolívar, T02-228 0940, http://alabado.org, Thu-Tue 0900-1730, Wed 1330-1730, closed 25 December and 1 January, US$6, concessions for students and seniors, 3 guided visits a day, 1 on Wed, cost extra*, with an excellent art shop. An impressive display of pre-Columbian art from all regions of Ecuador, among the best in the city.

Two blocks west of Cuenca on Rocafuerte (opposite San Roque church) is Mercado San Francisco, a market selling local food and medicina ancestral – potions and plants for every conceivable ailment, physical and psychological. The selection of produce is very good and it is a smart place, but it's best to go with a Quiteño/a.

North of San Francisco is the church of **La Merced** ① *Chile y Cuenca, 0630-1200, 1300-1800, free*, with many splendidly elaborate styles. Nearby is the **Museo de Arte Colonial** ① *Cuenca N6-15 y Mejía, T02-228 2297, Tue-Sat 0930-1700, US$2*, housed in a 17th-century mansion. It has a collection of colonial sculpture and painting as well as temporary exhibits and occasional concerts (free).

To the west of the city, the **Yaku Museo del Agua** ① *El Placer Oe11-271, T02-251 1100, www.yakumuseoagua.gob.ec, Tue-Sun 0900-1730, US$3, children US$1*, has lovely views. This interactive museum is great for kids of all ages. Its main themes are water and climate, also a self-guided trail: *eco-ruta*. To get there take a taxi to the main entrance or enter through the parking lot at the top of Calle Bolívar and take the lift up.

Southeast of Plaza de la Independencia

At **Plaza de Santo Domingo** (or Sucre), southeast of Plaza de la Independencia, is the church and convent of **Santo Domingo** ① *Mon-Sat 0600-1200, 1600-1930, Sun 0600-1300, 1700-1900*, with its rich wood carvings and a remarkable **Chapel of the Rosary** to the right of the main altar. In the convent is the **Museo Dominicano Fray Pedro Bedón** ① *T02-228 0518, Mon-Fri 0915-1300, 1400-1630, Sat 0900-1300, US$2, English-speaking guides available*, with another fine collection of religious art. In the centre of the plaza is a statue of Sucre, facing the slopes of Pichincha where he won his battle against the Royalists. Just south of Santo Domingo, in the old bus station, is **Parque Qmandá (Cumandá)** ① *Tue-Fri 0700-2000, Sat and Sun 0700-1800, busy at weekends*, with a pool, sport fields, climbing wall, gym and activities. **Museo Monacal Santa Catalina** ① *Espejo 779 y Flores, T02-228 4000, Mon-Fri 0900-1730, Sat 0900-1230, US$2.50*, said to have been built on the ruins of the Inca House of the Virgins, depicts the history of cloistered life. Many of the heroes of Ecuador's struggle for independence are buried in the monastery of **San Agustín** ① *Chile y Guayaquil, T02-295*

5525, Tue-Fri 0730-1200, 1500-1700, Sat and Sun 0800-1200, which has beautifully painted cloisters on three sides where the first act of independence from Spain was signed on 10 August 1809. Here is the **Museo Miguel de Santiago** ① *Chile 924 y Guayaquil, T02-295 1001, Mon-Fri 0900-1230, 1400-1700, Sat 0900-1230, US$2*, with religious art.

Northeast of Plaza de la Independencia

To the northeast of Plaza de la Independencia is **Plaza del Teatro** with the lovely neoclassical 19th-century **Teatro Sucre** ① *Manabí N8-131 y Guayaquil (see Entertainment, page 67)*. Further north, on Parque García Moreno, the **Basílica del Voto Nacional** ① *Carchi 122 y Venezuela, T02-228 9428, visits Mon-Fri 0700-0900, 1800-1900, Sat and Sun 0600-1830, US$2, Mass Sat 0700, 0800, 1700, 1830, Sun hourly 0600-1200 and 1830; bell tower open daily 0930-1730, US$2*, is very large, has many gargoyles (some in the shape of Ecuadorean fauna), stained-glass windows and fine, bas-relief bronze doors (begun in 1926; some final details remain unfinished due to lack of funding). Climbing to the top of the tower gives a 360-degree panorama of the city, as well as a good view of the interior from the choir on the way up. The **Centro de Arte Contemporáneo** ① *Luis Dávila y Montevideo, San Juan, T02-394 6990, Tue-Fri 1030-1730, Sat and Sun 0900-1730, free*, in the beautifully restored Antiguo Hospital Militar, built in the early 1900s, has rotating art exhibits.

East of the colonial city is **Parque Itchimbía** ① *T02-322 63638 2017, Facebook: ItchimbiaCentroCultural, park open daily 0600-1800, exhibits Tue-Sun 0900-1630*; a natural lookout over the city with walking and cycle trails and a cultural centre housed in a 19th-century 'crystal palace' which came from Europe and once housed the original Santa Clara market.

Modern Quito
the capital's main tourist and business area

Parque La Alameda and around

Parque La Alameda has South America's oldest **astronomical observatory** ① *T02-258 3451, ext 100, http://oaq.epn.edu.ec, museum Mon-Sat 0900-1300, 1400-1700, US$2, night observations Tue-Thu 1900-2030 weather permitting, US$3*, dating to 1873 (native people had observatories long before the arrival of the Europeans). There is also a splendid monument to Simón Bolívar, lakes and, in the northwest corner, a spiral lookout tower with a good view.

A short distance north of Parque La Alameda, opposite Parque El Ejido and bound by 6 de Diciembre, Patria, 12 de Octubre and Parque El Arbolito, is the **Casa de la Cultura**, a large cultural and museum complex. If you have time to visit only one museum in Quito, it should be the ★ **Museo Nacional** ① *entrance on Patria, T02-222 3258, Tue-Fri 0900-1700, Sat and Sun and holidays 1000-1600*, housed in the north side of the Casa de la Cultura. The **Sala de Arqueología** is particularly impressive with beautiful pre-Columbian ceramics; the **Sala de Oro** has a nice collection of prehispanic gold objects; and the **Sala de Arte Colonial** has religious art from the Quito School. On the east side of the complex are the museums administered by the **Casa de la Cultura** ① *entrance on 12 de Octubre, T02-222 1006, www. casadelacultura.gob.ec, Tue-Sat 0900-1300, 1400-1700, US$2*: the **Museo de Arte Moderno**, which has paintings and sculpture since 1830 as well as rotating exhibits, and the **Museo de Instrumentos Musicales**, an impressive collection of musical instruments, said to be the second in importance in the world. Also on the east side are an art gallery for temporary exhibits and the **Agora**, a large open space used for concerts. On the west side are halls for temporary art exhibits, in the original old building, and the entrance to the **Teatro Nacional**, with free evening performances. On the south side are the **Teatro Demetrio Aguilera Malta** and other areas devoted to dance and theatre. Near the Casa de la Cultura, in the Catholic University's **cultural centre** ① *12 de Octubre y Roca, www.centrocultural puce.org,* is the superb **Museo Jijón y Caamaño** ① *T02-299 1710, Mon-Fri 0900-1900, Sat 1900-1700, free,* with a private collection of archaeological objects, historical documents and art. The interactive displays and narration in Spanish are excellent. Here too are temporary exhibits and the **Museo Weilbauer** ① *same phone and hours, www.museoweilbauer.org,* with archaeological and photo collections and a *Sala Táctil* where the visually impaired can touch replicas of ceramics.

Between Parque La Alameda and Parque El Arbolito is the **Palacio Legislativo** ① *bounded by Montalvo, Gran Colombia, Piedrahita and Av 6 de Diciembre,* where the Asamblea Nacional has sat since 2009, replacing the Congreso Nacional under the 2008 Constitution. On the face of the building (1958-1960) is a mural depicting the history of the country by Víctor Mideros. The Salón de Pleno has a mural by Guayasamín (see below).

La Floresta

In La Floresta further northeast is **Casa Cultural Trude Sojka** ① *Toledo N24-569 y Coruña, entrance from Pje Moeller, T09-9873 3572, https://casaculturaltrudesojka. wordpress.com, daily from 1000 by arrangement, US\$3,* a cultural centre which promotes peace, tolerance and art. It exhibits the works of Trude Sojka (1909-2007), a Czech-born painter and sculptor, and a Jewish survivor of the Holocaust who emigrated to Ecuador. The centre also includes a Holocaust memorial, temporary exhibits and a library, and offers art workshops.

La Mariscal

A focal point in La Mariscal, north of Parque El Ejido, is **Plaza Foch** (Reina Victoria y Foch), also called **Plaza del Quinde**, a popular meeting place surrounded by cafés and restaurants. At the corner of Reina

3 **La Floresta & around**

Where to stay 🛏
Casona de Mario 1

Bars & clubs 🎵
La Juliana 7

Restaurants 🍴
Chez Jérôme 1
La Briciola 2
La Gloria 4
Pekín 5
Urko 6

Victoria and La Niña is the excellent **Museo Mindalae** ① *T02-223 0609, www.mindalae. com.ec, Mon-Sat 0930-1730, US$3,* which exhibits Ecuadorean crafts and places them in their historical and cultural context, as well as temporary exhibits and a good Fairtrade, non-profit shop. (For another handicrafts museum and shop, see **Folklore**, page 69.)

North of La Mariscal is the large **Parque La Carolina**, a favourite recreational spot at weekends. Around it is the banking district, several shopping malls, hotels and restaurants. In the park is the **Jardín Botánico** ① *T02-333 2516, http://jardinbotanicoquito.com, Mon-Fri 0800-1645, Sat-Sun 0900-1645, US$3.50,* which has a good cross section of Andean flora. Also here is the **Vivarium** ① *T02-227 1799, www.vivarium.org.ec, Tue-Sun 0930-1300, 1330-1730, US$3.25,* dedicated to protecting endangered snakes, reptiles and amphibians, and the **Museo de Ciencias Naturales** ① *T02-244 9825, Mon-Fri 0800-1300, 1345-1630, US$2.* Beyond La Carolina, on the grounds of Quito's former airport, is **Parque Bicentenario** ① *daily 0430-1800,* with sports fields and a great cycling track, right on the old tarmac.

Quito suburbs

modern art, archaeological remains and a cable car

Eastern suburbs

Built by indigenous slaves in 1693, the **Santuario de Guápulo** ① *Mass Mon-Fri 1900, Sat 0700, Sun 0700-1200, 1600-1700,* perched on the edge of a ravine east of the city, is well worth seeing for its many paintings, gilded altars, stone carvings and the marvellously carved pulpit. The **Museo Fray Antonio Rodríguez** ① *Plaza de Guápulo N27-138, T02-258 1420, Mon-Fri 0800-1700, US$1.50,* has religious art and furniture, from the 16th to the 20th centuries. Guided tours (Spanish only) include a visit to the beautiful Santuario.

Overlooking the city from the northeast is the grandiose **Capilla del Hombre** ① *Lorenzo Chávez E18-94 y Mariano Calvache, Bellavista, T02-244 6455, www.guayasamin. org, daily 1000-1700, except holidays, US$8 (US$4 for disabled visitors and students), take a taxi, US$4, or Jesús del Gran Poder–Bellavista bus,* a monument to Latin America conceived by the internationally famous Ecuadorean artist Oswaldo Guayasamín (1919-1999) and completed after his death. This highly recommended museum includes a collection of murals depicting the fate of Latin America from pre-Columbian to modern times and, in Guayasamín's home and studio (guided tours only), his works, as well as pre-Columbian, colonial and contemporary art collections. Works of art, jewellery and clothing decorated with Guayasamín's art are for sale and there is a café.

The valleys east of the capital, towards the airport, are commuting districts, some very fashionable. The Valle de Los Chillos, in the south, and the Valle de Tumbaco, to the north, are separated by the eroded Volcán Ilaló, which is a good place for weekend activities, such as trekking and biking. Los Chillos valley goes via San Rafael and Sangolquí towards Cotopaxi. In the Tumbaco district are the new airport and surrounding towns (see box on Quito airport, page 61), while closer to Quito are Tumbaco itself, Nayón, the 'garden of Quito' with many plant nurseries, coastal seafood restaurants and an adventure park, and Cumbayá (see Restaurants, page 65).

Western suburbs

For spectacular views ride the ★ **TelefériQo** ① *Av Occidental above La Gasca, T02-222 2996, http://teleferico.com.ec, open daily 0800-2000, US$8.50, disabled, children and seniors*

4 Modern Quito

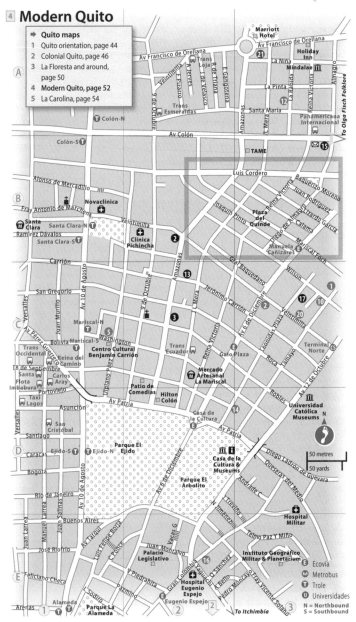

➡ **Quito maps**
1 Quito orientation, page 44
2 Colonial Quito, page 46
3 La Floresta and around, page 50
4 Modern Quito, page 52
5 La Carolina, page 54

Marriott Hotel
Holiday Inn
Av Francisco de Orellana
Trans Loja
La Niña
Mindalae 🏛
Veintimilla
R de Velasco
E Gangotena
Pizarro
La Pinta
Reina Victoria
Amazonas
Santa María
Panamericana Internacional
To Olga Fisch Folklore

Av Colón
TAME 🏛 ✉ **15**

Alfonso de Mercadillo
Luis Cordero
Baquerizo Moreno
Reina Victoria
Juan Rodríguez
Lizardo García
Calama
Wilson

Fray Antonio de Marchena
Novaclinica ✚
🅜 Santa Clara
Santa Clara-N 🅣
Ramírez Dávalos
Santa Clara-S 🅣
Veintimilla
Joaquín Pinto
Plaza del Quinde
Diego de Almagro
Manuela Cañizares
Mariscal Foch 🅔

Carrión
Clínica Pichincha ✚
Amazonas
2
Gral Baquedano

San Gregorio
Av 10 de Agosto
Juan Murillo
6 de Octubre
13
Jerónimo Carrión
Mera
3
2
17
10
Versalles

Mariscal-N 🅣
Washington
5
Centro Cultural Benjamín Carrión
Reina Victoria
Galo Plaza
Fernández Plaza
Veintimilla
Roca
Tamayo
Terminal Norte 🅔

Juan Pérez Guerrero
Bolívar Mariscal-S 🅣
Trans Occidental
Reina del Camino
Mariscal-S
18 de Septiembre
Santa Flota Imbabura
Carlos Aray
Portoviejo
🚕 Taxi Lagos
Asunción
Urbano Páez
Trans Ecuador
Mercado Artesanal La Mariscal 🏛
Robles
Av 6 de Diciembre
An 12 de Octubre
🏛 Universidad Católica Museums
N

Patio de Comedias
Hilton Colón
Casa de la Cultura 🅔
Av Patria
Diego Ladrón de Guevara
Queseras del Medio
50 metres
50 yards

San Cristóbal
Santiago
Caracas
Bogotá
Río de Janeiro
Ejido-S 🅣
🅣 Ejido-N
Parque El Ejido
Av 10 de Agosto
Av 6 de Diciembre
Casa de la Cultura & Museums 🏛 ℹ
Parque El Arbolito
Andrade C
Treviño

Manuel Larrea
Juan Larrea
José Riofrío
Feliciano Checa
Buenos Aires
Luis Felipe Borja
C Ponce
V Piedrahita
Pazmiño
Vaca G
Juan Montalvo
Palacio Legislativo
16
N Jiménez
Telmo Paz Y Miño
🕇 Hospital Militar
Instituto Geográfico Militar & Planetarium
🅔 Ecovía
🅜 Metrobus
🅣 Trole
🅤 Universidades

Arenas
Alameda 🅣
1
Parque La Alameda
Sodiro
Gran Colombia
Eugenio Espejo
Hospital Eugenio Espejo 🕇
Aguirre
O Sánchez
A Bello
Pedro Moncayo Fray Vicente Solano
To Itchimbía
2
3
N = Northbound
S = Southbound

US$6.50. The cable car is part of a complex with an amusement park, shops and food courts. It climbs to 4050 m on the flanks of Pichincha, where there are walking trails, including one to the summit of Rucu Pichincha, and horse riding just past the fence. The area below is not safe so it's best to get there by taxi (US$1.50 from América y Colón).

Tip...
The Chaquiñán is a 20-km walking and cycle path from Cumbayá via Tumbaco to Puembo on an old railway track, including three tunnels. It has seven rest stops.

Parque Arqueológico y Ecológico Rumipamba ① *east side of Av Occidental just north of Mariana de Jesús, T02-224 2313, Wed-Sun 0830-1630, free, some English-speaking guides*, is a 32-ha park on the slopes of Pichincha, where vestiges of human occupation of several pre-Inca periods, dating from 1500 BC to AD 1500, have been found. There are walking trails in some pockets of native vegetation. Northwest of Rumipamba, at north end of El Ejido–San Vicente bus line in the neighbourhood of San Vicente de la Florida, is **Museo de Sitio La Florida** ① *C Antonio Costas y Román, T02-380 3043/224 2313, Wed-Sun 0900-1630, free, some English-speaking guides*. At this necropolis of the Quitus people, 10 17-m deep burial chambers, dating to AD 220-640, have been excavated. The elaborate dress and jewellery found in the tombs suggests most were prominent citizens.

La Mariscal detail

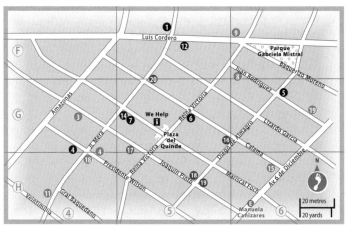

Where to stay 🛏	Hostal de la Rábida **12** *A3*	Restaurants 🍴	The Magic Bean **14** *G5*
Anahi **1** *C3*	La Cartuja **14** *D3*	Chandani Tandoori **1** *F5*	Yu Su **15** *B3*
Casa Helbling **2** *C3*	La Casa Sol **15** *H6*	El Hornero **2** *B2*	
Casa Joaquín **3** *G4*	L'Auberge Inn **16** *E2*	Ethnic Coffee **3** *C2*	Bars & clubs 🍸
City Art Hotel Silberstein **4** *G4*	Mansión del Angel **17** *G5*	Kallari **4** *G4*	Bungalow Six **16** *G5*
Cultura Manor **5** *C1*	Marquíz **18** *H4*	La Petite Mariscal **5** *G6*	Cafelibro **17** *C3*
El Arupo **8** *F6*	Posada del Maple **19** *G6*	Mama Clorinda **6** *G5*	Cherusker **18** *H5*
El Cafecito **9** *F6*	Sierra Madre **20** *C3*	No Sé Pizzería & Bar **7** *G5*	Finn McCool's **19** *H5*
Fuente de Piedra I **10** *C3*		Chez Alain **12** *F5*	No Bar **20** *F5*
Fuente de Piedra II **11** *H4*		Sakti **13** *C2*	Turtle's Head **21** *A3*

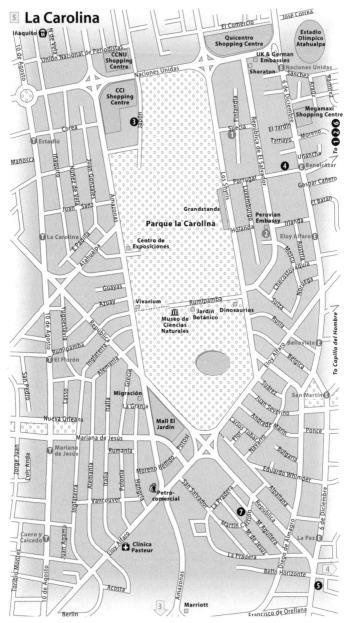

Iñaquito

10 de Agosto

N de Vela

José Correa

El Comercio

Unión Nacional de Periodistas

Quicentro Shopping Centre

Estadio Olímpico Atahualpa

CCNU Shopping Centre

UK & German Embassies

Naciones Unidas

Naciones Unidas

CCI Shopping Centre

Sheraton

Sánchez

Arauz

Palmira

6 de Diciembre

Corea

3

Finlandia

Suecia

El Jardín

Megamaxi Shopping Centre

Tamayo

Moreno

To **1 2 6**

Estadio

Inaquito

Juan González

Manosca

Azuero

Juan Sanz

República de El Salvador

Portugal

Los Shyris

Unancha

Benalcázar

4

Gaspar Cañero

El Batán

La Carolina

Atahualpa

F Padilla

Luxemburgo

Grandstands

Parque la Carolina

Holanda

Peruvian Embassy

Irlanda

Eloy Alfaro

2

Guayas

Azuay

Centro de Exposiciones

Mosca

Noruega

Checoslovaquia

El Florón

Yugoslavia

Rumipamba

República

Indiaterra

Alemania

Grecia

Vivarium

Rumipamba

Dinosaurios

Museo de Ciencias Naturales

Jardín Botánico

Suiza

Rusia

Eloy Alfaro

Bélgica

Bellavista

To Capilla del Hombre

San Pedro

Oslo

Lasso

Italia

Migración

La Granja

San Martín

Suárez

Juan Severino

Andrade Marín

Flor Tobar

Navarro

Ponce

Jorge Juan

Luis Anda

Mariana de Jesús

Nueva Orleans

Mariana de Jesús

Alemania

Italia

Polonia

Rumania

Mariana de Jesús

Mall El Jardín

Potosí

Carlos Tobar

Bulgaria

Eduardo Whimper

Albaniana

6 de Diciembre

Cuero y Calcedo

Juan Agama

Ingleterra

Vancouver

Eloy Alfaro

Moreno Bellido

Humana

Petro-comercial

San Salvador

La Pradera

7

Martín C M de Jesús

República

M Aguilera

Diego de Almagro

La Paz

4

Clínica Pasteur

La Pradera

Bello Horizonte

5

Torbio Montes

10 de Agosto

Acosta

Amazonas

3

Marriott

Berlín

Francisco de Orellana

Tourist information

**Empresa Metropolitana Quito Turismo/
Quito Visitor's Bureau**
*HQ at Parque Bicentenario (old airport),
T02-299 3300, info@quito-turismo.gob.ec,
www.quito.com.ec. Mon-Fri 0830-1700.*
Has information offices with English-
speaking personnel, brochures and maps,
and an excellent website.

Airport, in Arrivals area, T02-255 1566,
Mon-Fri 0600-2200, Sat-Sun 0700-1900. **Bus
station**, Terminal Quitumbe, T02-382 4815,
daily 0800-1800. **Colonial Quito**, **El Quinde
Visitors Centre**, Plaza de la Independencia,
at Palacio Municipal, Venezuela y Espejo,
T02-257 2445, Mon-Fri 0900-1800, Sat
0900-2000, Sun 1000-1700; also offers
booking services and walking tours, and
has storage lockers. In the premises are
also crafts and chocolate shops, tour
operators and sale points for double-
decker bus tours, see page 70, Mitad del
Mundo, train tours and travel insurance.
Best Trip Ecuador in El Quinde, T02-243
5458, www.besttripecuador.com, as well
as selling Quito Bus tours, has a map with a
free-to-download app with 3D descriptions,
videos and adverts, also interactive cards.
La Mariscal, at Ecuador Gourmet, Reina
Victoria N24-263 y Lizardo García, T02-223
9469, Mon-Sat 0900-1730. To file a complaint
about services contact the **Quito Visitor's
Bureau** headquarters (see above).

Ministerio de Turismo
*Av Gran Colombia y Briceño, T02-399 9333
or T1-800-887476, www.ecuador.travel,
www.turismo.gob.ec. Mon-Fri 0815-1700.*
Offers information at the reception desk.

Servicio de Seguridad Turística
*HQ at Reina Victoria y Roca, Edif de Relaciones
Exteriores, La Mariscal, T02-254 3983.
Open 0800-1800 for information, 24 hrs for
emergencies. Other offices at: Plaza Grande,
north side, Casa de los Alcaldes, Chile entre
Venezuela y García Moreno, T02-295 5785,
0800-2400; La Ronda, Calle La Ronda 925, p 2,
entre Morales y Guayaquil, T02-295 6010, Sun-
Tue 0800-2300, Wed-Sat 0800-0400; Terminal
Quitumbe, T02-382 4765, daily 0900-1900.*
In order to file an online police report on
a robbery, go to www.gestiondefiscalias.
gob.ec/rtourist.

**Sistema de Museos y Centros Culturales
Quito**
*Calle el Placer Oe11-271, Yaku Museo del Agua,
T02-251 1100 ext 101, www.museosquito.gob.ec.*
Offers useful information about museums and
cultural centres throughout Quito. Good website.

Where to stay

Large international chain hotels are
represented in the city and meet their
international standards. For more
information see: www.bestwestern.com,
www.hotelquito.com, www.hotelesdann.
com, www.hilton.com, www.holidayinn.
com, www.hiexpress.com (**Holiday Inn
Express**), www.marriott.com.mx,
mercure.com, www.starwoodhotels.com
(Sheraton), www.swissotel.com, and www.
wyndhamhotels.com. See box, Choosing a
hotel in Quito, page 57.

N

300 metres
300 yards

Colonial Quito

$$$$ Casa El Edén
Esmeraldas Oe3-30 y Guayaquil, T02-228 1810,
www.casaeleden.com.
Beautiful old home restored to save original murals and painted ceilings, convenient location, 6 well-appointed heated rooms, rooftop views.

$$$$ Casa Gangotena
Bolívar Oe6-41 y Cuenca, T02-400 8088,
www.casagangotena.com.
Superb location by Plaza San Francisco, luxury accommodation in beautifully refurbished classic family home with a variety of rooms and suites, fine restaurant specialiazing in the use of Ecuadorean ingredients.

$$$$ La Casona de La Ronda
Morales Oe1-160 y Guayaquil, T02-228 7501,
www.lacasonadelaronda.com.
Tastefully refurbished colonial house in the heart of La Ronda, comfortable rooms and suite, includes buffet breakfast, restaurant serves Ecuadorean specialities and some international dishes.

$$$$ Mama Cuchara
Vicente Rocafuerte E3-250 Y Chávez, T02-381 3400, www.arthotelsecuador.com.
Brand new coversion by Arthotels of a 100-year-old house at the end of a cul-de-sac at the top of La Loma Grande and built into the hillside. Rooms in the historic part and a new wing have locally made furniture, there's a covered patio for restaurant, rooftop terrace and bar with 360-degree views. It's very tasteful with a focus on art and culture and a gallery for Ecuadorean artists. 24-hr security.

$$$$ Patio Andaluz
García Moreno N6-52 y Olmedo, T02-228 0830, www.hotelpatioandaluz.com.
Beautifully reconstructed 16th-century mansion with large arches, balconies and patios, breakfast extra, exclusive restaurant with Ecuadorean and Spanish cuisine, library, gift shop.

$$$$ Plaza Grande
García Moreno N5-16, Plaza de la Independencia, T02-251 0777, www.plazagrandequito.com.
Exclusive top-of-the-line hotel with an exceptional location, 15 suites including a presidential suite for US$2000, jacuzzi in all rooms, climate control, 2 restaurants, including **La Belle Epoque**, gourmet French cuisine and a wine cellar, mini-spa.

$$$ Casa Gardenia
Benalcázar N9-42 y Oriente, T02-295 7936, www.hotelcasagardenia.com.
Nice 9-room B&B in a 19th-century house in a quiet location, buffet breakfast, lovely views from the terrace, sitting room, personalized service, garage. The neighbourhood is being upgraded and it's a 5-block walk to Plaza Independencia.

$$$-$$ San Francisco de Quito
Sucre Oe3-17 y Guayaquil, T02-295 1241, www.sanfranciscodequito.com.ec.
Converted colonial building, breakfast served in attractive patio or underground cloisters, restaurant, suites are particularly good value, well run by owners.

$$ Quito Cultural
Flores N4-160 y Chile, T02-228 8084, www.hostalquitocultural.com.
Nicely refurbished colonial house, bright, colourful rooms, rooftop terrace with nice views, patio with plants, café, tours arranged.

$$-$ Community Hostel
Cevallos N6-78 y Olmedo, T09-5904 9658, www.communityhostel.com.
Popular hostel with 2 double rooms and dorms for 4-6 (US$10-12.50 pp), comfy beds, shared bath (may have to wait for toilet in the morning), good showers, very clean and efficient, nice sitting area, breakfast extra, communal kitchen, yoga classes, helpful staff.

There are a great many hotels in Quito, of which we list a small fraction. With so much accommodation being offered, you can find a good place to stay regardless of your taste or budget, but the large selection can be bewildering. So narrow your search by reading up on the city, its neighbourhoods and hotels before you arrive.

Modern Quito has the greatest number of hotels. Many are concentrated in **La Mariscal**, Quito's tourist neighbourhood par excellence, the place for those who want to be in the heart of the action. Here you will be surrounded by restaurants, bars, nightlife, tour agencies, craft shops, Spanish schools, and even launderettes. Many budget hotels are in this area. With so much going on, it is not surprising that parts of La Mariscal are noisy, nor that this is where thieves and drug dealers can find the highest concentration of tourists.

La Floresta and other neighbourhoods to the east of La Mariscal, as well as **La Carolina** to the north, offer a variety of good accommodation in more relaxed residential surroundings. This is also where a number of the international hotels are located, while in the suburbs and to the west along the flanks of Pichincha are a handful of stylish hotels in rural settings not far from the city.

For those who prefer to stay in the historical heart of the city, there are a number of hotels in restored buildings in **colonial Quito**. Several posh places are by the main plazas and this area has some good mid-range hotels and B&Bs as well. The cheap hotels in this district tend to cater to short-stay couples and are not recommended.

Between colonial and modern Quito are ageing residential neighbourhoods with neither the charm of the old city, nor the vibrant scene of La Mariscal. The sector is nonetheless conveniently located and has some good-value accommodation.

For lodgings near the airport, see page 60. Near the Quitumbe (south) bus terminal are a few simple establishments catering to short-stay customers and there is one simple *hostal* ($ **Madrid**) opposite the Carcelén (north) bus terminal, along busy Avenida Eloy Alfaro. There is not much of interest here, so it's only worth staying if you are taking another bus early the next day.

$$-$ Huasi Continental
Flores N3-08 y Sucre, T02-295 7327,
www.hotelhuasi.com.
Colonial house, a bit dark, restaurant serves good breakfast and lunch (both extra), private or shared bath, parking, good service and value.

Between colonial and modern Quito

$$$$ Mansión del Angel
Los Ríos N13-134 y Pasaje Gándara, T02-255 7721, www.mansiondelangel.com.ec.

Luxurious hotel decorated with antiques in a beautifully renovated mansion, 14 ample rooms and a palatial suite, afternoon tea and dinner available, nice gardens, lovely atmosphere, spa.

$$-$ Guayunga
Antepara E4-27 y Los Ríos, T02-228 8544,
http://guayunga.com.
Attractive hostel with a few double rooms, with and without bath, and dorms for 3-9 (US$14 pp), breakfast, snacks and drinks available, kitchen and laundry service,

interior patio, rooftop terrace with great views, parking; travel agency.

$$-$ L'Auberge Inn
Gran Colombia N15-200 y Yaguachi, T02-255 2912, www.auberge-inn-hostal.com.
Nice spacious rooms, duvets, private or shared bath, excellent hot water, buffet breakfast and restaurant with vegetarian options, cooking facilities, Spanish lessons, parking, lovely garden, terrace and communal area, helpful, English spoken, good atmosphere. Highly recommended.

$$-$ Secret Garden
Antepara E4-60 y Los Ríos, T02-295 6704, www.secretgardenquito.com.
Well-decorated house, some rooms small and dark, lovely rooftop terrace restaurant, private or shared bath, US$10-12 pp in dorm, breakfast extra, pleasant atmosphere, very popular meeting place. Ecuadorean/Australian-owned, also run a rustic lodge between Pasochoa and Cotopaxi, www.secretgardencotopaxi.com.

Modern Quito

$$$$ Cultura Manor
Jorge Washington E2-43 y Páez, T02-222 4271, www.culturamanor.com.
Brand new luxury hotel to replace old favourite **Café Cultura**, incorporating historic Quito architecture and Renaissance style ('Boticelli meets magic realism') in a 1933 monument, award-winning restoration, high-end **Renaissance** and **Historical** suites (more rooms to be added, including **Explorer** style), good restaurant (0700-1500), bar, terrace, spa, wood-panelled library with fireplace, garden, very attentive service, secure parking, tours arranged. Opened 2017. Holds an annual classical music concert in conjunction with the Hungarian Embassy at the end of summer.

$$$$ Le Parc
República de El Salvador N34-349 e Irlanda, T02-227 6800, www.leparc.com.ec.
Modern hotel with 30 executive suites, full luxury facilities and service, restaurant, spa, gym, parking.

$$$ Anahi
Tamayo N23-95 y Wilson, T02-250 1421, www.anahihotelquito.com.
Very nice tastefully decorated suites, each one is different, ample bathrooms, buffet breakfast, safety box, fridge, terrace with nice views, good value.

$$$ Casa Joaquín
Pinto E4-376 y JL Mera, T02-222 4791, www.hotelcasajoaquin.com.
Nicely refurbished hotel in the heart of La Mariscal, covered patio makes it warm, good service, Belgian-run. Also owns **La Petite Mariscal** restaurant, Almagro N24-304 y Rodríguez, T02-604 3303, www.lapetitemariscal.com.

$$$ City Art Hotel Silberstein
Wilson E5-29 y JL Mera, T02-515 1651, www.cityartsilberstein.com.
10 comfortable rooms and suites in an attractively refurbished building, includes buffet breakfast, tours available.

$$$ Finlandia
Finlandia N35-129 y Suecia, north of centre, T02-382 0860, www.hotelfinlandia.com.ec.
Pleasant hotel in residential area, buffet breakfast, restaurant, spacious rooms, sitting room with fireplace, small garden, parking, helpful staff.

$$$ Fuente de Piedra I & II
Wilson E9-80 y Tamayo, T02-255 9775 and JL Mera N23-21 y Baquedano, T02-290 0323, www.ecuahotel.com.
Well-decorated modern hotels, comfortable, some rooms are small, nice sitting areas, pleasant.

$$$ Hostal de la Rábida
La Rábida 227 y Santa María, T02-222 2169,
www.hostalrabida.com.
Lovely converted home, bright comfortable
rooms, good restaurant for breakfast and
dinner (both extra), parking, Ecuadorean/
Italian-run. Recommended.

$$$ La Cartuja
Plaza N20-108 y 18 de Septiembre, T02-
252 3721, www.hotelacartuja.com.
In the former British Embassy, beautifully
decorated, spacious comfortable rooms,
cafeteria, parking, lovely garden, very helpful
and hospitable. Highly recommended.

$$$ Marquíz
JL Mera N23-106 y Wilson, T02-252 2873,
www.hotelmarquiz.com.ec.
Nice modern hotel in the heart of
La Mariscal, safe, comfortable rooms,
attractive public spaces, café, bar, jacuzzi,
helpful staff, good value.

$$$ Sierra Madre
Veintimilla E9-33 y Tamayo, T02-250 5687,
www.hotelsierramadre.com.
Fully renovated villa, comfortable rooms,
includes buffet breakfast, restaurant, nice
sun roof, English spoken.

$$$-$$ La Casa Sol
Calama 127 y 6 de Diciembre, T02-223 0798,
www.lacasasol.com.

Attractive small hotel with courtyard, very
helpful, English and French spoken, also
run **Casa Sol** in Peguche near Otavalo.
Recommended.

$$ El Arupo
Rodríguez E7-22 y Reina Victoria, T02-
255 7543, www.hostalelarupo.com.
Good hotel, cooking facilities, English and
French spoken. Recommended. One of
several *hostales* in the same block of this
tree-lined, semi-pedestrian street.

$$-$ Casa Helbling
Veintimilla E8-152 y 6 de Diciembre,
T02-256 5740, www.casahelbling.de.
Very good, popular hostel, spotless,
breakfast extra, private or shared bath,
also 6-bed dorm, laundry and
cooking facilities, English and German
spoken, pleasant atmosphere, reliable
information, luggage storage, parking.
Highly recommended.

$$-$ Posada del Maple
Rodríguez E8-49 y 6 de Diciembre, T02-
254 4507, www.posadadelmaple.com.
Popular hostel, private or shared bath, also
8-bed dorm (US$9 pp), cooking facilities,
warm atmosphere, free tea and coffee.

$ Casona de Mario
Andalucía 213 y Galicia (La Floresta), T02-
254 4036, www.casonademario.com.

Popular hostel, shared bath, laundry facilities, no breakfast, well-equipped kitchen, parking, sitting room, nice garden, book exchange, long-stay discounts, Argentine owner. Repeatedly recommended.

$ El Cafecito
Cordero E6-43 y Reina Victoria,
T02-223 0922, www.cafecito.net.
Popular with backpackers, cheaper in dorm (US$9.50, shared bath), 2 small rooms with bath, breakfast extra, good café with coffee from owner's own Finca Maputo (you can learn about the full process), meals including soups, pizza, salads, sandwiches, relaxed atmosphere, volunteer opportunities. Also has art exhibitions and good music.

Quito suburbs

$$$$ Hacienda Rumiloma
Obispo Díaz de La Madrid, T02-254 8206,
www.rumiloma.com.
Luxurious hotel in a 40-ha hacienda on the slopes of Pichincha. Sumptuous suites with lots of attention to detail, lounges with antiques, good restaurant, bar with fireplace, spa, nice views, personalized attention from owners, ideal for a luxurious escape not far from the city.

$$$ Hostería San Jorge
Km 4 via antigua Quito–Nono, to the
west of Av Mariscal Sucre, T02-339 0403,
www.eco-lodgesanjorge.com.
Converted 18th-century hacienda on an 80-ha private reserve on the slopes of Pichincha, full board available, good pricey restaurant, heating, pool, sauna and jacuzzi, horse riding and birdwatching. Operates 7 nature reserves and offers bird and wildlife photography tours in many different ecosystems. 5- to 18-day packages available.

Near the airport
Tababela
There are several places to stay in the town and a good place to eat before a flight is **Bella Italia** (24 de Septiembre, T09-8585 5753), Italian-owned, great pizza, pasta and gnocchi.

$$ Hostería San Carlos
Justo Cuello Oe1-245 y Maldonado, T02-359
9057, www.hosteriasancarlostababela.com.
Hacienda-style inn with ample grounds, spacious rooms, 2 standards, breakfast included, other meals in restaurant, pool and waterslide, jacuzzi, airport transfers US$5 pp.

$$ Quito Airport Suites
Alfonso Tobar 971 y Tulio Guzmán, 1 block
from the plaza, T02-359 9110 or T09-8889
9774, airporthotelquito.com.
Room price includes breakfast which can be a box breakfast in case of an early departure, good dinner extra, English spoken; free phone calls to US or Canada, will print boarding passes etc. Rooms available for day use between flights ($); luggage storage US$1 per case, per day, available to non-guests US$2; long-term parking; airport transfers US$5.

$$-$ Chester's Pizzería and B&B
29 de Abril E1-53 y 24 de Septiembre, T02-
359 9044, www.chesterspizzas.com.
A popular place either to stay or to have a pizza and hang out while waiting for a flight.

$$-$ Hostal Colibrí
Pje Tobías Trujillo, 3 blocks downhill from the
Tababela plaza, T02-215 0100, or 09-9547
0312, www.hostalcolibriaeropuerto.com.
Quite rustic place with "tiny suites", private rooms and dorm (US$15 pp), includes breakfast, dinner extra, garden with pool and jacuzzi, plenty of information, also arrange excursions; airport transfers US$8 for 2 passengers.

Quito airport: how to get there and where to stay

There are three access roads to **Mariscal Sucre Airport**: the most direct from the city centre is the **Ruta Viva** which starts on Avenida Simón Bolívar (the inner eastern ring road) and goes through the suburbs of Cumbayá, Tumbaco and Puembo. The **Vía Interoceánica** originates in Plaza Argentina, northeast of La Mariscal, and goes through the Oswaldo Guayasamín tunnel before heading east to join the Ruta Viva beyond Tumbaco; the joint route then merges with the E-35 highway at **Pifo** and, at the airport roundabout (with the World Mirror statue), turns north 7 km to the airport. The third road is the **Vía Collas**, a dual-carriageway which heads south about 2 km past the Oyacoto toll booth on the Panamericana, north of Quito beyond Calderón.

Where to stay

The Wyndham Quito Airport ($$$$ www.wyndham.com) luxury hotel is 500 m from the airport terminal and is reported as good. Some five minutes from the airport by its own shuttle is Hotel Alpachaca ($$ Conector Alpachaca, just off airport road, T02-309 5014, Facebook: hotelalpachaca.quitoairport, meals available). At the World Mirror roundabout is the EB Hotel ($$$ Eurobuilding, www.ebhotels.com), eight minutes away.

Towns near the airport with accommodation include:
Tababela, access road at the World Mirror roundabout on highway E-35, 10 minutes from the airport (airport taxi US$10).
Pifo by the junction of the E-35 and the Ruta Viva/Vía Interoceánica, also about 10 minutes from the airport (taxi US$10). This is the best place for bus connections (see below).
Puembo, on the opposite side of the highway to Pifo, is 20 minutes from the airport (taxi US$10-15).
Oyambarillo, southeast of the airport off the E-35, is 10 minutes away (taxi US$10).

See main listings for hotels in these towns. There are places to eat in Tababela and Puembo and a food court in the shopping area opposite the airport.

Getting there

Regional buses to the airport and to **Pifo, Puembo** and **El Quinche** go from the Terminal Río Coca (on the Ecovía system). For **Tababela** town, get out at the World Mirror roundabout and take a taxi (US$1). Taxi drivers may not be familiar with the hotels in these towns, so print the hotel's map before travelling, or arrange transport with the hotel itself.

If going to the airport from other cities, take a bus that bypasses Quito along highway E-35. The **Cita** bus company runs Ambato–Ibarra 12 times a day via Pifo (terminal A Gangotena 605 e Ignacio Jarrín, T02-238 2096, www.transportescita.com), Pifo–Ambato, three hours, US$3.80; Pifo–Ibarra, 2½ hours US$3.10. **Expreso Baños** (A Gangotena 242 y D Vásquez Cépeda, Pifo, T02-238 2742) has three buses a day Baños-Pifo–Ibarra, four a day Ibarra–Pifo–Baños (Pifo–Ibarra US$3.15, two hours; Pifo–Baños US$5, four hours). If coming from the east (Papallacta, Baeza or Oriente), go to Pifo and transfer to another bus or taxi there.

Puembo

$$$$-$$$ Casa de Hacienda Su Merced
Julio Tobar Donoso 12, Chiche Obraje,
Puembo, T02-389 5351, www.sumerced.com.
Beautifully refurbished 18th-century hacienda
house, well-appointed rooms with bathtubs
and individual decor and hand-painted
linen, also has small family house to rent
($$$$), includes traditional breakfast, other
meals available on request in restaurant,
immaculate gardens, peaceful, airport
transfers US$5, can arrange trips into Quito.

Also in Puembo are the large, group- and
conference-oriented **Rincón de Puembo**
(in town, M Burbano N6-66 y F Ruiz, T02-239
1106, www.rincondepuembo.com) and **San
José de Puembo** (M Burbano s/n, T02-239
0264, http://sanjosedepuembo.com; based
at an hacienda, 4 ha of gardens), both **$$$$-
$$**, with restaurants, pools, activities, airport
and city transfers, both have wheelchair-
accessible rooms.

Elsewhere

$$$ Casa de Hacienda La Jimenita
1.2 km from highway in Pifo, T02-238 0253,
www.haciendajimenita.com.
In a renovated hacienda on 9-ha private
reserve on the canyon of the Río Chiche/
Chupahuayco, 15-20 mins from airport.
Rooms all styled differently, local
furnishings, sustainable practices, works
with communities, organic food, no TV but
Wi-Fi in rooms. Has an Inca tunnel, 97-m
long, 30-m deep, good birdwatching.

$$$ Posada Mirolindo
Lizardo Vega s/n y C Línea Férrea,
San José de Oyambarillo, T02-215 0363,
www.posadamirolindo.com.
Pleasant rooms and cottages, includes
transfers to and from the airport, breakfast
provided, other meals on request.

Eating out in Quito is excellent, varied
and increasingly cosmopolitan. There
are many elegant restaurants offering
Ecuadorean and international food, as
well as small simple places serving set
meals for US$2.50-5, the latter close by
early evening and on Sun.

Colonial Quito

Many restaurants serving economical
almuerzos (set lunches) post their daily
menu at the entrance; look for them along
Calles Benalcázar, García Moreno, Guayaquil
and Espejo.

$$$ El Ventanal
Carchi y Nicaragua, west of the Basílica,
in Parque San Juan, take a taxi to the
parking area and a staff member will
accompany you along a footpath to
the restaurant, T02-257 2232, www.el
ventanal.ec. Tue-Sat 1300-1500, 1800-2230.
International nouvelle cuisine with a varied
menu including a number of seafood
dishes, fantastic views over the city.

$$$ La Casa de los Geranios
Morales Oe1-134, T02-295 6035, www.
casalosgeranios.com.ec. Mon-Thu 0900-
0000, Fri-Sat 0900-0200, Sun 1000-2200.
Upscale *comida típica*, in a nicely restored
La Ronda house.

$$$ Octava de Corpus
Junín E2-167 y Ortiz, T02-295 2989,
octavadecorpus@yahoo.com. Mon-Sat for
lunch and dinner, reservation essential.
For an out-of-the-ordinary treat, this one-
man band of a restaurant serves à la carte
dishes from a menu of fish, seafood and
meat with organic vegetables and herbs, no
fats used, in a remarkable house crammed
full of artworks, fine glass and cutlery. Also
has a wine *cava*, mostly Argentine.

$$$ Theatrum
Plaza del Teatro, 2nd floor of Teatro Sucre,
T02-257 1011, www.theatrum.com.ec. Mon-Fri
1200-1500, 1800-2300, Sat-Sun 1800-2300.
Good Ecuadorean cuisine (seafood a
speciality) in the city's most important
theatre, excellent service, free transport.

$$$-$$ Hasta la Vuelta, Señor
Pasaje Arzobispal (Chile Oe4-56 y Venezuela),
3rd floor, T02-258 0887, https://hastalavuelta.
com. Mon-Sat 1100-2300, Sun 1100-2100.
A *fonda quiteña* perched on an indoor balcony
with *comida típica* and snacks, try *empanadas*
(pasties) or a *seco de chivo* (goat stew). Also
at La Niña E6-13 in La Mariscal. (There are
other places to eat in this smart little mall.)

$$ Vista Hermosa
Mejía Oe4-45 y García Moreno, T02-295 1401,
http://vistahermosa.ec. Mon-Sat 1300-2400,
Sun 1200-2000.
Good meals, drinks, pizza, live music
at weekends, lovely terrace-top views;
there is a lift up to the restaurant.

$$-$ San Ignacio
García Moreno N2-60, at Museo María
Agusta Urrutia, T02-258 4173, see Facebook.
Mon-Tue 0800-2100, Wed-Sat 0800-2200,
Sun 0800-1600.
Excellent popular set lunch (US$4.50) with
a choice of dishes and buffet salad bar;
à la carte in the evening.

$ Govindas
Esmeraldas Oe3-119 y Venezuela, T09-
9193 4095, Facebook: Govindas Quito.
Mon-Sat 0800-1800.
Vegetarian dishes, good-value economical
set lunch and à la carte snacks, also breakfast
and yoga and cultural centre.

Cafés

El Palomar
García Moreno N9-59 y Oriente, T09-9191
2587, Facebook: ElPalomarChocolateria.
Mon-Sat 1500-2100.

Café serving chocolate to eat and drink,
coffee, teas, juices, sandwiches and desserts
in a colonial house.

Heladería San Agustín
Guayaquil N5-59 y Chile. Mon-Fri 1000-1730,
Sat-Sun 1030-1600.
Coffee, traditional home-made cakes, ices
and lunch, a Quito tradition since 1858.

Modern Quito
There are at least 25 restaurants ($$$-$$)
and cafés within a block of Plaza Foch.
There are many restaurants serving good
economical set lunches along both Pinto
and Foch, between Amazonas and Cordero.
A number of restaurants can be found in
La Floresta, east of La Mariscal, near Parque
La Carolina and along Av Eloy Alfaro, some
of which fall outside the scope of our map.
Also in La Floresta, in Parque Navarro at
Ladrón de Guevara y Lérida, stalls sell local
food every evening, *fritadas*, *tortillas*, *sopas*
and other dishes, all about US$3-4.

$$$ Carmine
Catalina Aldaz N34-208 y Portugal, T02-
333 2829, www.carmineristorante.com.
Mon-Sat 1200-2300, Sun 1230-1700.
Creative international and Italian gourmet
cuisine, exclusive and very expensive.

$$$ Chez Jérôme
Whymper N30-96 y Coruña, T02-223 4067,
www.chezjeromerestaurante.com.
Mon-Fri 1230-1500, 1930-2300.
Excellent traditional and modern French
cuisine, with local ingredients, good
ambiance and service.

$$$ Il Risotto
Eloy Alfaro N34-447 y Portugal, T02-224 6852
7, see Facebook. Mon-Fri 1130-1530, 1830-
2300, Sat 1130-2300, Sun 1130-2200.
Very popular and very good Italian cooking.
A Quito tradition.

$$$ La Briciola
Isabel la Católica y Salazar (esquina), T02-254 5157, www.labriciola.com.ec. Mon-Sat 1200-2300, Sun 1200-2200. Also in Cumbayá.
Extensive Italian menu, excellent food, very good personal service.

$$$ La Gloria
Valladolid N24-519 y Salazar, La Floresta, T02-252 7855, www.lagloria.com.ec. Mon-Fri 1230-2300, Sat-Sun 1200-1600.
Very innovative Peruvian and international cuisine, excellent food and service. Also has a terrace and bar.

$$$ San Telmo
Portugal 440 y Casanova, T02-225 6946, Facebook: santelmouio. Daily 1200-2300.
Good Argentine grill, seafood, pasta, pleasant atmosphere, great service.

$$$ Urko
Isabel La Católica N24-862 y Zaldumbide, T02-256 3180, www.urko.rest. Restaurant Tue-Sat 1300-1600, 1900-2300, tasting menus Thu-Sat 1900-2300.
Dishes and tasting menus derived from all 4 regions of the country, contemporary, imaginative use of local ingredients, English spoken.

$$$ Zazu
Mariano Aguilera 331 y La Pradera, T02-254 3559, www.zazuquito.com. Mon-Fri 1130-1500, 1830-2300, Sat 1830-2300.
Very elegant and exclusive dining. International and Peruvian specialities, tasting menu US$70, extensive wine list, attentive service, reservations required.

$$$-$$ No Sé Pizzería Bar
Foch E5-24 y JL Mera, T09-9944 4817, Facebook: nosequito. Mon-Sat 1200-2400.
Pizzas and pastas, includes vegetarian and vegan options, salads, *menú del día* US$7.99, with terrace at the front, pleasant atmosphere.

$$ Chez Alain
Cordero E5-36 y JL Mera, T02-290 6204. Mon-Sat 1200-150, and Tue-Fri 1830-2200.
Choice of good 4-course set lunches, pleasant relaxed atmosphere, monthly dinner/show specials. Recommended.

$$ The Magic Bean
Foch E5-08 y JL Mera, daily 0800-2200, and Portugal y El Salvador, daily 0800-1730, T02-256 6181, http://magicbeanquito.com.
Fine coffees and natural food, more than 20 varieties of pancakes, good salads, large portions, outdoor seating.

$$ Mama Clorinda
Reina Victoria N24-150 (11-44) y Calama, T02-254 4362, www.restaurantemama clorinda.com. Daily 1100-2345.
Ecuadorean cuisine à la carte and set meals, filling, good value.

$$ Mr Bagel
Portugal E10-95 y 6 de Diciembre, Facebook: MisterBagelCoffeShop. Mon-Fri 0700-1500, Sat-Sun 0730-1500.
Very popular breakfast and lunch restaurant, 17 varieties of bagel and many spreads, sandwiches, soups, salads, desserts, also take away, Wi-Fi and book exchange.

$$ Pekín
Whymper N28-42 y Orellana, T02-223 5273, www.restaurante-pekin.com. Mon-Sat 1200-1530, 1800-2230, Sat closes 2200, Sun 1200-2000.
Excellent Chinese food, very pleasant atmosphere.

$$-$ El Hornero
Veintimilla 1149 y Amazonas, República de El Salvador 1047 y Naciones Unidas, González Suárez 1070 y Bejarano and other branches throughout the country, www. pizzeriaelhornero.com.ec. Daily 1100-2200.
Very good wood-oven pizzas, try one with *choclo* (fresh corn). Recommended.

$$-$ Las Palmeras
Japón N36-87 y Naciones Unidas, opposite Parque la Carolina, and 11 other branches, www.laspalmeras.com.ec. Mon-Thu 0900-1730, Fri-Sun 0830-1730.
Very good *comida Esmeraldeña*, try their hearty *viche de pescado* soup, outdoor tables, popular, good value. Recommended.

$$-$ Rincón Ecuatoriano Chileno
6 de Diciembre N28-30 y Belo Horizonte, T02-250 9462, Facebook: Rincon EcuatorianoChileno. Mon 1200-1800, Tue-Sat 1200-2000, Sun 1200-1700.
Good tasty home cooking, Chilean specialities including *empanadas*, large portions, efficient service, some tables in the back garden.

$$-$ Sakti
Carrión E4-144 y Amazonas, T02-252 0466, http://sakti-quito.com. Mon-Fri 0830-1730.
Good-quality vegetarian food, tasty healthy breakfast, daily specials, fruit juices, great desserts (also has a shop and rooms around a small garden, $$). Recommended.

$ Chandani Tandoori
JL Mera 1312 y Cordero, T02-222 1053. Mon-Thu 1100-2300, Fri 1100-0200, Sat 1300-0200.
Good authentic Indian cuisine, economical set meals, popular, good value. Recommended.

$ Yu Su
Colón E7-60 y Almagro, edif Torres de Almagro, T02-223 5001, see Facebook. Mon-Sat 1200-1600, 1800-2100.
Very good sushi bar, pleasant, Korean-run, takeaway service.

Cafés

Ethnic Coffee
Amazonas entre Robles y Roca, Edif Hotel Mercure, local 3, www.ethniccollection.com. Mon-Fri 0930-2100.
Nice popular café with gourmet coffee as well as a wide range of desserts, meals ($$) and drinks.

Kallari
Wilson E4-266 y JL Mera, T02-223 6009, www.kallari.com.ec. Open 0900-1800.
Fairtrade café, breakfast, snacks, salad and sandwich set lunches, organic coffee and chocolate, crafts, run by an association of farmers and artisans from the Province of Napo working on rainforest and cultural conservation.

Sweet & Coffee
This chain of coffees shops has branches throughout the city (and the country), selling coffee sourced from Ecuadorean growers, snacks and cakes; works with disabled people.

Quito suburbs
The plaza in Cumbayá is surrounded by restaurants and the town is a popular place for Sun lunch. Between Cumbayá and Tumbaco is the the Scala shopping centre, with a good food court, including a branch of the Colombian Crepes y Waffles.

Bars and clubs

Colonial Quito
In the old city, much of the nightlife is concentrated along La Ronda.

Bandidos
Olmedo E1-136 y Cevallos, T02-228 6504, http://bandidobrewing.com. Mon-Fri 1600-2300, Sat 1400-2300.
Very popular pub, partly housed in an old chapel, serves a choice of excellent microbrews and snacks.

Modern Quito

Bungalow Six
Almagro N24-139 y Calama, Facebook: Bungalow6. Wed-Sat 2000-0300.
US-style sports bar and club. Popular place to hang out and watch a game or a film, dancing later on, varied music,

covercharge, ladies' night on Wed, different themes other nights.

Cafelibro
L Plaza N23-56 entre Veintimilla y Wilson, T02-250 3214, www.cafelibro.com. Tue-Sat, lunch served 1230-1430, evening events and classes at different times – see website.
Well-established spot for music, tango (including classes), dancing, talks and exhibitions. Lunch costs US$5; for other events prices vary.

Cherusker
Pinto E7-85 y Diego de Almagro, T02-601 2142, http://cherusker.com. Mon 1600-2400, Tue-Wed 1500-2400, Thu-Sat 1200-0200.
Various microbrews and German food. Also has a branch in Baños.

Finn McCool's
Almagro N24-64 y Pinto, T02-252 1780, www.irishpubquito.com. Mon-Wed 1200-0100, Thu 1200-0300, Fri-Sat 1100-0300, Sun 1100-1900.
Irish-run pub, Irish and international food, darts, pool, table football, sports on TV, Wi-Fi, popular meeting place.

La Juliana
Av 12 de Octubre N24-722 y Coruña, T02-604 1569, www.lajuliana.com.ec. Fri-Sat 2100-0300.
Popular club, live music, Latin, urban, DJ sets.

No Bar
Calama E4-381 y JL Mera, T02-254 5145, Facebook: nobarquito. Wed-Sat 2000-0300.
Good mix of Latin and Euro dance music, busy at weekends. Nightly specials on drinks, see Facebook.

Turtle's Head
La Niña 626 y JL Mera, T02-256 5544, Facebook: TurtlesHeadQuito. Mon-Wed 1600-2345, Thu-Sat 1600-0200.
Microbrews, fish and chips, curry, pool table, darts, fun atmosphere.

Entertainment

There are always many cultural events taking place in Quito, especially at fiesta times and often free of charge. Ask around as few are widely publicized.

Cinema
There are several multiplexes, eg **Cinemark**, www.cinemark.com.ec, and **Multicines**, www.multicines.com.ec.
Casa de la Cultura, *Av 6 de Diciembre N16-224 y Patria, T02-290 2272, http://www.cinematecaecuador.com.* Shows foreign films, often has documentaries, film festivals, free.
Ocho y Medio, *Valladolid N24-353 y Vizcaya, La Floresta, T02-290 4720, www.ochoymedio.net.* Cinema and café, good for art films. Ticket office Tue-Sun 1500-2100, tickets US$5.

Dance
Casa de la Danza, *Junín E2-186 y Javier Gutiérrez, Parque San Marcos in colonial city, T02-295 5445, www.casadeladanza.org.* Run by the well-known Ecuadorean dancer Susana Reyes, this is the venue for dance festivals and events. Also has **Museo del Danzante**, an exhibit about Ecuadorean folk dance, and hosts other exhibits and folk dance presentations on Thu or Sat night. Enquire ahead.

Dance schools 1-to-1 or group lessons are offered for US$4-6 per hr.
Ritmo Tropical, *Amazonas N24-155 y Calama, T02-255 7094, www.ritmotropicalsalsa.com.* Salsa, capoeira, merengue, tango and more.
Salsa y Merengue School, *Foch E4-256 y Amazonas, T09-9880 5372, Facebook: tropicaldancing.* Also cumbia.

Ecuadorean folk ballet Ballet Andino Humanizarte (Casa 707, Morales 707, La Ronda, T09-8750 0595, see Facebook, Fri-Sat 2130, US$5), plays and comedies are also often in their repertoire, restaurant on the premises. **Jacchigua** (at **Teatro**

Demetrio Aguilera Malta, Casa de la Cultura, 6 de Diciembre y Patria, T02-295 2025, www.jacchigua.org. Wed at 1930). Entertaining, colourful and touristy, reserve ahead, US$35, see website for offers, dinner and transfers. Other dance groups highlighting Ecuadorean traditions and folklore are **Saruymanda** (T02-295 5445, www.saruymanda.com) and **Danzando Tierra** (at Casona del Centro de Desarrollo Comunitario de San Marcos, T09-9574 9756, Facebook: danzandotierraquito).

Literature
Centro Cultural Benjamín Carrión, *Jorge Washington E2-42 y Ulpiano Páez, T02-222 1895, www.ccbenjamincarrion.com (opposite Cultura Manor).* For literary events, meetings with authors, exhibitions and conferences.

Music
Classical The **Orquesta Sinfónica Nacional** (T02-250 2815), performs at **Teatro Sucre**, **Casa de la Música**, **Teatro Escuela Politécnica Nacional**, **Teatro México**, in the colonial churches and regionally. **Casa de la Música** (Valderrama N32-307 y Mariana de Jesús, T02-226 1965, www.casadelamusica. ec), concerts by the Orquesta Sinfónica Nacional, Orquesta Filarmónica del Ecuador, Orquesta de Instrumentos Andinos and invited performers. Excellent acoustics.

Folk Folk music is popular in *peñas* which come alive after 2230:
Ñucanchi, *Av Universitaria Oe5-188 y Armero, T02-254 0967, Facebook: niucanchi. Fri-Sat 1945-0245.* Ecuadorean and other music, including Latin dance later in the night, entry US$7.50-15.

Theatre
Agora (open-air theatre), **Teatro Nacional** (large) and **Prometeo** (informal), all at Casa de la Cultura, stage plays and concerts. For upcoming events, see www.casadelacultura.gob.ec.

Patio de Comedias, *18 de Septiembre E4-26 entre Av Amazonas y 9 de Octubre, T02-256 1902, Facebook: teatropatiodecomedias.* Plays, stand-up, performance art and children's events, Wed-Sat 1830-2030, Sun 1700-1830. Also has dancing and a restaurant, Creperola del Teatro, which is open in the day.
Teatro Bolívar, *Espejo Oe243 y Guayaquil, T02-257 1911, www.teatrobolivar.org.* Reopening after restoration, tours available, tickets available online or at box office Mon-Fri 0900-1730.
Teatro Sucre, *at Plaza del Teatro, T02-295 1661, www.teatrosucre.org (includes programme).* Beautifully restored 19th-century building, the city's classical theatre.

Festivals

New Year Años Viejos: life-size puppets satirize politicians and others. At midnight on 31 Dec a will is read, the legacy of the outgoing year, and the puppets are burnt; good at Av Amazonas, where a competition is held, very entertaining and good humoured. On New Year's Day everything is shut.
6 Jan (may be moved to the weekend) Colourful **Inocentes** procesion from Plaza de Santo Domingo at 1700.
8 Mar International Women's Day, marks the start of **Mujeres en la Danza**, a week-long international dance festival organized by Casa de la Danza, see above.
Mar-Apr Música Sacra, a 10-day religious music festival is held before and during Easter week. **Palm Sunday**, colourful procession from the Basílica, 0800-1000. The solemn **Good Friday** processions are most impressive.
24 May Independence, commemorating the Battle of Pichincha in 1822 with early morning cannon-fire and parades. Everything closes.
Aug Agosto Arte y Cultura (El Mes de los Artes), organized by the municipality, daily cultural events, dance and music in different places throughout the city.

1-6 Dec **Día de Quito**. The city's main festival celebrated, commemorates the foundation of the city with elaborate parades, bullfights, performances and music in the streets, very lively. Hotels charge extra, everything except a few restaurants shuts on 6 Dec.

25 Dec Foremost among **Christmas** celebrations is the **Misa del Gallo**, midnight Mass. Nativity scenes can be admired in many public places.

Shopping

Shops open generally 0900-1900 on weekdays, some close at midday and most shut Sat afternoon and Sun. Shopping centres are open at weekends. In modern Quito much of the shopping is done in malls. Be aware that over Christmas, Quito is crowded and the streets are packed with vendors and shoppers. For purchasing maps see Practicalities, page 389.

Bookshops

The following have a selection of books in English:

Confederate Books, *Amazonas N24-155 y Calama, upstairs, www.confederatebooks.com.* Used books.

Libri Mundi, *Urbanización San José del Valle, 2 Transversal, lote 121, T02-382 4190, Facebook: LibrimundiEC, has shops at Quicentro Shopping, other malls and the airport.*

Mr Books, *Mall El Jardín, p3 and Scala and El Condado shopping centres, www. mrbooks.com.*

The English Bookshop, *Venezuela N8-42 y Manabí, see Facebook.* Used books sales and exchange, new book rental; other languages too.

Camping

Camping gas is available in many of the shops listed below, white gas is not.

Aventura Sport, *Quicentro Shopping, loc 18, T02-292 4372, http://aventurasport.ec.* Tents, good selection of glacier sunglasses,

Ecuadorean and imported outdoor clothing and gear.

Equipos Cotopaxi, *Zaruma S9-80 Caranqui, T02 252 6725, http://equiposcotopaxi.com. Stocks the same products as Aventura Sport, see above.*

Explorer, *Plaza Foch and all main shopping centres in the city, www.explorer-ecuador.com.* Clothing and equipment for adventure sports.

Mono Dedo, *Rafael León Larrea N24-36 y Coruña, La Floresta, T02-290 4496, www. monodedoecuador.com.* Climbing equipment. Part of a rock climbing club, lessons.

Tatoo, *Av de los Granados y 6 de Diciembre and CC Scala in Cumbayá, www.tatoo.ws. Daily from 1000.* Quality backpacks and outdoor clothing.

Chocolate

Ecuador has exported its fine cacao to the most prestigious chocolatiers around the world for over 100 years. Today, quality chocolate is on offer in specialized shops and food stores.

Cacao & Cacao, *JL Mera N21-241 y Roca, T02-222 4951, plus 3 shops, http://cacaoshopcacao. com.* Shop and café featuring many brands of Ecuadorean chocolate and coffee.

Galería Ecuador, *Reina Victoria N24-263 y García, http://galeriaecuador.com.* Shop and café featuring Ecuadorean gourmet organic coffee and chocolate as well as some crafts.

Kallari, *see Modern Quito, Cafés, page 65.*

Pacari, *Zaldumbide N24-676 y Miravalle, www.pacarichocolate.com.* Factory outlet for one of the most highly regarded manufacturers. They have won more international chocolate awards than any other company in the world. Also have an organic products market on Tue.

República del Cacao, *Venezuela N5-44 y Chile; Reina Victoria y Pinto, Plaza Foch; Morales Oe1-166, La Ronda, El Jardín and Scala malls and at the airport, www.republica delcacao.com.* Chocolate boutique and café, also sell Panama hats. The Venezuela

N5-44 branch in the coloial city has a Museo del Cacao with tours and guided tastings (US$5). It also has chocolate-making classes, US$80 per group.

Handicrafts

There are controls on export of arts and crafts: unless they are obviously new handicrafts, you may have to get a permit from the **Instituto Nacional de Patrimonio Cultural** (Colón Oe1-93 y 10 de Agosto, T02-254 3527, http://patrimoniocultural.gob.ec, offices also in other cities) before you can mail or take things home; permits take time.

A wide selection can be found at the **Mercado Artesanal La Mariscal** (Jorge Washington, between Reina Victoria and JL Mera, daily 1000-1800), interesting and worthwhile.

At weekends, crafts are sold in stalls at **Parque El Ejido**, and along the **Av Patria** side of this park artists sell their paintings. There are souvenir shops on **García Moreno** in front of the Palacio Presidencial and crafts and art shops along **La Ronda** (see Colonial Quito, page 43), which has a collective of traditional artisans called Manos en La Ronda (see Facebook, open 1000-1800), which groups together jewellers, cabinet makers (José Luis Jiménez), toy makers (Zabala), artists and foods such as chocolate, honey (Api Real) and ice cream (Dulce Placer).

Recommended shops with an ample selection are:

Camari, Marchena Oe2-38 y Versalles, T02254 9407, www.camari.org. Fairtrade shop run by an artisan organization.

Colaciones Cruz Verde, Bolívar Oe8-97 y Chimborazo, T02-295 6654, Facebook: colcruzverdeuio1915, closed Sun. A little shop selling traditional, sugar-based sweets which have been made the same way for over 100 years.

EBD Carmal, Amazonas N24-126 y Foch, T09-9780 8098, www.ebdcarmal.com. Panama and fedora hats.

Ethnic Collection, Amazonas y R Hotel Mercure, www.ethniccollect Wide variety of clothing, leathe jewellery and ceramic items. Also ca 2 doors south.

Folklore, Colón E10-53 y Caamaño, T02-256 3085, Facebook: olgafisch. The store of the late Olga Fisch, who for decades encouraged craftspeople to excel. Attractive selection of top-quality, pricey handicrafts and rugs. Small museum upstairs includes a very good collection of pre-Columbian ceramics.

Galería Latina, JL Mera 823 y Veintimilla. Daily 1000-1900, Sun 1100-1800. Fine selection of alpaca and other handicrafts from Ecuador, Peru and Bolivia, visiting artists sometimes demonstrate their work.

Hilana, 6 de Diciembre N23-10 y Veintimilla, Mon-Fri 0900-1900, Sat 1000-1300. Beautiful unique 100% wool blankets, ponchos and clothing with Ecuadorean motifs, also cotton garnments, excellent quality.

Kallari. Crafts from Oriente at the café, page 65.

K Dorfzaun. Fine Panama hats are sold at the **República del Cacao** shops, see under Chocolate, above.

Mindalae. Nice crafts are sold at the museum, page 51.

Productos Andinos, Urbina 111 y Cordero, T02-222 4565. Artisan's co-op, good selection, unusual items.

Saucisa, Amazonas N22-118 y Veintimilla, T02-222 4174, Facebook: SaucisaTienda. Very good place to buy Andean music and instruments.

Jewellery

Ariu, Bolívar Oe6-33 y Benalcázar, Plaza San Francisco, T02-228 4157, see Facebook. Daily 1000-1800. Fine silver with ancestral motifs.

Taller Guayasamín, at the Capilla del Hombre, see page 51. Jewellery with native designs.

Birdwatching and nature

The following are specialized operators:
Andean Birding, www.andeanbirding.com;
Birdsexplore, www.exploraves.com;
Ecuador Experience, part of Nature
Experience, www.nature-experience-group.
com (in French); **Mindo Bird Tours**, www.
mindobirdtours.com; **Neblina Forest**,
www.neblinaforest.com; **Real Nature**,
www.realnaturetravel.com. Local birding
guides are also available in Mindo.

City tours

Quito Tour Bus, *T02-245 8010, www.
quitotourbus.com*. Tours on double-decker
bus, stops at 11 places of interest, it starts
and ends at Av Naciones Unidas, south side.
You can start at any stop along the route
and can alight at a site and continue later
on another bus. Hourly, 0900-1600, 3-hr
ride, US$15, children and seniors US$7.50,
ticket valid all day. Night tour Fri, Sat and
holidays at 1900, US$15, with a 1½-hr stop at
La Ronda. Mitad del Mundo and Pululahua
tour, daily 1200, US$30, children and seniors
US$20, includes museum entrance fees,
7 hrs. They also offer daily tours to Nayón
adventure park (US$55) and weekly tours to
Otavalo, Cotopaxi, Papallacta and Quilotoa
(US$60-70). Reservations required; see
website for details including points of sale;
also buy online.

A **Ruta Turística** walking tour of historic
buildings in the colonial city, led by English-
or French-speaking officers of the Policía
Metropolitana, starts at the Plaza de la
Independencia El Quinde Visitors Centre,
Venezuela y Espejo, T02-257 2445. It is called
Ruta de Fachadas, 2 hrs, US$8.50. Reserve
24 hrs in advance from 0900-1400, minimum
of 2 passengers required. **Quito Eterno**
(www.quitoeterno.org) a programme
rescuing the city's identity, offers tours in
which Quito's legendary characters guide

you through their city, most on Sat 1900-
2000, US$8-10.

Climbing, trekking and walking

The following Quito operators specialize
in this area, most also offer conventional
tours and sell Galápagos and jungle tours.
Note that no one may climb without a
licensed guide employed by an authorized
agency. Independent climbers and guides
are refused entry to national parks, but
exceptions may be made for internationally
(UIAA) certified guides and members of
Ecuadorian climbing clubs. The **Asociación
Ecuatoriana de Guías de Montaña
(ASEGUIM)** is at Cordero E12-22 e Isabel
La Católica, p12c, T02-254 0599, https://
aseguim.org.

Campus Adventures, *Joaquina Vargas 99 y
A Calderón, Conocoto, T02-234 0601,
www.campus-trekking.com*. Good-value
trekking, climbing and cultural tours, 8- to
15-day biking trips, tailor-made itineraries.
Also run **Hostería Pantaví**, near Ibarra;
8 languages spoken.

Climbing Tours, *Amazonas N21-221 y
Roca, T02-381 4960, www.climbingtour.com*.
Climbing, trekking and other adventure
sports, also tours to regional attractions,
jungle tours and Galápagos. Well-
established operator.

Condor Trekk, *Reina Victoria N24-281
y J Rodríguez, T02-222 6004, www.
condortrekkexpeditions.com*. Climbing,
trekking and fishing trips, 4WD transport,
equipment rentals and sales.

Cotopaxi Cara Sur, *contact Eduardo Agama,
T09-9800 2681, eagamaz@gmail.com*. Offers
climbing and trekking tours, runs **Refugio
Cotopaxi Cara Sur** (see Facebook).

Gulliver, *Foch E738 y Reina Victoria, T02-
252 9297, https://gulliver.com.ec, Mon-Fri
0830-1730*. Climbing and trekking and
a wide range of economical adventure
and traditional tours. Operate **Hosterías
PapaGayo** at Cotopaxi and in Quito.

High Summits, *Pinto E5-29 y JL Mera, p2, T02-254 9358, www.climbing-ecuador.com.* Climbing specialists for over 40 years, Swiss/Ecuadorean-run.

Latitud 0°, *Mallorca N24-500 y F Salazar, La Floresta, T02-254 7921, www.latitud0.com.* Climbing specialists, German spoken.

Original Ecuador, *Av Francisco de Orellana E6-07 y El Ceibo, Cumbayá, T02-204 1684, or 09-9554 5821, www.originalecuador.com.* Runs 1- to 7-day highland tours which involve walking several hours daily, land-based tours in the Galápagos, also custom-made itineraries.

TribuTrek, *Llano Chico Pasaje B 456 y Espejo, T09-9282 5404, http://tributrek.com.* Hiking and trekking, cultural and budget tours.

Cycling and mountain biking

Quito has many bike paths and bike lanes on city streets, but mind the traffic and aggressive drivers. The city organizes a *ciclopaseo*, a cycle day, every Sun 0800-1400. Key avenues are closed to vehicular traffic and thousands of cyclists cross the city in 29 km from north to south. This and other cycle events are run by **Fundación Ciclópolis** (Queseras del Medio E11-253 y Andalucía, T02-604 2079, Facebook: ciclopolis.ecuador). Rentals from **La Casa del Ciclista** (República 770 y Eloy Alfaro, near the *ciclopaseo* route, T02-254 2852, Facebook: Lacasadelciclistaecuador, US$3 per hr, US$12 per day) and **Cicleadas El Rey** at **El Cafecito** (see Where to stay, page 60), Facebook: CicleadasElRey, from US$8. If staying a long time in the city, sign up with **BiciQuito** (www.biciquito.gob.ec), to use their bikes stationed throughout town. **Biciacción** (www.biciaccion.org), has information about routes in the city and organizes trips outside Quito.

Mountain bike tours Many operators offer bike tours, the following are specialists:
Aries, *in Barrio La Libertad on road to Pifo,*

T02-389 5712, or 09-9981 6603, w bikecompany.com. 1-day tours provided. Also has a cabin for

Biking Dutchman, *La Pinta E-731 y Reina Victoria, T02-256 8323, after hours T09-9420 5349, www.bikingdutchman.com.* 1- and several-day tours, great fun, good food, very well organized, English, German and Dutch spoken, pioneers in mountain biking in Ecuador.

Horse riding

Horse-riding tours are offered on Pichincha above the gate of the TelefériQo (see page 51).

Green Horse Ranch, *see page 91.*
Ride Andes, *T09-9973 8221, www.rideandes. com.* Private and set date tours in the highlands including stays in haciendas, also in other South American countries.

Language courses

Andean Global Studies, *www.andean globalstudies.org.*
Beraca, *www.beracaspanishschool.com.*
Cristóbal Colón, *www.colonspanish school.com.*
Equinox, *www.ecuadorspanish.com.*
Instituto Superior, *www.superior spanishschool.com.*
La Lengua, *http://la-lengua.com.*
Sintaxis, *www.sintaxis.net.*
South American, *http://spanishschool southamerican.com.*
Universidad Católica, *T02-299 1700 ext 1388, www.puce.edu.ec (go to Idiomas section, Español para extranjeros).* Group lessons.
Vida Verde, *www.vidaverde.com.*

Motorbiking

Freedom Bike Rental, *Finlandia N35-06 y Suecia, T02-600 4459, www.freedombikerental. com.* Motorcycle rentals US$95-225 per day, scooter US$35, good equipment, also 4WD rentals and mountain bikes US$25 per day, GPS, route planning, also guided and self-guided tours.

agliding

cuela Pichincha de Vuelo Libre, *Carlos Endara Oe3-60 y Amazonas, T02-225 6592 (office hours), T09-9993 1206, Facebook: parapentepichincha.* Offers complete courses for US$450 and tandem flights for US$65-US$105 (Pichincha).

Quito Paragliding, *T09-9830 8325, http://quitoparagliding.com.* Tandem flights, beginner and extension courses.

Tour operators

Most operators also sell Galápagos cruises and jungle tours.

Advantage Travel, *Gaspar de Villarroel N40-143, T02-336 0887, https://advantage-travel-ecuador.com.* Tours on the Anakonda and Manatee floating hotels on Río Napo and to Manatraya resort, Machalilla.

Adventure Journeys, *República E7-03 y Eloy Alfaro, of 307, T02-254 8293, www.adventurejourneys.com.* Adventure and traditional tours in Ecuador, the Galápagos and in Colombia and Peru.

Andando Tours, *Moreno Bellido E6-167 y Amazonas, T02-323 7330, https://visit galapagos.travel.* Operate the *Mary Anne* sailing vessel, *Anahi* catamaran, *Passion* motor yacht and others, as well as LGBT cruises and tours.

Andean Travel Company, *Guipuzcoa E13-117 y Lugo, La Floresta, T02-222 8385, www.andeantc.com.* Dutch/Ecuadorean-

Language schools

Quito is one of the most important centres for Spanish language study in Latin America with some 80 schools operating. There are also other schools around the country, including in Baños and Cuenca. There is a great variety to choose from. Identify your budget and goals for the course: rigorous grammatical and technical training, fluent conversation skills, getting to know Ecuadoreans or just enough basic Spanish to get you through your trip.

Visit a few places to get a feel for what they charge and offer. Prices vary greatly, from US$5 to US$22 per hour. There is also tremendous variation in teacher qualifications, infrastructure and resource materials. **Internacional de Español (IE)**, www.diplomaie. com, trains teachers who offer tuition in Spanish as a second language and maintains a list of qualified schools and teachers. Schools usually offer courses of four to seven hours per day. Many readers suggest that four hours is enough. Some schools have packages which combine teaching in the morning and tours in the afternoon, others combine teaching with travel throughout the country. A great deal of emphasis has traditionally been placed on one-to-one teaching, but a well-structured small classroom setting is also recommended.

The quality of homestays offered as part of language study packages likewise varies. The cost including half board is US$16-20 per day (more for full board). Try to book just one week at first to see how a place suits you. For language courses as well as homestays, deal directly with the people who will provide services to you, avoid intermediaries and always get a detailed receipt.

If you are short on time it can be a good idea to make your arrangements from home, either directly with one of the schools or through an agency, who can offer you a wide variety of options. If you have more time and less money, then it may be more economical to organize your own studies after you arrive. See What to do, page 71, for schools in Quito.

owned operator, wide range of tours including trekking and cruises on the *Nemo I* catamaran and *San José* and *Odyssey* motor yachts and *Treasure of the Galápagos* catamaran.

Andes Overland, *Santa Fe N43-106 y Río Coca, T02-512 3358, www.andesoverland. com*. A 72-day tour through Bolivia, Peru, Ecuador and Colombia, offered with 2 levels of comfort, which you can join or leave at any point. Part of an international group, which guarantees departure.

Creter Tours, *Pinto E5-29 y JL Mera, T02-254 5491, www.cretertours.com.ec*. Offers cruises on several mid- and upper-class yachts and catamarans in the Galápagos, also a wide range tours on Ecuador mainland and in South America.

Dracaena, *Pinto E4-375 y Amazonas, T02-290 6644, www.amazondracaena.com*. Runs good budget jungle tours to **Nicky Lodge** in Cuyabeno, 4- to 8-day itineraries, popular.

EcoAndes/Unigalapagos, *JL Mera N23-36 y Baquedano, T02-222 0892, www.ecoandes travel.com*. Classic and adventure tours in Ecuador, Bolivia, Chile and Peru. Also operate hotels in Quito and Galápagos cruises.

Ecoventura, *La Niña E8-52 y Almagro, T02-323 7393, www.ecoventura.com*. Operate first-class Galápagos cruises on the *Eric*, *Letty* and *Origin* motor yachts and *Galápagos Sky* dive boat, and sell mainland tours and to Peru.

Ecuador Expat Journeys, *T02-603 5548, www. ecuadorexpatjourneys.com*. Adventure tours to off-the-beaten-path destinations, day tours, treks to volcanoes, tours to expat hotspots.

Ecuador Galapagos Travels (EGT), *Veintimilla E10-78 y 12 de Octubre, Edif El Girón, Torre E, of 104, T02-254 7286, www.galapagos-cruises.ec, www.ecuadortravels.ec*. Wide range of traditional and adventure tours throughout Ecuador; tailor-made itineraries.

Ecuador Nature, *Jiménez de la Espada N32-156 y González Suárez, T02-222 2341, www.ecuadornature.com*. Offers a variety of mainland and Galápagos tours, can arrange kosher food.

Ecuador Treasure, *Wilson E4-266 y JL Mera, T02-255 9919, http://ecuadortreasure.com*. Daily tours, climbing, hiking, biking, trekking, horse riding and transport including a shuttle service to Lago Agrio, see page 265. Run **Chuquiragua Lodge**, near Reserva Los Ilinizas.

Enchanted Expeditions, *de las Alondras N45-102 y Los Lirios, T02-334 0525, www.enchantedexpeditions.com*. Operate the *Cachalote* and *Beluga* Galápagos vessels, sell jungle trips to Cuyabeno and highland tours. Very experienced.

Equateur Voyages Passion, *Gran Colombia N15-220 y Yaguachi, next to L'Auberge Inn, T02-322 7605, www.magical-ecuador. com*. Full range of adventure tours, run in highlands, coast and jungle. Also custom-made itineraries.

Galacruises Expeditions, *9 de Octubre N22-118 y Veintimilla, pb, T02-252 3324, www.islasgalapagos.travel*. Galápagos cruises on the *Archipel I and II* and other vessels and diving tours on the *Pingüino Explorer*. Also island hopping and land tours on Isabela, mainland and South America packages.

Galasam, *Cordero N24-214 y Amazonas, T02-290 3909, www.galasamecuador.com*. Has a fleet of boats in different categories for Galápagos cruises, including the *Humboldt Explorer* diving yacht. City tours, full range of highland tours and jungle trips to **Siona** in Cuyabeno and other lodges.

Galextur, *De los Motilones E14-58 y Charapa, T02-292 1739, http://galextur.com*. Run land-based Galápagos tours with daily sailings and island hopping. Sell live aboard and diving tours from the Silberstein Dive Center. Operate **Hotel Silberstein** in Puerto Ayora and **City Art Hotel Silberstein** in Quito. Good service.

Geo Reisen, *Av de los Shyris N37-27 y Naciones Unidas, T02-292 0583*, www.georeisen-ecuador.com. Specializing in cultural, adventure and nature tours adapted for individuals, groups or families.

Happy Gringo, *Catalina Aldaz N34-155 y Portugal, Edif Catalina Plaza, of 509, T02-512 3486, www.happygringo.com*. Tailor-made tours throughout Ecuador, Quito city tours, Otavalo, sell Galápagos, jungle and other destinations, good service. Recommended.

Klein Tours, *Eloy Alfaro N34-111 y Catalina Aldaz, T02-226 7000, www.gogalapagos.com*. Operate the *Galapagos Legend* and *Coral I* and *II* cruise ships. Also run community-based tours in Imbabura and highland tours with tailor-made itineraries, English, French and German spoken.

Latin Trails, *T02-286 7832, https://latintrails. com*. Run cruises in various Galápagos vessels including the *Seaman Journey* and *Sea Star Journey*; offer a variety of land trips in Ecuador and Peru and operate **Hakuna Matata Lodge** in Archidona.

Metropolitan Touring, *Av de las Palmeras N45-74 y de las Orquídeas, T02-298 8312, www. metropolitan-touring.com*. A large organization operating in Ecuador, Peru and Colombia. Run 3 luxury Galápagos vessels, the **Finch Bay Hotel** in Puerto Ayora, **Casa Gangotena** in Quito and **Mashpi Lodge** west of Quito. Also adventure, cultural and gastronomy tours.

Positiv Turismo, *Jorge Juan N33-38 y Atahualpa, T02-252 7305, http://positiv turismo.com*. Cultural trips, Cuyabeno, trekking and special interest tours, Swiss-run.

Pure! Ecuador, *Santa Fe N43-106 y Río Coca, T02-512 3358, www.pure-ecuador.com*. A Dutch/Ecuadorean operator offering tours throughout Ecuador and the Galápagos, trips to Amazon and cloudforest lodges, Pacific coast, the Andes and tailor-made tours.

Pushaq's Headquarters: Av. Circunvalación 151, Guayaquil/Guayas/Ecuador
Pushaq's Office: Av. de los Reyes 23, 170170, Cumbayá/Pichincha/Ecuador
T: (593) 99 436 5622   E: jose@pushaq.com   W: www.pushaq.com

2018 & 2019 NET SERVICE RATES
FOR FOOTPRINT TRAVELERS

PRIVATE SERVICE	RATE PER SERVICE	SERVICE CAPACITY
City transfers (Quito and Guayaquil)	48 USD	From 1 to 4 guests
Daily tours (8 hours service)	179 USD	From 1 to 4 guests
Weekly tours (6 days service)	969 US	From 1 to 4 guests

* Rates include: Private guidance and transportation
* Rates do not include: Accommodation, meals and entrance fees
* For larger groups & combined tours, please inquire with us
* Service is always subject to availability

Pushaq, *Av de los Reyes 23, Cumbayá, T09-9436 5622, www.epushaq.com.* Tailor-made tours throughout Ecuador, including the coast, can arrange car hire with GPS, hotels and petrol stations mapped out. Personal service, English, French, German and Spanish spoken. Efficient, enthusiastic, knowledgeable. Recommended.

Quasar Expeditions, *Ponce Carrasco E8-06 y Almagro, T02-382 5680, T1-800 247 2925 (USA), www.quasarex.com.* Offer 7-day naturalist and diving Galápagos cruises on yachts *Evolution* and *Grace*; also mainland extensions.

Rain Forestur, *Amazonas N21-108, T02-527970, www.*rainforestur.com. Offer climbing, rafting, canyoning, primary forest and jungle tours as well as day tours from Quito. Also 5-day Galápagos tours to 3 islands from US$870.

Rolf Wittmer Turismo/Tip Top Travel, *Foch E7-81 y Almagro, T02-2563181, www.*rwittmer.com. Run first-class yachts: *Tip Top II, III* and *IV*, plus the dive boat *Nortada*. Also tailor-made tours throughout Ecuador.

South America for All, *T02-237 7430, www.southamericaforall.com.* Specialized tours to all regions of Ecuador for the mobility and hearing-impaired traveller, also chocolate tours. Also operate in Peru.

Surtrek, *San Ignacio E10-114 y Caamaño, T02-250 0660, T1-866-978 7398 in the US, www.surtrek.com.* Wide range of tours in all regions, helicopter and ballon flights, birdwatching, rafting, horse riding, mountain biking and jungle tours, arrange last-minute Galápagos tours, also sell domestic flights and run **Las Cascadas Lodge**.

Tierra de Fuego, *Amazonas N23-23 y Veintimilla, T02-250 1418, www.ecuador tierradefuego.com.* Provide transport and tours throughout the country,

book domestic flight tickets and make Galápagos bookings.

Tropic Ecuador, *Pasaje Sánchez Melo Oe1-37 y Av Galo Plaza, T02-240 8741, http://destinationecuador.com and www. tropiceco.com.* Environmental and cultural tours, Quito, coast and highland tours, lodge-to-lodge mountain treks (based at Chilcabamba Mountain Lodge near Cotopaxi), Amazon lodges and Galápagos land-based tours (Floreana, Isabela and Santa Cruz –Magic Galápagos safari camp). Community-based tourism working with and donating a percentage of all profits to **Conservation in Action**. Winner of awards for responsible tourism.

Yacu Amu Experiences, *Amazonas N25-23 y Colón, Edif España, p 5, T02-255 0558, www. yacuamu.com.* Tailor-made adventure, nature and cultural trips for active couples, families and small groups.

Zenith Travel, *Pinto E4-358 y Amazonas, T02-252 9993, www.zenithecuador.com.* Good-value Galápagos cruises as well as various land tours in Ecuador and Peru. Multilingual service, knowledgeable helpful staff, good value.

Train rides

The lovely refurbished train station, **Estación Eloy Alfaro (Chimbacalle)**, with a railway museum and working concert hall, is 2 km south of the colonial city at Maldonado y Sincholagua, T1-800-873637, T02-265 0421, www.trenecuador.com, Mon-Fri 0800-1630. *Tren Crucero*, a luxury tourist train, runs about twice per month in either direction between Quito and Durán, outside Guayaquil, part of the route is run with a historic steam locomotive. The complete route takes 4 days and costs US$1735 one way (double room; US$2322 gold class); you can also take it for segments 1-3 days. The tour includes visits to places of interest and accommodation in luxury inns. See http://trenecuador.com/es/tren-crucero/

for details. Tourist trains run Fri-Sun and holidays from Quito to **El Boliche** and **Machachi** (0800, US$55 includes lunch, US$38 children, seniors and disabled people). A farm is visited in Machachi.

Near El Boliche station is **Area Nacional de Recreación El Boliche**, a protected area bordering Parque Nacional Cotopaxi, where the tour includes a walk. There are lovely views of Cotopaxi and Los Ilinizas. Purchase tickets in advance by phone, internet, at the station or **El Quinde Visitors Centre**, Palacio Municipal, Venezuela y Espejo. You need each passenger's passport number and age to purchase tickets. Boarding 30 mins before departure, you can visit the railway museum before boarding.

Whitewater rafting

Río Blanco/Toachi tours cost US$87.

Ríos Ecuador, *T02-234 4798 in Quito, www. riosecuador.com.* Rafting and kayaking trips of 1-6 days, also have an office in Tena and run trips in Oriente.

Transport

Air

Details of internal air service are given under the respective destinations. Quito's **Mariscal Sucre Airport** (T02-395 4200, www.quitoairport.aero for information about current arrival and departures, airport services and airlines) is in Tababela, off Highway E-35, about 30 km northeast of the city, at 2134 m above sea level. There are ATMs and a *casa de cambio* for exchange in the Arrivals level and banks and ATMs in the shopping mall across the street. Luggage storage and lockers downstairs at Arrivals, www.bagparkingquito.com, US$8-15 per case per day; see also **Quito Airport Suites** hotel, page 60. The information office (Arrivals level, see Tourist information, page 55), will assist with hotel bookings. The airport taxi cooperative, T02-281 8021, www.taxienquitoecuador.com, has set rates to different zones of the city; these are posted by Arrivals (US$25 to La Mariscal, US$26 to colonial Quito, US$33 to Quitumbe bus station, US$26.50 to Carcelén station); taxi rates from the city to the airport are about 10% cheaper. **Aero Servicios** express bus, T02-604 3500, T1-800-237673, www.aeroservicios.com.ec, runs almost 24 hrs per day, between the new airport and the old airport in northern Quito (Parque Bicentenario), US$8 (US$6 with boarding pass). From the airport, departures are Mon-Fri 0430-0040 every 30 mins, Sat 0500-2230 and Sun 0500-2330; from Quito, departures are 30 mins 0330-2300, Sat 0400-2130, Sun 0400-2330. They also offer transfers between the old airport and other locations in the city. Taking a transfer service or a taxi from the old airport to your hotel is recommended. Regional buses with limited stops run every 15 mins, 0530-2200, between the airport and Terminal Río Coca in the north (see Ecovía, below) and 0530-1700 to Terminal Quitumbe in the south, US$2. Private van services are good value for groups, but require advanced arrangements, eg **Trans-Rabbit**, T02-290 2690, www.transrabbit.com.ec, US$30 for 2 passengers, US$5 per additional person, and **Achupallas Tours**, T02-255 1614, www.achupallastour.amawebs.com. Both also offer trips in Quito and out of town.

Note It takes at least 45 mins to reach the airport from Quito, but with traffic it can be much longer; allow 1½ hrs.

Bus

Local Quito has 5 parallel mass transit lines running from north to south mostly on exclusive lanes, covering almost the length of the city. There are several transfer stations where you can switch from one line to another without cost. At rush hour there are express buses with limited stops. Feeder bus lines (*alimentadores*) go from the terminals to outer suburbs. Within the city the fare is US$0.25, students and seniors US$0.12, disabled people US$0.10; the combined fare to some suburbs is US$0.40. Public transit is not designed for carrying heavy luggage and is often crowded. **Trole** (T02-266 5015, www.trolebus.gob.ec, Mon-Fri 0500-0030, weekends and holidays 0600-2200, plus hourly overnight service with limited stops) is a system of trolley buses which runs along Av 10 de Agosto in the north of the city, C Guayaquil (southbound) and C Flores (northbound) in colonial Quito, and mainly along Av Maldonado and Av Teniente Ortiz in the south. The main northern terminus is north of 'La Y', the junction of 10 de Agosto, Av América and Av de la Prensa, although 1 service, C5, goes to Carcelén bus terminal; south of the colonial city are important transfer stations at El Recreo and Morán Valverde; the southern terminus for 2 services is at the Quitumbe bus station. Trolleys do not necessarily run the full length of the line, the destination is marked in front of the vehicle. Trolleys have a special entrance for wheelchairs. **Ecovía** (Mon-Fri 0500-2145, Sat 0600-2045, Sun and holidays 0600-2020), articulated buses, runs along Av 6 de Diciembre from Terminal Río Coca, at C Río Coca east of 6 de Diciembre, in the north, to La Marín transfer station and on either to Quitumbe bus terminal, or to the Terminal Sur in the south of the city. Again, not all buses run the full length of the line. Troncal Occidental routes are either **Metrobús** (Mon-Fri 0530-2230, weekends and holidays 0600-2100) articulated buses run along Av de la Prensa and Av América from Terminal La Ofelia in the north to La Marín in the south, or **Sur Occidental** buses run from the Seminario Mayor interchange (Av América y Colón) in the north, along Av América, Av Universitaria and Av Occidental to Terminal Quitumbe in the south; an interchange on this route is at La Magdalena, south of San Diego; several routes branch out from Hospital del IESS station in the north. **Universidades** (or Escolar) articulated buses run from 12 de Octubre y Veintimilla in the north to Quitumbe bus terminal. There are also 2 types of **city buses**: *Selectivos* are red, and *Bus Tipo* are royal blue, both cost US$0.25. Many bus lines go through La Marín and El Playón Ecovía/Metrobús stations. Extra caution is advised here: pickpockets abound and it is best avoided at night.

Regional Outer suburbs are served by green *Interparroquial* buses. Those running east to the valleys of Cumbayá, Tumbaco and the airport leave from the Estación Río Coca (see Ecovía, above). Buses southeast to Valle de los Chillos leave from El Playón Ecovía/Metrobús station, from Isabel La Católica y Mena Caamaño, behind Universidad Católica and from Alonso de Mercadillo by the Universidad Central. Buses going north (ie Calderón, Mitad del Mundo) leave from La Ofelia Metrobús station. Regional destinations to the north (ie Cayambe) and northwest (ie Mindo) leave from a regional station adjacent to La Ofelia Metrobús station. Buses west to Nono from the Plaza de Cotocollao, to Lloa from C Angamarca in Mena 2 neighbourhood. Buses south to Machachi from El Playón, La Villaflora and Quitumbe. Buses to **Papallacta**, **Baeza** and **El Chaco** leave from Chile E3-22 y Pedro Fermín Cevallos, near La Marín.

Long distance Quito has 2 main bus terminals: **Terminal Quitumbe** in the southwest of the city, T02-290 7005 ext 31222, serves destinations south, the coast via Santo Domingo, Oriente and Tulcán (in the north). It is served by the Trole (line C4: El Ejido–Quitumbe, best taken at El Ejido) and the Sur Occidental and Universidades buses; however, it is advisable to take a taxi, about US$6, 30-45 mins to the colonial city,

US$8-10, 45 mins-1 hr to La Mariscal. Arrivals and tourist information are on the ground floor. Ticket counters (destinations grouped and colour coded by region), and departures in the upper level. Left luggage (US$0.90 per day) and food stalls are at the adjoining shopping area. The terminal is large, allow extra time to reach your bus. Terminal use fee US$0.20. Watch your belongings at all times. On holiday weekends it is advisable to reserve the day before. The smaller **Terminal Carcelén**, Av Eloy Alfaro, T02-290 7005 ext 31273, where it meets the Panamericana Norte, serves destinations to the north (including Otavalo) and the coast via the Calacalí–La Independencia road. It is served by the Trole and by feeder buses from Terminal La Ofelia; a taxi costs about US$5, 30-45 mins to La Mariscal, US$7, 45 mins-1 hr to colonial Quito. There is no direct bus between Quitumbe and Carcelén; take the Trole to La Y and change to an Express service there. Ticket counters are organized by destination. See under destinations for fares and schedules; these are also listed in http://andestransit.com and www.multipasajes.com, where you can also purchase tickets on line for buses leaving Quito. A convenient way to travel between Quitumbe and Carcelén is to take a bus bound for Tulcán, **Trans Vencedores** or **Unión del Carchi** (Booth 12), every 30 mins during the day, hourly at night, US$1, 1 hr; from Carcelén to Quitumbe, wait for a through bus arriving from the north; a taxi between terminals costs US$15.

All long-distance buses depart from either Quitumbe or Carcelén; the following companies also have ticket sales points in modern Quito: **Flota Imbabura**, Larrea 1211 y Portoviejo, T02-256 9628, http://flota-imbabura.com, for **Cuenca**, **Guayaquil**, **Manta** and **Tulcán**; **Transportes Ecuador**, JL Mera N21-44 y Washington, T02-222 5315 (terminal Quitumbe T02-382 4851), www.transportesecuador.com.ec, hourly to **Guayaquil**; **Trans Esmeraldas**, Santa María y 9 de Octubre, T02-250 5099, www.transportesesmeraldas.com, for **Esmeraldas**, **Atacames**, **Coca**, **Lago Agrio**, **Manta**, **Guayaquil** and **Huaquillas**. **Reina del Camino**, Larrea y 18 de Septiembre, T02-321 6633/5824, for **Bahía**, **Puerto López** and **Manta**; **Transportes Loja**, Orellana N41-38 y Juan de Velasco, T02-222 4306, http://cooperativaloja.com.ec, for **Loja** and **Lago Agrio**, they offer transport from their office to Quitumbe for US$2.50 pp (minimum of 4 passengers); **Transportes Baños**, Santa María E5-37 y JL Mera, T02-223 2752, www.cooperativabanos.com.ec, for **Baños** and **Oriente** destinations. **Panamericana Internacional**, Colón E7-31 y Reina Victoria, T02-255 7133, ext 127 for national routes, ext 125 for international, www.panamericana.ec, for **Huaquillas**, **Machala**, **Cuenca**, **Loja**, **Manta**, **Guayaquil** and **Esmeraldas**.

Car hire

All the main international car rental companies are at the airport. For rental procedures see Getting around, page 387. A local company is: **Simon Car Rental**, Los Shyris 2930 e Isla Floreana, T02-243 1019, www.simoncarrental.com, good rates and service.

Metro

Construction has begun on a metro system, from Quitumbe in the south to El Labrador in the north. 15 stations are planned and the line is due to start operating in 2019. At Plaza San Francisco, in the colonial city, work caused major disruption and the line had to be moved following archaeological discoveries. In Dec 2017, it was reported that work was progressing as planned and on schedule. For more information see www.metrodequito.gob.ec.

Taxi

Taxis are a cheap and efficient way to get around the city, but for safety it is important to know how to select a cab. Authorized taxis have orange license plates or white plates with an orange stripe on the upper edge; they display stickers with a unit number on the windshield, the front doors and back side-windows; the name of the company should be displayed on the back doors, the driver's photograph in the interior and they should have a working meter. Taxis with a red and blue 'Transporte Seguro' sticker on the windshield and back doors should have cameras and red panic buttons linked to the 911 emergency system. At night it is safer to use a radio taxi (*taxi ejecutivo*), such as **American Taxi**, T02-252 6000, www.americantaxi.com.ec; **Fast Line**, T02-222 2222, www.fastline.com.ec; **Llamada Fácil**, T02-266 6666, http://taxillamadafacil.com. All have apps for reservations. Make sure they give you the taxi number and description so that you get the correct vehicle, some radio taxis are unmarked. All taxis should use a meter, negotiate the price ahead if they refuse to use it. The minimum daytime fare is US$1.45, US$1.75 after 1900. Note the registration and the licence plate numbers if you feel you have been seriously overcharged or mistreated. You may then complain to the municipal police or tourist office. To hire a taxi by the hour costs from US$8 in the city, more out of town. For trips outside Quito, agree the fare beforehand: US$70-85 a day. Outside luxury hotels cooperative taxi drivers have a list of agreed excursion prices and most drivers are knowledgeable.

Long-distance taxis and vans Shared taxis and vans offer door-to-door service to some cities and avoid the hassle of reaching Quito's bus terminals. Some companies have set departures, others travel according to demand; at weekends there are fewer departures. Reserve at least 2 days ahead. There is service between Quito and Otavalo, Ibarra, Latacunga, Ambato, Riobamba, Cuenca, Baños, Puyo, Lago Agrio, Santo Domingo and Esmeraldas. For details, see Transport under the corresponding destination.

Train
There is no regular passenger service. For tourist rides, see Train rides, page 76.

Around
Quito

Despite Quito's bustling big city atmosphere, it is surrounded by pretty and surprisingly tranquil countryside, with many opportunities for day trips as well as longer excursions. A combination of city and regional buses and pick-up trucks will get you to most destinations. Excursions are also offered by Quito tour operators. The monument on the equator (see Mitad del Mundo, opposite page) is just a few minutes away; there are nature reserves, craft-producing towns, excellent thermal swimming pools, walking and climbing routes and scenic train rides (see page 76). To the west of Quito on the slopes of Pichincha is a region of spectacular natural beauty with many crystal-clear rivers and waterfalls, worth taking several days to explore. Visit www.pichincha.gob.ec (click on 'Turismo en Pichincha') for some attractions near Quito.

★ Mitad del Mundo

place a foot in each hemisphere

The location of the equatorial line here (23 km north of central Quito) was determined by Charles-Marie de la Condamine and his French expedition in 1736, and agrees to within 150 m with modern GPS measurements.

The monument forms the focal point of **Ciudad Mitad del Mundo** ① *T02-239 4803, www.mitaddelmundo.com, 0900-1800 daily (very crowded on Sun), entry to complex and 5 pavilions US$3.50, all the facilities US$7.50, all facilities plus a bar of chocolate US$10,* a leisure park built as a typical colonial town, with restaurants, a Plaza de Cacao, gift shops, post office and travel agency. In the interior of the equatorial monument is the very interesting Museo Etnográfico, with displays about Ecuador's indigenous cultures. Each of the nations which participated in the 18th-century expedition has a pavilion with exhibits which include an interesting **model of old Quito**, about 10 m sq, with artificial day and night and an **insectarium**. The **Museo Inti-Ñan** ① *200 m north of the monument, T02-239 5122, www.museointinan.com.ec, daily 0930-1700, US$4,* is eclectic, very interesting, has lots of fun things and issues equator certificates for visitors. Research about the equator and its importance to prehistoric cultures is carried out near Cayambe, by an organization called **Quitsato** ① *www.quitsato.org, daily 0800-1700, US$2.* Beyond Mitad del Mundo is Pululahua, see below.

Listings Mitad del Mundo

What to do

Calimatours, *30 m east of monument, Mitad del Mundo, T02-239 4796, www.mitaddelmundotour.com.* Tours to Pululahua and other sites in the vicinity.

Transport

Bus
From Quito take a 'Mitad del Mundo' feeder bus from La Ofelia station on the Metrobús (transfer ticket US$0.15), or from the corner of Bolivia y Av América (US$0.40). Some buses continue to the turn-off for Pululahua or Calacalí beyond.

Taxi
An excursion by taxi to Mitad del Mundo (with 1-hr wait) is US$25, or US$30 to include Pululahua. Just a ride from La Mariscal costs about US$15.

★ Papallacta

one of Ecuador's best hot springs

This small village high in the hills (3200 m), 64 km east of Quito, has thermal pools and walking opportunities. During the holidays and at weekends the hotels can get very busy. It is conveniently placed, 30 km east of the airport, so it is quite possible to relax at the baths and go directly to the airport, without returning to the city (taxis can be arranged at the village).

Termas de Papallacta
2 km from the town of Papallacta, T02-250 4787 (Quito), www.termaspapallacta.com.

These, the best-developed hot springs in the country, consist of nine thermal pools, all different in size and temperature, with varying hydromassages and four cold plunge pools. There are two public complexes of springs: the regular **pools** ⓘ *daily 0600-2100, US$8.50*, and the **spa centre** ⓘ *Sun-Thu 0900-2000, Fri, Sat and hols 0900-2100, US$22 (massage and other special treatments extra)*. There are additional pools at the Termas' hotel and cabins (see Where to stay, below) for the exclusive use of their guests. The complex is tastefully done and recommended.

In addition to the *termas* there are nice municipal pools in the village of Papallacta: **Santa Catalina** ⓘ *daily 0800-1800, US$3*, and several more economical places to stay (some with pools) on the road to the Termas and in the village. The view, on a clear day, of Antisana while enjoying the thermal waters is superb. Along the highway to Quito, are several additional thermal pools. There are a number of walking paths in the **Rancho del Cañón private reserve** ⓘ *behind the Termas, US$2 for use of a short trail; to go on longer walks you are required to take a guide for US$8 pp*.

To the north of this private reserve is **Reserva Cayambe-Coca** ⓘ *T02-211 0370, http://areasprotegidas.ambiente.gob.ec*. A scenic road starts by the Termas information centre, crosses both reserves and leads, in 45 km, to Oyacachi. A permit from Cayambe-Coca headquarters is required to travel this road even on foot; write ahead. It is a lovely two-day walk, there is a ranger's station and camping area 1½ hours from Papallacta. Reserva Cayambe-Coca is also accessed from La Virgen, the pass on the road to Quito, where there is a ranger's station. **Ríos Ecuador**, see Whitewater rafting, page 76, offer a hiking tour here which can be combined with rafting.

Listings Papallacta

Where to stay

$$$$ Hotel Termas Papallacta
At the Termas complex, T06-289 5060.
Comfortable heated rooms and suites, good expensive restaurant, thermal pools set in a lovely garden, nice lounge with fireplace, some rooms with private jacuzzi, also cabins for up to 6, transport from Quito extra. Guests have access to all areas in the complex and get discounts at the spa. For weekends and holidays book 1 month in advance. Recommended.

$$$ Guango Lodge
Near Cuyuja, 9 km east of Papallacta, T02-289 1880 (Quito), www.guangolodge.com.

In a 350-ha temperate forest reserve along the Río Papallacta. All meals extra, or go for full board ($$$$), good food and facilities, excellent birdwatching. Day visits US$5. Reserve ahead. Taxi from Papallacta US$10.

$$$-$$ Hostería Pampallacta
On the road to Termas, T06-289 5022, www.pampallactatermales.com.
A variety of rooms with bathtubs, pools for exclusive use for guests, higher prices at the weekend, restaurant.

$$$-$$ La Choza de Don Wilson
At turn-off for Termas, T06-289 5027, www.hosteriachozapapallacta.com.
Rooms with good views of the valley, fancier rooms have hot tubs and heaters, cheaper

rooms are small and heaters extra, good popular restaurant, pools (US$5 for non-residents), attentive.

$$ Coturpa
Next to the Santa Catalina baths in Papallacta town, T06-289 5040, www.hostalcoturpa.com.
A variety of rooms, some with hot tubs, heaters, restaurant.

$$-$ El Leñador
By entrance to Termas, T09-9825 8821, see Facebook.
Simple rooms with electric shower, skylights make it bright and warm, restaurant, breakfast extra.

Transport

Papallacta
Bus and taxi
From **Quito**, buses bound for Tena or Lago Agrio from Terminal Quitumbe, or buses to Baeza from near La Marín (see page 78), 2 hrs, US$2.50. The bus and taxi stop is at El Triángulo, east of (below) the village, at the junction of the main highway and the old road through town. A taxi to **Termas** costs US$1 pp shared or US$2.50 private. The access to the Termas is uphill from the village, off the old road. The complex is a 40-min walk from town. To return to Quito, most buses pass in the afternoon; travelling back at night is not recommended. Taxi to Quito starts at US$50, to the airport US$40. **Transporte Santa Catalina** taxis in Papallacta, T09-8510 2556.

Western slopes of Pichincha

an ideal destination for nature lovers

Despite their proximity to the capital (two hours from Quito), the western slopes of Volcán Pichincha and its surroundings are surprisingly wild, with fine opportunities for walking and birdwatching (the altitude ranges from 1200-2800 m). This scenic area known as El Noroccidente has lovely cloudforests and many nature reserves. The main tourist town in this region is Mindo. To the west of Mindo is a warm subtropical area of clear rivers and waterfalls, with a number of reserves, resorts and lodges.

Ecoruta

Two roads go from Quito over the western Cordillera before dropping into the northwestern lowlands. The old route via **Nono** (the only town of any size along this route) and **Tandayapa** is dubbed the Ecoruta or **Paseo del Quinde** (Route of the Hummingbird). It begins towards the northern end of Avenida Mariscal Sucre (Occidental), Quito's western ring road, at the intersection with Calle Machala. With increased awareness of the need to conserve the cloudforests of the northwest slopes of Pichincha and of their potential for tourism, the number of reserves here is steadily growing. Keen birdwatchers are no longer the only visitors and the region has much to offer all nature lovers. Infrastructure at reserves varies considerably. Some have comfortable upmarket lodges offering accommodation, meals, guides and transport. Others may require taking your own camping gear, food and obtaining a permit. There are too many reserves and lodges to mention here.

Above Tandayapa along the Ecoruta is **Bellavista Cloud Forest Reserve** ① *T02-361 3447 (lodge), 09-9416 5868 (cell phone), www.bellavistacloudforest.com*, a 700-ha private reserve at about 2200 m, rich in flora and fauna, including the olinguito (*Bassaricyon neblina*), a mammal new to science, first identified in 2013 (you can see it near the lodge most evenings). Birdwatching is excellent (it's the easiest place to see the plate-billed mountain-toucan) in lovely scenery, including waterfalls; on-site guides are knowledgeable and enthusiastic. There are 10 km of well-maintained trails ranging from easy to slippery/suicidal; you can take three pre-arranged guided walks a day, or set off on your own.

Day-visits from Quito include transport, two meals and guided walks. The new Sunrise View bamboo restaurant is open to non-guests. There are several access routes: from Quito, the fastest is to take the new road to km 52, from where it is 12 km uphill to Bellavista, and from Mindo, take the new route towards Quito for 2 km and then the Ecoruta. For lodge information, see Where to stay, below.

The new route

From the Mitad del Mundo monument (see above) the road goes past **Calacalí**, also on the equator, whose plaza has an older monument to the Mitad del Mundo. Beyond Calacalí, at Km 15, a road turns south to Nono and north to **Yunguilla**, which has a community tourism project (T09-99954 1537, www.yunguilla.org.ec, with the **Tahuallullo Lodge**, camping or homestays, day- and longer tours, volunteering; pick-up from Calacalí, US$4). The road at Km 52 that goes to Bellavista (see above) also goes to Tandayapa. The main road, with heavy traffic at weekends, continues to Nanegalito (Km 56), Miraflores (Km 62) where another road goes to the Ecoruta, the turn-off for a third road to the Ecoruta at Km 77 and the turn-off for Mindo at Km 79. For places beyond here, see West of Mindo, below.

Pululahua ⓘ *park office by the rim lookout, T02-239 6543, http://areasprotegidas.ambiente.gob.ec, 0800-1700, free*, is a geobotanical reserve in an inhabited, farmed volcanic caldera. A few kilometres beyond Mitad del Mundo, off the road to Calacalí, Mirador Ventanillas, a lookout on the rim of Pululahua gives a great view, but go in the morning, as the cloud usually descends around 1300. You can go down to the reserve and experience the rich vegetation and warm microclimate inside. From the mirador, walk down 30 minutes to the agricultural zone then turn left. There are picnic and camping areas and the **$$-$ Hostal Pululahua** (www.pululahuahostal.com, has lots of information). A longer road allows you to drive down a steep, twisting road into the crater via **Moraspungo**, where there is a recreational area (US$5 entry). To walk out this way, starting at the mirador, continue past the village in the crater, turn left and follow the unimproved road up to the rim and back to the main road; it's a 15- to 20-km round trip. From Moraspungo a road goes west to San José de Niebli and out of the crater, from where an old road goes to Yunguilla (see above). At **Nanegalito**, the transport hub for this area, is the turn-off to Nanegal and the cloudforest in the 18,500-ha **Maquipucuna Biological Reserve** ⓘ *www.maqui.org, knowledgeable guides: US$25 (Spanish), US$100 (English) per day for a group of 9*, which contains a tremendous diversity of flora and fauna, including the spectacled bear, which can be seen when the *pacche/aguacatillo* trees are in fruit (any time between July and February) and about 400 species of bird. The reserve has 40 km of trails (US$10 per person) and a lodge (see below).

Next to Maquipucuna is **Santa Lucía** ⓘ *T02-215 7242*. Access to this reserve is 30 minutes by car from Nanegal and a walk from there. Day tours combining Pululahua, Yunguilla and Santa Lucía are available. **Bosque Nublado Santa Lucía** is a community-based conservation and ecotourism project protecting a beautiful 650-ha tract of cloudforest.

Look at the website of any lodge in Ecuador's northwestern cloudforests or Amazon rainforests and it will tell you about the abundance of wildlife to be seen. It will talk about mammals big and small, birds (hundreds of species in many cases), butterflies and plants. These are not idle boasts and, unless you are extraordinarily unlucky, a visit to either type of forest will yield rich rewards. But which to choose if you don't have time to visit both? Neither is 'better' than the other, but what are the differences?

Richard Parsons of Bellavista Cloud Forest Reserve writes: tropical/subtropical rainforests grow at altitudes from near sea level up to approximately 2500 m in the Andes of Ecuador, on both sides of the mountain range. Millions of years ago, but recently in geological time, the area of South America where today we find the Andes was flat and the vast Amazon River flowed west out to the Pacific. As the Andes began to rise, pushed upwards by the subducting oceanic Nazca Plate, on the plate boundary with the continental South American Plate, so the essentially uniform lowland rainforests with time adapted to higher altitude. And the Amazon River now flows east.

There are similarities between lowland forests and higher-elevation cloudforests. Plants often have large, fleshy leaves, providing plenty of surface area to capture the dim sunlight that penetrates to the forest floor. Because of the high rainfall in both types of forest, leaves usually curve somewhat downwards, and have 'pinched-together' drip tips. Both of these adaptations make the excess water run off. Root systems are generally shallow and nutrients are in the biomass of the plants, rather than the soil.

The differences, however, are significant and are most deeply reflected in the totally different species found in a lowland forest as compared with high-elevation cloudforest. Ecuador is the most biodiverse country on the planet, boasting

The area is very rich in birds (there is a cock-of-the-rock lek) and other wildlife. There are waterfalls and walking trails and a lodge (see below).

At Armenia (Km 60), a few kilometres beyond Nanegalito, a road heads northwest through **Santa Clara**, with a handicrafts market on Sunday, to the village and archaeological site of **Tulipe** (14 km; 1450 m). The site consists of several man-made 'pools' linked by water channels. A path leads beside the Río Tulipe in about 15 minutes to a circular pool amid trees. The site **museum** ① *T02-285 0635, US$3, Wed-Sun 0900-1730, guided tours (arrange ahead for English),* has exhibits in Spanish on the Yumbos culture and the *colonos* (contemporary settlers). There is also an orchid garden.

The Yumbos were traders who linked the Quitus with coastal and jungle peoples between AD 800 and 1600. Their trails, called *culuncos*, are 1-m wide and 3-m deep, covered in vegetation for coolness. Several treks in the area follow them. Also to be seen are raised earth platforms called *tolas*; there are some 1500 around Tulipe. **Turismo Comunitario Las Tolas** ① *6 km from Tulipe, T02-286 9488,* offers lodging, food, craft workshops and guides to *tolas* and *culuncos*.

To the northwest of Tulipe are **Gualea** and **Pacto**, beyond which is the secluded, luxurious $$$$ **Mashpi Lodge** (T02-400 8088, www.mashpilodge.com, open to lodge over 1600 bird species, the highest number per square kilometre of any country in the world. A bird or mammal list from a lodge/reserve in Ecuador's Amazon Basin, shares few species with a lodge/reserve in Ecuador's northwest (also called the Noroccidente, or the Chocó at lower elevations). The same is true of orchids, butterflies, moths and so much more. Just as an example, in the private **Bellavista Cloud Forest Reserve** in 2015, 70 new species of *Noctuidae* moths were identified to science in just nine months!

Differences in temperature mean different food availability, different dominant species, etc. Lowland rainforests frequently have large rivers, whereas higher-elevation forests tend to have an abundance of waterfalls. Root systems in Amazon forest are often so shallow that merely to remove the leaves is to expose humus-poor lateritic soil. In cloudforests, a surprisingly high percentage of the vegetable biomass is found in epiphytes (air plants), living up on the branches and in the canopy, with no need for roots to the ground to supply their nutrients... an ecosystem of its own.

Another significant difference is that lowland forests, notably Amazon forests, are generally much flatter and so the canopy tends to be closed. As a result, the forest floor is frequently quite open and young trees need light gaps created by fallen trees to start their push up towards the light of the forest canopy. Higher-elevation Andean cloudforests, on the other hand, often have steep slopes, so the canopy is much more open and vegetation on the forest floor flourishes.

For the visitor, the ideal is to experience both ecosystems; a lowland, perhaps Amazonian rainforest, and a high-elevation cloudforest up in the Andes. Both are easily accessible, although it has to be said that, taking the city of Quito as your starting point, you'll need longer to get into an Amazon reserve.

See also Wildlife and vegetation, page 368.

guests only), at the heart of a 3000-ha private **reserve** which protects both rain- and cloudforest. The five-star, award-winning and proudly contemporary lodge is at the centre of a research project which aims to understand and preserve the diversity of the surrounding forest. There is also close cooperation with local communities. Activities include hiking trails, visits to waterfalls, birdwatching – the list is estimated at 500 species, a 26-m observation tower, a canopy cable car, the Sky Bike ride and a spa. Programmes are for three days/two nights. Back along the main road, by Miraflores, turn north at Km 63.5 **Tucanopy** (T09-9531 1625, www.tucanopy.com), a reserve, Intillacta, with lodging, trails, canopy zip-lines and conservation volunteer opportunities. At Km 79 is the turn-off for Mindo.

★ Mindo

Mindo is a small town at 1250 m surrounded by dairy farms and lush cloudforest climbing the western slopes of Pichincha. Bird- and butterfly watching, walks and gentle adventure are the main draws and the town gets very crowded with Quiteños at weekends and holidays. During the week it is quite quiet. See What to do in Mindo, page 91. The rainy season is October to May. There is one ATM, Nexo, at the corner of the plaza.

This is the main access point for the 19,200-ha **Bosque Protector Mindo-Nambillo**. The reserve, which ranges in altitude from 1400 m to 4780 m, is administered by the state but 50% of it was donated by three different haciendas. It features beautiful flora (many orchids and bromeliads), fauna (butterflies, frogs, about 450 species of bird including the cock-of-the-rock, golden-headed quetzal and toucan-barbet) and spectacular cloudforest, rivers and waterfalls. Access to the reserve is restricted to scientists, but there are several private reserves with lodges bordering the Bosque Protector. The region's rich diversity is threatened by proposed mining in the area.

West of Mindo

The road continues west beyond the turn-off to Mindo, descending to the subtropical zone north of Santo Domingo de los Tsáchilas. It goes via **San Miguel de los Bancos**, a pleasant market town perched on a ridge above the Río Blanco, **Pedro Vicente (PV) Maldonado** and **Puerto Quito** (on the lovely Río Caoni) to join the Santo Domingo–Esmeraldas road just north of La Independencia and the larger town of La Concordia. From San Miguel de Los Bancos a newly paved road also goes to Santo Domingo. The entire area is good for birdwatching, swimming in rivers and natural pools, walking, kayaking, or simply relaxing in pleasant natural surroundings. There are many reserves, resorts, lodgings and places to visit along the route, of particular interest to birdwatchers. There are tours from Quito, see Birdwatching, page 70, and What to do, page 91. See Where to stay, below, for resorts.

Listings Western slopes of Pichincha

Tourist information

Mindo

Municipal Tourist Information
Quito y 9 de Octubre, by the plaza,
turismo.municipiosmb@gmail.com.
Wed-Sun 0730-1300, 1430-1700.
Plenty of local information and
pamphlets, sketch map, some
English spoken, very helpful.

Where to stay

Ecoruta

$$$$ Tandayapa Bird Lodge
T02-243 3676 (Quito, Mon-Fri 0900-1800),
www.tandayapa.com.
Designed and owned by birders. Full board, comfortable rooms, some have a canopy platform for observation, large common area; wide variety of packages which include guide and transport from Quito. Reserve in advance.

$$$$-$$ Bellavista Cloud Forest
T02-361 3447 (lodge), in Quito T02-223 2313,
www.bellavistacloudforest.com.
A dramatic lodge perched in beautiful cloudforest, includes unique geodesic dome. A variety of comfortable rooms with wonderful views ranging from large suites and new superior rooms (good for families) to rooms with shared bath, heaters, 1 wheelchair-accessible room, dormitory and camping (US$9 pp). All prices per person and can include 3 excellent meals (with vegetarian options, dishes are home-made), in new bamboo dining room. Bilingual guide service costs US$18; 3 guided walks a day. Good research station with dorms and kitchen facilities (US$21 pp). Package tours with guide and transport from Quito are the best option. Local tours to Mindo and other reserves are available. Restaurant open to non-guests for breakfast and lunch. Best booked in advance. Very good service. Warmly recommended.

$$$ San Jorge

T02-339 0403, www.eco-lodgesanjorge.com.
A series of reserves with lodges in bird-rich
areas. One is 4 km from Quito (see **Hostería
San Jorge**, page 60), 1 in Tandayapa at
1500 m and another in Milpe, off the new
road near San Miguel de los Bancos, at
900 m. Advanced reservations required.

The new route

$$$$ Santa Lucía

T02-215 7242, www.santaluciaecuador.com.
The lodge with panoramic views is a 1½-hr
walk from the access to the reserve. Price
includes full board with good food and
guiding. There are cabins with private bath,
rooms with shared composting toilets and
hot showers and dorms ($ pp including food
but not guiding).

$$$$-$$$ Maquipucuna Lodge

T02-250 7200, 09-9421 8033, www.maqui.org.
Comfortable rustic lodge, includes full board
with good meals using ingredients from
own organic garden (vegetarian and vegan
available). Rooms range from shared to
rooms with bath, hot water, electricity. 1- to
4-night packages available, with birding,
community, adventure and cloudforest
tours. Campsite is 20 mins' walk from main
lodge, under US$6 pp (food extra), cooking
lessons, chocolate massages.

$$$ Hostería Sumak Pakari

*Tulipe, 200 m from the village, T02-361 3121,
www.hosteriasumakpakari.com.*
Cabins with suites with jacuzzi and rooms
set in gardens, includes breakfast and
museum fee, terraces with hammocks,
pools, restaurant, sports fields.

$ Posada del Yumbo

Tulipe, T02-286 0121.
Up a side street off the main road. Cabins in
large property with river view, also simple
rooms, electric shower, pool, horse riding.
Also run **Restaurant La Aldea**, by the
archaeological site.

Mindo

$$$$ Casa Divina

*1.2 km on the road to Cascada de Nambillo,
T09-8659 4965, www.mindocasadivina.com.*
Comfortable 2-storey cabins, lovely location
surrounded by 2.7 forested ha, includes
breakfast, lunch and dinner on request,
bathtubs, guiding extra, US/Ecuadorean-run.

$$$$ El Monte

*2 km from town on road to CEA, then
opposite Mariposas de Mindo, cross river on
tarabita (rustic cable car), T02-217 0102, T09-
9308 4675, www.ecuadorcloudforest.com.*
Beautifully constructed lodge in 44-ha
property, newer cabins are spacious and
very comfortable, includes 3 meals (mostly

vegetarian), swimming, birdwatching and nature walks with a *guía nativo*, other adventure sports and horse riding are extra, some solar power, reserve in advance. Recommended.

$$$ Séptimo Paraíso
2 km from Calacalí–La Independencia road along Mindo access road, then 500 m right on a small side road, well signed, T09-9368 4417, www.septimoparaiso.com.
All-wood lodge in a 420-ha reserve, comfortable, restaurant with good choice of set meals including vegetarian, warm and spring-fed pools and jaccuzi, parking, lovely grounds, great birdwatching, walking trails open to non-guests for US$10. Recommended.

$$ Caskaffesu
Sixto Durán Ballén (the street leading to the stadium) y Av Quito, T02-217 0100, www.caskaffesu.net.
Pleasant *hostal* with nice courtyard, no breakfast, good coffee at café/bar, live music Tue-Sat (US$3 cover), US/Ecuadorean-run.

$$ Dragonfly Inn
On Av Quito (main street), 1st block after bridge, T02-217 0319, www.mindo.biz.
Popular hotel, comfortable rooms with balcony and hammock, café and restaurant serving local and international food, vegetarian options. Can arrange local tours.

$$ Hacienda San Vicente
(Yellow House)
Entrance is 25 m south of the plaza, then 500 m along a pretty drive, T02-217 0124, www.ecuadormindobirds.com.
Family-run lodge set in 200 ha of very rich forest, includes excellent breakfast served on the hummingbird terrace, nice rooms, also has cabins for long stay, good walking trails open to non-guests for US$6, reservations required, good value. Highly recommended for nature lovers.

$$ Mindo Real
Vía al Cinto (extension Av Sixto Durán) 500 m from town, T02-217 0120, www.mindoreal.com.
Cabins and rooms in lovely extensive gardens on the banks of the Río Mindo, camping with good facilities US$5 pp, pool, trails.

$$-$ El Descanso
C Colibríes (1st right after Río Canchupi bridge at entrance to town), 5 blocks from Av Quito, T09-9482 9587, see Facebook (Hostal El Jardín del Descanso).
Nice house with comfortable rooms, cheaper in loft with shared bath, ample parking. Recommended. Good birdwatching in garden, open to non-guests for US$5, cafeteria open to the public for breakfast.

$$-$ Jardín de los Pájaros
C Colibríes 415, T02-217 0159, 09-9422 7624, www.hostaljardindelospajaros.com.
Family-run hostel, several types of rooms, includes good breakfast, small pool, parking, large covered terrace with hammocks, good value. Recommended.

$ Charito
C Colibríes, 2 blocks from Av Quito, T02-217 0093, www.charitodemindo.com.
Family-run hostel in a wooden house, cheaper without breakfast, nice rooms, newer ones at the back overlook the Río Canchupi, use of kitchen, lunch and dinner on request, good value.

$ Rubby
5 blocks past the plaza along C Quito, T09-9193 1853, Facebook: hostalrubby.
Family-run *hostal* on the outskirts of town, nice rooms, kitchen and laundry facilities, good value. English spoken, owner Marcelo Arias is a birding guide.

West of Mindo

$$$$ Arashá
4 km west of PV Maldonado, Km 121, T02-390 0007, Quito T02-244 9881 for reservations, www.arasharesort.com.
Resort and spa with pools, waterfalls (artificial and natural) and hiking trails. Comfortable thatched cabins, price includes all meals (world-class chef), use of the facilities (spa extra) and tours, can arrange transport from Quito, attentive staff, popular with families, elegant and very upmarket.

$$$ Selva Virgen
At Km 132, east of Puerto Quito, T02-390 1317, Facebook: hosteriaselvavirgenoficial. Wed-Sun, Mon-Tue with advanced booking only.
Nice *hostería* in a 100-ha property owned by the Universidad Técnica Equinoccial (UTE, www.ute.edu.ec). Staffed by students. Restaurant, rooms with ceiling fan and spacious comfortable cabins for 4 with fan, fridge, jacuzzi and a nice porch, 3 pools, lovely grounds, part of the property is forested and has trails, facilities also open to restaurant patrons.

$$ Mirador Río Blanco
Av 17 de Julio L20 y El Cisne, SanMiguel de los Bancos, at the east end of town, T02-277 0307, www.miradorrioblanco.com.
Popular hotel/restaurant serving tropical dishes ($$), vegetarian options, good coffee, rooms in *cabañas* overlooking the river, breakfast extra, parking, terrace with bird feeders (many hummingbirds and tanagers) and magnificent views of the river.

Restaurants

Mindo

$$$-$$ El Quetzal
9 de Octubre, 3 blocks from the park, T02-217 0034, wwwelquetzaldemindo.com. Daily 0800-2030.

Nice restaurant serving Ecuadorean/North American food with vegetarian options, microbrews, local chocolate and other sweets for sale, Wi-Fi. Hourly chocolate tours daily 1000-1700, US$10. Also has **Hostería** ($$$), rooms with balcony.

$$ Fuera de Babilonia
9 de Octubre y Los Ríos, 2 blocks from the park, no sign. Daily 1400-2100.
A la carte international dishes, set lunch US$8.50, trout, pizza, pasta, good food, music and nice atmosphere.

$$-$ Mishqui Quinde
Vicente de Aguirre y Gallo de la Peña, T09-8489 9234, see Facebook.
Vegetarian and vegan food based on quinoa, including soups, burgers, home-made ice cream, artesan beer. On the street known as 'Gourmet Avenue'; there are several other places to eat here.

$$-$ La Sazón de Marcelo
Av Quito past the plaza, opposite the children's playground. Daily 0730-1900.
Set meals, US$3, and à la carte including vegetarian dishes; *bandeja mindeña* a dish for 2 with trout and tilapia is one of their specialities. Very popular.

What to do

The new route: Pululahua
Green Horse Ranch, *Astrid Müller, T09-8612 5433, www.horseranch.de.* 1- to 9-day rides, Bellavista is included in one of the options, but also Pululahua, Río Guayllabamba and much more.

Mindo
Birdwatching
Stroll along any of the roads out of town; the access road into town is particularly good for birdwatching, as are the private 'Yellow House Trail' at **Hacienda San Vicente** and the garden at **El Descanso**, see Where to

stay, page 90. Also good is the **Estación Biológica Río Bravo**, US$8, beyond the Balneario Nambillo (see below), 15 km from Mindo, taxi US$12, a 3000-ha private reserve with 3 waterfalls in primary forest.

Dani Jumbo, *T09-9328 0769*. A recommended birding guide.

Julia Patiño, *T09-8616 2816, juliaguideofbirds@ gmail.com*. A recommended English-speaking birding guide.

Mindo Xtrem Birds, *Sector Saguambi 36, just out of town, T02-217 0188, www. mindoxtreme.com*. Birdwatching with Luis Pérez and Fernanda Villamil, regattas, cycling, hiking, waterfalls, horse riding, English spoken, very helpful.

Vinicio Pérez, *T09-9947 6867, www.bird watchershouse.com*. Is a recommended birding guide, he speaks some English and has his own reserve by Santa Rosa, 600 m from the Ecoruta, 6 km from the main highway.

Butterfly watching

250 species of butterfly have been identified around Mindo, and butterfly farms are good places to see them.

Mariposas de Mindo, *2 km from town in La Yaguira, near the Río Mindo, T09-9920 2124, www.mariposasdemindo.com*. This is a good butterfly farm with restaurant and lodging, US$6.

Nathaly, *100 m from the main plaza*. A small, simple butterfly farm and orchid garden, US$5.

Innertubing

A very popular activity in the Mindo area is *regattas*, the local name for innertubing: floating down a river on a raft made of several inner tubes tied together. The number of tubes that can run together depends on the water level. Several local agencies and hotels offer this activity on the Río Mindo for US$6-35 depending on the level, but experts also run the Río Blanco, where competitions are held during local holidays.

Orchids

Jardín de Orquídeas, *Lluvia de Oro y Sixto Durán, 2 blocks from the church, by the stadium, T02-217 0131, www.birdingmindo. com*. A fine collection of the region's orchids can be seen at this orchid garden, US$3 with guide. They also have **Cabañas Armonía** and a restaurant.

Mindo Lago, *300 m from town on the road to Quito, T02-217 0201, www.mindolago.com.ec*. Day visit (US$1) has trails and cabins around a pretty pond, where you can listen to the frogs' concert around sunset (US$5).

Tour operators

There are tour operators offering trips to local sites all along C Quito. They also offer **canyoning** (US$15 plus transport), **horse riding** (US$12) and **bicycle rentals** (see **Endemic Tours**, below). There are tours to **chocolate factories** through **Yumbos Chocolate** (Av Quito, T09-9063 6345, www. yumboschocolate.com), and **El Quetzal** (see Restaurants, above), both US$10. Also to **coffee farms**, US$6.50, 2 hrs.

Endemic Tours, *Av Quito y Gallo de la Peña, T09-9888 5801, romelly85@hotmail.com*. Bicycle rentals US$5/2 hrs, US$10 per full day, hiking, regattas and other adventure activities.

Waterfalls

Several waterfalls can be visited, all on private land.

Balneario Nambillo, *on the Río Nambillo, 8 km, 2½ hrs' walk from town, taxi US$8*. With natural swimming holes and slides on the river, US$3.

Santuario de Cascadas, *T09-9949 5044, or 02-256 9312 (Quito), 6 km walk, 2 hrs, taxi US$6*. There are 7 falls on a tributary of the Nambillo, with the added attraction of a 530-m-long *tarabita* (cable car) to cross the river that runs 0830-1700 (US$5); tickets sold at either end of the *tarabita* and at agencies in town; if you do not want to use the *tarabita*, you can still visit the falls crossing on a bridge (same price).

Zip-wiring

Canopy zip-lines are available on the way to **Santuario de Cascadas** for US$20: **Mindo Canopy**, *T09-9453 0624, www. mindocanopy.com*, with 3500 m of lines. **Mindo Ropes & Canopy**, *T09-9440 8662, www.mindoziplines.com*, with 2650 m of lines.

Transport

The new route: Pululahua
Bus

From **Quito**, La Ofelia Metrobús terminal, take a 'Mitad del Mundo' bus. When boarding, ask if it goes as far as the Pululahua turn-off (some end their route at Mitad del Mundo, others at the Pululahua Mirador turn-off, others continue to Calacalí). It is a 30-min walk from the turn-off to the rim.

The new route: Tulipe
Bus

From **Quito**, Estación La Ofelia, 0630 to 1830, US$2.25, 1¾ hrs: **Transportes Otavalo**, 7 daily, continue to Pacto (US$2.50, 2 hrs) and **Transportes Minas** 5 daily, continue to Chontal (US$3.15, 3 hrs). To **Las Tolas**, **Transportes Minas**, daily at 1730, US$2.50, 2½ hrs or take pick-up from Tulipe, US$5.

Mindo
Bus and taxi

Buses in Mindo park on C Quito, some 4 blocks from the plaza, opposite restaurant La Sazón de Marcelo; get on here or at the plaza. From **Quito**, Estación La Ofelia, **Coop Flor del Valle**, T02-217 0171, Mon-Fri 5 a day, Sat and Sun 7 a day; Mindo–Quito: Mon-Fri 5 a day, Sat and Sun 6 a day; US$3.10, 2½ hrs; weekend buses fill quickly, buy ahead (office in Mindo on C Quito next to **American World Tours**). Going to Mindo you can also take any bus bound for Esmeraldas or San Miguel de los Bancos (see below) and get off at the turn-off for Mindo from where there are taxis until 1930, US$0.50 pp or US$3 without sharing. Taxis wait opposite the church at Sixto Durán y Quito, T02-217 03745; also T02-217 0305. Fare to **Quito airport** US$80; to **La Mariscal** US$70. **Cooperativa Kennedy** to/from **Santo Domingo** 5 daily via La Concordia, US$5, 3½ hrs (1100 bus from Mindo connects to Guayaquil, 8 hrs, US$11).

West of Mindo
Bus

From **Quito**, Terminal Carcelén, departures every 30 mins (**Cooperativa Kennedy** and associates) to Santo Domingo via: **Nanegalito** (US$2, 1½ hrs), **San Miguel de los Bancos** (US$3-4, 2½ hrs), **Pedro Vicente Maldonado** (US$4, 3 hrs) and **Puerto Quito** (US$4-5, 3½ hrs). **Trans Esmeraldas** frequent departures from Terminal Carcelén also serve these destinations along the Quito–Esmeraldas route.

Northern
highlands

North from Quito to the border with Colombia is an area of great natural beauty and cultural interest. The landscape is mountainous, with views of Cotacachi, Imbabura and Chiles volcanoes, as well as the glacier-covered Cayambe, interspersed with lakes.

This is also a region renowned for its *artesanía*. Countless villages specialize in their own particular craft, be it textiles, hats, woodcarvings, bread figures or leather goods. And, of course, there is Otavalo, with its outstanding market, a must on everyone's itinerary.

The Pan-American Highway, fully paved, runs northeast from Quito to Otavalo (94 km), Ibarra (114 km) and Tulcán (240 km), from where it continues to Ipiales in Colombia. Secondary roads go west from all these cities, and descend to subtropical lowlands. From Ibarra a paved road runs northwest to the Pacific port of San Lorenzo and south of Tulcán a road goes east to Lago Agrio. Parque Nacional Cayambe Coca and Reservas Cotacachi Cayapas and El Angel protect this region's natural wonders.

Best for
Boat rides ■ Climbing ■ Indigenous crafts ■ Trekking

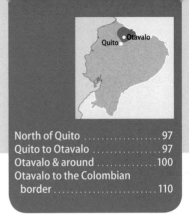

Footprint
picks

★ Parque Arqueológico Cochasquí, page 97

Among the many pre-Inca structures found in northern Ecuador,
these pyramids are the most elaborate.

★ Otavalo market, page 100

Featuring a dazzling array of indigenous textiles and crafts, Otavalo's
Saturday market is second to none.

★ Laguna Cuicocha, page 110

Walk around the rim of Cuicocha crater lake for fantastic views of the
surrounding volcanoes and the lake's two islands.

★ Helados de paila, pages 111 and 122

Enjoy the delicious fresh fruit sorbets made in a copper kettle, an
Ibarra speciality.

★ Reserva Ecológica El Angel, page 114

Admire Ecuador's largest stand of velvety leaved *frailejón* plants in
the high-altitude El Angel Reserve.

★ Tulcán cemetery, page 115

In Tulcán's cemetery, the art of topiary is taken to incredible extremes.

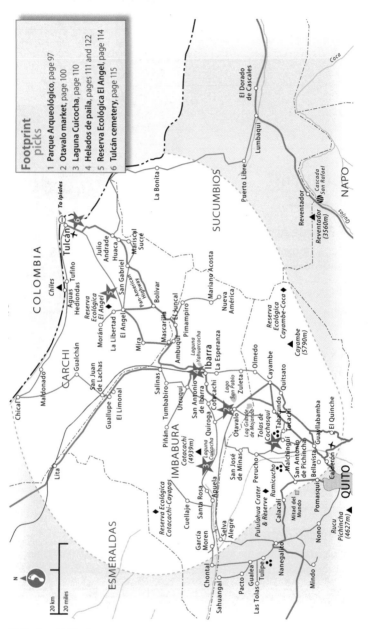

Footprint picks

1 Parque Arqueológico, page 97
2 Otavalo market, page 100
3 Laguna Cuicocha, page 110
4 Helados de paila, pages 111 and 122
5 Reserva Ecológica El Angel, page 114
6 Tulcán cemetery, page 115

To Ipiales

COLOMBIA

Chiles

Tufiño
Aguas Hediondas
Tulcán
Maldonado
Gualchán
San Juan de Lachas
Chical

CARCHI

Julio Andrade
Huaca
San Gabriel
Bolívar
El Angel
La Libertad
Morán
El Angel
Mira
Mariscal Sucre
La Bonita

Reserva Ecológica El Angel

Pan-American Highway

Mascarilla
El Juncal
Ambuquí
Pimampiro
Mariano Acosta
Nueva América

SUCUMBIOS

La Bonita

Puerto Libre

El Dorado de Cascales

Lita
Guallupe
El Limonal
Salinas
Tumbabiro
Urcuquí
Piñán
San Antonio de Ibarra
Quiroga

IMBABURA

Cotacachi (4939m)

Reserva Ecológica Cotacachi-Cayapas

Laguna Cuicocha

Apuela
Santa Rosa
Cuellaje
García Moren
Selva Alegre
San José de Minas

Laguna Yahuarcocha
Ibarra
La Esperanza
Olmedo
Cotacachi
Zuleta
Lago San Pablo
Otavalo
Lago Grande de Mojanda
Tolas de Cochasquí
Tabacundo
Cayambe
Quitsato
Guayllabamba
El Quinche

Reserva Ecológica Cayambe-Coca

Cayambe (5790m)

Reventador (3560m)

Cascada San Rafael

NAPO

Coca

Quijos

Salado

Peruchо
Rumicucho
Malchinguí
San Antonio de Pichincha
Calderón
QUITO

Pululahua Crater & Reserve
Calacalí
Mitad del Mundo
Pomasqui
Nono
Rucu Pichincha (4627m)

ESMERALDAS

Chontal
Pacto
Gualea
Las Tolas
Tulipe
Sahuangal
Nanegalito
Bellavista
Mindo

20 km
20 miles

N

North of
Quito

The area north of Quito to the Colombian border is outstandingly beautiful. The landscape is mountainous, with views of the Cotacachi, Imbabura, and Chiles volcanoes, as well as the glacier-covered Cayambe, interspersed with lakes. The region is also renowned for its *artesanía*.

Quito to Otavalo
straddling the equator, a good area for crafts, trekking and pre-Inca pyramids

On the way from the capital to the main tourist centre in northern Ecuador, the landscape is dominated by the Cayambe volcano.

Quito to Cayambe
At **Calderón**, 32 km north of the centre of Quito but now a suburb of the city and on one of the routes to the new airport, you can see the famous bread figurines being made. Prices are lower than in the city centre. On 1-2 November, the graves in the cemetery are decorated with flowers, drinks and food for the dead. The Corpus Christi processions are very colourful. To get there take a bus at La Ofelia Metrobus terminal.

The Pan-American Highway goes to **Guayllabamba**, home of the Quito zoo (www.quitozoo.org) and renowned for avocadoes and *locro* (Típico Locro is recommended – see Food and drink, page 33), where it branches, one road going through Cayambe and the second, a new dual-carriageway, through Tabacundo before rejoining at Cajas. By the Río Pisque bridge, a road to the left is signed to **Parque Recreacional y Bosque Protector Jerusalem** ① *open 0800-1630, US$2 for foreigners, camping US$1, www.pichincha.gob.ec*, a dry forest reserve at over 2000 m. It is beside the old road to Otavalo, now called the Ruta Escondida, which goes through the villages of Puéllaro, Perucho and San José de Minas. The reserve is 28 km from Quito, 4 km off the main road.

At Km 10 past Guayllabamba on the road to Tabacundo, just north of the toll booth, a cobbled road to the left (signed Pirámides de Cochasquí) leads to Tocachi and further on to the ★ **Parque Arqueológico Cochasquí** ① *T09-9822 0686, Quito T02-399 4405, 0800-1630, last entry 1500, US$3, entry only with a 1½-hr guided tour every 15 mins, Spanish only.* The protected area contains 15 truncated clay pyramids (*tolas*), nine with long ramps, built between AD 950 and 1550 by the Cara or Cayambi-Caranqui people. Festivals with dancing take place at the equinoxes and solstices. There is a site museum, a model of a typical house, native crops, llamas, alpacas and vicuñas; views from the pyramids, south to Quito, are marvellous. The site is said to have mystical properties and is popular for star-gazing and UFO-watching.

Uphill from the park entrance is **Camping Cochasquí** ① *T09-9491 9008, US$3 pp for camping (US$10 if hiring a tent, take sleeping bag), US$10 pp in cabins, meals available US$3 each, gates open 0600-1800.* Wooden cabins are set in lovely gardens with great views; contact the Consejo Provincial de Pichincha to make reservations, eight days in advance for weekends, website as above. The road beyond Cochasquí goes to the Lagunas de Mojanda (see page 104), but this is not the official entrance. On the other road, 8 km before Cayambe, a globe carved out of rock by the Pan-American Highway is at the spot where the French expedition marked the equator (small shops sell drinks and snacks). A few metres north is **Quitsato** ① *T02-361 0908, www.quitsato.org, US$2, open daily 0830-1730,* where studies about the equator and its importance to ancient cultures are carried out. There is a sun dial, 54 m in diameter, and a solar culture exhibit, with information about indigenous cultures and archaeological sites along the equator; here too there are special events for the solstices and equinoxes.

Cayambe *Colour map 1, B5.*

Cayambe, on the eastern (right-hand) branch of the highway, 25 km northeast of Guayllabamba, is overshadowed by the snow-capped volcano of the same name. The surrounding countryside consists of a few dairy farms and many flower plantations. The area is noted for its *bizcochos* (biscuits) served with *queso de hoja* (string cheese). At the Centro Cultural Espinoza-Jarrín, is the **Museo de la Ciudad** ① *Rocafuerte y Bolívar, Wed-Sun 0800-1700, free,* with displays relating to the Cayambi culture and ceramics found at **Puntiachil**, an important but poorly preserved archaeologic site at the edge of town. There is a fiesta in March for the equinox with plenty of local music; also Inti Raymi solstice and San Pedro celebrations in June. Market day is Sunday. A community tourism project, **Camino del Cóndor Paquiestancia** ① *Terán S0-54 y Sucre, T02-212 9022, https://caminodelcondorec.jimdo.com,* provides lodging ($$-$), food, cultural events and trekking, riding and mountain biking in the highlands of the Cayambe Coca reserve.

Reserva Ecológica Cayambe Coca
Rocafuerte y Puerto Baquerizo, Cayambe, T02-211 0370, werner.barrera@ambiente.gob.ec.

Cayambe is a good place to access the western side of Reserva Ecológica Cayambe-Coca, a large park which spans the Cordillera Oriental and extends down to the eastern lowlands. **Volcán Cayambe**, Ecuador's third highest peak, at 5790 m, lies within the reserve. It is the highest point in the world to lie so close to the equator (3.75 km north). The equator goes over the mountain's flanks. About 1 km south of the town of Cayambe is an unmarked cobbled road heading east via Juan Montalvo, leading in 26 km to the **Ruales-Oleas-Berge refuge** ① *T09-5955 9765, rooms for 4-10 passengers take sleeping bag, US$14 pp with use of kitchen or US$30 with dinner and breakfast,* at 4600 m. The standard climbing route, from the west, uses the refuge as a base. There is a crevasse near the summit which can be very difficult to cross if there isn't enough snow, ask the refuge keeper about conditions. There are good acclimatization hikes around the refuge. Otavalo and Quito operators offer tours here.

To the southeast of Cayambe, also within the reserve and surrounded by cloudforest at 3200 m, is **Oyacachi** ① *T06-299 1846, oyacachi@gmail.com*, a traditional village of farmers and woodcarvers, with thermal baths (US$3). Accommodation (**$$-$**) is available at **Cabañas Oyacachi** (*T06-299 1846, www.cabanasoyacachi.com*) and in family *hospedajes*. There is good walking in the area, including a two-day walk to Papallacta and a three-day walk to El Chaco in the lowlands; these require a permit from the reserve, write ahead.

Listings Quito to Otavalo

Where to stay

Cayambe

$$$ Hacienda Guachalá
South of Cayambe on the road to Cangahua, T02-361 0908, www.guachala.com.
The first hacienda in Ecuador, nicely restored, the chapel (1580) is built on top of a pre-Inca structure. Simple but comfortable rooms in older section and fancier ones in newer area, fireplaces, delicious meals, covered swimming pool, parking, attentive service, good walking, horses for rent, excursions to nearby ruins, small museum.

$$-$ Mitad del Mundo
Av Natalia Jarrín S7-74 y Córdova Galarza, T02-236 0226, see Facebook (Hostería Mitad del Mundo Ecuador).
Modern building, simple rooms, indoor pool, restaurant and parking, popular for group events.

$ La Gran Colombia
Panamericana y Calderón, T02-236 1238.
Modern multi-storey building, restaurant, parking, traffic noise in front rooms.

Restaurants

Cayambe

$$$ Casa de Fernando
Panamericana Norte Km 1.5, T02-236 0262, www.casadefernando.com. Tue-Sun from 1230.
Varied menu, good international food. Also has **Café Encuentro**.

$$-$ Aroma
Bolívar 404 y Ascázubi, T02-236 1773, see Facebook. Open 0700-2100, except Wed and Sun 0800-1600.
Large choice of set lunches and à la carte, variety of desserts, very good.

Festivals

Mar Fiesta for the equinox with plenty of local music.
Jun Inti Raymi solstice and San Pedro celebrations.

Transport

Quito to Cayambe
Cochasquí
Bus
From Terminal Carcelén, Quito, be sure to take a bus that goes on the Tabacundo road and ask to be let off at the turn-off, from where it's a pleasant 8-km uphill walk, or get out at the Cochasquí toll booth and take a pick-up; 1¾-2 hrs from the city. Alternatively, from Terminal La Ofelia, take a bus to **Malchinguí** (hourly, US$1.50, 2 hrs) and a pick-up to Cochasquí (US$3, 15 mins) or a taxi (US$6). There are also buses between Malchinguí and Cayambe which go by Cochasquí.

Cayambe
Bus
Flor del Valle, from La Ofelia, **Quito**, every 7 mins 0530-2100, US$1.50, 1½ hrs. Their Cayambe station is at Montalvo y Junín.

To **Otavalo**, from roundabout at Bolívar y Av N Jarrín, every 15 mins, US$0.95, 45 mins.

Reserva Ecológica Cayambe Coca Road

To **Volcán Cayambe**, most vehicles can go as far as the **Hacienda Piemonte El Hato** (at about 3500 m) from where it is a 3- to 4-hr walk, longer if heavily laden or if it is windy, but it is a beautiful walk. Regular pick-ups can often make it to 'la Z', a sharp curve on the road 30-mins' walk from the *refugio*. 4WDs can often make it to the *refugio*. Pick-ups can be hired by the market in Cayambe, Junín y Ascázubi, US$45, 1½-2 hrs. Arrange ahead for return transport. A milk truck runs from Cayambe's hospital to the hacienda at 0600, returning between 1700 and 1900. To **Oyacachi**, from the north side of Cayambe, near the Mercado Mayorista, Mon, Wed, Sat at 1500, Sun at 0800, US$2.50, 1½ hrs; return to Cayambe Wed, Fri, Sat at 0400, Sun at 1400.

Otavalo and around   *Colour map 1, B5.*

a town famous for its markets in a beautiful area of mountains and lakes

Otavalo, only a short distance from the capital, is a must on any tourist itinerary in Ecuador. The Tabacundo and Cayambe roads join at Cajas, then cross the *páramo* and suddenly descend into the land of the Otavaleños, a thriving, prosperous group, famous for their prodigious production of woollens. The town itself, consisting of rather functional modern buildings, is one of South America's most important centres of ethno-tourism and its enormous Saturday market, featuring a dazzling array of textiles and crafts, is second to none and not to be missed. Set in beautiful countryside, the area is worth exploring for three or four days.

Otavalo

Men here wear their hair long and plaited under a broad-brimmed hat and wear white, calf-length trousers and blue ponchos. The women's colourful costumes consist of embroidered blouses, shoulder wraps and many coloured beads. Indigenous families speak Quichua at home, although it is losing some ground to Spanish with the younger generation.

The ★ **Saturday market** comprises four different markets in various parts of the town with the central streets filled with vendors. The *artesanías* market is held 0700-1800, based around the Plaza de Ponchos (Plaza Centenario). The livestock section is open from 0500 until 0900, outside the centre, west of the Panamericana; go west on Calderón from the town centre. There are also stalls selling foodstuffs, hardware and more, but in small quantities. The produce market, Mercado 24 de Mayo, at the old stadium, west of the centre, lasts from 0700 until 1400. The *artesanías* industry is so big that the Plaza de Ponchos is filled with vendors every day of the week. The selection is better on Saturday but prices are a little higher than other days when the atmosphere is more relaxed. Wednesday is also an important market day with more movement than other weekdays. Polite bargaining is appropriate in the market and shops. Otavaleños not only sell goods they weave and sew themselves, but they bring crafts from throughout Ecuador and from Peru and Bolivia.

The **Museo Viviente Otavalango** ⓘ *Vía Antigua a Quiroga 1230, antigua Fábrica San Pedro, Barrio San Juan, T06-290 3879, https://otavalango.wordpress.com, Mon-Sat 0900-1700, call ahead for tours in English or special demonstrations, US$5*, has displays on all cultural aspects of Otavaleño life and is worth a visit; it has live presentations of local traditions for groups. You can get there by taxi (US$1.50) or by bus (route explained on website). There are good views of town from the cultural centre **Kinti Wasi (La Casa del Colibrí)** ⓘ *C Morales past the railway line (Kinti Wasi-Otavalo on Facebook)*.

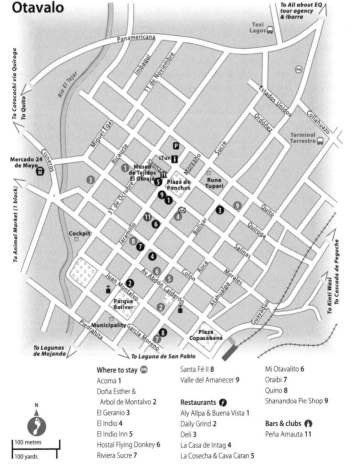

Otavalo

Where to stay 🛏
Acoma **1**
Doña Esther &
 Arbol de Montalvo **2**
El Geranio **3**
El Indio **4**
El Indio Inn **5**
Hostal Flying Donkey **6**
Riviera Sucre **7**

Santa Fé II **8**
Valle del Amanecer **9**

Restaurants 🍴
Aly Allpa & Buena Vista **1**
Daily Grind **2**
Deli **3**
La Casa de Intag **4**
La Cosecha & Cava Caran **5**

Mi Otavalito **6**
Oraibi **7**
Quino **8**
Shanandoa Pie Shop **9**

Bars & clubs 🍸
Peña Amauta **11**

Around Otavalo

Otavalo weavers come from dozens of communities. Many families weave and visitors should shop around as the less known weavers often have better prices and some of the most famous ones only sell from their homes, especially in Agato and Peguche. The easiest villages to visit are **Ilumán** (there are also many felt hatmakers in town and *yachacs*, or shamen, mostly north of the plaza – look for signs); **Agato**; **Carabuela** (many homes sell crafts, including wool sweaters); and **Peguche**. These villages are only 15-30 minutes from Otavalo bus services are good; buses leave from the Terminal and stop at Plaza Copacabana (Atahualpa y Montalvo). You can also take a taxi (US$2).

To reach the lovely **Cascada de Peguche**, from Peguche's plaza, facing the church, head right and continue straight until the road forks. Take the lower fork to the right, but not the road that heads downhill. There is a small campsite at the falls, as well as a small information centre (contributions are appreciated). From the top (left side, excellent views) you can continue the walk to Lago San Pablo. The 11-day **Pawkar Raymi** festival is held in Peguche (see Festivals, page 107).

The **Ciclovía** is a bicycle path which runs along the old railway line 21 km between Eugenio Espejo de Cajas and Otavalo. Because of the slope, it is better to start in Cajas. You can take a tour or hire a bike and take a bus bound for Quito to the bike path.

Around Otavalo

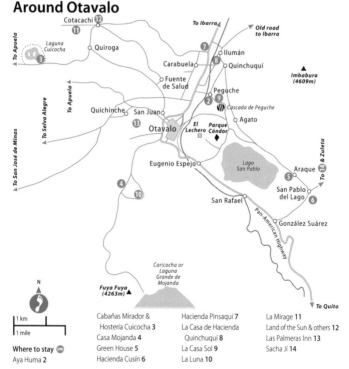

Where to stay

Aya Huma 2	Hacienda Pinsaquí 7	La Mirage 11
Cabañas Mirador &	La Casa de Hacienda	Land of the Sun & others 12
Hostería Cuicocha 3	Quinchuquí 8	Las Palmeras Inn 13
Casa Mojanda 4	La Casa Sol 9	Sacha Jí 14
Green House 5	La Luna 10	
Hacienda Cusín 6		

ON THE ROAD

The Otavaleños

The Otavaleños are a proud and prosperous people who have made their name not only as successful weavers and international business people, but also as unsurpassed symbols of cultural fortitude. Today, they make up the economic elite of their town and its surroundings and provide an example which other groups have followed. The Otavalo dialect of Quichua, the highland native tongue, has been adopted as the national standard.

There is considerable debate over the origin of the Otavaleños. In present-day Imbabura, pre-Inca people were Caranquis, or Imbaya, and, in Otavalo, the Cayambi. They were subjugated by the Caras who expanded into the highlands from the Manabí coast. The Caras resisted the Incas for 17 years, but the conquering Incas eventually moved the local population away to replace them with vassals from Peru and Bolivia. One theory is that the Otavaleños are descended from these forced migrants and also Chibcha salt traders from Colombia, while some current-day Otavaleños prefer to stress their local pre-Inca roots.

Otavalo men wear their hair long and plaited under a white trophy hat. They wear white, calf-length trousers and blue ponchos. The women's colourful costumes consist of embroidered blouses, shoulder wraps, a plethora of gold-coloured necklace beads and red bead bracelets. Their ankle-length skirts, known as *anacos*, are fastened with an intricately woven cloth belt or *faja*. Traditional footwear for both genders is the *alpargata*, a sandal whose sole was originally made of coiled hemp rope, but today has been replaced by rubber.

Perhaps the most outstanding feature of the Otavaleños is their profound sense of pride and self-assurance. This is aided not only by the group's economic success, but also by achievements in academic and cultural realms. In the words of one local elder: My grandfather was illiterate, my father completed primary school and I finished high school in Quito. My son has a PhD and has served as a cabinet minister!

Southeast of Otavalo, at the foot of Cerro Imbabura and just off the Panamericana, is Lago San Pablo, the largest natural lake in the country. Along the secondary road which circumnavigates the lake are several villages and a number of upmarket *hosterías*. Mats and other crafts are made with *totora* reeds from the lake. There is a network of old roads and trails between Otavalo and Lago San Pablo, none of which takes more than two hours to explore. It is worth walking either to or back from the lake for the views. Going in a group is recommended for safety. A good half-day excursion is via Cascada de Peguche, **Parque Cóndor** ① *on a hill called Curyloma, near the community of Pucará Alto, T06-304 9399, www.parquecondor.com, Wed-Sun and holidays 0930-1700, raptor flight demonstrations at 1130 and 1530, US$4.50, crowded at weekends*, a reserve and birds of prey rehabilitation centre, and then back via **El Lechero**, a lookout by a tree considered sacred among local indigenous people.

From **San Pablo del Lago** it is possible to climb **Imbabura** volcano (4630 m, a serious climb and frequently under cloud); allow at least six hours to reach the summit and four hours for the descent. Alternative access is from La Esperanza or San Clemente (see page 112). Easier, and no less impressive, is the nearby **Cerro Huarmi Imbabura**, 3845 m; it is not signed but several paths lead there. Take a good map, food and warm clothing.

Southwest of Otavalo are the impressive **Lagunas de Mojanda**, accessed by cobbled roads from Otavalo or Tabacundo, or by tracks from Cochasquí or Tocachi. Otavalo agencies offer tours. **Caricocha** (or Laguna Grande de Mojanda) is a crater lake 18 km from and 1200 m higher than Otavalo. About 25 minutes' walk above Caricocha is the smaller **Laguna Huarmicocha** and a further 25 minutes is **Laguna Yanacocha** (Laguna Negra). The Pedro Moncayo municipal government has a *refugio* between Caricocha and Yanacocha. There are cabins which must be reserved in advance ($$-$) and it is a recommended place to camp, US$4.20 (check in advance which days it is attended, in Tabacundo T02-383 6560 ext 177, www.pedromoncayo.gob.ec). Take a warm jacket, food and drinks, a tent and warm sleeping bags if camping. From Caricocha a trail continues south about 5 km before dividing: the left-hand track to **Tocachi**, the right-hand one to Cochasquí (see page 97), both about 20 km from Caricocha. You can climb **Fuya Fuya** (4263 m), a popular acclimatization ascent, and **Yanaurco** (4259 m).

Listings Otavalo and around *maps pages 101 and 102.*

Tourist information

Dirección de Turismo
Corner of Plaza de Ponchos, Jaramillo y Quiroga, T06-292 7230, www.otavalo.travel. Mon-Fri 0800-1730, Sat 0800-1600.
Local and regional information, English spoken Mon-Fri, helpful; the website is good, multilingual and gives a list of community tourism projects.

Where to stay

Otavalo
In town
Hotels may be full on Fri night before market.

$$$-$$ Acoma
Salinas 07-57 y 31 de Octubre, T06-292 6570, www.acomahotel.com.
Lovely rebuilt home in colonial style, parking, comfortable rooms, some with balcony, 1 room with bathtub, 2 suites with kitchenette.

$$$-$$ Doña Esther
Montalvo 4-44 y Bolívar, T06-292 0739, www.otavalohotel.com.

Nicely restored colonial house, a hotel for over 100 years, very good restaurant (**Arbol de Montalvo**, see Restaurants, below), rooms with lovely wooden floors, colourful decor, pleasant atmosphere, transfers to Quito or airport.

$$$-$$ El Indio Inn
Bolívar 9-04 y Calderón, T06-292 2922, www.hotelelindioinn.com.
Modern hotel, carpeted rooms and simple suites, restaurant, parking, use of spa US$6.50.

$$ El Indio
Sucre 12-14 y Salinas, near Plaza de Ponchos, T06-292 0060, www.hotelelindio.com.
In multi-storey building, ask for a room with balcony, simple restaurant, parking, helpful service.

$$ Riviera Sucre
García Moreno 380 y Roca, T06-292 0241, www.rivierasucre.com.
Traditional hotel with ample renovated and new rooms, good breakfast available, cafeteria, private or shared bath, kitchen facilities, book exchange, bookshop with

good selection of English and German titles, pleasant common areas, garden and courtyard, good meeting place. Good value and recommended.

$$-$ Santa Fé
Roca 7-34 y García Moreno, T06-292 3640, www.hotelsantafeotavalo.com.
Modern, attractive pine decoration, breakfast available, restaurant, run by indigenous Otavaleños, good value. Also **Santa Fé II** (Colón 507 y Sucre, T06-292 0161), same web page, same price and facilities.

$$-$ Valle del Amanecer
Roca y Quiroga, T06-292 0990, http://valledelamanecer.com.
Small rustic rooms, some with thin walls, private or shared bath, pleasant courtyard with hammocks, popular.

$ El Geranio
Ricaurte y Morales, T06-292 0185, www.hostalelgeranio.com.
2 types of room, smaller ones with electric shower and no TV are cheaper, laundry facilities and use of kitchen, parking, quiet, family-run, popular, runs trips, good value. Recommended.

$ Flying Donkey
Abdón Calderón 510 y Bolívar, upstairs, T06-292 8122, www.flyingdonkeyotavalo.com.
Popular backpacker's hostel, rooms with private bath, US$12 pp in dorm, free coffee and fruit, no breakfast, kitchen facilities and terrace.

Out of town

$$$ Hacienda Pinsaquí
Panamericana Norte Km 5, 300 m north of the turn-off for Cotacachi, T06-294 6116, www.haciendapinsaqui.com.
Converted hacienda dating to 1790, with 30 suites, 1 with jacuzzi, restaurant with lovely dining room, lounge with fireplace, beautiful antiques, colonial ambience, gardens, horse riding.

$$$ Las Palmeras Inn
Vía Quichinche Km 2, 15 mins by bus from Otavalo, T06-266 8067, www.laspalmerasinn.com.
Cabins with terrace and fireplace in a rural setting, restaurant, parking, nice grounds and views, pool table and ping-pong, British-owned, airport transfers arranged. Sister hotel is **Hacienda Cusín**, see below.

Around Otavalo
Ilumán

$$ La Casa de Hacienda Quinchuquí
Vía Ilumán, entrance at Panamericana Norte Km 3, then 300 m east, T06-269 0245, www.casahaciendaquinchuqui.com.
Tasteful cabins with fireplace, restaurant, parking, horse riding.

Peguche

$$$-$$ La Casa Sol
Near the Cascada de Peguche, T06-269 0500, or Quito 02-223 0798, www.lacasasol.com.
Comfortable rustic lodge set on a hillside. Bright cosy rooms and suites with balcony, some with fireplace, lovely attention to detail, restaurant and conference room.

$$ Aya Huma
On the railway line in Peguche, T06-269 0333, www.ayahuma.com.
In a country setting between the railway tracks and the river. Quiet, pleasant atmosphere, kitchen facilities, restaurant for breakfast and dinner, dormitory US$7 pp, camping US$4 pp, organizes ancestral ceremonies, Dutch/Ecuadorean-run, popular. Recommended.

Lago San Pablo

$$$$ Sacha Jí
Vía del Cóndor y Angel Vaca, San Pablo, T06-304 9474, www.mysachaji.com.

A wellness and yoga retreat on a hilltop overlooking Lago San Pablo and Imbabura volcano, a long way from the village. Spacious rooms with heating, organic orchard and gardens planted with native species, restaurant with holistic dining (all local ingredients), outdoor hot tub, yoga and breathing classes, and a variety of therapies. Packages available, either B&B or half-board; reserve in advance.

$$$$-$$$ Hacienda Cusín
By the village of San Pablo del Lago to the southeast of the lake, T06-291 8013, www.haciendacusin.com.
A converted 17th-century hacienda with lovely courtyard and well-established garden with old trees, flowers and cobbled paths. Has 2 parts, the **Hacienda** (rooms with fireplace, huge beds) and El **Monastrerio de Cusín** (http://elmonasteriodecusin.com), which is slightly less grand, but still very comfortable. Fine restaurant, decorations throughout have a religious theme, sports facilities (horses, bikes, squash court, games room), Spanish classes, library, book in advance, British-run. Recommended.

$$ Green House
C 24 de Junio, Comunidad Araque, by the east shore of the lake, northwest of San Pablo del Lago, T06-291 9298, www.araquebyb.hostel.com.
Family-run *hostal*, some rooms with bath, others with detached bath, dinner on request, sitting room with fireplace, rooftop terrace with views, Quito airport pick-up.

Lagunas de Mojanda

$$$$-$$$ Casa Mojanda
Vía a Mojanda Km 3.5, T09-8033 5108, www.casamojanda.com.
Comfortable cabins set on a beautiful hillside. Includes breakfast prepared with ingredients from own organic garden, use

of outdoor hot tub with great views and short guided hike to waterfall (the dogs will take you). Each room is decorated with its own elegant touch, other meals extra, quiet, good library, horse riding, local tours, transfer from Quito and airport. Recommended.

$$ La Luna
Mojandita Curubi, on a side road going south off the Mojanda road at Km 4, T09-9315 6082, www.lalunaecuador.info.
Pleasant hostel in attractive surroundings, some rooms with fireplace, heater and private bath, others with shared bath, US$14-17 pp in dorm, camping US$8 pp, terrace with hammocks, pleasant dining room-lounge, transport information on hostel's website, excursions arranged, popular, British/Ecuadorean-owned. Recommended.

Restaurants

Otavalo

$$$-$$ Arbol de Montalvo
Montalvo 4-44 y Bolívar, in Hotel Doña Esther, T06-292 0739, www.otavalohotel. com. Tue-Thu 1800-2100, Fri-Sat 0715-2100, Sun 0715-2100.
Wide variety of dishes including excellent wood-oven pizzas.

$$$-$$ Quino
Roca 7-40 y García Moreno, T06-292 4994. Mon-Sat 1000-2200.
Traditional coastal cooking, good seafood and some meat dishes, pleasant seating around patio, popular.

$$ Aly Allpa
Salinas 509 at Plaza de Ponchos, T06-292 0289. Daily 0800-1700.
Good-value set meals, breakfast and à la carte including trout, vegetarian and meat. Recommended.

$$ Buena Vista
Salinas entre Sucre y Jaramillo, p2, www.buenavistaotavalo.com. Sun-Mon 1300-2200, Wed-Thu 1000-2200, Fri 1100-2300, Sat 0900-2300.
Bistro with balcony overlooking Plaza de Ponchos. Good international food, sandwiches, salads, vegetarian options, trout, good coffee, Wi-Fi.

$$ Mi Otavalito
Sucre y Morales. Daily 1200-2100
Good for set lunch and international food à la carte. Popular with tour groups.

$$ Oraibi
Sucre y Colón. Tue 0900-1800, Wed-Fri 0930-2000, Sat 0700-2000.
Vegetarian food in pleasant patio setting, pizza, salads, pasta, Mexican, breakfast, Swiss-owned.

$$-$ Deli
Quiroga 12-18 y Bolívar. Daily 1130-2100.
Economical set lunch, plus good Mexican food, international and pizza à la carte, nice desserts, pleasant atmosphere, family-run, good value.

Cafés

Daily Grind
Sucre y Juan Montalvo, Parque Bolívar, see Facebook. Daily 0830-2030.
Small outdoor café with very good coffee, muffins and other treats.

La Casa de Intag
Colón 465 y Sucre. Mon 0900-1730, Tue-Sat 0830-1730.
Fairtrade cafeteria/shop run by Intag coffee growers and artisans associations. Good organic coffee, breakfast, pancakes, sandwiches, sisal crafts, fruit pulp and more.

La Cosecha
Jaramillo y Salinas, upstairs, T06-292 4520, www.lacosechaec.com. Daily 0900-2000.
Great modern café and bakery overlooking Plaza de Ponchos. Excellent coffee, sandwiches and bagels. English and French spoken. Recommended. Downstairs is **Cava Caran** "beer experience", selling craft brews and light meals, 5 taster beers for US$5, see Facebook. Also has an organic market on Sat.

Shenandoa Pie Shop
Salinas y Jaramillo. Mon-Fri 1300-2100.
Good fruit pies, milk shakes and ice cream, popular meeting place, an Otavalo tradition.

Bars and clubs

Otavalo
Otavalo is generally safe but avoid deserted areas at night. Nightlife is concentrated at Morales y Jaramillo and C 31 de Octubre. *Peñas* are open Fri and Sat from 1930, entrance US$3.

Peña Amauta
Morales 5-11 y Jaramillo, T06-292 2435, Facebook: amautabar. Fri and Sat 1800-0200.
Good local bands, welcoming, mainly foreigners. Upstairs is **Napolitano** Italian restaurant (open Sun-Fri 0700-2300, Sat 0700-2300).

Festivals

Otavalo and around
Jan-Feb **Pawkar Raymi**, www.otavalo.travel. The 11-day festival is held in Peguche before carnival.
End of Jun **Inti Raymi** combines celebrations of the summer solstice (21 Jun), with the **Fiesta de San Juan** (24 Jun) and the **Fiesta de San Pedro y San Pablo** (29 Jun). These combined festivities are known as **Los San Juanes** and participants are mostly indigenous. They take place in the smaller communities surrounding Otavalo, each one celebrates separately on different dates, some for a full week. The celebration begins with a ritual bath; the Peguche waterfall

Ecuadorean ball games

Like in all of Latin America, *fútbol* (football or soccer) is played by young and old throughout Ecuador. In addition, there are a number of traditional ball games which are part of the fabric of the country, either unique to Ecuador or shared with one of its neighbours. It is generally men who play and a fair bit of swearing accompanies the action. In many cases betting among the spectators make the game all the more exciting.

Walk by a park in any city or town in the late afternoon and you will see a crowd cheering around a volleyball court. If you pay close attention, you will see that there are only three players on either side of the court and that the ball is handled in a way not permitted in ordinary volleyball. This is *ecuavolley* or *voli*, Ecuador's very own sport.

A unique form of paddle ball most commonly played in the northern and central highlands is *pelota nacional* (the 'national' ball game), requiring considerable strength. It is also known as *pelota de tabla* (board ball) for its impressive paddles or *tablas*. A 1-m-long square wooden paddle with rubber spikes weighing about 1.5 kg is used for batting and another, up to 6 kg, for returning the heavy natural rubber ball. The paddle is secured to the forearm with a leather glove. There are five players on either side of the court and the rules are like those of tennis. *Pelota nacional* is played in the afternoons in the Yacucalle neighbourhood of Ibarra, south of the bus station, and in Quito at weekends at Parque La Carolina and in the southern neighbourhoods of Mena 2 and Quito Sur.

A similar game, also played in the north is *pelota de guante* (glove ball), where the 'glove' is really a wooden disk around 35 cm in diameter, covered in leather and studded with thick nails on one surface. Also similar is *pelota de mano* (hand ball), where a rubber or leather ball is struck with the hand.

Bolas is yet another popular game. The term refers to marbles, also known as *canicas*. These are placed inside a circle and each player tries to hit the opponent's pieces. In a similar fashion, large steel balls (*bolas de acero*) are propelled from about 50 m away to a court with an inner circle of small balls or palm fruits (*coquitos*). This game called *bolas* or *cocos*, is played in the central highlands and in Quito at Parque El Ejido.

is used by Otavalo residents (a personal spiritual activity, best carried out without visitors and certainly without cameras). In Otavalo, indigenous families have costume parties, which at times spill over onto the streets. In the San Juan neighbourhood, near the Yanayacu baths, there is a week-long celebration with food, drink and music.
1st 2 weeks of Sep Fiesta del Yamor and **Colla Raymi** feature local dishes, funfairs, bands in the plaza and sporting events.
Oct Mes de la Cultura, cultural events throughout the month.

Last weekend of Oct Mojanda Arriba is an annual full-day hike from Malchinguí over Mojanda to reach Otavalo for the foundation celebrations.

What to do

Otavalo
Horse riding
Several operators offer riding tours. Half-day trips to nearby attractions cost US$40-50. Full-day trips such as Cuicocha or Mojanda run at US$60-70.

Language schools

Instituto Superior de Español, *Jaramillo 6-23 y Morales, T06-292 7354, www.superiorspanishschool.com.*

Mundo Andino Internacional, *Bolívar 8-16 y Abdón Calderón, p3, T06-292 1864, www. mandinospanishschool.com.* Cooking classes, tours and other activities offered.

Mountain bikes

Several tour operators rent bikes and offer cycling tours at US$35-110 for a day trip (price depends on number of people). See also **Ciclovía**, page 102. Rentals cost US$10-12 per day. **Taller Ciclo Primaxi**, Ricaurte y Morales and in Peguche.

Tour operators

Most tours are to indigenous communities, Cuicocha and Mojanda, US$25-85 pp.
All about EQ, *Los Corazas 433 y Albarracín, at the north end of town, T06-292 3633, www.all-about-ecuador.com.* Interesting itineraries, trekking and horse-riding tours, climbing, cycling, trips to Intag, Piñán, Cayambe, Oyacachi, volunteering on organic farms. English and French spoken. Recommended.
Ecomontes, *Sucre y Morales, T06-292 6244, www.ecomontestour.com.* A branch of a Quito operator (JL Mera N24-91 y Mcal Foch, T02-290 3629), trekking, climbing, rafting, also sell tours to Cuyabeno and Galápagos.
Runa Tupari, *Sucre 14-15 y Quito, T06-292 2320, www.runatupari.com.* Arranges indigenous homestays in the Cotacachi area, also the usual tours, trekking, horse riding and cycling trips and transport.

Train rides

Beautifully restored historic train station at Guayaquil entre Calderón y J Montalvo, T1-800-873637, www.trenecuador.com, Wed-Thu 0800-1700, Fri-Sat 0700-1700, Sun 0700-1300. Train ride to **Salinas** (57 km away) and back, *El Tren de la Libertad II*, US$53. Departures Fri-Sun 0800, returning 1755; on Sun return from Ibarra to Otavalo is by bus. Includes stops at San Roque, Andrade Marín (with **Museo Textil**) and San Antonio de Ibarra. You can continue by bus from Salinas to **San Lorenzo**, see page 256.

Transport

Otavalo
Bus
Terminal at Atahualpa y Ordóñez (no departures after 1930). The Ibarra Terminal offers many more destinations. To **Quito** 2 hrs, US$2.50, every 10 mins; all depart from Terminal Carcelén in Quito, **Coop Otavalo** and **Coop Los Lagos** go into Otavalo, buses bound for Ibarra or Tulcán drop you off at the highway, this is inconvenient and not safe at night. From **Quito** or airport by taxi takes 1½ hrs, US$60 one way; shared taxis with **Taxis Lagos/Serviquito**, in Quito, Asunción 3-82, T02-256 5955; in Otavalo, Av Los Sarances y Corazas, T06-292 3203, www. serviquito.com, who run a hotel to hotel service (to/from modern Quito only) and will divert to resorts just off the highway; Mon-Sat hourly, 6 departures on Sun, 1½ hrs, US$15 pp, buy ticket at least 1 day ahead; they also go from Quito to Ibarra. Tour operators also offer transfers. Bus to **Ibarra**, every 4 mins, US$0.55, 40 mins. To **Peguche**, Imbaburapac city bus on Av Atahualpa, every 10 mins, bus stops in front of the terminal and at Plaza Copacabana, US$0.35; taxi US$3. To **Apuela** in the Intag region, **Trans Otavalo**, T06-292 0405, daily at 0730, 1000 and 1400, US$2.50, 2 hrs. To **Ambato** bypassing Quito, US$5.65, see Ibarra Transport (page 123), **CITA** buses from Ibarra stop along the Panamericana, enquire locally where to wait for them, and note that this is not safe after dark.

Around Otavalo
Bus
From Otavalo to **San Pablo del Lago** every 25 mins, more often on Sat, US$0.35, 30 mins; taxi US$4. Also buses to many nearby communities.

Northwest of Otavalo is Cotacachi from where a road goes west to the Cotacachi-Cayapas reserve and the subtropical Intag region. The main highway goes north to the city of Ibarra and beyond into the hot Chota Valley from where a branch road goes west to the subtropical valley of the Río Mira and the coastal town of San Lorenzo. The Panamericana reaches the border at the busy town of Tulcán, with its fantastic cemetery topiary.

Cotacachi

West of the road between Otavalo and Ibarra is Cotacachi. There is also access along a secondary road from Otavalo through Quiroga. Cotacachi, home to a growing expatriate community, produces and sells many leather goods.

The **Casa de las Culturas** ① *Bolívar 1334 y 9 de Octubre*, a beautifully refurbished 19th-century building, is a monument to peace. It houses the post office, a library, gallery and radio station. The **Museo de las Culturas** ① *García Moreno 13-41 y Bolívar, T06-255 4155, Mon-Fri 0800-1800, Sat-Sun 0930-1400, free*, has good displays of early Ecuadorean history and regional crafts and traditions. For local festivals, see page 122.

★Laguna Cuicocha and Intag

15 km from Cotacachi, the visitor centre has good natural history and cultural displays, daily 0800-1700.

This crater lake (altitude 3070 m) is part of the **Reserva Ecológica Cotacachi-Cayapas**, which extends from Cotacachi volcano to the tropical lowlands on the Río Cayapas in Esmeraldas. It is a crater lake with two islands, which are closed to the public to protect the native species. There is a well-marked 8-km path around the lake, which takes four to five hours and is best done anticlockwise. It provides spectacular views of the Cotacachi, Imbabura and, occasionally, Cayambe peaks. The best views are in the morning, when condors can sometimes be seen. There is a lookout at Km 3, two hours from the start. Take water and a waterproof jacket. Note that the path is not recommended for vertigo sufferers. There is a shorter trail which takes 40 minutes. Motor boat rides are available around the islands, US$3.25 per person for minimum eight persons.

To the northwest of Otavalo lies the lush subtropical region of **Intag**, reached along a paved road that follows the southern edge of Cuicocha, crosses the Cordillera Occidental and gradually descends to the southwest. It passes the hamlet of Santa Rosa, 35 km from Cuicocha, near which are several reserves in primary cloudforest which are good for birdwatching and nature observation. See for example **El Refugio de Intag** (www.elrefugiocloudforest.com) and **Intag Cloud Forest Reserve** (www.intagcloudforest.com). The town of **Apuela** is 46 km from Cuicocha. The region's primary cloudforest is threatened by a proposed large-scale copper mine, vigorously opposed by local communities. See **Defensa y Conservación Ecológica de Intag** ① *www.decoin.org*, and **Codelco Out Of Intag** ① *http://codelcoecuador.com*, for local conservation and community development projects. The area's rivers will also be affected by an irrigation and hydroelectric scheme in the Piñán area, see Northwest of Ibarra, page 113. The **Asociación Agroartesanal** de Café Río Intag (AACRI) ① *C García Moreno, Apuela, T06-256 6029, www.aacri.com*, a Fairtrade organic coffee grower's association, offers tours of coffee, sisal and sugar cane plantations and processing plants, also lodging and volunteer opportunities. Beyond are pleasant thermal baths at **Nangulví** ① *5 km from Apuela, T06-305 2024, http:// termasnangulvi.blogspot.co.uk*, with lodging, five hot pools and a large cold plunge pool. After Nangulví the road continues southwest to Aguagrún, where it joins a road to the region from Otavalo to Selva Alegre. The **Junín Cloud Forest Reserve** ① *1 hr from García Moreno by pick-up, 3 hrs on foot, T09-8887 1860 (Rosario), www.junincloudforest.com*, is an 800-ha reserve at 1500-2000 m with a lodge and hiking in the forest. The community is at the forefront of the struggle against the mining in the area. On the southwest boundary of the Cotacachi-Cayapas reserve is **Los Cedros Research Station** ① *2 hrs' walk from the road, T06-301 6650, T09-9277 8878, http://reservaloscedros.org*, 6400 ha of pristine cloudforest, with abundant orchids and bird life. Full board is available (**$$$** range) as well as volunteering opportunities; reservations necessary. **Cloud Forest Adventure** (Finca San Antonio, Cuellaje, transport details on website, T06-301 7543, www.cloudforestadventure. com) offers accommodation, tours and volunteer opportunities in the Intag region. The Intag road joins the San Miguel de los Bancos–La Independencia road at Pedro Vicente Maldonado (see page 88), having passed through Magdalena and Cielo Verde.

★ **Ibarra and around** *Colour map 1, B5.*
Ibarra, the provincial capital, is the main commercial centre and transport hub of the northern highlands. The city has an interesting ethnic mix, with blacks from the Chota valley and Esmeraldas alongside Otavaleños and other highland *indígenas*, mestizos and Colombian immigrants.

On **Parque Pedro Moncayo** stand the Catedral, the Municipio and Gobernación. One block away, at Flores y Olmedo, is the smaller Parque 9 de Octubre or **Parque de la Merced** (after its church). Beyond the railway station, to the south and west of the centre, is a busy commercial area with several markets, beyond which is the bus terminal. At the Centro Cultural Ibarra, the **Museo Regional Sierra Norte** ① *Sucre 7-21 y Oviedo, T06-260 2093, Mon-Sat 0830-1330, 1430-1630, Sun and holidays 1400-1600, US$1*, has interesting archaeological displays about cultures of northern Ecuador, colonial and contemporary art as well as temporary exhibits. **Bosque Protector Guayabillas** ① *Urbanización La Victoria, on the eastern outskirts of town, T09-8691 9891, Facebook: GuayabillasIBARRA, Tue-Sun 0900-1700*, is a 54-ha park on a hill which offers great views over the city. There are trails amid the eucalyptus forest. For Festivals, see page 122.

Off the main road between Otavalo and Ibarra is **San Antonio de Ibarra**, well known for its wood carvings (San Antonio is almost part of Ibarra now). It is worth seeing the range of styles and techniques and shopping around in the galleries and workshops. Further west is the town of **Atuntaqui**, famous for clothing and *fritadas* (see Food and drink, page 33; eat them at the best-known **Fritadas Amazonas**). On the opposite side of the Panamericana and along the railway line is Andrade Marín, home of the **Museo Fábrica Textil Imbabura** ① *T06-253 0240, Wed-Sun 0900-1600, US$3, knowledgeable guides*, which has a good display of machinery of the most important producer and employer in the area between 1926 and 1966; included in train tours.

About 8 km from Ibarra on the road south to Olmedo is **La Esperanza**, a pretty village in beautiful surroundings. Some 15 km further along, by Angochagua, is the community of **Zuleta**. The region is known for its fine embroidery. West of La Esperanza, along a road that starts at Avenida Atahualpa, and also 8 km from Ibarra, is the community of **San Clemente**, which has a very good grassroots tourism project, Pukyu Pamba (www. sclemente.com), see **Tradiciones San Clemente**, page 118. From either La Esperanza or San Clemente you can climb **Cubilche** volcano and **Imbabura**, more easily than from San Pablo del Lago. From the top you can walk down to Lago San Pablo (see page 103). *Guías nativos* are available for these climbs.

Ibarra to the coast The spectacular train ride from Ibarra to San Lorenzo on the Pacific coast no longer operates. A tourist train runs on a small section of this route, see pages 109 and 123.

Some 24 km north of Ibarra is the turn-off west for **Salinas**, a mainly Afro-Ecuadorean village with a Museo de la Sal, an ethnographic cultural centre and a restaurant offering local cuisine, and the very scenic road beside the Río Mira down to San Lorenzo. The road winds its way down along the cultivated valley beneath steep, dry mountains. At Km 41 from the turn-off are the villages of **Guallupe**, **El Limonal** (both bypassed – see

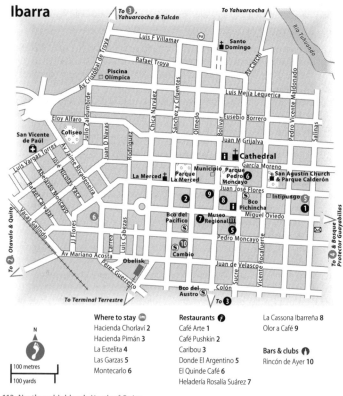

Ibarra

Where to stay
Hacienda Chorlaví **2**
Hacienda Pimán **3**
La Estelita **4**
Las Garzas **5**
Montecarlo **6**

Restaurants
Café Arte **1**
Café Pushkin **2**
Caribou **3**
Donde El Argentino **5**
El Quinde Café **6**
Heladería Rosalía Suárez **7**

La Cassona Ibarreña **8**
Olor a Café **9**

Bars & clubs
Rincón de Ayer **10**

Where to stay, pages 118 and 119), and **San Juan de Lachas**, in a lush subtropical area. Ceramic masks and figurines are produced at San Juan de Lachas, from where a road goes northeast 8 km to Gualchán. Here it divides, one branch going north to Chical by the Colombian border (see page 116), the second continuing northeast to Las Juntas, in an area with waterfalls. In **Lita**, 33 km from Guallupe, there is good swimming in the river. Beyond is the Río Chuchubi with waterfalls and swimming holes; here you'll find **Las Siete Cascadas resort** ⓘ *entry from 0900, US$10, guide US$10 per group* (see Where to stay, page 119). The closer to the coast, the greater is the extraction of timber and the planting of oil palm. There is a pleasant avenue of trees after Carondelet. A few kilometres further on is the bridge over the Río Tululbí, then **Calderón**, 66 km from Lita, where this road meets the coastal highway coming from Esmeraldas. Two kilometres before the junction, on the Río Tululbí, is **Tunda Loma** (see Where to stay, page 259). About 12 km beyond is San Lorenzo (see page 256).

Northwest of Ibarra Along a secondary road to the northwest of Ibarra is the town of **Urcuquí** with a basic hotel. Nearby is **Yachay**, a university and national research and technology centre, in a beautiful historic hacienda. From just south of Urcuquí, a road leads via Irunguicho towards the **Piñán lakes**, a beautiful, remote, high *páramo* region, part of the Reserva Ecológica Cotacachi-Cayapas. The local community of **Piñán** (3112 m) has a tourism programme (www.pinantrek.com), with a well-equipped refuge (US$12 per person, meals available), *guías nativos* (US$15 per day) and muleteers (US$12 per day, per horse). Another access to the hamlet of Piñán is via **La Merced de Buenos Aires**, a village reached from either Tumbabiro (see below) or San Gerónimo, near Guallupe (on the road to the coast). Along the Tumbabiro access is the community of **Sachapamba**, where muleteers and mules can be found. The nicest lakes, Donoso and Caricocha, are one-hour walk from the community. They can also be reached walking from either Chachimbiro (see below), Irubí or Cuellaje in the Intag area. Otavalo agencies and hotels in Chachimbiro and Tumababiro also offer trekking tours to Piñán. Note that a proposed irrigation and hydroelectric scheme will affect this beautiful area.

Beyond Urcuquí is the friendly town of **Tumbabiro**, which has with a mild climate and makes a good base from which to explore this region; it can also be reached from Salinas on the road to the coast. Some 8 km from Tumbabiro along a side road, set on the slopes of an extinct volcano, is **Chachimbiro**, a good area for walking and horse riding, with several resorts with thermal baths. The largest one, run by the provincial government, is **Santagua Chachimbiro** ⓘ *T06-293 6060, www.santagua.com.ec, 0730-2400, entry to recreational pools US$5, to medicinal pools and spa US$10,* with several hot mineral pools, lodging, restaurants, zip-line and horses for riding; weekends can be crowded.

North to Colombia

From Ibarra the Pan-American highway goes past **Laguna Yahuarcocha** (with a few hotels, a campsite (see Where to stay, Ibarra), and many food stalls, busy at weekends) and then descends to the hot dry **Chota valley**, a centre of Afro-Ecuadorean culture. Beyond the turn-off for Salinas and San Lorenzo, 30 km from Ibarra, the highway divides. The western branch follows an older route through Mira and El Angel to Tulcán on the Colombian border; the eastern route, the Pan-American Highway, goes to Tulcán via Bolívar, San Gabriel and Huaca. A paved road between El Angel and Bolívar connects the two branches.

Western route to Tulcán At **Mascarilla**, 1 km after the roads divide, ceramic masks are made. The women's crafts association here is called **Grupo Artesanal Esperanza Negra (GAEN)** ⓘ *T09-9316 1621, https://gaen.weebly.com*, produces sculptures, jewellery and bags, as well as masks. Some 16 km further on is **Mira** (2400 m), where fine woollens are made. This road is paved and in good condition as far as **El Angel** (3000 m), where the main plaza retains a few trees sculpted by José Franco (see Tulcán cemetery, page 115); market day is Monday. Beyond El Angel to Tulcán the road north goes through beautiful *páramo* but it is poor and you'll need a 4WD; it's a great mountain bike route.

The nearby ★ **Reserva Ecológica El Angel** ⓘ *T06-297 7597, office in El Angel near the Municipio; best time to visit May-Aug, see http://areasprotegidas.ambiente.gob.ec*, protects 16,451 ha of *páramo* ranging in altitude from 3400 m to 4768 m. The reserve contains large stands of the velvet-leaved *frailejón* plant, also found in the Andes of Colombia and Venezuela. Also of interest are the spiny *achupallas*, bromeliads with giant compound flowers. The fauna includes *curiquingues* (caracara), deer, foxes and a few condors. From El Angel follow the poor road north towards Tulcán for 16 km to **El Voladero** ranger station/shelter, where a self-guided trail climbs over a low ridge (30 minutes' walk) to two crystal-clear lakes. Pick-ups or taxis from the main plaza of El Angel charge US$25 return with a one-hour wait for a day trip to El Voladero. A longer route to another area follows an equally poor road to Cerro Socabones, beginning at **La Libertad**, 3.5 km north of El Angel (transport El Angel–Cerro Socabones, US$30 return), which also has some topiary in the main plaza. It climbs gradually through San Francisco and Jesús del Gran Poder to reach the high *páramo* at the centre of the reserve and, in 40 minutes, the **El Salado** ranger station. From Socabones the road descends to the village of **Morán** (lodging and guides, transport with Sr Calderón, T09-9128 4022), the start of a good three-day walk down to Guallupe, on the Ibarra–San Lorenzo road. Note, roads in this area are very poorly signed; ask directions frequently.

Eastern route to Tulcán From Mascarilla, the Panamericana runs east through the warm Chota valley. Just past the Ambuquí toll, heading north, is an unsigned turning east to **Tunas y Cabras** and **Pimán** (see Where to stay, page 120). The unpaved road climbs up an arid valley into the hills and, beyond Pimán, an alternative route heads back to Ibarra in about 20 minutes via Yahuarcocha. The Panamericana continues to **El Juncal**, after which the highway turns northeast to **Bolívar**, a neat little town where the houses and the interior of its church are painted in lively pastel colours; there is also a huge mural by the roadside. At the **Museo Paleontológico** ⓘ *by the north entrance to town, US$2*, you can see the remains of a mammoth, found nearby. There is a Friday market.

Some 16 km north of Bolívar is **San Gabriel**, an important commercial centre. The 60-m-high **Paluz** waterfall is 4 km north of town, beyond a smaller waterfall. To the southeast, 11 km from town on the road to Piartal is **Bosque de Arrayanes**, a 16-ha mature forest with a predominance of myrtle trees, some reaching 20 m, taxi US$5.

Some 20 km east of San Gabriel is the tiny community of **Mariscal Sucre**, also known as Colonia Huaqueña, the gateway

> **Fact...**
> El Juncal has a football academy and stadium in recognition of the fact that most of Ecuador's talented soccer players come from the Chota valley.

Tulcán

N
100 metres
100 yards

to the **Guandera Reserve and Biological Station** ⓘ *the reserve is part of Fundación Jatun Sacha. Reservations should be made at the Quito office, T02-331 7163, www.jatunsacha.org.* You can see bromeliads, orchids, birds and other wildlife in ancient high-altitude forest and *frailejón páramo*. From San Gabriel, take a taxi beyond Mariscal Sucre, one hour, then walk 30 minutes to the reserve, or make arrangements with Jatun Sacha.

Between San Gabriel and Tulcán are the towns of Huaca, site of a pre-Inca settlement and many archaeological finds, and Julio Andrade, with **$$-$ Hotel Naderik**, T06-220 5433 or 09-9956 3323, and a Sunday market and, afterwards, paddleball games. This is the beginning of the road east to La Bonita, Lumbaqui and Lago Agrio. The road follows the border for much of the route. Enquire locally about safety before embarking on this beautiful route.

Tulcán *Colour map 1, A6.*

The chilly city of Tulcán (altitude 2960 m) is the busy capital of the province of Carchi. The eastern and western roads from the south join at Las Juntas, 2 km south of the city. There is a great deal of informal trade here with Colombia, a textile and dry goods fair takes place on Thursday and Sunday. There is also a permanent clothing market at Sucre y Chimborazo. The Mercado Central, entrances on Bolívar, Boyacá and Sucre, is covered, with a well-organized central area; economical meals and juices are sold here. In the ★ **cemetery** ⓘ *daily 0800-1800*, two blocks from Parque Ayora, the art of topiary is taken to beautiful extremes. Cypress bushes are trimmed into archways, fantastic figures and geometric shapes in *haut* and *bas* relief. To see the stages of this art form, go to the back of the cemetery where young bushes are being pruned. The artistry, started in 1936, is that of the late Sr José Franco, born in El Angel (see above), now buried among the splendour he created. The tradition is carried on by his sons. Around the cemetery is a promenade with fountains, souvenir and flower stalls and the **tourist office**, see below, which is helpful and has toilets. Ask here about a guided tour of the cemetery. Two blocks south is the **Museo de la Casa de la Cultura** ⓘ *Mon-Fri 0730-1300, 1500-1800*, with a collection of pre-Inca ceramics.

West of Tulcán

To the west of Tulcán, along the Colombian border, lies a scenic area of rivers, lakes and waterfalls, followed by *páramos* with geothermal activity at the foot of Volcán Chiles and, further on, tropical lowlands. The main road west is the northern border of the Reserva Ecológica El Angel, see page 114. As it is a border area, there are police and military checkpoints. Tufiño, 18 km from Tulcán, is just on the border. Two blocks downhill from the main park is a museum with archaeological and ethnographic displays (free, ask around for the caretaker). By far the best hot springs of the region are **Aguas Hediondas** (stinking waters) ⓘ *US$2, food available at weekends*, a complex of indoor and outdoor pools fed by a stream of boiling sulphurous mineral water in an impressive valley. The area around the water source is walled off because of lethal sulphur fumes; the baths are deserted on weekdays. Access is 3 km past Tufiño, from where a road goes to the right, 8 km through strange scenery, to the magnificent natural hot river. A shared taxi from Tulcán to Tufiño will cost US$0.75; you can arrange for the taxi to continue to the baths.

Past the turn-off for Aguas Hediondas the road climbs to the *páramo* on the southern slopes of **Volcán Chiles**, about one hour from Tulcán. The border with Colombia crosses at the summit. Chiles, 5300 m, can be climbed in about five hours; ask about guides at the Municipio in Tulcán. There is a basic *refugio* with toilets. To the south, also within the reserve, is an area of lovely lakes, the **Lagunas Verdes**. The road then begins its long descent to the west. **Maldonado**, already in a subtropical area descending to the coast, is 57 km from Tufiño and **Chical**, 12 km beyond (bus from Tulcán). From Chical a road goes south to Gualchán (see page 113) and on to Salinas and Ibarra.

Border with Colombia: Tulcán–Ipiales

The border is at **Rumichaca** (stone bridge), 5 km from Tulcán. Border posts with immigration, customs and agriculture control are on either side of a concrete bridge over the Río Carchi, to the east of the natural stone bridge. This well-organized border is open 24 hours. On the Ecuadorean side, next to immigration (T06-298 6169), is a **tourist information office**. Colombian consulate in Tulcán ⓘ *Olmedo y 10 de Agosto, Edif La Catedral, T06-225 2458, ctulcan@cancilleria.gov.co, Mon-Fri 0800-1300*. Visas require three days. Money changers hang about in Plaza Independencia, Tulcán; ask for their ID and watch out for short-changing. There are money changers also at the bus terminal and the border. Ipiales, with all services, is 2 km from the border.

Tourist information

Cotacachi

Alcaldía de Cotacachi
González Suárez y García, T06-291 5115,
http://cotacachi.gob.ec.
Turismo page of the website has lots
of information. Tourist information also
at **Hostería Cuicocha**, http://turismo
cotacachi.com, see below.

Ibarra

Dirección de Turismo del Municipio
Sucre y Oviedo, T06-260 8489, Facebook:
IbarraPuroEncanto. Mon-Fri 0800-1230,
1400-1730, holidays 0900-1500.
City map, pamphlets, English spoken,
free Wi-Fi.

Tulcán

Unidad de Turismo
Entrance to the cemetery, 1st floor, T06-
298 5760, turismo@gmtulcan.gob.ec.
Daily 0800-1800.
Helpful, has toilets.

Where to stay

Cotacachi

$$$$ La Mirage
500 m west of town on C 10 de Agosto,
T06-291 5237, www.mirage.com.ec.
Luxurious converted hacienda with elegant
suites and common areas, includes breakfast
and dinner, excellent restaurant, pool, gym
and spa (treatments extra), beautiful gardens,
tours arranged.

$$$-$$ Land of the Sun
García Moreno 13-76 y Sucre, T06-291 6009,
http://landofthesunhotel.com.

Refurbished colonial house in the heart of
town, rooms with balcony, internal ones
are cheaper, breakfast served in lovely
patio, local specialities in restaurant,
request dinner in advance, sauna, parking.
Recommended.

$$ Runa Tupari
www.runatupari.com.
A system of homestays in nearby villages.
Visitors experience life with an indigenous
family by taking part in daily activities.
The comfortable rooms have space for 3,
fireplace, bathroom and hot shower, and
cost US$38 pp in a double room, including
breakfast, dinner and transport from Otavalo.
Arrange with **Runa Tupari** or other Otavalo
tour operators.

$$-$ La Cuadra
Peñaherrera 11-46 y González Suárez,
T06-291 6015, www.lacuadra-hostal.com.
Modern comfortable rooms, good
matresses, private or shared bath, no
breakfast, kitchen facilities.

$ Casa Residencial Bachita
Sucre 16-82 y Peñaherrera, T06-291 5063.
Simple place, private or shared bath, no
breakfast, quiet.

Laguna Cuicocha

$$$ Hostería Cuicocha
Laguna Cuicocha, by the pier, T06-301 7218,
www.cuicocha.org.
Rooms overlooking the lake, internal ones
are cheaper, includes breakfast and dinner,
restaurant, no overnight staff.

$$-$ Cabañas Mirador
On a lookout above the pier, follow the
trail or by car follow the road to the left
of the park entrance, T09-9055 8367,
miradordecuicocha@yahoo.com.

Rustic cabins with fireplace and modern rooms overlooking the lake, good economical restaurant, trout is the speciality, parking, transport provided to Quiroga (US$5), Cotacachi (US$5) or Otavalo (US$10); owner Ernesto Cevillano is knowledgeable about the area and arranges trips.

Ibarra

$$$ Hacienda Chorlaví
Panamericana Norte Km 4.5, T06-293 2222, www.haciendachorlavi.com.
In a historical hacienda dating to 1620, comfortable rooms, very good restaurant, excellent *parrillada*, pool and spa, parking, busy on weekends, folk music and crafts on Sat.

$$$ La Estelita
Km 5 Vía a Yuracrucito, T06-304 7079, www.laestelitahosteria.com.
Modern hotel 5 km from the city, high on a hill overlooking town and Laguna Yahuarcocha. Rooms and suites with lovely views, good restaurant, pool, spa, can arrange paragliding.

$$ Montecarlo
Av Jaime Rivadeneira 5-55 y Oviedo, near the obelisk, T06-295 8266, www.hotelmontecarloibarra.ec.
Pleasant comfortable rooms, buffet breakfast, restaurant, heated pool open at weekends, parking.

$ Las Garzas
Flores 3-13 y Salinas, T06-295 0985.
Simple comfortable rooms, no breakfast, sitting room.

Around Ibarra

$$$$ Hacienda Zuleta
By Angochagua, along the Ibarra–Cayambe road, T06-266 2232, http://zuleta.com.
A 2000-ha working historic hacienda, among the nicest in the country. Superb

accommodation and food, 15 rooms with fireplace, price includes all meals (prepared with organic vegetables, trout and dairy produced on the farm) and excursions, advance reservations essential.

$$$ Tradiciones San Clemente
In San Clemente, T06-266-0045, 09-9776 1524, www.sanclementetours.com.
Part of a community-run programme. Attractively built cottages with hot water on family properties, cheaper in more humble family homes, price includes 3 tasty meals and a guided tour. Opportunities to participate in daily activities in the field and kitchen and learn about local traditions and celebrations. Options for hiking, horse riding and climbing Imbabura volcano.

$$ Casa Aída
C Galo Plaza Lasso 19-291, in La Esperanza village, T06-266 0221, or 09-6858 9026, Facebook: casa.aida.imbabura.
Simple rooms with good beds, includes dinner and breakfast, restaurant, shared bath, hot water, patios, some English spoken, meeting place for climbing Imbabura.

$$ Finca Sommerwind
Autopista Yahuarcocha Km 8, T09-3937 1170, www.finca-sommerwind.info.
A 12-ha ranch by Laguna Yahuarcocha with cabins and campsite, US$6 pp, electricity, hot shower, laundry facilities, German, English and Spanish spoken.

Ibarra to the coast

$$$$ Hacienda Primavera
North of Guallupe on the road to Chical, T09-9370 8571, www.haciendaprimavera.com.
8 rooms in a beautiful forest setting, pool, includes full board, guided hiking and horse riding, packages of 3, 4 and 6 nights available.

$$$ Las Siete Cascadas
Vía Ibarra–San Lorenzo Km 66.5, 15 km past Lita, T09-8261 1195, http://las7cascadas.com.
A-frame cabins with balconies in a 204-ha reserve, price includes full board and excursions to waterfalls and the forest, reserve well ahead.

$$-$ Parque Bambú
In El Limonal, about 600 m uphill from the main square, T06-301 6606, www.bospas.org.
Family-run farm with splendid views of the valley and many birds. Private rooms with terrace, US$14 pp in dorm, good breakfast, tasty meals available, camping U$3 pp, trekking. Run by Belgian Piet Sabbe, a permaculture landscape designer, and his daughters; Piet will share his knowledge and experience in landscape restoration and welcomes volunteers with a green thumb (arrange ahead). Recommended.

Northwest of Ibarra

$$$ Aguasavia
In Chachimbiro,15-min walk from Santa Agua complex, T06-304 8347, www.aguasavia.com.
Community-run modern hotel in a beautiful setting in the crater of La Viuda Volcano, includes 3 meals, rooms on ground floor with jacuzzi, thermal pools, trips. See website for midweek deals.

$$$ Hacienda San Francisco
In the community of San Francisco, 5 km past Tumbabiro on the road to Chachimbiro, T06-304 8232, www.hosteriasanfrancisco.com.
Intimate family-run inn in tastefully converted hacienda stables, includes breakfast, Ecuadorean and international restaurant, full-board packages available, small thermal pool, attractive grounds, good walking, horse riding, tennis court, excursions to Piñán, best Thu to Sun when owners are in.

$$$ Santagua Chachimbiro
Part of the recreational complex, T06-293 6060, www.santagua.com.ec.
Rooms and cabins (some with jacuzzi), includes 3 meals and access to spa and pools, restaurant, good, busy at weekends, reserve ahead.

$$$-$$ Hostería Spa Pantaví
7 km from Salinas, at the entrance to Tumbabiro, T06-293 4185, Quito reservations T02-234 0601 ext 105, www.hosteriapantavi.com.
Stylish inn in a tastefully restored hacienda. Very comfortable rooms, decorated with the owner's original works of art (www.camiloandrade.com), includes nice breakfast, good restaurant, pool, spa, jacuzzi, attractive gardens, attentive service, bikes and horses for rent, tours.

$ Tío Lauro
1 block from plaza, Tumbabiro, T06-293 4148.
Pleasant *residencial*, simple rooms, meals on request, parking, friendly owner.

North to Colombia
El Angel

$$$$-$$ Polylepis Lodge
Abutting the reserve, 14 km from El Angel along the road to Socabones, turn off after Jesús del Gran Poder (road is signed but it is unpaved and poor, high-clearance advisable, US$15 from La Libertad), T06-263 1819, www.polylepislodgeec.com.
Set in a lovely 12-ha ancient polylepis forest at 3582 m, these rustic cabins with fireplace in stone rooms have electric blankets (it is very cold at night) and include 3 set meals (vegetarian on request) and 3 guided walks in the forest and *fraijejón*-covered *páramo* (1½-3 hrs), spa, Wi-Fi in lounge, helpful staff. Also has bunk rooms in a big building with living room and shared bath (**$$** pp all-inclusive) and backpacker bunk loft (US$30 pp with breakfast, take sleeping bag).

$$ Las Orquídeas
In the village of Morán, T09-8641 6936, castro503@yahoo.com.
Mountain cabin with bunk beds, shared bath, includes 3 meals, horse riding and guide, run by Carlos Castro, a local guide and conservation pioneer.

$ Blas Angel
C Espejo, facing the roundabout by the entrance to El Angel, T06-297 7346.
Private or shared bath, parking, a good economical option.

Eastern route to Tulcán

$$$$-$$$ Tunas y Cabras
Pimán Chico on the old Ibarra–Chota– Tulcán road, T06-263 1819 or 09-9522 7472, www.tunasycabras.com.
A green oasis in the arid hills at 1950 m, gardens with lots of birds, swimming pool, outdoor jacuzzi, good views, walks around and beyond the property. Various types of cabin, some with jacuzzi, some family rooms with bunks, includes 3 meals, good food in small restaurant, has its own water treatment and its own toiletries made from aloe. A different experience.

$$$ Hacienda Pimán
Aloburo Km 9 Principal s/n, 9 km northeast of Ibarra, above Pimán Chico, T06-304 6854, Quito T02-256 6090, www.haciendapiman.com.
Luxuriously restored 17th-century hacienda with beautiful buildings and gardens. Rooms in the original house have antique furniture, wooden floors, some with original wallpaper, also modern rooms in cabins, small pool, massage, dining room and bar. Price includes breakfast and dinner. Trails for walking, cycling or horse riding. All-inclusive 2- and 3-day packages with a train ride and visit to El Angel Reserve.

POLYLEPIS
LODGE

www.polylepis.com

San Gabriel

$$ Gabrielita
Mejía y Los Andes, above the agricultural supply shop, T06-229 1832.
Modern hostel, includes breakfast, parking, best in town.

Tulcán

$$$ Palacio Imperial
Sucre y Pichincha, T06-298 0638, www.hotelpalacioimperial.com.
Modern hotel in contemporary Chinese style, with ample rooms with wood floors, suites with jacuzzi, warm blankets, includes buffet breakfast, rooftop spa, gym, parking. Recommended.

$$ Grand Hotel Comfort
Colón y Chimborazo, T06-298 1452, www.grandhotelcomfort.com.
Modern high-rise hotel with rooms and suites with jacuzzi, fridge, safety box, with breakfast, restaurant with set lunch and à la carte (closed Sat and Sun evening), parking.

$$-$ Los Alpes
JR Arellanoy Centenario, next to bus station, T06-298 2235.
Best option near the bus terminal, breakfast extra, restaurant, good value.

$$-$ Sara Espíndola
Sucre y Ayacucho, on plaza, T06-298 2464, http://hotelsaraespindiol.wixsite.com/hotelespindola.
Comfortable rooms in purple and turquoise building, with breakfast, spa, parking, helpful.

$$-$ Torres de Oro
Sucre y Rocafuerte, T06-298 4660, www.hoteltorresdeoro.com.
Modern, nice, restaurant, parking.

$ Florida
Sucre y Ayacucho, T06-298 3849.
Simple, clean, shared bath, no breakfast, a good economy option.

Restaurants

Cotacachi
A local speciality is *carne colorada* (spiced pork).

$$ D'Anita
10 de Agosto y González Suárez.
Daily 0800-2100.
Good set meal of the day, local and international dishes à la carte, popular, English spoken, good value.

$$-$ La Vaca Gorda
10 de Agosto entre Rocafuerte y Pedro Moncay, Facebook: lavacagordacotacachi.
Open 1200-2100.

TUNAS & CABRAS
www.tunasycabras.com

Grilled meats, burgers, wings, fries and beer, popular with expats.

Café Río Intag
Imbabura 8-63, on Plaza San Francisco. Daily 0800-2100.
The best coffee, snacks and a good meeting place.

Ibarra

$$ Caribou
Pérez Guerrero 5-37 y Sucre and Av Rafael Sánchez 9-56 y Ricardo Sánchez, south of the bus terminal, T06-260 5137, see Facebook. Mon 1730-2300, Tue-Thu 1300-2300, Fri-Sat 1300-0030.
Excellent meat specialities, including burgers, salads, bar, Canadian-owned. Recommended.

$$ Donde El Argentino
Sucre y P Moncayo, at Plazoleta Francisco Calderón. Tue-Sun.
Good mixed grill and salads, small, pleasant, outdoor seating.

$$-$ La Cassona Ibarreña
Bolívar 6-47 y Oviedo, T06-260 7752, Facebook: LaCassonaIbarra. Mon-Thu 1100-1800, Fri-Sat 0900-2200.
In a nice colonial patio, international, seafood and local dishes, also set lunch.

Cafés and heladerías

Café Arte
Salinas 5-43 y Oviedo, Facebook: cafearte696. Thu-Sat 1730-0200 (till 1200 on Thu).
Café-bar with character, drinks, Mexican snacks, sandwiches, live music Fri-Sat night.

Café Pushkin
Olmedo 7-64 y Oviedo. Open 0700-1700.
For breakfast, snacks, coffee. An Ibarra classic, very popular.

El Quinde Café
Sucre 5-62 y Flores, Facebook: elquindecafe. Mon-Fri 1100-2100.
A good place for late breakfast, coffee, cake, snacks.

★ Heladería Rosalía Suárez
Oviedo 7-82 y Olmedo, T06-295 8772, Facebook: HELADOSROSALIASUAREZ.
Excellent home-made *helados de paila* (fruit sherbets made in large copper basins), an Ibarra tradition since 1896. Highly recommended.

Olor a Café
Flores y Bolívar.
Café/bar/cultural centre in a historic home, music, library.

Tulcán
Look for stickers on restaurant windows for Huecas de Tulcán, the organization of local eating places.

$ Café Estación 3-18
Sucre entre Junín y Ayacucho, Facebook: Estacion318. Mon-Sat 1500-2200.
New in 2017, good café and pub.

$ Café Tulcán
Sucre 52-029 y Ayacucho. Open 0800-1800.
Café, snacks, desserts, juices, set lunches. A Tulcán classic.

$ Pack Choy
Sucre y Pichincha, at Hotel Palacio Imperial, T06-298 2713.
Extremely popular for Chinese and international dishes, also sandwiches. Good food and excellent value. Under same ownership is **Casa China**, on Av Veinitimilla, next to Atahualpa taxi building, opposite bus station, T06-298 4699, similar prices but more specialized dishes.

Bars and clubs

Ibarra
Plazoleta Francisco Calderón on Sucre y Pedro Moncayo has several café-bars with outdoor seating and a pleasant atmosphere.

Rincón de Ayer
Olmedo 9-59 y Velasco. Mon-Sat 1400 till late. A bar with lots of character, attractively restored.

Festivals

Cotacachi
Jun **Inti Raymi/San Juan**.
Sep **Jora** during the Sep equinox.

Ibarra
16 Jul **Virgen del Carmen** festival.
Last weekend of Sep **Fiesta de los Lagos**, coincides with the founding of the city (28 Sep) around which there are many events including a gastronomic show and the **Cacería del Zorro**, a horse race with some 500 riders chasing a rider dressed as El Zorro (the film character). The winner becomes next year's Zorro.

What to do

Ibarra
Paragliding
Fly Ecuador, *R Troya 5121 y J Vinueza, T06-295 3297 or T09-8487 5577, www.flyecuador.com. ec.* Tandem flight US$67-90, course US$336, arrange ahead.

Pelota nacional
A unique form of paddle ball, *pelota nacional*, is played in the afternoon at Yacucalle, south of the bus station. Players have huge studded paddles for striking the 1-kg ball.

Tour operators
Intipungo, *Rocafuerte 6-08 y Flores, T06-295 7766, http://intipungo.com.ec.* Regional tours and travel agency.

Train rides
A tourist train, *El Tren de la Libertad I*, runs from Ibarra to **Salinas**, 29 km away, Thu-Sun and holidays at 1125, returning 1640, US$30 one way. When there is high demand, there is also *ferrochiva* (open-sided motorized railcar) service at 1030, US$15 one way, US$20 return. Purchase tickets in advance. Ibarra station at Acosta y Espejo, Mon-Sat 0800-1700, Sun 0800-1300, or through T1-800-873637; you need each passenger's passport number and date of birth to purchase tickets. The ride takes 2 hrs with stops. You can continue by bus from Salinas to **San Lorenzo**, see page 256.

Transport

Cotacachi
Bus and taxi
Terminal at 10 de Agosto y Salinas by the market. Every 10 mins to/from **Otavalo** terminal, US$0.35, 25 mins; service alternates between the Panamericana and the Quiroga roads; taxi US$5. To **Ibarra**, every 15 mins, US$0.50, 40 mins; service alternates between the Panamericana and Imantag roads.

Laguna Cuicocha
Bus and pick-ups
Pick-ups from **Otavalo** US$10. From **Cotacachi**, US$5 one way, US$10 return with short wait. From **Quiroga** US$5. Return service from the lake available from **Cabañas El Mirador**, same rates.

Intag Trans Otavalo run buses from Otavalo to villlages such as **Apuela**, **Cuellaje** (3 hrs, daily 1700), **García Moreno** (3½ hrs, 3 a day, US$3), **Magdalena** and **Cielo Verde**.

Los Cedros Research Station From Estación La Ofelia in Quito, **Trans Minas**, daily at 0615, 1000, 1530, 1800 to **Magdalena Alto**, US$4.50, 3½ hrs; then a 2-hr **walk**; arrange with the station for mules to carry luggage up. If the road is passable, 2 daily buses from Otavalo, pass **Chontal** on route to Cielo Verde. Take a pickup from Chontal to Magdalena Alto or it is a 5-hr walk from Chontal to Los Cedros.

Ibarra
Bus and taxi
Terminal is at Av Teodoro Gómez y Av Eugenio Espejo, southwest of the centre, T06-264 4676. Most inter-city transport runs from here. There are no ticket counters for regional destinations, such as Otavalo, proceed directly to the platforms. City buses go from the terminal to the centre or you can walk in 15 mins. To/from **Quito**, Terminal Carcelén, every 10 mins, US$3, 2½ hrs. Shared taxis with **Taxis Lagos/Serviquito** (Quito address under Otavalo Transport, page 109, in Ibarra at Flores 9-24 y Sánchez y Cifuentes, near Parque La Merced, T06-260 6858), buy ticket at least 1 day ahead, US$15 pp, 2½ hrs. To **Tulcán**, with **Expreso Turismo**, 9 daily, US$3, 2½-3 hrs. To **Otavalo**, platform 12, every 4 mins, US$0.55, 40 mins. To **Cotacachi**, platform 15, every 15 mins, US$0.50, 40 mins, some continue to **Quiroga**. To the coast, several companies, some go all the way to **San Lorenzo** US$7, 4 hrs, others only as far as **Lita**, US$4.50, 2 hrs. To **Ambato**, **CITA** goes via the World Mirror roundabout and Pifo, bypassing Quito, 12 daily, US$6.25, 5½ hrs. To **Baños**, **Expreso Baños**, also through Pifo and bypassing Quito, at 0500, 0550, 1430, 2100, US$7.50, 6 hrs (2 hrs, US$3.15 to Pifo). To **Lago Agrio**, **Valle de Chota**, at 0900, US$14, via La Bonita. To **Tumbabiro** via Urcuquí, **Coop Urcuquí**, hourly, US$1, 1 hr. To **Chachimbiro**, **Coop Urcuquí**, at 0700, 0730 and 1200, returning Mon-Fri at 1215 (Sat-Sun at 1300), 1530 and 1630, US$1.60, 1½ hrs, taxi US$40 return. Buses to La Esperanza, Zuleta and San Clemete leave from **Parque Germán Grijalva** (east of the Terminal Terrestre, follow C Sánchez y Cifuentes, south from the centre). To **La Esperanza**, every 20 mins, US$0.35, 30 mins. To **Zuleta**, hourly, US$0.65, 1 hr. To **San Clemente**, frequent, weekdays 0650-1840, Sat-Sun 0720-1500, US$0.35, 30 mins. For nearby destinations such as **San Antonio de Ibarra**, city buses run along Pérez Guerrero.

Train
See What to do, above.

North to Colombia
Bus and taxi
Western route to Tulcán From **Ibarra** Terminal Terrestre to **Mira**, every 30 mins, US$1.25, 1 hr; to **El Angel**, hourly, US$1.75, 1½ hrs. El Angel to **Mira**, every 30 mins, US$.50, 20 mins. El Angel to **Tulcán**, US$1.75, 1½ hrs. El Angel to **Quito**, US$5, 4 hrs.

Eastern route to Tulcán From **San Gabriel** to **Tulcán**, vans and jeeps US$0.75, shared taxis US$1, 30 mins, all from the main plaza. From San Gabriel to **Ibarra**, buses, US$2, 2 hrs. From San Gabriel to **Quito**, buses, US$4.50, 3½ hrs.

Tulcán
Air
There is an airport, but no commercial flights were operating in 2017.

Bus
The bus terminal is 1.5 km uphill from centre; best to take a taxi, US$1.25. All buses heading south are checked at the narcotics control a few kilometres out of town. To **Quito**, US$6, 5 hrs, every 15 mins, service to Terminal Carcelén, some continue to Quitumbe; from Quito, service from both terminals. To **Ibarra**, 2½ hrs, US$3. **Otavalo**, US$4, 3 hrs (they don't go in to the Otavalo Terminal, alight at the highway turn-off where taxis are available or transfer in Ibarra). To **Guayaquil**, 20 a day, 13 hrs, US$17.25-21. To **Lago Agrio via La Bonita**,

3 a day with **Putumayo** and 2 daily with **Coop Petrolera**, US$9, 7 hrs, spectacular.

Border with Colombia
Bus and taxi
Minivans (US$0.75, 0600-1900) and shared taxis (US$1 pp, 0430-2100) leave when full from Parque Ayora (near the cemetery); private taxi US$3.50. Taxi from the bus terminal to the border US$3, shared US$1.25 pp; taxi from terminal to Parque Ayora, US$1.25, city bus US$0.25. **Note** These vehicles do not cross the international bridge; after visiting Ecuadorean immigration, walk over to the Colombian side, where onward transport waits. *Colectivo* border–Ipiales, US$0.50, taxi US$3.

Central highlands

South of Quito is some of the loveliest mountain scenery in Ecuador. This part of the country was named the 'Avenue of the Volcanoes' by the German explorer Alexander Von Humboldt, and it is easy to see why. An impressive roll call of towering peaks lines the route south: Cotopaxi, the Ilinizas, Carihuayrazo and Chimborazo, to name but a few.

This area obviously attracts its fair share of trekkers and climbers, while the less sporty tourist can browse through the many teeming markets and colonial towns that nestle among the high volcanic cones.

After you have explored the mountains to your heart's delight, rest up and pamper yourself in one of the lovely haciendas which have opened their doors to visitors, or in Baños, named and famed for its thermal baths. Situated on the main road from the central highlands to the Oriente jungle, it is also the base for activities ranging from adrenalin sports and mountain biking to café lounging and Ecuador's special attraction: volcano watching.

Best for
Climbing ▪ Markets ▪ Mountain biking ▪ Trekking

Footprint
picks

★ Parque Nacional Cotopaxi, page 130
The perfect cone of Cotopaxi is the second highest peak in Ecuador and one of the highest active volcanoes in the world.

★ Quilotoa Circuit, page 136
This popular 200-km round trip can be done in two to three days by bus and it is also a great route for biking.

★ Thursday market in Saquisilí, page 139
Famous for its seven plazas jam-packed with people, the great majority of them wearing red ponchos and narrow-brimmed felt hats.

★ El Pailón del Diablo, page 151
The 'Devil's Cauldron' is probably the most spectacular of the many waterfalls in the Pastaza Basin around Baños.

★ Reserva Faunística Chimborazo, page 159
Visit the graceful vicuñas which inhabit the plateau at the base of Ecuador's highest summit.

★ The Devil's Nose, page 160
Touristy or not, this train ride takes you over an internationally acclaimed fantastic piece of railway engineering.

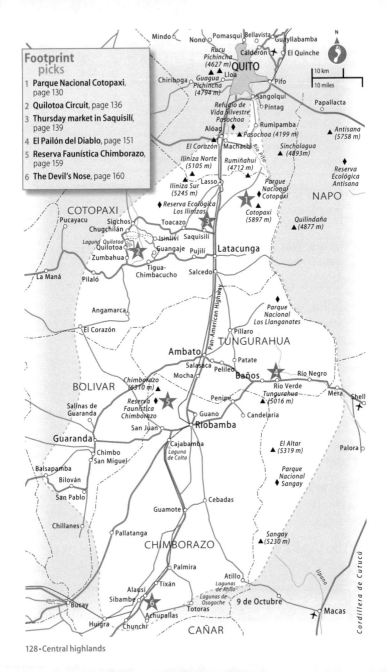

Cotopaxi, Latacunga & Quilotoa

From Quito, the six lanes of the Pan-American Highway head south towards the central highlands' hub of Ambato. The route is lined with impressive mountain scenery; the perfect cone of Cotopaxi volcano is ever-present and is one of the country's main tourist attractions. Machachi and Latacunga are good bases from which to explore the region and provide access to the beautiful Quilotoa Circuit of small villages and vast expanses of open countryside.

Cotopaxi

some nine volcanoes dominate this area, one towering above the others

Quito to Cotopaxi

From the capital to the Cotopaxi area, urban motorways head south or southeast eventually to meet the Panamericana Sur, the E35, at Sangolquí or Tambillo. The highway then continues south to **Alóag**, where an important road goes west to Santo Domingo and the coast, then to Aloasí and the turn-off to Machachi, 16 km from Tambillo.

An alternative is the cobbled road sometimes called the Avenida de los Volcanes on the east flank of Pasochoa that goes south from El Colibrí interchange near Sangolquí through Selva Alegre, San Fernando, La Moca, which has a natural bridge, Jatumpungo and Rumipamba/El Vallecito, then along the canyon of the Río Pita. It leads to the Pedregal entrance to the Cotopaxi National Park (see below). This road gives access to a number of waterfalls, including Cóndor Machay (80 m), Vilatuña and Pita (60 m; see www.ruminahui. gob.ec for details). Trails to some of the falls start at Rumipamba. The Cascada de Pita trail starts near Molinuco bridge at the entrance to the Tomo de Agua for Quito, where there is a restaurant at weekends. This beautiful, quite easy trail can be followed to El Pedregal, best to take a guide (for example from Chilcabamba, see page 134). The Pita valley is also popular for horse riding, cycling (there is a Cicloruta de los Volcanes) and other weekend activities, including at **Hacienda Santa Rita** ① *T09-9924 4940, Facebook: reservasantarita, closed Mon*, a private reserve with camping, zip-lines, hiking and cycling trails.

Machachi

In a valley between the summits of Pasochoa, Rumiñahui and Corazón, lies the town of Machachi, famous for its farming and dairies, mineral water springs and crystal-clear swimming pools. The water, 'Agua Güitig', is bottled in a plant 4 km from the town at

Tesalia, where there is also a sports/recreation complex with one warm and two cold pools, entry US$5. It gets very busy at weekends. The region claims to produce 70% of Ecuador's milk and 30% of its vegetables. Market day is Sunday, at various locations in town. The local cowboy (*chagra*) culture is celebrated at an annual highland 'rodeo', see page 135. Horse riding is an obvious activity, but there are also cycling and trekking routes and rural tourism projects. Full details from the tourist information office on the plaza (see page 132). Since 2017 an annual festival has been held in February, **El Quesotón** (see Festivals, page 135).

Refugio de Vida Silvestre Pasochoa

45 mins southeast of Quito by car, busy at weekends; park office at El Ejido de Amaguaña, T09-9894 5704, http://areasprotegidas.ambiente.gob.ec.

This natural park is set in humid Andean forest between 2800 m and 4210 m. The reserve has more than 120 bird species (unfortunately some of the fauna has been frightened away by the noise of the visitors) and 50 tree species. There are six walks ranging from 900 m to an eight-hour hike to the summit. There is a picnic and camping area at the interpretation centre. Take a good sleeping bag, food and water.

Reserva Ecológica Los Ilinizas

Machachi is a good starting point for a visit to the northern section of the Reserva Ecológica Los Ilinizas. Below the saddle between the two peaks, at 4740 m, is the **Refugio Nuevos Horizontes** ① *reserve ahead at office on the plaza in El Chaupi or Ilinizas Climbing, Guayaquil 6-74 y Sánchez de Orellana, Latacunga, T09-8133 3483, or T02-367 4125, www.ilinizasclimbing. com, or contact Andes Alpes Café y Hostal in El Chaupi, US$15 per night, US$7.50 for each meal, take sleeping bag*, a shelter with capacity for 25. The campsite beside the refuge, US$5, allows use of refuge's facilities. **Iliniza Norte** (5105 m) although not a technical climb, should not be underestimated, a few exposed, rocky sections require utmost caution. Some climbers suggest using a rope, and a helmet is recommended if other parties are there because of falling rock; allow two to four hours for the ascent from the refuge. **Iliniza Sur** (5245 m) involves ice climbing despite the deglaciation; full climbing gear and experience are absolutely necessary. All visitors must register and be accompanied by an authorized mountain guide for both ascents; maximum three climbers per guide on Iliniza Norte, two per guide on Iliniza Sur.

Access to the reserve is through a turn-off west of the Panamericana 6 km south of Machachi, then it's 7 km to the village of **El Chaupi**, which is a good base for day-walks and climbing **Corazón** (4782 m, not trivial). A dirt road continues from El Chaupi past the Guardianía Pilongo gateway and on to 'La Virgen' (statue), 9 km from El Chaupi. Near La Virgen car park is an area where you can camp (no facilities). El Chaupi hotels arrange for horses with muleteer (US$25 per animal, one way).

★ Parque Nacional Cotopaxi *Colour map, 3, A6.*

Visitors to the park must register at the entrance. Park gates are open 0800-1500, although you can stay until 1700. Visitors arriving with guides not authorized by the park are turned back at the gate. The park administration, a small museum (daily 0800-1530) and snack bar are 10 km from the park gates. La Rinconada shelter and camping area are 5 km beyond, just before lake Limpio Pungo. (See also Transport section, page 136.) The museum has a 3D model of the park, information about the volcano and stuffed animals.

Cotopaxi volcano (5897 m) is at the heart of a much-visited national park. This scenic snow-covered perfect cone is the second highest peak in Ecuador. Cotopaxi, one of the highest active volcanoes in the world, resumed activity in 2015, see box, page 150. Volcanic material from former eruptions can be seen strewn about the *páramo* surrounding Cotopaxi. The northwest flank is most often visited. Here is a high plateau with a small lake (Laguna Limpio Pungo), a lovely area for walking and admiring the delicate flora, and fauna including wild horses and native bird species such as the Andean lapwing and the Chimborazo hillstar hummingbird. The lower slopes are clad in planted pine forests, where llamas may be seen. The southwest flank, or Cara Sur, has not received as much impact as the west side. Here too, there is good walking, and you can climb **Morurco** (4881 m) as an acclimatization hike; condors may sometimes be seen. Just north of Cotopaxi are the peaks

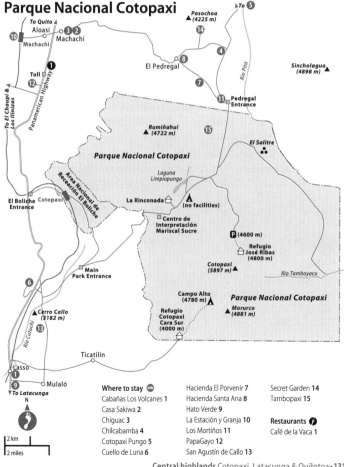

Parque Nacional Cotopaxi

Where to stay 🛏
Cabañas Los Volcanes **1**
Casa Sakiwa **2**
Chiguac **3**
Chilcabamba **4**
Cotopaxi Pungo **5**
Cuello de Luna **6**

Hacienda El Porvenir **7**
Hacienda Santa Ana **8**
Hato Verde **9**
La Estación y Granja **10**
Los Mortiños **11**
PapaGayo **12**
San Agustín de Callo **13**

Secret Garden **14**
Tamboxpaxi **15**

Restaurants 🍴
Café de la Vaca **1**

of **Rumiñahui** (4722 m), **Sincholagua** (4873 m) and **Pasochoa** (4225 m). To the southeast, beyond the park boundary, are **Quilindaña** (4890 m) and an area of rugged *páramos* and mountains dropping down to the jungle. To visit this area, contact **Hacienda Yanahurco** ($$$$-$$, http://cotopaxihaciendayanahurco.com) which has its own 26,000-ha wildlife reserve and has various levels of accommodation and offers tours.

The **main entrance** to Parque Nacional Cotopaxi is approached from Chasqui, 25 km south of Machachi, 6 km north of Lasso. Once through the national park gates, go past Laguna Limpio Pungo to a fork, where the right branch climbs steeply to a parking lot (4600 m). From here it's a 30-minute to one-hour walk to the José Ribas refuge, at 4800 m; beware of altitude sickness. Walking from the highway to the refuge takes an entire day or more. The **El Pedregal entrance**, from the northwest, is accessed from Machachi via Santa Ana del Pedregal (21 km from the Panamericana), or from Sangolquí via Rumipamba and the Río Pita Valley. From Pedregal to the refuge car park is 14 km. There are infrequent buses to Pedregal (two a day) then the hike in is shorter but still a couple of hours. The **Ticatilín access** leads to the southwest flank. Just north of Lasso, a road goes east to the village of San Ramón and on to Ticatilín (a contribution of US$2 per vehicle may be requested at the barrier here, be sure to close all gates) and Rancho María. From the south, San Ramón is accessed from Mulaló. Beyond Rancho María is the private **Refugio Cotopaxi Cara Sur** (4000 m, see Where to stay, below). Walking four hours from here you reach **Campo Alto** (4760 m), a climbers' tent camp. Note The summit of Cotopaxi was reopened in October 2017 after volcanic activity, but climbers should seek local advice before ascending.

Lasso

Some 30 km south of Machachi is the small town of Lasso, on the railway line and off the Panamericana. In the surrounding countryside are several *hosterías*, converted country estates, offering accommodation and meals. Intercity buses bypass Lasso.

Listings Cotopaxi *map page 131.*

Tourist information

Machaci

Tourist information office
*Mejía E-50 y Colón T02-381 9250 ext 163,
Facebook: ViajaporMejia. Mon-Fri 0800-
1700, Sat-Sun 0900-1700.*

Where to stay

There are many places to stay in this region, ranging from haciendas to climbing lodges. Of those listed below all have something different to recommend them. Those in the national park and near El Pedregal are good for acclimatization at altitudes between 3100 m and 3800 m.

Quito to Cotopaxi

$$$$ Hacienda La Alegría
*West of the Panamericana, about
3 km from Alóag, T09-9980 2526,
http://haciendalaalegria.com/web.*
A working hacienda on the railway line with its own stop, full of character and one the best places for horse riding, programmes from 1 to 12 days (rides up to 10 days), trekking, tours and painting workshops arranged, large comfortable rooms, good food, very welcoming, transport from Quito can be arranged.

$$$$-$$$ Sierra Alisos
*Outside Tambillo, T09-8940 5064,
http://sierra-alisos.com.*

Modern house in traditional style in its own 19-ha nature reserve with 11 km of trails, dairy farm, pretty gardens, cosy rooms, restaurant with all local produce, packed lunches available, horse riding, birdwatching and cycling can be organized, motorcycle-friendly, very helpful owner.

$$$ Cotopaxi Pungo
Av de los Volcanes, about 15 km from El Colibrí roundabout at Sangolquí, T09-9955 1216, www.cotopaxipungo.com.
Purpose-built hotel in a commanding position with fabulous views, large rooms, picture windows, breakfast extra, first-class restaurant, small reserve with walking trails, spa under construction, activities can be arranged.

Machachi

$$$ La Estación y Granja
3 km west of the Panamericana, by railway station outside the town of Aloasí, T09-9508 6721, Facebook: Hostería La Estación.
Rooms in a lovely old home and newer section, also cabins, fireplaces, meals available (produce from own garden), parking, family-run, hiking access to Volcán Corazón (guides arranged), reserve ahead.

$$$ PapaGayo
In Hacienda Bolívia, west of the Panamericana at Km 26, take a taxi fom Machachi, T02-231 0002, https://hosteria-papagayo.com.
Nicely refurbished hacienda, pleasant communal areas with fireplace and library, restaurant, jacuzzi, parking, central heating, cosy, horse riding, biking, tours, popular.

$$$ Puerta al Corazón
500 m south of the train station, T02-230 9858, www.puertaalcorazon.com.
Cosy lodge, located near the railway line with good views of the mountains, small restaurant, price includes dinner and breakfast. A good base for mountain trips.

$$$-$$ Casa Sakiwa
De Los Mortiños y Las Pantzas, Sector El Complejo, 8 blocks from Panamericana, T09-9266 8619, www.casasakiwa.com.
Family-owned and run hotel, light airy rooms up to family size, all with bath, buffet breakfast, restaurant serves own produce, new menu daily (*menú* US$10, open to non-guests with reservation), cycle hire US$5 per hr, US$10 per day, tours arranged.

$$-$ Chiguac
Los Caras 0-35 y Colón, 4 blocks east of Machachi's plaza, T02-231 0396, or 09-9867 0413, germaniamor@hotmail.com.
Family-run hostel, comfortable rooms, good breakfast, dinner available (US$8), shared bath, helpful owners and mountain guiding.

Reserva Ecológica Los Ilinizas

$$$ Ilinizas Lodge
Inside the park, just beyond Guardianía Pilongo, T09-9453 9412, www.illinizas lodge.com, or Viajes por Ecuador, www. viajesporecuador.com.
Rooms with heaters for up to 6 people, families welcome, packages include 2 meals a day, spa planned, offers team-building challenges and educational programmes, warm and welcoming.

$$$-$$ Chuquiragua Lodge
500 m before El Chaupi, then 200 m on a cobbled road, T02-367 4046, Quito T02-603 5590, www.chuquiragualodgeandspa.com.
Inn with lovely views, a variety of rooms and prices, restaurant with roaring fireplace. US$18 pp in dorm, camping US$10 pp with hot shower (bring your own tent). Spa, horse riding, trekking, climbing, bike tours and transport from Quito available, advance booking advised.

$$-$ Andes Alpes Café y Hostal
El Chaupi, T02-367 4125, or 09-8813 0143, https://andesalpescafe.com.

Adventure hostel in the centre of the village, climbing information and tours, café serves breakfast, vegetarian meals, coffee, desserts and drinks.

$$-$ La Llovizna
100 m behind the church in El Chaupi, on the way to the mountain, T02-367 4076, Facebook: hosterialallovizna.
Pleasant hostel, sitting room with fireplace, includes breakfast and dinner, cheaper without meals and includes use of kitchen, private or shared bath, ping pong, horse, bike and gear rentals, helpful owner, climbing guides, transport to Ilinizas, book in advance.

$$-$ Nina Rumy
Near the bus stop in El Chaupi, T02-367 4088, or 09-8777 2120.
Includes breakfast and supper, cheaper without meals, simple rooms, private or shared bath, hot water, family-run and very friendly.

Parque Nacional Cotopaxi

$$$-$$ Tambopaxi
3 km south of the El Pedregal access (1-hr drive from Machachi, 2 hrs' walk from El Pedregal) or 4 km north of the turn-off for the climbing shelter, T02-600 0365 (Quito), www.tambopaxi.com.
Comfortable straw-bale mountain shelter at 3750 m. 6 'VIP' rooms and several dorms (US$20 pp), duvets, camping US$12.95 pp, restaurant, excellent horse riding with advance notice.

$$ Refugio Cotopaxi Cara Sur
At the southwestern end of the park, at the end of the Ticatilín road, T09-9800 2681, eagamaz@gmail.com.
Very nice mountain shelter at 4000 m, day use US$1. Includes breakfast and dinner, use of kitchen, some cabins with private bath, hot shower, transport from Quito and climbing tours available, equipment rental. **Campo Alto** is a very basic tent camp

(4780 m, US$8 pp), 4 hrs' walk from the shelter, horse to take gear to Campo Alto US$15, muleteer US$15.

Near El Pedregal entrance to the park

$$$$ Hacienda Santa Ana
3 km from north entrance to Cotopaxi National Park, T02-250 5687, www.santaanacotopaxi.com.
17th-century former Jesuit hacienda in beautiful surroundings. 7 comfortable rooms with fireplaces, central heating, great views, horse riding, hiking, trekking, climbing, price includes breakfast and packed lunch for activities. Also run **Hotel Sierra Madre** in Quito.

$$$$-$$$ Los Mortiños
2 km from Pedregal entrance, T02-334 2520 or 09-9043 6396, www.losmortinos.com.
Purpose-built lodge in the *páramo* with beautiful views, rooms in separate buildings with stoves, trekking, cycling, horse riding, tours to Quilotoa, spa. Closest to northern entrance.

$$$$-$$ Hacienda El Porvenir
T09-9498 0115/0121, Quito T02-600 9533, www.tierradelvolcan.com.
A working ranch by Rumiñahui between El Pedregal and the northern access to the park, family-run, 3 types of rooms from suites to shared bath (US$39), includes breakfast, restaurant serves traditional, locally sourced food. Focus on 'multi-adventure', horse rides, mountain bikes for hire (US$45 per day), spa, works with local communities. Tierra del Volcán also has the more remote, rustic **Hacienda El Tambo** by Quilindaña, southeast of the park, local-style rooms with shared bath. Offers many adventure activities in the park, full details of packages on website.

$$$ Chilcabamba
Loreto del Pedregal, near the northern access to the national park, T09-9875 9033,

T02-240 8741 (Mon-Fri 0830-1730), http://chilcabamba.com/.
Rustic mountain lodge with rooms and family suites in 3 blocks, some rooms with shared bath, all with heating, magnificent views, short trails on property, fire pit in afternoon, can arrange riding, cycling and Río Pita treks. Good restaurant, **Nuna**, uses local ingredients. Helpful staff, good value.

$$$ Secret Garden
T09-9357 2714, www.secret gardencotopaxi.com.
Rooms, cabins and dorms (US$35 pp), includes 3 meals, hot drinks, good common areas with fireplace, indoor jacuzzi with views of Cotopaxi. Offer hiking tours, horse riding and transport (US$5 from Quito). Good value, popular.

Near the main entrance to the park

$$$$ Hacienda San Agustín de Callo
2 access roads from the Panamericana, 1 just north of the main park access (6.2 km); the 2nd, just north of Lasso (4.3 km), T03-271 9160, Quito T02-290 6157, www.incahacienda.com.
Exclusive hacienda, the only place in Ecuador where you can sleep and dine in an Inca building, the northernmost imperial-style Inca structure still standing. Rooms and suites with fireplace and bathtub, includes breakfast and dinner, horse rides, treks, bicycles and fishing. Restaurant (**$$$**) and buildings open to non-guests (US$5-10).

$$$-$$ Cuello de Luna
2 km northwest of the park's main access on a dirt road, T09-9838 1129, www.cuellodeluna.com.
Comfortable rooms with fireplace, includes breakfast, other meals and half-board available, US$20 pp in dorm (a low loft). Can arrange riding, cycling, tours and transfers.

Lasso

$$$$ Hacienda Hato Verde
Panamericana Sur Km 331, by entry to Mulaló, southeast of Lasso, T03-271 9348, www.haciendahatoverde.com.
Lovely old hacienda and working dairy farm near the south flank of Cotopaxi, tastefully restored. 10 rooms with wood-burning stoves, includes breakfast, other meals available; horse riding (for experienced riders), trekking, trip up Cotopaxi Cara Sur, charming hosts.

$$$$-$$$ Hostería La Ciénega
2 km south of Lasso, T03-271 9093, www.haciendalacienega.com.
A historic hacienda with nice gardens, rooms with heater or fireplace, good expensive restaurant, can arrange a variety of activities.

$ Cabañas Los Volcanes
At the south end of Lasso, opposite Parmalat, T09-9869 8125, maexpediciones@yahoo.com.
Small hostel, nice rooms, private or shared bath, meals available. Climbing Cotopaxi and other tours.

Restaurants

Machachi
There are a few simple places in town.

$$$-$$ Café de la Vaca
4 km south of town on the Panamericana. Daily 0800-1730.
Very good meals using produce from their own farm, owned by same family as Sierra Alisos (see page 132), popular.

Festivals

Machachi
Feb El Quesotón, an annual festival celebrating cheese and dairy products, with culinary demonstrations and horse riding. **3rd week Jul** The local cowboy (*chagra*) culture is celebrated at an annual highland 'rodeo', **El Chagra**.

Transport

Machachi

Bus

To **Quito**, from El Playón behind the stadium, every 20 mins to Terminal Quitumbe, 1 hr, US$0.55, every 30 mins to Villa Flora and El Trebol, all US$1, 1½ hrs. To **Latacunga**, from the monument to El Chagra at the Panamericana, US$0.75, 1 hr.

Refugio de Vida Silvestre Pasochoa

Bus

From **Quito** buses run from El Playón to Amaguaña US$0.50 (ask the driver to let you off at the 'Ejido de Amaguaña'); from there follow the signs. It's about an 8-km walk, with not much traffic except at weekends, or book a pick-up from Amaguaña, **Cooperativa Pacheco Jr**, T02-287 7047, about US$6.

Reserva Ecológica Los Ilinizas

Bus

From El Playón in Machachi, to **El Chaupi** (every 30 mins, US$0.35, 40 mins), from where you can walk to the *refugio* in 7-8 hrs. A pick-up from El Chaupi to 'La Virgen' costs US$5 pp from the *refugio* office on north side of plaza or Andes Alpes, from Machachi

US$25. It takes 3 hrs to walk with a full pack from 'La Virgen' to the *refugio*.

Parque Nacional Cotopaxi

Bus

For the main park entrance and Refugio Ribas, take a Latacunga bus from **Quito** and get off at the main access point, where there is a large overpass. Do not take an express bus as you can't get off before Latacunga. At the overpass there are usually pick-up trucks which go to the park, US$20 to Laguna Limpio Pungo for up to 4 passengers, or US$3 to the main park entrance where other vehicles offer half-day guided tours for US$60. From **Machachi**, pick-ups go via the cobbled road to El Pedregal and on to Limpio Pungo and the *refugio* parking lot, US$40. From **Lasso**, a full-day trip to the park, US$50 return, with **Cabañas Los Volcanes**. From **Latacunga**, see Tour operators.

To **Cara Sur** from Quito, **Cotopaxi Cara Sur** offer transport to the **Refugio Cara Sur**, US$60 per vehicle up to 5 passengers. Alternatively take a Latacunga-bound bus and get off at **Pastocalle**, and take a pick-up from there, US$15 per vehicle.

All prices subject to considerable variation, ask around and negotiate politely. All lodges arrange transfers.

★ Latacunga and Quilotoa Circuit

a challenging but rewarding hike, or bike ride

The popular and recommended 200-km round trip from Latacunga to Pujilí, Zumbahua, Quilotoa crater, Chugchilán, Sigchos, Isinliví, Toacazo, Saquisilí and back to Latacunga, can be done in two to three days by bus. It is also a great route for biking and only a few sections of the loop are cobbled or rough. Hiking from one town to another can be challenging, especially when the fog rolls in. For these longer walks hiring a guide might not be unreasonable if you don't have a proper map or enough experience.

Latacunga *Colour map, 3, A6.*

The capital of Cotopaxi Province is a place where the abundance of light grey pumice has been artfully employed. Volcán Cotopaxi is much in evidence, though it is 29 km away.

Provided they are not hidden by clouds, which unfortunately is all too often, as many as nine volcanic cones can be seen from Latacunga; try early in the morning. The colonial character of the town has been well preserved. The central plaza, **Parque Vicente León**, is a beautifully maintained garden (locked at night). There are several other gardens in the town including **Parque San Francisco** and **Lago Flores** (better known as 'La Laguna'). **Casa de los Marqueses de Miraflores** ⓘ *Sánchez de Orellana y Abel Echeverría, Mon-Fri 0800-1700, free*, in a restored colonial mansion has a modest museum, with exhibits on Mama Negra (see Festivals, page 142), colonial art, archaeology, numismatics, a library and the Jefatura de Turismo, see below.

    Casa de la Cultura ⓘ *Antonia Vela 3-49 y Padre Salcedo T03-281 3247, Tue-Sat 0900-1300, 1400-1800, US$1*, built around the remains of a Jesuit Monastery and the old Monserrat watermill, houses a nice museum with pre-Columbian ceramics, weavings, costumes and festival masks; also gallery, library and theatre. It has week-long festivals with exhibits and concerts. There is a Saturday **market** on the Plaza de San Sebastián (at Juan Abel Echeverría). Goods for sale include *shigras* (fine stitched, colourful straw bags) and homespun wool and cotton yarn. The produce market, El Salto, has daily trading and larger fairs on Tuesday, Friday and Saturday.

Latacunga to Zumbahua

A fine paved road leads west from Latacunga to **Pujilí** (15 km, bus US$0.35), which has a beautiful church. There is a good market on Sunday, a smaller one on Wednesday, and the Corpus Christi celebrations are colourful. Beyond Pujilí, many interesting crafts are practised by the *indígenas* in the **Tigua valley**: paintings on leather, hand-carved wooden masks and baskets. **Chimbacucho**, also known as Tigua, is home to the Toaquiza family, most famous of the Tigua artists. The road goes on to Zumbahua, then over the Western

Latacunga

Where to stay 😴
Central **1**
Endamo **2**
Rodelú **3**

Tiana &
  Tovar Expediciones **5**
Villa de Tacvnga **6**

Restaurants ❼
Chifa Dragón **1**
Cunani **2**
Gamber Rosso **3**

Guadalajara Grill **4**

Cordillera to La Maná and Quevedo. This is a great paved downhill bike route. It carries very little traffic and is extremely twisty in parts but is one of the most beautiful routes connecting the highlands with the coast. Beyond Zumbahua are the pretty towns of **Pilaló** (two restaurants, small *hostal* and petrol pumps), **El Tingo-La Esperanza** (two restaurants and three hotels) and **La Maná** (two hotels).

Zumbahua *Colour map 3, A5.*

Zumbahua lies 800 m from the main road, 62 km from Pujilí. It has an interesting Saturday market (starts at 0600) for local produce, and some tourist items. Just below the plaza is a shop selling dairy products and cold drinks. Friday nights involve dancing and drinking. Take a fleece, as it can be windy, cold and dusty. There is a good hospital in town, Italian-funded and run. The Saturday trip to Zumbahua market and the Quilotoa crater makes an excellent excursion.

Quilotoa

Zumbahua is the point to turn off for a visit to Quilotoa, a volcanic crater filled by a beautiful emerald lake. From the rim of the crater (3850 m) several snow-capped volcanoes can be seen in the distance. The crater is reached by a paved road which runs north from Zumbahua (about 12 km, three- to five-hours' walk). There's a 300-m drop down from the crater rim to the water. The hike down takes about 30 minutes (an hour or more to climb back up, mind the altitude). The trail starts at the village of Quilotoa, up the slope from the parking area, then down a steep canyon-like cut. You can hire a mule to ride up from the bottom of the crater (US$10), best arrange before heading down. There is a basic hostel

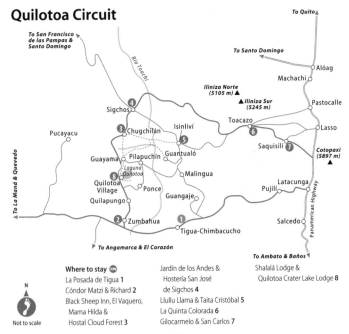

Quilotoa Circuit

Where to stay
La Posada de Tigua 1
Cóndor Matzi & Richard 2
Black Sheep Inn, El Vaquero,
   Mama Hilda &
   Hostal Cloud Forest 3

Jardín de los Andes &
   Hostería San José
   de Sigchos 4
Llullu Llama & Taita Cristóbal 5
La Quinta Colorada 6
Gilocarmelo & San Carlos 7

Shalalá Lodge &
   Quilotoa Crater Lake Lodge 8

Not to scale

by the lake and kayaks for rent (US$5 per hour). Everyone at the crater tries to sell the famous naïve Tigua pictures and carved wooden masks, so expect to be besieged (also by begging children). To the southeast of the crater is the village of **Macapungo**, which runs the Shalalá Lodge, see Where to stay, below. The **Mirador Shalalá** platform offers great views of the lake. To hike around the crater rim takes 4½ to six hours in clear weather. Be prepared for sudden changes in the weather, it gets very cold at night and can be foggy. Never deviate from the trail. For a shorter loop (three to four hours), start on the regular circuit going right when you reach the rim by Quilotoa village and follow it to Mirador Shalalá, a great place for a picnic; then backtrack for about five minutes and take the path down to the lake. To return, follow a path near the lake until you reach the large trail which takes you back up to Quilotoa village. If you are tired, you can hire a horse to take you up.

Chugchilán, Sigchos and Isinliví

Chugchilán, a lovely scenic village, is 16 km by paved road from Quilotoa. An alternative to the road is a five- to six-hour walk around part of the Quilotoa crater rim, then down to Guayama, and across the canyon (Río Sigüi) to Chugchilán, 11 km. Outside town is a cheese factory and nearby, at Chinaló, a woodcarving shop. The area has good walking.

Continuing from Chugchilán the road, newly paved, runs to **Sigchos** (market on Sunday), the starting point for the Toachi Valley walk, via Asache to San Francisco de las Pampas (0900 bus daily to Latacunga). There is also a vehicle road to Las Pampas, with two buses from Sigchos. Southeast of Sigchos is **Isinliví**, on the old, unpaved route to Toacazo and Latacunga. It has a fine woodcarving shop and a pre-Inca *pucará*. Trek to the village of Guantualó, which has a fascinating market on Monday. You can hike between Isinliví and Chugchilán (four to six hours), Isinliví and Sigchos (three to four hours), or from Quilotoa to Isinliví in seven to nine hours.

From Sigchos, a paved road with many curves leads to **Toacazo** ($$$-$$ La Quinta Colorada, T03-238 2202, or 09-9904 9927, www.quintacolorada.com, price includes breakfast and dinner) and on to Saquisilí.

Saquisilí

Some 16 km southwest of Lasso and 4 km west of the Panamericana is the important market town of Saquisilí. Its ★ **Thursday market** (0500-1400) is famous throughout Ecuador for the way in which its seven plazas and some streets become jam-packed with people, the great majority of them local *indígenas* with red ponchos and narrow-brimmed felt hats. The best time to visit the market is 0900-1200 (before 0800 for the animal market). Be sure to bargain, as there is a lot of competition. This area has colourful Corpus Christi processions.

Listings Latacunga and Quilotoa Circuit *maps pages 137 and 138.*

Tourist information

Latacunga

Cámara de Turismo de Cotopaxi
Quito 14-38 y General Maldonado, Latacunga,
T03-280 1112, Facebook: capturcotopaxi.
Mon-Fri 0900-1300, 1400-1700.

Local and regional information, Spanish only.

Jefatura de Turismo
Casa de los Marqueses, T03-370 0440
ext 1303, http://amalatacunga.com.
Mon-Fri 0800-1700.
Local and regional information and maps.

Where to stay

Latacunga

$$$-$$ Villa de Tacvnga
Sánchez de Orellana 16-15 y Guayaquil,
T03-281 2352, info@villadetacvnga.com.
Well-restored colonial house built of
Cotopaxi pumice stone. Comfortable rooms
and suites with fireplace, also has cheaper
rooms, restaurant.

$$ Endamo
2 de Mayo 4-38 y Tarqui, T03-280 2678,
www.hotelendamo.com.
Modern hotel with nice rooms and a small
restaurant, good value, central, helpful.

$$ Rodelú
Quito 16-31 y Salcedo, T03-281 2341,
www.rodelu.com.ec.
Popular hotel, restaurant, suites and rooms
(some are very small, look before taking a
room), breakfast included from the 2nd day.

$$-$ Tiana
Luis F Vivero N1-31 y Sánchez de Orellana,
T03-281 0147, www.hostaltiana.com.
Includes breakfast, drinks and snacks
available, private or shared bath, US$10.50-
11.50 pp in dorm, pleasant patio, kitchen
facilities, luggage store US$1.50 per day,
popular backpackers' meeting place. Tour
agency **Tovar Expediciones**, see page 142.

$ Central
Sánchez de Orellana 15-01 y Padre Salcedo,
T03-280 2912, www.hosteltrail.com/hostels/
hotelcentral.
A multi-storey hotel in the centre of town,
breakfast extra, simple adequate rooms,
very helpful, will store luggage.

Latacunga to Zumbahua

$$ La Posada de Tigua
3 km east of Tigua-Chimbacucho,
400 m north of the road, T03-305 6103,
posadadetigua@yahoo.com.

On a working dairy ranch, 6 rooms, wood-
burning stove, includes tasty home-cooked
breakfast and dinner, pleasant family
atmosphere, horse riding, trails, nice views.

Zumbahua

$ Cóndor Matzi
C Angel María Umajinga, overlooking
the market area, T03-267 2094,
Facebook: hostalcondormatzi.
No frills, best in town, shared bath, hot
water, with breakfast and Wi-Fi, dining room
with wood stove, kitchen facilities, best to
reserve ahead, if closed ask at **Restaurante
Zumbahua** on the plaza. Good for
information on local excursions.

$ Richard
Opposite the market on the road in to town,
T09-9015 5996.
Basic shared rooms and 1 shower with hot
water, cooking facilities, parking.

Quilotoa

$$ Shalalá Lodge
In Macapungo, T03-280 0215, or 09-8813
0143, www.quilotoashalala.com.
Community-run lodge in a lovely 35-ha
cloudforest reserve. Nice cabins, 1 with
wheelchair access, includes breakfast and
dinner, restaurant, trails. Offers 1- and 2-day
tours from Quito.

$$ Quilotoa Crater Lake Lodge
On the main road facing the access
to Quilotoa, T03-305 5816, http://
quilotacraterlodge.hlsecuador.com.
Hacienda-style lodge, includes breakfast
and dinner, dining room, views.

Humberto Latacunga, a good painter
who also organizes treks, runs 3 hostels,
T03-305 5805 or 09-9212 5962, all offer
breakfast and dinner: **$$ Hostería Alpaka**
(http://hosteria-alpakaquilotoa.com), the
most upmarket, rooms with wood stoves;

$ pp **Cabañas Quilotoa** (on the access road to the crater, www.hosteltrail.com/hostels/hostalcabanas), private or shared bath, wood stoves; $ pp **Hostal Pachamama** (at the top of the hill by the rim of the crater).

Chugchilán

$$$$-$$$ Black Sheep Inn
Below the village on the way to Sigchos, T03-270-8077, http://blacksheepinn.com.
A lovely eco-friendly resort which has received international awards. Includes 3 excellent vegetarian meals, private and shared bath, US$35 pp in dorms, spa, water slide, zip-line, arrange excursions.

$$$-$$ Hostal Mama Hilda
On the road in to town, T03-270 8005.
Pleasant family-run hostel, warm atmosphere, large rooms some with wood stoves, includes good dinner and breakfast, private or shared bath, camping, parking, arranges trips.

$$ El Vaquero
Just outside town on the road to Quilotoa, T03-270 8003, www.hostalelvaquero.com.
Variety of rooms with bath, US$20 pp in dorm, great views, includes generous breakfast, tours on horseback or by vehicle arranged, transport to Quilotoa available (US$20).

$$ Hostal Cloud Forest
At the entrance to town, T03-270 8016, www.cloudforesthostal.com.
Simple popular family-run hostel, sitting room with wood stove, includes dinner and great breakfast, restaurant open to public for lunch (US$3), private or shared bath, also dorm (US$15 pp), trekking information, parking, very helpful, great value.

Sigchos

$$ Hostería San José de Sigchos
1.5 km south of town, Quito T02-280 0793 (Mon-Fri 0830-1700), or 09-9467 6413, www.sanjosedesigchos.com.

Comfortable rooms on a 150-ha working hacienda with heated pool, spa, restaurant, karaoke, horse riding, day visit US$20.

$ Jardín de los Andes
Ilinizas y Tungurahua, on plaza 22 de Septiembre, T03-271 4114 or 09-7924 9020, see Facebook.
Basic but quite clean and friendly, with bath, Wi-Fi, parking.

Isinliví

$$$-$$ Llullu Llama
T09-9258 0562, www.llullullama.com.
Farmhouse with cosy sitting room and wood stove, tastefully decorated rooms, cheaper in dorm (US$19 pp), shared ecological bath. Also cottages with bath, fireplace and balcony. All options include good hearty dinner and breakfast, hiking information. Warm and relaxing atmosphere, a lovely spot. Recommended.

$ pp Taita Cristóbal
T09-9137 6542, taitacristobal@gmail.com.
Simple, helpful economy hostel with rooms and dorms, includes dinner and breakfast, good food.

Saquisilí

$$ Gilocarmelo
By the cemetery, 800 m from town on the road north to Guaytacama, T09-9966 9734, T02-340 0924.
Restored hacienda house in a 4-ha property. Plain rooms with fireplace, restaurant, pool, sauna, jacuzzi, nice garden.

$ San Carlos
Bolívar y Sucre, opposite the Parque Central, T03-272 1981, see Facebook: Hostal SAN Carlos.
A multi-storey building, electric shower, parking, good value, but watch your valuables. Will hold luggage for US$1 while you visit the market.

Restaurants

Latacunga

Few places are open on Sun. Many along the Panamericana specialize in *chugchucaras*, a traditional pork dish. *Allullas* biscuits and string cheese are sold by the road.

$$ Chifa Dragón
Amazonas y Pastaza. Daily 1100-2300.
Chinese food, large portions, popular.

$$ Gamber Rosso
Quito y Padre Salcedo, T03-281 3394. Mon-Sat 1600-2200.
Good pizzas, antipasto and lasagne.

$$-$ Guadalajara Grill
Quijano y Ordóñez y Vivero, T03-281 0950.
Economical set lunch Mon-Fri 1200-1500, good Mexican food 1800-2200.

Cunani
Vivero y Quijano y Ordóñez. Mon-Fri 1300-2100.
Cosy café/restaurant serving home-made ravioli, *humitas* and excellent hot chocolate. Also a handicraft store.

Festivals

Latacunga

23-24 Sep La Mama Negra, in homage to the Virgen de las Mercedes. There are 5 main characters in the parade and hundreds of dancers, some representing black slaves, others the whites. Mama Negra (portrayed by a man) is a slave who dared to ask for freedom in colonial times. The colourful costumes are called La Santísima Trajería. **1st or 2nd Sat in Nov** (but not 2 Nov, Día de los Muertos). The civic festival of **La Mama Negra**, with a similar parade. It is part of the **Fiestas de Latacunga**, 11 Nov.

What to do

Latacunga

All operators offer day trips to **Cotopaxi** and **Quilotoa** (US$50 pp, includes lunch and a visit to a market town if on Thu or Sat, minimum 2 people). Trekking trips US$80 pp per day. **Note** Many agencies require passport as deposit when renting gear.

Greivag, *Guayaquil y Sánchez de Orellana, Plaza Santo Domingo, L5, T03-281 0510, www.greivagturismo.com*. Day trips.

Neiges, *Sánchez de Orellana 17-38 y Guayaquil, Plaza Santo Domingo, T03-281 1199, Facebook: neigestours@hotmail.com*. Day trips and climbing. Also has a café.

Tovar Expediciones, *at Hostal Tiana, T03-281 1333*. Climbing and trekking, a good source of information for the Quilotoa Circuit.

Transport

Latacunga
Bus

Buses leave from the terminal just south of 5 de Junio. At night (1900-0700) they enter the city to pick up passengers if they have space available. **Transportes Santa** has its own terminal at Eloy Alfaro y Vargas Torres, T03-281 1659, serving **Cuenca**, US$11, **Loja**, US$15, **Guayaquil**, US$10; 5 daily to each, 2 a day to **Machala**, US$11. Other companies from the main terminal: to **Quito**, every 15-30 mins, 2 hrs, US$2.50. To **Ambato**, 1 hr, US$1.25. Through buses, which are more frequent, do not stop at Latacunga Terminal. During the day they stay on the 'Paso Lateral', the city bypass of the Panamericana, and stop at the roundabout at the road to Pujilí; taxi from town US$3. For long-haul service southbound, it may be easiest to take a local bus to Ambato and transfer there. To **Otavalo** and **Ibarra**, bypassing Quito, see **Cita Express** (Los Nevados y Av Río Cutuchi, T03-280 9264) under Ambato; also with **Expreso Baños**. To **Baños**, US$2.25, 2 hrs, every 20 mins from the Paso Lateral. To **Saquisilí**, every 20 mins (see below). Buses on the Zumbahua, Quilotoa, Chugchilán, Sigchos circuit are given below. **Note** On Thu most buses to nearby communities leave from Saquisilí market instead of Latacunga.

Zumbahua
Bus
Many daily on the Latacunga–Quevedo road (0500-1900, US$1.50, 1½ hrs). Buses on Sat are full, get your ticket on Fri. A pick-up truck can be hired from Zumbahua to **Quilotoa** for US$5-10 depending on number of passengers; also to **Chugchilán** for around US$30. On Sat mornings there are many trucks leaving the Zumbahua market for Chugchilán which pass Quilotoa. Pick-up Quilotoa–Chugchilán US$25.

Taxi
Day-trip by taxi to Zumbahua, Quilotoa, and return to **Latacunga** is about US$60.

Quilotoa
Bus
From the terminal terrestre in Latacunga **Trans Vivero** daily at 1000, 1130, 1230 and 1330, US$2.50, 2 hrs. Note that this leaves from Latacunga, not Saquisilí market, even on Thu. Return bus direct to Latacunga at 1300. Buses returning at 1400 and 1500 go only as far as Zumbahua, from where you can catch a Latacunga-bound bus at the highway. Also, buses going through Zumbahua bound for Chugchilán will drop you at the turn-off, 5 mins from the crater, where you can also pick them up on their way to Zumbahua and Latacunga. Taxi from Latacunga, US$40 one way. For **Shalalá**, **Trans Iliniza** from Latacunga to **Macapungo** at 1300, US$2, or go to Zumbahua and take a pick-up from there, US$5. From Macapungo it is a 30-min walk to the cabins.

Chugchilán
Bus
From **Latacunga**, daily at 0700 with **14 de Octubre** via Zumbahua and at 1130 (except Thu) via Sigchos, and 1145 and 1300 via Zumbahua with Trans Iliniza; on Thu from **Saquisilí market** via Sigchos around 1130, US$3, 3 hrs. Buses return to Latacunga at 0400 via Sigchos, at 0500, 0600 and 1300 via Zumbahua. On Sun there are extra buses to Latacunga leaving at 0900, 1000, 1100 and 1330. On Sat also pick-ups going to/from market in Zumbahua and Latacunga. From **Sigchos**, through buses as above, US$0.75, 1 hr. Pick-up hire to Sigchos US$20, up to 5 people, US$5 additional person. Pick-up to **Quilotoa** US$25, up to 5 people, US$5 additional person. Taxi from Latacunga US$50; to **Isinliví**, taxi US$30. Transport information on http://blacksheepinn.com.

Sigchos
Bus
From **Latacunga** almost every hour, 0500-2000; returning to Latacunga 0500-1700; US$3.50, 2 hrs. From **Quito** direct service daily 1400 and 1830 (plus Mon 0800 and Fri 1745i), Sigchos–Quito 0430, 1415, plus Fri 1245 and Sun 1130 and 1500, all with **Reina de Sigchos**; also Fri 1700 with **Iliniza**; US$3.75, 3 hrs. To **La Maná** on the road to Quevedo, via Chugchilán, Quilotoa and Zumbahua, Fri at 0500 and Sun at 0830, US$4.50, 6 hrs (returns Sat at 0730 and Sun at 1530). To **Las Pampas**, at 0400, 1000 and 1430, US$3.25, 3 hrs; these continue to **Santo Domingo**, plus 0400 and 0600 Las Pampas–Santo Domingo, US$3.25, 3 hrs.

Isinliví
Bus
From **Latacunga** daily (except Thu), via Sigchos at 1215 (**14 de Octubre**) and direct at 1300 (**Trans Vivero**), on Thu both leave from Saquisilí market 14 de Octubre at 1200,

Vivero at 1100, on Sat the direct bus leaves at 1100 instead of 1300, US$2.50, 2½ hrs. Both return to Latacunga 0300-0330, except Wed at 0700 direct, Sun 1245 direct and Mon 1500 via Sigchos. Buses fill quickly, be early. Connections to Chugchilán, Quilotoa and Zumbahua can be made in Sigchos. For bus schedules, see www.llullullama.com.

Saquisilí
Bus
Frequent service between **Latacunga** and Saquisilí, US$0.50, 20 mins; many buses daily to/from **Quito** (Quitumbe), 0530-1300, US$2.50, 2 hrs. Buses and trucks to many outlying villages leave from 1000 onwards. Bus tours from Quito cost US$45 pp, taxis charge US$80, with 2 hrs' wait at market.

Ambato and around   *Colour map 3, B5.*

service and transport hub of the area

Almost completely destroyed in the great 1949 earthquake, Ambato lacks the colonial charm of other Andean cities, though its location in the heart of fertile orchard-country has earned it the nickname of 'the city of fruits and flowers'. It is also a transport hub and the principal commercial city of the central highlands, with a large Monday market and smaller ones on Wednesday and Friday.

Ambato
The modern cathedral faces **Parque Montalvo**, where there is a statue of the writer Juan Montalvo (1832-1889); **Montalvo's house** ⓘ *Bolívar y Montalvo, T03-282 4248, www.casademontalvo.gob.ec, US$1, Mon-Fri 0930-1700, Sat 1000-1500,* can be visited. The **Museo de la Provincia** in the Casa del Portal (built 1900), facing Parque Montalvo, has a photo collection.

Northeast of Ambato is the colonial town of **Píllaro**, gateway to **Parque Nacional Los Llanganates**, a beautiful rugged area (for tours, see **Sachayacu Explorer**, page 156). The town is known for its colourful festivals (see page 147).

Ambato to Baños
To the east of Ambato, an important road leads to **Salasaca**, where the *indígenas* sell their weavings; they wear distinctive black ponchos with white trousers and broad white hats. Further east, 5 km, is **Pelileo**, the blue jean manufacturing capital of Ecuador with good views of Tungurahua. There are opportunities for cultural tourism, walking and paragliding in the area (see www.turismopelileo.com, website of Pelileo municipality, T03-287 1121 ext 223). From Pelileo, the road descends to Las Juntas, where the Patate and Chambo rivers meet to form the Río Pastaza. About 1 km east of Las Juntas bridge, the junction with the road to Riobamba is marked by a large sculpture of a macaw and a toucan (locally known as Los Pájaros – the lower bird was destroyed by the volcano). It is a favourite volcano-watching site. The road to Baños then continues along the lower slopes of the volcano.

Eight kilometres northeast of Pelileo on a paved sideroad is **Patate**, centre of the warm, fruit-growing Patate valley. There are excellent views of Volcán Tungurahua from town. The fiesta of **Nuestro Señor del Terremoto** is held on the weekend leading up to 4 February (see Festivals, page 147).

Ambato to Riobamba and Guaranda

After Ambato, the Pan-American Highway runs south to Riobamba (see page 157). About half way is **Mocha**, where guinea pigs (*cuy*) are bred for the table. You can sample roast *cuy* and other typical dishes at stalls and restaurants by the roadside, **Mariadiocelina** is recommended. The highway climbs steeply south of Mocha and at the pass at **Urbina** there are fine views in the dry season of Chimborazo and Carihuayrazo.

To the west of Ambato, a paved road climbs through tilled fields, past the *páramos* of Carihuayrazo and Chimborazo to the great Arenal (a high desert at the base of the mountain), and down through the Chimbo valley to Guaranda (see page 158). This spectacular journey reaches a height of 4380 m and vicuñas can be seen.

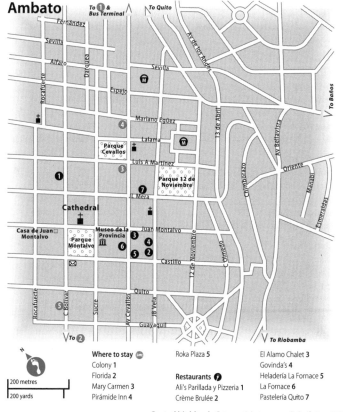

Ambato

Where to stay
Colony 1
Florida 2
Mary Carmen 3
Pirámide Inn 4
Roka Plaza 5

Restaurants
Ali's Parillada y Pizzeria 1
Crème Brulée 2
El Alamo Chalet 3
Govinda's 4
Heladería La Fornace 5
La Fornace 6
Pastelería Quito 7

Where to stay

$$$ Florida
Av Miraflores 1131, T03-242 2007,
www.hotelflorida.com.ec.
Pleasant hotel in a lovely setting, restaurant with good set meals, weekend discounts.

$$$ Mary Carmen
Av Ceballos y Martínez, T03-242 0908,
http://hotelboutiquemc.com.
Very nice boutique hotel with Café del Parque, gym, spa and parking.

$$$ Roka Plaza
Bolívar 20-62 y Guayaquil, T03-242 3845,
www.hotelrokaplaza.com.
Stylish hotel in a refurbished colonial house in the heart of the city, sushi restaurant.

$$-$ Colony
12 de Noviembre 124 y Av El Rey, near the bus terminal, T03-282 5789, see Facebook.
A modern hotel with large rooms, parking, spotless.

$$-$ Pirámide Inn
Cevallos y Mariano Egüez, T03-242 1920.
Comfortable hotel, cafeteria, English spoken.

Ambato to Baños
Salasaca and Pelileo

$$ Runa Huasi
In Salasaca, 1 km north off main highway, T09-9984 0125, www.hostalrunahuasi.com.
Simple hostel, includes breakfast and fruit, other meals on request, cooking facilities, nice views, guided walks.

$ Pensión Pelileo
Eloy Alfaro 641, T03-287 1390.
Shared bath, hot water, simple.

Patate

$$$$-$$$ Hacienda Manteles
In the Leito valley on the road to El Triunfo, Patate, T09-8821 9095, Quito T02-254 9559, www.haciendamanteles.com.
Converted hacienda with views of Tungurahua and Chimborazo, includes breakfast, dinner, snacks, walk to waterfalls, hiking, horse riding and birdwatching (part of **Bird Life International**). Day trips to Baños possible. Reserve ahead.

$$$ Hacienda Leito
Km 8.5 on Vía Ecológica Patate–Baños, T03-306 3196, www.haciendaleito.com.
Classy hacienda with spacious rooms and great views of Tungurahua, *parrilla*-style restaurant, spa, activities include cycling, walking and horse riding.

$$$ Hostería Viña del Río
3 km from town on the old road to Baños, T03-287 0139, www.hosteriavinadelrio.com.
Cabins on a 22-ha ranch, restaurant, various pools, spa and mini golf, US$7 for day use of facilities.

$ Hostal Casa del Valle
Juan Montalvo y Ambato, 2 blocks from plaza, T09-8150 1062, see Facebook.
A good simple place right in town.

Restaurants

$$$-$$ Ali's Parrillada y Pizzería
Bolívar 16-36 y JL Mera, also in Ficoa neighbourhood and opposite Mall de los Andes, www.alisparrilladas.com. Open 1030-2230.
Good pizzas and international meat dishes.

$$$-$$ La Fornace
Cevallos 1728 y Montalvo. Mon-Thu 1000-2200, Fri-Sun 1000-2300).

Wood-oven pizza. Opposite is **Heladería La Fornace**, Cevallos y Castillo. Snacks, sandwiches, ice cream, very popular.

$$ El Alamo Chalet
Cevallos 1719 y Montalvo. Open 0930-2200.
Ecuadorean and international food. Set meals and à la carte, Swiss-owned, good quality.

$$-$ Govinda's
JB Vela entre Montalvo y Castillo, see Facebook. Mon-Sat 0800-1600.
Vegetarian set meals and à la carte, also a meditation centre (T09-9893 2027).

Cafés

Crème Brulée
Juan B Vela 08-38 y Montalvo. Mon-Sat 0830-2100.
Very good coffee, chocolate and pastries, also breakfast and lunches.

Pasterlería Quito
JL Mera y Cevallos. Daily 0700-2100.
Coffee, pastries, good for breakfast.

Festivals

Ambato
Ambato is known for its colourful festivals.
1-6 Jan La Diablada (devils' parade).
Feb/Mar Ambato has a famous festival, the **Fiesta de Frutas y Flores**, during carnival, when there are 4 days of festivities and parades (best Sun morning and Mon night). Must book ahead to get a hotel room.
May/Jun Corpus Christi.

Ambato to Baños
Patate
Weekend leading up to 4 Feb Fiesta de Nuestro Señor del Terremoto features a parade with floats made with fruit and flowers.

Shopping

Ambato is a centre for leather: shoe shops on Bolívar; jackets, bags, belts on Vela between Lalama and Montalvo. Take a bus up to the leather town of Quisapincha for the best deals, every day, but big market on Sat.

What to do

Train rides
The *Tren de Hielo II* runs from Ambato to **Urbina** and back via **Cevallos**, Fri-Sat at 0800, US$23, snack lunch and demonstration of collection of glacial ice at Urbina station. The train station is at Av Gran Colombia y Chile, near the Terminal Terrestre, T03-252 2623; Wed-Thu 0800-1800, Fri 0700-1700, Sat 0700-1400, Sun 0700-1300.

Transport

Bus
The main bus station is on Av Colombia y Paraguay, 2 km north of the centre. City buses go there from Plaza Cevallos in the centre, US$0.25. Buses to **Quito**, 3 hrs, US$3.25; also door to door shared taxis, US$12, with **Delux**, T09-3920 9827or 09-8343 0275, Facebook: DELUX.vip, and others. Buses to **Cuenca**, US$9, 6½ hrs. To **Guayaquil**, 6 hrs, US$8.25. To **Riobamba**, US$1.25, 1 hr. To **Guaranda**, US$2.50, 3 hrs. To **Ibarra**, via Pifo and bypassing Quito, **CITA**, 12 daily, 5½ hrs, US$6.25. To **Santo Domingo de los Tsáchilas**, 4 hrs, US$5. To **Tena**, US$6.25, 4½ hrs. To **Puyo**, US$3.75, 2½ hrs. To **Macas**, US$8, 5½ hrs. To **Esmeraldas**, US$10, 8 hrs. To **Baños**: either take a bus from the terminal on the Ambato–Puyo/Tena route and get out at Baños, or other services leave from the Mercado Mayorista, Av El Cóndor y Tres Caravelas, southeast of the centre, and then stop at the edge of town, 1 hr, US$1.10. Through buses do not go into the terminal, they take the Paso Lateral bypass road.

Baños
& Riobamba

Baños and Riobamba are both good bases for exploring the Sierra and their close proximity to high peaks gives great opportunities for climbing, cycling and trekking (but check about Tungurahua's volcanic activity before you set out). The thermal springs at Baños are an added lure and the road east is a great way to get to the jungle lowlands. South of Riobamba, Alausí offers the opportunity to ride the train on the famous section of the line from the Andes to Guayaquil, around the Devil's Nose.

Baños and around   *Colour map 3, B6.*

hot baths, adventure sports and hospitality from near and far

Baños de Agua Santa (to give it its full name) is nestled between the Río Pastaza and the Tungurahua volcano, only 8 km from its crater. Baños bursts at the seams with hotels, *residenciales*, restaurants and tour agencies. Ecuadoreans flock here at weekends and onholidays for the hot springs, to visit the Basílica and enjoy the local *melcochas* (toffees), while escaping the Andean chill in a subtropical climate (wettest in July and August). Foreign visitors are also frequent; using Baños as a base for trekking, organizing a visit to the jungle, making local day trips or just plain hanging out.

Sights
The **Manto de la Virgen** waterfall at the southeast end of town is a symbol of Baños. The **Basílica** attracts many pilgrims. The paintings of miracles performed by Nuestra Señora del Agua Santa are worth seeing. There are various thermal baths in town. The **Termas de la Virgen** ⓘ *by the waterfall, Wed-Sun and holidays 0900-1800, US$6, children US$3,* is the amalgamation of the Baños de la Virgen with the neighbouring **Piscinas Modernas** in 2017. There are 10 pools, eight of them thermal, a wave pool, a waterslide and children's area. They get busy so best visit early. There are plans to develop the complex still further. **El Salado baths** ⓘ *daily 0500-1600, weekends also 1800-2100, US$4,* consist of several hot pools, plus icy cold river water, repeatedly destroyed by volcanic debris (not safe when activity is high), 1.5 km out of town off the Ambato road. The **Santa Ana baths** ⓘ *Fri-Sun*

and holidays 0830-1700, US$2, have hot and cold pools in a pleasant setting, just east of town on the road to Puyo. All the baths can be very crowded at weekends and on holidays; the brown colour of the water is due to its high mineral content. The **Santa Clara baths** ① *C Velasco Ibarra behind Parque Montalvo, daily 0900-1700, US$4,* are not natural springs but have clean heated pools as well as a nice large cold pool for swimming laps.

As well as the medicinal baths, there are various spas, in hotels, as independent centres and massage therapists. These offer a combination of sauna, steam bath (Turkish or box), jacuzzi, clay and other types of bath, a variety of massage techniques (Shiatsu, Reiki, Scandinavian) and more.

Around Baños

There are many interesting **walks** in the Baños area. The **San Martín shrine**, a 45-minute easy walk from town, overlooks a deep rocky canyon with the Río Pastaza thundering below. Beyond the shrine, crossing to the north side of the Pastaza, is the **Ecozoológico San Martín** ① *T03-274 1966, http://ecozoosanmartin.com, 0800-1700, US$3,* with the

Baños

Where to stay
Casa del Molino Blanco 1 *C1*
El Belén 2 *B2*
Erupción Art Hostel 3 *B2*
Erupción Backpackers 4 *B2*
Finca Chamanapamba 5 *A4*
Hostal Ilé 6 *C3*
Isla de Baños 7 *C2*
La Casa Verde 8 *A4*
La Chimenea 9 *nC4*
La Floresta 10 *C2*

Los Pinos 12 *B4*
Luna Runtún 13 *A3*
Plantas y Blanco 14 *C3*
Posada del Arte 15 *C4*
Princesa María 16 *B1*
Puerta del Sol 17 *B4*
Samari 18 *A4*
Sangay 19 *C4*
Santa Cruz 20 *C3*
Transilvania 21 *B3*
Volcano 23 *C4*

Restaurants
Ali Cumba 1 *C3*
Café Blah Blah 2 *B2*
Café Hood 3 *B2*
Café Honey 16 *B2*
Casa Hood 4 *C3*
El Castillo 5 *C4*
Jota Jota 6 *C3*
Mariane 7 *C2*
Pancho's 8 *C2*
Rico Pan 9 *B2*

Sativa 10 *C3*
Swiss Bistro 11 *C3*

Bars & clubs
Buena Vista 12 *B3*
Ferchos 13 *B3*
Jack Rock 14 *B3*
Leprechaun 15 *B3*

ON THE ROAD

Active volcanoes

In 1999, after over 80 years of dormancy, Tungurahua became active again and remains so. The level of activity is variable; the volcano can be quiet for weeks or months between bursts of energy. Baños continues to be a safe and popular destination unless and until the level of volcanic activity greatly increases. The volcano is closed to climbers but all else is normal. In 2015, after 135 years of tranquility, it was Cotopaxi's turn and this volcano also remains active. The level of activity diminished through 2016 and 2017, so much so that restrictions on climbing to the summit were lifted in October 2017. You should be prepared to leave immediately, however, in the event of an alarm. Also under surveillance are Cayambe, which showed signs of increased activity in 2016, and Reventador, which has been erupting since 2002 and had a significant event in December 2017. Since the level of volcanic activity can change, you should enquire locally before visiting any of these mountains and surrounding areas. Reports from the National Geophysical Institute are posted daily on www.igepn.edu.ec.

Serpentario San Martín ⓘ *daily 0700-1800, US$2*, opposite. Some 50 m beyond is a path to the **Inés María waterfall**, cascading down, but polluted. Further, a *tarabita* (cable car) and zip-lines span the entrance to the canyon. You can also cross the Pastaza by the **Puente San Francisco** road bridge, behind the kiosks across the main road from the bus station. From here a series of trails fans out into the hills, offering excellent views of Tungurahua from the ridge-tops in clear weather. A total of six bridges span the Pastaza near Baños, so you can make a round trip.

On the hillside behind Baños are a series of interconnecting trails with nice views. It is a pleasant 45-minute hike to the **statue of the Virgin**; go to the south end of Calle JL Mera, before the street ends, take the last street to the right (Misioneros Dominicanos) at the end of which are stairs leading to the trail. A steep, narrow path continues along the ridge, past the statue. Another trail also begins at the south end of JL Mera and leads to the Hotel Luna Runtún, continuing on to the village of Runtún (five- to six-hour round trip). Yet another trail starts at the south end of Calle Maldonado and leads in 45 minutes to the **Bellavista cross**, from where you can also continue to Runtún. Another popular attraction in this area is the **Casa Del Arbol** ⓘ *daily, there may be queues when a bus or tour arrives, staff on hand, US$1*, a tree house originally set up as a seismic observatory of Tungurahua (of which there are great views on a clear day), which has a swing out towards the valley – the famous **Swing at the End of the World** – more swings, a small zip-line and a café. Tours from town go frequently and cost about US$9, otherwise take a taxi for US$15, bus for US$2 (four a day from Rocafuerte y Pastaza), or hike for about three or four hours up (don't go alone).

The scenic road to **Puyo** (58 km) has many waterfalls tumbling down into the Pastaza. Many *tarabitas* (cable cars) and zip-lines span the canyon offering good views. By the Agoyán dam and bridge, 5 km from town, is **Parque de la Familia** ⓘ *Wed-Fri 1000-1800, Sat, Sun and holidays 0800-1800, entry free, parking US$1*, with orchards, gardens, paths and domestic animals. Beyond, the paved road goes through seven tunnels between Agoyán and Río Negro. The older gravel road runs parallel to the paved road, directly above the

Río Pastaza, and is the preferred route for cyclists who, coming from Baños, should only go through one tunnel at Agoyán and then stay to the right avoiding the other tunnels. Between tunnels there is only the paved road, cyclists must be very careful as there are many buses and lorries. The area has excellent opportunities for walking and nature observation.

At the junction of the Verde and Pastaza rivers, 17 km from Baños, is the town of **Río Verde** with snack bars, restaurants and a few places to stay. The Río Verde has crystalline green water and is cold but nice for bathing. The paved highway runs to the north of town, between it and the old road, the river has been dammed forming a small lake where rubber rafts are rented for paddling. Near the paved road is **Orquideario** ① *T03-249 3166, Facebook: OrquidearioVerde, 0900-1700 (but may close Mon-Tue at certain times of year), US$1.50*, with pretty regional orchids. Before joining the Pastaza, the Río Verde tumbles down several falls, the most spectacular of which is ★ **El Pailón del Diablo** (the Devil's Cauldron). Cross the Río Verde on the old road and take the path to the right after the church, then follow the trail down towards the suspension bridge over the Pastaza for about 20 minutes. Just before the bridge take a side trail to the right (signposted) which leads you to **Paradero del Pailón**, a pleasant restaurant, and trails to viewing platforms above and below the falls (US$1.50): the former goes over a hanging bridge, the latter through a natural tunnel. Be prepared to get wet. The **San Miguel Falls**, smaller but also nice, are some five minutes' walk from the town along a different trail. Cross the old bridge and take the first path to the right, here is **Falls Garden** (US$1.50), with lookout platforms over both sets of falls. Cyclists can leave bikes at one of the snack bars while visiting the falls and return to Baños by bus.

Listings Baños and around *map page 149.*

Tourist information

iTur
Oficina Municipal de Turismo, at the Municipio, Halflants y Rocafuerte, opposite Parque Central, Baños, T03-274 0483. Mon-Fri 0800-1230, 1400-1730. See www.banios.com or http://banos-ecuador.com.

Where to stay

Baños has plenty of accommodation but can fill during holiday weekends.

$$$$ Luna Runtún
Vía a Runtún Km 6, T03-274 0309, or 09-8557 4069, www.lunaruntun.com.
A classy hotel in a beautiful setting overlooking Baños. Includes dinner, breakfast and use of pools (spa extra), very comfortable rooms with balconies and superb views, lovely gardens. Good service,

English, French and German spoken, tours, nanny service.

$$$$ Samari
Vía a Puyo Km 1, T03-274 1855, www.samarispa.com.
Upmarket resort opposite the Santa Ana baths, nice grounds, tastefully decorated hacienda-style rooms and suites, pool and spa (US$24.50 for non-residents, daily 0800-2000), fine upmarket restaurant.

$$$$-$$$ Sangay
Plazoleta Isidro Ayora 100, next to waterfall and thermal baths, T03-274 0490, www.sangayspahotel.com.
Traditional Baños hotel with rooms and bungalows in 3 areas, buffet breakfast, good restaurant specializes in Ecuadorean food, pool and spa, parking, tennis and squash courts, games room, bicycle hire, attentive service, midweek discounts, British/Ecuadorean-run.

$$$ Finca Chamanapamba
On the east shore of the Río Ulba, a short ride from the road to Puyo, T03-277 6241, www.chamanapamba.com.
2 well-finished wooden cabins in a spectacular location overlooking the Río Ulba and just next to the Chamanapamba waterfalls, very good café-restaurant serves German food.

$$$ La Floresta
Halflants y Montalvo, T03-274 1824, www.laflorestahotel.com.
Lovely hotel with large comfortable rooms set around a pretty garden, excellent buffet breakfast, wheelchair accessible, craft and book shop, parking, attentive service. Warmly recommended.

$$$ Posada del Arte
Pasaje Velasco Ibarra y Montalvo, T03-274 0083, www.posadadelarte.com.
Cosy inn, restaurant with vegetarian options, pleasant sitting room, more expensive rooms have fireplace, terrace, US-run.

$$$ Volcano
Rafael Vieira y Montalvo, T03-274 2140, www.volcano.com.ec.
Spacious modern hotel, large rooms with fridge, some with views of the waterfall, buffet breakfast, restaurant, heated pool, massage, nice garden.

$$$-$$ Isla de Baños
Halflants 1-31 y Montalvo, T03-274 1511, www.isladebanios.com.
Well-decorated comfortable hotel, includes European breakfast and steam bath, spa operates when there are enough people, pleasant garden.

$$ Hostal Ilé
12 de Noviembre y Montalvo, T03-274 2699, www.facebook.com/hostalile.
Rustic feel with lots of wood, ample comfortable rooms, Mexican restaurant.

$$ La Casa Verde
In Santa Ana, 1.5 km from town on Camino Real, a road parallel and north of the road to Puyo, T03-274 2671, www.lacasaverde.com.ec.
Spacious hotel decorated in pine, the largest rooms in Baños, laundry and cooking facilities, very quiet, yoga, communal kitchen, New Zealand/Australian-run.

$$-$ El Belén
Reyes y Ambato, T03-274 1024, www.hotelelbelen.com.
Nice hostel, cooking facilities, spa, parking, helpful staff.

$$-$ Los Pinos
Ricardo Zurita y C Ambato, T03-274 1825, www.greathostels.com.ec.
Large hostel with double rooms and dorms (US$9-13.50 pp), includes breakfast, camping area, spa, kitchen and laundry facilities, bar, pool table, Argentine-run, great value.

$$-$ Puerta del Sol
Ambato y Arrayanes (east end of C Ambato), T03-274 2265, Facebook: HotelPuertasDelSolBanos.
Modern hotel, better than it looks on the outside, large well-appointed rooms, includes breakfast, pleasant dining area, laundry facilities, parking.

$ Casa del Molino Blanco
Misioneros Dominicanos y JL Mera, Barrio San José, T03-274 1138, www.casamolinoblanco.com.
Located in a quiet area, with bath, US$11 pp in dorm, spotlessly clean, includes buffet breakfast, German and English spoken.

$ Erupción Art Hostel
Halflants y Ambato (corner of the Plaza), T03-274 3254, www.hostalerupcion.com.
Busy hostel with private rooms and dorms (US$9 pp), nice social area, restaurant/bar. Has a 2nd branch, **Erupción Backpackers** (Maldonado y Espejo, T03-274 3475, same website), which is simpler and

a bit cheaper (dorm US$7 pp). Both are popular meeting places, with kitchen facilities, can arrange tours.

$ La Chimenea
Martínez y Rafael Vieira, T03-274 2725, www.hostalchimenea.com.
Nice hostel with terrace café, breakfast available, private or shared bath, US$8.50 pp in dorm, small pool, jacuzzi extra, parking for small cars, quiet, helpful and good value. Recommended.

$ Plantas y Blanco
12 de Noviembre y Martínez, T03-274 0044, www.plantasyblanco.com.
Pleasant popular hostel decorated with plants, private or shared bath, US$9-10 pp in dorm, excellent breakfast available, rooftop cafeteria, steam bath, classic films, good restaurant (open 1700-0100), bakery, French-owned, good value. Recommended.

$ Princesa María
Rocafuerte y Mera, T03-274 1035, www.hostalprincesamaria.com.
Spacious rooms, US$8 pp in dorm, laundry and cooking facilities, parking, popular budget travellers' meeting place, helpful and good value.

$ Santa Cruz
16 de Diciembre y Martínez, T03-274 3527, www.santacruzbackpackers.com.
Large rooms, US$10.50 pp in dorm, fireplace in lounge, small garden with hammocks, kitchen facilities, mini pool on roof.

$ Transilvania
16 de Diciembre y Oriente, T03-274 2281, www.hostal-transilvania.com.
Multi-storey building with simple rooms, includes breakfast, US$8.50 pp in dorm, Middle Eastern restaurant, nice views from balconies, large TV and movies in sitting room, pool table, popular meeting place.

Around Baños

$$$ Miramelindo
Río Verde, just north of the paved road at Km 15 on Baños–Puyo road, T03-249 3004 or 09-9587 3307, http://miramelindo.com.
Lovely hotel and spa, well-decorated rooms, good restaurant, pleasant gardens include an orchid collection with over 1000 plants.

Restaurants

$$$ Mariane
On a small lane by Montalvo y Halflants, T03-274 1947, http://hotelmariane.com. Mon-Sat 1300-2200.
Excellent authentic Provençal cuisine, generous portions, lovely setting, popular, slow service. Highly recommended. **Hotel Mariane ($$)** at the same location.

$$$ Swiss Bistro
Martínez y Alfaro, T03-274 2262, www.swiss-bistro.com. Daily 0730-2230.
International dishes and Swiss specialities, open for breakfast and coffee, Swiss-run.

$$ Café Hood
Montalvo y Vieira, T03-274 1609, http:// cafehoodecuador.com. Daily 1200-2200.
Mainly vegetarian but also some meat dishes, excellent food, English spoken, always busy. Also rents rooms.

$$ Casa Hood
Martínez between Halflants and Alfaro, T03-274 2668, Facebook: banos.ec. Open 1200-2215.
Largely vegetarian, juices, milkshakes, varied menu including Indonesian and Thai, good set lunch and desserts. Travel books and maps sold, book exchange, cinema, cultural events, nice atmosphere. Popular and recommended.

$$ Sativa
Martínez y Eloy Alfaro, www.sativa studiocafe.com. Mon-Sat 1100-2300.

Wholesome food, some organic ingredients from their own garden, Caribbean influence, also has pottery studio.

$ El Castillo
Martínez y Rafael Vieira, in hostel, T03-274 0285, see Facebook. Open 0800-1000, 1200-1330.
A favourite for a good filling set lunch.

Cafés

Ali Cumba
12 de Noviembre y Martínez, T03-274 3413, see Facebook. Daily 0800-2000.
Excellent breakfasts, salads, good coffee (filtered, espresso), muffins, cakes, home-made bread, large sandwiches, book exchange. Danish/Ecuadorean-run.

Café Blah Blah
Halflants y Martínez. Daily 0800-2000.
Cosy, popular café serving very good breakfasts, coffee, cakes, snacks and juices.

Café Honey
Maldonado y Rocafuerte at the Parque Central, T09-9860 9450, www.honey coffeeandtea.com. Daily 0730-2200.
Fine modern café with all kinds of coffees, teas and pastries, very good.

Jota Jota
Martínez y Halflants. Tue-Sun to 1000-2200.
Great choice of coffees and cocktails, book exchange. German-run.

Pancho's
Rocafuerte y Maldonado at Parque Central. Daily 1530-2200.
Hamburgers, snacks, sandwiches, coffee, large-screen TV for sports and other events.

Rico Pan
Ambato y Maldonado at Parque Central, T03-274 0387. Daily 0700-2100.
Good breakfasts, hot bread (including whole wheat), fruit salads and pizzas, also meals.

Bars and clubs

Eloy Alfaro, between Ambato and Oriente has many bars including:

Buena Vista
Alfaro y Oriente, T09-9858 6762, Facebook: buenavistadiscotec.
A good place for salsa and other Latin music.

Ferchos
Alfaro y Oriente. Tue-Sun 1600-2400.
Café-bar, modern decor, snacks, cakes, good varied music, German-run.

Jack Rock
Alfaro y Oriente 5-41, T03-274 1329, Facebook: JackRockCafe.
A favourite traveller hangout.

Leprechaun
Alfaro y Oriente, T09-8459 3829, Facebook: LeprechaunBarBanios. Mon-Sat 0800-0200.
Popular for dancing, bonfire on weekends, occasional live music.

Entertainment

Chivas, open-sided buses, cruise town playing music; they take you to different night spots and to a volcano lookout when Tungurahua is active (T03-274 1024, www. alquilerdeciva.com).

Festivals

During Carnival and Holy Week hotels are full and prices rise.

Oct Nuestra Señora de Agua Santa. Daily processions, bands, fireworks, sporting events and partying through the month.
15 Dec Verbenas. A night-time celebration when each barrio hires a band and parties.
16 Dec The town's anniversary, with parades, fairs, sports, cultural events leading up to this date.

Shopping

Look out for jaw-aching toffee (*melcocha*) made in ropes in shop doorways, or the less sticky *alfeñique*.

Handicrafts

Crafts stalls at Pasaje Ermita de la Vírgen, off C Ambato, by the market. Tagua (vegetable ivory made from palm nuts) crafts on Maldonado y Martínez. Leather shops on Rocafuerte between Halflants and 16 de Diciembre.

Latino's Boutique, *Ambato 8-56 y Reyes*. For T-shirts, jeans and other clothing.

Librería Vieira Arte-Ilusiones, *Halflants y Martínez*. Bookstore with a café, Wi-Fi, nice meeting place.

What to do

Adventure sports are popular in Baños, including mountaineering, whitewater rafting, canyoning, canopying and bridge jumps. Safety standards vary greatly. There is seldom any recourse in the event of a mishap so these activities are at your own risk. For example, in mid-2017 the municipality suspended puenting from San Francisco bridge for 10 days after the death of a bungee jumper.

Bus tours

The *chivas* (see Entertainment) and a **double-decker bus** (C Ambato y Halflants, T03-274 0596, US$8) visit waterfalls and other attractions. Check destinations if you have a specific interest such as El Pailón falls.

Canopying or zip-lining

Involves hanging from a harness and sliding on a steel cable. Prices vary according to length, up to US$20. Cable car, US$1.50.

Canyoning

Many agencies offer this sport, rates US$30 half day, US$50-65 full day.

Climbing and trekking

There are countless possibilities for walking and nature observation near Baños and to the east. Tungurahua has been officially closed to climbers since 1999, but there are other rock-climbing opportunities, about US$30. Operators offer trekking tours for US$60-80 per day.

Cycling

Many places rent bikes, quality varies, US$5-10 per day; check brakes and tyres, find out who has to pay for repairs, and insist on a helmet, puncture repair kit and pump. The following have good equipment:

Carrillo Hermanos, *Av Oriente diagoanal al Cuerpo de Bomberos (fire station), T09-9992 8377, see Facebook*. Rents mountain bikes, motorcycles (reliable machines with helmets, US10 per hr) and vehicles.

Hotel Isla de Baños, rentals, US$10 per day.

Horse riding

There are many places but check their horses as not all are well cared for. Rates around US$10 per hr (minimum 2 hrs), US$40 per day. The following have been recommended: **Antonio Banderas** (Montalvo y Halflants, T03-274 2532). **José & Two Dogs** (Maldonado y Martínez, T09-8420 6966, Facebook: JoseTwoDogsBanos), flexible hours, also arranges other adventures.

Language schools

Spanish schools charge US$8-10 per hr, many also offer homestays. **Baños Spanish Center** (www.spanishcenter.banios. com). Runtún **Home Stay Baños** (https://runtunhomestaybanos.wordpress.com). **Mayra's** (www.mayraspanishschool.com). **Raíces** (www.spanishlessons.org).

Paragliding

See www.aeropasion.net; US$60 per flight.

Puenting

Many operators offer this bungee-jumping-like activity from the bridges around Baños, US$10-20 per jump, heights and styles vary.

Tour operators

There are many tour agencies in town, some with several offices, as well as 'independent' guides who seek out tourists on the street (the latter are generally not recommended). Quality varies considerably; to obtain a qualified guide and avoid unscrupulous operators, it is best to seek advice from other travellers who have recently returned from a tour. We have received some critical reports of tours out of Baños, but there are also highly respected and qualified operators here. Most agencies and guides offer trips to the jungle (US$55-80 per day pp). There are also volcano-watching, trekking and horse-riding tours, in addition to the day trips and sports mentioned above. Several companies run tours aboard a *chiva* (open-sided bus). The following agencies and guides have received positive recommendations, but the list is not exhaustive and there are certainly others.

Expediciones Amazónicas, *Oriente 11-68 y Halflants, T09-9299 1109, http://expedicionesamazonicas.com.*

Geotours, *Ambato y Halflants, next to Banco Pichincha, T03-274 1344, Facebook: GeotoursBanosEcuador.* Good rafting trips and paragliding for US$60.

Imagine Ecuador, *16 de Diciembre y Montalvo, T03-274 3472, www.imagineecuador.com.*

Natural Magic, *Martínez y 16 de Diciembre, T09-5879 6043, www.naturalmagic.travel.*

Sachayacu Explorer, *Bolívar 229 y Urbina, in Píllaro, T03-387 5316 or T09-8740 3376, http://llanganati.wixsite.com/ecuador.* Trekking in the Llanganates, jungle tours in Huaorani territory, Yasuní and as far as Peru, English spoken.

Wonderful Ecuador, *Maldonado y Oriente, T03-274 1580, www.wonderfulecuador.org.* Good for whitewater rafting.

Whitewater rafting

Rates US$30 for half day, US$70 for full day. The Pastaza river is the most used for rafting, but also the Chambo and Patate. None is pollution free. Fatal accidents have occurred, but not with the agencies listed above.

Transport

Bus

City buses run from Alfaro y Martínez east to Agoyán and from Rocafuerte by the market, west to El Salado and the zoo. The long-distance bus station is on the Ambato–Puyo road (Av Amazonas). It gets very busy at weekends and on holidays; buy tickets in advance. To **Río Verde** take any Puyo-bound bus, through buses don't go in the station, 20 mins, US$0.65. To **Quito**, US$4-5, 3 hrs, frequent service; going to Quito sit on the right for views of Cotopaxi; also shared taxis US$20, eg with **Delux**, see under Ambato, page 147. To **Ambato**, 1 hr, US$1.10. To **Riobamba**, some buses take the direct Baños–Riobamba road but most go via Mocha, 1½ hrs, US$2. To **Latacunga**, 2 hrs, US$2. To **Otavalo** and **Ibarra** direct, bypassing Quito via Pifo, **Expreso Baños**, at 0400, 1350 and 1440, US$7.50, 6 hrs; 0400 bus stops in Ambato (Baños–Pifo, 4 hrs, US$5). To **Guayaquil**, 1 bus per day and 1 overnight, US$11, 6-7 hrs; or change in Riobamba. To **Puyo**, 1½ hrs, US$2.40. Sit on the right. You can cycle to Puyo and take the bus back (passport check on the way). To **Tena**, 3½ hrs, US$5. To **Misahuallí**, change at Tena. To **Macas**, 4½ hrs, US$7-9 (sit on the right).

Tip...
Buses on the Baños–Quito route are targeted by thieves; take a shared taxi or a bus to Ambato and transfer there.

Guaranda and Riobamba are good bases for exploring the Sierra. Riobamba is the bigger of the two and is on the famous railway line from Quito to Guayaquil. Many indigenous people from the surrounding countryside can be seen in both cities on market days. Because of their central location Riobamba and the surrounding province are known as 'Corazón de la Patria' – the heartland of Ecuador – and the city boasts the nickname 'La Sultana de Los Andes' in honour of lofty Mount Chimborazo.

Riobamba *Colour map 3, B5. See map, page 162.*

The capital of Chimborazo Province has broad streets and many ageing but impressive buildings. The main square is **Parque Maldonado** around which are the cathedral, the **municipality** and several colonial buildings with arcades. The **cathedral** has a beautiful colonial stone façade and an incongruously modern interior. Four blocks northeast of the railway station is the **Parque 21 de Abril**, named after the Batalla de Tapi, 21 April 1822, the city's independence from Spain. The park, better known as **La Loma de Quito**, affords an unobstructed view of Riobamba and Chimborazo, Carihuayrazo, Tungurahua, El Altar and occasionally Sangay. It also has a colourful tile tableau of the history of Ecuador but is a bit run-down (2017). **Convento de la Concepción** ① *Orozco y España, entrance at Argentinos y J Larrea, T03-296 5212, Tue-Sat 0900-1230, 1500-1730, US$5*, has a religious art museum. **Museo de la Ciudad** ① *Primera Constituyente y Espejo, Parque Maldonado, T03-294 4420, daily 0700-1900, free*, in a beautifully restored colonial building, has an interesting historical photograph exhibit, a few religious items and furniture, models of local traditional dances (the sound works on some of them) and temporary displays.

Riobamba is an important **market centre** where people from many communities congregate. Saturday is the main day when the city fills with colourfully dressed *indígenas* from all over Chimborazo, each wearing their distinctive costume; trading overflows the markets and buying and selling go on all over town. Wednesday is a smaller market day. The **'tourist' market** ① *Orozco y Colón, Sat and Wed 0800-1500*, in the small **Plaza de la Concepción** or **Plaza Roja**, is a good place to buy local handicrafts and authentic *indígena* clothing. The main **produce market** ① *San Alfonso, Argentinos y 5 de Junio*, also sells clothing, ceramics, baskets and hats. Other markets in the colonial centre are **La Condamine** ① *Carabobo y Colombia, daily*, largest market on Fridays, **San Francisco** and **La Merced**, near the churches of the same name.

Eight kilometres north of Riobamba, **Guano** is a carpet-weaving, sisal and leather-working tow. Many shops sell rugs and you can arrange to have these woven to your own design. To get there, take a bus from the Mercado Dávalos (García Moreno y New York, every 15 minutes, US$0.30, last bus back at 1900). A taxi costs US$5.

Guaranda *Colour map 3, B5.*

This quaint town, capital of Bolívar Province, proudly calls itself 'the Rome of Ecuador' because it is built on seven hills. There are fine views of the mountains all around and a colourful market. Locals traditionally take an evening stroll in the palm-fringed main plaza, **Parque Libertador Simón Bolívar**, around which are the municipal buildings and a large stone **cathedral**. Towering over the city, on one of the hills, is an impressive statue of **El Indio Guaranga**; museum (free) and art gallery. There is also a small local museum at the **Casa de la Cultura** ① *Sucre entre Manuela Cañizares y Selva Alegre.*

Tip...
Although not on the tourist trail, there are many sights worth visiting in the province, for which Guaranda is the ideal base. Of particular interest is the highland town of Salinas, with its community development projects (accommodations and tours available, see Where to stay, below, and foods such as chocolate, dairy products and meats, see www.salinerito.com), as well as the *subtrópico* region, the lowlands stretching west towards the coast.

Market days are Friday (till 1200) and Saturday (larger), when many indigenous people in typical dress trade at the market complex at the east end of Calle Azuay, by Plaza 15 de Mayo (9 de Abril y Maldonado), and at Plaza Roja (Avenida General Enríquez).

Guaranda

Where to stay 🛏
Bolívar **1**
El Angel **6**
El Marquez **2**
La Casa de las Flores **3**
La Colina **4**

Oasis **5**

Restaurants 🍴
Cafetería 7 Santos **6**
Chifa Gran Cangrejo Rojo **1**
La Bohemia **2**

La Estancia **3**
Pizza Buon Giorno **4**
Salinerito **5**

200 metres
200 yards

★ Reserva Faunística Chimborazo

Information from Ministerio del Ambiente, Av 9 de Octubre y Duchicela, Quinta Macají, Riobamba, T03-261 0029, ext 110, Mon-Fri 0800-1300, 1400-1700. Ranger station T03-302 7358, daily 0800-1700.

The most outstanding features of this reserve, created to protect the camelids (vicuñas, alpacas and llamas) which were re-introduced here, are the beautiful snow-capped volcanos of **Chimborazo** and its

Tip...

Look out for the endemic hummingbird, estrella de Chimborazo.

neighbour **Carihuayrazo**. Chimborazo, inactive, has five summits, the uppermost of which is the highest peak in Ecuador (6263 m), while Carihuayrazo, 5020 m, is dwarfed by its neighbour. Day visitors can enjoy lovely views, a glimpse of the handsome vicuñas and the rarefied air above 4800 m. There are great opportunities for trekking on the eastern slopes, accessed from **Urbina**, west of the Ambato–Riobamba road, and of course climbing Ecuador's highest peak. Horse-riding and trekking tours are offered along the Mocha Valley between the two peaks and downhill cycling from Chimborazo is popular. The biking trail can be very slippery with loose ash, sand and gravel. An alternative is the dirt and asphalt road to San Juan.

To the west of the reserve runs the Vía del Arenal which joins San Juan, along the Riobamba–Guaranda road, with Cruce del Arenal on the Ambato–Guaranda road. A turn-off from this road leads to the main park entrance and beyond to the visitor centre at 4386 m (open 0800-1600), with a shop selling handicrafts and toilets. You must take a guide beyond here (although Ecuadorean families appear not to), US$30 per group. From the visitor centre it is 8 km to the **Refugio Hermanos Carrel**, a shelter at 4800 m, from where it is a 45-minute walk to **Refugio Whymper** at 5040 m. This is a popular day trip, but respect the altitude and the sun's radiation, the highest on the planet. The Carrel shelter is modern, warm and has 36 dorm beds, shared bath, no shower, US$30 pp including dinner and breakfast (advise rangers that you want to stay overnight when entering the reserve, or contact T09-7908 4401, refugioschimborazo@gmail.com); there is a cafeteria serving hot drinks and snacks, which is closed on Monday. There are no cooking facilities. The Whymper refuge opens only 0900-1600 for day visits. The path between the two refuges goes beside the memorial plaques to those who have died on the mountain.

The access from Riobamba (51 km) is very beautiful. It is paved to the park entrance: turn right off the Panamericana at Calpe, south of Riobamba; 31 km to the reserve.

Fact...

Four hundred and fifty vicuñas were introduced into the reserve when it was founded in 1987. Now there are over 5000. The vicuña, hunted to extinction in Ecuador by the Spanish, were replaced with sheep, which ate everything. Now sheep are kept out of the park, allowing vicuñas, which are more selective feeders, to thrive.

Along the Vía del Arenal past San Juan are a couple of small indigenous communities which grow a few crops and raise llamas and alpacas. They offer lodging and *guías nativos*, the area is good for acclimatization. The last community is **Pulinguí San Pablo** at 3840 m, which has the **Casa Cóndor** hostal (see Where to stay, page 164). The *arenal* is a large sandy plateau at about 4400 m, to the west of Chimborazo, just below the main park entrance. It can be a harsh, windy place, but it is also very beautiful; take the time to admire the tiny flowers which grow here. This is the best place to see vicuñas, which hang around either in family groups, one male and its harem, or lone males which have been expelled from the group.

Climbing Chimborazo At 6263 m, this is a difficult climb owing to the altitude. Climbers must go with a certified guide working for an operator who has a special permit (*patente*). Rope, ice-axe, helmet and crampons must be used. It is essential to have at least one week's acclimatization above 3500 m. Chimborazo can be climbed all year round but the weather is unpredictable. It is best to avoid late July and August, when it can be very windy. Of several routes, the two most used are **El Castillo** from the Whymper refuge and the slightly longer **Guargualla** route from the Carrel refuge (which does not pass the Whymper refuge). Deglaciation is making the climb more difficult and rock falls may occur year-round, especially on the Castillo route, which is often closed. For this reason, the safer Guargualla route is used with increasing frequency and climbing tours start from Carrel. Start at 2230-2300 to avoid rock avalanches and to reach the top before the clouds roll in. Note that ice pinnacles, *penitentes*, sometimes obstruct the final section between the two main summits, Veintimilla and Whymper.

Carihuayrazo This is a small volcano with a collapsed crater. Its highest peak is 5020 m. It's not a technical climb, but is good for beginners.

Alausí Colour map 3, C5.
This picturesque town perched on a hillside 96 km south of Riobamba is where many passengers take the train for the amazing descent over *La Nariz de Diablo* to Sibambe. There is good walking, a Sunday market and a **Fiesta de San Pedro** on 29 June.

★ The Devil's Nose Train
This spectacular ride is popular with Ecuadorean and foreign tourists alike. Tourist trains run between Alausí and Sibambe, the most scenic part of the trip including the **Devil's Nose**. (From Riobamba itself there is only a train north to Urbina.) For details see What to do, page 168.

Parque Nacional Sangay
Information from Ministerio del Ambiente, see Reserva Chimborazo, above.

Riobamba provides access to the central highland region of Sangay National Park, a beautiful wilderness area with excellent opportunities for trekking and climbing. A spectacular road, good for downhill biking, runs from Riobamba to Macas in the Oriente, cutting through the park. Near **Cebadas** (with a good cheese factory) a branch road joins from **Guamote**, a quiet, mainly indigenous town on the Pan-American highway, which comes to life during its colourful Thursday market. At **Atillo**, south of Cebadas, an area of lovely *páramo* dotted with lakes, there is lodging (US$7 per person) and restaurant at Cabaña Saskines (T03-301 4383, atillosaskines@hotmail.com). **Sangay** (5230 m) is an active volcano; access to the mountain takes at least three days and is only for those who can endure long, hard days of walking and severe weather. Climbing Sangay can be dangerous even when volcanic activity seems low and a helmet to protect against falling stones is vital. November to January is a good time to climb it. Agencies in Quito

ON THE ROAD

The railway that refused to die

As you climb aboard for the *Devil's Nose*, consider the rich history of this train. What is today a popular and exhilarating tourist ride was once the country's pride and joy. Its construction was internationally acclaimed, the 11-year US$26 million project of Ecuadorean president Eloy Alfaro and US entrepreneur Archer Harman. A spectacular 464-km railway line (1.067-m gauge), which ran from Durán (outside Guayaquil) up to Riobamba, was opened in 1908. It passed through 87 km of delta lands and then, in another 80 km, climbed to 3238 m. The highest point (3619 m) was reached at Urbina, between Riobamba and Ambato. It then fell and rose before reaching Quito at 2850 m.

This was one of the great railway journeys of the world and a fantastic piece of engineering, with a maximum gradient of 5.5%. Rail lines also ran from Riobamba south to Cuenca, and from Quito north to Ibarra, then down to the coast at San Lorenzo. There were even more ambitious plans, never achieved, to push the railhead deep into the Oriente Jungle, from Ambato as far as Leticia (then Ecuador, today Colombia). Time and neglect subsequently took their toll and by the turn of the millennium only a few short segments remained in service, basically as cheap tourist rides. There was often talk of reviving the Ecuadorean railway as a whole but it never seemed to happen.

Between 2007 and 2013 however, the Ecuadorean government undertook a complete restoration of the line from Quito to Durán, which was re-opened with much fanfare. From new concrete ties to modern rolling stock, it was a formidable achievement. However, many feel disappointed that it isn't a real railway. Rather it is a series of seven short (but no longer cheap) tourist rides with cutesy names like *Tren de la Dulzura* (the 'sweetness train', because it runs through sugar cane fields), and a lavish multi-day excursion for railway buffs offered a few times a year.

We can't help but ask what happened to the dream of Eloy Alfaro and Archer Harman, which seems to have derailed along the way. Surely they envisaged a working railway to transport passengers and freight, efficiently serving the needs of Ecuador today as well as it did in the past? That vision, like the railway itself, refuses to die.

---

and Riobamba offer tours or you can organize an expedition independently. A guide is essential; porters can be hired in the access towns of **Alao** and **Guarguallá**. The latter has a **community tourism project** ⓘ *T03-302 6688, T09-9121 3205, accommodation in Guarguallá Chico US$15 pp, US$23 pp with dinner and breakfast (reserve in advance), kitchen facilities US$5 per group. Guías nativos, US$65 per day plus US$110 for ascent; porters and horses US$20 per day.*

Also in Sangay National Park is the beautiful **El Altar** volcano (5315 m), whose crater is surrounded by nine summits. The northernmost is **El Canónigo** at 5260 m and the southernmost is **El Obispo**, which is also the highest, at 5315 m. Ascents start from Italian Camp at 4500 m, best accessed from Boca Toma. A popular climbing and trekking route begins beyond Candelaria (3100 m) at **Hacienda Releche** (see **Hostal Capac Urcu**, Where to stay, page 165). It is about six hours from Candelaria to the Collanes plain, where there is a *refugio* (see **Hostal Capac Urcu**, page 165), and another two hours to the crater.

Tourist information

Riobamba

iTur
Av Daniel León Borja y Brasil, Riobamba, T03-296 3159. Mon-Fri 0830-1230, 1430-1800.
Municipal information office, English spoken.

Guaranda

Oficina Municipal de Turismo
García Moreno entre 7 de Mayo y Convención de 1884, T03-298 0321, www.guaranda.gob.ec (in Spanish). Mon-Fri 0800-1200, 1400-1800.
Provides information in Spanish and maps.

Where to stay

Riobamba

$$$$-$$$ Abraspungo
Km 3 on the road to Guano, T03-236 4275, http://haciendaabraspungo.com.
Nice country hotel, comfortable rooms, includes buffet breakfast, excellent restaurant concentrating on local ingredients, activities include horse riding and cycling, handicraft shop, parking, attentive service. Recommended.

$$$$-$$$ La Andaluza
16 km north of Riobamba along the Panamericana, in Chuquipoguio, T03-233 3000, www.hosteriaandaluza.com.
At a 16th century hacienda, rooms have heaters and roaring fireplaces, includes buffet breakfast, good restaurant (**El Establo**), café and bar, lovely views, good walking and horse riding.

$$$ Mansión Santa Isabella
Veloz 28-48 y Carabobo, T03-296 2947, www.mansionsantaisabella.com.
Lovely restored house with pleasant patio, some rooms in modern wing behind the older part, comfortable rooms with

Where to stay
Abraspungo 1
La Andaluza 2
Mansión Santa Isabella 3
Metropolitano 4
Oasis 5
Rincón Alemán 6
San Pedro de Riobamba
& La Fogata Restaurant 7
Tren Dorado 8

Restaurants
Café París 1
Frida 2
Jamones La Andaluza
& Naranjo's 3

duvets, most with bathtub, includes buffet breakfast, restaurant serves set lunches and à la carte, bar in stone basement, spa under construction in basement too (2017), parking, attentive service, British/Ecuadorean-run. Recommended.

$$$ San Pedro de Riobamba
Daniel L Borja 29-50 y Montalvo, opposite the train station, T03-294 1359, see Facebook.
Elegant hotel in a beautifully restored house in the centre of town, ample comfortable rooms, bathtubs, cafeteria, parking, covered patio, reservations required. Recommended.

$$ Rincón Alemán
Remigio Romero y Alfredo Pareja, Ciudadela Arupos del Norte, T03-260 3540, www.hostalrinconaleman.com.
Family-run hotel in a quiet residential area north of the centre, laundry and cooking facilities, parking, fireplace, sauna, gym, garden, terrace, good views, German spoken.

La Abuela Rosa **4**
Mónaco Pizzería **5**
Tradiciones de Paila **6**
Zen Wei **7**

$$ Tren Dorado
Carabobo 22-35 y 10 de Agosto, near station, T03-296 4890, www.hoteltrendorado.com.
Modern hotel with nice large rooms, buffet breakfast available (starting 0730, open to non-guests), restaurant, reliable hot water, good value. Recommended.

$$-$ Oasis
Veloz 15-32 y Almagro, T03-296 1210, www.oasishostelriobamba.com.
Small, quiet, family-run hostel, laundry facilities, some rooms with kitchen and fridge, shared kitchen for the others, parking, nice garden, Wi-Fi US$1 per day, popular with backpackers. Recommended.

$ Metropolitano
Daniel L Borja y Lavalle, near the train station, T03-296 1714.
One of the oldest hotels in Riobamba, built in 1912 and nicely restored. Ample rooms, convenient location, no breakfast.

Guaranda

$$$ La Colina
Av Guayaquil 117, on the road to Ambato, T03-298 0666, www.complejolacolina.com.
Nicely situated on a quiet hillside overlooking the city. Bright spacious rooms, nice views, gardens, parking, tours available.

$$ El Angel
Km Vía Guaranda Riobamba, T03-222 5075, www.hosteriaelangel.com.
Just outside town on old road to Riobamba, hacienda-type accommodation with comfortable rooms, restaurant, gardens and parking. A good option.

$$ Oasis
Gen Enríquez y García Moreno, T03-255 0229, Facebook: hostaloasisguaranda.
Modern multi-storey building on Plaza Roja, with large, bright and clean rooms.

$$-$ Bolívar

Sucre 704 y Rocafuerte, T03-298 0547,
http://hotelbolivar.wordpress.com.
Pleasant hotel with courtyard, small modern
rooms, best quality in the centre of town.
Restaurant next door open Mon-Fri for
economical breakfasts and lunches.

$ El Marquez

10 de Agosto y Eloy Alfaro, T03-298 1306/1101.
Pleasant hotel with family atmosphere,
newer rooms with private bath are clean and
modern, older ones with shared bath are
cheaper, parking.

$ La Casa de las Flores

Pichincha 402 y Rocafuerte, T03-298 5795.
Renovated colonial house with covered
courtyard and flowers, private bath,
hot water, simple economical rooms,
no breakfast.

Salinas

$$ Hotel Refugio Salinas

45 mins from Guaranda, T03-221 0044,
www.salinerito.com.
Pleasant community-run hotel, economical
meals on request, private or shared bath,
dining/sitting area with fireplace, visits to
community projects, walking and horse-
riding tours, packages available, advance
booking advised.

$$-$ La Minga

By the main plaza, T09-8626 7586,
www.laminga-hostal.com.
Simple rooms with bath and dorms, hostal
and pizzeria with famous Salinerito cheese,
offer full board packages including tour.

Reserva Faunística Chimborazo

The following are all good for
acclimatization; those in Urbina can be
reached by train from either Riobamba
or Ambato.

$$$ Chimborazo Lodge

Operated by Expediciones Andinas,
see Tour operators, page 168.
Comfortable cabins in a beautiful
location on the south flank of
Chimborazo, includes dinner and
breakfast, advance booking required.

$ Casa Cóndor

In Pulinguí San Pablo, Vía del Arenal,
T09-8650 8152.
Basic community-run hostel, dinner and
breakfast available, use of cooking facilities
extra, tours in the area. Popular with
climbers for acclimatization.

$ Chakana Templo de Montaña

Vía del Arenal at La Chorrera, T03-3013104,
T09-68297999.
Price includes dinner and breakfast, 1 room
with private bath and 3 with shared bath,
hot water.

$ Posada de la Estación

Opposite Urbina train station, T09-9969 4867.
Comfortable rooms with heaters, shared
bath, meals available or cooking facilities
(US$5 per group), wood stoves, magnificent
views, trips and equipment arranged, tagua
workshop, helpful. Also run **$ Urcu Huasi**,
cabins at 4150 m, 10 km (2½ hrs walking)
from Urbina, in an area being reforested
with polylepis trees.

Alausí

$$$ El Molino

Sucre N141 y Bolívar, T03-293 1659,
http://hotelelmolino.com.ec.
Comfortable rooms in a restored historical
home, 1 block from station, pleasant common
areas, includes buffet breakfast, free calls to
USA. Recommended as best in town.

$$$ Posada de las Nubes

On the north side of the Río Chanchán,
7 or 11 km from Alausí depending on the
route, best with 4WD, pick-up from Alausí

US$7, T03-302 9362 or T09-9315 0847,
www.posadadelasnubes.com.
Rustic hacienda house in cloudforest at
2600 m. Rooms are simple to basic for the
price, some with bath, includes dinner and
breakfast, hiking and horse riding, advance
booking required.

$$ Europa
5 de Junio 175 y Orozco, T03-293 0200.
One of the older hotels in town, recently
refurbished, nice rooms, good value.

$$ Gampala
*5 de Junio 122 y Loza, T03-293 0138,
www.hotelgampala.com.*
Well-refurbished modern rooms and 1 suite
with jacuzzi (**$$$**), restaurant and bar with
pool table.

$$-$ San Pedro
*5 de Junio y 9 de Octubre, T03-293 0196,
hostalsanpedro@hotmail.com.*
Simple comfortable rooms, a few cheaper
rooms in older section, restaurant downstairs,
parking, nice owner.

Parque Nacional Sangay

$ Hostal Capac Urcu
*At Hacienda Releche, near the village of
Candelaria, T03-301 4067.*
Basic rooms in small working hacienda.
Use of kitchen (US$10) or meals prepared
on request, rents horses for the trek to
Collanes, US$45 per horse, plus US$45 per
muleteer, round trip. Also runs the *refugio*
at Collanes (same price), by the crater of
El Altar: thatched-roof rustic shelters with
solar hot water. The *refugio* is cold, take
a warm sleeping bag. Rubber boots are
indispensable for the muddy trail.

Guamote

$$$-$ Sisa Art Guesthouse
*Vargas Torres y García Moreno,
T03-291 6529, www.intisisa.com.*

Cosy, pleasant guesthouse, part of a
community development project, most
rooms with bath, US$25 pp in dorm,
includes breakfast, other meals available,
dining room and communal area with
fireplace, decorative paintings, horse riding
and community tours to highland villages,
reservations necessary.

$$ Chuza Longa
*García Moreno y Manabí, T03-291 6567,
www.chuzalonga.com.*
Good place to stay, rooms with bath,
breakfast included, other meals on request,
can organize local tours,

Restaurants

Riobamba
Many places close after 2100 and on Sun.

$$ Mónaco Pizzería
*Av de la Prensa y Francisco Aguilar.
Mon-Fri 1500-2200, Sat-Sun 1200-2200.*
Delicious pizza and pasta, nice salads, good
food, service and value. Recommended.

$$-$ Frida
*Av DL Borja y Duchicela (beside Hotel Zeus),
T03-239 5625, Facebook: Frida Riobamba.*
Mexican restaurant, good food
and atmosphere.

$ La Fogata
*Daniel L Borja y Carabobo, opposite the train
station. Wed-Mon 0730-2115, Tue 0730-1500.*
Simple but good local food, economical set
meals and breakfast.

$ Naranjo's
*Daniel L Borja 36-20 y Uruguay. Tue-Sun
1200-1500.*
Excellent set lunch, friendly service, popular.

$ Zen Wei
*Princesa Toa 43-29 y Calicuchima.
Mon-Sat 1200-1500.*
Oriental restaurant serving economical
vegetarian and vegan set meals.

Cafés and bakeries

Café París
Daniel L Borja y Juan Montalvo.
Mon-Sat 0800-2200.
Small popular meeting place serving
excellent coffees and snacks.

Jamones La Andaluza
Daniel L Borja y Uruguay. Daily 0830-2300.
Indoor and outdoor seating, good set
lunches, coffee, sandwiches, salads,
variety of cold-cuts, cheeses and tapas.

La Abuela Rosa
Brasil y Esmeraldas. Mon-Sat 1600-2100.
Cafetería in grandmother's house serving
typical Ecuadorean snacks. Nice atmosphere
and good service.

Tradiciones de Paila
Espejo y 10 de Agosto. Daily 0900-1900.
Excellent home-made ice cream, coffee,
sweets, sandwiches and juices, popular.

Guaranda
Most places close on Sun.

$$$-$$ Pizza Buon Giorno
Sucre at Parque Bolívar. Tue-Sun 1100-2200.
Pizza and salads.

$$ La Bohemia
Convención de 1884 y 10 de Agosto.
Mon-Sat 0800-2100.
Very good economical set meals and pricier
international dishes à la carte, nice decor and
ambiance, very popular. Recommended.

$$ La Estancia
García Moreno y Sucre. Mon 1200-1500,
Tue-Sat 1200-2100.
Excellent buffet lunch for quality, variety
and value, à la carte in the evening, nicely
decorated, pleasant atmosphere, popular.

$$-$ Chifa Gran Cangrejo Rojo
10 de Agosto y Convención de 1884.
Open 1100-2200.
Good Chinese food.

Cafés

Cafetería 7 Santos
Convención de 1884 y Olmedo.
Mon-Sat 1000-2200.
Pleasant café and bar with open courtyard.
Good coffee and snacks, fireplace, live music
Fri and Sat, popular.

Salinerito
Plaza Roja. Daily 0800-1300, 1430-1900.
Salinas cheese shop also serves coffee,
sandwiches and pizza.

Alausí

$$ Bukardia
Guatemala 107. Open 1300-2200, closed Wed.
Meat specialities, snacks and drinks.

$$ El Mesón del Tren
Ricaurte y Eloy Alfaro. Tue-Sun 0700-0930,
1200-1430.
Good restaurant, popular with tour groups,
breakfast, set lunch and à la carte.

$ La Higuera
Av 5 de Junio y Ricaurte. Daily 0630-2200.
At corner of train station, cheap set lunches,
tasty *locros*.

$ Tikal Cocina Café
Eloy Alfaro y Bolivia. Open 0800-2100,
closed Mon.
Guatemalan/Ecuadorean-run, good choice
of meals, including vegetarian.

Bars and clubs

Riobamba

La Rayuela
Daniel L Borja 36-30 y Uruguay.
Mon-Sat 1200-2200, Sun 1200-1600.
Trendy bar/restaurant, sometimes live music
on Fri, sandwiches, coffee, salads, pasta.

San Valentín

Daniel L Borja y Vargas Torres. Mon-Thu 1800-2400, Fri-Sat 1800-0200.
Very popular bar, good pizzas and Mexican dishes.

Entertainment

Riobamba

Casa de la Cultura, *10 de Agosto y Rocafuerte, T03-296 0219.* Cultural events, cinema on Tue.

Festivals

Riobamba

Dec-Jan Fiesta del Niño Rey de Reyes, street parades, music and dancing, starts in Dec and culminates on 6 Jan.
Apr Independence celebrations around 21 Apr lasting several days, hotel prices rise.
29 Jun Fiestas Patronales in honour of San Pedro.
11 Nov Festival to celebrate the first attempt at independence from Spain.

Guaranda

Feb Carnival in Guaranda is among the best known in the country.

Alausí

29 Jun Fiesta de San Pedro.

Shopping

Riobamba
Camping gear
Some of the tour operators listed below hire camping and climbing gear.
Marathon Explorer, *Multiplaza mall, Av Lizarzaburu near the airport.* High-end outdoor equipment and clothing.
Protección Industrial, *Rocafuerte 24-51 y Orozco, T03-296 3017.* Outdoor equipment, rope, fishing supplies, rain ponchos.

Handicrafts
Crafts are sold at Plaza Roja (Concepción) on Wed and Sat.
Almacén Cacha, *Colón y Orozco, next to the Plaza Roja.* A cooperative of indigenous people from the Cacha area, sells woven bags, wool sweaters, and other crafts, good value (closed Sun-Mon).

What to do

Riobamba
Mountain biking
Guided tours with support vehicle average US$55-65 pp per day.
Julio Verne, *see Tour operators.* Very good tours, equipment and routes.
Pro Bici, *Primera Constituyente 23-51 y Larrea, T03-295 1759, www.probici.com.* Tours and rentals.

Tour operators

Most companies offer climbing trips (US$250-270 pp for 2 days to Chimborazo or Carihuayrazo), trekking (US$100-125 pp per day) and day hikes (US$60-70 pp).

Andes Trek, *Esmeraldas 21-45 y Espejo, T03-2951275, www.goandestrek.com.* Climbing and trekking, transport, equipment rental. Also runs an office and hostel in Quito.

Expediciones Andinas, *Vía a Guano, Km 3, across from Hotel Abraspungo, T03-236 4278, www.expediciones-andinas.com.* Climbing expeditions run by Marco Cruz, a guide certified by the **German Alpine Club**, operate **Chimborazo Lodge** (see Where to stay, page 164). Recommended.

Incañán, *Brasil 20-28 y Luis A Falconí, T03-294 0508, http://incanian2011.blogspot.com.* Trekking, cycling and cultural tours.

Julio Verne, *Brasil 22-40 between Daniel L Borja and Primera Constituyente, T03-296 3436, www.julioverne-travel.com.* Climbing, trekking, cycling, jungle and Galápagos trips, transport (with TAAP Transfers), equipment rental, English spoken, Ecuadorean/Dutch-run, very conscientious and reliable. Uses official guides. Highly recommended.

The Devil's Nose Train

The Devil's Nose Train departs from Alausí, Tue-Sun at 0800 and 1100, 2½ hrs return, US$33, includes a snack and folklore dance. A *Tren de Hielo I* runs from Riobamba to Urbina (Fri-Sun at 0800, US$28), dress warmly; the trip includes a short walk, demonstration of the collection of glacial ice from Chimborazo, lunch at La Moya and café service. Returns to Riobamba at 1430. Purchase tickets well in advance for weekends and holidays at any train station (Riobamba, T03-296 1038, Mon-Wed 0800-1630, Thu-Fri 0700-1630, Sat-Sun 0700-1300; Alausí, T03-293 0126, Tue-Sun 0700-1530), through the call centre (T1800-873637) or by email (info@trenecuador.com, then you have to make a bank deposit). Procedures change frequently, so enquire locally and check www.trenecuador.com. Riobamba station has a railway museum, handicraft stalls and a café.

Transport

Riobamba
Bus

Terminal Terrestre on Epiclachima y Av Daniel L Borja for all long-distance buses including to Baños and destinations in Oriente. Not all buses go to the terminal, but drop passengers on the outskirts; ask if the bus to Riobamba goes to the station. There are lots of hotels and *hostales* by the terminal. **Terminal Oriental**, Espejo y Cordovez, only for local services to Candelaria and Penipe. **Terminal Intercantonal**, Av Canónigo Ramos about 2.5 km northwest of the Terminal Terrestre, for Guamote, San Juan and Cajabamba (Colta). Taxi between terminals US$1.50-2. To **Quito**, US$4.75, 4 hrs, about every 30 mins; also shared taxis with: **Montecarlo Trans Vip**, T03-296 8758 or T09-8411 4114, 7 daily, US$18 (US$5 extra for large luggage) and **Delux**, T09-3920 9827 or T09-8343 0275, every 2 hrs, US$20. To **Guaranda**, US$2.50, 2 hrs (sit on the right). To **Ambato**, US$1.25, 1 hr. To **Alausí**, see below. To **Cuenca**, 8 a day via Alausí, 5½ hrs, US$8. To **Guayaquil** via Pallatanga, frequent service, US$7, 5 hrs, spectacular for the first 2 hrs. To **Baños**, US$2, 1¼ hrs on new road – but if there's heavy rain, buses use the old road, 2 hrs – good views of Tungurahua. To **Puyo** US$4, 4 hrs. To **Macas** via Parque Nacional Sangay, 8 daily, 4 hrs, US$6.25 (sit on the left).

Guaranda
Bus

Terminal at Eliza Mariño Carvajal, on road to Riobamba and Babahoyo; if you are staying in town get off closer to the centre. Many daily buses to: **Ambato**, US$2.50, 2 hrs. **Riobamba**, see above. **Babahoyo**, US$3.75, 3 hrs, beautiful ride. **Guayaquil**, US$5, 5 hrs. **Quito**, US$6.25, 5 hrs.

Reserva Faunística Chimborazo

There are no buses to the shelters. Take a tour or arrange transport with a Riobamba tour operator (US$35 one way, US$45 return with wait) or take a Riobamba–Guaranda bus, alight at the turn-off for the refuges and walk the remaining steep 8 km (5 km taking short cuts) to the first shelter. For the eastern slopes, take a trekking tour, arrange transport from an agency or take a bus between Riobamba and Ambato, get off at the turn-off for **Posada La Estación** and Urbina and walk from there.

Alausí

Bus

To **Riobamba**, 1½ hrs, US$2.50, 84 km. To **Quito**, from 0600, 8 a day, 6 hrs, US$7.50, often have to change in Riobamba. To **Cuenca**, 4 hrs, US$6.50. To **Ambato** hourly, 3 hrs, US$4. To **Guayaquil**, 4 a day, 4 hrs,

US$6.50. **Coop Patria**, Colombia y Orozco, 3 blocks up from the main street (buses to Cuenca stop opposite; this is by the road signed to Huigra and Guayaquil – the same road that goes to the station); **Trans Alausí**, 5 de Junio y Loza. Many through buses don't go into town, but have to be caught on the highway, taxi from town US$1.

Parque Nacional Sangay

Bus

To **Atillo** from Parque La Dolorosa, Puruhá y Primera Constituyente, 15 daily 0400-1845, US$2.50, 2 hrs. Also Riobamba–**Macas** service goes through Atillo, see above. To **Alao**, from Parque La Dolorosa, hourly 0700-2300, US$1.50, 1½ hrs. To **Guarguallá Grande** from Parque La Dolorosa daily at 1345 (return to Riobamba at 0545), US$2 (Grande), 2 hrs; also a milk truck from La Dolorosa to Guargualla at 0530, US$2. To **Candelaria**, from Terminal Oriental, daily 0600, 0800, 1100, 1500 and 1615, US$1.25, 1½ hrs. Alternatively, take a bus from the same terminal to Penipe, every 30 mins, US$0.40, 40 mins, and hire a pick-up truck from there to Candelaria, US$15, 40 mins.

Southern highlands

the ancient Andes

The convoluted topography of the southern highlands, comprising the provinces of Cañar, Azuay and Loja, reveals an ancient non-volcanic past distinct from its northern Sierra neighbours.

This region is home to many treasures. Here is Ecuador's prime Inca site, two of its most spectacular national parks, and Cuenca – the nation's most congenial city and focal point of El Austro, as southern Ecuador is called. Cuenca boasts some of the country's finest colonial architecture, and the Cuenca basin is a major *artesanía* centre, producing ceramics, baskets, gold and silver jewellery and textiles, as well as the famous Panama hat.

In addition to Cuenca's cultural attractions, a pleasant climate and magnificent scenery make the southern highlands prime walking country. Vilcabamba, south of Loja, is a particularly suitable base for trekking and horse-riding excursions, with nearby undisturbed *páramo* and cloudforest, home to many birds and other wildlife.

The southern highlands have an extensive road network and there is access to the Peruvian border at several different points.

Best for
Crafts ▪ Relaxing ▪ Walking

Footprint picks

★ **Cuenca's cathedral**, page 175

One of the largest in South America, this imposing blue-domed cathedral is built on the foundations of an Inca structure.

★ **Pumapungo Museum**, page 175

The extensive holdings include a special collection of *tsantsas*, shrunken heads from the Shuar people of Oriente.

★ **Ingapirca**, page 185

Ecuador's most important archaeological site was home to the Cañari people before it was conquered by the Incas in the 15th century.

★ **Parque Nacional Cajas**, page 186

This high, cold, wet and wild area is easily reached from Cuenca.

★ **Parque Nacional Podocarpus**, page 191

With its broad range of altitudes and remote hinterlands, this is one of the most diverse protected areas in the world.

★ **Horse riding from Vilcabamba**, page 197

Saddle up for a ride through some of the prettiest countryside in Ecuador.

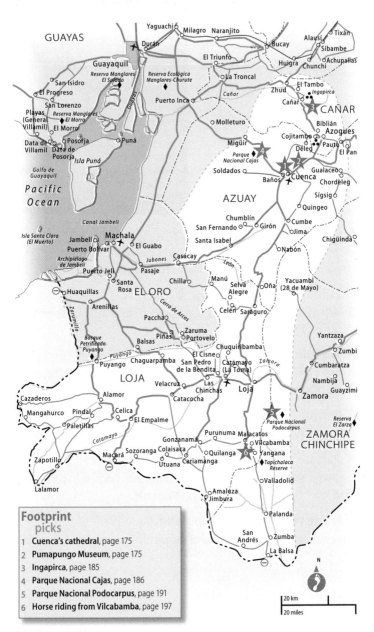

GUAYAS

Yaguachi
Milagro
Naranjito
Bucay
Alausí
Tixán
Sibambe
Achupallas
Durán
El Triunfo
Huigra
Chunchi
Guayaquil
Reserva Manglares
El Salado
Reserva Ecológica
Manglares-Churute
La Troncal
El Tambo
Zhud
Ingapirca
Cañar
CAÑAR

San Isidro
El Progreso
San Lorenzo
Playas
(General
Villamil)
Reserva Manglares
El Morro
El Morro
Posorja
Puná
Data de
Villamil
Data de
Posorja
Isla Puná
Puerto Inca
Molleturo
Miguir
Parque
Nacional Cajas
Soldados
Baños
Cuenca
Biblián
Cojitambo
Azogues
Déleg
Paute
El Pan
Gualaceo
Chordeleg
Sígsig

Golfo de
Guayaquil
Pacific
Ocean
AZUAY
Quingeo

Canal Jambelí
Isla Santa Clara
(El Muerto)
Jambelí
Puerto Bolívar
Machala
El Guabo
Casacay
Chumblín
San Fernando
Girón
Cumbe
Jima
Chigüinda

Archipiélago
de Jambelí
Puerto Jeli
Santa
Rosa
Pasaje
Chilla
Jubones
Manú
Selva
Alegre
Celén
Saraguro
León
Santa Isabel
Nabón
Oña
Yacuambi
(28 de Mayo)

Huaquillas
EL ORO
Arenillas
Paccha
Cerro de Arcos
Zamora
Yantzaza
Zumbi
Cumbaratza

Zaruma
Portovelo
Chuquiribamba
Nambija
Guayzimi

Bosque
Petrificado
Puyango
Piñas
Balsas
Puyango
El Cisne
San Pedro
de la Bendita
Catamayo
(La Toma)
Chaguarpamba
Zamora
ZAMORA

Cazaderos
Mangahurco
Pindal
Celica
El Empalme
Paletillas
Zapotillo
Lalamor
Alamor
Velacruz
Las
Chinchas
Catacocha
Loja
Parque Nacional
Podocarpus
Reserva
El Zarza
ZAMORA
CHINCHIPE

Catamayo
Gonzanamá
Purunuma
Malacatos
Vilcabamba
Yangana
LOJA
Sozoranga
Colaisaca
Quilanga
Cariamanga
Tapichalaca
Reserve
Macará
Utuana

Amaluza
Jimbura
Valladolid
Palanda

San
Andrés
Zumba
La Balsa

N

20 km
20 miles

Cuenca
& around

Cuenca is capital of the province of Azuay and the third largest city in Ecuador, with something of a European flavour. The city has preserved much of its colonial ambience, with many of its old buildings originally constructed from the travertine quarried nearby and elegantly renovated. Most Ecuadoreans consider this their finest city and few would disagree. Its cobble-stone streets, flowering plazas and whitewashed buildings with old wooden doors and ironwork balconies make it a pleasure to explore. In 1999 Cuenca was designated a World Heritage Site by UNESCO.

As well as being the economic centre of El Austro, as southern Ecuador is called, Cuenca is also an intellectual centre. It has a long tradition as the birthplace of notable artists, writers, poets and philosophers, earning it the title 'The Athens of Ecuador'. It remains a rather formal city, loyal to its conservative traditions. Many places close for lunch between 1300 and 1500 and on Sunday.

Cuenca is home to a growing expat retiree community. The city and surrounding areas are known for their crafts.

Essential Cuenca

Finding your feet

The **Terminal Terrestre** is on Avenida España, 15 minutes' ride northeast of the centre, T07-282 4811. The **airport**, T07-286 7120, www.aeropuertocuenca.ec, is five minutes beyond the Terminal Terrestre. Both can be reached by city bus, but best take a taxi at all hours (US$1.50-2.50 to the centre). The **Terminal Sur** for regional buses is by the Feria Libre El Arenal on Avenida Las Américas. Many city buses pass here. See Transport, page 184, for details.

The city is bounded by Río Machángara to the north and ríos Yanuncay and Tarqui to the south. The Río Tomebamba separates the colonial heart from the newer districts to the south. Avenida Las Américas is a ring road around the north and west of the city and the *autopista*, a multilane highway, bypasses the city to the south.

Getting around

The narrow streets of colonial Cuenca are clogged with cars on weekdays. Sunday is more tranquil and an excellent time to enjoy the colonial city. It is hoped that a new tram system (still unfinished in 2017) will alleviate some of the congestion.

Safety

Though safer than Quito or Guayaquil, routine precautions are advised. Outside the busy nightlife area around Calle Larga, the city centre is deserted after 2300, taking a taxi is recommended. The river banks, the Cruz del Vado area (south end of Juan Montalvo), the Terminal Terrestre and all market areas are not safe after dark.

Best restaurants

Tiestos, page 180
Raymipampa, page 181
Good Affinity, page 181
Tutto Freddo, page 181

When to go

If you're here over Christmas, Cuenca has perhaps the largest and finest Christmas parade in the country on 24 December, Pase del Niño Vlajero.

Best places to stay

Forum, page 177
Posada del Angel, page 177
Macondo, page 179
Posada Todos Santos, page 179

Weather Cuenca

January	February	March	April	May	June
20°C 9°C 60mm	19°C 10°C 69mm	19°C 10°C 75mm	17°C 9°C 99mm	17°C 9°C 72mm	18°C 8°C 27mm

July	August	September	October	November	December
6°C 8°C 18mm	17°C 8°C 30mm	19°C 9°C 48mm	19°C 9°C 99mm	20°C 9°C 48mm	18°C 9°C 66mm

Sights

On the main plaza, **Parque Abdón Calderón**, are the Old Cathedral, ★ **El Sagrario** ⓘ *daily guided visits 0830-1700, ask for door to Terraza de Santa Ana to be opened (155 steps up), US$2*, begun in 1557, and the immense 'New' **Catedral de la Inmaculada**, started in 1885. The latter contains a famous crowned image of the Virgin, a beautiful altar and an exceptional play of light and shade through modern stained glass. Other churches which deserve a visit are **San Blas**, **San Francisco** and **Santo Domingo**. Close to the southwest corner of La Inmaculada, the church of **El Carmen de la Asunción**, has a flower market in the tiny **Plazoleta El Carmen** in front. There is a colourful daily market in **Plaza Rotary** where pottery, clothes, guinea pigs and local produce, especially baskets, are sold. Thursday is the busiest.

Tip...
Many churches are open at irregular hours only and for services.

The **Museo del Monasterio de las Conceptas** ⓘ *Hermano Miguel 6-33 entre Pdte Córdova y Juan Jaramillo, T07-283 0625, Mon-Fri 0900-1830, Sat and holidays 1000-1300, US$2.50*, in a cloistered convent founded in 1599, houses a well-displayed collection of religious and folk art, in addition to an extensive collection of lithographs by Guayasamín.

★ **Pumapungo** ⓘ *C Larga y Huayna Capac, T07-283 1521, Tue-Fri 0800-1730, Sat, Sun and holidays 1000-1600*, is a museum complex on the edge of the colonial city, at the actual site of Tomebamba excavations of a Cañari and a later Inca settlement. Part of the area explored is seen at **Parque Arqueológico Pumapungo**. The **Sala Arqueológica** section contains all the Cañari and Inca remains and artifacts found here, as well as history of the other pre-Inca cultures of the region. Other halls in the premises house the **Sala Etnográfica**, with information on different Ecuadorean cultures, including a special collection of *tsantsas* (shrunken heads from the Oriente), the **Sala de Arte Religioso**, the **Sala Numismática** and temporary exhibits. There are also book and music libraries, free cultural videos and music events. Three blocks west of Pumapungo, **Museo Manuel Agustín Landívar** ⓘ *C Larga 2-23 y Manuel Vega, T07-282 1177, Mon-Fri 0800-1630, free*, is at the site of the small Todos los Santos ruins, with Cañari, Inca and colonial remains; ceramics and artifacts found at the site are also displayed.

The **Museo de las Culturas Aborígenes** ⓘ *C Larga 5-24 y Hermano Miguel, T07-283 9181, Mon-Fri 0830-1800, Sat 0900-1400, US$4, craft shop*, the private collection of Dr J Cordero Íñiguez, has an impressive selection of pre-Columbian archaeology. The **Museo Remigio Crespo Toral** ⓘ *C Larga 7-25 y Borrero (you can also enter from riverside level), Tue-Fri 1000-1300, 1500-1800, Sat-Sun 1000-1400, free*, in a beautifully refurbished colonial house, has sections on early 20th-century history, prominent Cuencanos, art and fashion, an important archaeology collection as yet largely undisplayed, and a café. The **Museo del Sombrero de Paja Toquilla** ⓘ *C Larga 10-41 y Gral Torres, T07-283 1569, Mon-Fri 0900-1800, Sat 0930-1700, Sun 0930-1330, free tour in Spanish or English*, a shop in Barranco belonging to the familia Paredes Roldán, has all the old factory machines for hat finishing. There's also a café and mirador overlooking the river. The Municipalidad also has a **Casa del Sombrero** ⓘ *Rafael María Arízaga 7-95, see Facebook: economuseocasadelsombrero*, as does **Homero Ortega** (see Shopping, page 183).

BACKGROUND

Cuenca

From AD 500 to around 1480, Cuenca was a Cañari settlement, called Guapondeleg, which roughly translates as 'an area as large as heaven'. The suffix 'deleg' is still found in several local place names, a vestige of the now extinct Cañari language.

Owing to its geographical location, this was among the first parts of what is now Ecuador to come under the domination of the Inca Empire, which had expanded north. The Incas settled the area around Cuenca and called it Tomebamba, which translates as 'Valley of Knives'. The name survives as one of the region's rivers. Some 70 km north of Cuenca, in an area known as Jatun Cañar, the Incas built the ceremonial centre of Ingapirca, which remains the most important Inca site in the country (see page 185). Ingapirca and Tomebamba were, for a time, the hub of the northern part of the Inca Empire.

The city as it is today was founded by the Spanish in 1557 on the site of Tomebamba and named Santa Ana de los Cuatro Ríos de Cuenca. Cuenca then became an important and regional centre in the crown colony governed from Quito. The conquistadors and the settlers who followed them were interested in the working of precious metals, for which the region's indigenous peoples had earned a well-deserved reputation. Following independence from Spain, Cuenca became capital of one of three provinces that made up the new republic, the others being Quito and Guayaquil.

On Plaza San Sebastián, the **Museo Municipal de Arte Moderno** ⓘ *Sucre 1527 y Talbot, T07-283 1027, Mon-Fri 0900-1730, Sat-Sun 0900-1300, free*, has a permanent contemporary art collection and art library. It holds a biennial international painting competition and other cultural activities. Across the river from the Museo Pumapungo, the **Museo de Artes de Fuego** ⓘ *Las Herrerías y 10 de Agosto, T07-288 3061, Mon-Fri 0900-1300, 1500-1800, free except for special events*, has a display of wrought ironwork and pottery. It is housed in the beautifully restored Casa de Chaguarchimbana. At the University of Cuenca is an **Orquideario** ⓘ *Av Víctor Manuel Albornoz, Quinta de Balzay, Mon-Fri, 0800-1200, 1400-1800*, displaying hundreds of species of orchid. South of city, accessed via Avenida Fray Vicente Solano and beyond the football stadium, is **Turi church**, orphanage and mirador; a tiled panorama explains the magnificent views.

Listings Cuenca *map page 178.*

Tourist information

To locate an establishment see www.ubicacuenca.com.

Cámara de Turismo Azuay
Padre Aguirre 16-50 y Héroes de Verdeloma, T07-284 5657, http://camaradeturismoazuay.com. Information about the city and province.

Fundación Municipal Turismo
Bolívar 8-44 y Benigno Malo, on Parque Calderón next to the Municipio, T07-284 0383, www.cuencaecuador.com.ec. Mon-Fri, 0800-2000, Sat 0900-1600, Sun 0830-1330. Helpful. Free walking tours Tue-Sat 1000-1200, see Facebook: FreeWalkingTourCuencaOficial to sign up, or ask at the tourist office or hotels.

iTur
Sucre entre Benigno Malo y Luis Cordero,
T07-282 1035, itur@cuenca.com.ec.
Mon-Fri 0800-2000, Sat-Sun 0830-1330.
With offices at the airport and the Terminal
Terrestre (closed Sun).

Where to stay

There is a large number of hotels, many in
refurbished colonial buildings and, hence,
in similar styles; some more 'boutique'
than others; many have a restaurant or
café. Shop around from this list or on the
internet before going.

$$$$ Carvallo
Gran Colombia 9-52, entre Padre
Aguirre y Benigno Malo, T07-283 2063,
www.hotelcarvallo.com.ec.
Combination of an elegant colonial-
style hotel and art/antique gallery. Very
comfortable rooms all have bath tubs,
buffet breakfast, cafeteria.

$$$$ Mansión Alcázar
Bolívar 12-55 y Tarqui, T07-282 3918,
www.mansionalcazar.com.
Beautifully restored house, a mansion
indeed, central, very nice rooms, restaurant
serves gourmet international food, lovely
gardens, quiet relaxed atmosphere.

$$$$ Oro Verde
Av Ordóñez Lazo, northwest of the
centre towards Cajas, T07-409 0000,
www.oroverdecuenca.com.
Elegant hotel, buffet breakfast, excellent
international restaurant (buffet Sun lunch),
small pool, parking.

$$$$ Santa Lucía
Borrero 8-44 y Sucre, T07-282 8000,
www.santaluciahotel.com.
A stylish renovated colonial house, very nice
comfortable rooms, around the courtyard, safe
deposit box, excellent Italian restaurant and La
Placita café with cocktails and traditional food.

$$$ Forum
Borrero 10-91 y Lamar, T07-282 8801,
http://forumhotel.ec.
Stylish modern rooms in a converted
building, comfortable, safe in room,
courtyards and public areas retain historic
elements, French/Ecuadorean restaurant
La Brasserie, German-owned, English and
German spoken. At the same location is
Alfredo's (T09-6899 0513), serving mostly
cazuelas, organic ingredients, desserts,
drinks and wine list.

$$$ Inca Real
Gral Torres 8-40 entre Sucre y Bolívar, T07-
282 3636, http://hotelincareal.com.ec.
Refurbished colonial house with
comfortable rooms around patios,
breakfast available, good Spanish
restaurant (**Akelarre**), parking.

$$$ Posada del Angel
Bolívar 14-11 y Estévez de Toral, T07-284 0695,
www.hostalposadadelangel.com.
A nicely restored colonial house,
comfortable rooms, good Italian restaurant
(**Mangiare Bene**), parking, patio with plants,
some noise from restaurant, English spoken,
helpful staff. Recommended.

$$$ Victoria
C Larga 6-93 y Borrero, T07-283 1120,
www.hotelvictoriaecuador.com.
Elegant refurbished hotel on 5 floors
overlooking the river, comfortable modern
rooms, attractive social areas, renowned
restaurant (**El Jardín**, www.eljardincuenca.
com), good views. Recommended.

$$$-$$ Casa Ordóñez
Lamar 8-59 y Benigno Malo, T07-282 3297,
www.hotelcasaordonez.com.
Well-renovated colonial house with wood
floors and 3 inner patios, attractively
decorated rooms and common areas,
down duvets, no smoking.

$$ La Orquídea

Borrero 9-31 y Bolívar, T07-282 4511,
www.laorquidea.com.ec.

Refurbished colonial house, bright rooms,
fridge in some rooms, other rooms quite
basic, some are up several flights of stairs,
low-season and long-term discounts,
good value, very helpful staff, continental
breakfast included, pay extra for American
breakfast and healthy options.

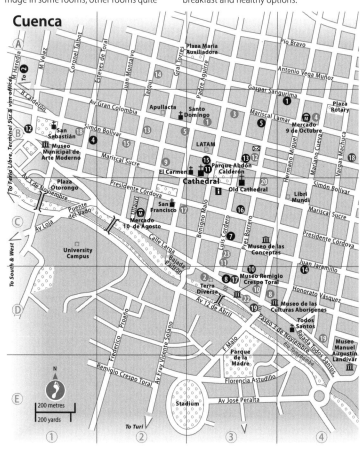

Cuenca

Where to stay
Carvallo **1** *B3*
Casa del Barranco **2** *D3*
Casa Ordóñez **3** *B3*
El Cafecito **4** *B4*
Forum & Alfredo's
  Restaurant **5** *B3*
Hogar Cuencano **8** *D3*
Inca Real **9** *B2*
La Casa Cuencana **10** *D3*
La Cigale **11** *C3*
La Orquídea **12** *B3*
La Posada Cuencana **13** *B2*
Macondo **14** *A2*
Mansión Alcázar **15** *B2*
Milán **17** *C2*
Oro Verde **16** *A6*
Posada del Angel &
  Mangiare Bene
  Restaurant **18** *B1*
Posada Todos Santos **19** *D4*
Santa Lucía **20** *C3*
Victoria **22** *D3*
Yakumama **23** *C3*

Restaurants
Balcón Quiteño **1** *B4*
El Carbón **5** *B3*
El Maíz **6** *E5*
El Mesón Español &
  Hotel Príncipe **7** *C3*
Good Affinity **2** *A1*
Goza **8** *D3*
Mixx Gourmet **9** *C5*
Moliendo Café **10** *D3*
Monte Bianco **3** *C5*
Pedregal Azteca **4** *B1*
Raymipampa **11** *B3*
San Sebas **12** *B1*

$$ La Posada Cuencana
Tarqui 9-46 y Bolívar, T07-282 6831,
www.laposadacuencana.com.ec.
Small family-run hotel with beautiful colonial-style rooms, has **La Cena** café/restaurant.

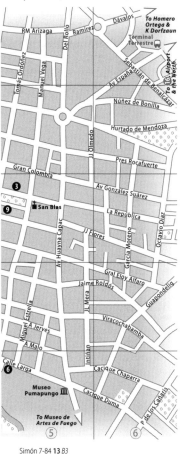

$$ Macondo
Tarqui 11-64 y Lamar, T07-282 1700,
www.hostalmacondo.com.
Attractive restored colonial house, large rooms, buffet breakfast, cooking facilities, pleasant patio with plants, garden, very popular, US-run. Highly recommended.

$$ Posada Todos Santos
C Larga 3-42 y Tomás Ordóñez, near the Todos Santos church, T07-282 4247, see Facebook.
Tranquil hostel decorated with murals, good views of the river, very good, attentive service, English spoken, group discounts.

$$-$ Casa del Barranco
Calle Larga 8-41 y Luis Cordero, T07-283 9763,
http://casadelbarranco.com.
Tastefully restored colonial house, some rooms with lovely views over the river, cafeteria overlooking the river.

$$-$ El Cafecito
Mariano Cueva 11-28 y Lamar, T07-411 4765, http://elcafecitohostel.wixsite.com/elcafecito/cuenca.
Opposite Mercado 9 de Octubre, private rooms with bath and dorm with bath (US$10 pp), café with vegan options, teas, coffees, bar, tours booked, English spoken.

$$-$ La Casa Cuencana
Hermano Miguel 4-45 y Larga, T07-282 6009,
https://lacasacuencana.wordpress.com.
Private rooms and dorms (US$10 pp) in 3 buildings, good backpacker hostal with a range of options including suites and kitchenette, family-run, also has a restaurant.

$$-$ Milán
Pres Córdova 9-89 y Padre Aguirre, T07-283 1104, www.hotelmilan.com.ec.
Multi-storey hotel with views over the market, popular and with a restaurant.

$ Hogar Cuencano
Hermano Miguel 4-36 y C Larga, T07-283 4941, celso3515@yahoo.com.

Well-furnished family-run central *hostal*,
private or shared bath, US$10 pp in dorm,
cafeteria, breakfast available, cooking facilities.

$ La Cigale
*Honorato Vásquez 7-80 y Cordero, T07-
283 5308, www.hostallacigale.com.*
Very popular hostel with private rooms and
dorms (US$8 pp), breakfast available, very
good restaurant (**$$-$**), hostel can be noisy
until midnight.

$ Yakumama
*Cordero 5-66 y Honorato Vásquez, T07-
283 4353, www.hostalyakumama.com.*
Popular hostel, 2 private rooms and dorms
with 2-6 beds US$8-10 pp, restaurant with
Ecuadorean and Swiss dishes, bar, patio with
plants and lounging area, terrace with skate
ramp, can get noisy.

Restaurants

There is a wide selection and fast turnover
of restaurants. Some places are closed on
Sun evening, but quite a few, especially
those associated with hotels, are open all
day Sun. In the cathedral precinct next
to **Raymipampa** is a cloister with Italian,
French and other restaurants, as well as
shops and toilets.

There are several restaurants of all types,
some very new, on Honorato Vásquez,
6 blocks between Hermano Miguel and
Borrero. There are cheap *comedores* at the
Mercados 9 de Octubre and 10 de Agosto.

$$$ Tiestos
*J Jaramillo 4-89 y M Cueva, T07-283 5310.
Tue-Sat 1230-1500, 1830-2200, Sun 1230-1500.*
Superb international cuisine prepared on
tiestos, shallow clay pans, comfortable homely
atmosphere, very popular, reserve ahead.

$$$-$$ Balcón Quiteño
*Sangurima 6-49 y Borrero, and BQ Sport,
Av Ordóñez Lazo 311 y los Pinos, T07-283*

*1928, www.balconquiteno.com.
Daily 1000-0100.*
Good Ecuadorean and international food
and service, 1960s decor. Popular with locals
after a night's partying.

$$$-$$ El Carbón
*Borrero 10-69 y Lamar, in Hotel Cuenca,
T07-283 3711, www.hotelcuenca.com.ec.
Daily 0700-2300.*
Excellent charcol-grilled meat served with a
choice of fresh salads, seafood, wide choice
of dishes and breakfasts, large portions
enough for 2.

$$$-$$ El Maíz
*C Larga 1-279 y C de los Molinos, T07-284
0224, www.elmaizrestaurante.com. Mon-Fri
1200-2100, Sat 1200-1600, 1900-2100.*
Good traditional Ecuadorean dishes with
some innovations, salads.

$$$-$$ Mangiare Bene
*Estévez de Toral 8-91 y Bolívar, at Posada del
Angel, T07-282 1360. Mon-Sat 1200-1500,
1730-2230, Sun 1200-1500.*
Excellent Italian food, home-made pasta,
good value, very popular with locals.

$$$-$$ Pedregal Azteca
*Esteves de Toral 8-60 y Bolívar, T07-282 3652,
www.pedregalazteca.com. Tue-Sat 1200-
1500, 1830-2230, Sun 1200-1500.*
Nicely decorated restaurant with very good
authentic Mexican food.

$$$-$$ Simón 7-84
*Luis Cordero 9-14 y Bolívar (another entrance
on Bolívar), T07-283 7285. Sun-Wed 0800-
2200, Thu-Sat 0800-2330.*
Mixed menu of Ecuadorean and
international food, generous portions,
mostly meat (ribs a speciality) and fish,
tables in covered courtyard, music on Fri.

$$ El Mesón Español
*Luis Cordero y Jaramillo (in courtyard
restaurant of Hotel Príncipe, T07-284 7287,*

www.hotelprincipe.com.ec), T09-3934 2714,
jazzsocietyofecuador@gmail.com.
Tapas bar and restaurant with small menu
of paella, pizza, burgers and drinks. Wed-Sat
free music evenings by **Jazz Café Society**,
1830-2200 (not necessarily jazz), donations
for the music goes towards music education.

$$ Raymipampa

Benigno Malo 8-59, at Parque Calderón,
T07-283 4159, raymi859@hotmail.com.
Mon-Fri 0830-2300, Sat-Sun 0930-2230.
Good typical and international food in a nice
central location, inexpensive set lunch on
weekdays, fast service, very popular, at times
it is hard to get a table.

$$-$ Viejo Rincón

Pres Córdova 7-46 y Borrero. Mon-Fri 0900-
2100, Sat 0900-1500.
Tasty Ecuadorean food, very good
economical set lunch and à la carte, popular.

$ Good Affinity

Capulíes 1-89 y Gran Colombia, T07-283 2469,
see Facebook. Mon-Sat 0930-1530.
Very good vegetarian food, vegan options,
cheap set lunch, pleasant garden seating.

$ Moliendo Café

Honorato Vásquez 6-24 y Hermano Miguel,
T07-282 8710, see Facebook (also on
Ordóñez Lasso, opposite Oro Verde).
Mon-Sat 0900-2100.
Tasty Colombian food including set lunch,
friendly service.

Cafés

Goza

Borrero 4-11 y Larga, Plaza de la Merced,
Facebook: gozaespresso. Mon-Thu 0800-
2300, Fri-Sat 0800-2400, Sun 0800-2200.
Very popular café/restaurant with a varied
menu; one of the few places in Cuenca with
outdoor seating.

Mixx Gourmet

Parque San Blas 2-73 y Tomás Ordóñez.
A variety of fruit- and liquor-flavoured ice
cream, popular. Several others nearby.

Monte Bianco

Bolívar 2-80 y Ordóñez, Parque San Blas,
and a couple of other locations.
Good ice cream and cream cakes,
good value.

San Sebas

San Sebastián 1-94 y Sucre, Parque San
Sebastián, www.sansebascuenca.com.
Wed-Sun 0830-1500.
Outdoor café, popular for breakfast, good
selection of giant sandwiches and salads.

Tutto Freddo

Bolívar 8-09 y Benigno Malo and several
other locations. Daily 0900-2200.
Good ice cream, crêpes, pizza, sandwiches,
sweets and coffee, reasonable prices, very
popular. On the opposite corner at B Malo
y Bolívar (under Hotel del Parque) is **Tutto
Freddo Gourmet**, with more exotic flavours.

Bars and clubs

Calle Larga is a major destination for
nightlife, with bars serving snacks and
some restaurants. Av 12 de Abril, along the
river near Parque de la Madre, and to the
west of the centre, Plaza del Arte, Gaspar
de Sangurima y Abraham Sarmiento,
opposite Plazoleta El Otorongo, are also
popular. There are also several bars serving
craft beer. Most bars open Wed-Thu until
2300, Fri-Sat until 0200.

La Compañía Brewhouse

Borrero 4-58 to 4-66 y H Vásquez, Facebook:
La Compania BrewPub. Mon-Thu 1600-2400,
Fri-Sat 1600-0200.
Microbrewery with several brews, in bottle
or on draught, taster selection, beer and
other cocktails, non-alcoholic drinks, no
credit cards.

La Mesa Salsa & Son
Gran Colombia 3-35 entre Vargas Machuca y Tomás Ordóñez (no sign), Facebook: lamesa salsayson. Wed and Fri 2100-0200 or 0300.
Latin music, salsa, popular among travellers and locals, young crowd.

Wunderbar
Entrance from stairs on Hermano Miguel y C Larga, T07-283 1274, Facebook: wunderbarcuenca. Mon-Wed 1200-2300, Thu 1200-2400, Fri 1200-0200, Sat 1500-0200.
A café-bar-restaurant, drinks, good coffee and food including some vegetarian. Nice atmosphere, book exchange, German-run.

Entertainment

Cinemas
Multicines, *Milenium Plaza, Av José Peralta y Cornelio Merchá,* and at Mall del Río, Av Felipe II y Circunvalación Sur. Both multi-screen complexes in shopping malls.

Dance classes
Cachumbambé, *Padre Julio Matovelle y Miguel Díaz, T09-9845 1217, see Facebook. Mon-Wed 1600-2100, Thu 1700-2000.* Salsa, merengue and a variety of other rhythms, group and individual classes.

Festivals

Mar/Apr Good Friday. There is a fine procession through the town to the Mirador Turi.
12 Apr Foundation of Cuenca.
May-Jun Septenario, the religious festival of Corpus Christi, lasts a week.
Oct-Dec Bienal de Cuenca, an internationally famous art competition. The next one is due in late 2018. Information from Bolívar 13-89, T07-283 1778, www.bienaldecuenca.org.
3 Nov Independence of Cuenca, with street theatre, art exhibitions and night-time dances all over the city for 4 days.

24 Dec Pase del Niño Viajero, probably the largest and finest Christmas parade in all Ecuador. Children and adults from all the barrios and surrounding villages decorate donkeys, horses, cars and trucks with symbols of abundance. Little children in colourful indigenous costumes or dressed up as biblical figures ride through the streets accompanied by musicians. The parade starts at about 1000 at San Sebastián, proceeds along C Bolívar and ends at San Blas about 5 hrs later. In the days up to, and just after Christmas, there are many smaller parades.

Shopping

Books
Carolina Bookstore, *Hermano Miguel 4-46 y C Larga.* Good selection of English books for sale and exchange. Friendly service.
Librimundi, *Hermano Miguel 8-14 y Sucre, Facebook: librimundicuenca.* Nice bookshop with good selection and a café/reading area.

Camping equipment
Cikla, *Av Remigio Tamariz 1-144 y Federico Proaño, T07-288 5430, http://cikla.net.* Specialists in cycling equipment.
Explorer, *at Mall del Río, www.explorer-ecuador.com.* Sporting goods, clothing. Several other shops near the university, on or near Av Remigio Crespo. Equipment rental from **Apullacta**, see Tour operators, page 184.

Handicrafts
There are many craftware shops along Gran Colombia, Benigno Malo and Juan Jaramillo alongside Las Conceptas. There are several good leather shops in the arcade off Bolívar between Benigno Malo and Luis Cordero. Lots of jewellery shops around Gran Colombia y Luis Cordero junction. Others dotted about the centre. *Polleras*, traditional skirts worn by indigenous women are found along Gral Torres, between Sucre and Pres Córdova, and on Tarqui, between Pres

Córdova and C Larga. Small crafts market in the **Plaza Santa Ana** at Benigno Malo y Lamar, open daily 0700-2200. Handicrafts are sold by the **Asociación El Otorongo**, in Plaza Otorongo, Av 3 de Noviembre, Facebook: feriasartesanalescuenca. For basketwork, take a 15-min bus ride from the Feria Libre (see Markets, below) to the village of **San Joaquín**.

Artesa, *L Cordero 10-31 y Gran Colombia and in CC Plaza de Las Américas, several branches in the country, www.artesa.com.ec.* Modern ceramic tableware; factory is at Isabel La Católica 1-102 y Av de Las Américas, T07-405 6352.
Centro Artesanal Municipal 'Casa de la Mujer', *Gral Torres 7-33 y Pres Córdova*. Crafts market with a great variety of handicrafts.
Colecciones Jorge Moscoso, *J Jaramillo 6-80 y Borrero, Facebook:* jorgemoscoso galeria. Weaving exhibitions, ethnographic museum, antiques and crafts.
El Barranco, *Av 3 de Noviembre Escalinata (stairs below Larga, by Hermano Miguel), Facebook: galeriaelbarranco.* Wed-Sun 1000-1900. Artisans' cooperative selling a wide variety of crafts.
El Tucán, *Borrero 7-35 y Pres Córdova*. Good selection. Recommended.
La Esquina de las Artes, *in Galería Manos del Mundo 12 de Abril y Agustín Cueva, open daily from 1000*. Shops with exclusive crafts including textiles and foodstuffs; also cultural events.

Jewellery
Galería Claudio Maldonado, *Bolívar 7-75 y Cordero*. Has unique pre-Columbian designs in silver and precious stones.

Markets
Feria Libre, *Av Las Américas y Av Remigio Crespo, west of the centre*. The largest market, also has dry goods and clothing, busiest Wed and Sat.

Mercado 9 de Octubre, *Sangurima y Mariano Cueva*. Daily, busiest on Thu, on 3 levels for produce and prepared foods. Nearby at **Plaza Rotary** (Sangurima y Vargas Machuca), crafts are sold, best selection on Thu.
Mercado 10 de Agosto, *C Larga y Gral Torres*. Daily market for produce and dry goods, with a prepared foods and drinks section on the 2nd floor.

Panama hats
Manufacturers have displays showing the complete hat making process, see also **Museo del Sombrero**, page 175.
Homero Ortega P e Hijos, *Av Gil Ramírez Dávalos 3-86, near bus station, T07-280 9000, www.homeroortega.com*. Good quality, with museum; also has a shop at Hermano Miguel 6-84 y Pres Córdova.
K Dorfzaun, *Gil Ramírez Dávalos 4-34, near bus station, T07-286 1707, www.kdorfzaun. com. Mon-Fri 0800-1600*. Good quality and selection of hats and straw crafts, nice styles, good prices. English-speaking guides.
Sombreros Vélez, *Larga 6-42 y Hermano Miguel, T09-8861 1069, see Facebook*. Small selection of fine hats, a bit pricier than others.

What to do

Language courses
Rates US$6-7 per hr shared lessons, US$8-12 per hr private.
Centro de Estudios Interamericanos (CEDEI), *Gran Colombia 11-02 y General Torres, T07-283 9003, www.cedei.org*. Spanish and Quichua lessons, immersion/volunteering programmes, also run the attached **Hostal Macondo**. Recommended.
Estudio Internacional Sampere, *Hermano Miguel 3-43 y C Larga, T07-284 2659, www.sampere.com*. At the high end of the price range.
Sí Centro de Español e Inglés, *Bolívar 13-28 y Juan Montalvo, T09-9918-8264, www.sicentrospanishschool.com*. Good

teachers, competitive prices, homestays, volunteer opportunities, helpful and enthusiastic, tourist information available. Recommended.

Tours

City tours cost about US$25 pp. Day tours to Ingapirca, Cajas or to Gualaceo and Chordeleg run about US$50 pp. Trekking in Cajas about US$60-100 pp per day, depending on group size.

Apullacta, *Gran Colombia 11-02 y Gral Torres, p 2, T07-283 7681, www.apullacta.com*. Run city and regional tours (Cajas, Ingapirca, Gualaceo and Chordeleg), also adventure tours (cycling, horse riding, canopy, canyoning), sell jungle, highland and Galápagos trips; also hire camping equipment.

Metropolitan Touring, *Sucre 6-62 y Borreo, T07-284 3223, or 09-9859 0166, www. metropolitan-touring.com*. A branch of the Quito operator, also sells airline tickets.

TerraDiversa, *C Larga 8-41 y Luis Cordero, T07-282 3782, www.terradiversa.com*. Lots of useful information, helpful staff. Ingapirca, Cajas, community tourism in Saraguro, jungle trips, horse riding, mountain biking and other options. The more common destinations have fixed departures. Also sell Galápagos tours and flights. Recommended.

Van Service, *Hermano Miguel y Pres Córdova, T07-282 3231, or 07-281 6409, www.vanservice. com.ec*. City tours on a double-decker bus. The 1¾-hr tour includes the main attractions in the colonial city and El Turi lookout. US$8, hourly departures 1000-2000 (Sun 0900-1600) from the Old Cathedral. Also double-decker bus tours to the north of the city, day tours outside the city, and vans with driver.

Air

The airport is about a 20-min ride northeast of the centre. To **Quito** with **LATAM** (Bolívar 9-18, T1-800-000527) and **TAME** (Av España,

by airport, T07-280 7072). Also to **Guayaquil** with TAME.

Bus

City buses US$0.25. For the local **Baños**, city buses every 5-10 mins, 0600-2230, buses 12 or 100 pass the front of the Terminal Terrestre, cross the city on Vega Muñoz and Cueva, then down Todos los Santos to the river, along 12 de Abril and onto Av Loja. A tram system is under construction, but had not started operating in 2017; some streets are closed due to the construction, adding to the traffic chaos in the centre: allow extra time.

Regional Buses to nearby destinations leave from **Terminal Sur** at the Feria Libre on Av Las Américas. Many city buses pass here, but it is a very busy area so watch your bags.

Long distance The **Terminal Terrestre** is on Av España, 15 mins by taxi northeast of centre; terminal tax US$0.10. Take daytime buses to enjoy scenic routes. To **Riobamba**, 6 hrs, US$8. To **Baños** (Tungurahua), transfer in Riobamba. To **Ambato**, 6½ hrs, US$9. To **Quito**, Terminal Quitumbe, US$12, 9½ hrs. To **Alausí**, 4 hrs, US$6; all Riobamba- and Quito-bound buses pass by, but few enter town. To **Loja**, 4 hrs, US$7.50, see www.viajerosinternacional.com; transfer here for Vilcabamba. **Viajeros Internacional** also to **Saraguro**, US$5, 2½ hrs, Zamora (3 a day), Yantzaza and El Cisne (2 a day). To **Machala**, 4 hrs, US$5.50, at least half-hourly, sit on the left, wonderful scenery; to **Huaquillas**, 5 hrs, US$7, 8 a day, both with **Trans Azuay** (www.transportesazuay.com). To **Guayaquil**, via Cajas and Molleturo, 4 hrs, or via Zhud, 5 hrs, both US$8.25. To **Macas** via Paute and Guarumales or via Gualaceo and Plan de Milagro, 6-7 hrs, US$11; spectacular scenery but prone to landslides, check in advance if roads are open. To **Gualaquiza**, in the southern Oriente, via Gualaceo and Plan de Milagro or via Sígsig, 6 hrs, US$8.75.

International To **Chiclayo** (Peru) via Tumbes, **Máncora** and **Piura**, with **Super Semería**, at 2200, US$20, 11 hrs (US$17 as far as Piura or Máncora); also with **Azuay** at 2100; and **Pullman Sucre**, connecting with CIFA in Huaquillas; or go to Loja and catch a bus to Piura from there.

Car rental
Bombuscaro, España 11-20 y Elia Liut, opposite the airport, T07-286 6541, www.driving bombuscar.com. Also international companies.

Taxi
All taxis are required to use meters, US$1.50 is the minimum fare; approximately US$2 from the centre to the bus station; US$2.50 to airport; US$5 to Baños. There are also unmarked taxis, eg from the van companies, which charge more to the centre.

Long-distance taxis and vans Several offices on Av Remigio Crespo, near Feria Libre (see above). To **Guayaquil**, **Operazuaytur**, Av Remigio Crespo y Edwin Sacoto, 1 block from Feria Libre, T07-420 3537, www. operazuaytur.com, every 30 to 60 mins, US$13. To **Machala**, **Tinamu**, Av Remigio Crespo 18-50 y Brasil, T07-288 7372, US$12, 24-hr service. To **Loja**, **Elite Tours**, Remigio Crespo 14-08 y Santa Cruz, T07-420 3088, also **Ecuavantur**, Remigio Crespo y Brasil, T07-404 4771, US$12, 3¼ hrs, 0400-2000 hourly; also go to Vilcabamba, US$15, and Zamora, US$15 (they have a *hostal* above the office, US$15 pp). To **Vilcabamba**, van service daily at 1300 from Hostal La Cigale, Honorato Vásquez y Luis Cordero, US$16, 5 hrs, reserve ahead at Izhcayluma in Vilcabamba, T07-302 5162, www.izhcayluma.com.

sulphur baths, Inca remains, lakes and hiking

Baños
There are **sulphur baths** ⓘ *entry US$3-10*, at Baños, with a domed, blue church in a delightful landscape, 5 km southwest of Cuenca. These are the hottest commercial baths in Ecuador. Above the Plaza Central are four separate complexes of warm baths with spa and lodging, **Agapantos** (T07-289 2493), **Rodas** (www.hosteriarodas.com), **Durán** (see Where to stay) and **Piedra de Agua** (www.piedradeagua.com.ec). (There is a map on http://parroquiabanos.gob.ec.) The latter two are better maintained and more exclusive. The country lanes above the baths offer some pleasant walks and the town is worth a visit.

★ Ingapirca *Colour map 5, A4.*
Open 0800-1800, US$2, including museum and tour in Spanish or English; bags can be stored, ATM; bar/restaurants and handicrafts outside the ticket office.

Ecuador's most important Inca ruin, at 3160 m, lies 8.5 km east of the colonial town of **Cañar** (*hostales* in $ range). Access is from Cañar, **El Tambo** or via an unmade road from the Panamericana to the paved road from Cañar through the village of **San José** (this takes about 1¼ hours from Cuenca, compared with two hours via Cañar). The Inca Huayna Capac took over the site from the conquered Cañaris when his empire expanded north into Ecuador in the third quarter of the 15th century. Ingapirca was strategically placed on the Capac Ñan, the Great Inca Road that ran from Cuzco to Quito, see Inca Trail, below. The site shows typical imperial Cuzco-style architecture, such as tightly fitting stonework and trapezoidal doorways, a small portion of Inca road and, in the round foundations of buildings, remains of Cañari buildings. The central structure may have been a solar observatory. A 10-minute walk away from the site is the **Cara del Inca**, or 'face of the Inca', an immense natural formation in the rock looking over the landscape. Nearby is a throne cut into the rock, the **Sillón del Inca** (Inca's Chair) and the **Ingachugana**, a large rock with carved channels. On Friday there is an interesting indigenous market at Ingapirca village.

About 1.5 km from El Tambo is the small Cañari-Inca archaeological site of **Baños del Inca** or **Coyoctor** ⓘ *site open daily 0800-1700, US$1*, a massive rock outcrop carved to form baths, showers, water channels and seats overlooking a small amphitheatre. There is an interpretation centre with information about the site, a hall with displays about regional fiestas and an audiovisual room with tourist information about all of Ecuador. You can get there from the El Tambo–Ingapirca road, or along the currently unused railway line from El Tambo to Coyoctor.

Inca Trail to Ingapirca

The three-day hike to Ingapirca starts at **Achupallas** (lively Saturday market, one hostel), 25 km from Alausí (see page 160). The walk is covered by three 1:50,000 *IGM* sheets, Alausí, Juncal and Cañar. The Juncal sheet is most important, the name Ingapirca does not appear on the latter, you may have to ask directions near the end. Also take a compass and GPS. Good camping equipment is essential; the altitude of the route ranges from 3100 to over 4000 m. Take all food and drink with you as there is nothing along the way. A shop in Achupallas sells basic foodstuffs. Don't take unnecessary valuables, leave nothing unattended on the hike and be prepared for begging. Tour operators in Riobamba offer this trek for about US$350 per person (two passengers, less for a larger group), three days, with everything included; tours from Cuenca cost between US$400-570 per person (group of two).

East of Cuenca

Northeast of Cuenca, on the paved road to Méndez in the Oriente, is **Paute**, with a pleasant park and modern church. South of Paute, **Gualaceo** is a rapidly expanding modern town set in beautiful landscape, with a charming plaza and Sunday produce market. The iTur (see page 188) is very helpful, English spoken. A scenic road goes from Gualaceo to Limón in Oriente. Many of Ecuador's 4000 species of orchid can be seen at **Ecuagénera** ⓘ *Km 2 on the road to Cuenca, T07-225 5237, www.ecuagenera.com, Mon-Fri 0730-1600, Sat 0730-1700, Sun 0900-1700, US$5 (US$3 pp for groups of 3 or more)*.

South of Gualaceo is **Chordeleg**, a touristy village famous for its crafts in wood, silver and gold filigree, pottery and Panama hats. At the **Museo Municipal** ⓘ *C 23 de Enero, Mon-Fri 0800-1300, 1400-1700, Sat-Sun 1000-1600*, is an exhibition hall with fascinating local textiles, ceramics and straw work, some of which are on sale at reasonable prices. It's a good uphill walk from Gualaceo to Chordeleg, and a pleasant hour downhill in the other direction. South of Gualaceo, 83 km from Cuenca, is **Sígsig**, an authentic highland town where women can be seen weaving hats 'on the move'. It has a Sunday market, two *residenciales* and an archaeology museum. A scenic road goes from Sígsig to Gualaquiza in Oriente, paved as far as Chigüinda, two-thirds of the way.

★ Parque Nacional Cajas

The park entrance is at Laguna Sorocucho, T07-237 0127, Mon-Fri 0800-1600. The administration office and visitors' centre are at Luguna Toreadora. Entry free, overnight stay US$4 per night (see Where to stay, below).

ON THE ROAD

Trekking in Cajas

For day walks, there are some marked trails near the visitor centre but they tend to peter out quickly. For overnight treks, adequate experience and equipment are necessary. Open fires are not permitted, so take a stove. A very strong hiker with a good sense of direction can cross the park in two days. Independent trekkers must register with the rangers.

On the opposite side of Laguna Toreadora from the *refugio* is **Cerro San Luis** (4200 m), which may be climbed in a day; the views are excellent. From the visitor centre go anticlockwise around the lake; after crossing the outflow look for a sign 'Al San Luis', follow the yellow and black stakes to the summit and beware of a side trail to dangerous ledges.

Beyond Laguna Toreadora on a paved road is the village of **Migüir**, from where you can follow a trail past several lakes and over a pass to Soldados (two days). It is also possible to follow the **Ingañán Trail**, an old Inca road that used to connect Cuenca with the coast. It is in ill repair or lost in places but there are interesting ruins above **Laguna Mamamag**. You can access the Ingañán from the park headquarters or from Migüir, from where it is two to three days' trekking to **Laguna Llaviuco**. From Llaviuco you might get a ride with fishermen back to Cuenca or you can walk to the main road in about an hour.

Northwest of Cuenca, Cajas is a 29,000-ha national park with over 230 lakes. The park is being diligently conserved by municipal authorities both for its environmental importance and because it is the water supply for Cuenca. The *páramo* vegetation, such as chuquiragua and lupin, is beautiful and the wildlife interesting. Cajas is very rich in birdlife; 125 species have been identified, including the condor and many varieties of hummingbird (the violet-tailed metaltail is endemic to this area). On the lakes are Andean gulls, speckled teal and yellow-billed pintails. On a clear morning the views are superb, even to Chimborazo, some 300 km away.

There are two access roads. The paved road from Cuenca to Guayaquil via Molleturo (E582) goes through the northern section and is the main route for Laguna Toreadora, the visitor centre and Laguna Llaviuco. There are various *paradores*, *miradores* and restaurants on this route. Skirting the southern edge of the park is a gravel secondary road, which goes from Cuenca via San Joaquín to the Soldados entrance and the community of Angas beyond (see Transport, below.) There is nowhere to stay after the *refugio* at Laguna Toreadora (see Where to stay, below) until you reach the lowlands between Naranjal and La Troncal.

The park offers ideal but strenuous walking, at 3150-4450 m altitude, and the climate is cold and wet. There have been deaths from exposure. The best time to visit is from August to January, when you may expect clear days, strong winds, night-time temperatures to -8°C and occasional mist and rain. From February to July temperatures are higher but there is much more fog, rain and snow. Arrive in the early morning if possible since it can get very cloudy, wet and cool after about 1300. It is best to get the *IGM* maps in Quito (Chaucha, Cuenca, San Felipe de Molleturo, and Chiquintad 1:50,000) and take a compass and GPS. It is easy to get lost.

Tourist information

East of Cuenca

iTur Gualaceo
At the Municipio, Gran Colombia y 3 de
Noviembre, Parque Central, T07-225 5131.
Mon-Fri 0800-1300, 1400-1700.
Very helpful, English spoken

Where to stay

Baños

There are also a couple of cheap *residenciales* in town.

$$$ Caballo Campana
Vía Misicata–Baños Km 4, Sector Huizhil,
on an alternative road from Cuenca to
Baños (2 km from Baños, taxi US$5 from
the centre of Cuenca), T07-412 8769,
www.caballocampana.com.
Nicely rebuilt colonial hacienda house
in 28 ha with gardens and forest, heated
rooms, suites and cabins, includes buffet
breakfast, Ecuadorean and international
cuisine, horse riding and lessons, sports
fields, discounts for longer stays.

$$$ Hostería Durán
Km 8 Vía Baños, T07-289 2301,
www.hosteriaduran.com.
Includes buffet breakfast, restaurant,
parking, has well-maintained, very clean
pools (US$3-7 for non-residents), gym
and steam bath.

Ingapirca

There are good economical meals at
several places by the entrance to the
archaeological site.

$$ Posada Ingapirca
600 m uphill from the ruins, for
reservations T07-283 1120 (Cuenca),
www.posadaingapirca.com.

Pretty converted hacienda, comfortable,
spacious rooms, heating, includes typical
breakfast, excellent restaurant and bar with
fireplace and views to the ruins and beyond,
specializes in local ingredients, good service,
Wi-Fi, guided trek or horse ride to Paredones
ruins and La Laguna de Culebrillas.

$$-$ Cabañas del Castillo
Opposite the ruins, T09-9998 3650,
cab.castillo@hotmail.com.
3 simple cabins, heating and restaurant.

El Tambo

This is the nearest town to Ingapirca on the
Panamerican Highway.

$ Chasky Wasy
Behind Banco del Austro, which is on the
Pananericana 1 block from the park, T07-223
8766 or 09-9883 0013, http://chaskywasy.com.
Nice hostel with ample rooms, no
breakfast, parking nearby. Also has
a branch in Cuenca, Gran Colombia
y Miguel Morocho, T07-282 6889.

$ Sunshine
Panamericana y Ramón Borrero, at north
end of town, T07-223 8394.
Simple, family-run, not always staffed,
private or shared bath, restaurant nearby,
traffic noise.

Inca Trail to Ingapirca

$ Ingañán
Achupallas, T03-293 0663.
Basic, with bath, hot water, meals on
request, camping.

East of Cuenca
Paute

$$$$ Hostería Uzhupud
Km 32 Vía a Paute, T07-370 0860.

Set in the beautiful Paute valley 10 km from town, deluxe, relaxing, rooms at the back have the best views, swimming pools and sauna (US$15 for non-residents), sports fields, horse riding, gardens, lots of orchids. Recommended.

Gualaceo

$$ Peñón de Cuzay
Sector Bullcay El Carmen on the main road to Cuenca, T07-217 1515, see Facebook.
In one of the weaving communities, spa, pool and water park, restaurant. Fills up at weekends, book ahead.

$ Hostal El Jardín
On the corner next to bus terminal, T09-9814 1126, Facebook: hjardingualaceo.
Very clean ample rooms with private or shared bath, no breakfast, a simple decent place.

Parque Nacional Cajas
There is a *refugio* at **Laguna Toreadora** (US$4 pp, reserve ahead at T07-283 1900), cold (take sleeping bag), cooking facilities, and camping at **Laguna Llaviuco**. Other shelters in the park are primitive.

$$$$-$$$ Hostería Dos Chorreras
Km 21 Vía al Cajas, sector Sayausí, T07-404 1824, www.hosteriadoschorreras.com.
Hacienda-style inn outside the park. Heating, restaurant serves excellent fresh trout, buffet breakfast, reservations advised, horse rentals with advanced notice. A good place to stop on the way down from Cajas to Cuenca.

Transport

Ingapirca
Bus and pick-up
Direct buses **Cuenca** to Ingapirca with **Transportes Cañar** daily at 0900, returning 1300, US$3.50, 2½ hrs. Buses run from Cuenca to Cañar (US$2.15) and El Tambo

(US$2.50) every 15 mins. From **Cañar**, corner of 24 de Mayo and Borrero, Trans Inga local buses leave every 15 mins for Ingapirca, 0600-1800, US$0.75, 45-50 mins; last bus returns at 1700. The same buses from Cañar go through **El Tambo**, US$0.75, 20 mins. If coming from the north, transfer in El Tambo. Pick-up taxi from Cañar US$10, from El Tambo US$6.25.

Inca Trail to Ingapirca
Bus and pick-up
From **Alausí to Achupallas**, small buses and pick-ups leave as they fill between 1100 and 1600, US$1.50, 1 hr. Alternatively, take any bus along the Panamericana to **La Moya**, south of Alausí, at the turn-off for Achupallas, and a shared pick-up from there (best on Thu and Sun), US$0.50. To hire a pick-up from Alausí costs US$12-15, from La Moya US$10.

East of Cuenca
Bus
From Terminal Terrestre in Cuenca: to **Paute**, every 15 mins, US$1.50, 1 hr; to **Gualaceo**, every 15 mins, US$1, 50 mins; to **Chordeleg**: every 15 mins from Gualaceo, US$0.45, 15 mins, or direct bus from Cuenca, US$1.50, 1 hr; to **Sígsig**, every 30 mins via Gualaceo, US$2 (US$0.75 from Gualaceo), 1½ hrs.

Parque Nacional Cajas
Bus
From Cuenca's Terminal Terrestre take any **Guayaquil** bus that goes via Molleturo (not Zhud), US$2, 30 mins to turn-off for Llaviuco, 45 mins to Toreadora. **Coop Occidental** to Molleturo, 8 a day from the Terminal Sur/Feria Libre, this is a slower bus and may wait to fill up. For the Soldados entrance, catch a bus from Puente del Vado in Cuenca, daily at 0600, US$2.15, 1½ hrs; the return bus passes the Soldados gate at about 1600.

impressive scenery on the way to and beyond an Andean indigenous community

From Cuenca various routes go to the Peruvian border, fanning out from the pleasant city of Loja, due south of which is Vilcabamba, famous for its invigorating climate and lovely countryside.

South to Loja

The Pan-American Highway divides about 20 km south of Cuenca. One branch runs south to Loja, the other heads southwest through **Girón**, the **Yunguilla valley** (with a small bird reserve, see www.fjocotoco.org) and **Santa Isabel** (several hotels with pools and spas; cloudforest and waterfalls). The last stretch through sugar cane fields leads to **Pasaje** and **Machala**. The scenic road between Cuenca and Loja undulates between high, cold *páramo* passes and deep desert-like canyons.

Saraguro *Colour map 5, B3.*

On the road to Loja is this old town, where the local people, the most southerly indigenous Andean group in Ecuador, dress all in black. The men are notable for their black shorts and the women for their pleated black skirts, necklaces of coloured beads and silver *topos*, ornate pins fastening their shawls. The town has a picturesque Sunday market and interesting Mass, Easter and Christmas celebrations. Traditional festivities are held during solstices and equinoxes in surrounding communities, Inti Raymi (19-21 June) being the most important. Necklaces and other crafts are sold near the church. Saraguro has a community tourism programme (**Red de Turismo Comunitario Saraguro Rikuy**) with tours and homestay opportunities with indigenous families (US$35 per person full board). Contact local tour operator **Saraurku** ① *18 de Noviembre y Av Loja, T07-220 0331, Facebook: saraurku-turismo saraguro*, or the **Oficina Municipal de Turismo** (see page 193). See also www.saraguro.gob.ec/turismo for general information on some of the sites in the area. **Bosque Washapampa** ① *entry free*, 6 km south, has good birdwatching.

Loja *Colour map 5, B3.*

This friendly, pleasant highland city, encircled by hills, is an important transport hub, of particular interest to travellers en route to and from Peru. If spending any time in the area then the small town of Vilcabamba, 40 km to the south (see page 197), is a more interesting place to hang out but Loja makes a practical overnight stop with all facilities and services.

Housed in a beautifully restored house on the main park is the **Centro Cultural Loja** home of the **Museo de la Cultura Lojana** ① *10 de Agosto 13-30 y Bolívar, T07-257 0001, closed 2018 for renovation*, with well-displayed archaeology, ethnography, art, and history halls as well as temporary exhibits. **Parque San Sebastián** at Bolívar y Mercadillo and the adjoining Calle Lourdes preserve the flavour of old Loja and are worth visiting. Loja is famed for its musicians and has a symphony orchestra. Cultural evenings with music and dance are held at Plaza San Sebastián, on Thursday 2000-2200 all year round. The **Museo de Música** ① *Valdivieso 09-42 y Rocafuerte, Mon-Fri 0830-1300, 1500-1800, free*, honours 10 Lojano composers.

Parque Universitario Francisco Vivar Castro (**Parque La Argelia**) ① *on the road south to Vilcabamba, Tue-Sun 0800-1700, US$1*, has trails through the forest to the *páramo*.

Across the road is the **Jardín Botánico Reynaldo Espinosa** ⓘ *Mon-Fri 0730-1230, 1500-1800, Sat-Sun 1300-1800, US$1*, which is nicely laid out. To get there, take the city bus marked 'Capulí-Dos Puentes' to the park or 'Argelia' to the Universidad Nacional and walk from there.

Fact...
On a ridge to the west of the city is the largest wind farm in Ecuador.

Ruta de la Cascarilla

This 37-km trail from Loja (by Parque Lineal La Tebaida, opposite Supermaxi) to Vilcabamba is good for walking and mountain biking. Signed also as 'Sendero Ecológico', it runs near the highway, uphill for the first 9 km to **Cajanuma** (the turn-off for Podocarpus National Park), then mostly downhill to **Malacatos** and up and down from there to Vilcabamba.

★ Parque Nacional Podocarpus

Podocarpus (950 m to 3700 m) is one of the most diverse protected areas in the world. It is particularly rich in birdlife, including many rarities, and includes one of the last major habitats for the spectacled bear. The park protects stands of *romerillo* or podocarpus, a native, slow-growing conifer. Podocarpus is divided into two areas, an upper premontane section with many lakes, spectacular walking country, lush cloudforest and excellent birdwatching; and a lower subtropical section, with remote areas of virgin rainforest and unmatched quantities of flora and fauna. Both zones are wet (wellies are recommended) but there may be periods of dry weather October to January. The upper section is also cold, so warm clothing and waterproofs are indispensable year-round.

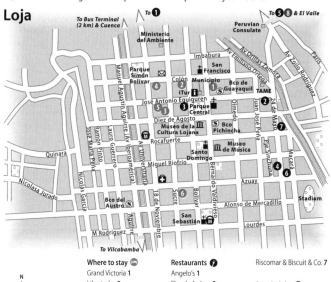

Loja

Where to stay 😴
Grand Victoria **1**
Libertador **2**
Londres **3**
Real Colón **4**
Romar Royal **5**
Vinarós **6**

Restaurants 🍴
Angelo's **1**
Flor de Azúcar **2**
Jugo Natural **3**
Lecka **4**
Mama Lola **5**
Pizzería Forno di Fango **6**

Riscomar & Biscuit & Co. **7**

Bars & clubs 🍸
Zarza **8**

200 metres
200 yards

Cajanuma is the trailhead for the demanding eight-hour hike to Lagunas del Compadre, a series of beautiful lakes set amid rock cliffs, camping is possible there (no services). Another trail from Cajanuma leads in one hour to a lookout with views over Loja. At San Francisco, the *guardianía* (ranger's station) is closed. You must contact park headquarters before visiting this area. They might send a ranger to accompany visitors.

This section of the park is a transition cloudforest at around 2200 m, very rich in birdlife. This is the best place to see podocarpus trees: a trail (four hours return) goes from the shelter to the trees. The Bombuscaro lowland section, also very rich in birdlife, has several trails leading to lovely swimming holes on the Bombuscaro River and waterfalls; Cascada La Poderosa is particularly nice.

Routes to the Peruvian border

Of all the crossings from Ecuador to Peru, by far the most efficient and relaxed is the scenic route from Loja to Piura via Macará (see below). Other routes are from Vilcabamba to La Balsa (see page 198), Huaquillas on the coast (page 223) and along the Río Napo in the Oriente (see page 272). There are smaller border crossings at Lalamor/Zapotillo, west of Macará, and Jimbura, southeast of Macará. The latter has immigration but no customs service. If arriving with a vehicle, cross at one of the other border posts.

Leaving Loja on the main paved highway going west, the airport at La Toma (1200 m) is reached after 35 km. La Toma is also called Catamayo, where there is lodging. At Catamayo, where you can catch the Loja–Macará–Piura bus, the Pan-American Highway divides: one branch runs west, the other south.

On the western road, at San Pedro de La Bendita, a road climbs to the much-venerated pilgrimage site of El Cisne, dominated by its large incongruous French-style Gothic church. Vendors and beggars fill the town and await visitors at festivals (see page 196). Continuing on the western route, Catacocha is spectacularly placed on a hilltop. Visit the Shiriculapo rock for the views. There are pre-Inca ruins around the town and the small archaeological **Museo Hermano Joaquín Liebana** ⓘ *T07-268 3201, 0800-1200, 1400-1800*. From Catacocha, the road runs south to the border at Macará.

Another route south from Catamayo to Macará is via **Gonzanamá**, a small city (basic *hostales*), famed for the weaving of beautiful *alforjas* (multi-purpose saddlebags), and **Cariamanga**, a regional centre with various hotels and services. From here the road twists along a ridge westwards to **Colaisaca**, before descending steeply through forests to **Utuana** with a nature reserve (www.fjocotoco.org) and **Sozoranga** (one hotel), then down to the rice paddies of **Macará**, on the border. There is a choice of accommodation here and good road connections to Piura in Peru.

Macará–La Tina The border is at the international bridge over the Río Macará, 2.5 km from town, taxi US$1.50. An integrated border complex was being built on the Ecuadorean side in 2017-2018. Until its completion, immigration, customs and other services are housed in temporary quarters. The border is open 24 hours. Formalities are straightforward, it is a much easier crossing than at Huaquillas. In Macará, at the park where taxis leave for the border, there are money changers dealing in soles, but no changers at the bridge. On the Peruvian side, minivans and cars run to Sullana but it is safer to take a bus from Loja or Macará directly to Piura. **Peruvian consulates in Loja** ⓘ *Zoilo Rodríguez 03-05, T07-258 7330, Mon-Fri 0900-1500*; in Macará ⓘ *Bolívar y 10 de Agosto, Barrio JM Cantón, T07-269 4030*, consuladoperu-macara@rree.gob.pe; see www.consulado.pe.

Listings Cuenca to the Peruvian border *map page 191.*

Tourist information

Saraguro

Oficina Municipal de Turismo
C 10 de Marzo y Av Loja, T07-220 0100 ext 155. Sun-Fri 0800-1300, 1400-1700.

Loja

iTur
José Antonio Eguiguren y Bolívar, Parque Central, T07-257 0407 ext 202. Mon-Fri 0800-1800, Sat 0800-1600, Sun 0900-1700.
Local information and map, monthly cultural agenda, English spoken, helpful.

Ministerio de Turismo
Sucre s/n y Quito, T07-257 2964, ext 2768. Mon-Fri 0815-1700.
Regional information for Loja, Zamora and El Oro.

Where to stay

Saraguro

$$ Achik Huasi
Intiñan s/n, La Luz, on a hillside above town, T07-220 0058, or through Fundación Kawsay, T07-220 0331.
Community-run *hostería* in a nice setting, lovely views from breakfast room, other meals on request, good service, private bath, hot water, parking, views, tours, taxi to centre US$1.

$ Saraguro
Loja 03-2 y A Castro, T07-220 0286.
Private or shared bath, hot water, no breakfast, attractive courtyard, family-run, basic, good value.

Loja

International chain hotels include **Howard Johnson** (www.hojo.com).

$$$$ Grand Victoria
B Valdivieso 06-50 y Eguiguren, ½ a block from the Parque Central, T07-258 3500, www.grandvictoriabh.com.
Rebuilt early 20th-century home with 2 patios, comfortable modern rooms and suites, restaurant, small pool, spa, gym, business centre, frigobar, safety box, parking, long-stay discounts.

$$$ Libertador
Colón 14-30 y Bolívar, T07-257 8278, www.hotellibertador.com.ec.
A very good hotel in the centre of town, comfortable rooms and suites, includes buffet breakfast, good restaurant (*menú ejecutivo* US$5), indoor pool (Tue-Fri 1500-2000, Sat-Sun 1000-1900, open to non-guests US$6), spa, parking.

$$$ Romar Royal
José A Eguiguren y 18 de Noviembre, T07-258 2888, www.romarroyalhotel.com.
Comfortable rooms and suites in modern hotel with safe deposit box, frigobar and coffee maker, buffet breakfast, cafeteria, indoor parking, good service, opened 2016.

$$-$ Real Colón
Colón 15-54 entre 18 de Noviembre y Sucre, T07-257 7826.
Modern centrally located multi-storey hotel, parking, decent value for this price range, breakfast included.

$ Londres
Sucre 07-51 y 10 de Agosto, T07-256 1936.
Economical hostel in a well-maintained old house, shared bath, hot water, no breakfast, basic, clean.

$ Vinarós
Sucre 11-30 y Azuay, T07-258 4015, hostalvinaros@hotmail.com.
Pleasant hostel with simple rooms, private bath, electric shower, no breakfast, good value.

Parque Nacional Podocarpus

At **Cajanuma**, there are cabins with beds for US$3, bring warm sleeping bag, stove and food. At **Bombuscaro** there are cabins with beds US$3 and an area for camping (note that it rains frequently).

Routes to the Peruvian border
Catamayo

$$ MarcJohn's
Isidro Ayora y 24 de Mayo, at the main park, T07-267 7631, granhotelmarcjohns@hotmail.com.
Modern multi-storey hotel, rooms with fan or a/c, includes breakfast from 0700 or set dinner, restaurant, attentive service.

$$ Rosal del Sol
A short walk from the city on the main road west of town, T07-267 6517.
Ranch-style building, comfortable rooms with fan, restaurant not always open, small pool, parking, includes airport transfer, welcoming owner.

$ Reina del Cisne
Isidro Ayora at the park, T07-267 7414.
Simple adequate rooms, hot water, cheaper with cold water, fan, no breakfast, pool, gym, parking, good value.

Macará

$ Bekalus
Valdivieso y 10 de Agosto, T07-269 4043.
Simple hostel, a/c, cheaper with fan, cold water, no breakfast.

$ El Conquistador
Bolívar y Abdón Calderón, T07-269 4057.
Comfortable hotel, some rooms are dark, request one with balcony, includes simple breakfast Mon-Sat, electric shower, a/c or fan.

Restaurants

Saraguro

Several restaurants around the main plaza serve economical meals.

$$$ ShamuiCo

10 de Marzo, next to the tourist information office, at the main park, T07-220 0590. Wed-Sun 1000-2100.

Popular tapas bar and gourmet European/Ecuadorean fusion cuisine, run by a Saraguro-born celebrity chef, Samuel Ortega, who trained in Spain. Good, creative dishes served in a nice setting with a patio, attentive service. An unexpected treat for Saraguro.

$ Tupay

10 de Marzo y Vivar, at the main park, T09-6971 4663. Sun-Fri 0800-2200.

Good set meals, also breakfast. Knowledgeable, helpful owners. Restaurant overlooks the main square.

Loja

There are a number of new restaurants along 24 de Mayo worth browsing.

$$$ Riscomar

Rocafuerte 09-00 y 24 de Mayo, T07-257 4965, www.riscomarloja.com. Tue-Sat 1000-1600, 1900-2200, Sun 1000-1600.

Extensive choice of good seafood and meat dishes. Pleasant atmosphere and very good service.

$$ Lecka

24 de Mayo 10-51 y Riofío, T07-256 3878, Facebook: LECKA Bistro Alemán. Mon-Fri 1700-2230.

Small quaint restaurant serving German specialities, very good food, friendly German/Ecuadorean owners. Recommended.

$$ Mama Lola

Av Salvador Bustamante Celi y Santa Rosa, T07-2614381. Mon-Sat 1200-2200, Sun 1200-1600.

Popular place for typical *lojano* specialities such as *cecina* and *cuy*. Portions are large; they also serve half portions.

$$-$ Pizzería Forno di Fango

24 de Mayo y Azuay, T07-258 2905. Tue-Sun 1200-2230.

Excellent wood-oven pizza, salads and lasagne. Forno di Fango is a Loja tradition, the pizza has a thick crust. Large portions, home delivery, good service and value.

$ Angelo's

18 de Noviembre y José Félix de Valdivieso, at Hotel Floy's. Mon-Sat 0700-1600, 1800-2100.

A choice of good-quality set meals and à la carte dishes, also breakfast, pleasant atmosphere, quiet (no TV), friendly service.

Cafés

Biscuit & Co.

24 de Mayo y Rocafuerte. Mon-Sat 1100-2100.

Nice café with good French-style sandwiches, snacks, sweets and coffee.

Flor de Azúcar

José A Eguiguren y 24 de Mayo. Mon-Fri 1100-2100.

Café and pastry shop with innovative savoury snacks and sweets, cappuccino and other drinks. Attractively decorated, pleasant atmosphere, good service.

Jugo Natural

José A Eguiguren14-20 y Bolívar, near the main park. Mon-Fri 0700-1900, Sat 0800-1800, Sun 0800-1400.

Small popular café with a choice of fresh fruit juices, snacks (try their *empanadas*), coffee, salads, vegetarian soups and lunches, cake, ice cream.

Bars

Zarza

Esmeraldas y Puerto Bolívar, esq El Valle, T07-257 1413, www.zarzabrewing.com. Mon-Wed 1600-2400, Thu-Sat 1600-0200.

Microbrewery with a range of beers. Also restaurant serving Tex-Mex food. Rock and other music, live bands every second Sat, US/Ecuadorean-run. Second location featuring burgers and a choice of kebabs on Av Salvador Bustamante y Segundo Cueva Celi, Ciudadela Zamora.

Festivals

Loja

Aug-Sep **Fiesta de la Virgen del Cisne**. Thousands of faithful accompany the statue of the Virgin in a 3-day 74-km pilgrimage from El Cisne to Loja cathedral, beginning 16 Aug. The image remains in Loja until 1 Nov when the return pilgrimage starts. Town is crowded Aug-Sep.

Nov **Festival Internacional de Artes Vivas** (www.festivaldeloja.com). An international arts festival in the last 2 weeks of Nov with events in theatres and in the streets.

What to do

Loja

Birdsexplore, *Lourdes 14-80 y Sucre, T07-258 2434, T09-8515 2239, www.exploraves.com*. Specializes in birdwatching tours throughout Ecuador, overnight trips to different types of forest, about US$150 pp per day. Pablo Andrade is a knowledgeable English-speaking guide.

Transport

Saraguro
Bus

To **Cuenca** US$5.40, 2½ hrs. To **Loja**, US$2.10, 1½ hrs. Check if your bus leaves from the plaza or the Panamericana.

Loja
Air

The airport is at La Toma (Catamayo), 35 km west (see Routes to the Peruvian border, page 192): taxi from airport to Catamayo

town US$2, to Loja shared taxi US$5 pp, to hire US$20 (cheaper from Loja) eg with Jaime González, T07-256 3714 or Paul Izquierdo, T07-256 3973; to Vilcabamba, US$40. There are 2 daily flights to **Quito** and 1 flight Mon-Fri to **Guayaquil** with **TAME** (24 de Mayo y E Ortega, T07-257 0248).

Bus

All buses leave from the Terminal Terrestre at Av Gran Colombia e Isidro Ayora, at the north of town, 10 mins by city bus from the centre; left luggage; US$0.10 terminal tax. Taxi from centre, US$1.50. To **Cuenca**, almost every hour (www.viajerosinternacional.com), 4 hrs, US$7.50. Van service with **Elite Tours**, Av Bracamoros 04-23 y Av Orillas del Zamora, Ciudadela las Palmas, T07-256 5064, elitetoursdelaustro@hotmail.com, and **Ecuavantur**, Pío Jaramillo y Amazonas, T07-260 7588, ecuavantur@outlook.com, US$12, 3 hrs; also to **Vilcabamba** and **Zamora**. **Machala**, many daily, 5-6 hrs, US$7 (3 routes, all scenic: via Piñas, partly unpaved and rough; via Balsas, paved; and via Alamor, for Puyango petrified forest). To Portovelo for **Zaruma** with TAC 1245, 1700; with **Piñas** 0600, 0915, 1500, US$6. **Quito**, Terminal Quitumbe, **Transportes Loja** regular 0800, 1230, 1730, US$17; *semi-cama/especial* 5 departures 1910-2200, US$21, 12 hrs; *bus cama* and their own terminal (Av Orellana y 9 de Octubre), US$40. **Guayaquil**, **Transportes Loja** 6 daily US$12 regular, US$14 *semi-cama/especial* 2200, 2400, 8 hrs. To **Huaquillas**, **Transportes Loja** 1230, 2315, US$7, 6 hrs direct. To **Zumba** (for Peru, paved to Palanda), 11 daily, US$10, 7 hrs; **Sur Oriente** at 0500 continues to La Balsa (border), US$12.25, 9 hrs; Unión **Cariamanga** at 0900, to make connections to Peru the same day. To **Catamayo** (for airport) every 15 mins 0630-1900, US$1.30, 1 hr. To **Macará**, see below. To **Piura (Peru)**, **Loja Internacional**, via Macará, at 0700 and 2300 daily, US$14, 8-9 hrs including border formalities. Also **Unión Cariamanga** at 2400. To **Zamora**, frequent service, 1½-2 hrs, US$3.

Parque Nacional Podocarpus
Bus and taxi

For **Cajanuma**, take a Vilcabamba-bound bus, get off at the turn-off, US$1, it is a pretty 8-km walk from there. Direct transport by taxi to Cajanuma, about US$10 (may not be feasible in the rainy season) or with a tour from Loja. You can arrange a pick-up later from the guard station. Pick-up from Vilcabamba, US$20. To the **San Francisco section**, take any bus between Loja and Zamora, make sure you alight by the Arcoiris

guardianía and not at Estación Científica San Francisco which is 10 km east. To the **lower section**: Bombuscaro is 6 km from Zamora, take a taxi US$6 to the entrance, then walk 1 km to the visitor centre.

Routes to the Peruvian border
Macará

Bus Transportes Loja and **Cariamanga** have frequent buses, daily from Macará to **Loja**; 5-6 hrs, US$7.40. Direct Loja–**Piura** buses can also be boarded in Macará, US$5 to Piura, 3 hrs. **Transportes Loja** also has service to **Quito**, US$19, 15 hrs, and **Guayaquil**, US$14, 8 hrs.

Vilcabamba to Peru

a beautiful, tranquil area popular with tourists and expats

★ **Vilcabamba** *Colour map 5, C3. See map, page 200.*

Once an isolated village, Vilcabamba (population around 5000) is today a colourful and eclectic cross between a resort town and a thriving expatriate community. It is popular with travellers and a good place to stop on route between Ecuador and Peru. The whole area is beautiful, with an agreeable climate. There are many nice places to stay and good restaurants. The area offers many great day-walks and longer treks, as well as ample opportunities for horse riding and cycling. As part of the **Ruta de la Cascarilla (Sendero Ecológico)** there are now several trails running along the river banks in the area. For information on this and on many other walking, mountain biking and motorcycling routes around town, go to www.vilcahike.com.

A number of lovely private nature reserves are situated east of Vilcabamba, towards Parque Nacional Podocarpus. Trekkers can continue on foot through orchid-clad cloudforests to the high *páramos* of Podocarpus. Artisans from all over Latin America sell their crafts in front of the school at weekends and there is an organic produce market by the bus terminal on Saturday morning, in addition to the regular Sunday market. **Craig's Book Exchange**① *in Yamburara, 1 km east of town, follow Diego Vaca de Vega*, has 2500 books in 12 languages and a small art gallery and pottery studio.

It's a 10-minute walk northeast of town **to Rumi Wilco** ① *US$2 valid for 3 visits*, a 40-ha private nature reserve with several signed trails. Many of the trees and shrubs are labelled with their scientific and common names. There are great views of town from the higher trails, and it is a very good place to go for a walk. Over 100 species of birds have been identified here. Volunteers are welcome. To get there, take Calle Agua de Hierro towards Calle La Paz and turn left, then follow the signs. **Sacred Sueños** ① *a 1½-hr walk in the hills above town, T09-8931 3698, www.sacredsuenos.wordpress.com*, is a grassroots permaculture community which accepts volunteers, two weeks' minimum commitment.

The Vilcabamba syndrome

At the time a tiny isolated village, Vilcabamba captured international attention in the 1960s when researchers announced that it was home to one of the oldest living populations in the world. It was said that people here often lived well over 100 years, some as old as 135.

Although doubt was subsequently cast on some of this data, there is still a high incidence of healthy, active elders in Vilcabamba. Such longevity and vitality has been ascribed to the area's famously healthy climate and excellent drinking water, but other factors must also be involved: perhaps physical activity, diet and lack of stress.

Attracted in part by Vilcabamba's reputation for nurturing a long and tranquil life, outsiders – both Ecuadoreans and foreigners – began to arrive; among the first was Doctor Johnny Lovewisdom, a California-born ascetic who arrived in 1969 to establish his Pristine Order of Paradisiacal Perfection.

Where he led, others followed, drawn by a succession of fashions: a hallucinogenic cactus extract called San Pedro (flashbacks associated with its use became known as the 'Vilcabamba syndrome'); UFO sightings; raw-food diets; a safe haven from the impending Mayan 'end of the world' in 2012; or simply a nice place to retire. With the rise in foreign residents, real-estate speculation has been rife and brokers' offices line the plaza alongside the cafés where the expats congregate. In a delightfully ironic reversal of roles, urban middle-class Ecuadoreans come to spend their holidays and watch the colourful gringos. Today's Vilcabamba syndrome has more to do with postmodern colonialism than hallucinogenic cactus juice.

Climbing **Mandango**, 'the sleeping woman' mountain is a scenic half-day walk. The signed access is along the highway, 250 m south of the bus terminal. Be careful on the higher sections when it is windy and enquire beforehand about public safety as there have been assaults. South of Vilcabamba, 45 km on the road to Zumba, is the 3500-ha bird- and orchid-rich **Reserva Tapichalaca** ① *T07-250 5212, www.fjocotoco.org, entry for day visits US$15*, with a lodge ($$$).

Border with Peru: La Balsa

Many daily buses run on the scenic road from Loja via Vilcabamba to **Zumba** (see Loja, Transport, page 196), 112 km south of Vilcabamba. It is a 1½-hour rough ride by *ranchera* (open-sided bus) from Zumba to the border at La Balsa; there is a control on the way, keep your passport to hand. La Balsa is just a few houses on either side of the international bridge over the Río Canchis; there are simple eateries, shops and money changers (no banks here or in Zumba). The closest decent accommodation is in **Sol de la Frontera** and there are basic places in **Namballe**. It is a relaxed border, Ecuadorean customs and immigration are officially open 24 hours. The Peruvian border post is open 0730-1430, 1600-1930; on entering Peru, visit immigration (see page 193 under Macará–La Tina for Peru's consulate in Loja). On the Peruvian side, cars run to Namballe and **San Ignacio** when full, two hours, from where there is transport to **Jaén**.

GOING FURTHER

The yellow forest

Mangahurco is a quiet end-of-the-road town nestled between two protected areas, Reserva Mangahurco in Ecuador and Parque Nacional Cerros de Amotape, across the border in Peru. This forgotten land in the southwest corner of the province of Loja comes to life once a year when thousands of visitors flock here to see a marvellous natural phenomenon, the flowering of the guayacanes.

Guayacán is a term used in the Neotropics to refer to many hardwood trees in four different genera. In the case of Ecuador, it refers to *Tabebuya chrysantha*, a deciduous tree of the dry tropical forest, 12 to 15 m high, found at elevations between 200 and 1200 m. Following the first rains of the year, usually in December or January (but sometimes as early as November and as late as March), the forest lights up with the beautiful yellow blossoms of the guayacán, which stand in contrast with giant green-barked ceibos (kapok). Around Mangahurco and Cazaderos, a village to the north, are 40,000 ha of forest, making it the best place to admire this phenomenon, but there are stands of guayacanes near Zapotillo, also in Loja, and in dry areas of the provinces of El Oro, Santa Elena and Manabí (here the trees may bloom as early as October). A week or two after the first rains the forest is at its prime and just a few days later the flowers start dropping, leading to another beautiful sight, a yellow carpet of flowers and the appearance of the first leaves.

Several driving circuits and trails allow visitors to admire the forest which is magnificent well beyond the guayacanes. Ravines provide welcome swimming holes and the opportunity to see water fowl such as rosiate spoonbills; there are also many endemic land birds. Among the mammals are howler monkeys and down river in Quebrada Cazaderos crocodiles may be seen.

In Mangahurco there are three hotels, Cabañas Mamilú, on a hill above town (T07-309 7970, 07-310 0293); Mangahurco, on the plaza (no sign, T07-310 0532); Guayacanes, on the plaza (T07-310 0520). None has hot water. There is also a basic hotel in Cazaderos (Marcial y Eva Rueda, T07-310 0303). Locals offer rooms in their homes and many people end up camping. There is no cell phone coverage in the area, but there are CNT rural wireless phones. Information from the parochial government, T07-310 0500.

Listings Vilcabamba to Peru *map page 200.*

Tourist information

Vilcabamba

iTur
Diego Vaca de Vega y Bolívar, on the corner of the main plaza, T07-264 0090. Daily 0800-1300, 1500-1800.
Has various pamphlets and local map of the town and surrounding attractions, helpful, Spanish only.

Where to stay

Vilcabamba

$$ Cabañas Río Yambala
Yamburara Alto, 4 km east of town (taxi US$3.50), T09-9106 2762, www.vilcabamba-hotel.com.
Cabins with cooking facilities in a beautiful tranquil setting on the shores of the Río Yambala, private or shared bath, hot water,

sauna, weekly and monthly rates available. No shops or restaurants nearby, bring food. Tours to Las Palmas private nature reserve. Family-run, English spoken.

$$-$ Izhcayluma
2 km south on road to Zumba, T07-302 5162, www.izhcayluma.com.
Popular inn with comfortable rooms and 2 types of cabin with terrace and hammocks. Very good buffet breakfast available, excellent restaurant with wonderful views, private or shared bath, also dorm US$9.50 pp, very nice grounds, pool, massage centre, yoga centre and lessons,

lively bar, billiards, ping-pong, parking, bird observation platform, walking trails, map and route descriptions, English and German spoken, helpful. Highly recommended.

$$-$ Las Margaritas
Sucre y Clodoveo Jaramillo, T07-272 1815, sole.toledo.cueva@gmail.com.
Small family-run hotel with comfortable well-furnished rooms, includes good breakfast, solar-heated water, parking, pool, garden.

$$-$ Le Rendez-Vous
Diego Vaca de Vega 06-43 y La Paz, T09-9219 1180, www.rendezvousecuador.com.

Vilcabamba

Where to stay 🛏
Cabañas Río Yambala **1**
Hostal Taranza **2**
Izhcayluma **3**
Las Margaritas **4**

Le Rendez-Vous **5**
Rumi Wilco **6**
Valle Sagrado **7**
Vilcabamba Camping
Inca Cara **8**

Restaurants 🍴
La Baguette **1**
Murano **2**
Natural Yogurt **3**
Pizzería La Casetta **4**

Shanta's **5**
Vilcabamba Juice
Factory **6**

Simple, comfortable rooms with terrace and hammocks around a lovely garden. Private or shared bath, pleasant atmosphere, attentive service, French and English spoken. Recommended.

$$-$ Rumi Wilco
10-min walk northeast of town, take C Agua de Hierro towards C La Paz and turn left, follow the signs from there, www.rumiwilco.com.
Private cabins or shared adobe houses in the Rumi Wilco reserve. Lovely setting on the shores of the river, very tranquil, laundry facilities, fully furnished kitchens, discounts for long stays and volunteers, camping US$5 pp, friendly Argentine owners, English spoken. Recommended.

$ Hostal Taranza
1 km from the main park on the way to Yamburara, T07-302 5144, on Facebook, erenatomauricio@gmail.com.
Brightly painted hostel, economical rooms, private or shared bath, cooking facilities, breakfast on request, terrace, hammocks, pool, jacuzzi, parking.

$ Valle Sagrado
Av de la Eterna Juventud y Luis Fernando de Vega, T07-272 1424, miriantaday@outlook.com.
Simple economical rooms around a large garden, private or shared bath, electric shower, laundry and cooking facilities, bar, no food, parking, family-run.

$ Vilcabamba Camping Inca Cara
1.5 km south of town, Barrio Izhcayluma, T09-6945 1518, http://vilcabambacamping. wixsite.com/vilcabambacamping.
On a hill with good views, hot shower, kitchen facilities, British/Belgian-run.

Border with Peru

$$-$ Emperador
Colón y Orellana, Zumba, T07-230 8063.
Rooms with private bath, a/c, no breakfast.

$ San Luis
12 de Febrero y Brasil, Zumba, T07-230 8017.
Rooms on top floor are nicer, private or shared bath, no breakfast, attentive service.

Restaurants

Vilcabamba
Around the Parque Central are many café/ bar/restaurants with pleasant outdoor seating; too many to list. All those below are recommended.

$$ Izhcayluma
At the hotel of the same name, see above. Daily 0800-2000.
Excellent international food, German specialities and several vegetarian options, served in a lovely open-air dining room with gorgeous views and attentive service.

$$ Murano
Sucre y Diego Vaca de Vega, T09-8592 7081. Tue-Sun 1200-2000.
Bright, nicely decorated with a couple of tables on the pavement, extensive choice of Mediterranean dishes, meat, seafood and vegetarian, choice of set meals 1200-1500 ($), pleasant service.

$$ Pizzería La Casetta
Sucre 13-13 y Clodoveo Jaramillo, T07-264 0339. Sun 1200-2000. Mon and Tue, Thu-Sat 1700-2100.
Intimate restaurant with a wood-fired oven, excellent calzone and thin-crust pizza.

$$ Shanta's
Off Av Loja, 700 m north of the main park, T09-5949 1012. Wed-Sat 1300-2100, Sun 1300-2000.

Tip...
Try the local microbrews, **Sol del Venado** (www.soldelvenado.com) and **Viqueña** (German style), which are served by many establishments.

Excellent pizza, trout, filet mignon and *cuy* (with advance notice). Also pasta and vegetarian options, good fruit juices and drinks. Nicely decorated rustic setting, pleasant atmosphere and attentive service.

$ Natural Yogurt
Bolívar y Diego Vaca de Vega.
Daily 0800-2100.
Very popular economical restaurant, breakfast, home-made yoghurt, a variety of savoury and sweet crêpes, pasta, Mexican dishes, hamburgers, vegetarian options.

$ Vilcabamba Juice Factory
Sucre y Luis Fernando de Vega,
Parque Central. Tue-Sat 0800-1600,
Sun 0800-1400.
Healthy juices, soups and salads, vegan food available, waffles at weekends, run by a naturopath, sells natural food products, very popular with expats.

Cafés

La Baguette
Diego Vaca de Vega y Av de la Eterna Juventud. Wed-Sat 0700-1700, Sun 0700-1400.
French bakery and café, great bread and pastries, crêpes, selection of breakfasts.

What to do

Vilcabamba
See Where to stay, above, for more options.

Cycling
El Chino, *Sucre y Diego Vaca de Vega, T09-8187 6347, chinobike@gmail.com.* Mountain-bike tours (US$25-35), including to the Cajanuma sector of Podocarpus National Park, rentals (US$2-3 per hr, US$10-15 per day) and repairs. Also see **La Tasca Tours**, below.

Horse riding
Prices per person for group of 2: 1 hr US$10, 2 hrs US$20, 4 hrs US$30, 6 hrs/full day with box lunch US$40.

Gavilán Tours, *Sucre y Diego Vaca de Vega, 09-8133 2806 (Gavin Moore), gavilanhorse@yahoo.com.* Run by a group of experienced horsemen.
H y CH, *Diego Vaca de Vega y Valle Sagrado, T09-9152 3118.* Alvaro León, good horses and saddles.
La Tasca Tours, *Sucre at the Plaza, T09-8556 1188, latascatours@yahoo.com.* Horse and bike tours with experienced guides, René and Jaime León. They also organize tours (Ruta del Café, Ruta de la Panela) with downhill cycling (Cerro Toledo in Podocarpus National Park south of Vilcabamba) and a 4-day camping tour combining car, cycling and walking (in Yacuri National Park).
Vilca Adventure, *Fernando de la Vega y La Paz, 3 blocks from the park, T07-264 0088, www.vilcaadventure.com.* Trips around Vilcabamba and Zamora, tours to archaeological sites near Valladolid, south of Vilcabamba, hiking in Podocarpus National Park, tubing, camping, full moon tours. Run by Danny Toledo.
Vilcabamba Exploring, *T09-9020 8824.* Julio Ocampo, horse-riding tours, also guided hike to waterfall.

Language courses
Spanish classes with Vilcabamba Spanish School, run by Marleen Couwenbergh (T09-9845 1692, www.vilcabambaspanishschool.com).

Transport

Vilcabamba
Bus and taxi
Loja to Vilcabamba, a nice 1½-hr bus ride; from Loja's Terminal Terrestre, **Vilcabambaturis** and **Tursur** buses alternate every 15 mins, 0545-2115 (0510-2015 Vilcabamba–Loja), US$1.25, 1½ hr. **Taxiruta Loja** (shared taxis) from Manuel José Aguirre y Mercadillo, 0530-1800, US$2, 1 hr; taxi,

US$20. To **Loja**, buses and shared taxis leave from the small terminal behind the market. Taxi from Vilcabamba to Loja (Catamayo) airport US$35-40. For **Parque Nacional Podocarpus**, taxis charge US$20 each way (plus US$10/hr waiting time), taking you right to the trailhead at Cajanuma. To **Cuenca** vans at 0800 from Hostería Izhcayluma, US$15 for guests, US$16 for others, 5 hrs, Cuenca stop at Hostal La Cigale (no discount for their guests). To **Zumba** buses originating in Loja pass Vilcabamba about 1 hr after departure and stop along the highway in front of the market (1st around 0600 continues to La Balsa, next 1000), US$8.75, 6 hrs. To Catamayo airport, taxi US$40, 1½ hrs. To **Quito** (Quitumbe) **Transportes Loja** (tickets sold for this and other routes at Movistar office, Av de la Eterna Juventud y Clodoveo Jaramillo) at 1900, with a stop in Loja, US$22, 13-14 hrs.

Border with Peru
Bus

Terminal Terrestre in Zumba, 1 km south of the centre. From Zumba to **La Balsa**, *rancheras* at 0800, 1430 and 1730, US$2.25, 1½-2 hrs. From La Balsa to Zumba at 1200, 1730 and 1900. Taxi Zumba–La Balsa, US$30. From La Balsa to **Loja** (via Vilcabamba), **Sur Oriente** at 1000, US$12.25, 9 hrs; to **Vilcabamba** US$11, 8 hrs. From Zumba to **Loja**, see Loja Transport, above. In Zumba, petrol is sold 0700-1700. In Peru, shared taxi La Balsa–San Ignacio, US$4.66 pp.

Guayaquil & south to Peru

Ecuador's metropolis

Guayaquil, the largest and most dynamic industrial and commercial centre in the country, is also Ecuador's chief port. The city's influence extends all along the coast and beyond.

This 'working Ecuador' is more frequently seen by business visitors than tourists, but Guayaquil has its attractions. Trips to the Galápagos can be organized from here and the city is a logical starting point for travels north along the coast and south to Peru. The coastal plains nearby are the agro-industrial heartland of Ecuador. Rice, sugar, coffee, African palm, mango and other fruit, cacao and shrimp are produced in these hot and humid lowlands and processed or exported through Guayaquil.

To the south of the city, thriving banana plantations are the economic mainstay of the coastal area bordering the east flank of the Gulf of Guayaquil. Machala is the main centre here and nearby Puerto Bolívar is the port through which the oro verde (green gold) is shipped out to the world. Mangroves and islands characterize the coast leading south to Huaquillas, the main coastal border crossing to Peru. Inland from Machala, in the uplands of El Oro, is one of the best hidden treasures of Ecuador – the colonial mining town of Zaruma.

Best for
Dining ▪ Nature reserves ▪ Museums ▪ Nightlife

Footprint
picks

★ **Malecón 2000 and Cerro Santa Ana**, page 209

No visit to Guayaquil is complete without a stroll along its breezy riverside promenade. Don't miss the views from Cerro Santa Ana.

★ **MAAC Museum**, page 209

The Museo Antropológico y de Arte Contemporáneo is the place to learn about 10,000 years of Ecuadorean culture, as well as the country's modern art.

★ **Parque Histórico**, page 211

A pocket of 19th-century Guayaquil in an urban park across the river.

★ **Isla Santay**, page 213

Ride a bicycle through this protected wetland and admire its rich birdlife and flora.

★ **Reserva Ecológica Manglares-Churute**, page 213

Mangroves and dry tropical forest are the highlights of this nature reserve, not far from Guayaquil.

★ **Zaruma**, page 222

A colonial gem, off the beaten path in the beautiful uplands of El Oro.

Guayaquil

Guayaquil, Ecuador's largest city (population 2,700,000), lies on the west bank of the chocolate-brown Río Guayas, some 56 km from its outflow into the Gulf of Guayaquil. Industrial expansion and migration continually fuel the city's growth. The city has always been an intense political rival to Quito. Guayaquileños are certainly more lively, colourful and open than their Quito counterparts. Since 2000, Guayaquil has cleaned up and 'renewed' some of its most frequented downtown areas. It boasts modern airport (with a new one planned west of the city) and bus terminals, and the Metrovía transit system. In and around the city are various parks which provide its residents and visitors with much-needed relief from the heat.

Essential Guayaquil

Finding your feet

José Joaquín de Olmedo international airport is 15 minutes' drive north of the city centre. Not far from the airport is the Terminal Terrestre long-distance bus station. Opposite this is Terminal Río Daule, an important transfer station on the Metrovía rapid transit system. See also Transport, page 220.

Getting around

A number of hotels are centrally located in the downtown core, along the west bank of the Río Guayas, where you can get around on foot. The city's suburbs sprawl to the north and south of the centre, with middle-class neighbourhoods and some very upscale areas in the north, where some elegant hotels and restaurants are located, and poorer working-class neighbourhoods and slums to the south. Road tunnels under Cerro Santa Ana link the northern suburbs to downtown. Outside downtown, addresses are hard to find; ask for a nearby landmark to help orient your driver.

When to go

From May to December the climate is dry with often overcast days but pleasantly cool nights, whereas the

Best places to stay
Las Peñas, page 214
El Manso, page 215
Macaw, page 215
Hotel del Parque, page 215

hot rainy season from January to April can be oppressively humid.

Safety

The Malecón 2000, parts of Avenida 9 de Octubre, Las Peñas and Malecón del Estero Salado are heavily patrolled and reported safe. The rest of the city requires precautions. Do not go anywhere with valuables. Parque Centenario is also patrolled, but the area around it requires caution. 'Express kidnappings' are of particular concern in Guayaquil; do not take a taxi outside the north end of the Malecón 2000 near the MAAC museum, walk south along the Malecón as far as the Hotel Ramada, where there is a taxi stand; whenever possible, call for a radio taxi.

Best restaurants
Lo Nuestro, page 216
La Parrilla del Ñato, page 216
La Canoa, page 216
California, page 217

Weather Guayaquil

January	February	March	April	May	June
31°C 24°C 160mm	30°C 24°C 257mm	31°C 24°C 252mm	31°C 24°C 113mm	30°C 23°C 65mm	29°C 22°C 69mm

July	August	September	October	November	December
28°C 21°C 111mm	29°C 20°C 135mm	29°C 21°C 84mm	29°C 21°C 75mm	30°C 22°C 93mm	31°C 23°C 116mm

★ Malecón 2000
Daily 0700-2400.

The riverfront along this avenue is an attractive promenade, known as Malecón 2000, where visitors and locals can enjoy the fresh river breeze and take in the views. There are gardens, fountains, childrens' playgrounds, monuments, *miradores* and an electric vehicle for the disabled (daily 1000-2000, US$2). You can dine at upmarket restaurants, cafés and food courts.

At the south end is the Mercado Artesanal, with terraced gardens outside and, next to it, the **Palacio de Cristal** (prefabricated by Eiffel 1905-1907), originally a market and now a gallery housing temporary exhibits and events. Moving north is the Patio de Comida and then the Centro Comercial which stretches as far as Calle Colón. Most of the outlets are below the street and for those on a riverside walk there are lots of steps up and down. In the central part is a Moorish clocktower, the old Yacht Club and La Rotonda, a monument marking the meeting between independence leaders Simón Bolívar and José de San Martín in 1822.

At the north end of the Malecón, at end of Calle Loja, is **La Perla** ⓘ *www.laperla deguayaquil.com, Sun-Thu 1000-2200, Fri and Sat 1000-2400, general ticket Mon-Fri US$3.50, Sat-Sun US$5 (express with no queue US$7/10),* a 57-m-high ferris wheel – the largest in Latin America. Rides last 15 minutes, with six people per cabin; a good time to go is around 1750 when the city lights are coming on; it's busiest after 1900. Nearby is a 3D, large-screen cinema and, downstairs, the **Museo Miniatura** ⓘ *Tue-Sun 0900-1330, 1600-2000, US$3,* with miniature historical exhibits. Lastly, the **Centro Cultural Simón Bolívar,** better known as ★ **MAAC,** houses the **Museo Antropológico y de Arte Contemporáneo** ⓘ *T04-230 9400, Mon-Fri 0830-1630, Sat-Sun 0900-1700, free,* with excellent collections of ceramics and gold objects from coastal cultures and an extensive modern art collection.

Las Peñas
North of the Malecón 2000 is the old district of Las Peñas, the last picturesque vestige of colonial Guayaquil with its brightly painted wooden houses and narrow, cobbled main street (Numa Pompilio Llona). It is an attractive place for a walk to ★ **Cerro Santa Ana**, which offers great views of the city and the mighty Guayas. It has a bohemian feel, with bars and restaurants. A large open-air exhibition of paintings and sculpture is held here during the **Fiestas Julianas** (24-25 July). North of La Peñas is **Puerto Santa Ana**, with a luxury hotel, upmarket apartments, a promenade and **three museums**: to the romantic singer Julio Jaramillo, to beer in the old brewery, and to the Barcelona and Emelec football clubs (all open Wednesday-Saturday 1000-1300, 1400-1700, Sunday 1000-1500, free).

Cathedral and around
By the pleasant, shady **Parque Seminario** (or Bolívar because of the equestrian statue) stands the **cathedral** (Chimborazo y 10 de Agosto), in Gothic style, inaugurated in the 1950s. In the park are many iguanas and it is popularly referred to as Parque de las Iguanas. The nearby **Museo Municipal** ⓘ *in the Biblioteca Municipal, Sucre y Chile, Tue-Fri 0830-1630, Sat and Sun 1000-1400, free,* has paintings, gold and archaeological collections, shrunken heads, a section on the history of Guayaquil and a good newspaper library.

Between the Parque Seminario and the Malecón is the **Museo Nahim Isaías** ① *Pichincha y Clemente Ballén, T04-232 4182, temporarily closed in late 2017, free*, a colonial art museum with a permanent religious art collection and temporary exhibits.

Avenida 9 de Octubre

Avenida 9 de Octubre, the city's main artery with banks, ATMs, airline offices and large shops, runs west from the Malecón. Halfway along it is **Parque Centenario** with a towering monument to the liberation of the city erected in 1920. Overlooking the park is the **Casa de la Cultura** ① *9 de Octubre 1200 y P Moncayo, T04-230 0500, Mon-Fri 0900-1800, Sat 0900-1500, free*, which holds concerts, plays, films and exhibitions.

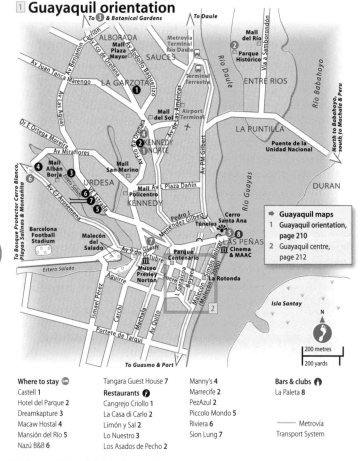

Guayaquil orientation

Where to stay 🛏
Castell 1
Hotel del Parque 2
Dreamkapture 3
Macaw Hostal 4
Mansión del Río 5
Nazú B&B 6

Tangara Guest House 7

Restaurants 🍴
Cangrejo Criollo 1
La Casa di Carlo 2
Limón y Sal 2
Lo Nuestro 3
Los Asados de Pecho 2

Manny's 4
Marrecife 2
PezAzul 2
Piccolo Mondo 5
Riviera 6
Sion Lung 7

Bars & clubs 🍸
La Paleta 8

––––– Metrovía
Transport System

BACKGROUND

Guayaquil

Santiago de Guayaquil had a complicated start. It was founded as Santiago de Quito (sic) in 1534 by Diego de Almagro up in the Sierra, by the chilly shores of Laguna de Colta. It was subsequently moved four times until, in 1547, it found its definitive location near the native settlement of Chief Guayaquile. Colonial Guayaquil with its bamboo and wood houses was repeatedly sacked and burnt by pirates. Throughout the colonial and republican periods, Guayaquil always retained its strategic importance as Ecuador's main port. The current Puerto Marítimo, opened in 1964, handles three-quarters of the country's imports and almost half of its exports. It has been a frequent bone of contention between costeños and serranos that Guayaquil is not given better recognition of its importance in the form of greater local authority and more central government funds. The city's mayor, Jaime Nebot, currently in his third term of office, is a leading national figure who has at times challenged the authority of the Quito government.

West of Parque Centenario, the **Museo Presley Norton** ⓘ *Av 9 de Octubre y Carchi, T04-229 3423, Tue-Fri 0830-1630, Sat and Sun 1000-1600, free*, has an interesting collection of coastal archaeology in a beautifully restored house. At the west end of 9 de Octubre are **Plaza Baquerizo Moreno** and the **Malecón del Estero Salado**, another pleasant waterfront promenade along a brackish estuary. It has various monuments, eateries specializing in seafood, and rowing boats and pedal-boats for hire. North of here, on the east side of the estuary, is the Urdesa residential neighbourhood, which has lots of restaurants of all types.

Around the city

parks and gardens

★ Parque Histórico Guayaquil
Vía Samborondón, near Entreríos, T04-283 2958, Wed-Sun 0900-1600, free; CISA buses to Samborondón leave from the Terminal Terrestre every 20 mins, US$0.25.

The park has several parts: a garden with flowers, vegetables, herbs and fruiting trees; a section with typical houses of the different classes and a chocolate finca from the end of the 19th century; and a natural area mostly in and around the river mangroves, with flora and fauna (a zoo in other words) with signs in Spanish, English, Quichua and braille. There is also an urban section with old wooden architecture, which adjoins the Casa Julián restaurant of the Hotel del Parque (see page 215), and a jetty into the river. At the entrance is a map and toilets. It's a pleasant place for a family outing; go in the morning when there are fewer people and the animals are not sleeping.

Botanical Gardens
Northwest of the city on Av Francisco de Orellana, in Ciudadela Las Orquídeas (bus line 63), T04-289 9689, daily 0800-1600, US$3, guiding service for up to 5 visitors US$10 (English available).

There are over 300 plant species, including exhibitions of some 50 species of Ecuadorean orchids (most flower August to December). There are plants from other parts of the world, too. Birds and butterflies can be seen and one area emulates the Amazon rainforest and has monkeys and other animals.

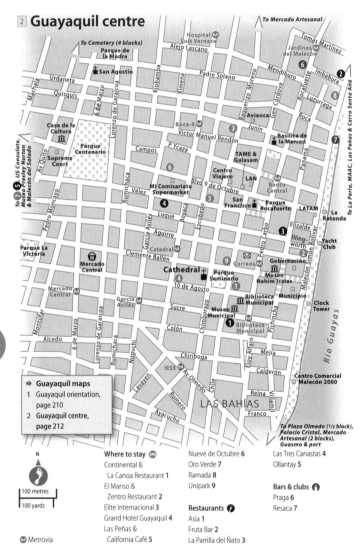

2 Guayaquil centre

Where to stay			
Continental &		Nueve de Octubre 6	Las Tres Canastas 4
La Canoa Restaurant 1		Oro Verde 7	Ollantay 5
El Manso &		Ramada 8	
Zentro Restaurant 2		Unipark 9	**Bars & clubs**
Elite Internacional 3			Praga 6
Grand Hotel Guayaquil 4		**Restaurants**	Resaca 7
Las Peñas &		Asia 1	
California Café 5		Fruta Bar 2	
		La Parrilla del Ñato 3	

Guayaquil maps
1 Guayaquil orientation, page 210
2 Guayaquil centre, page 212

100 metres
100 yards

Metrovía

Bosque Protector Cerro Blanco

Vía a la Costa, Km 16, T09-8622 5077 (Spanish), fundacionprobosque@ymail.com, http:// bosquecerroblanco.org, US$4, additional guiding fee US$12-20 depending on trails visited, camping US$28 for group of 10.

The reserve, run by **Fundación Pro-Bosque**, is set in tropical dry forest with an impressive variety of birds (over 200 species), many reptiles and with sightings of monkeys and other mammals. Unfortunately, it is getting harder to see the animals due to human encroachment in the area. Reservations are required during weekdays, for groups larger than eight at weekends, and for birders wishing to arrive before or stay after normal opening hours (0800-1600). Take a **CLP** bus from the Terminal Terrestre, a **Cooperativa Chongón** bus from Antepara y 10 de Agosto (hourly) or a taxi (US$8-10). On the other side of the road, at Km 18, is **Puerto Hondo**, where there are **canoe trips** through the mangroves (daily 0800-1600, T09-9140 0186, US$15 for a group of up to seven, one hour), and also kayak hire (US$4) and swimming.

★ Area Nacional de Recreación Isla Santay

www.islasantay.info, open 0600-1800, bicycle rental US$4 for 3 hrs.

On the Río Guayas, opposite downtown Guayaquil, is this Ramsar wetland rich in fauna and flora. Two pedestrian drawbridges link the island with the mainland, one from Calle El Oro, south of Malecón 2000 (open 0600-2100, but last permitted entry 1700 and return to the city 1800), the second from the city of Durán. A boardwalk/cycle path joins the two and makes a circuit of the island. By the local village, **San Jacinto**, 2.8 km from the Guayaquil bridge and 5.3 km from the Durán bridge, is the **Eco Aldea**, with a crocodile breeding centre (open 0600-1700), a cabin and restaurant run by the local community (meals cost US$2.50-8). Boat services operate to the Eco Aldea from **Cooperativa las Palmeras** (T09-8654 7034) or the **National Parks Service** (T04-268 3995, ext 3542, or T09-8709 1469), US$5 per person return, on Saturday and Sunday and sometimes Friday at 1000; they depart every 1½ hours from the Yacht Club. **Note** In October 2017 the El Oro bridge was damaged when hit by a boat; it was not known when it would reopen. Also, some parts of the boardwalk were closed for repair.

★ Reserva Ecológica Manglares Churute

Free entry, camping and use of basic cabins; for information and reservations contact the Dirección Provincial del Ambiente in Guayas, T04-232 0391, www.ambiente.gob.ec. Buses (CIFA, Ecuatoriano Pullman, 16 de Junio) leave the Terminal Terrestre every 30 mins, going to Naranjal or Machala; ask to be let off at the Churute information centre.

Heading east then south from Guayaquil, 22 km beyond the main crossroads at Km 49 on the road to Machala, lies this rich natural area with five different ecosystems created to preserve mangroves in the Gulf of Guayaquil and forests of the Cordillera Churute. Many waterbirds, monkeys, dolphins and other wildlife can be seen. There are five trails through the tropical forest from 300 m to 2.6 km, including to **Laguna Canclón** (1 km), a large lake where ducks nest. There are also two boat trips, of one and three hours, on the Ríos Ulpiano and Churute (US$20-40 depending on group size).

Tourist information

Empresa Pública Municipal de Turismo
C 10 de Agosto y Malecón, in the Municipio,
1st floor, T04-259 4800. Mon-Fri 0930-1700,
www.guayaquilesmidestino.com (in Spanish
and English).
Has information about the city. There is also an
information booth at the Terminal Terrestre.

Immigration
Av Benjamín Rosales s/n, opposite the bus
terminal, T04-213 0010.

Ministerio de Turismo
Subsecretaría del Litoral, Av Francisco de
Orellana y Justino Cornejo, Edif Gobierno
del Litoral, 8th floor and counter on the
ground floor, Ciudadela Kennedy, T04-206
8501, www.turismo.gob.ec and www.
ecuador.travel. Mon-Fri 0900-1700.
Information about the coastal provinces of
Ecuador and whale-watching regulations.

Where to stay

Guayaquil has some of the best top-class
accommodation in Ecuador.

For major chain hotels see: www.hilton.
com (**Hilton Colón**, excellent), www.
oroverdehotels.com (**Oro Verde**, **Unipark**
and **Hotel del Parque** – see below),
www.marriott.com, www.sheraton.com and www.
sonesta.com/guayaquil and www.
wyndhamhotels.com (Wyndham Guayaquil,
excellent location in Puerto Santa Ana and
views of the river and Wyndham Garden/
Howard Johnson by Mall del Sol).
There are several mid-range (**$$**) hotels on
Junín between Gen Córdova and Escobedo
but decent economy places are few and
far between; the latter are concentrated
around Parque Centenario, not a safe area at
any time and travellers have been mugged.

Many hotels here are used by short-stay
couples, and they are noisy and run-down.

$$$$ Mansión del Río
Numa Pompilio Llona 120, Las Peñas, T04-
256 6044, www.mansiondelrio-ec.com.
Elegant boutique hotel in a 1926 mansion,
period European style, river view, buffet
breakfast, airport transfers, 10 mins from
city centre.

$$$ Continental
Chile 512 y 10 de Agosto, on
Parque Seminario, T04-232 9270,
www.hotelcontinental.com.ec.
Rooms are plain but comfortable, with
a view of the park, iguanas and the
cathedral. Central, helpful staff, good
buffet breakfast in **La Canoa** (see page 216),
also has **El Fortín** international restaurant
and **El Astillero** bar.

$$$ Grand Hotel Guayaquil
Boyacá 1615 y Clemente Ballén, T04-232
9690, www.grandhotelguayaquil.com.
A traditional Guayaquil hotel in a modern
building, central, includes buffet breakfast,
good restaurants, pool, gym and sauna.

$$$ Las Peñas
Escobedo 1215 y Vélez, T04-232 3374,
www.hlpgye.ec.
Nice hotel in a refurbished part of
downtown, ample modern rooms, cafetería,
a/c, quiet despite being in the centre of
town, good value. Recommended.

$$$ Nazú B&B
Ciudadela La Cogra, Manzana 1, Villa 2, off
Av Carlos Julio Arosemena Km 3.5 (taxi from
bus terminal or airport US$6-8, Metrovía
'28 de Mayo' stop, best without luggage),
T04-462 2523, www.nazuhouse.com.
Lovely suburban guesthouse with a variety
of rooms and suites with a/c, includes dinner

and breakfast, pool, parking, terrace with views of the city, English and German spoken.

$$$ Ramada
Malecón 606 e Imbabura, T04-256 5555, www.hotelramada.com.
Excellent location right on the Malecón, rooms facing the river are more expensive, includes buffet breakfast, restaurant, a/c, pool, spa.

$$$-$ El Manso
Malecón 1406 y Aguirre, upstairs, T04-252 6644, http://manso.ec.
Nicely refurbished hostel in a great location opposite the Malecón. Rooms vary from fancy with a/c, private bath and breakfast (**$$$**), to simpler with shared bath and fan (**$$**), and 3- to 4-bed dorms with lockers (US$15 pp); interior rooms are quieter but have no river view. English spoken. See **Zentro** restaurant, page 217. Also arranges Urban Ecotourism Packages to fishing communities in the mangroves (US$49 pp) and the Afro-Ecuadorean community of Isla Trinitaria (US$27 pp).

$$ Elite Internacional
Baquerizo Moreno 902 y Junín, T04-256 5385/09-9477 8901, Facebook: hoteleliteinternacional.
Completely refurbished old downtown hotel, comfortable rooms with a/c and hot water, parking.

$$ Tangara Guest House
Manuela Sáenz y O'Leary, Manzana F, Villa 1, Ciudadela Bolivariana, T04-228 4445, www.tangara-ecuador.com.
Comfortable hotel in a pleassant area by the university and near the Estero Salado, a/c, fridge, low-season discounts, convenient for airport and bus terminal, also runs nationwide tours, including community tourism.

$$-$ Dreamkapture
Juan Sixto Bernal, Alborada Etapa 12, mz 2 villa 21, T04-227 1938, www.dreamkapture.com.

Hostel with private rooms and shared and single-sex dorms (US$9.50-11 pp), some with bath and a/c, fans, breakfast included, kitchen, garden and plunge pool. Also has travel agency for mainland and Galápagos tours, www.dreamkapturetravel.com. US$5 taxi ride from bus and airport terminals and centre.

$ Nueve de Octubre
9 de Octubre 736 y García Avilés, T04-256 4222.
Busy 8-storey hotel in a central location. Simple functional rooms, those facing the street are larger but noisy, restaurant, private bath, cold water, a/c, parking extra. Fills early and does not accept reservations. Good value.

Around Mall del Sol

$$$ Castell
Av Miguel H Alcivar y Ulloa, by Parque Japonés, Kennedy Norte, T04-268 0190, www.hotelcastell.com.
Modern comfortable hotel in a quiet location in the north of the city, includes buffet breakfast, restaurant (on Sat-Sun open for breakfast only), a/c, safe in room, convenient for the airport (taxi US$3-4, US$2.50 minimum elsewhere). Check for weekend promotions.

$$$ Macaw Hostal
Víctor Hugo Sicouret, Cdla Guayaquil, Mz 11 V 8, north of the centre, T04-228 1842, www.hostalmacaw.com.
Good comfortable a/c rooms, family-style service, breakfast included, evening meal on request, luggage store, laundry service, book exchange, very helpful; convenient for airport, Mall del Sol and restaurants. Recommended. Also owns Galanet Galápagos tour operator, www.galapagosnet.com (general manager Fanny Paltán).

Around the city

$$$$ Hotel del Parque
Av Río Esmeraldas, in the Parque Histórico, member of the Oro Verde group, T04-500 0111, www.hoteldelparquehistorico.com.

Excellent hotel in a historic building moved here from the city centre, 6 types of room, very spacious, 1 specifically for disabled guests, but all have wide doors, welcome lemonade and chocolate bar, fridge, safe and umbrella in room, big bathrooms, mixture of antique and modern fittings, lounge/business centre, spa, tours arranged. There are 2 courtyards separated by a chapel, one with orchids and saman trees, where breakfast is served, the other with fountains. Superb in every respect.

Restaurants

The main areas for restaurants are the centre, with many in the larger hotels around Urdesa, and the residential and commercial neighbourhoods to the north.

In the area around the Macaw Hostal/Hilton Colón/Mall del Sol, there are several places to eat, as well as the Mall's own busy *patio de comida*:

$$$ Cangrejo Criollo
Av Principal de La Garzota, T04-262 9006, Facebook: elunicocangrejocriollo. Tue-Fri from 1000, Sat-Mon from 1100, closes 0100 on Fri, 2000 on Sun.
Excellent, varied seafood menu.

$$$ Lo Nuestro
VE Estrada 903 e Higueras, Urdesa, T04-462 7233, http://lonuestro.com.ec. Daily 1200-2300.
Luxury restaurant with typical coastal cooking, good seafood platters and stuffed crabs, colonial decor, live music Fri-Sun.

$$$ Manny's
Av Miraflores 112 y C Primera, Miraflores, T04-463 2872; also on VE Estrada 920, Urdesa, and Av CL Plaza Dañín 320, Kennedy, Facebook: CangrejalMannys. Daily 1000-2400.
Well-known crab house with specialities such as *cangrejo al ajillo* (crab in garlic butter), good quality and value.

$$$ Riviera
VE Estrada 707 y Ficus, Urdesa, T04-460 2628, and in Samborondón, Av Río Esmeraldas y C Vehicular, www.rivieraecuador.com. Daily 1230-2330.
Extensive Italian menu, good pasta, antipasto, salads, bright surroundings, good service.

$$$-$$ La Parrilla del Ñato
VE Estrada 1219 y Laureles in Urdesa; Av Francisco de Orellana opposite the Hilton Colón; Luque y Pichincha downtown; and several other locations, www. parilladelnato.com. Daily 1200-2300.
Large variety of dishes, salad bar, also pizza by the metre, good quality, generous portions. Try the *parrillada de mariscos*, available only at the Urdesa and Kennedy locations. Recommended.

$$$-$$ Piccolo Mondo
Bálsamos 504 y las Monjas, Urdesa, T04-238 7079, http://latrattoria.com.ec. Mon-Sat 1230-2330, Sun 1230-2200.
Very exclusive Italian restaurant since 1980, the best in food and surroundings, good antipasto.

$$$-$$ Sion Lung
VE Estrada 621 y Ficus, Urdesa, T04-454 9319, also Mz 71, Solar 1 esq Peatonal, Entre Ríos, T04-283 6159, www.sionlung.com. Daily 1200-2200.
Cantonese food, a variety of rice (*chaulafán*) and noodle (*tallarín*) dishes.

$$ Asia
Sucre 321 y Chile, downtown, T04-232 8088, also 9 de Octubre y Rumichaca and VE Estrada 508 y Las Monjas, Urdesa (there are other Chinese places in this block), http:// salonasia.ec. Daily 1100-2100 at Sucre, later at other branches.
Chinese food, large portions, popular.

$$ La Canoa
Hotel Continental, see Where to stay, above. Open 24 hrs.

ON THE ROAD

Dining out in Guayaquil

Dining out can be the highlight of a visit to Guayaquil. The city's unique culinary traditions go back to the days when typical foods were sold from wooden carts along the Malecón. They made up in flavour for whatever they may have lacked in hygiene but the carts were eventually banned by municipal authorities. Undeterred, their owners found simple locales for their establishments which became known as *huecas*, the quintessential hole-in-the-wall eateries. *Huecas* have always been popular but in recent years they have even become fashionable and attract diners from all walks of life.

Given the city's coastal location, it is not surprising that many typical dishes offered by the *huecas* feature seafood. These include *encebollado*, a tasty fish and *yuca* chowder served with pickled onions, and of course the ubiquitous *ceviche*. Another speciality is *carne asada con arroz, menestra y patacones* (grilled meat with rice, beans and fried bananas), also a perennial favourite.

Drawing on the same local gastronomic traditions as the *huecas*, but in an entirely different price category, many upmarket Guayaquil restaurants offer their delicacies in elegant air-conditioned surroundings. Some are located in the city's best hotels while others have become traditions in their own right. They are generally worth the price, perhaps for a special last night out on the town.

Juice bars are understandably popular in Guayaquil's warm climate and often serve typical snacks like *empanadas de verde* (a fried ground plantain shell filled with cheese, meat or shrimp) as well as a wide variety of refreshing fresh fruit juices.

For additional details about Guayaquil's gastronomy and dining, see www. guayaquilesmidestino.com/es/gastronomia.

Rare regional dishes, with different specials during the week, a Guayaquil tradition.

$$-$ Zentro
Malecón 1406 y Aguirre, at the Hotel Manso. Mon-Fri 1230-2200, Sat 1830-2200.
Small dining area serving innovative set lunches with vegetarian options, à la carte dishes and snacks (*agroecológico*). One table on the balcony, others inside, some with river view, good value.

$ Ollantay
Tungurahua 508 y 9 de Octubre, near Estero Salado west of downtown, T04-236 1436, Facebook: c.i.ollantay. Mon-Sat 0700-2000.
Good vegetarian and vegan food. Also runs courses, dance, yoga and has exhibitions.

California
Escobedo 1215 y Vélez, beside and part of Hotel Las Peñas. Mon-Fri 0700-2030.
Good and popular for breakfast, snacks, lunch, drinks, sweets and à la carte meals.

Fruta Bar
Malecón e Imbabura, VE Estrada 608 y Monjas, Urdesa.
Excellent fruit juices and snacks, unusual African decor, good music.

Sweet & Coffee Co
9 de Octubre 111, www.sweetandcoffee.com. Mon-Thu 0730-2200, Fri 0730-2300, Sat 0900-2300, Sun 1000-2200. Also on Malecón and at Centro de Convenciones.
Good Ecuadorean coffees, cakes and desserts, a/c, part of the nationwide chain.

Las Tres Canastas
*Vélez y García Avilés, Ballén y Carbo,
and several other locations.*
Breakfast, snacks, safe fruit juices
and smoothies.

Around Mall del Sol
In the area around the **Macaw Hostal/
Hilton Colón/Mall del Sol**, there are several
places to eat, as well as the mall's own busy
patio de comida:

$$ La Casa di Carlo
*E Soro Lenti, Cdla Guayaquil Norte, Mz 19,
villa 9, T04-228 2009, www.lacasadicarlo.
com. Mon-Fri 1200-1600, 1900-2300,
Sun 1200-1600, Sat closed.*
Italian, serving pizza, pasta and seafood.

$$ Los Asados de Pecho
*Víctor Hugo Sicouret y Emma Ortiz,
Cdla Guayaquil, T04-505 0134.*
Pork, chicken or guinea pig on the
parrilla, with rice, *menestra* and local
side dishes, a/c, take away available,
popular Sun lunchtime.

$$ Marrecife
*AV Miguel H Alcívar y Av F de Orellana,
Cdla Guayaquil, Mz 03 Solar 08,
T04-600 7570, www.marrecife.com.*
Seafood specialities, very popular
Sun lunchtime.

$$-$ Limón y Sal
*Av Emma Ortiz y Calle 13, Facebook:
limonysalcevicheria. Tue-Sun 0830-1500.*
Good for ceviche.

$$-$ Pez Azul
*Víctor Hugo Sicouret, 1 block from Los
Asasdos de Pecho. Daily 0800-1430.*
Local food, especially seafood.

Guayaquil nightlife is not cheap. There are
clubs and bars in most of the major hotels,
as well as in the northern suburbs, especially
at the Kennedy Mall. Also in vogue are
the Las Peñas area, and the Zona Rosa,
bounded by the Malecón Simón Bolívar and
Rocafuerte, C Loja and C Roca. Both these
areas are considered reasonably safe but
always take a radio taxi back to your hotel.

La Paleta
*Numa Pompilio Llona 180, Las Peñas, T09-
9091295, Facebook: lapaleta.enlasrocas.
Tue-Sat from 2000.*
Good music, great drinks and snacks. US$10-
15 cover Fri and Sat, popular, reserve.

Praga
*Rocafuerte 624 y Tomás Martínez, T09-9646
1932, Facebook: pragadiscotecazr. Tue and
Wed 1700-2400, Thu-Sat 1700-0300.*
US$5-15 cover, live music Fri-Sat. Pleasant
atmosphere, several halls, varied music.

Resaca
*Malecón 2000, at the level of Junín, T09-
9942 3390, Facebook: Resaca.restaurant.
Daily 1130-2400.*
Lovely setting, live tropical music Fri and Sat
nights. Also serves set lunches on weekdays,
regional dishes and pricey drinks.

Cinema
Cinemas are at the main shopping centres
and cost US$4-8. The 3D Cinema, Malecón
2000, projects impressive films on its
oversize screen.

Theatre
Centro Cívico, *Guaranda y García Goyena,
Parque Forestal, south of the centre.* Excellent
theatre/concert facility, home to the Guayaquil
Symphony which gives free concerts.

Festivals

24-25 Jul The foundation of Guayaquil, **Fiestas Julianas**.
9-12 Oct The **city's independence**. Cultural happenings are prolonged throughout Oct. Both holidays are lively and there are many public events.

Shopping

Handicrafts
In Albán Borja Mall are: **El Telar** with a good variety of *artesanías* and **Ramayana**, with nice ceramics. **Mall del Sol** (near the airport). Has craft shops.
Mercado Artesanal del Malecón 2000, *at the south end of the Malecón*. Has kiosks selling varied crafts.
Mercado Artesanal, *Baquerizo Moreno between Loja and J Montalvo*. Greatest variety, almost a whole block of stalls with good prices.

Markets
La Bahía, *on Chile from Olmedo to Huancavilca*. Several blocks of mainly clothing and other wholesale goods.

Shopping malls
There are many shopping malls (eg **Malecón 2000**, south end of Malecón and the huge **San Marino**, Av Francisco de Orellana y L Plaza Dañín) which are noisy but have a/c for cooling off on hot days.

What to do

Boat tours
Gulf islands The gulf islands and mangroves can be visited on tours from Guayaquil, Puerto Hondo or Puerto El Morro. **Isla Puná**, the largest of the islands has a community tourism programme. Contact the village of **Subida Alta**, T04-511 3759, or 09-9710 3462. Access is by boat from Data de Posorja.
River tours **El Morgan**, *Muelle Malecón y Sucre, below McDonald's*, T04-251 7228, see

Facebook: Barco Morgan. 1-hr tours on the river with good city views, Tue-Thu at 1600, 1800 and 1930, Sat and Sun at 1230, 1400, 1600, 1800 and 1930, Fri and Sat also at 2130; US$7. Also 2-hr party cruises, Thu 2130-2330, Fri-Sat from 2330-0200, US$20, with live music, open bar and dancing.
Turismo En El Golfo, boat trips from the Malecón 2000 (same place as boats to Isla Santay – see page 213), passing some of the sights of the city, Mon-Fri between 1200 and 1800, 45 mins, US$3, and to the railway station in Durán, Sat, Sun and holidays, 1000-1800, 1½ hrs, US$4.

Tour operators
A 3-hr city tour costs about US$14 pp in a group. Tours to coastal haciendas offer a glimpse of rural life.
Centro Viajero, *Baquerizo Moreno 1119 y 9 de Octubre, of 805*, T04-230 1283, T09-9235 7745 24-hr service, www.centroviajero.com. Custom-designed tours to all regions, travel information and bookings, flight tickets, car and driver service, well informed about options for Galápagos, helpful, English, French and Italian spoken. Recommended.
Galasam, *Edif Gran Pasaje, 9 Octubre 424 y Córdova, ground floor*, T04-230 4488, www. galasam.com.ec. Cruises and land-based tours in the Galápagos.
Guayaquil Visión, *ticket booth at Olmedo y Malecón*, T09-6882 3935, Facebook: GuayaquilVision. City tours on a double-decker bus, from US$7, departs from Plaza Olmedo and the Rotonda, Malecón at the bottom of 9 de Octubre. Also tours to attractions outside the city and night-time party tours.
La Moneda, *Av de las Américas 406, Centro de Convenciones Simón Bolívar, of 2*, T04-292 5660, www.lamoneda.com.ec. City and coastal tours, whale watching, also other regions.
Metropolitan Touring, *Francisco De Orellana, Edif World Trade Center, CC Millenium Galery, PB*, T04-263 0900, or 09-9992 9985, www.

metropolitan-touring.com. High-end land tours and Galápagos cruises.

Train rides

The train station is in Durán, across the river from Guayaquil, reservations T1800-873637, www.trenecuador.com, Mon-Fri 0800-1630, Sat-Sun 0700-0900. For information on the luxury *Tren Crucero* from Durán to Quito, see page 76. *Tren de la Dulzura* day trips to Bucay, 88 km away, Fri and every other Sat-Sun, cost US$30. Other fortnightly weekend itineraries go to Naranjito (*Tren de la Dulzura Plus*, with a visit to a sugar hacienda, US$53) and San Antonio (*Tren del Cacao*, to Hacienda La Danesa, US$112); lunch included. Durán–Alausí on Sat, 0800, Alausí–Durán Sun at 0700, US$69, US$121 return. Tickets are also sold at the railcar on Malecón 2000, Malecón e Icaza, Mon-Fri 0900-1230, 1330-1800, Sat-Sun 1000-1200, 1330-1600.

Transport

Air

José Joaquín de Olmedo is a modern airport with all services, including Banco Bolivariano ATM upstairs (claims to take all cards), a *cambio*, car hire and luggage storage. The information booth outside international arrivals (T04-216 9000, open 24 hrs) has flight, hotel and transport information. It is minimum 15 mins to the city centre by taxi, US$5, 5-10 mins to the bus terminal, US$3, and north Guayaquil, US$3-5. Fares from the airport to other areas are posted at exit doors and on www. taxiecuadorairport.com. Official airport taxis are safer than those out on the street. The **Coop de Taxis** desk is opposite the exit from Customs. It is along line 2 of the Metrovía, but neither the Metrovía nor buses to the centre (eg Línea 130 'Full 2') are practical with luggage. For groups, there are van services such as **M&M**, T04-226 1777, www.vansertrans.com, US$15 to centre.

Many flights daily to **Quito** (sit on the right for the best views) and **Galápagos**, see page 300, with **Avianca** (office in Hotel Hilton Colón, T1-800-003434), **LATAM** (9 de Octubre 101-103 y Malecón, and in Mall del Sol, T1-800-000527) and **TAME** (9 de Octubre 424 y Chile, T04-256 0728 and in Mall del Sol and San Marino shopping centres, T1-700-500800). **TAME** also flies to **Cuenca** and **Loja**.

Bus

Local Metrovía (T04-213 0402, www. metrovia-gye.com.ec, US$0.30) is an integrated system of articulated buses on exclusive lanes and *alimentadores* (feeder buses) serving suburbs from the terminuses. Line 1 runs from the Terminal Río Daule, opposite the Terminal Terrestre in the north, to the Terminal El Guasmo in the south. In the city centre it runs along Boyacá southbound and Pedro Carbo northbound. Line 2 goes from the Terminal Río Daule along Av de las Américas past the airport, then through the centre and on to 25 de Julio terminal in the southern suburb of Sopeña. Line 3 goes from the centre (transfer points to line 1 at Biblioteca Municipal and IESS; to line 2 at Plaza La Victoria) along C Sucre to the northwest as far as Bastión. Provides access to neighbourhoods such as Estero Salado, Urdesa, Miraflores and Los Ceibos. The Metrovía is a good way of getting around without luggage or valuables. You need a prepaid card to board; some stations have kiosks where you can buy them, some just have ticket machines.

City buses (US$0.30) are only permitted on a few streets in the centre; northbound buses go along Rumichaca or the Malecón, southbound along Lorenzo de Garaicoa or García Avilés. Buses and Metrovía get very crowded at rush hour.

Long distance The **Terminal Terrestre**, just north of the airport, is off the road to the Guayas bridge. The Metrovía, opposite the bus station, and many city buses (eg Línea 84 to Parque Centenario) go from to the city centre but these are not practical with luggage; take a taxi (US$3-5). There is a dispatcher at the taxi rank who will find a taxi for you and tell you the price. The bus station doubles as a shopping centre with supermarket, shops, banks, ATMs, post office, calling centres, internet, food courts, etc. Incoming buses arrive on the ground floor, where the ticket offices are also located. Regional buses depart from the 2nd level and long-distance (*interprovincial*) buses depart from the 3rd level. The terminal is very large, so you need to allow extra time to get to your bus. Check the board at the entrance for the location of the ticket counters for your destination, they are colour coded by region.

Several companies to **Quito**, 8 hrs, US$10.25, US$15 for express buses which go at night; also non-stop, a/c services, eg **Transportes Ecuador**. To **Cuenca**, 4 hrs via Molleturo/Cajas, 5 hrs via Zhud, both US$8.25, both scenic; also hourly van service, 0500-2100, with Operazuaytur, Centro de Negocios El Terminal, Bloque A, of 1-2, Av de las Américas y entrada a Bahía Norte, T04-213 0837, www.operazuaytur. com, US$13, 3 hrs, reserve ahead; others at the same address, departures every hour. **Riobamba**, 5 hrs, US$7-7.25; to Guaranda, US$5.25; to **Ambato**, 6 hrs, US$8.25; to **Baños**, US$11. To **Santo Domingo de los Tsáchilas**, 5 hrs, US$7. **Manta**, 4 hrs, US$6.25. **Esmeraldas**, 8 hrs, US$11.25. To **Bahía de Caráquez**, 6 hrs, US$7-10. Frequent buses to **Playas**, 2 hrs, US$3; and to **Salinas**, 2½ hrs, US$4.75 (you may have to change in Santa Elena or La Libertad). To **Santa Elena**, 2 hrs, US$4.15, change here for **Puerto López**. To **Montañita** and **Olón**, CLP, 17 a day, 3¼ hrs, US$6.25. For the Peruvian border, to **Huaquillas** direct, 4½-5 hrs, US$7.50; van

service with **Transfrosur**, Chile 616 y Sucre, T04-232 6387, hourly 0500-2000, Sun 0700-2000, 4 hrs, US$13.50; to **Machala**, 3 hrs, US$5, also hourly with **Oro Guayas**, Gonzalo Zaldumbide y Av Carlos Plaza Dañín, T04-239 0280, see Facebook, US$10. To **Zaruma**, 8 buses daily, US$8.15, 6 hrs. To **Loja**, with **Trans Loja**, 6 *regular* daily, US$12, 2 *semi-cama* at night, US$14, 9-10 hrs.

International (Peru) CIFA, T04-213 0379, www.cifainternacional.com, from Terminal Terrestre to **Tumbes** 6 daily, 6 hrs, US$10 *ejecutivo*, US$15 *bus-cama*; to **Piura** via **Máncora** (9 hrs, same price as Piura), 5 a day, 10-11 hrs, US$15; also with **CIVA**, T04-213 1199, www.civa.com.pe, daily at 2100, *semi-cama* US$17, *cama* US$25, continues to Chiclayo, US$25 and US$35 respectively, and Lima US$70, 90 and 120 for suite. To **Chiclayo** with **Super Semeria**, at 2200 daily, US$25, 12 hrs (also to Piura US$20). To **Lima** with **Cruz del Sur**, of 88, T04-213 0179, www. cruzdelsur.com.pe, Tue, Wed, Fri, Sun at 1400, US$85 *semi-cama*, US$120 *cama* (including meals), 27 hrs (stops in Trujillo). With **Ormeño**, Centro de Negocios El Terminal (near Terminal Terrestre), Of C33-34, T04-213 0847, daily at 1130 to **Lima**, US$70.

Taxi
Using a radio taxi, such as **Samboroncar**, T04-284 3883, https://samboroncargye. wordpress.com, or **Vipcar**, T04-259 3400, www.vipcar.com.ec, is recommended (ask restaurant or hotel for recommendation). Short trips cost US$2.50, fares from the centre to Urdesa, Policentro or Alborada are around US$4-5, about 50% more for a hotel or radio taxis. Taxis are supposed to use a meter, but not all drivers comply.

Train
See Train rides under What to do, above.

South to
Peru

Thriving banana plantations and other agro-industry are the economic mainstay of the coastal area bordering the east flank of the Gulf of Guayaquil. The Guayas lowlands are subject to flooding, humidity is high and biting insects are fierce. Mangroves characterize the coast leading south to Huaquillas, the main coastal border crossing to Peru.

Machala

The capital of the province of El Oro (altitude 4 m) is a booming agricultural town in a major banana-producing and exporting region. In recent years there has been some regeneration of parts of the city and construction of new parks, but it can be oppressively hot. For the tourist, the main reasons for stopping here are to go to the beautiful tranquil uplands of El Oro, and to catch a through **CIFA** bus to Peru (also runs from Guayaquil) for the beaches around Máncora. Some 30 km south along the road to Peru is **Santa Rosa** with the regional airport.

Puerto Bolívar

Puerto Bolívar, on the Estero Jambelí among mangroves, is a major export outlet for over two million tonnes of bananas annually. From the old pier canoes cross to the beaches of **Jambelí** (every 30 minutes, 0730-1500, US$4 return, 30-minute crossing) on the far side of the mangrove islands which shelter Puerto Bolívar from the Pacific. The beaches are crowded at weekends, but deserted during the week. Boats can be rented for excursions to the **Archipiélago de Jambelí**, a maze of islands and channels just offshore, stretching south between Puerto Bolívar and the Peruvian border. These mangrove islands are rich in birdlife (and insects for them to feed on; take repellent), the water is very clear and you may also see fish and reefs.

★ Zaruma

Southeast from Machala is the delightful old gold-mining town of Zaruma (118 km). It is reached from Machala by paved road via Piñas, by a scenic dirt road off the main Loja–Machala road, or via Pasaje and Paccha on another scenic dirt road off the Machala–Cuenca road.

Founded in 1549, Zaruma is perched on a hilltop, with steep, twisting streets and painted wooden buildings. Next door to the tourist office (see page 224), the small **Museo Municipal** ① *Wed-Fri 0800-1200, 1400-1800, Sat 0900-1600, Sun 0900-1300, free*, has a collection of local historical artifacts.

The Zaruma area has a number of prehispanic archaeological sites and petroglyphs. Tours with **Oroadventure** ⓘ *Parque Central, T09-9309 4707, Facebook: Vive Zaruma*; English-speaking guide **Ramiro Rodríguez** ⓘ *T07-297 2523, kazan_rodríguez@yahoo.com*; or Patricio Toledo, president of the **Casa de Cultura** ⓘ *T09-6850 6767*. Zaruma is also known for its excellent Arabica coffee freshly roasted in the agricultural store basement; the proud owner will show you around if the store isn't busy. On top of the small hill beyond the market is a public swimming pool (US$1), from where there are amazing views over the hot, dry valleys. For even grander views, walk up **Cerro del Calvario** (follow Calle San Francisco); go early in the morning as it gets very hot. At **Portovelo**, south of Zaruma, is the largest mine in the area. Its history is told inside a mine shaft at the **Museo Magner Turner** ⓘ *T07-294 9345, daily 0900-1730, US$2*. In addition to the the minerals on display, there are archaeological pieces; the owner is knowledgeable about sites in this region.

Piñas and around

Piñas, 19 km west of Zaruma along the road to Machala, is a pleasant town which conserves just a few of its older wooden buildings. Northwest of Piñas, 20 minutes along the road to Saracay and Machala, is **Buenaventura**, to the north of which lies an important area for bird conservation, with some 330 bird species recorded, including many rare ones. The **Jocotoco Foundation** ⓘ *http://jocotoursecuador.com, entry US$15, open 0700-1530*, protects a 1350-ha forest in this region, with 12 km of trails. Advance booking is required to stay at their Umbrellabird Lodge ($$$$, see website).

Bosque Petrificado Puyango

110 km south of Machala, west of the Arenillas–Alamor road, T07-293 2106 (Machala), bosquepuyango@hotmail.com, 0800-1700, US$1 (under new administration in 2017; contact numbers may change).

At Puyango, a dry-forest reserve, a great number of petrified trees, ferns, fruits and molluscs, 65 to 120 million years old, have been found and over 120 bird species can be seen. There is a camping area, no accommodation in the village, but ask around for floor space or try at the on-site information centre. If not, basic accommodation is available in **Las Lajas**, 20 minutes north (one *residencial*) and **Alamor**, 20 km south (several hotels, eg $ Rey Plaza, T07-268 0256/0168).

Huaquillas

The stiflingly hot Ecuadorean border town of Huaquillas is something of a shopping arcade for Peruvians. The border runs along the Canal de Zarumilla and is crossed by two international bridges, one at the western end of Avenida La República in Huaquillas and a second newer one further south.

Border with Peru: Huaquillas–Tumbes

The best way to cross this border is on one of the international buses that run between Ecuador and Peru. Border formalities are only carried out at the new bridge, far outside the towns of Huaquillas (Ecuador) and Aguas Verdes (Peru). There are two border complexes called CEBAF *(Centro Binacional de Atención Fronteriza)*, open 24 hours, on either side of the bridge; they are about 4 km apart. Both complexes have Ecuadorean and Peruvian customs and immigration officers so you get your exit and entry stamps in the same place. There is a **Peruvian Consulate in Machala** ⓘ *Urb Unioro, Mz 14, Villa 11, near*

Hotel Oro Verde, T07-298 1719, www.consulado.pe/es/Machala, Mon-Fri 0800-1300, 1500-1800, Sat 0800-1300. If crossing with your own vehicle, you have to stop at both border complexes for customs and, on the Ecuadorean side, you also have to stop at the customs (*aduana*) post at Chacras, 7 km from the Ecuadorean CEBAF, on the road to Machala. If you do not take one of the international buses, transport between the two sides via the new bridge is inconvenient and expensive. A taxi from Huaquillas to the Ecuadorean CEBAF costs US$2.50, to the Peruvian CEBAF US$5. In addition, it can be a hot and troublesome crossing as there are countless scams on both sides. Thefts, muggings and shakedowns by minor officials have frequently been reported. Never leave your baggage unattended and do you own arithmetic when changing money. Banks do not change money in Huaquillas. Many street changers deal in soles and US dollars cash. Do not change more US dollars than you need to get to Tumbes, where there are reliable *cambios*, but get rid of all your soles here as they are difficult to exchange further inside Ecuador. Only clean, crisp US dollar bills are accepted in Peru. Those seeking a more relaxed crossing to or from Peru should consider Macará (see page 193) or La Balsa (see page 198).

Listings South to Peru

Tourist office

Machala

Ministerio de Turismo
25 de Junio y 9 de Mayo, Municipio, www.machala.gob.ec. Mon-Fri 0800-1300, 1430-1730.
Spanish only.

Zaruma

Tourist office
Plaza de la Independencia y Calle 9 de Octubre, in the Municipio, T07-297 3033/3101, www.zaruma.gob.ec. Mon-Fri 0800-1200, 1330-1730, Sat 0900-1600.
Very friendly and helpful. They can arrange for guides and accommodation with local families.

Where to stay

Machala

$$$$ Oro Verde
Gral Telmo Sandoval y Av Edgar Córdova Polo, east of centre in Unioro, T07-298 0074, http://oroverdemachala.com.

Includes buffet breakfast, 2 restaurants and piano bar, nice pool, beautiful gardens, tennis courts, full luxury. Best in town.

$$ Oro Hotel
Sucre 1002 y Juan Montalvo, T07-293 0032, www.orohotel.com.
Includes breakfast, pricey restaurant, a/c, fridge, parking, nice comfortable rooms but those facing the street can be noisy, helpful staff. Recommended.

$ San Miguel
9 de Mayo y Sucre, T07-292 0474.
Good quality and value, some rooms without windows, hot water (request), no meals, a/c, cheaper with fan, fridge, helpful staff.

Zaruma

$$ Hostería El Jardín
Av Ayora, Barrio Limoncito, 10-min walk from centre (taxi US$1.50), T07-297 2706, www.hosteriaeljardinzaruma.com.
Lovely palm garden and terrace with views, internet, parking, comfortable rooms, breakfast extra, family-run. Recommended.

$$ Roland
Av Alonso de Mercadillo, at the
entrance to town on the road from
Portovelo, T07-297 2800.
Comfortable rooms (some are dark) and
nicer more expensive cabins around the
pool, no breakfast, parking.

$$-$ Zaruma Colonial
Sucre y El Sexmo, T07-297 2742,
www.hotelzarumacolonial.com.
Modern hotel, comfortable, ample bright
rooms, those to the back have mountain
views, no meals.

$ Blacio
El Sexmo 015 y Sucre, T07-297 2045,
see Facebook.
Modern, ask for rooms with balcony, internal
rooms cheaper than those facing the street,
no meals.

$ Romería
On Plaza de la Independencia 45 y 9 de
Octubre, facing the church, T07-297 3618.
Wooden house with balcony, a treat, nicely
refurnished, restaurant downstairs for
breakfast (not included in price), owner
is knowledgeable and helpful.

Huaquillas

$$-$ Hernancor
1 de Mayo entre Av Hualtaco y
10 de Agosto, T07-299 5467,
grandhotelhernancor@gmail.com.
Nice rooms with a/c, includes
breakfast, parking.

$$-$ Sol del Sur
Av La República y Chiriboga, T07-251 0898,
www.soldelsurhotel.com.
Attractive rooms, includes breakfast, a/c,
small bathrooms, parking.

$ Vanessa
1 de Mayo y Av Hualtaco, T07-299 6263.
A/c, internet, fridge, parking, pleasant.

Restaurants

Machala
The best food is found in the better hotels.

$$ Mesón Hispano
Av Las Palmeras y Sucre.
Very good grill, attentive service, outstanding.

$ Chifa Gran Oriental
25 de Junio entre Guayas y Ayacucho.
Good food and service, clean. Recommended.

Zaruma

$$-$ Café Zarumeño
Av Honorato Márquez, uphill from bus
station, T07-297 2600, see Facebook.
Mon-Sat 0730-2200, Sun 0800-1600.
Good seafood and regional dishes (*tigrillo* –
plantain, eggs and fresh cheese scrambled
together – is a speciality), open for breakfast,
also bar.

$ Cafetería Uno
C Sucre, T07-297 2440. Open 0730-1800.
Good for breakfast and Zaruma specialities,
best *tigrillo* (see above) in town.

Transport

Machala
Air
The regional airport is at Santa Rosa, 28 km
south of Machala. 1 or 2 flights a day to
Quito with TAME (Montalvo entre Bolívar y
Pichincha, T07-293 0139).

Bus
There is no Terminal Terrestre, but a
new one, with shopping mall, is under
construction (2017). Do not take night buses
into or out of Machala as they are prone
to hold-ups. To **Quito**, with **Occidentales**
(Buenavista entre Sucre y Olmedo), 10 hrs,
8 daily, or **Panamericana** (Colón y Bolívar),
9 daily, from US$14. To **Guayaquil**, 3 hrs,
US$5, at least hourly, several companies
including **CIFA** (Guayas entre Bolívar y

Pichincha); also hourly vans with **Oro Guayas**, Guayas y Pichincha, T07-293 4382, US$10, 3 hrs. There are 3 different scenic routes to **Loja**, each with bus service. They are, from north to south: via **Piñas** and **Zaruma**, partly paved and rough; via **Balsas**, fully paved; and via **Arenillas** and **Alamor**, for **Puyango** petrified forest. Fare to **Loja**, US$7, 5-6 hrs, 13 daily with **Trans Loja** (Tarqui y Bolívar). To **Zaruma**, see below. To **Cuenca**, at least half-hourly with **Trans Azuay** (Sucre entre Tarqui y Junín) via Pasaje, 4 hrs, US$5.50. **Van service** with Tinamu (Guayas y Pichincha, T07-296 8998), US$12. To **Huaquillas**, with **CIFA**, direct, 1½ hrs, US$2.50, every 20 mins till 2000. To **Piura**, in Peru, with **CIFA**, 5 a day, US$10-15, 6 hrs, via **Máncora**, US$9-14, 5 hrs and **Tumbes**, 7 daily, US$5, 3 hrs.

Zaruma
Bus
To/from Machala with **Trans Piñas** or **TAC**, half-hourly 0300-1800, US$4, 3 hrs; both companies have terminals about 10 blocks from centre on road to Portovelo; take a taxi. To **Piñas**, take a Machala-bound bus, US$1.25, 1 hr. To **Guayaquil**, 6 buses daily US$8.15, 6 hrs. To **Quito**, 8 daily, US$15.20, 12 hrs; to **Cuenca**, 4 daily, **TAC** at 0030, US$8.75, 6 hrs; to **Loja**, 0500 with TAC, 0730 Piñas, US$6, 5 hrs (or take a taxi to Portovelo and change there: 0300, 0600 with **TAC**, 0200, 0830 and 1245 with Piñas).

Puyango
Bus and pick-up
Puyango is west of the Arenillas–Alamor highway: get off the bus by the turn-off at the bridge over the Río Puyango. Bus from **Machala**, Trans Loja at 0930 and 1300, **CIFA** at 0600, US$3.50, 2½ hrs. From **Loja**, Trans Loja 0900, 1400 and 1930, US$7, 5 hrs. From **Alamor**, Trans Loja at 0730, 1000 and 1300, US$1.50, 1 hr. From **Huaquillas**, CIFA at 0500, **Trans Loja** at 0740 and **Unión Cariamanga** at 1130, US$2.50, 1½ hrs. You might be able to hire a pick-up from the main road to the park, US$3. Pick-up from Alamor to Puyango US$25 return, including wait.

Huaquillas
Bus
There is no Terminal Terrestre, each bus company has its own office, many on Teniente Cordovez. If you are in a hurry, it can be quicker to change buses in Machala or Guayaquil. To **Machala**, with **CIFA** (Santa Rosa y Machala), direct, 1½ hrs, US$2.50, every 20 mins; via Arenillas and Santa Rosa, 2 hrs, every 10 mins. To **Quito**, with **Occidentales**, 5 a day, 12 hrs, US$12.50; with **Panamericana**, 11½ hrs, 8 daily via Santo Domingo; 1 daily via **Ambato**, 12 hrs. To **Guayaquil**, frequent service with **CIFA** and **Ecuatoriano Pullman**, 4½-5 hrs, US$7.50, take a direct bus; van service to downtown Guayaquil with **Transfrosur**, Santa Rosa/Machala y Benalcázar, T07-299 5288, hourly 0500-2000, Sun 0700-2000, 4 hrs, US$13.50. To **Cuenca**, 8 daily, 5 hrs, US$7. To **Loja**, **Trans Loja** twice daily, 6 hrs, US$7. If not on an international bus service to Peru (recommended), there are several bus services to Piura (US$7-8.50), **Chiclayo** (US$9) and points south from Tumbes.

Northern
Pacific lowlands

This vast tract of Ecuador covers everything west of the Andes and north of the Guayas delta. Although overlooked by some foreign visitors, this area offers great natural beauty, diversity and a rich cultural heritage.

You can surf, watch whales at play, visit ancient archaeological sites or enjoy some of the country's best cuisine. The jewel in the coastal crown, Parque Nacional Machalilla, protects an important area of primary tropical dry forest, pre-Columbian ruins, coral reef and a wide variety of wildlife. Further north, in the province of Esmeraldas, are unique ecosystems and the Afro-Ecuadorean way of life.

Even if your time is limited, the coast is easily accessible from Quito, making it an ideal short break from the Andean chill. The water is warm for bathing and there are a number of attractive beaches. Coastal tourism is hugely influenced by national holidays: the super-high seasons are carnival, New Year and public holiday weekends such as 1-2 November; the high *temporada de playa* for Ecuadoreans is December to April; July and August are busy with people from the Sierra and foreigners and, continuing to October, whale watchers; October and November are the lowest season, with reduced prices, but more rain.

Best for
Beaches ▪ Seafood ▪ Surfing ▪ Whale watching

Footprint
   picks

★ **The Montañita surf scene**, page 233

A major resort, packed with everything for surfers and their entourage.

★ **Whale watching from Puerto López**, page 234

From mid-June to September, this is the place to spot humpback whales.

★ **Parque Nacional Machalilla**, page 235

This beautiful park preserves marine ecosystems as well as the dry
tropical forest and archaeological sites on shore.

★ **Air sports at Crucita**, page 246

A popular beach with ideal conditions for paragliding, hang-gliding
and kitesurfing.

★ **Canoa**, page 248

On a splendid 200-m-wide beach, Canoa is recovering from the 2016
earthquake with fun places to stay and lots to do in and out of the sea.

★ **Surfing at Mompiche**, page 254

The town combines great waves with a laid-back atmosphere.

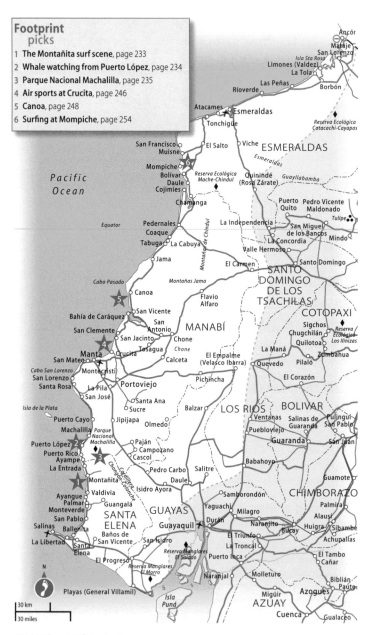

Ancón
Mataje
San Lorenzo
Isla Sta Rosa
Limones (Valdez)
La Tola
Las Peñas
Borbón
Rioverde
Atacames
Esmeraldas
Tonchigüe

Reserva Ecológica Cotacachi-Cayapas

ESMERALDAS

San Francisco
Muisne
El Salto
Viche
Esmeraldas
Mompiche
Bolívar
Daule
Cojimíes
Chamanga

Reserva Ecológica Mache-Chindul

Quinindé (Rosa Zárate)
Guayllabamba

Puerto Quito
Pedro Vicente Maldonado
Tulipe

Pacific Ocean

Equator

Pedernales
Coaque
Tabuga   La Cabuya
Jama

La Independencia
San Miguel de los Bancos
La Concordia
Valle Hermoso
El Carmen
Mindo

Montaña de Chindul

Santo Domingo

SANTO DOMINGO DE LOS TSACHILAS

Cabo Pasado
Canoa
Flavio Alfaro

Montañas Jama

San Vicente
San Antonio
Bahía de Caráquez
San Clemente
San Jacinto
Chone
Tosagua
Crucita
Calceta

Manta
San Mateo
Montecristi

Cabo San Lorenzo
San Lorenzo
Santa Rosa
La Pila
San José

Portoviejo

Santa Ana
Sucre

MANABÍ

Chone
El Empalme (Velasco Ibarra)
Pichincha

Balzar

COTOPAXI
Sigchos
Chugchilán
Quilotoa
La Maná
Quevedo
Pilaló
El Corazón

Reserva Ecológica Los Ilinizas
Zumbahua

LOS RIOS   BOLIVAR

Isla de la Plata

Puerto Cayo
Machalilla
Parque Nacional Machalilla
Puerto López
Puerto Rico
Ayampe
La Entrada
Montañita
Ayangue
Valdivia
Palmar
Monteverde
San Pablo
Salinas
Ballenita
La Libertad
Santa Elena
Baños de San Vicente
San Isidro

Jipijapa
Olmedo
Paján
Campozano
Cascol
Pedro Carbo
Daule
Salitre

Ventanas
Pueblo viejo
Babahoyo

Salinas de Guaranda
Guaranda

Pulinguí
San Pablo
San Juan

Guamote
CHIMBORAZO
Palmira
Alausí
Huigra
Bucay
El Tambo
Cañar
Biblián
Azogues

Cordillera Chongón-Colonche

Isidro Ayora
Samborondón
Yaguachi
Milagro
Naranjito
Guayaquil
Durán
El Triunfo
La Troncal
Puerto Inca

SANTA ELENA   GUAYAS

El Progreso

Reserva Manglares El Salado
Reserva Manglares El Morro

Naranjal
Molleturo
Migüir

Playas (General Villamil)

Isla Puná

N
30 km
30 miles

Sibambe
Achupallas

Paute
AZUAY
Cuenca
Gualaceo

Southwest of Guayaquil is the beach resort of Playas and, west of it, the Santa Elena Peninsula, with Salinas at its tip. From the town of Santa Elena, capital of the province of the same name, the coastal road stretches north for 737 km to Mataje on the Colombian border; along the way are countless beaches and fishing villages, and a few cities. Puerto López is the perfect base for whale watching and from which to explore the beautiful Parque Nacional Machalilla.

Playas and Salinas *Colour map 3, C1/C2.*

The beach resorts of Playas and Salinas remain as popular as ever with vacationing Guayaquileños. The paved toll highway from Guayaquil (US$0.25 toll) divides after 63 km at El Progreso (Gómez Rendón). One branch leads to Playas (General Villamil), 30 km, the nearest seaside resort to Guayaquil.

Playas Bottle-shaped ceibo (kapok) trees characterize the landscape as it turns into dry, tropical thorn scrub. In Playas a few single-sailed balsa rafts, very simple but highly ingenious and colourful, can still be seen among the motor launches returning laden with fish. In high season (*temporada* – December to April) and at weekends, Playas is prone to crowding, although the authorities try to keep the packed beaches clean and safe (don't leave belongings unattended). Out of season or midweek, the beaches are almost empty, especially north towards **Punta Pelado** (5 km). Playas has several good surf breaks. It also claims to have 320 days a year of sunshine. A new Malecón has been built and there are showers, toilets and changing rooms along the beach, with fresh water, for a fee. There are many hotels in our **$$-$** ranges. Excellent seafood and typical dishes are served from over 50 beach cafés (all numbered and named). Many close out of season. The beaches and other coastal and marine environments stretching south from Playas for 14 km to **Data de Posorja** are covered under the national system of protected areas. On the eastern side of the peninsula, best reached from Playas via El Morro is another reserve, the **Refugio de Vida Silvestre Manglares El Morro**, saltwater mangroves with significant populations of dolphins, frigate birds and other species. Boat trips with guides run from Puerto El Morro (http://areasprotegidas.ambiente.gob.ec).

From El Progreso the Vía a la Costa heads west towards Santa Elena. Just after Río Verde a turning left goes to Atahualpa, Ancón and Anconcito, leading to Punta Carnero (see below). Santa Elena itself, the provincial capital, is a crossroads: the '**Ruta del Spondylus**' turns north towards Puerto López, a road south goes to Ancón and the Vía a la Costa continues west for a few kilometres to La Libertad, which is contiguous with Salinas (see Transport, page 243).

Salinas and its beaches Salinas, surrounded by miles of salt flats and shrimp farms, is Ecuador's answer to Miami Beach. There are two urban beaches in the bay on the north side of the peninsula, **San Lorenzo** and **Chipipe**, both with safe swimming. They are lined with high-rise blocks of holiday flats and hotels and separated by the exclusive **Salinas Yacht Club**. Chipipe, to the west of the club, is the more appealing of the two.

In December-April it is overcrowded, its services stretched to the limit. Even in the off season it is not that quiet. The extreme westerly point (Puntilla) is La Chocolatera; it can be visited but you have to go through the military base to get there. The point and the entire south shore of the Santa Elena Peninsula forms the **Reserva Marino Costera Puntilla de Santa Elena**. Access to the shoreline is interrupted by the airport, after which is the long straight beach road, backed by salt pans and shrimp farms, of **Mar Bravo**. This is a good place to watch the sunset and migratory birds, but not swim – it's too dangerous because of strong currents. The sea is safe only at the southeastern end, near **Punta Carnero**, built on a cliff, with hotels in the $$$-$$ range. To get there take a bus from the El Paseo mall at the La Libertad/Salinas boundary towards Anconcito and get out at La Curva de Punta Carnero. In season whales may be seen from the beach and occasionally flamingos visit the salt pans.

North to Puerto López

North of Santa Elena, the '**Ruta del Spondylus**' to Puerto López in the province of Manabí parallels the coastline and crosses the Chongón-Colonche coastal range. Most of the numerous small fishing villages along the way have good beaches and are slowly being developed for tourism. Beware of rip currents and undertow. The first town is **Ballenita**, then **Punta Blanca** and **San Pablo**, which has restaurants all along the seafront. San Pablo and the Ruta can also be reached by a road heading north from the Vía a la Costa by the **Baños de San Vicente**, which misses Santa Elenta altogether. Between San Pablo and Monteverde are the **Ecuasal salt pans**, a recognized birdwatching area. The untidy town of Monteverde has an unused gas pier and a fish factory which can smell bad at times.

Valdivia

San Pedro village merges with Valdivia, a strung-out town which is not a beach stop, but has many fish stalls and a large fishing fleet. This is the site of the 5000-year-old Valdivia culture. Souvenir stalls along the main street of the northern part of town sell 'genuine' artefacts (it is illegal to export pre-Columbian items from Ecuador). Juan Orrala, who makes excellent copies, lives up the hill from the **Ecomuseo Venus de Valdivia** ① *northern end of town, open daily, US$1.50*, which has displays of original artefacts from Valdivia and other coastal cultures. There is also a handicraft section, where artisans may be seen at work, and lots of local information. At the museum is a restaurant and five rooms with bath to let. Another manufacturer of replicas is José Angel Yagual, who has an archaeological museum called **Las Calaveras** ① *Mon-Fri 0800-1800, US$1*. Most of the genuine artefacts discovered at the site are in museums in Quito and Guayaquil.

Manglaralto *Colour map 3, B1.*

Located 180 km northwest of Guayaquil, this is the main centre of the region north of Santa Elena. There is a tagua nursery; ask to see examples of the worked 'vegetable ivory' nuts. It is a nice place, with a quiet beach, good surf but little shade. **Pro-pueblo** is an organization working with local communities to foster family-run orchards and cottage craft industry, using tagua nuts, *paja toquilla* (the fibre Panama hats are made from), and other local products. They have an office and shop in San Antonio south of Manglaralto (T04-278 0230, daily 0900-1800 – in theory) and headquarters in Guayaquil (T04-268 3598, www.propueblo.com).

ON THE ROAD

Valdivia culture

The village of Valdivia gave its name to one of the earliest of Ecuador's cultures, famed for its ceramics and dating back to 3300 BC. In the 1950s and 1960s these were the earliest ceramics known in the Americas. The superficial similarities between Valdivia ceramics and those of the Jomon Culture of Japan led many archaeologists to the conclusion that the Valdivia ceramics were first introduced to the Americas by Japanese fishermen.

However, subsequent discoveries showed that ceramic manufacture in the Americas has its own long path of development and that the idea of a Japanese contribution to pre-European cultures in South America should be discarded.

A much more compelling notion is that ceramic production in Ecuador had its origins in the eastern Amazon basin. Findings at Brazilian sites place early pottery there at between 6000-5000 BC. It is possible that ceramic technology was transmitted from the Amazon basin through commerce or movement of people.

The third alternative is that the development of pottery occurred locally and may have accompanied the development of a more sedentary lifestyle on the Colombian, Venezuelan and Ecuadorean coasts.

The impressive Valdivia figurines are, in most cases, female representations and are nude and display breasts and a prominent pubic area. Some show pregnancy and in the womb of these are placed one or more seeds or small stones. Others have infants in their hands and some have two heads.

These figurines fill museum cases throughout the country (notably the excellent museums of the Ministerio de Cultura in Guayaquil, Quito and Cuenca). They are still being produced by artisans in the fishing village of Valdivia today and can be purchased here or at the museum in Salango, further north near Puerto López. In fact, according to the research of several Ecuadorean archaeologists, many of the figurines housed in the museum collections were made in the 1950s and 1960s because the archaeologists working at that time would pay for any figurines that were found.

(Jonathan D Kent, PhD, Associate Professor, Metropolitan State College of Denver).

Montañita and Olón

About 3 km north of Manglaralto, ★ **Montañita** has mushroomed into a major surf resort, packed with hotels, restaurants, surf-board rentals, tattoo parlours and craft/jewellery vendors. A new, raised Malecón has been built, with steps down to the beach. The main street, Guido Chiriboga, is two blocks from the Malecón; in the nightlife zone (at the northern end) you won't get any sleep Friday to Sunday. At the north end of the bay, 1 km away, is another hotel area with more elbow-room, Baja Montañita (or Montañita Punta, Surf Point). Between the two is a lovely beach where you'll find some of the best surfing in Ecuador. Various competitions are held during the year. Local advice is to avoid the town during carnival week and at local holidays when it becomes impossibly full.

Beyond an impressive headland and a few minutes north of Montañita is **Olón** (www.olon.ec), with a spectacular 4-km-long beach, still tranquil (how Montañita used to be), except on holidays. Even then you can walk along the beach to escape the crowds.

The seafront is lined with bars and *cabañas* serving food; ask for latest recommendations. There are also restaurants in town, eg **Spondylus**, behind Hotel La Corona, serving Venezuelan food, also Asian, burgers and pizza. There are two surf schools. About 1 km north is **El Cangrejal**, a 7-ha dry tropical forest

Tip...
A favourite stop in La Entrada is **Los Dulces de Benito** – a red house – which sells excellent cakes and desserts (also in Mall del Sol in Guayaquil).

with mangroves and a threatened species of blue crab. North of Olón the beach has various names: **Curia**, **San José**, **Núñez** and finally **La Entrada**.

Ayampe to Salango

After La Entrada the road climbs inland through the dripping forest of the westernmost hills of the **Cordillera Chongón-Colonche**. The mountain range, 800 m at its highest, stretches southeast to Guayas province. In Manabí it contains remnants of humid tropical forest, but the fringes (where they survive) are dry tropical forest. From the hills the road winds down, passing the entrance to the **$$$ Hostería Atamari** ① *Km 83 Vía Santa Elena–Puerto López, T09-8570 0667, www.hosteriatamari.com,* overlooking the ocean at the most southerly point of Manabí province. It has three lookout points and three trails (to the point, to a private beach and to Ayampe – not open in fog); all cabins have sea view, there are two restaurants open to non-guests, a pool and spa. Back at sea level the next village is **Ayampe**. Tourism is growing here, with many popular places to stay at the south end of the beach, but the village retains a peaceful atmosphere, thanks to the local Comité de Turismo. The surfing here is very good. Offshore is the twin rock formation called **Los Ahorcados**. The Río Ayampe flows into the sea through tropical forest which here comes down to the beach. The community has set up the **Ecoruta del Colibrí** trail and, just to the north, the **Fundación Jocotoco** has the Río Ayampe reserve (www.fjocotoco.org/ayampe.html) to protect the *estrellita esmeraldeña* hummingbird, in conjunction with the village of Las Tunas.

North of Ayampe are the villages of **Puerto Rico** and **Río Chico**. There are places to stay along this stretch of coast. Just north of Río Chico is **Salango**, with a fish processing plant at the south end and a very active *artesanal* fishing port at the north end. The town is worth visiting for the small but excellent **Salango archaeological museum** ① *at the north end of town by the Centro de Eventos, daily 0900-1700, US$2.50, signs in Spanish and English,* housing artefacts from excavations right in town. It also has a tourist office (see page 238), a craft shop and, at the back, nice rooms with bath in the $ range. There is a place for snorkelling offshore, by **Isla Salango**, where plenty of marine life can be seen: frigate birds, blue-footed boobies and pelicans. On the leeward north shore is a pink beach. Boat trips here last three hours and cost US$25.

★ Puerto López *Colour map 3, B1.*

This pleasant fishing town (population 18,000 including Machalilla and Salango) is beautifully set in a horseshoe bay. The Malecón extends through town to beyond the northern limit; it has a few parking places. The beach is best for swimming at the north end, away from the fleet of small fishing boats which congregates offshore towards the south. The town is popular with tourists for watching humpback whales from approximately mid-June to September. The beginning of the season is marked with the

Festival de la Observación de las Ballenas Jorobadas on 18 June. The other main reason for visiting is the Parque Nacional Machalilla and Isla de la Plata. There is a turtle rehabilitation centre 1.5 km north of town along the beach (ask at Mandála hotel for details). Banco de Pichincha has branches on Avenida Machalilla near the church, with ATM, and on the Malecón, near Calle Sucre.

★ Parque Nacional Machalilla

Park office in Puerto López, C Eloy Alfaro y García Moreno on Plaza Machalilla, T05-230 0170, http://areasprotegidas.ambiente.gob.ec, daily 0800-1700, no English spoken.

The park extends over 55,000 ha and preserves marine ecosystems as well as the dry tropical forest and archaeological sites on shore. It is divided into three sections: a marine section including Isla Salango, between Salango and Puerto López; the largest central section, on- and offshore, which includes Isla de la Plata, Los Frailes beach, Agua Blanca, Cerro San Sebastián and a portion of the Cordillera Chongón-Colonche; and the northernmost section, also on- and offshore, north of the town of Machalilla. The park is recommended for birdwatching, especially in the cloudforest of Cerro San Sebastián; there are also howler monkeys, several other species of mammal and reptile.

About 5 km north of Puerto López, at Buena Vista, a dirt road to the east leads to **Agua Blanca** (park kiosk at entry). Here, 5 km from the main road, in the national park, amid hot, arid scrub, is a small village and a fine, small **archaeological museum** ① *0800-1800, US$5 for a 2- to 3-hr guided tour of the museum, ruins (a 45-min walk), funerary urns and sulphurous lake*, containing some fascinating ceramics from the Manteño civilization. There is also a 5-km self-guided trail, **El Sendero de Sombra de los Algarrobos**. Horses can be hired at the museum, camping is possible and there's a cabin and one very basic room for rent above the museum (US$5 pp). **San Sebastián**, 9 km from Agua Blanca, is in tropical moist forest at 800 m; orchids and birds can be seen and possibly howler monkeys. Although part of the national park, this area is administered by the **Comuna de Agua Blanca**, which charges an entry fee; you cannot go independently. A tour to the forest costs US$35 per day

Puerto López

To ②, Machalilla & Manta
To ③⑤⑦ & Fish Market
Río Pital
María Immaculada Concepción
Abdón Calderón
González Suárez
Exploramar Diving
Lascano
Machalilla Tours
Malecón Julio Izurieta
Eloy Alfaro
Montalvo
Atahualpa
Machalilla
iTUR
Machalilla Nat Park Office
Eloy Alfaro
Plaza Machalilla
General Córdova
García Moreno
To Pier
Mariscal Sucre
To Montañita & Guayaquil

N
Not to scale

Where to stay
Itapoa 1
La Terraza 2
Mandála 3
Máxima 4
Nantu 5
Sol Inn 6
Víctor Hugo 7

Restaurants
Bellitalia 1
Carmita 2
La Casa Vecchia 3
Patacón Pisao 4

ON THE ROAD

A whale of a time

Whale watching is a major tourist attraction along Ecuador's coast. A prime site to see these massive mammals is around Isla de La Plata but whales travel the entire length of Ecuador's shores and well beyond.

Between June and September, each year, groups of up to 10 individuals of this gregarious species make the 7200-km-long trip from their Antarctic feeding grounds to the equator. They head for these warmer waters to mate and calve. Inspired by love – we presume – the humpbacks become real acrobats. Watching them breach (jump almost completely out of the water) is the most exciting moment of any tour. Not far behind, though, is listening to them 'sing'. Chirrups, snores, purrs and haunting moans are all emitted by solitary males eager to use their chat-up techniques on a prospective mating partner. These vocal performances can last half an hour or more.

Adult humpbacks reach a length of over 15 m and can exceed 30 tonnes in weight. The gestation period is about one year and newborn calves are 5-6 m long. The ventral side of the tail has a distinctive series of stripes which allows scientists to identify and track individual whales.

Humpbacks got their English name from their humped dorsal fins and the way they arch when diving. Their scientific name, *Megaptera novaeangliae*, which translates roughly as 'large-winged New Englanders', comes from the fact that they were first identified off the coast of New England, and from their very large wing-like pectoral fins. In Spanish they are called *ballena jorobada* or *yubarta*.

These whales have blubber up to 20 cm thick. Combined with their slow swimming, this made them all too attractive for whalers during the 19th and 20th centuries. During that period their numbers are estimated to have fallen from 100,000 to 2500 worldwide. Protected by international whaling treaties since 1966, the humpbacks are making a gradual recovery. Ironically, the same behaviour that once allowed them to be harpooned so easily makes the humpbacks particularly appealing to whale watchers today. The difference is that each sighting is now greeted with the shooting of cameras instead of lethal harpoons.

including guide and horses. Camping is possible (minimum two people), otherwise lodging is with a family at extra cost. Horse rides go to **La Bola de Oro**, the highest point in the park. Access to this part can also be made from **Pital** community, 10 km inland from Puerto López, from where trails start along the Río Blanco before climbing up to the cloudforest.

Los Frailes beach is clean and well cared for but gets busy at weekends and on holidays. From the entry point where visitors must register (on the main road about 3 km north of the Agua Blanca turn) you can drive 2.7 km to the car park, or take a 3.2-km self-guided trail to Los Frailes through the forest. This leads to two lookouts with great views to beaches and the town of Machalilla, before descending to the main beach. There are toilets and showers, water for sale, but prepared food, alcohol and smoking are not permitted.

About 24 km offshore (40 km by boat from Puerto López) is **Isla de la Plata**. Trips are popular because of the similarities with the Galápagos. Wildlife includes nesting colonies of waved albatross (April to November), frigates and three different booby species. Whales can be seen from June to September, as well as sea lions. It is also a pre-Columbian site with substantial pottery finds, and there is good diving and snorkelling, as well as four walks. Take a change of clothes, water, precautions against sun and seasickness (most agencies provide snorkelling equipment). You can only visit with a tour run by an authorized agent (do not buy a tour on the street) and staying overnight is not permitted.

Back on the mainland, in the northern section of the national park are **El Sombrerito** walking trail, a coastal walk through dry tropical forest which starts 4 km from Machalilla town (guide US$5), and **El Rocío** trail, near Pueblo Nuevo, 2 km long, with ocean views and dry tropical forest flora and fauna (guide US$5).

Puerto López to Manta

North of Machalilla, the road forks at **Puerto Cayo**, where whale-watching tours may be organized in July and August. One route heads inland through the trading centre of **Jipijapa** to **Montecristi**, below an imposing hill, 16 km before Manta. Montecristi is renowned as the centre of the Panama hat industry. Also produced are varied straw- and basketware, and wooden barrels which are strapped to donkeys for carrying water. Ask for José Chávez Franco (Rocafuerte 203), where you can see Panama hats being made. Some 23 km east of Montecristi is **Portoviejo**, capital of Manabí province, a sweltering, unappealing commercial city. The other road follows the coast to San José, near which a new road also heads to Montecristi, continuing to Rocafuerte, east of Manta. This route links the Ruta del Spondylus either side of Manta, bypassing the city.

Carrying on up the coast from San José, you pass **Cabo San Lorenzo** with its lighthouse (40 km from Puerto Cayo) and the **Refugio de Vida Silvestre Pacoche** ① *near El Aromo, 3 km off the road, look for the entrance to Sendero El Mono, T05-263 8857, http:// areasprotegidas.ambiente.gob.ec, 0900-1600.* Created in 2008, this land and marine reserve is a green oasis of coastal cloudforest in the midst of a dry forest zone. Howler monkeys may be seen (or heard), there is good birdwatching and from September to December marine turtles nest on San Lorenzo beach. There are walking trails of 1 km and 1.5 km. Santa Marianita/Playa Bonita, just before the town of San Mateo and 20 km from Manta, has a reputation as the best kite-surfing beach in Ecuador. The beach is 4 km long, with few facilities apart from some kite schools and seafood stalls and is ideal for all levels. Take a taxi or pick-up from Manta bus terminal.

Listings Guayaquil to Puerto López *map page 235.*

Tourist information

Playas

Turismo
On the Malecón. Tue-Fri 0800-1200, 1400-1800, Sat-Sun 0900-1600. Municipal office on 15 de Agosto, Plaza Cívica, www. municipioplayas.gob.ec.

Salinas

Turismo Municipal
Eloy Alfaro y Mercedes de Jesús Molina, Chipipe, T04-258 8563, www.salinas. gob.ec. Mon-Fri 0830-1730. See also www.infosalinas.com.

Salango

Centro Turístico Comunitario
At the north end of town by the Centro de
Eventos, T05-257 4304, or 09-9021 2880,
www.salango.com.ec.

Puerto López

Tourist office
Av Machalilla y Atahualpa in the centre,
T09-9475 0497, www.puertolopez.gob.ec.
Mon-Fri 0800-1700.

Where to stay

Salinas
There are about 100 places to stay; the
more expensive hotels are on the Malecón.
If you go 1 street (Gral Enríquez Gallo) or
more inland, there are cheaper places to
stay and eat.

$$ Francisco III
Malecón 231 y C 27, T09-9155 2127,
www.hotelfranciscoecuador.com.
Very nice, comfortable rooms, restaurant,
a/c, fridge, pool. There is also **Francisco II**
at Malecón y Las Palmeras, T04-277 3751.

Manglaralto

$$ Manglaralto Sunset
El Oro y Constitución, 1 block from
the Plaza, T04-290 1405, www.
hotelmanglaraltosunset.com.
Nice modern place, comfortable rooms
with a/c, hammocks, cafeteria bar, electric
shower, parking.

Montañita
There are many places to stay in town;
several on or near Guido Chiriboga have a
bar/restaurant as well and serving as party
places, such as Montezuma, Chiriboga y de
los Cócteles (10 de Agosto), T04-206 0122,
Facebook: montezumahostal. The quieter
ones are at Baja Montañita. For listings,

information, map, and transport, see www.
infomontanita.com. Prices below are for
low season; they rise by US$10-15 pp in high
season, but are negotiable in low season.

$$$-$$ Balsa Surf Camp
50 m from the beach in Baja Montañita,
T04-206 0075, 09-8971 4685,
www.balsasurfcamp.com.
Very nice spacious cabins with terrace,
hammocks in garden, fan, parking, yoga
included, surf classes (US$25-35) and rentals,
small well-designed spa, parking, good
restaurant, **L'Eden**, with local food, French/
Ecuadorean-run. Recommended.

$$ Galeón
C Pública y 10 de Agosto, T04-206 0109,
Facebook: galeon1940.
Prices rise at weekends and on holidays (to
$$$), rooms overlooking the river are quieter,
group rooms overlooking street are noisy,
good-quality fittings, neat. In same building
is **Pigro** Italian café/restaurant (closed Tue).

$$ La Casa del Sol
In Baja Montañita, T09-8251 1853,
www.casadelsolmontanita.com.
A/c, or fan, dorms US$15 pp, restaurant/bar,
surf classes and rentals, alternative medicine
and yoga classes (US$8), retreats and
teacher-training, www.yogamontanita.com.

$$ Pakaloro
In town at the end of C Guido Chiriboga,
T04-206 0092, www.pakaloro.com.
Modern 4-storey building with lots of wood,
ample rooms with balcony and hammock
(**$$$** in highest season), fan, shared kitchen,
nice setting by the river.

$$-$ Charo's
Between Malecón and 15 de Mayo, south of
centre, T04-206 0044, www.charoshostal.com.
Modern rooms in blocks with pool between
(pool open 0900-2100), basic breakfast
available, shared kitchen, bar/restaurant,
hammocks, fun atmosphere.

$$-$ Sole Mare

On the beach at the north end
of Baja Montañita, T04-206 0119,
www.solemare-ecuador.com.
In a lovely setting on the beach, fan, garden, parking, run by an attentive father-and-son, both called Carlos, English spoken, price includes full breakfast, long-stay rates available, good value.

Olón

$$$ Samai Ocean Lodge Spa

In San José, Km 700 Ruta del Spondylus,
on a hill 10 mins from Olón (taxi US$5),
T09-9462 1316, www.samailodge.com.
Cabins in a natural setting, great views, restaurant/bar, pool, jacuzzi, specializes in yoga, retreats, detox, advance booking required.

$$-$ Isramar

Av Sta Lucia y Rosa Mística, ½ block from
beach, T04-278 8096, 09-9712 1293,
hosteriaisramar@gmail.com.
Large place with rooms for 3 to 5 (US$15 pp), a/c, breakfast US$5, pizza served at night, restaurant/bar, small garden, friendly owner Doris Cevallos.

$$-$ La Mariposa

13 de Diciembre y Rosa Mística,
by church, T04-278 8120, 09-8017 8357,
www.lamariposahostal.com.
3-storey building, some rooms with a/c, no TV, breakfast extra, nice ocean views from top floor, Italian-run, English and French also spoken, good service and value.

Ayampe to Salango
Ayampe

Many of Ayampe's hotels are part-hidden by trees and have a relaxed atmosphere. Those in the upper bracket (**$$$**) include La Buena Vida (http://surflabuenavida.com) with surf school and spa, and El Espondylus (http://spondyluslodge.com), with surfing and yoga.

$$ Cabañas Tortuga

Ayampe, T09-9383 4825,
www.latortuga.com.ec.
Cabins on a beachfront property, with fan, shared kitchen, bar, pool, can arrange activities and excursions. Also has nearby **Tortuga Suites**, a little more expensive, with a/c, quiet and good for long stays.

$$-$ Cabañas de la Iguana

Ayampe, T05-257 5165,
www.hotelayampe.com.
Cabins for 4 (US$15 pp room only), mosquito nets, cooking facilities, quiet, relaxed family atmosphere, knowledgeable and helpful, organizes excursions, pleasant garden, laundry service, good choice. Swiss-owned.

Puerto Rico

$$$-$$ La Barquita

Puerto Rico, 4 km north of Ayampe, T05-234 7051, www.hosterialabarquita.com.
Restaurant and bar are in a boat on the beach with good ocean views, rooms with a/c and Wi-Fi, pool, spa, attractive garden, arranges tours and activities, Swiss-run.

Puerto López

$$$ La Terraza

On hill overlooking town, C San Francisco s/n, Ciudadela Luis Gencón (moto-taxi US$0.50), T05-230 0235, www.laterraza.de.
12 spacious a/c cabins in nice gardens with crystal-clear pool and jacuzzi, great views over the bay. Comfortable, well-appointed rooms, laundry service, includes good breakfast, restaurant for dinner and light lunch on request, parking, masses of tourist information, kind German owners, German, English and Spanish spoken. Recommended.

$$$-$$ Mandála

Malecón at north end of the beach, T05-230 0181, www.hosteriamandala.info.
Big cabins and superior rooms decorated with art, fully wheelchair accessible,

gorgeous tropical garden, good restaurant only for guests, fan (no a/c or TV), mosquito nets, safe, games, music room, great value, Swiss/Italian-run, English spoken, knowledgeable owners. Recommended.

$$$-$$ Víctor Hugo
Malecón north along the beach, T05-230 0054, www.victorhugohotel.com.ec.
Ample rooms with bamboo decor and balconies, suites and standard rooms, being expanded, offers packages up to 5 days.

$$ Itapoa
On a lane off Abdón Calderón, with an entrance on the Malecón, T05-230 0071, www.hosteriaitapoa.com.
Thatched cabins around large garden, hot water, cheaper in dorm, includes breakfast on a lovely terrace overlooking the sea, family-run, English spoken, café with organic produce from its own rainforest reserve in Puerto Quito (visits and local tours arranged).

$$ Nantu
Malecón at north end of the beach, T05-230 0040, www.hosterianantu.com.
Modern well-maintained rooms, a/c, small pool and garden, pizza restaurant, espresso and tequila bars overlooking the beach.

$ pp Máxima
González Suárez y Machalilla, T05-230 0310, www.hotelmaxima.org.

With bath, mosquito nets, same price high or low season, laundry and cooking facilities, hammocks, parking, modern, English spoken, good value, tours organized.

$ Sol Inn
Montalvo y Eloy Alfaro, T05-230 0234, http://hostalsolinn.machalillatours.org.
Bamboo and wood construction, private or shared bath (private rooms $$ in high season, dorm US$10 pp), hot water, fan, laundry and cooking facilities, camping in yard US$5, pool table, popular, relaxed atmosphere, offers tours, surfing and Spanish classes.

Puerto López to Manta

$$$-$$ Donkey Den Guesthouse & Café
In Santa Marianita, 20 mins from Manta, T09-9723 2026, http:// donkeydenguesthouse.com.
Good rooms right on the kite-surfing beach, private or shared bath, dorm for 5 US$16 pp, cooking facilities, breakfast, dinner and cocktails available, popular with US expats, taxi from Manta US$10.

Restaurants

Salinas
A couple of blocks inland from the Malecón at the west end of Plaza San Lorenzo between Calles Eladora Peña and Fidón

Hostería La Terraza
Teléfono: +593 5 2300235 · +593 9 88554887
info@laterrazabooking.com · www.laterrazabooking.com
Puerto López · Manabí · Ecuador

Tomalá, are many food stalls serving good ceviches and freshly cooked seafood, daytime only, eg **Cevichelandia**.

$$$ La Bella Italia
Malecón y C 17.
Good pizza and international food.

$$$-$$ Amazon
Malecón near Banco de Guayaquil, T04-277 3671.
Elegant upmarket eatery, grill and seafood specialities, pizza, good wine list.

$$ La Lojanita
Leonardo Avilés y Enríquez Gallo, T04-277 0819, www.cevicherialojanita.com. Daily 0800-2100, closes earlier Sat-Sun.
Takes up the best part of a block, renowned place for ceviches, seafood and fish, very popular, takes credit cards.

Montañita

$$$-$$ Tikilimbo
C Guido Chiriboga 2, www.tikilimbo.com.
Good quality, vegetarian dishes available. Also has hostel, bar and **Sumbawa** surf shop.

$$ Marea Pizzeria Bar
10 de Agosto y Av 2. Evenings only in the week, from midday Sat-Sun.
Real wood-oven pizza, very tasty. Recommended.

$$ Rocío
10 de Agosto y Av 2, inside eponymous hotel, www.rocioboutiquehotel.com.
Good Mediterranean food.

$ Govindaprasad
10 de Agosto, T09-9567 8278. Daily 1000-2100.
Vegetarian and vegan food. Next door is Solo Vida, with vegetarian dishes and organic food.

Ayampe to Salango
Salango

$$ El Delfín Mágico
Facing the Parque Central, T09-9114 7555, www.delfinmagico.com.ec. Open 1000-2000.
Excellent, order meal in advance or before visiting museum because all food is cooked from scratch, very fresh and safe.

Puerto López

$$$ Bellitalia
North toward the river, T09-9617 5183. Mon-Sat from 1800. Usually closed in May.
Excellent authentic Italian food, home-made pasta, attentive owners Vittorio and Elena. Reservations required in high season, but it can fill up at any time. Recommended.

$$$-$$ La Casa Vecchia
Eloy Alfaro 124, 100 m from Malecón, T09-8859 0932, casavecchiapizzeria@gmail.com.
Central trattoria/pizzeria with good choice of Italian dishes, pizzas recommended.

$$ Carmita
Malecón y General Córdova.
Tasty fish and seafood, a Puerto López tradition. Several others in the same block.

$$ Patacón Pisao
Gen Córdova, half a block from the Malecón.
Colombian food, giant *patacones* and *arepas*.

Festivals

Puerto López
Feb/Mar **Carnival**.
18 Jun **Festival de la Observación de las Ballenas Jorobadas** marks the beginning of the whale-watching season.
End-Jun **Fiestas de San Pedro y San Pablo**, take place at many coastal communities.
31 Aug **Cantón de Puerto López** is celebrated with music, dancing and games.

12 Oct Festival de la Balsa Manteña
features the decoration of traditional rafts,
singing and dancing.

What to do

Salinas
Tour guides
Ben Haase, *at Museo de Ballenas,
Av Enríquez Gallo entre C47 y C50, T04-
277 8329, bhaase2012@gmail.com, www.
museodeballenas.org. Daily 0700-2000,
phone in advance.* Expert English-speaking
naturalist guide runs birdwatching tours
to the Ecuasal salt ponds, US$50 for a small
group. Also whale watching and trips to a
sea lion colony. Also **Fernando Félix** (same
address, fefelix90@hotmail.com) English-
speaking marine biologist, can guide for
whale watching and other nature trips,
arrange in advance. The museum itself is
a private collection and research centre.

Montañita
Language courses
Montañita Spanish School, *on the main road
50 m uphill outside the village, T04-206 0116,
www.montanitaspanishschool.com.*

Surfing
Surfboard rentals all over town from
US$4 per hr, US$15 per day.

Ayampe to Salango
Joe Salango Tours, *Salango, T09-9399 8515,
joesalangotours@gmail.com.* Trips to islands
US$15 pp, with snorkelling, to see birds and
fish, 1½ hrs, life jacket provided. Also whale
and dolphin watching, US$50 for 2 people.
Sport fishing US$150.
Otra Ola, *beside Cabañas de la Iguana,
Ayampe, T09-8884 3278, www.otraola.com.*
Surf lessons and board rental, yoga and
Spanish classes and a café with organic
coffee and snacks (open 1030-1900, 1700
on Tue). Enthusiastic Canadian owners.

Puerto López
Language courses
La Lengua, *Abdón Calderón y García Moreno,
east of the highway, T09-9951 4389 or Quito
T02-250 1271, www.la-lengua.com.*

Whale watching
Puerto López is a major centre for trips from
Jun to Sep, with many more agencies than
we can list. Only 9, however, are licensed to
go to Isla de la Plata (ask to see authorization).
Whales can also be seen elsewhere, but most
reliably in Puerto López. There is a good fleet
of small boats (16-20 passengers) running
excursions, all have life jackets and a toilet,
those with 2 engines are safer. All agencies
offer the same tours for the same price.
Beware touts offering cheap tours to 'La Isla',
they take you to Isla Salango not Isla de la
Plata. In high season: US$40 pp for whale
watching, Isla de la Plata and snorkelling,
with a snack and drinks, US$25 for whale
watching only (available Jun and Sep).
Outside whale season, tours to Isla de la Plata
and snorkelling cost US$35. Trips depart from
the pier (US$1 entry fee) around 0800 and
last 2 to 4 hrs. A half-day boat tour including
Isla Salango costs US$25; inshore fishing trips
US$200, deep-sea US$350 for 1-5 people.
Agencies also offer tours to the mainland
sites of the national park. A guided tour to
Agua Blanca costs US$35 plus entry fee; a
guided tour to Los Frailes also costs US$35
pp. Horse-riding trips to La Bola de Oro cost
US$35 pp (6-7 hrs). There are also hiking,
birdwatching, kayaking, diving (be sure to
use a reputable agency) and other trips.
Aventuras La Plata, *on Malecón, T05-
230 0105, www.aventuraslaplata.com.*
Whale-watching tours.
Cercapez, *at the Centro Comercial on the
highway, T05-230 0173.* All-inclusive trips to
San Sebastián, with camping, local guide
and food at US$40 pp per day.
Exploramar Diving, *Malecón next
to Hotel Pacífico, T09-9950 0910, www.*

exploradiving.com. Quito-based (T02-256 3905). Have boats for 8-16 people and their own compressor. PADI divemaster accompanies qualified divers to various sites, but advance notice is required. Also diving lessons, whale watching and tours to Machalilla National Park. Recommended. **Machalilla Tours**, *Malecón y Eloy Alfaro, T05-230 0234, www.machalillatours.org*. Whale watching, tours to Machalilla National Park and diving.
Palo Santo, *Malecón y Abdón Calderón, T05-230 0312, http://whalewatchingecuador.com*. Whale-watching tours, also has a lodge and offers packages.

Transport

Playas
Bus and taxi
Trans Posorja and **Villamil** to **Guayaquil**, frequent, 2 hrs, US$3.25; taxi US$25.

Salinas
Air
Flights from Quito on Thu and Sun with **Tame**.

Bus and taxi
There are no direct buses from **Guayaquil**. Take a **Coop Libertad Peninsular** (**CLP**, Guayaquil T04-213 0175, http://libertad peninsular.com) bus to the Sumpa regional terminal between Santa Elena and Ballenita (T04-295 5048), US$4.50, from 0300-2200, 2½ hrs. Guayaquil–Santa Elena also with CICA. From Sumpa take a bus to Salinas, US$0.30, or taxi (recommended), US$5. For **Montañita**, **Puerto López** and points north, transfer to **Coop Manglaralto** (**CITM**) buses at Sumpa. **CLP** goes from Sumpa to Montañita and Olón.

Manglaralto
Bus
To **Santa Elena** and **La Libertad**, US$1.50, 1 hr with **Coop Manglaralto**. Transfer

at Sumpa, Santa Elena for Guayaquil. To **Guayaquil** direct, see Olón, below. To **Puerto López**, 1 hr, US$2.75.

Montañita and Olón
Bus and taxi
Montañita is just a few mins south of Olón, from where **CLP** has direct buses to **Guayaquil**, US$6.25, 3 hrs, buses run between 0500 and 1930 (earlier Mon-Thu); or transfer at Sumpa, Santa Elena (see above), US$2, 1½ hrs. Taxi Guayaquil airport–Montañita minimum US$80. To **Puerto López**, **Coop Manglaralto** every 15 mins, US$2.50, 45-60 mins. If heading north to Bahía de Caráquez and Canoa from here or Puerto López, consider going via Jipijapa and Portoviejo, rather than via Manta, because it is quicker.

Puerto López
Mototaxis in town US$0.25 pp, to districts above town and to bus terminal US$0.50, after 2000, US$1.

Bus and taxi
Bus terminal 2 km north of town. To **Santa Elena**, every 15 mins, US$4, 2 hrs with Coop Manglaralto. These buses go to **Montañita** and **Manglaralto**, US$2.50, 1 hr. To **Guayaquil**, also with **Coop Manglaralto** via Jipijapa, between 0400 and 1700, US$5.25, 3½ shrs; or transfer in Santa Elena (Sumpa terminal). To/from **Manta**, direct, same company, 3 with a/c (1¾ hrs), 6 without (slower), US$3.75; or change in Jipijapa. To **Quito** (Quitumbe) with **Reina del Camino** (T05-303 6002), daily 2030 each way, arrives 0530; and **CA Aray**, T05-303 6006, at 0505, 0915 and 1900, 9-10 hrs, from Quito at 1000 and 1900, 2 stops on night bus, 9 stops on day buses, US$14. To **Jipijapa**, on CA Aray buses, or **Coop Manglaralto**, US$2, 1 hr. Taxis and pick-ups for hire to nearby sites are on Plaza Machalilla and between the church and the bank on Av Machalilla.

Parque Nacional Machalilla
Bus

To **Los Frailes**: take a tour, or bus towards Manta or Jipijapa (US$0.75), mototaxi (US$5), or a pick-up (US$8), and alight at the turn-off just south of the town of Machalilla, then walk for 30 mins. No transport back to Puerto López after 2000 (but check in advance). To **Agua Blanca**: take tour, a pick-up (US$7), mototaxi (US$10 return with 2 hrs' wait) or a bus bound for Jipijapa (US$0.75); it is a hot walk of more than 1 hr

from the turning to the village. To **Isla de la Plata**: the island can only be visited on a day trip. Many agencies offer tours, see Puerto López, above.

Puerto López to Manta
Bus

From Jipijapa (terminal on the outskirts) to **Manglaralto** (2 hrs, US$2.50), to **Puerto López** (1 hr, US$2, these go by Puerto Cayo), to **Manta** (1 hr, US$1.25), to **Quito** (10 hrs, US$9).

Manta and Bahía de Caráquez
busy centres, wind and water sports and a route to the highlands

These are two quite different seaside places: Manta a rapidly growing port city, prospering on fishing and trade; Bahía de Caráquez a relaxed resort town and a pleasant place to spend a few days. It is proud of its 'eco' credentials. Just beyond Bahía, on the other side of the Río Chone estuary, is the popular resort village of Canoa, boasting some of the finest beaches in Ecuador.

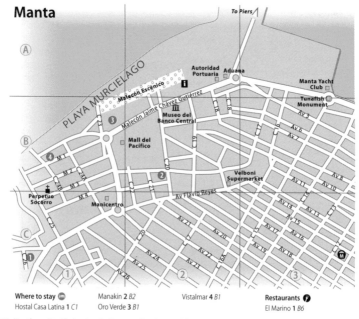

Where to stay ⬤	Manakin **2** B2	Vistalmar **4** B1	Restaurants ⬤
Hostal Casa Latina **1** C1	Oro Verde **3** B1		El Marino **1** B6

Manta and around *Colour map 3, A1.*

Ecuador's second port after Guayaquil is a busy town that sweeps round a bay filled with all sorts of boats. A constant sea breeze tempers the intense sun and makes the city's *malecones* pleasant places to stroll. At the gentrified west end of town is Playa Murciélago, a popular beach with wild surf (flags indicate whether it is safe to bathe), with good surfing from December to April. Here, the Malecón Escénico has a cluster of bars and seafood restaurants. It is a lively place especially at weekends, when there is good music, free beach aerobics and lots of action. West beyond El Murciélago, the Ruta del Spondylus is dual carriageway to San Mateo and being worked on towards Santa Marianita, San Lorenzo and Puerto Cayo (see above). The **Museo Centro Cultural Manta** ⓘ *Malecón y C 19, T05-262 6998, Mon-Fri 0830-1630, Sat-Sun 1000-1600, free,* has a small but excellent collection of archaeological pieces from seven different civilizations (Valdivia, Machalilla, Chorrera, Jama Coaque, Bahía, Guangala and Manteño) which flourished on the coast of Manabí between 3500 BC and AD 1530. It also holds tremporary exhibitions. At the port is a cruise ship terminal. Three bridges join the main town with **Tarqui**, which was flattened in the April 2016 earthquake. Nevertheless, Tarqui's beach with its associated fish market, seafood restaurants (El Parque del Marisco) and shipyards are operating. A new commercial centre, Nuevo Tarqui, housing Tarqui's traders, has been opened on Avenida La Cultura. The municipality is undertaking lots of urban improvement, with new roads, a hospital, bus terminal; see the Twitter page, https://twitter.com/Municipio_Manta. Enquire locally about changes to services and the current situation regarding public safety.

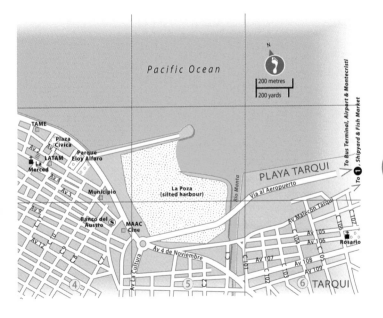

★ Crucita

A rapidly growing resort, 45 minutes by road from either Manta or Portoviejo, Crucita is busy at weekends and holidays when people flock here to enjoy ideal conditions for paragliding, hang-gliding and kite-surfing. The best season for flights is July to December. There is also an abundance of sea birds in the area. There are many restaurants serving fish and seafood along the seafront. A good one is **Motumbo**, try their *viche*, they also offer interesting tours and rent bikes.

North to Bahía

About 60 km northeast of Manta (30 km south of Bahía de Caráquez) are **San Clemente** and, 3 km south but basically all one town, **San Jacinto**. The ocean is magnificent but be wary of the strong undertow. The beach is lined with fishing huts and boats, with the usual mob of pelicans and frigate birds. Both places get crowded during the holiday season and have a selection of *cabañas* and hotels along the seafront. For example, **The Cottages by the Sea** ① *T09-8408 4211, www.thecottages.ec*, with fully-equipped cabins, pool and gardens; the upmarket hotel and spa, **Palmazul** ① *T05-267 3008, www. palmazulecuador.com*; and **San Jacinto** ① *T05-267 2516, www.hotelsanjacinto.com*, an older-style place, refurbished, with rooms, pool (US$3), restaurant, disco and karaoke. Some 3 km north of San Clemente is **Punta Charapotó**, a high promontory clad in dry tropical forest above a lovely beach. Here are some nice out-of-the-way places to stay and eat (eg Sabor de Bambú, sabor.debambu@hotmail.com, breakfasts, seafood and, after 1700, pizza, bar with craft beers, relaxed place, German and English spoken). On a 250-ha dry tropical forest reserve is **Peñón del Sol** ① *T09-9941 4149, penondelsol@hotmail.com*, with two walking trails and a big, rustic family house, lovely atmosphere and great views; they have three bamboo cabins ($$) being refurbished after the earthquake, camping and volunteering opportunities (includes breakfast, vegetarian/vegan meals on request).

Bahía de Caráquez and around *Colour map 3, A2.*

Set on the southern shore at the seaward end of the Chone estuary, Bahía has an attractive riverfront laid out with parks along the Malecón which goes right around the point to the ocean side. The beaches in town are nothing special, but there are excellent beaches nearby between San Vicente and Canoa and at Punta Bellaca (the town is busiest July and August). Bahía has declared itself an 'eco-city', with recycling projects, organic gardens and eco-clubs. Tricycle rickshaws called 'eco-taxis' are a popular form of local transport and keep the streets quiet. Information about the eco-city concept can be obtained from **Río Muchacho Organic Farm** in Canoa (see What to do, page 252) or the **Planet Drum Foundation** ① *www.planetdrum.org (information from 2015)*. The municipal website, www.sucre.gob.ec, also has information. Unfortunately, there was significant earthquake damage here in April 2016 and by late 2017 this was still much in evidence. The **Museo Bahía de Caráquez** ① *Malecón Alberto Santos y Aguilera*, with a collection of archaeological artefacts from prehispanic coastal cultures, was closed. Commercial activity, however, has returned to full operation. Bahía is a port for international yachts, with good service at **Puerto Amistad** ① *T05-269 3112, www.puertoamistad.com*.

The Río Chone estuary has several islands with mangrove forest. The area is rich in birdlife, and dolphins may also be seen. **Isla Corazón** has a boardwalk through an area of protected mangrove forest and there are bird colonies at the end of the island which can only be accessed by boat. It is reached from the village of **Puerto Portovelo**, which is involved in mangrove reforestation and runs an ecotourism project (tours with *guía nativo* US$5-15 per person for two to five people, www.islacorazon.com). You can visit independently, taking a Chone-bound bus from San Vicente or with an agency. Visits here are tide-sensitive, so even if you go independently, it is best to check with the agencies about the best time to visit. Inland near Chone is **La Segua** wetland, very rich in birds; Bahía agencies offer tours here. **Saiananda** ⓘ *5 km from Bahía along the bay, T05-239 8331, www.saiananda.com,* is a private park owned by biologist Alfredo Harmsen, with extensive areas of reforestation and a large collection of animals, a cactus garden and

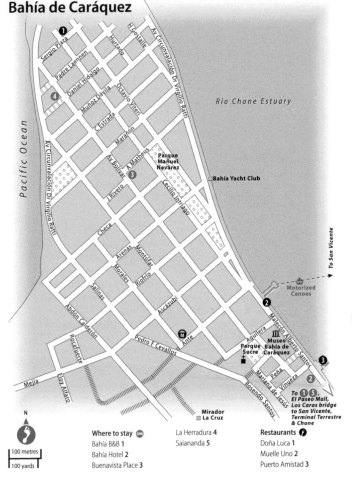

Bahía de Caráquez

Pacific Ocean

Río Chone Estuary

Sergio Plaza ❶

Padre Laennen

H Gostalle

Hurtado

Av Circunvalación Dr Virgilio Ratti

Daniel Hidalgo

Muñoz Dávila

Octavio Viteri

❹

C Estrada

Marañón

Av Circunvalación Dr Virgilio Ratti

Av Bolívar

A Matheus

Parque Manuel Nevárez

❸

Rivero

Cecilio Intriago

Bahía Yacht Club

Checa

Arenas

Montúfar

Riofrío

Salinas

Morales

To San Vicente

Abdón Calderón

Ascázubi

Motorized Canoes

Rocafuerte

Pedro F Cevallos

Ante

M

❷

Aguilera

Malecón Alberto Santos

Museo Bahía de Caráquez

Parque Sucre

Peña

Vinueza

❸

Mejía

Eloy Alfaro

Mariana de Jesús

Rosendo Santos

❷

To ❶❺, El Paseo Mall, Los Caras bridge to San Vicente, Terminal Terrestre & Chone

N

100 metres
100 yards

Mirador La Cruz

Where to stay 🛏
Bahía B&B **1**
Bahía Hotel **2**
Buenavista Place **3**

La Herradura **4**
Saiananda **5**

Restaurants 🍴
Doña Luca **1**
Muelle Uno **2**
Puerto Amistad **3**

spiritual centre. They also offer first-class accommodation ($$$ including taxes and breakfast), traditional Manabí meals served in an exquisite dining area over the water, tours and water sports. It can be reached by taxi or any bus heading out of town, US$2.

San Vicente and Canoa *Colour map 3, A2.*

On the north side of the Río Chone, **San Vicente** is reached from Bahía de Caráquez by the 2-km Los Caras bridge. Thanks to its construction, on 48 independently movable piles, it survived the 2016 earthquake, while San Vicente's Malecón has had to be rebuilt. Some 7 km beyond San Vicente is Briceño, whose beach is being developed and there are more new-builds going up on the 10-km stretch to ★**Canoa**. This was once a quiet fishing village with a splendid 200-m-wide beach, but grew rapidly and became very popular with Ecuadorean and foreign tourists. It is claimed that before the 2016 earthquake there were about 100 hotels in and around town. Only about 10 survived, but more are reopening. By late 2017, the town was picking up with lots of construction and repair work. The beach remains a wonderful attraction and it is a good base for plenty of activities. The sandy Malecón runs beside the beach, with small bamboo-and-thatch bars and snack-bars between road and beach. There are also attractive hostels along the Malecón, all with sea views. Two blocks back from the seafront is the market square, also sandy, with a few restaurants around it. The beautiful beach between San Vicente, Briceño and Canoa is a good walk, horse or bike ride. Horses and bicycles can be hired through several hotels. Surfing is good, particularly during the wet season, December to April. In the dry season there is good wind for windsurfing. Canoa is also a good place for hang-gliding and paragliding.

About 10 km north of Canoa is the turn-off (7 km) to the **Río Muchacho Organic Farm** ⓘ *www.riomuchacho.com, see What to do, page 252*, which accepts visitors and volunteers; it's an eye-opener to rural coastal (*montubio*) culture and to organic farming.

North to Pedernales *Colour map 1, B1.*

The coastal road cuts across Cabo Pasado, passing very few communities (a useful stop is Restaurante Maribel at Km 43 from San Vicente), to **Jama** (1½ hours). A new bridge crosses the river into town and there is a giant statue of a monkey. After Jama the road runs parallel to the beach past hotels and *balnearios*, the settlement of Don Juan where new houses have been built for those dispossessed by the 2016 earthquake, shrimp hatcheries, coconut groves and other crops. Just across the equator is **Pedernales**, a market town and crossroads with nice undeveloped beaches to the north. It was heavily damaged in the 2016 earthquake. A poor unpaved road goes north 35 km along the shore to Cojimíes, a fishing town at the end of the peninsula and at the mouth of the Río Mache. It's a popular beach resort with many good seafood restaurants, water sports and sunsets (the municipal website, http://gadcojimies.gob.ec, has some pictures and suggestions of places to stay). The main coastal road, fully paved, goes north, crossing into Esmeraldas province.

Santo Domingo de los Tsáchilas

From Pedernales, another important road goes inland to El Carmen; it divides at Puerto Nuevo: one branch to Santo Domingo de los Tsáchilas, another to La Concordia. The latter is the most direct route to Quito. In the hills above the western lowlands, Santo Domingo, 129 km from Quito, is an important commercial centre and transport hub. It is capital of the eponymous province. The city is big, noisy and unsafe, caution is recommended at all times in the market areas, including the pedestrian walkway along 3 de Julio and in peripheral neighbourhoods. Sunday is market day, shops and banks close Monday instead. It was known as 'Santo Domingo de los Colorados', a reference to the traditional red hair dye, made with *achiote* (annatto), worn by the indigenous Tsáchila men. Today the Tsáchila only wear their indigenous dress on special occasions. There are less than 2000 Tsáchilas left, living in eight communities off the roads leading from Santo Domingo towards the coast. Their lands make up a reserve of some 8000 ha. Visitors interested in their culture are welcome at the **Complejo Turístico Huapilú**, in the **Comunidad Chigüilpe**, where there is a small but interesting museum (contributions expected). Access is via the turn-off east at Km 7 on the road to Quevedo, from where it is 4 km. Tours are run by travel agencies in town. The Santo Domingo area also offers opportunities for nature trips and sports activities, such as rafting.

Listings Manta and Bahía de Caráquez *maps pages 244 and 247.*

Tourist information

Manta

Dirección Municipal de Turismo
At the Municipalidad, C9 y Av 4.
Mon-Fri 0800-1700.
Helpful and speak some English.

ITur Manta
Playa El Murciélago, diagonal al Estadio de Arena, T05-261 0171. Mon-Fri 0800-1700, Sat 1000-1700.

Where to stay

Manta and around
All streets have numbers; those above 100 are in Tarqui (those above C110 are not safe).

$$$$ Oro Verde
Malecón y C 23, T05-262 9200, www.ororodehotels.com.
Includes buffet breakfast, restaurant, pool, all luxuries.

$$$ Vistalmar
C M1 y Av 24B, at Playa Murciélago, T05-262 1671, www.hosteriavistaalmar.com.
Exclusive hotel overlooking the ocean. Ample cabins and suites tastefully decorated with art, a/c, pool, cabins have

kitchenettes, gardens by the sea. A place for a honeymoon.

$$ Hostal Casa Latina
C 26 y Av Flavio Reyes, Barrio Urmiña, T09-9682 7180, Facebook: casalatina2008.
Reopened in 2017 after earthquake damage, family-run, rooms with a/c or fan, bath, Wi-Fi, café, parking.

$$ Manakin
C 20 y Av 12, T05-262 0413, see Facebook.
A/c, comfortable rooms, small patio, café open for breakfast, nice common areas.

Crucita

$$-$ Cruzita
Malecón Sur y Sucre, towards the south end of the beach, T05-234 0068.
Pleasant hostel right on the beach with great views, meals on request, cold water, fan, pool, use of kitchen in the evening, parking, good value. Owner Raul Tobar offers paragliding flights and lessons. Recommended.

$$-$ Hostal Voladores
Nueva Loja y Principal, at the south end of the beach, T05-234 0200, www.parapentecrucita.com.
Simple but nice, restaurant, private bath, cheaper with cold water or shared bath,

small pool, sea kayaks available. Owner Luis Tobar offers paragliding flights and lessons.

Bahía de Caráquez

$$ Buenavista Place
Bolívar 701 y Matheus, T05-269 2400,
www.hotelbuenavistaplace.com
New hotel between the point and the commercial centre, convenient, with pool, parking and all services.

$$ Bahía B&B
Beyond El Paseo Shopping, by Puente Los
Caras access, 500 m from the Malecón,
T05-269 1880, http://ecuavacation.com.
A variety of different rooms in a modern building, a/c, parking, Canadian/Colombian-owned.

$$-$ La Herradura
Bolívar e Hidalgo, T05-269 0446,
www.laherradurahotelecuador.com.
Older well-maintained hotel, cheaper without a/c, nice common areas.

$ Hotel Bahía
Malecón y Vinueza, T05-269 3158,
or 09-5949 4073.
In an old building, with a variety of rooms, those at the back are nicer, cheaper without a/c, no meals.

Canoa

$$$ Hostería Canoa
At south end, about 500 m from centre of
town, T05-258 8180, www.hosteriacanoa.com.
Comfortable cabins and rooms, good restaurant and bar, a/c, pool, sauna, whirlpool.

$$ La Vista
On the beach next to Coco Loco, T05-
258 8108, www.lavistacanoa.com.
Wood and brick building with thatched roof, a/c rooms with seaview, hammocks on balconies, also has family rooms,

no breakfast or meals, can arrange all activities, parking.

$$-$ Baloo
On the beach at the south end of the village,
T09-8188 5048, www.baloo-canoa.com.
Wood and bamboo cabins, rooms with bath and fan, dorms US$8 pp with shared bath and use of kitchen, British-run. Nice quiet location, rebuilt after 2016 earthquake, also has a bar open Mon-Sat 1600-2130, Sun 2830-2130, parking.

$ Amalur
C San Andrés, opposite Plaza del Mercado
and football pitch, T09-8303 5039, www.
amalurcanoa.com.
Rooms and apartments ($$), brightly furnished, all with bath, welcoming, restaurant (see below), garden.
Yoga classes Mon, Wed, Fri at 0930.

$ pp Canoamar
On the beach toward the south end of town,
T09-6938 1673, www.canoamar.com.
Private, family and shared rooms with bath, mosquito nets, use of kitchen, breakfast on request US$3-3.50, book exchange, massage, tourist information and can organize surfing; helpful.

$ Casa Shangrila
A Aveiga 8, on main road 200 m
north of bridge, T09-9146 8470,
Facebook: casashangrilacanoa.
Inland, at north entrance to town, away from the buzz of the centre but only 5 mins' walk from a pleasant quiet stretch of beach. Rooms with fan and private bath, hot water, pretty garden, small pool, attentive service, good value.

$ Coco Loco
On the beach toward the south end of town,
T09-5910 4821, Facebook: hostelcocoloco.
Pleasant breezy hostel with nice views, under new ownership in 2017 and completely renovated with rooms with fan

and bath, dorms with shared bath, kitchen for guests, café serves breakfast (US$3-6) and family dinners (US$4-6 including vegetarian), new bar, live music, English spoken, popular, good information.

North to Pedernales
Jama

$$$$-$$$ Punta Prieta Guest House
By Punta Prieta, 14 km from Jama, 36 km from Pedernales, T09-8039 5972, Quito T02-286 2986, www.puntaprieta.com.
Gorgeous setting on a headland high above the ocean with access down to pristine beaches north and south (north is the safer of the 2). Has a variety of rooms and suites with fridge, balcony with hammocks, only breakfast available (restaurant for other meals temporarily closed), use of kitchen, pool overlooking south beach, nice grounds.

Pedernales

$$$ Cocosolo
On a secluded beach 20 km north of Pedernales on the road to Cojimíes (pick-ups from the main park US$1, 30 mins), T05-302 0708, or 09-9033 3306, http://cocosololodge.com.
A lovely hideaway set among palms. Cabins and rooms, backpackers' room US$20 pp, camping possible, excellent restaurant serving traditional Manabí fare, pool, boat trips, kayaks, fishing, walks and community visits, no Wi-Fi, no TV, no mobile signal.

Santo Domingo de los Tsáchilas

$$$ Zaracay
Av Quito 1639, 1.5 km from the centre, T02-275 0316, www.hotelzaracay.com.
Restaurant, gardens and swimming pool (US$5 for non-guests), parking, good rooms and service. Advance booking advised, especially at weekends.

$ Safiro Internacional
29 de Mayo 800 y Loja, T02-276 0706.

Comfortable modern hotel, cafeteria, hot water, a/c, good value.

Restaurants

Manta and around
Restaurants on Malecón Escénico serve local seafood.

$$ El Marino
Malecón y C 110, Tarqui. Lunch only.
Classic fish and seafood restaurant, for ceviches, *sopa marinera* and other delicacies.

Bahía de Caráquez
For reasonably priced fast food, go to the food court at El Paseo mall, which also has banks and ATMs.

$$ Puerto Amistad
On the pier at Malecón y Vinueza. Mon-Sat 1200-2400.
Nice setting over the water, international food and atmosphere, popular with yachties.

$$-$ Muelle Uno
By the pier where canoes leave for San Vicente. Daily 1000-2400.
Good grill and seafood, lovely setting over the water. This is the smartest of 3 places here; the other 2 are **La Terraza** and **Buen Sabor**.

$ Doña Luca
Cecilio Intriago y Sergio Plaza, towards the tip of the peninsula, no sign. Daily 0800-1800.
Simple little place serving local fare, including breakfasts and set lunches.

Canoa
For the local craft beer, go to **Beerkingo**, Río Canoa, near Finca Verde (see What to do, below), T09-8734 0472, see Facebook. Ask for Oswaldo.

$$-$ Amalur
See Where to stay, above. Daily 0800-1200 for breakfast, 1200-1500 and 1700-2200 for à la carte.

Fresh seafood and authentic Spanish and Mediterranean specialities, also vegetarian, attentive service.

$$-$ Saboréame
At the beach (2 locations) and on Plaza del Mercado. Open daily.
Good for *ceviche* and other local seafood dishes.

$$-$ Surf Shak
At the beach. Daily 0800-2400.
Good for pizza, burgers and breakfast, best coffee in town, Wi-Fi, popular hangout for surfers, English spoken.

What to do

Manta and around
Language courses
Academia Sur Pacífico, *C U8 entre Av Universitaria 2 y 3, Ciudadela Universitaria, T05-267 9206, www.surpacifico.k12.ec.* With a variety of programmes and activities.

Canoa
From Canoa you can arrange tours to Isla Corazón (see page 246); paragliding (US$40 tandem flight); surfboard rentals (US$5 per hr); trips with fishermen (US$25 pp) or to other beaches; visits to organic farms (see below) and more.
Canoa Thrills, *at the beach next to Surf Shak, T09-6744 4921, www.canoathrills.com.* Surfing tours and lessons, sea kayaking, paragliding, fishing trips. Also rent boards and bikes. English spoken.
Finca Verde, *7 km from town on the Río Canoa, Facebook: fincaverde.* Permculture project with lodging, horse riding (US$40), Canadian/Ecuadorean-owned, takes volunteers.
Río Muchacho Organic Farm Park & Lodge, *T05-302 0487, or 09-9277 7925 at 1200 or 1800, www.riomuchacho.com (limited internet access, allow a couple of days for email reply).* Fully operational and rebuilding after earthquake, this is a social enterprise and educational centre with accommodation, Ecuadorean/New Zealander-owned and run. There are trails to the pretty river and to a mirador, a children's park and 167 species of bird identified on regenerated and reforested land. Wooden cabins with composting toilets ($ pp); all food in the restaurant is home produced, absolutely fresh and organic, vegetarian, innovative, US$5 per meal, communal eating. Lots of activities with or without guides, recommended for families; classes include permaculture, Spanish, yoga and bamboo construction; volunteers welcome. Helpful with local information. Warmly recommended.

Transport

Manta and around
Air
Eloy Alfaro airport. **TAME** (T05-261 0100), **Avianca** (T05-262 8899) and **LATAM** (A2 No 1155) to **Quito** several daily.

Bus
The new busterminal (opened late 2017) is in El Palmar, 6 km from the centre, near the airport, T05-303 7681, Facebook: ttManta. To **Quito** Terminal Quitumbe, 9 hrs, US$11-13. **Guayaquil**, 4 hrs, US$6.25, hourly. **Esmeraldas**, 3 daily, 10 hrs, US$11. **Santo Domingo**, 6 hrs, US$7-8. **Portoviejo**, 45 mins, US$1-2, every 10 mins. **Jipijapa**, 1 hr, US$1, every 20 mins. **Bahía de Caráquez**, 3 hrs, US$3, hourly.

Crucita
Bus
Run along the Malecón. There is frequent service to **Portoviejo**, US$1.25, 1 hr and **Manta**, US$1.50, 1½ hrs.

North to Bahía
Bus and taxi
From San Clemente to **Portoviejo**, every 15 mins, US$1.50, 1¼ hrs. To **Bahía de Caráquez**, US$0.75, 30 mins, a few start in San Clemente in the morning or wait for a through bus at the highway. Mototaxis from San Clemente to Punta Charapotó, US$0.75.

Bahía de Caráquez
Boat
Motorized canoes (*lanchas* or *pangas*) cross the estuary to **San Vicente**, from the dock opposite C Ante, US$0.50.

Bus
The Terminal Terrestre is at the entrance to town, 3 km from centre, taxi US$2. To **Quito** Terminal Quitumbe, **Reina del Camino** at 0620, 0800, 2145 and 2220, 8 hrs, US$10-12.50. To **Santo Domingo**, 5 hrs, US$6. To **Guayaquil**, hourly, 6 hrs, US$7-10. To **Portoviejo**, 2 hrs, US$2.50. To **Manta**, 3 hrs. US$3. To **Puerto López**, change in Manta, or better yet Portoviejo or Jipijapa.

Canoa
Bus and taxi
Buses set down and pick up near Farmacia Cruz Azul, opposite which is a taxi stand. To/from **San Vicente**, every 30 mins, 0600-1900, 30 mins, US$0.75, Tosagua bus; taxi US$2.50. Tosagua bus also from Bahía's bus station, same price; taxi to/from Bahía de Caráquez, US$8. To **Pedernales**, every 30 mins 0600-1800, 1½ hrs, US$3.25 with **Coactur**, which also goes to **Guayaquil** (as does **Reina del Camino**). To **Quito**, direct with **Reina del Camino** at 1030, 2330 (from Quito 1200, 2330), US$12.50, 6 hrs; or transfer in Pedernales or Bahía.

Pedernales
Bus
To **Santo Domingo**, every 15 mins, 3½ hrs, US$4, transfer to Quito. To **Quito** (Quitumbe) direct with **Reina del Camino** and **Trans Vencedores**, 5-7 daily via Santo Domingo, US$7-9, 6 hrs; also starting in Jama 4 times a day. To **Chamanga**, hourly 0600-1700, 1½ hrs, US$2.50, change there for **Esmeraldas**, 3½ hrs, US$4.50. To **Bahía de Caráquez**, shared vans from Plaza Acosta 121 y Robles, T05-268 1019, 7 daily, US$5.75.

Santo Domingo de los Tsáchilas
Bus and taxi
The bus terminal is on Av Abraham Calazacón, at the north end of town, along the city's bypass. Long-distance buses do not enter the city. Taxi downtown, US$1, bus US$0.25. A major hub with service throughout Ecuador. To **Quito** via Alóag US$4-5, 3 hrs; via San Miguel de los Bancos, 5 hrs; also **Sudamericana Taxis**, Cocaniguas 218 y Río Toachi, T02-276 1462, www.sudaten.com, door to door shared taxi service, frequent departures via Alóag or Los Bancos, 0400-1900, US$15-17, 3-4 hrs. To Mindo, **Coop Kennedy** via La Concordia, 3½ hrs, US$5, 5 a day. To **Ambato** US$5, 4 hrs. To **Loja** US$21, 11 hrs. To **Guayaquil** US$7, 5 hrs. To **Esmeraldas** US$3-4, 3 hrs. To **Atacames**, US$5, 4 hrs. To **Manta** US$7-8, 6 hrs. To **Bahía de Caráquez** US$6, 6 hrs. To **Pedernales** US$4, 3½ hrs. To Sigchos (Quilotoa Circuit) via Las Pampas with Reina de Sigchos, daily 0600, 1100, 1200, 1400, US$6, 6 hrs.

A mixture of palm-lined beaches, mangroves (where not destroyed for shrimp production), tropical rainforests, Afro-Ecuadorean and Cayapa indigenous communities characterize this part of Ecuador's Pacific lowlands as they stretch north to the Colombian border.

North to Atacames

North of Pedernales the coastal highway veers northeast, going slightly inland, then crosses into the province of Esmeraldas near **Chamanga** (San José de Chamanga, population 4400), a village with houses built on stilts on the freshwater estuary. It was devastated in the April 2016 earthquake. The town is 1 km from the highway. Inland and spanning the provincial border is the **Reserva Ecológica Mache-Chindul**, a reserve with both humid and dry forest (access is from Quinindé on the Santo Domingo–Esmeraldas road, on the eastern side of the park, http://areasprotegidas.ambiente.gob.ec).

Thirty-one kilometres north of Chamanga and 7 km from the main road along a paved side road is ★ **Mompiche** with a lovely beach and one of Ecuador's best surfing spots. There are three surf schools and it's a laid-back, safe place. At night you can see phosphorescence in the sea. The main street runs down to the sea, parallel to which the front has been rather damaged. The fishing fleet comes in at the southwestern end of the beach, beyond which is a breakwater to stop the beach being eroded. Further on still is an animal refuge and, at low tide, you can walk around the southwestern point to see boobies. There is an international resort complex and holiday real estate development (Decameron) 2 km south, past Playa Arena Negra at Punta Portete, in front of which is the small Isla Portete. The nearest banks and ATMs are far away in Atacames and Pedernales. Take sufficient cash. *Colectivos* wait at the bus stop at the intersection on the main road. The fare to Mompiche should be US$1, but they usually ask US$3. In the daytime it's OK to wait here for transport in or out, but don't do so at night: it is not safe.

The main road continues through El Salto, 84 km from Pedernales, the crossroads for **Muisne**, a town part of which is on an island with a beach (strong undertow). A footbridge takes mototaxis and pedestrians to the island; on the landward side the main street is scruffy and car drivers are hustled by people offering to park the car (not a problem if you arrive by bus).

The fishing village of **Tonchigüe** is 25 km north of El Salto. A few kilometres south of it, a paved road goes west and more or less follows the line of the shore of the peninsula which includes **Punta Galera** and Cabo San Francisco. About 14 km from Tonchigüe is the entrance to the secluded beach of **Playa Escondida** (signpost on the main road, see Where to stay, below). The road eventually meets the access road to Muisne but is poor in parts south of Punta Galera. Offshore is the 54,604-ha **Reserva Marina Galera San Francisco**, which extends along 37 km of the coastline, protecting coastal and marine habitats, including reefs and islets. Forested hills come down to the sea and there are some lovely secluded beaches.

Three kilometres northeast of Tonchigüe is **Playa de Same**, with a beautiful, long, clean, grey sandy beach, safe for swimming. The accommodation here is mostly upmarket, intended for wealthy Quiteños, with white condos stretching up the hillside. It is wonderfully quiet in the low season. There is good birdwatching in the area and some of the hotels offer whale watching tours in season. Ten kilometres east of Same and 4 km west of Atacames, is **Súa**, a friendly little beach resort, set in a beautiful bay. The grey sand cove has cliffs at one end and the sea is calmer than on other ocean beaches. Boats make trips to the **Isla de los Pájaros** (US$25 for three passengers) to see the birds and, in season, whale-watching trips (US$20 per person, one hour; ask at **Hotel Chagra Ramos**). Damage from the 2016 earthquakes is slowly being repaired.

Atacames *Colour map 1, A2.*

One of the main resorts on the Ecuadorean coast, Atacames, 30 km southwest of Esmeraldas, is a real party town during the high season (July-September), at weekends and national holidays. Head instead for Súa or Playa Escondida (see above) if you want peace and quiet. The town itself has a busy commercial centre full of traffic and shops which is separated from the beach front by the green, mangrove-lined river. Cross the bridge and turn right to the hotel and restaurant zone, which has a Malecón del Río and a Malecón del Mar. There is no seafront boulevard to speak of because it is all taken up with thatched bamboo restaurants.

Some 12 km east of Atacames is Tonsupa (18 km from Esmeraldas), another resort favoured by Quiteños, with a collection of high-rise apartment blocks and hotels interspersed with empty lots. The pleasant beach sweeps along to the mouth of the river at Atacames.

After the damage caused by the April 2016 earthquake, the area around Atacames and Esmeraldas was further affected by a second earthquake in December 2016.

Esmeraldas *Colour map 1, A2.*

Capital of the eponymous province, Esmeraldas is a place to learn about Afro-Ecuadorean culture. Marimba groups can be seen practising in town, enquire about schedules at the tourist office. Ceramics from La Tolita culture (see below), as well as finds from other pre-Columbian periods and displays of current coastal cultures are all found at the **Museo Arqueológico Esmeraldas** ⓘ *Piedrahita 427 y Bolívar, T06-272 7076, Tue-Sun 0830-1630, US$1, English explanations.* It also has temporary exhibitions. If in the city this museum should not be missed. The main highway from San Lorenzo passes the airport at Tachina, then crosses a bridge over the Río Esmeraldas to enter the city. Turn right to go to the commercial centre, the ports for the fishing fleet and ocean-going vessels and Playa Las Palmas district, where the new Malecón Las Palmas has built beside the ocean, with open spaces, sports and entertainment areas, restaurants and bars. Turn left after the bridge for the bypass and roads to Santo Domingo and Atacames.

Despite its wealth in natural resources, Esmeraldas is among the poorest provinces in the country. Shrimp farming has destroyed much mangrove, and timber exports and African palm plantations are decimating Ecuador's last Pacific rainforest.

Insect-borne diseases including malaria are a serious problem in many parts of Esmeraldas province, especially in the rainy season (January to May). Most *residenciales* provide mosquito nets (*toldos* or *mosquiteros*) or you can buy one in the market.

> **Tip...**
> The main coastal road in Esmeraldas province is not as fast as in Manabí. It is paved, but the carriageway is narrower and roadside communities are closer together. Most of them have set up speed-restriction bumps. Allow more time for travelling in this part of the country.

North of Esmeraldas

From Esmeraldas, the coastal road goes northeast to Camarones, Palestina and Río Verde, with a nice beach, from where it goes east to **Las Peñas**, once a sleepy seaside village with a nice wide beach, now a holiday resort. With the paved highway from Ibarra, Las Peñas is the closest beach to the highland towns north of Quito, only four hours by bus. Ibarreños and Colombians pack the place at weekends and on holidays. From Las Peñas, a secondary road follows the shore north to **La Tola** (122 km from Esmeraldas) where you can catch a launch to Limones. Here the shoreline changes from sandy beaches to mangrove swamp; the wildlife is varied and spectacular, especially the birds. The tallest mangrove trees in the world (63.7 m) are found by **Majagual** to the south. To the northeast of La Tola and on an island on the northern shore of the Río Cayapas is **La Tolita**, a small, poor village, where the culture of the same name thrived between 300 BC and AD 700. Many remains have been found here, several burial mounds remain to be explored and looters continue to take out artefacts to sell.

Limones (also known as Valdez) is the focus of traffic downriver from much of northern Esmeraldas Province, where bananas from the Río Santiago are sent to Esmeraldas for export. The Cayapa people live up the Río Cayapas and can sometimes be seen in Limones, especially during the crowded weekend market, but they are more frequently seen at Borbón (see below).

Borbón and further north

Borbón, upriver from La Tola at the confluence of the Cayapas and Santiago rivers, is a lively, dirty, busy and somewhat dangerous place, with a high rate of malaria. The local fiestas are held in September (see page 260).

From Borbón, the coastal road goes northeast towards **Calderón** where it meets the Ibarra–San Lorenzo road. Along the way, by the Río Santiago, are the nature reserves of **Humedales de Yalare**, accessed from **Maldonado**, and Playa de Oro (see below). From Calderón, the two roads run together for a few kilometres before the coastal road turns north and ends at **Mataje** on the border with Colombia. The road from Ibarra continues to San Lorenzo.

San Lorenzo *Colour map 1, A4.*

Hot and humid San Lorenzo stands on the Bahía del Pailón, which is characterized by a maze of canals. It is a good place to experience the Afro-Ecuadorean culture including marimba music and dances. There is a local festival in August (see page 260) and groups practice throughout the year; ask around. At the seaward end of the bay are several beaches without facilities, including **San Pedro** (one hour away) and **Palma Real** (1¾ hours). Note that this is a tense border area with many police and other patrols, but also armed civilians and much contraband activity. Enquire about current conditions with the police or Navy (Marina). From San Lorenzo you can visit several natural areas; launches can be hired for excursions, see Transport, page 261. There are mangroves at **Reserva Ecológica Cayapas-Mataje**, which protects islands in the estuary northwest of town. **Reserva Playa de Oro**, see Where to stay, page 259, has 10,406 ha of Chocó rainforest, rich in wildlife, along the Río Santiago. Access is from **Selva Alegre** (a couple of basic *residenciales*), off the road to Borbón.

Border with Colombia: San Lorenzo–Tumaco

The Río Mataje is the border with Colombia. From San Lorenzo, the port of Tumaco in Colombia can be reached by a combination of boat and land transport. Because this is a most unsafe region, travellers are advised not to enter Colombia at this border. Go to Tulcán and Ipiales instead.

Tourist information

Atacames
Cámara de Turismo de Atacames
Vía Atacames–Súa, T06-273 1333,
Facebook: captur.atacames.

Esmeraldas

Alcaldía de Esmeraldas
Juan Montalvo y Pedro Vicente Maldonado,
T06-272 5263, http://turismo.esmeraldas.
gob.ec. Mon-Fri 0800-1700.
The website has information on places to visit, hotels and restaurants.

ITur
Bolívar y 9 de Octubre, T06-272 3150,
Facebook: turismociudadesmeraldas.
Mon-Fri 0800-1700, and at the airport.

Where to stay

North to Atacames
Mompiche
There are many economical places on C La Fosforera, with direct access to the beach and vehicular access from the street. They range from the smart **San Antonio Suite ($$$)** at the northeastern end to **Casa Coral** (Facebook:casacoralmompiche), **Kiwi Hostal** (Facebook: kiwimompiche) and **La Jungla** (3 tropical bungalows, www. lajunglabungalows.com), near where the fishing boats come in. Others can be found on the main street.

$$ Bam-Bú
C La Fosforera, T09-5978 09412,
www.bambu-hotel.com.
Built entirely of bamboo, this is a large place with rooms which have double bunks and singles with bath, fan, hammock area by bar, breakfast available, dinner of burgers and pizzas from 1900.

$ DMCA (de Mompiche con Amor)
C La Fosforera, T06-244 8022, see Facebook.
Surf hostel with private rooms and dorms (US$7 pp), some with sea view, shared bath, mosquito nets, hammock zone and guests' kitchen.

$ pp La Facha
C La Fosforera, T06-244 8024,
www.lafachahostel.com.
Hostel with private and shared rooms and a popular restaurant (**$$**) open for breakfast 0800-1030 and dinner 2000-2400, great seafood and vegetarian (try their veggie burgers), very creative and recommended. Argentine chef.

Punta Galera

$$ Playa Escondida
14 km west of Tonchigüe and 6 km east of
Punta Galera, T06-302 7483, T09-9650 6812,
www.playaescondida.com.ec.
A charming beach hideaway set in 100 ha with 500-m beachfront stretching back to dry tropical forest with guayacán trees. Entry to reserve US$5. Run by Canadian Judith Barett on an ecologically sound basis. Nice rustic rooms in main building and in other buildings of various sizes overlooking

a lovely little bay, private showers, shared composting toilets, mosquito nets, hammocks, some villas have kitchen and sun terrace, camping at sea level US$7 pp, excellent restaurant (**Caoba**, T09-8102 8703), all meals extra, good birdwatching, swimming and walking along the beach at low tide. Also offers volunteer opportunities.

Same

$$$ El Acantilado
By the cliff, Same, T06-302 7620,
www.elacantilado.net.
Comfortable rooms and cabins, pool, nice views, gardens, good restaurant, path to the beach. Also operate a camping area at Tongorachí, near Cabo San Francisco, US$30 pp including 3 meals prepared in the community, a private development project.

$$-$ La Terraza
On Same beach, T06-247 0320,
pepol@hotmail.es.
Pleasant rooms and cabins for 3-4 with balconies, hammocks and large terrace, spacious, hot water, a/c, fan, mosquito net, some rooms have fridge, good restaurant open in season, Spanish-run.

Súa

$ Chagra Ramos
On the Malecón, T06-247 3106
or 09-8012 7240, see Facebook.
Hotel with balconies overlooking the beach, many steps up hillside, tepid water, fan, no breakfast, restaurant and bar, parking, good service, being refurbished (2017).

$ pp Las Buganvillas
On the Malecón, T06-247 3008, see Facebook.
Basic, cold water, fans, room 10 has the best views, small pool, no breakfast, helpful owners. Reception is in **Bazaar Anita** shop beside the gate.

Atacames

Prices rise on holiday weekends, discounts may be available in low season. There are many more hotels than we can list.

$$$ Cielo Azul
Av 21 de Noviembre, towards the west end of the beach, entrance 1 block back from sea, T06-273 1813, www.hotelcieloazul.com.
Rooms with balconies and hammocks, comfortable, well cared for property leads through to beach, restaurant, small pool, very good, German-owned, Ecuadorean-run.

$$$ Juan Sebastián
Malecón de la Playa, towards the east end of the beach, T06-273 1606, www.hoteles-embassy.com/juansebastian/en/index.php.
Large upmarket low-rise hotel with cabins and suites, restaurant, a/c, 3 pools (US$5 for non-guests), fridge, parking, popular with Quiteños, major refurbishment underway in late 2017. In same group and close by, also **$$$**, is **Costa Paraíso**, Malecón de la Playa entre Coral Negro y Delfines, T06-276 0848, similar services but a bit cheaper than Juan Sebastián.

$$ Carluz
Barrio Nueva Granada, Av 21 de Noviembre, near Cielo Azul, T06-273 1456, www.hotelcarluz.com.
Good hotel in a quiet location, not on the beach. Comfortable suites for 4 and apartments for 6, good restaurant, a/c, fan, pool, fridge, parking.

Esmeraldas

$$$ Perla Verde
Piedrahíta 330 y Olmedo, T06-272 3820, www.hotelperlaverde.ec.
Good rooms with a/c and fridge, restaurant, bar, ATM, parking, in the city centre.

$$$-$$ Apart Hotel Esmeraldas
Libertad 407 y Ramón Tello, T06-272 0622, http://aparthotelesmeraldas.net.

Good restaurant, a/c, fridge, parking, excellent quality, in the city centre.

North of Esmeraldas
Las Peñas

$$$-$$ Cabañas Mikey
By the beach, north end, T06-279 3101, http://laspeñasesmeraldas.com/cabanas_mikey.html.
Cabins with kitchenettes, private bath, hot water, pool.

San Lorenzo

$$$ Playa de Oro
On the Río Santiago, upriver from Borbón, contact through Maquipucuna (see page 89), www.maquipucuna.org.
Basic cabins with shared bath, includes 3 meals and guided excursion. Advance booking required.

$$ Tunda Loma
Km 17 on the road to Ibarra (taxi from San Lorenzo US$5), T06-278 0367.
Beautifully located on a hill overlooking the Río Tululbí. Wood cabins, includes breakfast, restaurant, warm water, fan, organizes tubing trips on the river and hikes in the forest.

$$-$ Castillo Real
Camilo Ponce y Esmeraldas, T06-278 0152, see Facebook.
Rooms with private bath and a/c, cheaper with fan, good restaurant, parking.

Restaurants

North to Atacames
Mompiche

Several places on the main street serve cheap set meals, all much the same. Most hostels have a restaurant of some description. Water is in short supply; it comes from rain butts or deep wells and has chlorine added (sometimes too much, sometimes too little).

Same

$$$ El Nuevo Sea Flower
By the beach at the entrance road.
Excellent Mediterranean food.

$$-$ Azuca
By south entrance to town, T09-8882 9581, Facebook: AZUCA-Restaurante-Hostel.
Good creative food, also rents cheap rooms with shared or private bath.

Súa

$ Kikes
On the Malecón, T09-9355 8406.
Good local food, generous portions, good value, also rents rooms.

Atacames

The area between the Malecones del Río and del Mar is packed with bars and restaurants offering seafood, too many to list.

$$ Da Giulio
Malecón y Cedros. Weekdays 1700-2300, weekends from 1100.
Italian cuisine, good pasta and pizzas, some Spanish dishes, on 2 floors.

$$-$ La Ramada
On the Malecón del Mar opposite Hotel Playa Hermosa.
A group of kitchens specializing in ceviches and *encebollados*, good value. Open for breakfast. Similar is the **Asociación de Cevicheros** (12 de Octubre, opposite Hotel Juan Sebastián), also open from breakfast time.

Esmeraldas

There are restaurants and bars on the Malecón Las Palmas offering regional specialities.

$$ Chifa Asiático
Cañizares y Bolívar, T06-272 6888.
Chinese and seafood, a/c, excellent.

$$ La Casa del Chacal
Manabí y Alfaro, T09-9146 7531, Facebook:
La-Casa-Del-Chacal. Open 1700-2300.
Tasty à la carte meals, grill, popular with locals.

$$-$ Ceviches Maranatha
Quito y Olmedo, T09-9415 0681.
Good ceviche and other seafood.

$$-$ Parrilladas el Toro
Olmedo y 9 de Octubre, T06-272 3610,
Facebook: parrilladaeltoro. Open 1730-2300.
Popular meat and seafood grill.

Festivals

Borbon
1st week Sep Local fiestas with marimba music and other Afro-Ecuadorean traditions.

San Lorenzo
6-10 Aug Local festival; groups practice throughout the year; ask around.

Transport

North to Atacames
Bus and taxi
Hourly from **Chamanga** to **Esmeraldas**, US$6, 3½ hrs, and to **Pedernales**, US$2, 1½ hrs. **Mompiche** to/from **Esmeraldas**, 8 a day, US$4, 3 hrs, the last one from Esmeraldas about 1630. To **Playa Escondida**: take a *ranchera* or bus from Esmeraldas or Atacames for Punta Galera or Cabo San Francisco, 5 a day, US$2.50, 2 hrs. A taxi from Atacames costs US$15 and a pick-up from Tonchigüe US$6.25. To **Súa** and **Same**: Buses run every 30 mins to and from **Atacames**, 15 mins, US$0.50. Make sure it drops you at Same and not at **Club Casablanca**.

Atacames
Bus
To **Esmeraldas**, every 15 mins, US$1, 1 hr. To **Guayaquil**, US$12, 8 hrs, **Trans Esmeraldas** at 0830 and 2245. To **Quito**, various companies, about 10 daily, US$10, 7 hrs. To **Pedernales**, **Coop G Zambrano**, 4 daily, US$9, 4 hrs or change in Chamanga.

Esmeraldas
Air
The **airport** is along the coastal road heading north. A taxi to the city centre costs US$3, buses to the Terminal Terrestre from the road outside the airport pass about every 30 mins. If heading north towards San Lorenzo, you can catch a bus outside the airport. **TAME** (Bolívar y 9 de Octubre, under Palacio Municipal, T06-272 1913), 1-2 daily flights to **Quito**.

Bus
Terminal Terrestre by Redondel Petrolrios at Aki supermarket in Codesa district, some distance from centre, taxi to town US$3, to airport US$6. **Trans-Esmeraldas** (recommended) and **Panamericana** have *servicio directo* or *ejecutivo* to **Quito** and **Guayaquil**, a better choice as they are faster buses and don't stop for passengers along the way. Frequent service to **Quito** via Santo Domingo to Quitumbe or via San Miguel de Los Bancos to Carcelén, US$9, 6 hrs; ask which terminal they go to before purchasing tickets; also shared vans door-to-door via Los Bancos with (for example) **Robles y Robles**, Las Palmas, T09-9412 8500, 4 vehicles daily, 5 hrs, US$25, pay extra to/from the beaches. To **Santo Domingo**, US$4, 3 hrs. To **Ambato**, 6 a day, US$10, 8 hrs. To **Guayaquil**, hourly, US$11.25, *directo*, 8 hrs. To **Bahía de Caráquez**, via Santo Domingo, US$11, 9 hrs. To **Manta**, US$11, 10 hrs. La Costeñita and El Pacífico, both on Malecón, to/from **La Tola**, 8 daily, US$4.75, 3 hrs. To **Borbón**, frequent service, US$3-4, 3 hrs. To **San Lorenzo**, 8 daily, US$5, 4 hrs. To **Súa**, **Same** and **Atacames**, every 15 mins from 0630-2030, to Atacames US$1, 1 hr. To **Chamanga**, hourly 0500-1900, US$6, 3½ hrs, change here for points south.

North of Esmeraldas
Boat
There are launches between **La Tola** and **Limones** which connect with the buses arriving from Esmeraldas, US$4, 1 hr, and 3 daily Limones–**San Lorenzo**, 2 hrs US$3. You can also hire a launch to **Borbón**, a fascinating trip through mangrove islands, passing hunting pelicans, approximately US$10 per hr.

Borbón
Bus
To **Esmeraldas**, US$3-4, 3 hrs. To **San Lorenzo**, US$2, 1 hr.

San Lorenzo
Boat
Launch service with **Coopseturi**, T06-278 0161; and **Costeñita**, both near the pier. All services are subject to change and cancellation. To **Limones**, 4 daily, US$3, 2 hrs. To **La Tola**, US$6, 4 hrs. To **Palma Real**, for beaches, 2 daily, US$3, 2 hrs.

Bus
Buses leave from the train station or environs. To **Ibarra**, 10 daily, US$7, 4 hrs. To **Esmeraldas**, via Borbón, 8 daily, US$5, 4 hrs.

The Oriente

the vast green carpet of Amazonia

East of the Andes the hills fall away to El Oriente, the vast green carpet of Amazonia. Some of this beautiful wilderness remains unspoiled and sparsely populated, with indigenous settlements along the tributaries of the Amazon.

For the visitor, the Ecuadorean jungle, especially northern Oriente, has the advantage of being relatively accessible and tourist infrastructure here is well developed.

Most tourists love the exotic feeling of El Oriente, and El Oriente needs tourists. Large tracts of jungle are under threat; colonists have cleared many areas for agriculture, while others are laid waste by petroleum exploration or mining. The region's irreplaceable biodiversity and traditional ways of life can only be protected if sustainable ecotourism provides a viable economic alternative.

The eastern foothills of the Andes, where the jungle begins, offer a good introduction to the rainforest for those with limited time or money. Further east lie the remaining tracts of primary rainforest, teeming with life, which can be visited from several excellent (and generally expensive) jungle lodges. Southern Oriente is as yet less developed for tourism, it offers good opportunities off the beaten path but is threatened by large mining projects.

Best for
Ethno-tourism ▪ Jungle lodges ▪ Whitewater sports

Footprint
picks

★ Rafting and kayaking from Baeza or Tena,
pages 265 and 281
Both of these pleasant towns provide access to excellent white water tumbling down the eastern slopes of the Andes.

★ San Rafael Falls, page 265
This beautiful and impressive 145-m cascade is believed to be the highest in Ecuador.

★ Río Napo Jungle Lodges, pages 266, 277 and 286
Along the upper and lower reaches of the Napo River are some of the finest jungle lodges in the country, offering top-notch facilities surrounded by pristine rainforest.

★ Cuyabeno Wildlife Reserve, page 271
This is among the best places in Ecuador to see Amazon wildlife and offers a more economical jungle experience than many other areas of the Oriente.

★ Río Nangaritza Gorge, page 283
In the far south of Oriente, the upper Río Nangaritza flows through Shuar territory and a magnificent jungle-covered gorge with 200-m-high walls.

N

50 km
50 miles

COLOMBIA

Limones
(Valdéz)
Mataje
San Lorenzo
La Tola
Borbón
Maldonado
ESMERALDAS
Tulcán
Gualupe
Salinas
El Angel
Mira
San Gabriel
Bolívar
La Bonita
Gral Farfán
Putumayo
Puerto El Carmen
de Putumayo
IMBABURA
Ibarra
SUCUMBÍOS
Lago
Agrio
Tarapoa
Reserva
Faunística
Cuyabeno
Güeppi
Cayambe
Otavalo
Reventador
(3560m)
Shushifindi
Mindo
QUITO
Chiriboga
Sangolquí
El Chaco
Pan de Azúcar
Reventador
(3732m)
Coca
Limoncocha
Aguarico
Pañacocha
Zancudo
Santo Domingo
Machachi
Baeza
Sumaco
(3732m)
Pompeya
Napo
Tiputini
Tiputini
COTOPAXI
Lasso
Saquisilí
Narupa
Parque
Nacional Sumaco
Loreto
ORELLANA
Nuevo
Rocafuerte
Quilotoa
Sigchos
Latacunga
Archidona
Chontapunta
Parque
Nacional
Yasuní
Pilaló
Pujilí
Salcedo
Tena
Misahuallí
Ahuano
Nashiño
El Corazón
TUNGURAHUA
Puerto Napo
Tigüino
Cononaco
Cononaco
Ambato
Pelileo
Mera
Arajuno
Napo
BOLÍVAR
Baños
Shell
Puyo
PASTAZA
Curaray
Guaranda
Riobamba
Porvenir
Babonoza
Pintoyacu
Chimbo
Cajabamba
Conambo
Guamote
Corrientes
CHIMBORAZO
MORONA
SANTIAGO
Curaray
Sibambe
Atillo
Pastaza
Alausí
Cordillera de Cutucú
Macas
Morona
Río Corientes
El Tambo
Ishpingo
Cañar
Azogues
CAÑAR
Paute
Cuenca
Baños
Chordeleg
Limón
Puerto
Morona
Sigsig
AZUAY
Indanza
Girón
Jima
Oña
Nabón
Gualaquiza
Saraguro
El Pangui
Parque Binacional
El Cóndor
Yacuambi
Zumbi
Catamayo
ZAMORA
CHINCHIPE
PERU
Loja
Zamora
Malacatos
Reserva El Zarza
Vilcabamba
Yangana
Valladolid
Palanda
Zumba
La Balsa

Footprint
picks

1 **Rafting and kayaking from Baeza or Tena**, pages 265 and 281
2 **San Rafael Falls**, page 265
3 **Río Napo Jungle Lodges**, pages 266, 277 and 286
4 **Cuyabeno Wildlife Reserve**, page 271
5 **Río Nangaritza Gorge**, page 283

Much of the Northern Oriente is taken up by the Parque Nacional Yasuní, the Cuyabeno Wildlife Reserve and most of the Cayambe-Coca Ecological Reserve. The main towns for access are Baeza, Lago Agrio and Coca.

Quito to the Oriente

From Quito to Baeza, a paved road goes via the **Guamaní pass** (4064 m). It crosses the Eastern Cordillera just north of **Volcán Antisana** (5705 m), and then descends via the small village of **Papallacta** (hot springs, see page 82) to the old mission settlement of Baeza. The trip between the pass and Baeza has beautiful views of the glaciers of Antisana (clouds permitting), high waterfalls, *páramo*, cloudforest and a lake contained by an old lava flow.

★ Baeza *Colour map 1, C5.*

The mountainous landscape and high rainfall have created spectacular waterfalls and dense vegetation. Orchids and bromeliads abound. Baeza, in the beautiful Quijos valley, is about 1 km from the main junction of roads from Lago Agrio and Tena. The town itself is divided in two parts: a faded but pleasant **Baeza Colonial** (Old Baeza) and **Baeza Nueva** (New Baeza), where most shops and services are located. The trail/road from Baeza Vieja to Las Antenas has nice views, two hours return. There are excellent kayaking and rafting opportunities in the area, tours offered by **La Casa de Rodrigo** (see Where to stay, page 275) and operators in Quito and Tena (see pages 72 and 291).

Beyond Baeza

From Baeza a road heads south to Tena, with a branch going east via Loreto to Coca, all paved. Another paved road goes northeast from Baeza to Lago Agrio, following the Río Quijos past the villages of **Borja** (8 km from Baeza, very good *comedor* **Doña Cleo** along the highway, closed Sunday) and **El Chaco** (12 km further, basic accommodation) to the slopes of the active volcano **Reventador**, 3560 m (erupting since 2002). Check www.igepn. edu.ec and enquire locally about volcanic activity before trekking here; **Ecuador Journeys** offers tours, see page 73. Half a kilometre south of the bridge over the Río Reventador is signed access to the impressive 145-m ★ **San Rafael Falls** (part of Reserva Ecológica Cayambe-Coca), believed to be the highest in Ecuador. It is a pleasant 45-minute hike through cloudforest to a *mirador* with stunning views of the thundering cascade. Many birds can be spotted along the trail, including cock-of-the-rock, also monkeys and coatimundis. A large hydroelectric project has been built nearby. Although access to the falls is not restricted, the turbines use up to 70% of the water in the Río Quijos, leaving the remainder to go over the falls.

Lago Agrio *Colour map 2, B3. See map, page 271.*

The capital of Sucumbíos province is an old oil town which now lives mainly from commerce with neighbouring Colombia. The name comes from Sour Lake, the US headquarters of Texaco, the first oil company to exploit the Ecuadorean Amazon in the 1970s. It is also called Nueva Loja or just 'Lago'. If taking a Cuyabeno tour from Lago Agrio, it is worth leaving Quito a couple of days early, stopping en route at Papallacta, Baeza and San Rafael Falls (see above).

Essential Oriente

Finding your feet

There are commercial flights from Quito to Lago Agrio and Coca. From Quito, Macas and Shell, light aircraft can be chartered to any jungle village with a landing strip. Western Oriente is also accessible by scenic roads which wind their way down from the highlands. Quito, via Baeza, to Lago Agrio and Coca, Baños to Puyo, and Loja to Zamora are fully paved, as is the entire lowland road from Lago Agrio south to Zamora. Other access roads to Oriente (many are paved or in the process of being paved) include: Tulcán to Lago Agrio via Lumbaqui, Riobamba to Macas, and three different roads from Cuenca to Macas and Gualaquiza.

Tip...

There may be police and military checkpoints in the Oriente, so always have your passport handy .

Getting around

Some roads are narrow and tortuous and subject to landslides in the rainy season, but all have a regular bus service and all can be travelled in a 4WD or in an ordinary car with good ground clearance. Deeper into the rainforest, motorized canoes provide the only alternative to air travel.

★ Jungle lodges

These complexes are normally located in natural settings away from towns and villages and are in most cases built to blend into the environment through the use of local materials and elements of indigenous design. Some are owned by urban-based nationals or foreigners, have offices in Quito and often deal with national or international travel agencies. Others are joint ventures or owned outright by local communities.

Experiencing the jungle in this way usually involves the purchase of an all-inclusive package in Quito or abroad, including reasonably comfortable accommodation, three good meals a day, and a leisurely programme of guided activities suited to special interests such as birdwatching. Getting to the lodge may involve a long canoe ride, with a longer return journey upstream and perhaps a pre-dawn start. Standards of service are generally high. Most lodges employ well-qualified personnel and claim a high degree of environmental awareness. Many have made some sort of arrangement with neighbouring indigenous communities but their contribution to local employment and the local economy varies.

When staying at a jungle lodge, you will need to take a torch (flashlight), insect repellent, protection against the sun and a rain poncho. Rubber boots are usually provided, but very large sizes may not be available so ask in advance. Note that most lodges count travel days as part of their package, which means that a 'four-day/three-night tour' often spends only two days actually in the rainforest. Most lodges have fixed departure days and it may not be possible to arrange a special departure on another day; check before planning your trip. Advance bookings are mandatory at most jungle lodges and can usually be made on the internet and through most Quito agencies. For lists of jungle lodges, see pages 276, 277, 286 and 287.

River cruises

The river cruise experience is substantially different from that of a jungle lodge. It offers a better appreciation of the grandeur of

Amazonia, but less intimate contact with life in the rainforest. Passengers sleep and take their meals onboard comfortable river boats designed specifically for tourism, stopping en route to visit local communities and make excursions into the jungle. At present two such vessels sail the Río Napo downstream from Coca. When the water level is low, however, they may only be able to cover part of their usual routes. For further details about these cruise boats, see page 279.

Yet another experience may be had using public river transport along the lower Napo, from Coca to Nuevo Rocafuerte, with connections to Iquitos (Peru). This is much cheaper and less comfortable than a river cruise, and touring opportunities are limited. You can stop at communities along the way but facilities are basic at best. Plenty of time and patience are needed to travel the river in this way. For details of river travel to Peru, see page 274.

Guided tours

Guided tours of varying length are offered by tour operators, who should be licensed

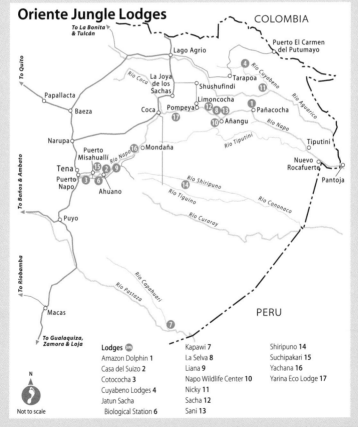

Oriente Jungle Lodges

COLOMBIA

To La Bonita & Tulcán

Puerto El Carmen del Putumayo

To Quito

Lago Agrio

Río Coca

La Joya de los Sachas

Tarapoa

Río Cuyabeno

④

Shushufindi

⑪

Río Aguarico

Papallacta

Baeza

Limoncocha

⑫

Coca   Pompeya   ⑧⑬

⑰

Pañacocha ①

Río Napo

⑩ Añangu

Narupa

Río Tiputini

Tiputini

Puerto Misahuallí

⑮②⑨

Río Napo

⑯ Mondaña

Nuevo Rocafuerte

Tena

⑮②⑨

Puerto Napo

③⑥

Ahuano

Río Shiripuno

⑭

Pantoja

Puyo

Río Tiguino

Río Curaray

Río Cononaco

To Riobamba

Río Capahuari

Río Pastaza

Macas

PERU

⑦

To Gualaquiza, Zamora & Loja

N

Not to scale

Lodges
Amazon Dolphin 1
Casa del Suizo 2
Cotococha 3
Cuyabeno Lodges 4
Jatun Sacha
   Biological Station 6

Kapawi 7
La Selva 8
Liana 9
Napo Wildlife Center 10
Nicky 11
Sacha 12
Sani 13

Shiripuno 14
Suchipakari 15
Yachana 16
Yarina Eco Lodge 17

by the Ecuadorean **Ministerio de Turismo**. Tour companies are mainly concentrated in Quito, Baños, Puyo, Tena, Misahuallí and Coca, and, to a lesser extent in Macas and Zamora. When shopping around for a guided tour ensure that the agency specifies the details of the programme, the services to be provided and whether payments to indigenous communities are included. Be especially prudent with cheaper tour agencies, some are good but we have also received negative reports. If possible, try to get a personal recommendation from a previous customer. Serious breaches of contract can be reported to the **Ministerio de Turismo**, but you should be reasonable about minor details. Most guided tours involve sleeping in simple shelters (open-sided raised platforms) or camping in tents or under plastic sheets.

Community ecotourism

A number of indigenous communities and families offer ecotourism programmes in their territories. These are either community-controlled and operated, or organized as joint ventures between the indigenous community or family and a non-indigenous partner. These programmes usually involve guides who are licensed as *guías nativos* with the right to guide within their communities. Accommodation is typically in simple native shelters of varying quality. Local food may be quite good, but keep an eye on hygiene. You should be prepared to be more self-sufficient on such a trip than on a visit to a jungle lodge or a tour with a high-end operator. Bring a light sleeping bag, rain jacket, trousers (not only shorts), long-sleeved shirt for mosquitoes, binoculars, torch (flashlight), insect repellent, sunscreen, hat, water-purifying tablets, and a first-aid kit. Keep everything in waterproof stuff-sacks or several plastic bags to keep it dry. Ask if rubber boots are provided.

Tours without a guide

Jungle travel without a guide is not recommended. Access to national parks and reserves is controlled, some indigenous groups prohibit the entry of outsiders to their territory, navigation in the jungle is difficult, and there is a variety of dangerous animals. For your own safety as well as to be a responsible tourist, the jungle is not a place to wander off on your own.

Choosing a rainforest

A tropical rainforest is one of the most exciting things to see in Ecuador, but it isn't easy to find a good one. The key is to have realistic expectations and choose accordingly. Think carefully about your interests. If you simply want to relax in nature and see some interesting plants, insects, small birds and mammals, you have many choices, including some that are quite economical and easily accessible. If you want to experience something of the cultures of rainforest people, you must go further. If you want the full experience, with large mammals and birds, you will have to go further still and spend more money, because large creatures have been hunted or driven out of settled areas.

A visit to a rainforest is not like a visit to the Galápagos. The diversity of life in a good rainforest far exceeds that of the Galápagos, but creatures don't sit around and let themselves be seen. Even in the best forests, your experiences will be unpredictable – none of this 'today is Wednesday, time to see iguanas'. A rainforest trip is a real adventure; the only guarantee is that the surprises will be genuine, and hence all the more unforgettable.

There are things that can increase the odds of really special surprises. One of the most important is the presence of a canopy tower or walkway. Even the most colourful rainforest birds are mere specks up in the branches against a glaring sky, unless you are above them looking down. Towers and walkways add an important dimension to bird and mammal watching. A good guide is another necessity. Avoid places that emphasize medicinal plants over everything else – this usually means that there isn't anything else around to show. If you are interested in exploring indigenous cultures, give preference to a guide from the same ethnic group as the village you will visit.

If you want to see real wilderness, with big birds and mammals, there are not many lodges you can drive to. Expect to travel at least a couple of hours in a motorized canoe, or pay extra to arrive in a small aircraft (when this option is available). Don't stay near villages even if they are in the middle of nowhere. In remote villages people hunt a lot for food, and animals will be scarce. Indigenous villages are no different in this regard; most indigenous groups (except for a very few that now specialize in ecotourism) are ruthlessly efficient hunters. See box, page 86.

Responsible jungle tourism

A few guides or their boatmen may try to hunt meat for your dinner – don't let them, and report such practices to the Ministerio del Ambiente. Don't buy anything made with animal or bird parts. Avoid making a pest of yourself in indigenous villages; don't take photographs or videos without permission, and don't insist. Try to minimize your impact on the forest and its people. Also remember when choosing a tour agency, that the cheapest is not the best. What happens is that agencies undercut each other and offer services that are unsafe or harm local communities and the environment. Do not encourage this practice.

A number of *centros de rescate* (wild animal rescue centres) exist in Oriente, ostensibly to prepare captive animals to return to their natural habitats. While this may seem laudable, it is not clear whether such efforts can in fact succeed. The *centros de rescate* are convenient for observing fauna close-up but, while some may have genuinely good intentions, others are really just zoos with small cages.

Health and safety

A yellow fever vaccination is required. Anti-malarial tablets are recommended, as is an effective insect repellent. There may be police and military checkpoints in the Oriente, so always have your passport handy. In the province of Sucumbíos, enquire about public safety before visiting sites near the Colombian border.

When to go

Heavy rain can fall at any time, but it is usually wettest from March to September.

ON THE ROAD
Orellana's River

The legends of the Incas fuelled the greed and ambition of the Spanish invaders, dreaming of untold riches buried deep in the Amazon jungle. The most famous and enduring of these was the legend of El Dorado, which inspired a spate of ill-fated expeditions deep into this mysterious and inhospitable world.

Francisco Pizarro, conqueror of the Incas, had appointed his younger brother, Gonzalo, as governor of Quito. Lured by tales of fresh lands to be conquered to the east and riches in cinnamon and gold, an expedition under the command of Gonzalo Pizarro left Quito at the end of February 1541. It was made up of 220 Spanish soldiers, 4000 indigenous slaves, 150 horses and 900 dogs, as well as a great many llamas and other livestock. They headed across the Andes not far from Papallacta and down through the cloudforest until they reached a place they called Zumaco. Here Pizarro was joined by Francisco de Orellana, founder of Guayaquil, accompanied by 23 more conquistadors who had left Quito a few weeks after the main expedition.

After proceeding to the shores of the Río Coca, the Spaniards began to run out of food and built a small ship, the *San Pedro*. Rumours that they would find food once they reached the Río Napo led Pizarro to dispatch Orellana and his men to look for this river and bring back provisions. Orellana and his party sailed down river in the San Pedro but found nothing for many days, and claimed they could not return against the current. Pizarro, for his part, was convinced that he had been betrayed and abandoned by Orellana.

On 12 February 1542, Orellana reached the confluence of the Napo and the Amazon – so called by him because he said he had been attacked by the legendary women warriors of the same name. Another name for the mighty new river, but one which never caught on, was *El Río de Orellana*.

On 26 August 1542, 559 days after he had left Guayaquil, Orellana and his men arrived at the mouth of the Amazon, having become the first Europeans to cross the breadth of South America and follow the world's greatest river from the Andes to the Atlantic. Totally lost, they then followed the coastline north and managed to reach the port of Cubagua in Venezuela. In the meantime, Gonzalo Pizarro had suffered enormous losses and limped back to Quito at about the same time, with only 80 starving survivors.

Orellana returned to Spain and, with great difficulty, organized a second expedition which sailed up the Amazon in 1544 only to meet with disaster. Three of his four vessels were shipwrecked and many of the survivors, including Orellana himself, died of fever.

Dominican friar Gaspar de Carvajal, who accompanied Orellana on his first voyage, penned a 31-page chronicle of this odyssey. Carvajal's manuscript survives to this day and the story has been retold countless times. Orellana is a national hero in Ecuador and his journey is a pillar of the country's assertion that it "is, was, and will be" an Amazonian nation.

★ Cuyabeno Wildlife Reserve

This large tract of rainforest, covering 603,000 ha, is located about 100 km east of Lago Agrio along the Río Cuyabeno, which eventually drains into the Aguarico. In the reserve are many lagoons and a great variety of wildlife, including river dolphins, tapirs, three species of caiman, ocelots, 11 species of monkey and some 680 bird species. This is among the best places in Ecuador to see jungle animals. The reserve is deservedly popular and offers a more economical jungle experience than many other areas in Oriente.

Access to most lodges is by paved road from Lago Agrio via Tarapoa as far as the bridge over the Río Cuyabeno, where there is a ranger station and visitors must register. Nobody is allowed to enter the reserve without a tour. From the bridge, transport is mainly by motorized canoe; **Magic River** also offers a worthwhile paddling alternative, see Cuyabeno jungle lodges, page 276. Most tours include a visit to a local Siona community.

The reserve can be visited year-round but the dry season (January and February) can bring low water levels and generally less wildlife, although certain species may be easier to see at this time. In order to see as many animals as possible and minimally impact their habitat, seek out a small tour group which scrupulously adheres to responsible tourism practices. Cuyabeno is close to the Colombian border and there have, in the past, been occasional armed robberies of tour groups. Do not take unnecessary valuables. Most Cuyabeno tours are booked through Quito agencies or online, see Cuyabeno jungle lodges, page 276.

South of Lago Agrio a paved road heads towards Coca. At Jivino, 25 km, a paved road turns east to Shushufindi, another oil producing and refining town, from where one road goes to the Río Napo at Pompeya and another new road goes 80 km to Puerto Providencia, which is 40 km east of Coca on the Napo. Puerto Providencia is part of an ambitious Ecuadorean/Brazilian project called **Manta-Manaos** which envisages a 'multimodal' transport corridor of river transport from Manaus on the Amazon via Nueva

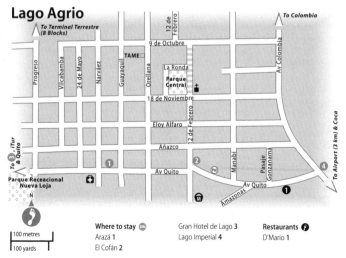

Where to stay 🛏
Arazá **1**
El Cofán **2**

Gran Hotel de Lago **3**
Lago Imperial **4**

Restaurants 🍴
D'Mario **1**

Rocafuerte (see below) to Puerto Providencia, then by road to the Pacific ports of Manta and Esmeraldas. In late 2017 Puerto Providencia's passenger facilities were open and being used by some river-cruise vessels.

Coca *Colour map 2, B3.*

Officially named **Puerto Francisco de Orellana**, Coca is a hot, noisy, bustling city at the junction of the Ríos Payamino and Napo, which has experienced exceptionally rapid growth from petroleum development. It is the capital of the province of Orellana and, for tourists, a launch pad to visit the lower Río Napo and jungle areas accessed from the Vía Auca, a road running south from the city. The view over the water is nice, and the remodelled riverfront **Malecón** can be a pleasant place to spend time around sunset; various indigenous groups have craft shops here. Hotel and restaurant provision is adequate but heavily booked and ironically for an oil-producing centre, petrol supplies are erratic.

Jungle tours from Coca The **lower Río Napo**, **Parque Nacional Yasuní** and **Huaorani Reserve**, all accessed from Coca, offer some of the finest jungle facilities and experiences in Ecuador. Wildlife in this area is nonetheless under threat; insist that guides and fellow tourists take all litter back and ban all hunting. Many tours out of Coca are booked through agencies in Quito but there are also a few local operators (see page 279).

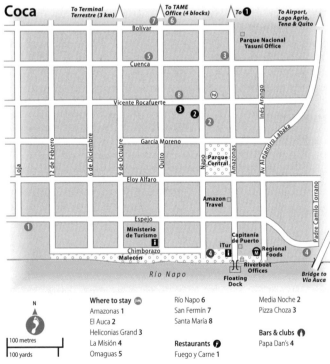

Coca

To Terminal Terrestre (3 km)
To TAME Office (4 blocks)
To ❶
To Airport, Lago Agrio, Tena & Quito

Parque Nacional Yasuní Office

Bolívar
❼ ❻
❺
Cuenca
❸
❽
Vicente Rocafuerte
❸ ❷
❷
García Moreno
Parque Central
Eloy Alfaro
Amazon Travel
Espejo
Ministerio de Turismo ℹ
Capitanía de Puerto
iTur ℹ
Regional Foods
Chimborazo
Malecón
Riverboat Offices
Floating Dock
Bridge to Vía Auca

Loja
12 de Febrero
6 de Diciembre
9 de Octubre
Quito
Napo
Amazonas
Inés Arango
Av Alejandro Labaka
Padre Camilo Torrano

Río Napo

N
100 metres
100 yards

Where to stay 🛏	Río Napo 6	Media Noche 2
Amazonas 1	San Fermín 7	Pizza Choza 3
El Auca 2	Santa María 8	
Heliconias Grand 3		**Bars & clubs** 🎵
La Misión 4	**Restaurants** 🍴	Papa Dan's 4
Omaguas 5	Fuego y Carne 1	

ON THE ROAD
The high price of petroleum

Coca and Lago Agrio are the main towns serving the petroleum industry operating in Oriente. Starting with Texaco from the USA, oil companies and their subcontractors have come from all over the world; today they are mostly from China. Large and powerful, they have turned the Ecuadorean Amazon into a place where barrels of oil mean more than biodiversity or human rights. Neither drawn-out international litigation by indigenous communities, nor protests by environmental groups, nor innovative but half-hearted attempts by the Ecuadorean government, have been able to halt their relentless advance.

Hundreds of thousands of barrels of oil flow out of the jungle every day through two pipelines that snake over the Andes and down to the coast for export. In their wake, feeder pipes crisscross the devastated terrain, toxic waste sumps contaminate watersheds and cancer rates run high among the local population. Oil spills have on occasion contaminated the Cuyabeno Wildlife Reserve or so badly polluted the Río Coca that they left the city of Coca without drinking water for weeks.

The natural habitat around Lago Agrio was the first to be decimated, followed by that along the Vía Auca, an oil company road running south from Coca into Huaorani territory. More recently the primary rainforest south of the upper Río Napo, between Coca and Misahuallí, has come under threat. Next in line are parts of Parque Nacional Yasuní.

Yet all the direct damage caused by the petroleum industry pales in comparison to that inflicted by the colonists who inevitably follow in its wake. The oil companies build access roads to their wells, and these become corridors of deforestation as settlers take out timber and introduce cattle and crops. Their agricultural practices are unsuited to the poor soils of the rainforest and are not sustainable. At the same time, the way of life of the native lowland people has been permanently altered. These issues are not unique to Ecuador but since the country's slice of the Amazon is among the smallest and biologically richest in South America, the prospect of catastrophe is all the more imminent. There are many campaigning websites such as www.accion ecologica.org, http://amazonwatch.org and www.sosyasuni.org; *Amazon Crude*, and other works by Judith Kimerling; and *Savages*, by Joe Kane.

Despite it all, the ongoing international demand for fossil fuels will continue to foster new exploration. And whatever the future price of a barrel of crude in London or New York, the price paid by the Ecuadorean Amazon has already been too high.

The paved road to Coca via Loreto passes through **Wawa Sumaco**, where a rough road heads north to **Sumaco National Park**; 7 km along it is $$$$ Wildsumaco ① *T06-301 8343, Quito office T02-202 2488, Mon-Fri 0900-1700, www.wildsumaco.com, reservations required*, a comfortable birdwatching lodge with full board, excellent trails and over 500 birds, including many rare species. Just beyond is the village of **Pacto Sumaco** from where a trail runs through the park to the *páramo*-clad summit of **Volcán Sumaco** (3732 m), six to seven days' round-trip. Local guides must be hired, there are three nice shelters along the route and a community-run hostel in the village (T06-301 8324, www.sumacobirdwatching. com) where you can see chestnut-fronted and military macaws.

ON THE ROAD

Parque Nacional Yasuní

Parque Nacional Yasuní was created in 1979 and was made a UNESCO Biosphere Reserve in 1989. Two uncontacted indigenous groups, the Tagaeri and Taromename, live within its boundaries and, according to the Ecuadorean constitution, their rights to live without interference are protected. The same can be argued about the wildlife and habitats within the park in that ecosystems are similarly protected from the destruction of species, ecosystems and natural cycles by outside agents. Nevertheless, parts of the park, notably so-called Block 31 and Ishpingo-Tambococha-Tiputini (ITT), are under serious threat from oil exploration and the land invasion that comes with it. In 2007 President Correa offered to leave the oil, of which there are huge reserves, in the ground if the global community raised US$3.6 bn in compensation for expected oil revenues. Only a small percentage of the money was forthcoming, Correa's plan was abandoned in 2013 and drilling for oil began. Correa's successor, Lenín Moreno, vowed to give the Amazon more protection and the 'intangible' area in Yasuní was expanded to 50,000 ha and the area open to drilling was reduced from 1030 to 300 ha. Nevertheless, oil exploration had begun and is not scheduled to stop. At risk is one of the most biodiverse areas of the planet. The park is largely rainforest, but being at the conjunction of Andean, Amazonian and equatorial ecosystems, the scale of life within it defies categorization. The numbers of mammals, birds, insects, amphibians, bats, trees and other plants is in the millions. There are countless discoveries yet to be made, not just in terms of animal and plantlife, but also in terms of the vast potential of medicinal and other benefits. It is therefore to be hoped that what oil drilling continues will be done without any of the catastrophic damage that has occurred in other jungle environments.

Coca to Nuevo Rocafuerte and Iquitos (Peru)

Pañacocha is halfway between Coca and Nuevo Rocafuerte, near a magnificent lagoon. It is a network of waterways surrounded by primary forest, covering 56,000 ha. There are a couple of **lodges** here (see Lodges on the Lower Napo, page 277) and Coca agencies also run tours to the area (see Jungle tours, page 279). Entry to Pañacocha reserve is US$10. There are basic places to stay and eat in Pañacocha village.

Following the Río Napo to Peru is rough, adventurous and requires plenty of time and patience. There are two options: by far the more economical is to take a motorized canoe from Coca to **Nuevo Rocafuerte** on the border. This tranquil riverside town has two simple hotels ($), places to eat, a phone office and basic shops. It can be a base for exploring the endangered southeastern section of **Parque Nacional Yasuní**; local guides are available, offering overnight camping trips. Make sure you go with a registered guide; unregistered guides can be dangerous as they do not know the jungle sufficiently well.

Ecuadorean immigration is two blocks from the pier, next to the Municipio. Peruvian entry stamps are given in **Pantoja**, where there is a decent municipal *hospedaje*, $ **Napuruna**. Shopkeepers in Nuevo Rocafuerte and Pantoja change money at poor rates; soles cannot be changed in Coca. In addition to immigration, you may have to register with the navy on either side of the border so have your passport to hand. See Transport, page 280, for Coca–Nuevo Rocafuerte boat services and onward to Pantoja and Iquitos.

The second option for river travel to Iquitos is to take a tour with a Coca agency, taking in various attractions en route, and continuing to Iquitos or closer Peruvian ports from where you can catch onward public river transport. These tours are expensive and may involve many hours sitting in small, cramped craft; confirm all details in advance.

Listings Northern Oriente *maps pages 267, 271 and 272.*

Tourist information

Lago Agrio

iTur
Av Quito y 20 de Junio, in the Parque Recreacional, T06-283 3951, www.turismo. lagoagrio.gob.ec. Mon-Fri 0800-1700.
Publishes an annual guide on things to do and places to visit in the and around the city.

Coca

iTur
Chimborazo y Amazonas, by the Malecón, T06-288 0532, www.orellanaturistica.gob.ec. Mon-Sat 0730-1630.
See also http://elcocavivelo.com for information on tours and services.

Ministerio de Turismo
Quito y Chimborazo, Ed Azriel Shopping, T06-288 1583.
The place to file any complaints regarding a jungle lodge or tour.

Where to stay

Baeza

$$-$ Gina
Jumandy y Batallón Chimborazo, just off the highway in the old town, T06-232 0471, restaurantgina@hotmail.com.
Hot water, parking, pleasant, busy restaurant and bar serving great trout and local tequila.

$$-$ Quinde Huayco
Gil Ramírez Dávalos, by the park in the old town, T06-232 0029, https://quindehuayco. wordpress.com.
Ample rooms, garden, restaurant, quiet location away from the main road, tours and volunteer opportunities available.

$ La Casa de Rodrigo
In the old town, T09-9963 8357, see Facebook.
Modern and comfortable, hot water, no breakfast, kitchen facilities, friendly owner offers rafting trips, kayak rentals and birdwatching. Good value and recommended.

Around Baeza

$$$$ Cabañas San Isidro
Near Cosanga, 19 km south of Baeza, T02-289 1880 (Quito), www.cabanasanisidro.com.
A 1200-ha private nature reserve with rich birdlife, comfortable accommodation in spacious cabins with views from porches and warm hospitality. Includes 3 excellent meals, reservations required.

$$ Hostería El Reventador
On main highway next to bridge over the Río Reventador, http://hosteriaelreventador.com.
Meals on request, pool, simple rooms, busy at weekends, a bit run-down and mediocre service but well located for San Rafael Falls and Volcán Reventador.

Lago Agrio

$$$ Gran Hotel de Lago
Km 1.5 Vía Quito, T06-283 2415, www.granhoteldelago.com.
Restaurant, rooms and suites designed for the business traveller or tourist, a/c, pool, parking, nice gardens, quiet, often full.

$$ Arazá
Quito 536 y Narváez, T06-283 1248,
http://araza-hotel.com.
Nice comfortable rooms, restaurant, a/c,
pool, fridge, parking.

$$ El Cofán
12 de Febrero 1915 y Quito, T06-283 0527,
Facebook.
Central, restaurant, a/c, fridge, parking, older
place but well maintained.

$$ Lago Imperial
Colombia y Quito, T06-283 0452, Facebook.
A/c, simple rooms, ample common areas,
pool, patio, restaurant, used for functions,
central location, good value.

Cuyabeno Wildlife Reserve
Lodges
There are over a dozen lodges operating
in Cuyabeno, more than we can list. The
following are all recommended. Prices range
from US$300-475 pp for 5 days/4 nights,
including transport from Lago Agrio,
accommodation, all meals and guiding. A
small community fee is charged separately.

Caiman Lodge
T06-282 8079, www.caimanlodge.com.
On Quebrada La Hormiga near the lagoon.
Well-maintained lodge, thatched 2-storey
cabins, rooms with 1-5 beds, with an
observation tower.

Cuyabeno Lodge
Operated by Neotropic Turis, Quito T02-292
6153, http://cuyabenolodge.com.ec.
On the lagoon. This was the 1st lodge in
the reserve, operating since 1988. Very well
organized and professional. Ample grounds,
comfortable accommodation in several price
categories, observation tower, and paddle
canoes for use of guests.

Guacamayo Ecolodge
Operated by Ara Expeditions, Quito, T02-
290 4765, www.guacamayoecolodge.com.

On the Río Cuyabeno near the lagoon.
Well-maintained lodge with simple
accommodation, friendly staff and an
observation tower.

Magic River
Lago Agrio, Calle Primero s/n y Pacayacu,
T09-9453 0593; Baños, 16 de Diciembre entre
Montalvo y Luís A Martínez, T03-274 3580,
www.magicrivertours.com.
On the Río Cuyabeno downstream from the
lagoon. Specialize in paddling trips (great
fun and wildlife watching without engine
noise) which spend the 1st night in a tent
camp in the jungle. Friendly atmosphere
at the lodge, good food and service.

Nicky Lodge
Operated by Dracaena, Quito T02-254 6590,
www.nickylodge.com.
On the lower Río Cuyabeno near its
confluence with the Aguarico, far from all
the other lodges. Good wildlife including
some species not easily seen elsewhere.
Rustic cabins on stilts connected by
boardwalks to main communal building.

Siona Lodge
Booked through Galasam, Quito T02-
290 3909, www.galasamecuador.com.
On the lagoon. Comfortable lodge with
very good infrastructure.

Tapir Lodge
Quito T02-380 1567, www.tapirlodge.com.
On the Río Cuyabeno downstream
from the lagoon. Known for high-quality
guiding. Rooms in towers to minimize
impact on environment.

Coca
Coca hotels are often full, best book
in advance.

$$$ Heliconias Grand
Cuenca y Amazonas, T06-288 2010,
http://heliconiasgrandhotel.com.ec.

Spacious rooms, includes buffet breakfast, pool and sauna. The most upmarket option but noisy with day visitors to the pool at weekends and service is patchy.

$$$-$$ El Auca
Napo entre Rocafuerte y García Moreno, T06-288 0127, www.hotelelaucacoca.com.
Large modern hotel with conference facilities. Restaurant, a/c, parking, a variety of different rooms and mini-suites. Rooms in the main building are better than in the *cabañas* on the noisy road. Attractive garden, English spoken. Popular, central, but can get noisy.

$$$-$$ Río Napo
Bolívar 7606 entre Napo y Quito, T06-288 0872, Facebook.
Modern rooms with a/c, good but a bit overpriced. Friendly staff, helpful service.

$$ La Misión
Padre Camilo Torrano, by riverfront 100 m downriver from the bridge, T06-288 0260, hotelamision@hotmail.com.
A larger hotel, restaurant, disco on weekends, a/c and fridge, pool (US$3 for non-guests), parking, a bit faded but adequate for a night.

$$ Omaguas
Quito 82-04 y Cuenca, T06-288 0136, www.facebook.com/hotelomaguaselcoca.
Very clean rooms with tiled floors, a/c, restaurant, parking, attentive service.

$$-$ Amazonas
12 de Febrero y Espejo, T06-288 0444, www.hosteriaamazonascoca.com.
Nice quiet setting by the river, away from centre, decent restaurant, electric shower, a/c, cheaper with fan, parking, tours.

$$-$ San Fermín
Quito 75-04 y Bolívar, T06-288 1848, robertvaca@wildlifeamazon.com.
Variety of different rooms, some with a/c, cheaper with fan, ample parking, popular and busy, good value, owner organizes tours.

$ Santa María
Rocafuerte 04-10 entre Quito y Napo, T06-288 0287.
Small adequate rooms with a/c or fan, private bath, cold water, good economy option.

★ Jungle tours from Coca
Lodges on the Lower Napo
All Napo lodges count travel days as part of their package, which means that a '3-day tour' spends only 1 day actually in the jungle. All prices given below are per person based on double occupancy, including transport from Coca. Most lodges have fixed departure days from Coca (eg Mon and Fri) and it is very expensive to get a special departure on another day. For lodges in Cuyabeno, see page 276; for lodges on the Upper Napo, see page 286, for southern Oriente lodges see page 287.

Amazon Dolphin Lodge
Quito T02-250 3225, www.amazondolphinlodge.com.
On Laguna de Pañacocha, 4½ hrs downriver from Coca. Special wildlife here includes Amazon river dolphins and giant river otters as well as over 500 species of bird. May be closed in dry season (Jan-Feb). Offers short trips and multi-day adventures. Cabins with private bath, US$600-900 for tours, Mon-Fri or Fri-Mon.

La Selva
Quito T02-394 9800, www.laselvajunglelodge.com.
An upmarket lodge and spa, 2½ hrs downstream from Coca on a picturesque lake. Surrounded by excellent forest, especially on the far side of Mandicocha. Bird and animal life is exceptionally diverse. Many species of monkey are seen regularly. A total of 580 bird species have been found, one of the highest totals in the world for a single

elevation. Comfortable cabins, excellent meals, massage treatments available at extra cost. High standards, canopy tower, most guides are biologists. US$1215 for 4 days.

Napo Wildlife Center
Quito T02-600-5819, www. napowildlifecenter.com.
Award-winning lodge operated by and for the local Añangu community, 2½ hrs downstream from Coca. Standard and new panoramic suites. This area of hilly forest is rather different from the low flat forest of some other lodges and the diversity is slightly higher. There are big caimans and good mammals, including giant otters, and the birdwatching is excellent with 2 parrot clay-licks and 2 canopy towers, 40 m high. From about US$1470 for 4 days. Recommended.

Sacha
Quito T02-256 6090, www.sachalodge.com.
A delightful upmarket lodge 2½ hrs downstream from Coca on a tranquil lake. Very comfortable cabins, excellent meals in 2 restaurants, laundry service, Wi-Fi extra. Good excursions on foot and by canoe in a private reserve, including canopy tower and 275-m canopy walkway. The bird list is outstanding; the local bird expert, Oscar Tapuy (Coca T06-2881486), can be requested in advance. Several species of monkey are commonly seen. Nearby river islands provide access to a distinct habitat. Full-day trips to Yasuní available and visits to a local community. Programmes from 4 to 15 days, US$1050 for 4 days. Recommended.

Sani
Quito T09-9434 1728, www.sanilodge.com.
All proceeds go to the Sani Isla community, who run the lodge with the help of outside experts. It is located on a remote lagoon which has 4- to 5-m-long black caiman. This area is rich in wildlife and birds, including many species such as the scarlet macaw which have disappeared from most other Napo area lodges. There is good accommodation and a 35-m canopy tower. The lodge is reached by canoe (total 3½ hrs from Coca) without a walk. US$1058 for 4 days. Recommended.

Yarina Eco Lodge
Quito T02-250 4037, www.yarinalodge.com.
A lodge 1 hr by motorized boat on the Napo from Coca, 20 cabins, with bath, electricity till 2200, 24-hr water. Long and short hikes, day and night activities, community visits, piranha fishing, caiman spotting, birdwatching, 100-ft observation tower.

Lodges in the Reserva Huaorani

Otobo's Amazon Safari
www.rainforestcamping.com.
Huaorani family-run 5-day/4-night or 8-day/7-night tailor-made camping expeditions usually once a month in Huaorani territory using lodges and thatched campsites. Fly from Shell-Puyo to Bameno (1 hr, US$770 for up to 5 passengers), then 2-hr motorized canoe ride to the main campsite of Boanamo. Access by road from Coca to the Río Shiripuno bridge (2 hrs), then all-day motorized canoe journey to Boanamo. All meals and guiding (bilingual and Huaorani) included. Excellent jungle with plenty of wildlife. US$200 pp per night.

Shiripuno
Quito T02-227 1094, www. shiripunolodge.com.
A lodge with capacity for 20 people, very good location on the Río Shiripuno, a 4-hr canoe ride downriver from the Vía Auca. Cabins have private bath. The surrounding area has seen relatively little human impact to date. From US$610 for 4 days, plus US$20 entry to Huaorani territory.

Restaurants

Baeza

$$-$ Kopal
50 m off the main road opposite the old town.
Good pizza, nice atmosphere, closes early.
Also has rooms for rent.

$ El Viejo
East end of Av de los Quijos, the road to
Tena in the new town. Daily 0700-2100.
Good set meals and à la carte.

Lago Agrio

There are good restaurants at the larger
hotels (see above).

$$-$ D'Mario
Av Quito 2-63 y Pasaje Gonzonamá,
T06-283 0172. Daily 0630-2200.
Set meals and à la carte, generous portions,
popular, meeting place for Cuyabeno groups
in hotel of same name.

Coca

$$ Fuego y Carne
Fernando Roy y Amazonas, T09-7915 5352.
Daily 1200-2300.
Upmarket for Coca, good grill and Italian
dishes. Wood-fired oven for good pizzas.

$$-$ Pizza Choza
Rocafuerte entre Napo y Quito,
T09-9887 3053. Daily 0800-2200.
Good pizza, 3 sizes, nice atmosphere,
eat in or take away.

$ Media Noche
Napo y Rocafuerte (no sign). Daily 1630-2400.
Only chicken in various dishes, large
portions, quick service, very popular,
a Coca institution.

Pappa Dan's Bar
Napo y Chimborazo, T06-288 1345,
Facebook. Daily 1700-0300.

A landmark watering-hole by the Malecón.
Cover charge for live music or DJ events.
Several other bars nearby.

What to do

Coca
Jungle tours
See also page 272.

Amazon Travel, *Amazonas y Espejo, in*
Hotel Safari, T06-288 2647, www.Amazon
TravelTours.com. Patricio Juanka runs
jungle tours throughout the region, very
knowledgeable and helpful.
Sachapi Amazon Outdoor Adventure,
T09-9547 2982, www.sachapi.com. Tours to
Yasuni, Panacocha and Cuyabeno. Day trips
or multi-day tours with camping.
Sachayacu Explorer, *in Píllaro near Baños*
(see page 156), T03-387 5316, Facebook.
Although not based in Coca, experienced
jungle guide Juan Medina offers
recommended jungle tours and trips to
Iquitos. Advance arrangements required.
Sumak Allpa, *Av Amazonas y*
Av Chimborazo, T09-737 1286, www.
sumakallpa.org. Sumak Allpa Biodiversity
Centre, Limoncochá Biological Reserve,
Yasuni National Park. This is a non-profit
foundation which welcomes volunteers.
3-day/2-night tours or longer.
Wildlife Amazon, *Napo y Rocafuerte,*
T09-9778 1798, www.amazonwildlife.ec.
Jungle tours and trips to Iquitos.

River cruises on the lower Río Napo
Manatee and Anakonda, *operated by*
Advantage Travel, Quito T02-336 0887,
www.manateeamazonexplorer.com, www.
anakondaamazoncruises.com. These
2 vessels travel along the Napo, offering
4-, 5- and 8-day itineraries, with lots of
excursions on shore or kayaking on lakes
and tributaries. First-class guides, excellent
food, en suite cabins.

Coca to Nuevo Rocafuerte and Iquitos
Juan Carlos Cuenca, *Nuevo Rocafuerte,*
T06-238 2257. A *guía nativo* who offers tours
to Parque Nacional Yasuní, about US$60 per
day, overnight camping, food and rubber
boots provided, no shade on his boat.
Fernando Sifuentes, *Nuevo Rocafuerte, T09-*
8051 9789, sifuentes.fede@gmail.com. Very
knowledgeable local guide accompanied
by his wife, Leiza, good service, good price,
you see lots of wildlife, tailor-made camping
tours to Parque Nacional Yasuní.

Transport

Baeza
Bus
Buses to and from **Tena** pass right through
town. If arriving on a **Lago Agrio** bus, get off
at the crossroads (La "Y") and walk or take a
pick-up for US$0.25. From **Quito**, Mon-Sat
at 1130, 1245, 1520, 1645, with **Trans Quijos**,
T02-295 0842, from Chile E3-22 y Pedro
Fermín Cevallos (near La Marín, an unsafe
area at night), US$4, 3 hrs. These continue to
Borja and **El Chaco**. To **Quito** from El Chaco
Mon-Sat at 0330, 0430, 0600, 0800, pass
Baeza about 20 mins later.

Lago Agrio
Air
Airport is 3 km southeast of the centre, taxi
US$1.50. **TAME** (Orellana y 9 de Octubre,
T06-283 0113) flies once or twice a day to
Quito. Book several days in advance. If there
is no space available to Lago Agrio then you
can fly to **Coca** instead, from where it is only
2 hrs by bus on a good road.

Bus
Terminal Terrestre, Manuela Sáenz y
Progreso, 8 blocks north of Av Quito,
taxi US$1.50-2 from the centre. To **Quito**
Terminal Quitumbe, frequent service with
several companies (**Trans Baños**, T06-283
0330, is good), US$10, 7-8 hrs; most buses go

via Reventador and El Chaco, but may take
the slightly longer route via Coca if there
are disruptions. To **Baeza** 5 hrs, pay fare to
Quito. To **Tena**, US$8.75, 6 hrs. To **Tulcán** via
La Bonita, US$8.75, 7 hrs. Several companies
offer service direct to **Guayaquil**, without
stopping in Quito, US$17.50, 14 hrs, as well as
other coastal cities. To **Coca**, every 15 mins
0800-1830, US$3.75, 2 hrs.

Coca
Air
Flights to **Quito** with **TAME** (C Quito y
Enrique Castillo, T06-288 0768) and **Avianca**
(at the airport T06-288 1742), several
daily, fewer on weekends, reserve as far in
advance as possible.

Bus
Long-distance buses, including those
to Lago Agrio, depart from the modern
Terminal Terrestre, 3 km north of centre,
taxi US$1.50. A small terminal on 9 de
Octubre serves only regional destinations.
Hotel San Fermín (T06-288 0802, see
page 277) will purchase bus tickets from
Coca for a small commission. To **Quito**
Terminal Quitumbe, US$12.50, 7 hrs via
Papallacta and Loreto (compared with 5 hrs
by private car), 9 hrs via Lago Agrio, several
daily. To **Baeza**, pay fare to Quito, 5 hrs. To
Tena, US$8.75, 4 hrs. To **Baños**, US$12.50,
7 hrs. To **Riobamba**, US$13.50, 9 hrs. To
Guayaquil, US$20, 15-16 hrs.

River
Down the Río Napo to **Nuevo Rocafuerte**
on the Peruvian border, 50-passenger
motorized canoes leave Coca daily except
Sat, 0730, arrive approximately 1500;
returning at 0530, arrive 1500 hrs; US$18.75.
Details change, enquire locally, buy tickets
at the dock a day in advance and arrive early
for boarding. **Transportes Fluvial Orellana**,
T06-288 2582, cfluvialorellana@yahoo.es,
and 2 others.

From Nuevo Rocafuerte boats can be hired for the 30-km trip downriver to the Peruvian border town of **Pantoja**, US$60 per boat, try to share the ride. Departure dates of riverboats from **Pantoja to Iquitos** are irregular, about once a month, be prepared for a long wait. Try to call Iquitos or Pantoja from Coca to enquire about the next sailing. For the journey, take a hammock, cup, bowl, cutlery, extra food and snacks, drinking water or purification, insect repellent, toilet paper, soap, towel, cash dollars and soles in small notes; soles cannot be purchased in Coca.

Central and southern Oriente
a whitewater rafting centre and off-the-beaten-track exploration

Quito, Baños, Puyo, Tena and Puerto Misahuallí are all starting points for central Oriente. Further south, Macas, Gualaquiza and Zamora are the main gateways. All have good road connections.

Archidona *Colour map 4, A2.*
Archidona, 65 km south of Baeza and 10 km north of Tena, has a striking, small painted church and not much else. Tours can be arranged to a private reserve on **Galeras Mountain** where there is easy walking as well as a tougher trek, the forest is wonderful; contact Elias Mamallacha, T09-8045 6942, mamallacha@yahoo.com.

★ Tena and around *Colour map 4, A2. See map, page 282.*
Relaxed and friendly, **Tena** is the capital of Napo Province. It occupies a hill above the confluence of the Ríos Tena and Pano, there are nice views of the Andean foothills often shrouded in mist. Tena is Ecuador's most important centre for whitewater rafting and also offers ethno-tourism. It makes a good stop en route from Quito to points deeper in Oriente. The road from the north passes the old airstrip and market and heads through the town centre as Avenida 15 de Noviembre on its way to the bus station, nearly 1 km south of the river. In August 2017 the city opened a new Malecón Escénico beside the rivers Napo and Pano, with bridges, water features, handicraft and food stalls, flowerbeds and children's play areas, all brightly lit at night. Tena is quite spread out. A couple of pedestrian bridges and a vehicle bridge link the two halves of town.

Misahuallí *Colour map 4, A2.*
This small port, at the junction of the Napo and Misahuallí rivers, is perhaps the best place in Ecuador from which to visit the 'near Oriente', but your expectations should be realistic. The area has been colonized for many years and there is no extensive virgin forest nearby (except at **Jatun Sacha** and **Liana Lodge**, see Lodges on the Upper Río Napo, page 286). Access is very easy, however, prices are reasonable and, while you will not encounter large animals in the wild, you can still see birds, butterflies and exuberant vegetation – enough to get a taste for the jungle.

There is a fine, sandy beach on the Río Misahuallí, but don't camp on it as the river can rise unexpectedly. A narrow suspension bridge crosses the Río Napo at Misahuallí and joins the road along the south shore. At Chichicorumi, outside Misahuallí, is **Kamak Maki** ① *US$3, T09-8415 3966, www.museokamakmaki.com*, an ethno-cultural museum run by the local Kichwa community. Tours with accommodation also available.

Puyo *Colour map 4, A2. See map, page 285.*

The capital of the province of Pastaza feels more like a lowland city anywhere in Ecuador rather than a typical jungle town. Visits can nonetheless be made to nearby forest reserves and tours deeper into the jungle can also be arranged from Puyo. It is the junction for road travel into the northern and southern Oriente (80 km south of Tena, 130 km north of Macas), and for traffic heading to or from Ambato and Riobamba via Baños; all on paved roads. The Sangay and Altar volcanoes can occasionally be seen from town.

Omaere ① *T06-288 3174, Tue-Sun 0900-1700, US$3, access by footbridge off the Paseo Turístico, Barrio Obrero*, is a 15.6-ha ethnobotanical reserve located in the north of Puyo. It has three trails with a variety of plants, an orchidarium and traditional indigenous homes. **Yana Cocha** ① *3 km from Puyo, 500 m off the road to Tena, T06-288 5641, daily 0800-1700, US$3*, is a rescue centre with good conditions for the animals, and you can see them close up. There are other private reserves of varying quality in the Puyo area and visits are arranged by local tour operators (see page 291). You cannot, however, expect to see large tracts of undisturbed primary jungle here.

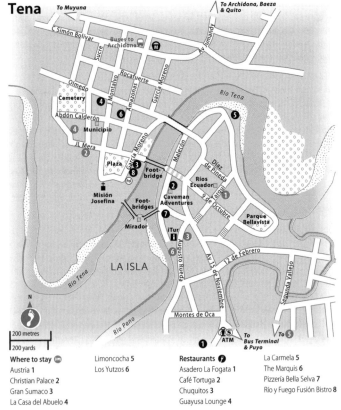

Where to stay 🛏
Austria **1**
Christian Palace **2**
Gran Sumaco **3**
La Casa del Abuelo **4**
Limoncocha **5**
Los Yutzos **6**

Restaurants 🍴
Asadero La Fogata **1**
Café Tortuga **2**
Chuquitos **3**
Guayusa Lounge **4**
La Carmela **5**
The Marquis **6**
Pizzería Bella Selva **7**
Río y Fuego Fusión Bistro **8**

Macas *Colour map 4, B1.*

Capital of Morona-Santiago province, Macas is situated high above the broad Río Upano Valley. It is a pleasant tranquil place, established by missionaries in 1563. **Sangay volcano** (5230 m) can be seen on clear mornings from the plaza, creating an amazing backdrop to the tropical jungle surrounding the town. The modern cathedral, with beautiful stained-glass windows, houses the much-venerated image of La Purísima de Macas. Five blocks north of the cathedral, at Don Bosco y Riobamba, the **Parque Recreacional**, which also affords great views of the Upano Valley, has a small orchid collection. The Sunday market on 27 de Febrero is worth a visit. **Fundación Chankuap** ① *Soasti y Bolívar, T07-270 1763, www.chankuap.org, Mon-Fri 0830-2030, Sat-Sun 0830-1430*, sells a nice variety of locally produced crafts and food products. Macas provides access to **Parque Nacional Sangay** ① *Macas office, Juan de la Cruz y Guamote, T07-270 2368, Mon-Fri 0800-1300, 1400-1700.* The lowland area of the park has interesting walking with many rivers and waterfalls. See also Sangay Transport (page 169) for notes on the road from Macas to Riobamba.

Macas to Gualaquiza

South of Macas lies one of Ecuador's least touristed areas, promising much to explore. **Sucúa**, 23 km from Macas, is the administrative centre of the Shuar indigenous people who inhabit much of southern Oriente. The town has most services and some attractions nearby; enquire at the **Tourist Office** in the Municipio. **Logroño**, 24 km further south, has a large limestone cave nearby (to visit contact Mario Crespo, T07-391 1013). It is another 31 km to (Santiago de) **Méndez**, a crossroads with a modern church. A paved road descends from Cuenca via Paute and Guarumales to Méndez, and another road heads east from Méndez via Patuca to Santiago and San José de Morona, near the Peruvian border. Some 26 km south of Méndez is **Limón** (official name General Leónidas Plaza Gutiérrez), a busy, friendly place, surrounded by impressive hills. From Limón the road climbs steeply 10 km to **Plan de Milagro**, another crossroads, where a great road for birdwatching (partly paved), descends from Cuenca via Gualaceo. Next are **Indanza**, 5 km south, then **San Juan Bosco**, 16 km further, with striking views of Cerro Pan de Azucar (2958 m) rising abruptly out of the jungle, before the road reaches Gualaquiza, 55 km ahead.

Gualaquiza *Colour map 5, B5.*

A pleasant town with an imposing church on a hilltop, Gualaquiza's pioneer-settlement charm is threatened by large mining projects in the area. Fortunately, tourism offers an alternative as there are also lovely waterfalls, good rivers for tubing, caves and undeveloped archaeological sites nearby. Information from Itur (see Tourist information, below), and from Leonardo Matoche at **Canela y Café**.

At Gualaquiza a road forks northwest to climb steeply to Cuenca via **Sígsig**. The road south from Gualaquiza passes El Pangui and Yantzaza (55 km), 8 km south of which is **Zumbi**, with basic hotels on the plaza. At Zumbi, a bridge crosses the Río Zamora and a side road goes southeast to Guayzimi and the beautiful **Alto Nangaritza** region, with **Reserva El Zarza**. The upper ★ **Río Nangaritza** flows through Shuar territory and a magnificent jungle-covered gorge with 200-m-high walls. There are also oilbird caves and other natural attractions. Buses run to the area from Zamora, and tours are available from **Cabañas Yankuam** (see Where to stay, page 288) and Zamora tour operators (page 291). South of Zumbi, the broad valley of the Río Zamora becomes progressively narrower, with forested mountains and lovely views. It is 35 km to Zamora.

Zamora *Colour map 5, B4.*

The colonial mission settlement of Zamora, at the confluence of the Ríos Zamora and Bombuscaro, today has a boom-town feeling due to large mining and hydroelectric projects in the area. It is reached by road from Gualaquiza (see above) or Loja, 64 km away. The road from Loja is beautiful as it wanders from *páramo* down to high jungle, crossing mountain ranges of cloudforest, weaving high above narrow gorges as it runs alongside the Río Zamora. The town itself is hilly, with a pleasant climate and a nice linear park along the river. It gives access to the **Alto Nangaritza** (see above) and is the gateway to the lowland portion of **Parque Nacional Podocarpus** (see page 191). Between town and the park is **Copalinga**, a bird-rich private reserve (see Where to stay, page 289). There are two private orchid collections that can be visited: **Pafinia** ① *Av del Ejército Km 2*, run by Marco Jiménez, mmjimenez473@gmail.com; and another belonging to **Padre Stanislau** ① *Av del Ejército, Cumbaratza, across from Hotel El Arenal.*

Listings Central and southern Oriente *maps pages 282 and 285.*

Tourist information

Tena

iTur and Ministerio de Turismo
Malecón, sector El Balnerio, T06-288 6452, www.tenaturismo.gob.ec. Mon-Fri 0730-1230, 1400-1700.

Puyo

iTur
Francisco de Orellana y 9 de Octubre, T06-288 5122. Daily 0800-1700. Also at Terminal Terrestre, T06-288 5122. Wed-Sun 0900-1600.

Macas

Ministerio de Turismo
Bolívar y 24 de Mayo, T07-270 1480. Mon-Fri 0800-1700.

Gualaquiza

Itur
Plaza Cívica, T07-278 1812, www.gadgualaquiza.gob.ec. Mon-Fri 0730-1230, 1330-1630.

Zamora

Ministerio de Turismo
José Luis Tamayo y Amazonas.
Mon-Fri 0815-1700.
English spoken.

Unidad de Turismo
Municipio, Diego de Vaca y 24 de Mayo, by the plaza, Zamora, T07-305 9386. Mon-Fri 0800-1230, 1400-1730.

Where to stay

Archidona

$$$$-$$$ Hakuna Matata
Vía Shungu Km 3.9, off the road between Tena and Archidona, T02-222 2119, or 06-288 9617, www.hakunamatata-ecuador.com.
Comfortable cabins in a lovely setting by the Río Inchillaqui. Includes 3 meals a day, walks, river bathing and horse riding.

$$$ Huasquila
Vía Huasquila, Km 3.5, Cotundo, T02-237 9200, T09-8764 6894, www.huasquila.com.
Wheelchair-accessible bungalows and Kichwa-style cabins, includes breakfast, various packages, full board available, jungle walks, caving, rock art.

$$$ Orchid Paradise
2 km north of town, T06-288 9232,
www.elparaisodelasorquideas.com.ec.
Cabins in nice secondary forest with lots of
birds, pool. Full board or cheaper with only
breakfast, owner organizes tours in the area.

$$-$ Hoteles Palmar del Río
Circunvalacion E45 y Transversal 16;
more economical branch on main street
4 blocks south of plaza, T06-287 7000;
www.hotelespalmardelrio.com.
Clean pleasant rooms with fan and parking.
Premium branch has pool, sauna, restaurant
and tour agency, includes breakfast.

Tena

$$$-$$ Los Yutzos
Augusto Rueda 190 y 12 de Febrero,
T06-288 6717.
Comfortable rooms and beautiful grounds
overlooking the Río Pano, central and family-
run. A/c, cheaper with fan, cramped parking.

$$ Christian Palace
JL Mera entre Sucre y Juan Montalvo,
T02-515 4324 (Quito) www.
hotelcristianresort.ec593.com.
Restaurant, a/c, pool, parking, modern and
comfortable. Also $$$ **Christian Resort**,
Km 5 on road to Puyo. Same website and
Quito phone number.

$$ La Casa del Abuelo
JL Mera 628, T06-288 6318, www.facebook.
com/LaCasaDelAbueloHostal.
Convenient place, comfortable rooms and
suites, small garden, hot water, ceiling fan,
good breakfast, parking, tours.

$$-$ Austria
Tarqui y Díaz de Pineda, T06-288 7205,
www.hostalaustriaecuador.com.
Spacious rooms, with a/c, cheaper
with fan, shared kitchen, ample parking,
quiet, good value.

$$-$ Gran Sumaco
Augusto Rueda y 15 de Nov, T06-288 8434,
www.hostalgransumaco.net.

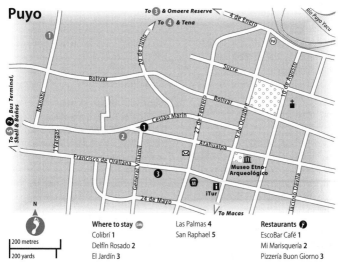

Puyo

N
200 metres
200 yards

Where to stay 🛏
Colibrí 1
Delfín Rosado 2
El Jardín 3

Las Palmas 4
San Raphael 5

Restaurants 🍴
EscoBar Café 1
Mi Marisquería 2
Pizzería Buon Giorno 3

Nice hotel in a good location, quiet, clean, bright, ample rooms, many with balcony and views. A/c, cheaper with fan, Wi-Fi, laundry service, very good value.

$ Limoncocha
Sangay 533, Sector Corazón de Jesús, on a hillside 4 blocks from the bus station, ask for directions, T06-284 6303, www. hostallimoncocha.com.
Concrete house with terrace and hammocks, some rooms with a/c, private or shared bath, US$7 pp in dorm, hot water, fan, laundry and cooking facilities, breakfast available, parking, German/Ecuadorean-run, enthusiastic owners organize tours. Out of the way in a humble neighbourhood, nice views, pleasant atmosphere, good value.

Misahuallí

$$$$ Hamadryade
Behind the Mariposario, 4 km from town, T09-8822 5413, www.hamadryade-lodge.com.
Luxury lodge in a 64-ha forest reserve, 5 designer wood cabins, packages include breakfast, dinner and excursions, French chef, pool, lovely views down to the river.

$$$ El Jardín Alemán
Jungle lodge on shores of Río Mishualli, 3 km from town, T06-306 2900, www. eljardinaleman.com.
Comfortable rooms with bath, hot water, set in protected rainforest. All-inclusive rate available ($$$$) with meals and daily guided tours.

$$$ Hostería Misahuallí
Across the river from town, T02-252 0043, www.hosteriasecuador.com/misahualli.
Cabins for up to 6 in a lovely setting, includes breakfast, other meals on request, electric shower, fan, pool and tennis court.

$$ Cabañas Río Napo
Cross the suspension bridge, then 100 m on the left-hand side, T06-289 0071.

Nice rustic cabins with thatched roof, private bath, hot water, ample grounds along the river, Kichwa-run, enthusiastic.

$$ El Paisano
Rivadeneyra y Tandalia, T06-289 0027, www.hostalelpaisano.com.
Restaurant, hot water, mosquito nets, helpful.

$$-$ Banana Lodge
500 m from town on the road to Pununo, T06-289 0190, www.bananalodge.com.
Sympathetically decorated hostel overlooking the river, ample rooms, huge garden with hammocks, breakfast available, cooking facilities, parking, US$4 pp for campervans, Russian/Ecuadorean-run.

$ Shaw
Santander, on the Plaza, T06-289 0163, hostalshaw@hotmail.com.
Good restaurant, hot water, fan, simple rooms, basic breakfast, tours, English spoken, very knowledgeable. Good value.

★ Lodges on the Upper Río Napo

Casa del Suizo
Quito T02-256 6090, www.casadelsuizo.com.
On north shore at Ahuano, resort with capacity for 200, comfortable rooms with fan and electricity, well-tended grounds, pool, gift shop, great views. Swiss/Ecuadorean-owned. All-inclusive packages, with or without transport; US$125 pp per night.

Cotococha Amazon Lodge
Km 10 on the Puerto Napo–Ahuano road, banks of Río Napo, T02-512 3358 (Quito office), www.cotococha.com.
Comfortable cabins. Packages with meals, entrance fees and local guides, excursions by dug-out canoe. US$440 for 4 days.

Jatun Sacha Biological Station
East of Ahuano and easily accessible by bus, Quito T02-243 2240, www.jatunsacha.org.
A 2500-ha reserve for education, research and tourism. 507 bird, 2500 plant and

765 butterfly species have been identified. Basic cabins with shared bath, cold water, good self-guided trails, canopy tower. US$30 per night, day visit US$6, guiding US$30 per group. Good value.

Liana Lodge
On Río Arajuno near confluence with the Napo, Tena T06-301 7702, www.selvaviva.ec.
Comfortable cabins with terraces and river views on a 1700-ha reserve. *Centro de rescate* has animals on site. US$388 for 4 nights/3 days. Also arranges stays at **Runa Wasi**, next door; basic cabins run by the local Kichwa community, US$32 pp per night with 3 meals, guiding extra.

Suchipakari Jungle Lodge
Pusuno Bajo, 25 mins by car from Misahuallí, then 15 mins' walk to lodge, T06-306 2864, or 09-8053 5854, Quito T02-295 9042, www.suchipakari.com.
Relatively isolated lodge in primary forest on a lake by a tributary of the Napo, rooms with fan, hot shower, balcony, hammocks, with electricity, Wi-Fi in public area. Staff from local communities, activities include hikes to waterfalls, kayaks (US$25), bikes (US$15), abseiling and rafting, nature and cultural visits, families catered for. 3- to 5-day packages (US$320-490 pp respectively), transport extra (US$35 pp in shared taxi from Misahuallí, US$120 private transfer).

Yachana
Quito T02-252 3777, www.yachana.com.
Near the village of Mondaña, 2 hrs downstream from Misahuallí or 2½ hrs upstream from Coca, also accessible by road (about 6 hrs from Quito). On a 2500-ha reserve, cabins on a bluff overlooking the Río Napo or further back in the forest. Proceeds help support community development projects. US$405 jungle view, US$504 river view for 4 days/3 nights.

Puyo

$$$ El Jardín
Paseo Turístico, Barrio Obrero, T03-289 2253, www.eljardinpuyo.com.
11 nice rooms and garden on the banks of the river in walking distance from town, good upmarket restaurant, bar, lounge, hot tub, bicycle hire.

$$ Delfín Rosado
Ceslao Marín y Atahualpa, T03-288 8757, www.hotel-delfinrosado.com.
Pool, sauna, modern rooms with a/c, parking.

$$ Las Palmas
4 de Enero 45 y 20 de Julio, 5 blocks from centre, T03-288 4832, www. hostallaspalmaspuyo.com.
Comfortable modern rooms with fridge, those at the back are quieter, excellent breakfast, friendly and helpful service, parking.

$ Colibrí
Av Manabí entre Bolívar y Galápagos, T03-288 3054, www.hostalelcolibripuyo.com.
Hot water, private bath, parking, away from centre, simple, good value, friendly and helpful.

$ San Raphael
Tte Hugo Ortiz y Juan de Velazco, 1½ blocks from bus station, T03-288 7275, Facebook.
Good choice for late arrivals or early departures. Clean rooms with private bath, hot water, good value.

Southern Oriente jungle lodges

Kapawi
T09-9260 5187, http://achuarlodge.com.
A top-of-the-line lodge located on the Río Capahuari near its confluence with the Pastaza, not far from the Peruvian border. Run by the local Achuar community and accessible only by small aircraft and motor canoe. The biodiversity is good, but more emphasis is placed on ethno-tourism here than at other

upmarket jungle lodges. From US$1068 for 3 nights/4 days, US$1298 for 4 nights/5 days includes land transport from Quito to Shell. Flight Shell–Kapawi US$222 return.

Macas

$$$ Arrayán y Piedra
Km 7 Vía a Puno, T07-304 5949, Facebook.
Large resort-style lodging, large, comfortable rooms, pool, sauna and hot tub, ample grounds with views of smoking Sangay and Río Upano, restaurant with very good food (particularly good breakfast), but slow service.

$$ Cabañas del Valle
Av 29 de Mayo, 1.5 km from town, T07-232 2282, http://hosteriacabanasdelvalle.com.
Comfortable rooms, pool, parking, sports areas, camping available, restaurant. Some noise from the Cuenca road.

$$ Casa Blanca
Soasti 14-29 y Sucre, T07-270 0195, Facebook.
Hot water, small pool, modern and comfortable, very helpful, good value.

$$ Nivel 5
Juan de la Cruz y Soasti, T07-270 1240, Facebook.
Nice modern multi-storey hotel, hot water, fan, pool, parking, helpful staff.

Macas to Gualaquiza
Sucúa
There are several other hotels ($) in town.

$$ Arutam
Vía a Macas Km 1, north of town, T07-274 0851, Facebook.
Restaurant, pool and sauna, parking, modern comfortable rooms, attractive grounds, sports fields, well suited to families.

$$ Luzcelinda
1 km vía a Cuenca, T07-274 2118, www.hosterialuzcelinda.com.

Comfortable rooms with fans, pool, sauna, limited restaurant but breakfast is included, gardens, parking.

Méndez

$ Interoceánico
C Quito on the plaza, T07-276 0245.
Hot water, parking, smart, good value.

Limón

$ Dream House
Quito y Bolívar, T07-277 0166.
With restaurant, shared bath, hot water, parking, adequate.

San Juan Bosco

$ Antares
On the Plaza, T07-270 7046.
Restaurant, hot water, indoor pool, simple functional rooms, helpful owner.

Gualaquiza

$ Gran Hotel
Orellana 08-33 y Gran Pasaje, T07-278 0722, julyconcepcion@hotmail.com.
Modern concrete building, hot water, fan, parking, small rooms, some windowless.

$ Wakiz
Orellana 08-52 y Domingo Comín, T07-278 0138.
Older simple place with small rooms, private or shared bath, hot water, parking, enthusiastic owner speaks English.

Alto Nangaritza

$$ Cabañas Yankuam
3 km south of Las Orquídeas, T09-9947 0740, www.lindoecuadortours.com.
Rustic cabins, includes breakfast, other tasty meals on request, private or shared bath, good walking in surrounding jungle-clad hills, organizes trips up the Río Nangaritza. Family-run. Reservations required.

Zamora

$$$ Copalinga
Km 3 on the road to the Bombuscaro
entrance of Parque Nacional Podocarpus,
T09-9710 1535, www.copalinga.com.
Reservations directly or through http://
jocotoursecuador.com.
Comfortable cabins with balcony in a lovely
setting (prices rise Oct-Apr), includes good
breakfast, other meals available if arranged
in advance; more rustic cabins with shared
bath are cheaper, but same price all year,
excellent birdwatching, walking trails,
English spoken. Operated by the **Jocotoco**
Foundation, reserve in advance, volunteer
opportunities available. Recommended.

$$ Samuria
24 de Mayo entre Diego de Vaca y Amazonas,
T07-260 7822, Facebook.
Modern bright hotel, comfortable well-
furnished rooms, a/c, cheaper with fan,
restaurant, parking.

$$ Wampushkar
Diego de Vaca y Pasaje Vicente Aldeán,
T07-260 7800, www.facebook.com/
wampushkarhotel.
Nice modern hotel, ample rooms, a/c,
cheaper with fan, hot water, parking, good
value, lovely view from rooftop restaurant.

$ Betania
Francisco de Orellana entre Diego de Vaca
y Amazonas, T07-260 7030, hotel-betania@
hotmail.com.
Modern and functional, breakfast available,
private bath, hot water, 4th-floor mirador,
communal kitchen, fridge, close to central
market and supermarket.

Tena

$$$ The Marquis
Amazonas 251 entre Calderón y Olmedo,
T06-288 6513. Daily 1200-1600, 1800-2200.
Upmarket restaurant serving good steaks.

$$ Chuquitos
García Moreno by the Plaza, T06-288 7630.
Mon-Sat 0700-2100, Sun 1100-2100.
Good food, à la carte only, seating on a
balcony overlooking the river. Pleasant
atmosphere, attentive service, popular
and recommended.

$$ Pizzería Bella Selva
García Moreno y Adbón Calderón, T06-288
8293; 2nd location at Av 15 de Noviembre,
diagonal a la Coop 29 de Octubre, T09-9850
1585. Daily 1100-2300.
Pizza and pasta.

$$ Río y Fuego Fusión Bistro
JL Mera y García Moreno, T09-8408 9689,
Facebook. Daily 1700-2200.
Asian and international dishes, sushi at
weekends, vegan and vegetarian options,
good juices and craft beers.

$$-$ Guayusa Lounge
Juan Montalvo y Olmedo, T06-288 8561,
Facebook. Tue-Sat 1600-2300.
Light meals, snacks and cocktails, good
meeting place, US-run, DJ at weekends.

$$-$ La Carmela
Av Francisco de Orellana y 15 de Noviembre,
T09 9811 3197, Facebook. Daily 1800-2400.
Café, restaurant and cultural centre. Italian
and local ingredients, good coffee and great
chocolate, artisanal beers, film club nights,
live music, popular with a young crowd.

$ Asadero La Fogata
Gil Ramírez Dávalos y Av Pano, T09-9204
2400, Facebook. Daily 1200-2200.

Tasty set meals, known for its tilapia, large portions, good value.

Cafés

Café Tortuga
Malecón south of the footbridge, T06-288 7304, Facebook. Mon-Sat 0700-1930, Sun 0700-1330.
Juices, snacks, good coffee, great breakfast, book exchange, handy bus timetable, Wi-Fi, nice location, friendly Swiss owner.

Misahuallí

$$$ El Jardín
300 m across bridge to Ahuano, T06-289 0219. Daily 1200-1600, 1800-2200.
Variety of dishes all very well cooked, beautiful garden setting.

$$ Parrillería Mesón Fasage
Guillermo Rivadeneyra, 1 block from the Plaza near Hotel El Paisano, T06-289 0192. Daily 1200-2400.
Good-quality grill.

$$-$ Bijao
Juan Arteaga y Guillermo Rivadeneira, T09-8735 7435. On the plaza. Daily 0800-2200.
Good set meals and *comida típica* à la carte. Can organize walks and canoe trips with guides.

Puyo

$$$-$$ Mi Marisquería
Orellana y Amazonas T03-288 5751, Facebook. Daily 0800-1800.
Very good fish and seafood, all cooked perfectly with lots of variety.

$$ Pizzería Buon Giorno
Orellana entre Villamil y 27 de Febrero T03-288 3841, Facebook. Mon-Sat 1200-2300, Sun 1400-2300.
Good pizza, lasagne and salads, pleasant atmosphere, lunch, supper, coffee and drinks, very popular.

EscoBar Café
Atahualpa y Ceslao Marín, T03-288 3008, Facebook. Mon-Sat 0630-2400.
Good for early breakfast, sandwiches, snacks and full meals, bar at night, craft beers, attractive bamboo decor, sit upstairs for good view of surroundings. Sometimes live music and cultural events.

Macas

$$ Jung+Lab
Bolívar entre Guamote y Amazonas, T07-270 2448, Facebook. Mon-Sat 1200-2245.
Delicious creative meals using local produce, also burgers, great desserts and cold beer.

$$-$ La Italiana
Soasti y Sucre, T07-270 2893, Facebook. Mon-Sat 1200-2300.
Great pizzas, pasta and salads.

$$-$ La Maravilla Guayusa Bar
Soasti y Sucre, across from Hotel Casa Blanca, T07-252 5533, Facebook. Tue-Sun 1200-0200.
Local food and drinks, try the fried yucca and the *guayusa* tea, very popular with locals, good meeting place, live music at weekends.

$ Rincón Manabita
Amazonas y Tarqui, T07-270 2340. Daily 0715-2200.
Good breakfasts and a choice of set meals which are delicious and filling. Also à la carte, local food.

Zamora

$$ Semillas
Pío Jaramillo y Jorge Mosquera, Diagonal Colegio Madre Bernarda, T07-260 5684.
Attentive service from the owner/host, who sources fresh, organic and tasty ingredients for his frequently changing and healthy menu.

$$ Terra Grill
Av del Maestro, T09-8867 4090, Facebook. Daily 1200-2300.

Burgers, wings and barbecued meats. Large portions, good value, friendly service.

Spiga Pan
Av del Maestro y Pío Jaramillo, T07-260 8088, Facebook. Daily 0700-2200.
Great bakery with a variety of hot bread, cream cakes and fresh fruit yoghurt.

What to do

Tena
Rafting tours cost US$40-80 per day, safety standards vary between operators. Avoid touts selling tours on the street.
Adventure River Amazonas (ARA), *María Vargas y Yuralpa, T06-284 7448, www.river amazonas.com.* Rafting, adventure sports and community cultural tours. Ecuadorean/French-run.
Caveman Adventures, *Bellavista Baja, Fco de Orellana 666 y Tarqui, T09-8420 0173, www.cavemanecuador.com.* Water sports and tours.
Limoncocha, *at Hostal Limoncocha (see Where to stay, above).* Rafting, kayaking and jungle, English and German spoken.
Ríos Ecuador, *Tarqui 230 y Díaz de Pineda, T09-9680 4046, www.riosecuador.com.* Rafting, kayaking, horse riding and hiking.
River People, *Vía a Inchillaqu, T09-8356 7307, www.riverpeopleecuador.com.* Rafting and kayaking.

Misahuallí
Jungle tours (US$45-80 pp per day) can be arranged by most hotels as well as:
Ecoselva, *Santander on the plaza, T06-289 0019, www.ecoselvapepetapia.com.* Recommended guide Pepe Tapia speaks English and has a biology background. Well organized and reliable. Bike rentals, US$10 per day.
Teorumi, *T06-289 0203, Facebook.* Community tourism. Offers tours to the Shiripuno Kichwa community.

Puyo
Selvavida Travel, *Ceslao Marín y Atahualpa, T03-288 9729, www.selvavidatravel.com.* Specializes in rafting, kayaking and Parque Nacional Yasuní.

Macas
Tours to indigenous communities and lowland portions of Parque Nacional Sangay, cost about US$50 per day.
Insondu Mundo Shuar, *Bolívar y Soasti, T07-270 2533.*
Real Nature Travel Company, *Av La Ciudad s/n, Barrio La Barranca, T07-252 5041, www.realnaturetravel.com.* Run by RhoAnn Wallace and professional birdwatching guide Galo Real, English spoken.
Tsuirim Viajes, *Don Bosco y Sucre, T07-270 1681, www.vivelaamazonia.com.* Owner Leo Salgado.

Zamora
Cabañas Yankuam, *see page 288.* Offer tours to the Alto Nangaritza.
Wellington Valdiviezo, *T09-9380 2211, http://lindozamoraturistico.blogspot. co.uk.* Tours to the Alto Nangaritza, Shuar communities, adventure sports, visits to shamans. Contact in advance.

Transport

Tena
Bus
Run-down Terminal Terrestre on 15 de Noviembre, 1 km from the centre (taxi US$1). To **Quito**, US$7.50, 5 hrs. To **Ambato**, via Baños, US$6.25, 4½ hrs. To **Baños**, US$6, 3½ hrs. To **Riobamba**, US$7.50, 5½ hrs. To **Puyo**, US$3.75, 2 hrs. To **Coca and Lago Agrio**, fares given above. To **Misahuallí**, see below. To **Archidona**, from Amazonas y Bolívar by market, every 20 mins, US$0.35, 15 mins.

Misahuallí
Bus
Buses run from the plaza. To **Tena**, hourly 0600-1900, US$1.25, 45 mins. Make long-distance connections in Tena. To **Quito**, 1 direct bus a day at 0830, US$8.75, 5 hrs.

River
No scheduled passenger service, but motorized canoes for 8-10 passengers can be chartered for touring.

Puyo
Air
The nearest airport to Puyo is at Shell, 13 km. Military flights to jungle villages are not open to foreigners, but light aircraft can be chartered starting around US$300 per hr.

Bus
Terminal Terrestre on the outskirts of town, a 10- to 15-min walk from the centre; taxi US$1. To **Baños**, US$2.50, 1½ hrs. To **Ambato**, US$3.75, 2½ hrs. To **Quito**, US$6.25, 5 hrs via Ambato; shared taxis with **Autovip**, T02-600 2582 or 09-9629 5406, US$40, 8 daily, fewer on weekends or **Delux**, T09-3920 9827 or 09-8343 0275, every 2 hrs, US$25. To **Riobamba**, US$5, 3½ hrs. To **Tena**, see above. To **Macas**, US$6, 2½-3 hrs. To **Coca**, US$11.25, 8hrs. To **Lago Agrio**, US$15, 11 hrs.

Macas
Air
Small modern airport within walking distance at Cuenca y Amazonas. Air taxis to jungle villages, US$600 per hr for 9 passengers.

Bus
Terminal Terrestre by the market. To **Puyo**, see above. To **Baños**, US$9, 4½ hrs. To **Quito**, via Puyo, Baños and Ambato, US$10, 8 hrs. To **Riobamba** through Parque Nacional Sangay, a beautiful ride, 6 daily, US$6.25, 4 hrs. To **Cuenca**, US$11, 6-7 hrs, via Guarumales and Paute or via Plan de Milagro and Gualaceo. To **Gualaquiza**, US$8, 8 hrs, where you can get a bus to Zamora and Loja (see below). To **Sucúa**, hourly, US$1.25, 30 min. To **9 de Octubre**, for **Parque Nacional Sangay**, US$2, 45 mins.

Gualaquiza
Bus
To **Macas**, see above. To **Cuenca**; via Sígsig, 4 daily, US$8.75, 6 hrs; or via Plan de Milagro and Gualaceo. To **Zamora**, US$4.50, 3½ hrs. To **Loja**, US$7.50, 5½ hrs.

Alto Nangaritza
Bus
To **Las Orquídeas**, with **Trans Zamora**, from Zamora at 0400, 0645, 1115 and 1230, US$4.75, 3½ hrs; from Yantzaza at 0440, 0740, 1150 and 1310, US$3.25, 3½ hrs; with **Unión Yantzaza**, from Yantzaza at 0430, 0930, 1130, 1430 and 1630; from Loja at 1415, 1510, US$7.75, 5½ hrs.

Zamora
Bus
Leave from Terminal Terrestre. To **Loja**, frequent service, 1½-2 hrs, US$3; to **Gualaquiza**, US$4.50, 3½ hrs, where you can transfer for Macas.

This is
Galápagos

A trip to the Galápagos is an unforgettable experience. As Charles Darwin put it: "the natural history of this archipelago is very remarkable: it seems to be a little world within itself". The islands are world renowned for their fearless wildlife but no amount of hype can prepare you for such a close encounter with nature.

Lying right on the equator, this ancient achipelago of harsh volcanic landscapes is ruled by animals, and human vistors are reduced to the role of voyeur. Here, you can snorkel with penguins and sea lions, watch 200-kg tortoises lumbering through giant cactus forest, and enjoy the courtship display of the blue-footed booby and frigate bird, all at startlingly close range. Both above and below water, sit back, wait patiently and allow the animals to come to you. They nearly always do.

On land, immerse yourself in another world. Sit beside newborn sea lion pups and their parents will simply lift their heads and give you a cursory glance. Marine iguanas bask by your toes, while birds pause on their backs doing daily clean-up duty.

Biodiversity figures are not as high as in some other places, yet the number of endemic species is unparalleled. Beneath the incessant waves, there are vast numbers of sharks, from the sleek silky to gentle whale sharks. Huge schools of hammerheads are the most common, yet they can also appear solo, drifting by your shoulder.

The Galápagos consist of six main islands: San Cristóbal, Santa Cruz, Isabela, Floreana, Santiago and Fernandina (Santiago and Fernandina are uninhabited). There are also 12 smaller islands as well as over 40 small islets, which can only be visited on cruises.

Despite their relative isolation and the cost of getting there, these islands are ever popular. A steady stream of people flies in daily, passing along well-trodden routes to witness the spectacular wildlife.

❶ North Seymour A good introduction to Galápagos wildlife, this small, flat island has sea lions, marine and land iguanas, blue-footed boobies and frigate birds. Dry landing on black basalt lava.

❷ South Plaza The jetty on South Plaza is often taken over by sea lions. Land iguanas are common. A trail leads across the island to seabird cliffs.

❸ Santa Fe From a sea lion-strewn bay on the northeast of Santa Fe, a trail winds through cactus forest home to land iguanas. Spot rays and turtles in the bay.

❹ Punta Pitt (San Cristóbal) A cliff trail provides encounters with all three species of booby: blue-footed, red-footed and Nazca.

❺ Gardner Bay (Española) Wade ashore on a dazzling 2-km-long coral-sand beach smothered in sea lions. Snorkelling around the offshore islet is excellent.

❻ Punta Suárez (Española) Spectacular rocky headland, often pounded by surf and the site of a blowhole on the southern coast. Wildlife is outstanding: marine iguanas, lava lizards, Nazca and blue-footed boobies, swallow-tailed gulls red-billed tropicbirds, three species of Darwin's finch, Galápagos hawks and (from April to December) a colony of waved albatross.

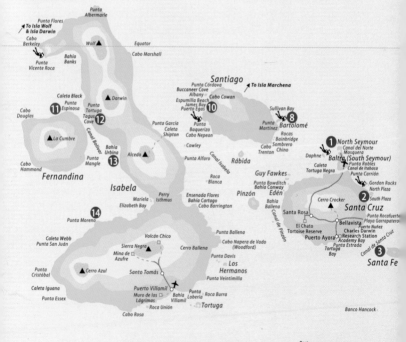

❼ Punta Cormorant (Floreana) Wet landing on olivine beach (you may see Galápagos penguins in the bay), followed by a trail that heads inland past a brackish lagoon (flamingos, stilts and other waders) to a sandy beach that's used as a nesting ground by green turtles. Look for stingrays in the shallows and lava lizards on the rocky headlands.

❽ Bartolomé A small island off the east coast of Santiago, Bartolomé has a boardwalk that climbs through a volcanic landscape of ash fields, lava tubes and cinder cones to a viewpoint overlooking Pinnacle Rock. You can snorkel at the Pinnacle, often with penguins and reef sharks.

Genovesa
❾
Bahía Darwin

Note Cruise itineraries are strictly controlled to avoid overcrowding or damaging the islands. As a result these landing sites are subject to change.

Pacific Ocean

San Cristóbal
Cabo Norte
Bahía Hobbs
Caleta Tortuga
Punta Dedo (Finger)
❹ *Punta Pitt*
Kicker Rock (Léon Dormido)
Canal de Santa Fé
Cerro Brujo
Bahía Stephens
Punta Bassa
I Lobos
Cerro San Joaquín
Bahía Rosa Blanca
Bahía Wreck
Puerto Baquerizo Moreno
El Junco
El Progreso
Roca Este
Punta Wreck
Puerto Chino
Roca Ballena (Whale)
Bahía Agua Dulce (Freshwater)

Arrecife Macgowen

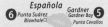

Española
❻ *Punta Suárez*
Blowhole
Gardner
❺
Gardner Bay
Punta Cevallos

❾ Genovesa Remote and spectacular, the flooded caldera of Genovesa has over a million nesting seabirds. Great frigate birds, red-footed boobies, lava and swallow-tailed gulls and yellow-crowned night herons are best seen around the sandy beach at Darwin Bay. At Prince Philip Steps a short climb leads onto basalt cliffs where daytime-hunting short-eared owls can be observed snatching white-vented storm petrels as they return to their nesting burrows. The trail also leads through dry woodland with nesting Nazca and red-footed boobies. Mockingbirds are common. Snorkel along the base of the cliffs near Prince Philip Steps to see large numbers of king angelfish, Moorish idols, yellow-tail surgeonfish and, possibly, a few Galápagos sharks and fur seals.

❿ Puerto Egas (James Bay, Santiago) Snorkelling from the black-sand beach is good, while a walking trail follows the coast to a series of tide pools teeming with marine iguanas and Sally Lightfoot crabs. Don't miss the fur seal grottoes.

⓫ Punta Espinosa The shield volcano of La Cumbre looms over black lava fields where the Galápagos' biggest concentration of marine iguanas can be found. Pioneer cactus, lava lizards and sally lightfoot crabs have also claimed the ropy coils of lava, while sea lions lounge on coves of crushed shell and pencil urchin spines. Look out for whales and dolphins in the Canal Bolívar.

⓬ Tagus Cove (Isabela) This sheltered, steep-sided bay is excellent for snorkelling – green turtles are abundant and you should also see flightless cormorants, penguins, sea lions, marine iguanas, large shoals of fish and even manta rays, sharks and dolphins. A *panga* ride along the shore will get you close to penguins and flightless cormorants, while a short hike above the bay has wonderful views across a flooded crater known as Darwin's Lake. Look for finches, flycatchers and yellow warblers in the surrounding woodland.

⓭ Urbina Bay (Isabela) Wet landing on a steep beach. Giant tortoise, land and marine iguanas, plus flightless cormorants.

⓮ Punta Moreno (Isabela) After navigating a maze of mangrove channels, you make a dry landing on pahoehoe lava before following a scant trail to a series of brackish lagoons – home to flamingos, pintail ducks and brown pelicans.

Galápagos calendar
Monthly guide to wildlife highlights

January As the rainy season starts, marine iguanas become brightly coloured and land birds begin nesting. Green turtles start egg laying and warming sea temperatures are ideal for snorkelling.

February Galápagos dove courtship is in full swing; flamingos and pintail ducks are also breeding, along with marine iguanas on Santa Cruz. Sea temperatures reach 25°C.

March Expect frequent downpours this month. Marine iguanas are nesting on Fernandina, but the big event in late March is the mass arrival of waved albatross to Española.

April Waved albatross waste no time in practising their courtship dances. Frigatebirds are also engaged in frenzied mating rituals. Green turtle and Isabela land iguana eggs hatch. As the rains come to an end, the islands are at their greenest.

May As North Seymour's blue-footed boobies begin their courtship, waved albatross are laying eggs on Española and turtle hatchlings are emerging. Marine iguana eggs are also hatching on Santa Cruz.

June The *garua* (mist) season begins as giant tortoises descend from the Santa Cruz highlands to find a nest. Seas can be choppy. This is a good month to spot migratory birds and humpback whales.

July Sea temperatures will drop to around 21°C this month. Everywhere you go, seabird colonies are a riot of courtship, egg-brooding and chick-feeding. It's another good month for whale watching.

August Sea temperatures fall to around 18°C. Sea lions begin to pup, and it's a good time to look for courting Galápagos hawks, nesting Nazca boobies and swallow-tailed gulls. Migrant shore birds arrive, while giant tortoises head back to the highlands.

September It's a good month to brave the waters around Bartolomé where Galápagos penguins are usually active. Most seabirds are also still busy nesting and rearing chicks. Male beachmaster sea lions start fighting over females.

October The *garúa* period is coming to an end. Galápagos fur seals start mating, lava herons begin nesting and blue-footed boobies have chicks on Española and Isabela.

November Seas are calmer and water temperatures start rising. Snorkellers can enjoy encounters with sea lion pups. Storm petrels are busy nesting on Genovesa and dodging the island's short-eared owls.

December Giant tortoise eggs hatch between now and April; green turtles are mating in offshore waters, while the first waved albatross chicks fledge.

Essential Galápagos

Finding your feet

There are no international flights to the Galápagos. Flights from Quito or Guayaquil arrive at two main airports: **Baltra**, across a narrow strait from Santa Cruz (the most populated island), and **Puerto Baquerizo Moreno**, on San Cristóbal. The two islands are 96 km apart and on most days there are flights between them, as well as to **Puerto Villamil** on Isabela. There is also a *lancha* (speedboat) service between **Puerto Ayora** (Santa Cruz) and the other populated islands. See Transport, page 342

Tour options

Live-aboard cruise The traditional and best way to visit the Galápagos is on a live-aboard cruise (*tour navegable*), where you travel and sleep on a yacht, tour boat or cruise ship. These vessels travel at night, arriving at a new landing site each day. Cruises range from three to 14 nights; seven is recommended. Itineraries are controlled by the national park to distribute cruise boats evenly throughout the islands. There is a vast range of options from economy to luxury and standards and prices vary considerably.

Island-hopping This is an alternative option for visiting Galápagos whereby you spend a night or two at hotels on the four populated islands, travelling between them in speedboats. You cover less ground than on a cruise, see fewer wildlife sites, and cannot visit the more distant islands. Island-hopping is sold in organized packages but visitors in no rush can also travel between and explore the populated islands independently at their leisure.

Day tours Day tours (*tour diario*) are based mostly out of Puerto Ayora. Some take you for day visits to national park landing sites on nearby unpopulated islands, such as Bartolomé, Seymour, Plazas and Santa Fe, and can be quite good. Others go for the day to the populated islands of Isabela or Floreana, with no stops permitted along the way. The latter require at least four hours of speedboat travel and generally leave insufficient time to enjoy visitor sites; they are not recommended.

When to go

The Galápagos climate can be divided into a hot season (December-May), when there is a possibility of heavy showers, and the cooler *garúa* (mist) season (June to November), when the days are generally more cloudy and there is often rain or drizzle. July and August can be windy, force four or five. The sea is cold July-October; underwater visibility is best January-March. Ocean temperatures are usually higher to the east and lower at the western end of the archipelago. Despite all these climatic variations, conditions are generally favourable for visiting Galápagos throughout the year.

High season for tourism is June-August and December-January, when last-minute arrangements are generally not possible. Some boats may be heavily booked throughout the year and you should plan well in advance if you want to travel on a specific vessel at a specific time.

Responsible tourism and safety

Never touch any of the animals, birds or plants.

Keep your distance from the male 'beach-master' sea lions, they have been known to bite.

Do not transfer sand, seeds or soil from one island to another.

Do not leave litter anywhere or take food onto the islands.

All areas of the national park are non-smoking.

Wildife **of**
the Galápagos

Over many hundreds of thousands of years, animals and plants migrated to the islands from across the sea and adapted themselves to the islands' conditions. Thus many of them are unique: a quarter of the species of shore fish, half of the plants and almost all the reptiles are found nowhere else. Plant and animal species in the Galápagos are grouped into three categories – endemic, native and introduced – terms you will hear often during your visit.

Reptiles

The reptiles found on the Galápagos islands are represented by five groups: iguana, lava lizards, geckos, snakes and, of course, the giant tortoise. Of the 27 species of reptile on the islands, 17 are endemic.

❶ Giant tortoise
Geochelone elephantopus

Sighting *In captivity on San Cristóbal, Isabela and Floreana, or in the wild at the tortoise reserve on Santa Cruz.*

The Galápagos are named after the saddle-back tortoise (*galápago* means saddle), one of 14 species of giant tortoise that have been discovered on the islands, although now only 10 survive (the famous Lonesome George – thought to be a subspecies all of his own – sadly died in 2012). Much prized by 17th- and 18th-century sailors as a source of fresh meat on long voyages, their eggs make a tasty snack for introduced species such as black rats, feral dogs and pigs. Numbers dwindled from an estimated 250,000 to just 15,000 in 1980. These days there are between 20,000 and 25,000 on the islands. The Darwin Research Station in Santa Cruz rears young for reintroduction to the wild, giving visitors the opportunity to see them close up. The tortoises mate during the wet season (January to March). Later, between February and May, the females amble down the coast where they bury up to 16 eggs in a nest about 30 cm deep. Three to eight months later, the eggs hatch, usually between mid-January and March.

■ *The oldest inhabitant of the Darwin Research Station may be 180 years old – old enough to have met Darwin himself.*

Species specifics

Endemic species Species which occur only in the Galápagos and nowhere else on earth.
Native species Species that are found in the Galápagos as well as other parts of the world. Although not unique to the islands, these native species have been an integral part of the Galápagos ecosystems for a very long time.
Introduced species These are very recent arrivals, brought by man, and inevitably the cause of much damage (see Tourists and settlers, page 347).

❷ Marine turtle
Chelonia mydas

Sighting *Caleta Tortuga Negra, at the northern tip of Santa Cruz, and the white-sand beach on Floreana.*

Of the eight species of marine turtle in the world only one is found on the islands: the Pacific green turtle. Mating turtles are a common sight in December and January. Egg-laying usually takes place between January and June, when the female comes ashore to dig a hole and lay 80 to 120 eggs under cover of darkness. After about two months the hatchlings emerge from their shells and scramble across the beach to the sea.

■ *Baby turtles always hatch at night to avoid crabs, herons, frigates and lava gulls on the lookout for a midnight feast as they make their perilous journey to the sea.*

❸ Marine iguana
Amblyrhynchus cristatus

Sighting *In the water or wandering around on most of the islands.*

The only sea-going lizard in the world, marine iguanas gather in huge herds on the coastal lava rocks. They vary in size, from 60 cm for the smallest variety (Isla Genovesa) up to 1 m for the largest (Isla Isabela). Their black skin acts as camouflage and allows them to absorb heat from the fierce equatorial sun, although those on Española have red and green coloration. The marine iguana's flat tail is ideal for swimming but, although they can dive to depths of 20 m and stay underwater for up to an hour at a time, they prefer to feed on the seaweed on exposed rocks at low tide.

■ *This prehistoric-looking endemic species could be as much as nine million years old, making it even older than the islands themselves.*

❹ Land iguana
Conolophus subcristatus, pallidus and rosada

Sighting *Conolophus subcristatus inhabits Santa Cruz, Plaza, Isabela and Fernandina; Conolophus pallidus is found only on Santa Fe; Conolophus rosada lives on Isabela.*

There are three endemic species of land iguana on the islands: *Conolophus subcristatus* is yellow-orange, *Conolophus pallidus* is whitish to chocolate brown and *Conolophus rosada* is pink. The biggest land iguanas weigh 6-7 kg and measure over 1 m in length. Their numbers have been greatly reduced over the years, as the young often fall prey to rats and feral animals; the chances of survival for a land iguana in the wild is less than 10%. It feeds mainly on the fruits and flowers of the prickly pear cactus.

■ *The land iguana is a friendly chap and can often be seen at close quarters.*

Birds

Sea birds were probably the first animals to colonize the archipelago. Half of the resident population of birds is endemic to the Galápagos, but only five of the 19 species of sea bird found on the Galápagos are unique to the islands. They are: the Galápagos penguin, the flightless cormorant, the lava gull, the swallowtail gull and the waved albatross. The endemism rate of land birds is much higher, owing to the fact that they are less often migratory. There are 29 species of land bird in the Galápagos, 22 of which are endemic, among them the 14 species of finch made famous by Darwin.

❺ Galápagos penguin
Spheniscus mendiculus

Sighting *In the water and around Fernandina and Isabela.*

The penguin population is small and fluctuates in response to the El Niño cycle. Breeding takes place on Fernandina and Isabela, where upwelling of the Cromwell Current cools the sea. These birds may appear ungraceful on land, hopping clumsily from rock to rock, but underwater they are fast and agile swimmers and can be seen breaking the surface, like dolphins.

■ *This is the world's most northerly species of penguin.*

❻ Flightless cormorant
Phalacrocorax harrisi

Sighting *Fernandina and Isabela*

This is one of the world's rarest birds, with an estimated population of 700 pairs. It is found only on Isla Fernandina and the west coast of Isla Isabela, where the nutrient-rich Cromwell Current brings a plentiful supply of fish from the central Pacific.

■ *Despite having lost the ability to fly, the cormorant still spreads its stunted wings to dry in the wind, proving that old habits die hard.*

❼ Waved albatross
Phoebastria irrorata

Sighting *Across the islands.*

The largest bird in the Galápagos, with a wingspan of 2.5 m, is a cousin of the petrels and puffins. It was not only endemic to the archipelago but also to Isla Española, until a few breeding pairs were found on Isla de la Plata off the Ecuadorean mainland (see page 236). Outside the April-December breeding season, the albatross glides majestically across the Pacific Ocean, sometimes as far as Japan. It returns after six months to begin a spectacular courtship display, a cross between an exotic dance and a fencing duel, which is repeated over and over.

■ *Not surprisingly, given the effort they put into their mating ritual, albatrosses stay faithful to their mate for life.*

❽ Frigate bird
Fregata minor and magnificens

Sighting *San Cristóbal, Genovesa and North Seymour.*

Both the great frigate bird and the magnificent frigate bird are found on the Galápagos. These 'avian pirates' have a wingspan to rival the albatross and spend much of their time gliding in circles with their distinctive long forked tail and angled wings. During the courtship display the males inflate a huge red sac under their throats, like a heart-shaped scarlet balloon, and flutter their spread wings. This seduces and attracts females to the nest, which the males have already prepared for mating. This amazing ritual can be seen in March and April on San Cristóbal and Genovesa, or throughout the year on North Seymour.

Unlike the great frigate bird, the magnificent frigate bird is an 'inshore feeder' and feeds near the islands. It is very similar in appearance, but the male has a purple sheen on its plumage and the female has a black triangle on the white patch on her throat.

■ *Having lost the waterproofing of their black plumage, the frigate never lands on sea; instead it pursues other birds and harasses them for food, or catches small fish on the surface of the water with its hooked beak.*

❾ Boobies
Sula nebouxii, Sula sula and Sula granti

Sighting *Common throughout the Galápagos.*

Three species of booby are found in the Galápagos. Most common is the blue-footed booby, *Sula nebouxii*. It can lay up to three eggs at a time, though if food is insufficient the stronger firstborn will kick its siblings out of the nest. Unlike its red-footed relative, the blue-footed booby fishes inshore, dropping on its prey like an arrow from the sky. It is best known for its comical and complicated courtship dance.

The red-footed booby, *Sula sula*, is the only Galápagos booby to nest in trees, thanks to feet that are adapted to gripping branches. Many are light brown in colour, although there is also a less common white variety. The largest colony of red-footed boobies is found on Isla Genovesa.

The Nazca booby, *Sula granti* (formerly called the masked booby), is the heaviest of the three boobies and has white plumage with a distinctive black mask on the eyes. Like its blue-footed cousin, the Nazca booby nests on the ground and surrounds its nest with waste. It chooses to fish between the other two boobies, thus providing an excellent illustration of the idea of the 'ecological niche'.

■ *The name 'booby' is thought to derive from pájaro bobo (silly bird); their extreme tameness once led to many being killed for sport.*

The number of native mammals in the archipelago is limited to two species of bat, a few species of rat and, of course, sea lions and seals. This is explained by the fact that the islands were never connected to the mainland. Since the arrival of man, however, goats, dogs, donkeys, horses and the black rat have been introduced and threaten the fragile ecological balance of the islands.

⑩ Sea lion
Zalophus wollebaeki

Sighting *Colonies on South Plaza, Santa Fe, Rábida, James Bay (Isla Santiago), Española, San Cristóbal and Isabela.*

Galápagos sea lions are common throughout the archipelago, gathering in large colonies on beaches or on the rocks. The male, distinguished from the female by its huge size and domed forehead, is very territorial, especially at the beginning of the May to January mating season. He patrols a territory of 40-100 sq m with a group of up to 30 females, chasing off intruders and keeping an eye on the young, who may wander too far from the safety of the beach. Males that are too tired or too old to hold a territory gather in bachelor clubs. The friendly, inquisitive females are one of the main tourist attractions, especially when cavorting with swimmers.

■ *The sea lions' favourite games are surfing the waves and playing 'water polo', using a marine iguana instead of a ball.*

⑪ Fur seal
Arctocephalus galapagoensis

Sighting *Santiago.*

Fur seals and sea lions both belong to the *otaridae* or eared seal family. Fortunately, these *lobos de dos pelos* (double-fur sea wolves), as they are known locally, survived and can be seen most easily in Puerto Egas on Santiago island, usually hiding from the sun under rocks or lava cracks. The fur seal is distinguished from the sea lion by its smaller size, its pointed nose, big round sad moist eyes, larger front flippers and more prominent ears.

■ *The fur seal's dense, luxuriant pelt attracted great interest and the creature was hunted almost to extinction at the beginning of the 20th century by whalers and other skin hunters.*

The Galápagos Islands are washed by three currents: the cold Humboldt and Cromwell currents, and the warm El Niño current. This provides the islands with diverse and unusual underwater fauna.

The number of species of fish could exceed 400, of which about 20% are endemic. Among the huge number of fish found in the islands' waters, there are 18 species of moray, five species of ray (stingrays, golden ray, marbled ray, spotted eagle ray and manta ray) and about 12 species of shark.

The most common sharks are the white-tip reef shark, the black-tip reef shark, two species of hammerhead, the Galápagos shark, the grey reef shark, the tiger shark, the hornshark and the whale shark. Among the marine mammals, at least 16 species of whale and seven species of dolphin have been identified.

The most common dolphins are the bottle-nosed dolphin, *Tursiops truncatus*, and the common dolphin.

Whales include the sperm whale, humpback whale, pilot whale, the orca and the false killer whale, sei whale, minke whale, Bryde's whale, Cuvier's beaked whale and the blue whale. These whales can be seen around all the islands, but most easily to the west of Isabela and Fernandina. The waters are also rich in starfish, sea urchins, sea cucumbers and crustaceans, including the ubiquitous and distinctive Sally Lightfoot crab.

A Galápagos
cruise

William Gray, author of Footprint's *Wildlife Travel*, gives a flavour
of his encounters with the animals.

On the island of Española, surf blooms white on the cliffs at Punta Suárez – a relentless procession of sinewy waves hurling themselves onto the rocks and filling the air with the salty sweat of their exertions. Anywhere else in the world and you would be spellbound by such a vibrant seascape. But this is the Galápagos and the boulder beach below us is twitching with sea lions and marine iguanas. Sally Lightfoot crabs daub the rocks with splashes of red and gold; waved albatross cartwheel overhead and Nazca boobies stand sentinel on rocky pedestals, their fluffy white chicks crouched in crevices like snagged cotton wool. The sea can flex its muscles all it likes, but it will never upstage the wildlife on Darwin's 'Enchanted Isles'.

Many places in the world have amazing wildlife. Some of them boast extraordinary biodiversity or a superabundance of animals. Others are renowned for endemic species, or allow intimate close-up encounters. It's a rare place, though, that combines all these attributes, and the Galápagos archipelago is one of them.

Punta Suárez on Española is only the third shore excursion on our week-long Galápagos cruise, but already we have seen several of the island's trademark wildlife highlights: blue-footed boobies dancing on North Seymour, hundreds of sea lions dozing on the beach at Gardner Bay, a Galápagos hawk feeding on one of Darwin's finches – evidence for the theory of natural selection ripped apart before our very eyes.

Over the next few days, our small expedition ship (with just 24 passengers onboard) loops through the archipelago. Each morning, we wake to find a new island. Zodiacs (or *pangas*) shuttle us ashore and we spend the next few hours walking slowly along trails that grapple with old lava flows or thread through forests of palo santo trees.

There is no need to walk far. At Punta Cormorant on Floreana Island (our fourth landing), we have barely strolled a dozen metres before our guide delivers a double whammy of Galápagos penguin and Caribbean flamingo. It's probably the only place in the world where the two can be seen together in the wild.

On Genovesa, there's another incongruous spectacle as we watch short-eared owls hunting storm petrels in broad daylight – the raptors waiting in ambush, perfectly camouflaged in clifftop lava fields, as swarms of the dainty seabirds return to their nesting burrows.

Then there are the Galápagos icons: flightless cormorants preening stubby wings; male frigate birds shaking bright red, party-balloon throat pouches in courtship frenzies; marine iguanas snorting salt from their nostrils and, of course, the high-stepping, head-bowing courtship dances of blue-footed boobies.

Then, just when you think the Galápagos has exhausted its cache of surprises, someone suggests you go snorkelling.

During an hour's drift along the rocky coast of Targus Bay on Isabela Island, we count 26 green turtles, sometimes in twos and threes, grazing on algae or drifting in watery space. Anywhere else in the world, this would be exceptional, but turtles are so common here they almost become part of the background. Sea lions steal the show in surging swim-pasts; penguins zip along at the surface like overwound bath toys, and flightless cormorants dive alongside you, their plumage wrapped in silver cocoons of trapped air.

And as if all this wasn't enough, the sea is squirming with fish – stately king angelfish parading from cover, vast shoals of yellowtail surgeonfish, wrasse, damselfish, parrotfish and even a brief encounter with an octopus.

Climbing into the zodiac and heading back to ship, I feel a warm glow of satisfaction. It's been another exceptional day of wildlife. I can't help but wonder whether the cruise will end in anticlimax, but early the next morning, the ship anchored in another pristine bay, I glance down and there, cruising off the stern, is an enormous manta ray.

The archipelago populated islands

'a little world within itself'

Santa Cruz: Puerto Ayora

Santa Cruz (population 16,600) is the most central of the Galápagos Islands and the main town is Puerto Ayora.

★Charles Darwin Research Station ⓘ *about 1.5 km from the pier at Academy Bay, www.darwinfoundation.org, office Mon-Fri 0730-1700, visitor areas 0600-1800 daily, free.* A visit to the station is a good introduction to the islands. Collections of several of the rare species of giant tortoise are maintained on the station as breeding nuclei, together with tortoise-rearing pens for the young.

The **Centro Comunitario de Educación Ambiental** ⓘ *west end of Charles Binford, Mon-Fri 0730-1200, 1400-1700, Sat morning only, free,* has an aquarium and exhibits about the Galápagos Marine Reserve.

★Tortuga Bay There is a beautiful beach at Tortuga Bay, 45 minutes' easy walk (2.5 km each way) west from Puerto Ayora on an excellent cobbled path through cactus forest. Start at the west end of Calle Charles Binford; further on there is a gate where you must register (open daily 0600-1700, free). Make sure you take a hat, sunscreen and drinking water; and beware of the very strong undertow. Do not walk on the dunes above

Santa Cruz best for ...

■ *visitor facilities: shops, hotels, restaurants, banks and tour operators*
■ *Charles Darwin Research Centre*
■ *beautiful Tortuga Bay*
■ *100-year-old wild giant tortoises*

the beach, which are a marine tortoise nesting area. At the west end of Tortuga Bay is a trail to a lovely mangrove-fringed lagoon, with calmer warmer water, shade, and sometimes a kayak for rent.

Las Grietas is a lovely gorge with a natural pool at the bottom which is popular (crowded on weekends) and splendid for bathing (open daily 0600-1700, free). Take a water taxi from the port to the dock at Punta Estrada (five minutes, US$0.80-1). It is a 10-minute walk from here to the **Finch Bay** hotel and 20 minutes further over lava boulders to Las Grietas – well worth the trip.

Puerto Ayora–Baltra The Puerto Ayora–Baltra road goes through the agricultural zone in the highlands. The community of **Bellavista** is 7 km from the port, and **Santa Rosa** is 15 km beyond. The area has national park visitor sites, walking possibilities and upmarket lodgings. **Los Gemelos** are a pair of large sinkholes, formed by collapse of the ground above empty magma chambers. They straddle the road to Baltra, beyond Santa Rosa. You can take a taxi or airport bus all the way; otherwise take a bus to Santa Rosa, then walk one hour uphill. There are several **lava tubes** (natural tunnels) on the island. Some are at **El Mirador**, 3 km from Puerto Ayora on the road to Bellavista. Two more lava tubes are 1 km from Bellavista. They are on private land, it costs US$5 (US$10 with torch – or bring your own) to enter the tunnels and it takes about 30 minutes to walk through them. Tours to the lava tubes can be arranged in Puerto Ayora.

Cerro Crocker The highest point on Santa Cruz Island is Cerro Crocker at 864 m. You can hike here and to two other nearby 'peaks' called **Media Luna** and **Puntudo**. The trail starts at Bellavista where a rough trail map is painted as a mural on the wall of the school. The round trip from Bellavista takes six to eight hours. A permit and guide are not required, but a guide may be helpful. Always take food, water and a compass or GPS.

El Chato Tortoise Reserve Another worthwhile trip is to the El Chato Tortoise Reserve, where giant tortoises can be seen in the wild during the dry season (June to February). In the wet season the tortoises are breeding down in the arid zone. Follow the road that goes past the Santa Rosa school to 'La Reserva'. At the end of the road (about 3 km) you reach a faded wooden memorial to an Israeli tourist who got lost here. Take the trail to the right (west) for about 45 minutes. There are many confusing trails in the reserve itself; take food, water and a compass or GPS. If you have no hiking experience, horses can sometimes be hired at Santa Rosa or arrange a tour from Puerto Ayora.

Tortoises can also be seen at **Cerro Mesa** and at several private ranches, some of which have camping facilities; eg **Butterfly Ranch** ⓘ *Hacienda Mariposa, entry US$5, access at Av Baltra Km 16, on the south side of the road just before the Hotel Royal Palm. The visiting area is 1 km off the main road, walk or take a taxi to the camping area. Camping US$25 for 2 including tent, US$30 with breakfast, make previous arrangements at Moonrise Travel, see page 339.*

San Cristóbal: Puerto Baquerizo Moreno

Puerto Baquerizo Moreno, on San Cristóbal island (population 7900), is the capital of the archipelago. Electrical energy here is provided by wind generators in the highlands.

The town's attractive *malecón* has many shaded seats shared by tourists, residents and sea lions. The **cathedral** ⓘ *on Av Northía y Cobos, 0900-1200, 1600-1800*, has interesting artwork combining religious and Galápagos motifs.

To the north of town, opposite **Playa Mann** (suitable for swimming), is the Galápagos National Park visitor centre or ★**Centro de Interpretación** ⓘ *T05-252 0138,*

San Cristóbal best for ...

- Intrepretation Centre
- *sailing or diving through Kicker Rock*
- *spotting three species of booby at Punta Pitt*

ext 123, daily 0700-1700, free. It has excellent displays of the natural and human history of the islands including contemporary issues, recommended. A good trail goes from the Centro de Interpretación to the northeast through scrub forest to **Cerro Tijeretas**, a hill overlooking town and the ocean, 30 minutes away. From here a rougher trail continues 45 minutes to **Playa Baquerizo**. Frigate birds nest in this area and can be observed gliding overhead; there

are sea lions on the beaches below. To go back from Cerro Tijeretas, if you take the trail which follows the coast, you will end up at **Playa Punta Carola**, a popular surfing beach, too rough for swimming. To the south of Puerto Baquerizo Moreno, 30 minutes' walk past the stadium and high school (ask for directions), is **La Lobería**, a rocky shore with sea lions, marine iguanas, and a rough trail leading to beautiful cliffs with many birds, overlooking the sea.

Four buses a day run the 6 km inland from Puerto Baquerizo Moreno to **El Progreso**, US$0.50, 15 minutes, then it's a 2½-hour walk to **El Junco lake**, the largest body of fresh water in Galápagos. At El Junco there is a path to walk around the lake in 20 minutes. The views are lovely in clear weather but it is cool and wet in the *garúa* season, so take adequate clothing. Pick-up trucks to El Progreso charge US$3, or you can hire them for touring: US$25 to El Junco (return with wait), US$50 continuing to the beaches at **Puerto Chino** on the other side of the island, past a man-made tortoise reserve. The beaches are white sand and sea lions can often be seen if the waves are not too rough. It is about a 1-km walk from the car park (toilets) to the beach where there are no facilities. Take snacks and drinks. A bus leaves the municipal market at 0800, US$2 to La Galapaguera, then 20 minutes' walk from there to Puerto Chino beach. The bus returns from the beach car park at 1600. A taxi costs about US$35 round trip. Camping is possible at Puerto Chino with a permit from the national park; take food and drinking water. Various small roads fan out from El Progreso and make for pleasant walking. **Jatun Sacha** (www.jatunsacha.org) has a volunteer centre on an old hacienda in the highlands beyond El Progreso, working on eradication of invasive species and a native plant nursery; US$15 taxi ride from town, take repellent.

Boats go to **Punta Pitt** at the northeast end of San Cristóbal where you can see all three species of booby. Off the northwest coast is **Kicker Rock** (León Dormido), the basalt remains of a volcanic plug; many seabirds, including Nazca and blue-footed boobies, can be seen around its cliffs (five-hour trip, including snorkelling, recommended).

Isabela (population 2500) is the largest island in the archipelago; at 120 km long it forms over half the total land area of the archipelago. It was formed by the coalesced lava flows of six volcanoes. Five are active and each has (or had) its own separate sub-species of giant tortoise. Isabela is also the island which is changing most rapidly, driven by growing land-based tourism. It remains a charming place but is at risk from uncontrolled development. Most residents live in Puerto Villamil. In the highlands, there is a cluster of farms at Santo Tomás. There are several lovely beaches right by town, but mind the strong undertow and ask locally about the best spots for swimming and surfing.

Isabela best for ...

■ *volcanic landscape of black lava fields*
■ *hiking to the caldera of Sierra Negra volcano*
■ *visiting massive colonies of marine iguanas and seabirds*

It is 8 km west to **Muro de las Lágrimas**, built by convict labour under hideous conditions. These days it makes a great day-hike or hire a bicycle (always take water). Short side-trails branch off the road to various attractions along the way, and a trail continues from the Muro to nearby hills with lovely views. Along the same road, 30 minutes from town, is the **Centro de Crianza**, a breeding centre for giant tortoises surrounded by lagoons with flamingos and other birds. In the opposite direction, 30 minutes east toward the *embarcadero* (pier) is **Concha de Perla Lagoon**, with a nice access trail through mangroves and a small dock from which you can go swimming with sea lions and other creatures. Tours go to **Las Tintoreras**, a set of small islets in the harbour where white-tipped reef sharks and penguins

may be seen in the still crystalline water (US$30 per person). There are also boat tours to **Los Túneles** at Cabo Rosa (US$65 per person, a tricky entrance from the open sea), where fish, rays and turtles can be seen in submerged lava tunnels.

★ **Sierra Negra Volcano** has the second-largest basaltic caldera in the world, 9 km by 10 km. It is 19 km (30 minutes) by pick-up truck to the park entrance (take passport and national park entry receipt), where you start the 1½-hour hike to the crater rim at 1000 m. It is a further 1½ hours' walk along bare brittle lava rock to **Volcán Chico**, with several fumaroles and more stunning views. Due to increased seismic activity of the Volcán Sierra Negra, a Yellow Alert was declared at the beginning of 2018, suspending all visits to the area of Volcán Chico. Visitors are currently only allowed to visit the areas of Mirador 1 and Mirador 2, and the surrounding trails in Sierra Negra. No visitors are allowed to explore closer towards Volcán Chico for safety reasons. Highland tours are available to **La Cueva de Sucre**, a large lava tube with many chambers, about 14 km from Puerto Villamil in the agricultural area; be sure to take a torch.

Floreana (population 160) is the island with the richest human history and the fewest inhabitants, most living in Puerto Velasco Ibarra. You can easily reach the island with a day-tour boat from Puerto Ayora, but these do not leave enough time to enjoy the visit. A couple of days' stay is recommended, however note that there may not always be space on boats returning to Puerto Ayora, so you must be flexible.

Community tourism is getting underway on Floreana but services are limited. One shop has basic supplies and there are a handful of places to eat and sleep, none is cheap (see Where to stay, page 337). Margaret Wittmer, one of the first settlers on Floreana, died in 2000, but you can meet her daughter and granddaughter.

Floreana best for ...

- ■ *Post Office Bay*
- ■ *snorkelling at Devil's Crown*
- ■ *pink flamingos and green sea turtles*

La Lobería is a beautiful little peninsula (which becomes an island at high tide), 15 minutes' walk from town, where sea lions, sea turtles, marine iguanas and various birds can be seen. The climate in the highlands is fresh and comfortable, good for walking and birdwatching. A *ranchera* runs up to **Asilo de La Paz**, with a natural spring and tortoise area (Monday to Saturday 0600 and 1500, returning 0700 and 1600; Sunday 0700 returning 1000). Or you can walk down in three to four hours, detouring to climb **Cerro Allieri** along the way.

★Post Office Bay, on the north side of Floreana, is visited by tour boats. There is a custom (since 1792) for visitors here to place unstamped letters and cards in a barrel, and deliver, free of charge, any addressed to their own destinations. Post Office Bay used to be accessible only by boat, but a trail has been opened from the highlands, allowing good birdwatching.

The archipelago
unpopulated
islands

It is not the strongest of the species that survives, nor the most intelligent, but the one most responsive to change

Baltra

Once a US Airforce base, Baltra is now a small military base for Ecuador and also the main airport into the islands. Also known as South Seymour, this is the island most affected by human presence. **Mosquera** is a small sandy bank just north of Baltra, home to a large colony of sea lions.

Bartolomé is a small island located in Sullivan Bay off the eastern shore of Santiago. It is probably the most easily recognized, the most visited and most photographed of all the islands in the Galápagos with its distinctive **Pinnacle Rock**. The trail leads steeply up to the summit, taking 30-40 minutes, from where there are panoramic views. At the second visitor site on the island there is a lovely beach from which you can snorkel or swim and usually see penguins

Bartolomé best for ...

■ *coloured rock formations, lava fields and craters*
■ *views from Pinnacle Rock or Cerro Bartolomé*
■ *excellent snorkelling*
■ *tropical fish, penguins, reef sharks*

Daphne Major

West of Baltra, Daphne Island has very rich birdlife, in particular the nesting boobies. Because of the possible problems of erosion, only small boats may land here and are limited to one visit each month.

Española best for ...

■ *white-sand beaches of Gardner Bay*
■ *large colony of waved albatross and other seabirds*
■ *dramatic kleef landscapes*

Española

This is the southernmost island of the Galápagos and, following a successful programme to remove all the feral species, is now the most pristine of the islands with many migrant, resident and endemic seabirds. **Gardner Bay**, on the north coast, is a beautiful white-sand beach with excellent swimming and snorkelling. **Punta Suárez**, on the western tip of the island, has a trail through a rookery. As well as a wide range of seabirds (including blue-footed and Nazca boobies) there is a great selection of wildlife including sea lions and the largest and most colourful marine iguanas of the Galápagos plus the original home of the waved albatrosses.

Fernandina

Fernandina is the youngest of the islands, at about 700,000 years old, and also the most volcanically active, with eruptions every few years. The visitor site of **Punta Espinosa** is on the northeast coast of Fernandina. The trail goes up through a sandy nesting site for huge colonies of marine iguanas. The nests appear as small hollows in the sand. You can also see flightless cormorants drying their atrophied wings in the sun and go snorkelling in the bay.

Fernandina best for ...

- ■ *dramatic coastline*
- ■ *impressive lava flows*
- ■ *penguins, marina iguanas, flightless cormorants*

Genovesa

Genovesa best for ...

- ■ *Prince Phillip's Steps*
- ■ *snorkelling with marine iguanas*
- ■ *the largest nesting colonies of red-footed boobies and frigate birds*

Located in the northeast of the archipelago, this is an outpost for many sea birds. It is an eight- to 10-hour all-night sail from Puerto Ayora. Like Fernandina, Genovesa is best visited on longer cruises or ships with larger range.

One of the most famous sites is **Prince Phillip's Steps**, an amazing walk through a seabird rookery that is full of life. You will see tropic birds, all three boobies, frigates, petrels, swallow-tailed and lava gulls, and many others. There is also good snorkelling at the foot of the steps, with lots of marine iguanas. The entrance to **Darwin Bay**, on the eastern side of the island, is very narrow and shallow and the anchorage in the lagoon is surrounded by mangroves, home to a large breeding colony of frigates and other seabirds.

Plaza Sur

One of the closest islands to Puerto Ayora is Plaza Sur. It's an example of a geological uplift and the southern part of the island has formed cliffs with spectacular views. It has a combination of both dry and coastal vegetation zones. Walking along the sea cliffs is a pleasant experience as swallowtail gulls, shearwaters and red-billed tropic birds nest here. This is the home of the **Men's Club**, a rather sad-looking colony of bachelor sea lions who are too old to mate and who get together to console each other. There are also lots of blue-footed boobies and a large population of land iguanas on the island.

Rábida

This island is just to the south of Santiago. The trail leads to a salt-water lagoon with an area of mangroves which are best explored by panga. The marshy lake is full of flamingos. This island is said to have the most diversified volcanic rocks of all the islands. It is a mating spot for green Pacific turtles and white-tipped sharks and mustard rays are found in the waters around the island. You can snorkel and swim from the dark red-sand beach populated with sea lions.

Santa Fe

This island is located on the southeastern part of Galápagos, between Santa Cruz and San Cristóbal, and was formed by volcanic uplift. The lagoon is home to a large colony of sea lions which are happy to join you for a swim. From the beach the trail goes inland, through a semi-arid landscape of cactus. This little island has its own species of land iguana.

Santiago

This large island, also known as James, is to the east of Isla Isabela. It has a volcanic landscape full of cliffs and pinnacles, and is home to several species of marine birds. **James Bay** is on the western side of the island, where there is a wet landing on the dark sands of **Puerto Egas**. The trail leads to the remains of an unsuccessful salt mining operation. Fur seals are seen nearby. **Espumilla Beach** is another famous visitor site. After landing on a large beach, walk through a mangrove forest that leads to a lake usually inhabited by flamingos, pintail ducks and stilts. There are nesting and feeding sites for flamingos. Sea turtles dig their nests at the edge of the mangroves. **Buccaneer Cove**, on the northwest part of

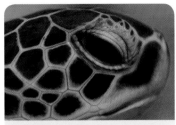

Santiago best for ...

- *marine iguanas sunbathing on black volcanic rocks*
- *swimming with fur seals*
- *hidden snorkelling spots and white-sand beaches*

the island, was a haven for pirates during the 1600s and 1700s. **Sullivan Bay** is on the eastern coast of Santiago, opposite Bartolomé Island. The visitor trail leads across an impressive lunar landscape of lava fields formed during eruptions in 1890.

North Seymour

Just north of Baltra, North Seymour is home to sea lions, marine iguanas, swallow-tailed gulls, magnificent frigate birds and blue-footed boobies. The trail leads through mangroves in one of the main nesting sites for blue-footed boobies and frigates in this part of the archipelago.

North Seymour best for ...

- *swimming with sea lions*

Sombrero Chino

This is just off the southeastern tip of Santiago, and its name refers to its shape. It is most noted for the volcanic landscape including sharp outcrops, cracked lava formations, lava tubes and volcanic rubble. This site is only accessible to smaller vessels.

Galápagos
cruises & tours

A visit to the islands doesn't come cheap. The return flight from Quito and national park fees add up to about US$600; plus around US$300 per person per day for sailing on an economy-class boat. There are few such inexpensive vessels and even fewer good inexpensive ones. Since you are already spending so much money, it is worth spending a bit more to make sure you sign up with a reputable agency on a better cruise, the quality of which is generally excellent.

Land-based and independent travel on the populated islands are alternatives, but there is simply no way to enjoy Galápagos on a shoestring. For those with a passion for nature, the once-in-a-lifetime Galápagos experience is well worth saving for. At the same time, high prices might be one way of keeping the number of visitors within sustainable levels. The islands have already suffered the impact of rapidly growing tourism and a viable mechanism is urgently needed to ensure their survival as the world's foremost wildlife sanctuary.

Choosing a boat *See also page 343.*

Most international visitors explore the islands on pre-arranged boat tours where you sleep on board overnight. Prices and standards vary substantially from small yachts with basic facilities to luxury cruise ships; both have their advantages and disadvantages. Captains, crews and guides regularly change on all boats. These factors, as well as the sea, weather and your fellow passengers will all influence the quality of your experience

The **least expensive boats** (economy class) cost around US$300 per person per day and a few of these vessels are dodgy. The boats are normally smaller and less powerful so you see less and spend more time travelling; also the guiding may be mostly in Spanish. There may be limitations for vegetarians on the cheaper boats.

The **more expensive boats** have air conditioning, hot water and private baths. **Tourist and tourist superior class cost** around US$300-600 per day and you will be on a better, faster boat which can travel more quickly between visitor sites, leaving more time to spend ashore.

Over US$600 per day are the **first-class and luxury brackets**, with far more comfortable and spacious cabins, as well as a superior level of service and cuisine.

Other considerations All cruises begin with a morning flight from the mainland on the first day and end on the last day with a midday flight back to the mainland. No boat may sail without a park-trained guide. All boats have to conform to certain minimum safety standards; more expensive boats are better equipped. Boats with over 20 passengers take quite a time to disembark and re-embark people, while the smaller boats have a more lively motion, which is important if you are prone to seasickness.

Time required

A seven-day cruise will allow time to get a good idea of the diversity of life and landscapes of the Galápagos and visit some of the outlying islands such as Genovesa, Española or Fernandina. Bear in mind that with any tour from the mainland, the first and last days will be spent travelling, which means that you should book a nine- or 10-day tour to allow enough time on the boat. Study the itinerary carefully. As a general rule, the better trips spend less time on the populated islands and more time further afield.

Fees and inspections

The islands are a national park. A US$20 fee is collected at Quito or Guayaquil airport, where a registration form must be completed. It is best to pre-register online at **www.gobiernogalapagos.gob.ec**, or ask your tour operator to do so for you. Bags are checked prior to flights to Galápagos. No live animals, meat, dairy products, fresh fruit or vegetables may be taken to the islands. On arrival, every foreign visitor must pay a US$100 national park fee. All fees are cash only. Be sure to have your passport to hand at the airport and keep all fee receipts throughout your stay in the islands. Bags are checked again on departure, as nothing may be taken off the islands. Puerto Villamil charges a US$10 port fee on arrival in Isabela.

Booking a tour

Galápagos is such a special destination for nature-lovers that most agree it is worth saving for and spending on a quality tour. You can book a Galápagos cruise in several different ways:

- Over the internet.
- From either a travel agency or directly though a Galápagos wholesaler in your home country.
- From one of the very many agencies found throughout Ecuador, especially in Quito (see page 72) but also in other tourist centres and Guayaquil (page 219).
- From local agencies, mostly in Puerto Ayora but also in Puerto Baquerizo Moreno (page 342).

The trade-off is always between time and money: booking from home is most efficient and expensive, last-minute arrangements in Galápagos are cheapest but most time-consuming (and the cost of staying in Puerto Ayora while you wait is high), while Quito and Guayaquil are intermediate. It is not possible to obtain discounts or make last-minute arrangements in high season (see When to go, page 17). Surcharges may apply when using a credit card to purchase tours on the islands, there are limits to ATM withdrawals and no cash advances in Galápagos, so take sufficient cash if looking for a last-minute cruise. Also, if looking for a last-minute sailing, it is best to pay your hotel one night at a time since hoteliers may not refund advance payments. Especially on cheaper boats, check carefully about what is and is not included (eg drinking water, snorkelling equipment, etc). Below is a selection of vessels which will give a good idea of the price category, what facilities to expect and the islands usually visited.

Making the most of your trip

▪ Always bring some US dollars cash to Galápagos. There are only a handful of ATMs in Puerto Ayora and **Puerto Baquerizo Moreno**, and they may not work with all cards. ATM withdrawals are limited to US$300-500 per day and cash advances on credit cards cannot be obtained in Galápagos.

▪ Daytime clothing should be lightweight and even on luxury cruises should be casual and comfortable. At night, particularly at sea and at higher altitudes, temperatures fall below 15°C and warm clothing is required.

▪ Bring good footwear, soles soon wear out on the abrasive lava terrain.

▪ A remedy for seasickness is recommended.

▪ A good supply of sun block and skin cream to prevent wind-burn and chapped lips is essential, as are a hat and good sunglasses.

▪ Be prepared for dry and wet landings. The latter involves wading ashore.

▪ Take plenty of memory cards for your camera. The animals are so tame that you will use far more than you expected. A telephoto lens is not essential, but bring it if you have one. An underwater camera is also an excellent idea.

▪ Snorkelling equipment is particularly useful as much of the sealife is only visible underwater. Few of the cheaper boats provide good snorkelling gear. If in doubt, bring your own, rent in Puerto Ayora or buy it in Quito.

▪ On most cruises a ship's crew and guides are usually tipped separately. The amount is a very personal matter; you may be guided by suggestions made onboard or in the agency's brochures, but the key factors should always be the quality of service received and your own resources.

▪ Raise any issues first with your guide or ship's captain. Additional complaints may be filed with the Ministerio de Turismo in Puerto Ayora or Puerto Baquerizo Moreno, see page 333.

Land-based tourism in the Galápagos

In the last few years there has been a radical shift in tourism in the Galápagos. Previously, the vast majority of visitors toured the islands on live-aboard cruise boats and land would be touched fleetingly, to visit wildlife and to disembark to connect with a flight. The change has come about through the increase in land-based tourism and the opportunities this has given for independent travel on the islands. On the four inhabited islands there are hotels and guesthouses which can be used as a base for visits to places of interest, day visits to nearby islands, activities such as trekking, biking, diving, kayaking and cultural experiences. Pick-up trucks and water taxis are an economical way of getting about and scheduled boats speed between the four main islands daily.

This does not mean that you can wander around at will on land. While stay-over visitors can go to places that cruise passengers will not, there is almost as much restriction outside as inside the national park. Within the national park you cannot wander about at liberty and have to stick to trails.

Whether there are advantages to opting for a land-based trip rather than a cruise depends on your interests and your pocket. If wildlife is the focus of your visit, a cruise is recommended because you will travel to more remote islands and see a greater variety of animals and birds. Day tours to uninhabited islands, on the other hand, go to the same places as cruise ships, are subject to the same regulations, cost from US$140 to US$200 per person and have to be booked in advance. When taking day trips you have to research which islands have the animals you most want to see. Also bear in mind that a day trip will probably not enable you to see animals and birds when they are most active, ie early morning or afternoon – those are the times you will be travelling.

There are hotels to suit most budgets, but the more journeys between islands and the greater number of day trips and excursions you take, the higher your costs will be. A cruise can be more restful, but the comfort and space of a hotel room may be more appealing than a cabin. If worried about seasickness, a cruise is not a good idea, but bear in mind that island-hopping can be a stomach-churning ride if the sea is rough. If wildlife is not your greatest priority, then a land-based holiday, staying on just one island even, could be just what you are looking for. Also note that most things that can be done independently can probably be covered by an organized package.

The hypothesis that cruises are the least harmful way of seeing the wildlife is not undermined by land-based tourism, but the latter adds new elements which raise serious questions. Most significant is whether land-based tourism is sustainable. It depends how it is managed and how much pressure from development and construction is put on the land. The bottom line is that if wildlife on the Galápagos Islands is degraded, they will lose their status as one of the prime nature destinations on the planet. It is in everyone's interest not to let that happen.

Listings Galápagos Islands map pages 334 and 336.

Tourist information

Santa Cruz

iTur
Av Charles Darwin y 12 de Febrero,
Puerto Ayora, T0-252 6153 ext 22. Mon-Fri
0730-1800, Sat 0830-1330, Sun 1300-1800.
Also at Baltra airport.
Has information about Puerto Ayora and
Santa Cruz Island.

Ministerio de Turismo
Charles Binford y 12 de Febrero, Puerto Ayora,
T05-252 6174. Mon-Fri 0830-1300, 1430-1730.
An administrative office but receives
complaints about agencies and vessels.

San Cristóbal

Ministerio de Turismo
12 de Febrero e Ignacio Hernández,
Puerto Baquerizo Moreno, T05-252 0704.
Mon-Fri 0830-1230, 1400-1730.
Operates as in Santa Cruz, above.

Municipal tourist office
Malecón Charles Darwin y 12 de Febrero,
Puerto Baquerizo Moreno, T05-252 0119
ext 120. Mon-Fri 0730-1230, 1400-1800.
Downstairs at the Municipio.

Isabela

Municipal tourist office
By the park, Puerto Villamil, T05-252 9002,
ext 113. Mon-Fri 0730-1230, 1400-1700.
Has local information.

Where to stay

Santa Cruz
Puerto Ayora

$$$$ Angemeyer Waterfront Inn
By the dock at Punta Estrada, T05-252 6561,
www.angermeyer-waterfront-inn.com.
Gorgeous location overlooking the bay
south of the centre. Includes buffet
breakfast, restaurant, comfortable modern
rooms and apartments, some with
kitchenettes, a/c, attentive service.

$$$$ Silberstein
Darwin y Piqueros, T05-252 6277, Quito
T02-292 1739, www.hotelsilberstein.com.
Modern and comfortable with lovely
grounds, pool in tropical garden, a/c, buffet
breakfast, restaurant, bar, spacious rooms
and common areas, very nice. Day tours by
boat and scuba diving.

$$$$ Solymar
Darwin y Berlanga, T05-252 6281,
www.hotelsolymar.com.ec.
Right in town but with a privileged location
overlooking the bay. Includes buffet
breakfast, restaurant, bar, pool, jacuzzi
and use of bicycles.

$$$ Estrella de Mar
By the water on a lane off 12 de Febrero, T05-
252 6427, www.estrellademarhostal.com.
Nice quiet location with views over the bay.
A/c, fan, fridge, spacious rooms, sitting area.

$$$ Jean's Home
Punta Estrada, T05-252 6446, T09-9296 0347,
www.jeans-home.com.
Comfortably refurbished home in a lovely
out-of-the-way location (short water taxi
ride south of town), a/c, family-run, English
and German spoken.

$$$ Lobo de Mar
12 de Febrero y Darwin, T05-252 6188, Quito
T02-250 2089, www.lobodemar.com.ec.
Modern building with balconies and rooftop
terrace, great views over the harbour. A/c,
small pool, fridge, modern and comfortable,
attentive service.

Puerto Ayora

Where to stay 🛏
España & Gardner **1**
Estrella de Mar **2**
Lobo de Mar **3**
Los Amigos **4**
Peregrina **5**
Silberstein **6**
Solymar **7**

Restaurants 🍴
El Descanso del Guía **1**
Il Giardino **2**
Isla Grill **3**
La Garrapata **5**
Los Kioskos **6**

$$$ Peregrina
Darwin e Indefatigable, T05-252 6323,
peregrinagalapagos@yahoo.com.
Away from the centre of town, a/c, nice
rooms and common areas, small garden,
family-run, homely atmosphere.

$$$-$$ Gardner
Berlanga y 12 de Febrero, T05-252 6979,
www.hostalgardnergalapagos.com.
A variety of comfortable rooms, cheaper
with fan, kitchen facilities, breakfast
available, good value.

$$ España
Berlanga y 12 de Febrero, T05-252 6108,
www.hotelespanagalapagos.com.
Pleasant and quiet, spacious rooms, a/c, small
courtyard with hammocks, good value.

$$-$ Los Amigos
Darwin y 12 de Febrero, T05-252 6265.
Small place, basic rooms with shared bath,
cold water, fan, laundry facilities, good value.

Highlands of Santa Cruz

$$$$ Galápagos Safari Camp
T09-8296 8228, www.galapagos
safaricamp.com.
Luxury resort with a central lodge and
comfortable, en suite tents. Includes
breakfast and dinner, swimming pool,
organizes tours and activities.

$$$$ Semilla Verde
T05-301-3079, www.gps.ec.
Located on a 5-ha property being reforested
with native plants, comfortable rooms and
common areas, includes breakfast, other
meals available or use of kitchen facilities,
British/Ecuadorean-run, family atmosphere,
yoga retreat.

$$$ Casa Natura Lodge
Bellavista, Vía al Camote, T04-450 5516,
www.casanaturahotel.com.
In the countryside outside the national park,
isolated and quiet. 14 light rooms of varying

sizes, with balcony, a/c, TV. Shuttle service to Puerto Ayora. Also Vía Natura, www.vianatura.com, for tours and packages.

$$$ Magic Galapagos Tented Camp
www.destinationecuador.com.
In the countryside on a private reserve where giant tortoises roam. 6 tents/cabins on wooden decks with en suite hot showers and 4 treehouses with en suite toilets but you have to descend for a shower some distance away, very good restaurant and 'lava lounge' bar in a lava tube.

San Cristóbal
Puerto Baquerizo Moreno

$$$$-$$$ Miconia
Darwin e Isabela, T05-252 0608, www.hotelmiconia.com.
Restaurant, a/c, small pool, large well-equipped gym, modern if somewhat small rooms, some with fridge.

$$$ Blue Marlin
Española y Northia, T05-252 0253, www.bluemarlingalapagos.ec.
Modern rooms, mostly wheelchair accessible, bathtubs, a/c, pool, fridge. Sport fishing.

$$$ Casablanca
Melville y Darwin, T05-252 0392, www.casablancagalapagos.com.
Large house with terrace and views of harbour. Each room is individually decorated by the owner who has an art gallery on the premises.

$$$ Mar Azul
Northía y Esmeraldas, T05-252 0139, http://hotelmarazulgalapagos.com.
Comfortable lodgings, electric shower, a/c and fan, fridge, pleasant. Same family runs 2 more expensive hotels.

$$ Casa de Nelly
Northía y Agama, T05-252 0112, www.casadenellygalapagos.com.ec.
3-storey building, quiet, bright comfortable rooms, a/c, kitchen facilities, family-run.

$ San Francisco
Darwin y Villamil, T05-252 0304.
Simple rooms with private bath, fan, kitchen facilities, good value.

El Progreso

$$ Casa del Ceibo
Progreso Km 7, Pto Baquerizo Moreno T09-9683 5088, Facebook.
A single unique room in the branches of a huge kapok tree. Private bath, hot water, advance booking required if you want to stay, US$2 to visit. Café for refreshments, walls made from bottles.

Isabela
Puerto Villamil

$$$$ Albemarle
On the beachfront in town, T05-252 9489, www.hotelalbemarle.com.
Attractive Mediterranean-style construction, restaurant, bright comfortable rooms with wonderful ocean views, a/c, small pool.

$$$$ IsaMar
On the beachfront in town, T09-9555 3718, http://isamargalapagos.com, or book through Tropic Ecuador, www.destinationecuador.com.
10 rooms, 3 of which have sea views, a/c, Wi-Fi, restaurant and bar, full range of activities on land and on water.

$$$$ La Casa de Marita
At east end of beach, T05-252 9301, www.galapagosisabela.com.
Tastefully chic, includes breakfast, other meals on request, a/c and fridge, very comfortable, each room is slightly different, some have balconies. Ocean or garden view or inland rooms. A little gem.

$$$ Casita de la Playa
On the beachfront in town, T09-9856 3802, Quito T02-250 4002, http://casaisabelaonthebeach.com.
Pleasant house on the beach, rooms with a/c, nice ocean views. Part of the **Casa Isabela on the Beach** group of hotels on the islands.

$$$ La Laguna
Los Flamencos y Los Petreles, T09-9137 2405, www.gruposanvicentegalapagos.com.

Pleasant rooms with a/c, attractive balconies and common areas, jacuzzi, rooftop terrace for good views.

$$$ San Vicente
Cormoran y Scalecias, T09-9137 2405, www.gruposanvicentegalapagos.com.
Very popular and well-organized hotel which also offers tours and kayak rentals, includes breakfast, other meals on request, a/c, jacuzzi, some rooms a bit small but nice, family-run.

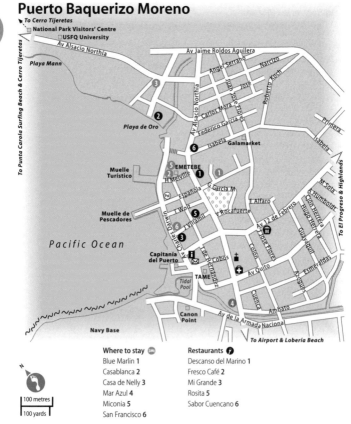

Puerto Baquerizo Moreno

To Cerro Tijeretas
National Park Visitors' Centre
USFQ University
Av Alsacio Northía
Av Jaime Roldos Aguilera
Playa Mann
Angel Serrano
Narcizo
To Punta Carola Surfing Beach & Cerro Tijeretas
Juan José de Flor
José
Roberto Koch
Carlos Mora
Av Alsacio Northía
Playa de Oro
Federico García
Isabela
Printera
Isabela Galamarket
Isabela
Muelle Turístico
EMETEBE
H Melville
C García M
M Sola
Española
Humboldt
Pol
F Alfaro
Chon Herrera
Muelle de Pescadores
T Wolf
J Villamil
Rocafuerte
Hugo Herrera
Av 12 de Febrero
Guayaquil
Pacific Ocean
José Flores
To El Progreso & Highlands
Colón
Esmeraldas
Capitanía del Puerto
J Hernández
Cobos
Roldos
Av Quito
TAME
Tidal Pool
Cuenca
Ambato
Canon Point
Av de la Armada Nacional
Navy Base
To Airport & Lobería Beach

Where to stay	Restaurants
Blue Marlin 1	Descanso del Marino 1
Casablanca 2	Fresco Café 2
Casa de Nelly 3	Mi Grande 3
Mar Azul 4	Rosita 5
Miconia 5	Sabor Cuencano 6
San Francisco 6	

100 metres
100 yards

$ Hostal Villamil
16 de Marzo y Antonio Gil, T09-9137 2405,
www.gruposanvicentegalapagos.com.
A/c, small patio with hammocks, family-run
and very friendly, good value.

$$ La Jungla
Off Antonio Gil at the west edge of town, T05-
301 6721, www.thejunglegalapagos.com.
Nice rooms with a/c, beach views, meals
on request, secluded non-central location.

Highlands of Isabela

$$$$ Scalesia Lodge
In the highlands 14 km from town,
T02-256 6090, www.scalesialodge.com.
Luxury lodge on 16 ha in the forest
with view of the coast. Dining room
and lounge in permanent building
while accommodation is in 16 large and
comfortable tents on timber platforms with
bathrooms. Lots of packages and activities
on offer, can be combined with lodges in
the Amazon and Andes.

$$ Campo Duro
T09-8545 3045, www.campo
duroecolodge.com.ec.
Camping (tents provided), includes
breakfast, nice ample grounds, giant
tortoises may be seen (US$3 to visit),
friendly owner. Taxi from Pto Villamil, US$8.

Floreana: Puerto Velasco Ibarra

$$$ Hotel/Pensión Wittmer
Right on Black Beach, T05-253 5013.
Lovely location, simple comfortable rooms,
electric shower, fan, very good meals
available, family-run, German spoken,
reservations required.

$$$ Lava Lodge
Vía la Lobería, 10 mins' walk from
town, book through Tropic Ecuador,
www.destinationecuador.com.

Simple wooden cabins on lava beach,
family-owned with food sourced from
their farm, breakfast included, other
meals available. Kayak, snorkel and SUP
equipment to rent, guided tours to wildlife
and historic sites, sea lions, turtles and crabs
outside your door.

Restaurants

Santa Cruz: Puerto Ayora

$$$ Il Giardino
Charles Darwin y Charles Binford, T05-252
6627, www.ilgiardinogalapagos.com.ec.
Open 0800-2330.
Very good international food, service and
atmosphere, excellent ice cream, very
popular, book in advance.

$$$ Isla Grill
Charles Darwin y Tomás de Berlanga, T09-
8462 7240, www.islagrillgalapagos.com.
Tue-Sun 1200-2200.
Upmarket grill, seafood and pizza, vegan
and vegetarian options.

$$$-$$ La Garrapata
Charles Darwin entre 12 de Febrero y
Tomás de Berlanga, T05-252 6264.
Mon-Sat 0900-2200.
Good food and drinks in an
attractive setting.

$$ Los Kioskos
Charles Binford entre Padre Herrera y
Rodríguez Lara.
Tasty local fare served from kiosks, including
a variety of seafood, outdoor seating, lively
informal atmosphere, busy at night. Also
beside the fishermen's dock at Pelican Bay,
evenings only.

$ El Descanso del Guía
Charles Darwin y Los Colonos, T05-252 6108.
Daily 0645-1945.
Good set meals, very popular with locals.

San Cristóbal: Puerto Baquerizo Moreno

Several simple places serving economical set meals ($) on Northia between Española and 12 de Febrero. Also Sun lunch up at El Progreso, good *comida del campo*.

$$$-$$ Descanso del Marinero
Northia y Española, T09-8728 2863. Wed-Mon 0800-2100.
Ceviches and seafood, outdoor seating. Decent portions but not cheap.

$$$-$$ Rosita
Ignacio Hernández y General Villamil. Daily 0930-1430, 1700-2230.
Old-time yachtie hangout, good food, large portions, nice atmosphere, à la carte and economical set meals.

$ Mi Grande
Villamil y Darwin, upstairs. Open from 0600.
Popular for set meals and good breakfast. Great *batidos*, juices and milkshakes.

Cafés and bakeries

Fresco Café
Av Jaime Roldós Aguilera, Facebook. Tue-Sat 0800-1600.
Waterfront open-sided café serving great vegetarian breakfasts, snacks and cakes. Excellent coffee, free, filtered water, good juices, lovely home-made sourdough bread.

Sabor Cuencano
Northía y Isabela. Closed Sun.
Good popular bakery.

Isabela: Puerto Villamil
Various outdoor restaurants around the plaza feature seafood on the menu; most offer an US$8 set lunch or à la carte ($$$-$$).

$$$ Isabela Grill
16 de Marzo y Flamencos, T09-9677 7918, Facebook.

Good choice for set lunch, dinner and à la carte. Charcoal grill for meats and seafood.

$$$-$$ Booby Trap
Antonio Gil, west end of town, T09-8864 6963, Facebook. Tue-Sat 1100-1400, 1700-2130, Sun-Mon 1700-2130.
Restaurant downstairs, bar upstairs with great view for sunset cocktails. Good fish and vegetarian dishes, some Asian flavours, great home-made chips, excellent desserts and a tasty range of drinks. Popular and dependable, attentive service.

$$-$ El Faro
Las Fragatas ½ block from the Plaza, T09-9978 3474. Daily 0700-2200.
Simple set lunch, grill at night, popular.

Floreana: Puerto Velasco Ibarra
$$$-$$ Meals available at hotels or from a couple of restaurants catering to tour groups, all require advance notice.

$$ Conchalagua
On the main road, T05-253 5048. Tue-Sun.
You can get a full meal, pizza, burger or snack here, the best option for eating out.

$ The Devil's Crown
100 m from the dock on road to the highlands.
Set lunch and dinner most days, ask in advance.

Shopping

Santa Cruz: Puerto Ayora
There is an attractive little **Mercado Artesanal** (craft market) at Charles Darwin y Tomás de Berlanga. **Proinsular**, opposite the pier, is the largest and best-stocked supermarket in Galápagos.

San Cristóbal: Puerto Baquerizo Moreno

Galamarket
Isabela y Juan José Flores.
A modern well-stocked supermarket.

What to do

Santa Cruz: Puerto Ayora
Cycling
Mountain bikes can be hired from travel agencies in town. Prices and quality vary, about US$15-20 for 3 hrs.

Diving
Only specialized diving boats are allowed to do diving tours. It is not possible to dive as part of a standard live-aboard cruise nor are dive boats allowed to call at the usual land visitor sites when they are diving. Some dive boats, however, might offer a week of diving followed by a week of cruising to land sites. National park rules prohibit collecting samples or souvenirs, spear-fishing, touching animals, or other environmental disruptions. Experienced dive guides can help visitors have the most spectacular opportunities to enjoy the wildlife. There are several diving agencies in Puerto Ayora, Baquerizo Moreno and Villamil (see Tour operators, below) offering courses, equipment rental, and dives; prices and quality vary. On offer in Puerto Ayora are diving day trips (2 dives, US$175-250) and daily tours for up to 1 week in the central islands. There is a hyperbaric chamber in Puerto Ayora at **Centro Médico Integral** (Marchena y Hanny, T05-252 4576, www.sssnetwork.com). Check if your dive operator is affiliated with this facility or arrange your own insurance from home.
Note To avoid the risk of decompression sickness, divers are advised to stay an extra day on the islands after their last dive before flying to the mainland, especially to Quito at 2840 m above sea level.

Dive Center Silberstein, *opposite Hotel Silberstein, T05-252 6277, www.divingalapagos. com.* Day tours in nice comfortable boat for up to 8 guests, English-speaking guides, good service, dive courses and trips for all levels of experience. Island-hopping dive tours and 8-day diving cruises are also organized.
Scuba Iguana, *Charles Darwin near the research station, T05-252 6497, www.scubaiguana. com.* Long-time reliable and recommended dive operator. Good safety, good equipment, good service. Courses up to PADI divemaster.

Snorkelling
Masks, snorkels and fins can be rented from travel agencies and dive shops, US$5 a day, deposit required. Las Grietas is a popular place to snorkel near Puerto Ayora.

Surfing
There is surfing at Tortuga Bay and at other more distant beaches accessed by boat. Look for the surf club office at Pelican Bay. There is better surfing near Puerto Baquerizo Moreno on San Cristóbal. The **Lonesome George** agency rents surfboards, see below.

Tour operators
See also Tour operators in Quito, page 72, and worldwide, page 399.
Lonesome George, *Av Baltra y Enrique Fuentes, T05-252 6245, www.lonesomegeorge. com.ec.* Run by Víctor Vaca. Sells tours and rents bicycles, surfboards, snorkelling equipment and motorcycles.
Moonrise Travel, *Av Charles Darwin y Charles Binford, T05-252 6348, www.galapagos moonrise.com.* Last-minute cruise bookings, day-tours to different islands, bay tours, flights, enquire about horse riding at ranches. They have eco-chalets on the other side of Academy Bay: Punta Estrada/Playa de los Alemanes with a capacity for 19 guests, private, on the water, next to Hotel Finch Bay. Also camping at Rancho Mariposa (Butterfly Ranch), see page 317. Owner Jenny Devine is knowledgeable and helpful.

ACTIVITY
Scuba diving

The Galápagos are among the most desirable scuba diving destinations in the world. At first look you might wonder why, with cold water, strong currents, difficult conditions and limited visibility (15 m or less). So what is the attraction?

Marine life
There is a profusion and variety of animals here that you won't find anywhere else, and so close up that you won't mind the low visibility. Not just reef fish and schooling fish and pelagic fish, but also sea lions, turtles, whalesharks, schools of hammerheads, flocks of several species of rays, diving birds, whales and dolphins; an exuberant diversity including many endemic species. You could be with a Galápagos marine iguana, the world's only lizard that dives and feeds in the sea, or perhaps meet a glittering man-sized sailfish. Make no mistake, this is no tame theme park: Galápagos is adventure diving, where any moment could surprise you.

Dive options
There are basically two options for diving in the Galápagos: live-aboard dive cruises and hotel-based day trips. Live-aboard operations usually expect the divers to bring their own equipment, and supply only lead and tanks. The day trip dive operators supply everything. Day trip diving is mostly offered by boats operating out of Puerto Ayora, as well as a couple of operators in Puerto Baquerizo Moreno and Puerto Villamil.

Live-aboard dive cruises (typically 10 days) can only be done on specialized boats, of which there are few and usually reserved far in advance. You cannot dive as part of an ordinary Galápagos cruise.

Day trip diving is more economical and spontaneous, often arranged at the dive shop the evening before. The distances between islands limit the range of the day trip boats to the central islands. Nevertheless, day boats can offer reliable service and superb dive locations including Gordon Rocks, world-famous for schooling hammerheads. The day trip dive boats cannot take passengers ashore at the usual visitors' sites but you can always do some diving day trips before or after a regular Galápagos cruise. A few live-aboard diving vessels may operate as dive boats for one week then as regular cruise boats the next, allowing for a combined experience.

See pages 339-342 for details of companies offering diving tours and services. Live-aboard diving cruises currently cost about US$800 per person per day.

General advice
Visitors should be aware of some of the special conditions in Galápagos. The national park includes practically all of the land and the surrounding waters. The national park prohibits collecting samples or souvenirs, spear-fishing, touching animals, or other

environmental disruptions. Guides apply the national park rules, and they can stop your participation if you do not cooperate. The experienced dive guides can help visitors have the most spectacular opportunities to enjoy the wildlife.

Nonetheless, diving requires self reliance and divers are encouraged to refresh their skills and have equipment serviced before the trip. Though the day-trip operators can offer introductory dives and complete certification training, this is not a place for a complete novice to come for a diving vacation. On many dives you could meet any combination of current, surge, cold water, poor visibility, deep bottom and big animals.

Like many exotic dive destinations, medical care is limited. There is a hyperbaric chamber in Puerto Ayora, the cost is high so you must carry adequate insurance or confirm with your tour operator whether they have coverage. To avoid the risk of decompression sickness, divers are advised to stay an extra day on the islands after their last dive before flying to the mainland, especially to Quito at 2840 m above sea level.

Dive sites

Santa Fe This site offers wall dives, rock reefs, shallow caves, fantastic scenery and usually has clear calm water. You can dive with sea lions, schooling fish, pelagic fish, moray eels, rays and Galápagos sharks. Like everywhere in Galápagos, you should expect the unexpected.

Seymour Norte You can see sea lions, reef fish, hammerhead sharks, giant manta rays and white tip reef sharks. Occasionally whalesharks, humpback whale and porpoises.

Floreana Island The dive sites are offshore islets, each with its own character and scenery. Devil's Crown is a fractured ring of spiked lava around coral reefs. **Champion** is a little crater with a nesting colony of boobies, sea lion beaches and underwater rocky shelves of coral and reef fish. Enderby is an eroded tuff cone where you often meet large pelagics: rays, turtles, tunas and sharks. **Gardner** has a huge natural arch like a cathedral's flying buttress. These and other islets offer diving with reef fish, schooling fish, sea lions, invertebrates, rays, moray eels, white tip reef sharks, turtles, big fish including amberjack, red snapper, and grouper. Sometimes you can see giant mantas, hammerheads, Galápagos sharks, whales, seahorses, and the bizarre red-lipped batfish.

Gordon Rocks Just north of the Plazas are two large rocks that are all that remains of the rim of a long-extinct volcano. On the inner side of the collapsed caldera rim the seabed is a mass of rocks jumbled over each other, while on the outer wall the sea drops away into thousands of feet of water. Currents here are exceptionally strong and the local name for the dive site is *La Lavadora* (washing machine). Here you can see schools of hammerheads, amberjacks and pompano, eagle rays, golden cowrays, whitetips and turtles.

Zenith Travel, *JL Mera N24-264 y Cordero, Quito, T02-252 9993, www.zenithecuador.com.* Good-value Galápagos cruises. All-gay Galápagos cruises available. Multilingual service, knowledgeable helpful staff, good value.

San Cristóbal: Puerto Baquerizo Moreno
Cycling
Bike rentals cost US$15 per half day, US$25 per day.

Diving
There are several dive sites around San Cristóbal, most popular being Kicker Rock, Roca Ballena and Punta Pitt.

Kayaking
Islanders Store, *Av J Roldós, above cargo pier, T05-252 0348.* Rentals US$10 per hr.

Surfing
There is good surfing in San Cristóbal, the best season is Dec-Mar. Punta Carola near town is the closest surfing beach; other spots are Canon and Tongo Reef, past the navy base. There is a championship during the local fiesta, the 2nd week of Feb.

Tour operators
Canon Point, *Armada Nacional y Darwin.* Rents bikes, skate boards and surfboards.
Chalo Tours, *Darwin y Villamil, T05-252 0953, chalotours@hotmail.com.* Specializes in diving and snorkelling, rents bikes and snorkelling gear.
Sharksky, *Darwin y Española, T05-252 1188, www.sharksky.com.* Highlands, snorkelling, diving, island-hopping, last-minute cruise bookings and gear rental. French/Ecuadorean-run, English, German and French spoken.
Wreck Bay Dive Center, *Darwin y Wolf, T05-252 1663, www.wreckbay.com.* Friendly and respectful of the environment as well as safety conscious. Divers and snorkellers on the same boat.

Puerto Villamil
Hotels also arrange tours. Kayak rentals at **Hotel San Vicente**.
Galapagos Bike & Surf, *Escalecias y Tero, T05-252 9509, www.galapagosbikeandsurf.com.* Lessons, tours and rentals. Highly regarded, friendly and helpful. Lots of different tours, with snorkelling, hiking and paddle boarding as well as bikes and surfing.
Galapagos Native, *Cormoran y 16 de Marzo, T05-252 9140, www.gruposanvicente galapagos.com.* Mountain biking downhill from Sierra Negra, full day including lunch, US$42. Also rentals: good bikes US$3 per hr, US$20 per day; snorkelling gear US$5 per day; surfboards US$4 per hr. Also on San Cristóbal and Santa Cruz.
Isabela Dive Center, *Escalecia y Alberto Gil, T05-252 9418, www.isabeladivecenter.com.ec.* Diving, snorkelling, land and boat tours.

Transport

Air
There are no international flights to Galápagos.

Airports at Baltra, across a narrow strait from Santa Cruz, and Puerto Baquerizo Moreno, on San Cristóbal, receive flights from mainland Ecuador. The 2 islands are 96 km apart and on most days there are local flights in light aircraft between them, as well as to Puerto Villamil on Isabela. There is also speedboat service between Puerto Ayora (Santa Cruz) and the other populated islands.

Avianca, LAN and **TAME** all fly from Quito and Guayaquil to Baltra or San Cristóbal. Baltra receives more flights but there is at least 1 daily to each destination. You can arrive at one and return from the other. You can also depart from Quito and return to Guayaquil or vice versa, but you may not buy a one-way ticket. The price of return fares varies considerably, depending on how far ahead and by what means you book. In 2017 regular low-season rates started at US$405 return from Guayaquil and US$445 from Quito (high-season fares are US$80-100 more).

Emetebe Avionetas, Boyacá 916 y Víctor Manuel Rendón, next to Hotel City Plaza, Guayaquil, T04-230 1277, www.emetebe. com.ec, offers inter-island flights in light aircraft. 2 daily flights except Sun between Puerto Baquerizo Moreno (San Cristóbal), Baltra and Puerto Villamil (Isabela). All fares US$165 one way; baggage allowance 25 lbs.

Boat

Lanchas (speedboats with 3 large engines for about 20 passengers) operate daily between Puerto Ayora and each of Puerto Baquerizo Moreno, Puerto Villamil, and Puerto Velasco Ibarra (Floreana); US$25-35 one way, 2 hrs or more depending on the weather and sea. Tickets are sold by several agencies in Puerto Baquerizo Moreno, Puerto Ayora and Puerto Villamil; purchase a day before travelling. This can be a wild ride in rough seas, life vests are provided, take drinking water.

Bus

Buses meet flights from the mainland at Baltra: some run to the port or *muelle* (10 mins, no charge) where the cruise boats wait; others go to Canal de Itabaca, the narrow channel which separates Baltra from Santa Cruz. It is 15 mins to the Canal, free, then you cross on a small ferry, US$1. On the other side, buses (US$2, may involve a long wait while they fill) and pick-up truck taxis (US$20 for up to 4 passengers) run to Puerto Ayora, 45 mins. For the return trip to the airport, buses leave the Terminal Terrestre on Av Baltra in Puerto Ayora (2 km from the pier, taxi US$1) daily at 0700, 0730 and 0830.

Taxi

Pick-up truck taxis These may be hired for transport throughout Puerto Ayora, US$1. A *ranchera* runs up to the highlands from the **Tropidurus** store, Av Baltra y Jaime Roldós, 2 blocks past the market: to **Bellavista** US$0.50, 10 mins; **Santa Rosa** US$1, 20 mins.

Water taxis (*taxis acuáticos*) From Puerto Ayora pier to Punta Estrada or anchored boats, US$0.80-1 during the day, US$2 at night.

Background Galápagos Islands

Geography and geology

Lying on the equator, 970 km west of the Ecuadorean coast, the Galápagos are not structurally connected to the mainland and, so far as is known, were never part of the South American Plate. They lie near the boundary between the Nazca Plate and the Cocos Plate to the north. A line of weakness, evidenced by a ridge of undersea lava flows, stretches southwest from the coast of Panama. This meets another undersea ridge running along the equator from Ecuador but separated from the continental shelf by a deep trench. At this conjuncture appear the Galápagos. Volcanic activity here has been particularly intense and the islands are the peaks of structures that rise over 7000 m from the deepest parts of the adjacent ocean floor. The oldest islands are San Cristóbal and Española in the east of the archipelago: three to 3½ million years old. The youngest ones, Fernandina and Isabela, lie to the west, and are between 700,000 and 800,000 years old. In geological terms, therefore, the Galápagos Islands have only recently appeared from the ocean and volcanic activity continues on at least five of them.

Evolution and wildlife

Galápagos has unique marine and terrestrial environments. This is due to the continuing volcanic formation of the islands in the west of the archipelago and its location at the nexus of several major marine currents, among other factors. Their interaction has created laboratory-type conditions where only certain species have been allowed access. Others have been excluded, and the resulting ecology has evolved in a unique direction, with many of the ecological niches being filled from some unexpected angles. A highly evolved sunflower, for instance, has in some areas taken over the niche left vacant by the absence of trees. There are also formidable barriers which prevent many species from travelling within the islands, hence a very high level of endemism. For example, each of the five main volcanoes on Isabela has evolved its own subspecies of giant tortoise.

Charles Darwin recognized this speciation within the archipelago when he visited the Galápagos on the Beagle in 1835 and his observations played a substantial part in his formulation of the theory of evolution. Since no large land mammals reached the islands (until they were recently introduced by man), reptiles were dominant just as they had been all over the world in the very distant past. Another extraordinary feature of the islands is the tameness of the animals. The islands were uninhabited when they were discovered in 1535 and the animals still have little instinctive fear of man.

Galápagos National Park and Marine Reserve

The Galápagos are a UNESCO World Heritage Site and 97% of the land area and 100% of the surrounding ocean are part of the Galápagos National Park and Marine Reserve. Within the park there are some 70 visitor sites, each with defined trails, so the impact of visitors to this fragile environment is minimized. There are also designated dive site in the marine reserve. These sites can only be visited with a national park guide as part of a cruise or tour.

Each of the visitor sites has been carefully chosen to show the different flora and fauna and, due to the high level of endemism, nearly every trail has flora and fauna that can be seen nowhere else in the world. The itineraries of tourist boats are strictly regulated in

Charles Darwin and the Galápagos

Without a doubt, the most famous visitor to the islands is Charles Darwin and his brief stay on the archipelago proved hugely significant.

In September 1835, Darwin sailed into Galápagos waters on board the HMS Beagle, captained by the aristocratic Robert FitzRoy whose job was to chart lesser-known parts of the world. FitzRoy had wanted on board a companion of his own social status and a naturalist, to study the strange new animals and plants they would find en route. He chose Charles Darwin to fill both roles.

Darwin was only 22 years old when he set sail from England in 1831 and it would be five years before he saw home again. They were to sail around the world, but most of the voyage was devoted to surveying the shores of South America, giving Darwin the chance to explore a great deal of the continent. The visit to the Galápagos was just a short stop on the return journey, by which time Darwin had become an experienced observer.

During the six weeks that the Beagle spent in the Galápagos, Darwin went ashore to collect plants, rocks, insects and birds. The unusual life forms and their adaptations to the harsh surroundings made a deep impression on him and eventually inspired his revolutionary theory on the evolution of species. The Galápagos provided a kind of model of the world in miniature. Darwin realized that these recently created volcanoes were young in comparison with the age of the Earth, and that life on the islands showed special adaptations. Yet the plants and animals also showed similarities to those from the South American mainland, where he guessed they had originally come from.

Darwin concluded that the life on the islands had probably arrived there by chance drifting, swimming or flying from the mainland and had not been created on the spot. Once the plants and animals had arrived, they evolved into forms better suited to the strange environment in which they found themselves. Darwin also noted that the animals were extremely tame, because of the lack of predators. The islands' isolation also meant that the giant tortoises did not face competition from more agile mammals and could survive.

On his return to England, Darwin in effect spent the rest of his life developing the ideas inspired by the Galápagos. It was, however, only when another scientist, named Alfred Russel Wallace, arrived at a similar conclusion to his own that he dared to publish a paper on his theory of evolution. Then followed his all-embracing The Origin of Species by means of natural selection, in 1859. It was to cause a major storm of controversy and to earn Charles Darwin recognition as the man who "provided a foundation for the entire structure of modern biology".

order to avoid crowding at the visitor sites and some sites are periodically closed by the park authorities in order to allow them to recover from the impact of tourism. Certain sites are only open to smaller boats and, additionally, limited to a maximum number of visits per month.

The 3% of Galápagos which is not national park is made up of towns and agricultural zones on four populated islands: Santa Cruz, San Cristóbal, Isabela and Floreana. However, there are also large restricted areas of national park land on these islands.

History of human settlement

The finding of fragments of ceramics suggests that the islands might have been visited by pre-Columbian sailors from the coast of Ecuador. They were uninhabited, however, when discovered accidentally by Tomás de Berlanga, the Bishop of Panama, in 1535. He was on his way to Peru when his ship was becalmed and swept 800 km off course by the currents. Like most of the early arrivals, Bishop Tomás and his crew arrived thirsty and disappointed at the dryness of the place. He did not even give the islands a name, although he did dub the giant tortoises *galápagos*.

The islands first appeared on a map in 1574, as Islands of Galápagos, which has remained in common use ever since. The individual islands, though, have had several names, both Spanish and English. The latter names come from visits by English buccaneers who used the Galápagos as a hideout, in particular a spot North of James Bay on Santiago Island, still known as Buccaneers' Cove. The pirates were the first to visit many of the islands and they named them after English kings and aristocracy or famous captains of the day.

The Spanish called the islands Las Encantadas, 'enchanted' or 'bewitched', owing to the fact that for much of the year they are surrounded by mists giving the impression that they appear and disappear as if by magic. Also, the tides and currents were so confusing that they thought the islands were floating and not real islands.

Between 1780 and 1860, the waters around the Galápagos became a favourite place for British and American whaling ships. At the beginning of the whaling era, in 1793, a British naval captain erected a barrel on Floreana Island to facilitate communication between boats and the land. It is still in Post Office Bay to this day.

The first island to be inhabited was Floreana, in 1807, by a lone Irishman named Patrick Watkins, who grew vegetables to trade for rum with passing ships. After two years he commandeered a lifeboat and a handful of sailors but later arrived in Guayaquil without his companions, who were never seen again. After his departure the Galápagos were again uninhabited for 25 years, but the bizarre episode set the tone for many more unusual colonists and nefarious events. Their story is told in *The Curse of the Giant Tortoise*, by Octavio Latorre.

In 1832, Ecuadorean General José Villamil founded a colony on Floreana, mainly composed of convicts and political prisoners, who traded meat and vegetables with whalers. The same year, following the creation of the young republic, Colonel Ignacio Hernández took official possession of the archipelago for Ecuador. Spanish names were given to the islands, in addition to the existing English ones, and both remain in use.

From 1880 to 1904 Manuel J Cobos ran a large sugar cane plantation and cattle ranch on San Cristóbal, notorious for mistreatment of its workers who eventually mutinied and killed him. The cruelty of prison colonies and slave farms like Cobos' cast a dark shadow over human presence in the archipelago.

There followed Norwegian fishermen and German philosophers, among others, many of whom met with some strange and tragic fate. Among the earliest colonists to endure were the Wittmer family on Floreana and the Angermeyers on Santa Cruz, whose story is beautifully told in *My Father's Island*, by Johanna Angermeyer.

From these small and erratic beginnings, Galápagos became the fastest growing province in Ecuador. In an attempt to protect the islands, controls on migration from the mainland were imposed in 2000 but these are frequently circumvented. Residents of the islands, now into their third and fourth generation, still call themselves *colonos* (colonists).

Tourists and settlers

The most devastating of the newly introduced species are human beings, both tourists and settlers. To a large degree, the two groups are connected, one supporting the other economically, but there is also a sizeable proportion who make an income independent of tourism by working the land or at sea.

While no great wealth has accumulated to those who farm, fortunes have been made by exporters and fishermen in a series of particularly destructive fisheries: black coral, lobster, shark fin, sea cucumber and sea horse. It is, however, farmers who are responsible for the largest number of introduced species. These include cattle, goats, donkeys, pigs, dogs, rats and ani (used to eat parasites living on cattle – although in the Galápagos it prefers baby finches when it can get them), and over 500 species of plants such as elephant grass (to provide pastures), guava trees (which have become a plague on Isabela) and tilapia in El Junco lake on San Cristóbal. The unchecked expansion of these introduced species has upset the natural balance of the archipelago and there have been campaigns to eradicate introduced species on some islands.

Galápagos is also a victim of its success as a tourist destination. The number of tourists has grown steadily: from 11,800 in 1979, to 68,900 in 2000, to approximately 225,000 in 2015. The prosperity achieved through tourism has created a strong demand for workers from the mainland and hence fuelled rapid population growth. The services required by these people (drinking water, sewage, electricity, transport, schools, hospitals) place a growing burden on the fragile natural environment. The islands and tour boats need fuel and there have been minor oil spills which, through good fortune alone, did not cause irreparable damage. With generous international financing, a wind-powered electric generating system was implemented on San Cristóbal, but even this is not without its environmental consequences, interfering as it does with the local petrel population.

Improve your travel photography

Taking pictures is a highlight for many travellers, yet too often the results turn out to be disappointing. Steve Davey, author of Footprint's *Travel Photography*, sets out his top rules for coming home with pictures you can be proud of.

Before you go

Don't waste precious travelling time and do your research before you leave. Find out what festivals or events might be happening or which day the weekly market takes place, and search online image sites such as Flickr to see whether places are best shot at the beginning or end of the day, and what vantage points you should consider.

Get up early

The quality of the light will be better in the few hours after sunrise and again before sunset – especially in the tropics when the sun will be harsh and unforgiving in the middle of the day. Sometimes seeing the sunrise is a part of the whole travel experience: sleep in and you will miss more than just photographs.

Stop and think

Don't just click away without any thought. Pause for a few seconds before raising the camera and ask yourself what you are trying to show with your photograph. Think about what things you need to include in the frame to convey this meaning. Be prepared to move around your subject to get the best angle. Knowing the point of your picture is the first step to making sure that the person looking at the picture will know it too.

Compose your picture

Avoid simply dumping your subject in the centre of the frame every time you take a picture. If you compose with it to one side, then your picture can look more balanced. This will also allow you to show a significant background and make the picture more meaningful. A good rule of thumb is to place your subject or any significant detail a third of the way into the frame; facing into the frame not out of it.

This rule also works for landscapes. Compose with the horizon two-thirds of the way up the frame if the foreground is the most interesting part of the picture; one-third of the way up if the sky is more striking.

Don't get hung up with this so-called Rule of Thirds, though. Exaggerate it by pushing your subject out to the edge of the frame if it makes a more interesting picture; or if the sky is dull in a landscape, try cropping with the horizon near the very top of the frame.

Fill the frame

If you are going to focus on a detail or even a person's face in a close-up portrait, then be bold and make sure that you fill the frame. This is often a case of physically getting in close. You can use a telephoto setting on a zoom lens but this can lead to pictures looking quite flat; moving in close is a lot more fun!

Interact with people

If you want to shoot evocative portraits then it is vital to approach people and seek permission in some way, even if it is just by smiling at someone. Spend a little time with them and they are likely to relax and look less stiff and formal. Action portraits where people are doing something, or environmental portraits, where they are set against a significant background, are a good way to achieve relaxed portraits. Interacting is a good way to find out more about people and their lives, creating memories as well as photographs.

Focus carefully

Your camera can focus quicker than you, but it doesn't know which part of the picture you want to be in focus. If your camera is using the centre focus sensor then move the camera so it is over the subject and half press the button, then, holding it down, recompose the picture. This will lock the focus. Take the now correctly focused picture when you are ready.

Another technique for accurate focusing is to move the active sensor over your subject. Some cameras with touch-sensitive screens allow you to do this by simply clicking on the subject.

Leave light in the sky

Most good night photography is actually taken at dusk when there is some light and colour left in the sky; any lit portions of the picture will balance with the sky and any ambient lighting. There is only a very small window when this will happen, so get into position early, be prepared and keep shooting and reviewing the results. You can take pictures after this time, but avoid shots of tall towers in an inky black sky; crop in close on lit areas to fill the frame.

Bring it home safely

Digital images are inherently ephemeral: they can be deleted or corrupted in a heartbeat. The good news though is they can be copied just as easily. Wherever you travel, you should have a backup strategy. Cloud backups are popular, but make sure that you will have access to fast enough Wi-Fi. If you use RAW format, then you will need some sort of physical back-up. If you don't travel with a laptop or tablet, then you can buy a backup drive that will copy directly from memory cards.

Available in both digital and print formats, Footprint's Travel Photography by Steve Davey covers everything you need to know about travelling with a camera, including simple post-processing. More information is available at www.footprinttravelguides.com

Background

History & politics

Earliest civilizations

The oldest archaeological artefacts that have been uncovered in Ecuador date back to approximately 10,000 BC. They include obsidian spear tips and belong to a pre-ceramic period during which the region's inhabitants are thought to have been nomadic hunters, fishers and gatherers. A subsequent formative period (4000-500 BC) saw the development of pottery, presumably alongside agriculture and fixed settlements. One of these settlements, known as Valdivia, existed along the coast of Ecuador and remains of buildings and earthenware figures have been found dating from 3500-1500 BC (see box, page 233).

Between 500 BC and AD 500, many different cultures evolved in all the geographic regions of what is today Ecuador. Among these were the Bahía, Guangalá, Jambelí and Duale-Tejar of the coast; Narrío, Tuncahuán and Panzaleo in the highlands; and Upano, Cosanga and Yasuní in Oriente. The period AD 500-1480 was an era of integration, during which dominant or amalgamated groups emerged. These included, from north to south in the Sierra, the Imbayas, Shyris, Quitus, Puruhaes and Cañaris; and the Caras, Manteños and Huancavilcas along the coast.

This rich and varied mosaic of ancient cultures is today considered the bedrock of Ecuador's national identity. It was confronted, in the mid-15th century, with the relentless northward expansion of the most powerful prehispanic empire on the continent: the Incas.

The Inca Empire

The Inca Kingdom already existed in southern Peru from the 11th century. It was not until the mid-15th century, however, that the empire began to expand northwards. Pachacuti Yupanqui became ruler of the Incas in 1428 and, along with his son **Túpac Yupanqui**, led the conquest of the Andean highlands north into present-day Ecuador. The Cañaris fiercely resisted for many years but were defeated around 1470. Their northern counterparts fought on for some decades, defeating various Inca armies.

Huayna Capac, Túpac Yupanqui's son, was probably born in Tomebamba (present-day Cuenca), although some claim he was born in Cuzco. Tomebamba eventually became one of the most important centres of the Inca Empire. Quito was finally captured in 1492 (a rather significant year) and became the base from which the Incas extended their territory even further north. A great road was built between Cuzco and Quito, but the empire was eventually divided; it was ruled after the death of Huayna Capac by his two sons, **Huáscar** at Cuzco and **Atahualpa** at Quito.

Conquest and colonial rule

Civil war broke out between the two halves of the empire and in 1532 Atahualpa secured victory over Huáscar and established his capital in Cajamarca, in northern Peru. In the same year, conquistador **Francisco Pizarro** set out from Tumbes, on the Peru-Ecuador border, finally reaching Cajamarca. There, he captured the Inca leader and put him to death in 1533. This effectively ended Inca resistance and their empire collapsed.

Pizarro claimed the northern kingdom of Quito, and his lieutenants **Sebastián de Benalcázar** and **Diego de Almagro** took the city in 1534. Pizarro founded Lima in 1535

BACKGROUND
Ecuador fact file

Population: 14.5 million (2010 census); estimates for 2017 are 16.3 million.
Urban population: 64.2%.
Population density: 59 inhabitants per sq km.
Population growth: 1.28%.
Infant mortality rate: 16.4 per 1000 live births.
Life expectancy at birth: 77 years.
Literacy: 94.4%.
Minimum wage: US$386 a month.
GDP per capita: US$11,200 (2017).

as capital of the whole region and four years later replaced Benalcázar at Quito with Gonzalo, his brother. **Gonzalo Pizarro** later set out on the exploration of the Oriente. He moved down the Napo river and sent **Francisco de Orellana** ahead to prospect. Orellana did not return. He drifted down the river finally to reach the mouth of the Amazon, thus becoming the first European to cross the continent in this way; an event which is still considered significant in the history of Ecuador (see box, page 270).

Quito became a *real audiencia* under the viceroyalty of Peru. For the next 280 years Ecuador reluctantly accepted the new ways brought by the conquerors. Gonzalo Pizarro had already introduced pigs and cattle; wheat was now added. The native people were Christianized and colonial laws, customs and ideas were introduced. The marriage of the arts of Spain to those of the Inca led to a remarkable efflorescence of painting, sculpture and building in Quito, one of the very few positive effects of conquest, which otherwise effectively enslaved the natives. In the 18th century, the production and export of cacao began and black slave labour was brought in to work cacao and sugar plantations.

Independence and the 19th century

Ecuadorean independence came about in several stages beginning in 1809, but was not completed until royalist forces were defeated by **Antonio José de Sucre** in the Battle of Pichincha in 1822. For the next eight years Ecuador was a province of Gran Colombia under the leadership of **Simón Bolívar**. As Gran Colombia collapsed in 1830, Ecuador at last became a fully independent nation.

Following independence, Ecuadorean politics were dominated by various elites. They were sometimes divided along regional lines (Quito and the highlands versus Guayaquil and the coast) and frequently fought among each other. Rule by rival oligarchies under the cloak of constitutional democracy or military dictatorship, has proved to be an enduring theme in Ecuadorean history.

Ecuador has had a great many presidents, but two diametrically opposed leaders are emblematic of their times. **Gabriel García Moreno** (president 1860-1865 and 1869-1875) was an arch-conservative, renowned for his cruel dictatorship and attempts to force Catholicism on the entire population; he denied citizenship to non-Catholics. He was eventually hacked to death by machete at the entrance of the presidential palace in Quito. **Eloy Alfaro** (1895-1901 and 1906-1911), was precisely the opposite, a liberal who sought to bring Ecuador into the modern world, based on revenues from the cacao boom. He introduced secular education, civil marriage and divorce, confiscated church lands and abolished capital punishment. Assassinated by his opponents, Alfaro's body was dragged through the streets of Quito before being publicly burned. García Moreno and Alfaro had more in common than their gruesome fate, both were *caudillos* (strong-men) who ruled by force of arms, as well as charisma. *Caudillismo* also remains an enduring feature of Ecuadorean public life.

The 20th century

Ecuadorean politics have long kept time with the country's fragile economy, with greater stability during occasional periods of prosperity and chaos during the more frequent lean years. The Great Depression exemplified the latter. Between 1931 and 1948 there were 21 governments, none of which succeeded in completing its term of office. "There were ministers who lasted hours, presidents who lasted for days, and dictators who lasted for weeks." (G Abad, *El proceso de lucha por el poder en el Ecuador*, Mexico 1970.) Political stability was only restored when the growth of coastal banana plantations created a fresh source of national revenue after the cacao boom had gone bust. The country's next larger-than-life president was **José María Velasco Ibarra**, a fiery orator who was elected four times in the 1950s and 1960s, and ousted each time by a military coup.

Like most other South American countries Ecuador experienced several periods of military rule during the 1960s and 1970s, but it did not suffer the widespread human rights abuses which took place in some other nations. Since 1979, Ecuador has enjoyed its longest period of civilian constitutional government since independence. In 1978 a young and charismatic **Jaime Roldós** was elected president, but died three years later in a still-mysterious plane crash. The following twenty years saw a series of governments which ostensibly alternated between the political right and left but, in practice, were little different from one another.

One of the outstanding personalities of this period was **León Febres Cordero** of the right-wing **Partido Social Cristiano**, strong-armed president 1984-1988, then twice popular mayor of Guayaquil and twice member of Congress. Equally newsworthy was **Abdalá Bucaram** of the populist **Partido Roldosista Ecuatoriano**, who was swept to power in 1996, but lasted barely six months. In 1997, following mass demonstrations, Congress voted to remove him on the grounds of 'mental incapacity'. Febres Cordero and Bucaram were Ecuador's late 20th century *caudillos* par excellence.

Jamil Mahuad of the **Democracia Popular** was narrowly elected president in 1998, amid border tensions with Peru. He diffused this explosive situation and signed a definitive peace treaty, putting an end to decades – even centuries – of conflict (see Peru, below). This early success was Mahuad's last, as a series of bank failures sent the country into an economic and political tailspin. In a desperate bid for stability, Mahuad decreed the adoption of the US dollar as the national currency in 1999. Less than a month later, in January 2000, he was forced out of office by Ecuador's indigenous peoples and disgruntled members of the armed forces. The coup lasted barely three hours before power was transferred to vice-president **Gustavo Noboa** and Mahuad joined the ranks of other Ecuadorean politicians in exile. Noboa, with assistance from the USA and the International Monetary Fund (IMF), was left to flesh out and implement the dollarization scheme.

Modern Ecuador

21st-century politics

In 2002 **Colonel Lucio Gutiérrez**, leader of the **Partido Sociedad Patriótica** (PSP) and leader of the 2000 coup, was elected president. He had run on a populist platform in alliance with the indigenous movement and labour unions, but began to change his stripes soon after taking office. In 2005, he became the third Ecuadorean president in eight years to be deposed by popular unrest. The colonel briefly took asylum in Brazil but soon returned home to again become an active political player.

In 2006, with disenchantment in the democratic process at an understandable high after so much political tragicomedy, **Rafael Correa**, a 43-year-old economics professor and leader of the **Alianza País** (**AP**) movement, was elected president. He came to office with a well-defined social and economic agenda and immediately convened a constituent assembly. The assembly drew up Ecuador's 19th constitution, which espouses *sumak kawsay* – a Quichua term roughly meaning 'quality of life' – as the fundamental goal of society. The new socially oriented charter was approved by nationwide referendum in 2008, and Correa was re-elected president in 2009 with a 52% majority and again in 2013 with 57%.

The Correa administration's affinity with other so called '21st-century socialist' governments (such as Venezuela, Bolivia and Nicaragua) drew international attention but there were no expropriations of property nor other drastic measures in Ecuador. Rather, the country entered another boom phase of it's cyclic development due mostly to high petroleum prices and even cacao exports once again flourished. The resulting revenues along with heavy borrowing from China allowed the Correa government to focus on long-neglected social issues. High levels of spending, an impressive growth in government bureaucracy and attempts to restrict the media were among the criticisms of Correa's opponents. Towards the end of his term of office, a fall in oil prices forced Correa to call for an expansion of oil drilling in the Amazon in order to fund his social programmes. In 2017, the support that Correa retained helped his preferred candidate, ex-vice-president Lenín Moreno, to gain victory in presidential elections. This did not guarantee a continuation of 'Correísmo', however. Much of his legacy was put under scrutiny, especially following the imprisonment of the new vice-president, Jorge Glas, Correa's second vice-president, for his involvement in the Odebrecht bribery scandal that was widely infecting Latin America. Moreno distanced himself from his former boss and in January 2018 a seven-question referendum overturned (among other things) the law permitting indefinite re-election of the president. Only one re-election will be allowed, thus preventing Correa from standing again.

Peru

After the dissolution of Gran Colombia in 1830 (largely present-day Venezuela, Colombia and Ecuador), repeated attempts to determine the extent of Ecuador's eastern jungle territory failed. While Ecuador claimed that its territory has been reduced from that of the old Real Audiencia de Quito by gradual Colombian and especially Peruvian infiltration, Peru insisted that its Amazonian territory was established in law and in fact before the foundation of Ecuador as an independent state.

In 1941 a war between the two countries ended with military defeat for Ecuador and the signing of the Rio de Janeiro Protocol of 1942 which allotted most of the disputed territory to Peru. Since 1960 Ecuador denounced the Protocol as unjust (because it was imposed by force of arms) and as technically flawed (because it refers to certain non-existent geographic features). According to Peru, the Protocol adequately demarcated the entire boundary.

Sporadic border skirmishes continued throughout subsequent decades. In January 1995 these escalated into an undeclared war over control of the headwaters of the Río Cenepa. Argentina, Brazil, Chile and the USA (guarantors of the Rio de Janeiro Protocol) intervened and subsequent negotiations led to a definitive peace treaty on 26 October 1998.

Under the terms of the agreement, Ecuador gained access to two Peruvian ports on the Amazon, Ecuador's navigation rights on the river were confirmed and, in the area of the most recent conflict, it was given a symbolic square kilometre of Peruvian territory as private property. In practice, Ecuador has yet to avail itself of any of the above. More significantly, however, relations have at last improved with new border crossings and new international bus routes. Adventurous travellers can now sail from the Ecuadorean Amazon to Peru, and tour operators offer a variety of packages involving both countries.

Colombia

Ecuador and Colombia have traditionally enjoyed excellent relations. Their larger, northern neighbour was for many decades a role model for Ecuadoreans. With escalating crime and violence in Colombia, however, that admiration gradually turned to fear, even though commercial ties remained very strong.

During the Correa governments, left-wing politics in Quito did not mesh well with the more right-wing Colombian administrations. Relations deteriorated dramatically in 2008, when the Colombian armed forces attacked from the air and on land a group of Colombian insurgents camped on Ecuadorean territory. Outraged by the violation of its sovereignty, Ecuador severed diplomatic ties which were re-established the following year. The two countries have since resumed excellent relations.

Government

There are 24 provinces, including the Galápagos Islands. Provinces are divided into *cantones* which are subdivided into *parroquias* for administration.

Under the 2008 constitution, all citizens over the age of 16 are entitled to vote. Between ages 18 and 65 voting is obligatory. The president and vice-president are elected for a four-year term and may be re-elected once. The unicameral *Asamblea Nacional* (National Assembly) has 137 members who are elected for a four-year term.

Culture

According to the latest census (2010, see www.ecuadorencifras.gob.ec), almost 72% of Ecuador's 14.5 million people consider themselves mestizos, descendants of *indígenas* and Spaniards. *Cholo* is another (mildly derogatory) term for this group, although infrequently used in Ecuador. Rural coastal dwellers are referred to as *montubios* and represent about 7.5% of the population. Roughly 7% of all Ecuadoreans today identify themselves as belonging to one of 14 different indigenous peoples.

Andean peoples

The largest indigenous group are the **Andean Quichuas**. The common language, Quichua, is closely related to the Quechua spoken in parts of Peru and Bolivia. Once

Indigenous cultures

Cultural groups

A Awa	**O** Otavaleño
Ac Achuar	**Qs** Quichua of the Sierra
Ch Chachi	**S** Salasaca
C Cofán	**Sa** Saraguro
E Epera	**Se** Secoya
H Huaorani	**Sh** Shuar
K Kichwa of the Oriente	**Si** Siona
N Negro-afroecuatoriano	**T** Tsachila
	Z Zápara

Not to scale

thought to have been imposed on conquered peoples by the Incas, Quechua/Quichua is now considered to have developed as a common trading language in the central Andes, long before the advent of the Inca Empire. Though Ecuador's highland natives all speak a similar language, indigenous dress differs from region to region. In the north, **Otavaleño** women are very distinctive with their blue skirts and embroidered blouses, while in the south the **Saraguros** traditionally wear black. A very important part of indigenous dress is the hat, which also varies from region to region.

Rainforest peoples

The largest indigenous groups in the Oriente are the **Kichwas**, in the north, and the **Shuar**, in the south. The Amazonian Kichwas speak a different dialect to their highland Quichua counterparts and their way of life is markedly distinct. Other Amazonian peoples of Ecuador include the **Achuar** and **Huaorani** as well as the **Cofán**, **Secoya**, **Shiwiar**, **Siona** and **Zápara**, all of whom are very few in number and in danger of disappearing.

Those very few jungle peoples who still maintain a traditional lifestyle, hunt and practise a form of itinerant farming which requires large areas of land, in order to allow the jungle to recover. Their way of life is under dire threat and many Amazonian indigenous communities are fighting for land rights in the face of oil exploration and colonization from the highlands.

There are also small groups of *indígenas* on the coastal plain. **Awas** live in Esmeraldas and Carchi provinces; **Chachis** and **Eperas** live nearer the coast and a little further south; **Tsáchilas**, formerly known as Colorados, live in the lowlands around Santo Domingo. These groups of coastal *indígenas* are also in danger of disappearing.

Afro-Ecuadoreans

The black population is estimated at about 7% of all Ecuadoreans. They live mostly in the coastal province of Esmeraldas and in neighbouring Imbabura and are descended from slaves who were brought from Africa in the 18th century to work on coastal plantations. Although the slave trade was abolished in 1821, slavery itself continued until 1852. Even then, freedom was not guaranteed until the system of debt tenancy was ended in 1881 and slaves could at last leave the plantations. However, the social status of Ecuador's black population remains low. They suffer from poor education and the racism endemic in all levels of society.

Religion

According to 2012 statistics, about 74% of the population belongs to the Roman Catholic faith. In recent decades a variety of Evangelical Protestant groups from the USA, Seventh-Day Adventists, Mormons and Jehovah's Witnesses have increased their influence. Freedom of worship is guaranteed by the Ecuadorean constitution.

Just as many of the great colonial churches of Ecuador are built over Inca and pre-Inca temples, the nation's impressive edifice of Roman Catholic faith rests firmly on pre-Christian foundations. The syncretism (mixing) of Catholic and earlier beliefs can be seen in many traditions and practices. One example is *fanesca*, a traditional soup eaten during Holy Week, made with salt fish and many different grains. The Catholic component is the lack of meat, which was not consumed during Lent, while the many grains came from native traditions to celebrate the beginning of the harvest at this time of year. The original native *fanesca* might have been made with *cuy*.

Ecuador is a shopper's paradise. Everywhere you turn there's some particularly seductive piece of *artesanía* being offered. This word loosely translates as handicrafts, but that doesn't really do them justice. The indigenous peoples make no distinction between fine arts and crafts, so *artesanía* is valued as much for its practical use as its beauty. See also Shopping tips, page 26.

Panama hats

Most people don't even know that the Panama hat, Ecuador's most famous export, comes from Ecuador. The confusion over the origin of this natty piece of headwear dates back over 100 years.

Until the 20th century, the Isthmus of Panama was the quickest and safest seafaring route to Europe and North America and the major trading post for South American goods, including the straw hats from Ecuador. In the mid-19th century, at the height of the California gold rush, would-be prospectors heading west to seek their fortune picked up the straw hats. Half a century later, when work on the Panama Canal was in full swing, labourers found the hats provided ideal protection against the fierce tropical sun and, like the gold-diggers before them, named them after the place they were sold rather than where they originated. The name stuck and, to Ecuador's eternal chagrin, the name of the Panama hat was born.

The plant from which these stylish titfers is made – *Carludovica palmata* (local name *paja toquilla*) – grows best in the low hills of the province of Manabí. The hats are woven from the very fine fronds of the plant, which are boiled, then dried in the sun before being taken to the various weaving centres – Montecristi and Jipijapa in Manabí and Azogues and Biblián in Cañar and Sigsig in Azuay. Montecristi, though, enjoys the reputation of producing the best *superfinos*. These are Panama hats of the highest quality, requiring many months' work. They are tightly woven, using the thinnest, lightest straw. When turned upside down they should hold water as surely as a glass, and when rolled up, should be able to pass through a wedding ring like silk. The whole process was added to UNESCO's Intangible Cultural Heritage of Humanity list in 2012. (As an aside, UNESCO included on the list Panama's own hat-making artesans from La Pintada in 2017.)

From the weaver, the hat passes to a middleman, who then sells it on to the factory. The loose ends are trimmed, the hat is bleached and the brim ironed into shape and then softened with a mallet. The hat is then prepared for export. The main export centre, and site of most of the finishing factories, is Cuenca, where countless shops also sell the *sombreros de paja toquilla* direct to tourists. The finest hats can be rolled into a cone and wrapped in paper in a balsawood box ready for travel. There are, however, many different styles, shapes and designs and not all are suitable for rolling. In general terms, the finest hats are *Técnica de la Costa* (made by weavers who stand, applying pressure to the work with their chest) as opposed to the less fine *Técnica de la Sierra* (the highland weavers sit to work). The hat-seller will advise on quality and the best way to transport and store your hat.

Weavers of Otavalo

During Inca times, textiles held pride of place and things are no different today. Throughout the highlands, beautiful woven textiles are still produced, often using techniques unchanged for centuries. One of the main weaving centres is Otavalo, which is a nucleus of trade for more than 75 scattered Otavaleño communities and home of the famous handicrafts market which attracts tourists in their thousands.

The history of weaving in Otavalo goes back to the time of conquest when the Spanish exploited the country's human resources through the feudal system of *encomiendas*. A textile workshop (*obraje*) was soon established in Otavalo using forced indigenous labour. *Obrajes* were also set up elsewhere in the region, for example in Peguche and Cotacachi, using technology exported from Europe: the spinning wheel and treadle loom. These are still in use today.

Though the *encomiendas* were eventually abolished, they were replaced by the equally infamous *huasipungo* system, which rendered the indigenous people virtual serfs on the large haciendas that were created. Many of these estates continued to operate weaving workshops, producing cloth in large quantities.

The Otavalo textile industry as it is known today was started in 1917 when weaving techniques and styles from Scotland were introduced to the native workers on Hacienda Cusín. These proved successful in the national market and soon spread to other families and villages in the surrounding area. The development of the industry received a further boost with the ending of the *huasipungo* system in 1964. The *indígenas* were granted title to their plots of land, allowing them to weave at home.

Today, weaving in Otavalo is almost exclusively for the tourist and export trades by which it is quite naturally influenced. Alongside traditional local motifs, are found many designs from as far afield as Argentina and Guatemala. The Otavaleños are not only renowned for their skilled weaving, but also for their considerable success as traders. They travel extensively, to Colombia, Venezuela, North America and Europe, in search of new markets for their products. As these begin to be saturated, Otavaleños are now peddling their wares in Asia.

Woodcarving

During the colonial era, uses of woodcarving were extended to provide the church with carved pieces to adorn the interiors of its many fine edifices. Wealthy families also commissioned work such as benches and chairs, mirrors and huge *barqueños* (chests) to decorate their salons.

In the 16th and 17th centuries woodcarvers from Spain settled north of Quito, where San Antonio de Ibarra has become the largest and most important woodcarving centre in South America. Initially the *mudéjar*, or Spanish-Moorish styles, were imported to the New World, but as the workshops of San Antonio spread north to Colombia and south to Chile and Argentina, they evolved their own styles. Today, everyone in San Antonio is involved with woodcarving and almost every shop sells carved wooden figures, or will make items to order.

Bags

Plant fibre is used not only for weaving but is also sewn into fabric for bags and other articles. In Cotopaxi province, *shigras*, bags made from sisal, were originally used to store dry foodstuffs around the home. It is said that very finely woven ones were even used to carry water from the wells, the fibres swelling when wet to make the bags impermeable. These bags almost died out with the arrival of plastic containers, until tourist demand ensured that the art survived. *Shigras* can be found at the market in Salcedo (early in the morning) and are also re-sold at tourist shops throughout the country.

Like the small backstrap looms and drop spindles of the Andes, the bags are portable and can be sewn while women are herding animals in the fields. Today, women's production is often organized by suppliers who provide dyed fibres for sewing and later buy the bags to resell. A large, blunt needle is used to sew the strong fibres and the finished article is likely to last a lot longer than the user.

Bread figures

The inhabitants of the town of Calderón, in the northeastern suburbs of Quito, know how to make dough. The main street is lined with shops selling the vibrantly coloured figures made of flour and water which have become hugely popular in recent years.

The origins of this practice are traced back to the small dolls made of bread for the annual celebrations of **Día de los Difuntos** (Day of the Dead, 2 November). The original edible figures, made in wooden moulds in the village bakery, were decorated with a simple cross over the chest in red, green and black, and were placed in cemeteries as offerings to the hungry souls of the dead. Gradually, different types of figures appeared and people started giving them as gifts for children and friends.

Primitivist paintings

In the province of Cotopaxi, near Zumbahua and the Quilotoa crater, a regional craft has developed specifically in response to tourist demand. It is the production of 'primitivist' paintings on leather, now carried out by many of the area's residents, depicting typical rural or village scenes and even current events. Following the 1999 volcanic eruptions of Tungurahua, these began to figure prominently in the Tigua paintings – named after the town where the work originated. The paintings vary in price and quality and are now also widely available in Quito, Otavalo and other tourist destinations.

Traditional music and dance

Culturally, ethnically and geographically, Ecuador is very much two countries – the Andean highlands with their centre in Quito and the Northern Pacific Lowlands behind Guayaquil. In spite of this, the music is relatively homogeneous and it is the Andean music that would be regarded as 'typically Ecuadorean'.

The principal highland rhythms are the Sanjuanito, Cachullapi, Albaza, Yumbo and Danzante, danced by *indígenas* and *mestizos* alike. These may be played by brass bands, guitar trios or groups of wind instruments, but it is the *rondador*, a small panpipe, that provides the classic Ecuadorean sound, although of late the Peruvian *quena* has been making heavy inroads via pan-Andean groups and has become a threat to the local instrument.

The coastal region has its own song form, the *Amorfino*, but the most genuinely 'national' song and dance genres, both of European origin, are the *Pasillo* (shared with Colombia) in waltz time and the *Pasacalle*, similar to the Spanish *Pasodoble*.

Music of the highland indigenous communities is, as elsewhere in the region, related to religious feasts and ceremonies and geared to wind instruments such as the *rondador*, the *pinkullo* and *pifano* flutes and the long *guarumo* horn with its mournful note. The guitar is also usually present and brass bands with well-worn instruments can be found in even the smallest villages.

There is one totally different cultural area, that of the black inhabitants of the Province of Esmeraldas and the highland valley of the Río Chota in Imbabura. The former is a southern extension of the Colombian Pacific coast negro culture, centred round the marimba, a huge wooden xylophone. The musical genres are also shared with black Colombians, including the *Bunde, Bambuco, Caderona, Torbellino* and *Currulao* dances and this music is some of the most African sounding in the whole of South America. The Chota Valley is an inverted oasis of desert in the Andes and here the black people dance the *Bomba*. It is also home to the unique Bandas Mochas, whose primitive instruments include leaves that are doubled over and blown through.

Literature

Much Ecuadorean literature has reflected political issues such as the rivalry between liberals and conservatives and between Costa and Sierra, and the position of the *indígenas* and other marginalized members of society, and many of the country's writers have adopted a strongly political line. Among the earliest were Francisco Eugenio de Santa Cruz y Espejo, who led a rebellion against Spain in 1795, José Joaquín de Olmedo, Federico González Suárez (archbishop of Quito) and Juan Montalvo.

The 19th century

José Joaquín de Olmedo (1780-1847) was a disciple of Espejo and was heavily involved first in the independence movement and then the formative years of the young republic. In 1825 he published *La Victoria de Junín, Canto a Bolívar*, a heroic poem glorifying the Liberator. His second famous poem was the *Canto al General Flores, Al Vencedor de Miñarica* (Juan José Flores was the Venezuelan appointed by Bolívar to govern Ecuador). He also wrote political works.

Juan Montalvo (1832-1889) was an essayist who was influenced by French Romantics such as Victor Hugo and Lamartine. One of his main objectives as a writer was to attack what he saw as the failings of Ecuador's rulers, but his position as a liberal, in opposition to conservatism such as García Moreno's, encompassed a passionate opposition to all injustice. His *Capítulos que se le olvidaron a Cervantes* (1895) was an attempt to imitate the creator of Don Quijote, translating him into an Ecuadorean setting.

Montalvo's contemporary and enemy, **Juan León Mera** (1832-1894), did write a book about the *indígena, Cumandá*. This dealt with the unsubjugated Amazonians, *los errantes y salvajes hijos de las selvas* (the wandering and savage sons of the jungles), a book which created much debate.

The 20th century and beyond

In 1904 **Luis A Martínez** (1869-1909) published *A la costa*, which attempts to present two very different sides of the country (the coast and the highlands) and the different customs and problems in each. *Plata y bronce* (1927) and *La embrujada* (1923), both by **Fernando Chávez** (1902-1999), portray the gulf between the white and the indigenous communities.

For the next 15 to 20 years, novelists in Ecuador produced a realist literature which was heavily influenced by writers like Zola and Sinclair Lewis. This was realism at the expense of beauty. The novelists in this period wrote politically committed stories about marginalized people in crude language and stripped-down prose. Among the more prominent writers in this era are José de la Cuadra (1903-1941), Alfredo Pareja D (1908-1993) and Demetrio Aguilera M (1909-1981). Continuing the realist literature and with a predominately indigenous theme are authors like Humberto Mata (1904-1988) and Jorge Icaza (1906-1978). Icaza's novel *Huasipungo* (1934) has been described as "the most contoversial novel in the history of Latin American narrative". Unlike some indigenist fiction, there is no attempt to portray the life on the Indians as anything other than brutal, inhuman, violent and hopeless.

The 1960s ushered in the so-called boom, with writers such as Gabriel García Márquez and Mario Vargas Llosa, gaining international recognition for the Latin American novel. At the same time, the Ecuadorean poet, essayist and novelist **Jorge Enrique Adoum** (1923-2009) wrote *Entre Marx y una mujer desnuda* (1976). This extraordinary novel is a dense investigation of itself, of novel-writing, of Marxism and politics, sex, love and Ecuador. Adoum has also written *Ciudad sin angel* (1995), plays (eg *El sol bajo las patas de los caballos* – 1972) and several collections of poetry, which is also intense and inventive (eg *No son todos los que están, 1949-1979*); his essay, *Ecuador: señales particulares* (1998), is a profound reflection on the Ecuadorean identity.

Among contemporary authors, **Alicia Yánez Cossío** (born 1928), in a long and productive career has delved into all aspects of Ecuadorean society. Among her best-known works are the novels *Bruna, soroche y los tíos* (1971) and *Más allá de las islas* (1980 – about the Galápagos). Her 12th novel, *Memorias de la Pivihuarmi Cuxirimay Oclo* (2008), is based on the life and tribulations of an Inca princess married to Atahualpa. Other prominent writers and their recent works include: **Jorge Dávila Vásquez** (born 1947), *María Joaquina en la vida y en la muerte* (1976) and many collections of stories, such as *Este mundo es el camino* (1980); **Modesto Ponce** (born 1938), *La casa del desván* (2008) and *Adela* (2017); **Gabriela Alemán** (born 1968), *Fuga permanente* (2002), *Poso Wells* (2007) and *Humo* (2017); and **Javier Vásconez** (born 1946), *El viajero de Praga* (1996), *La sombra del apostador* (1999), *La piel del miedo* (2010) and *Hoteles del silencio* (2016).

Poetry

The major figure, perhaps of all Ecuadorean poetry, was **Jorge Carrera Andrade** (1903-1978). He was involved in socialist politics in the 1920s before going to Europe. In the 1930s and 1940s, Carrera Andrade moved beyond the socialist realist, revolutionary stance of his contemporaries and of his own earlier views, seeking instead to explore universal themes. His first goal was to write beautiful poetry. He published many volumes, including the haiku-like *Microgramas* (see *Registro del mundo: antología poética*; 1922-1939), *El alba llama a la puerta* (1965-1966), *Misterios naturales* and others. Contemporary poets include: **Juan Carlos Morales M** (born 1967), *La campana en el espejo, El poeta y la luna* (2015) and others; **María Fernanda Espinosa** (born 1964), *Antología* (2005), *Geografías torturadas* (2013); **Francisco Granizo** (1925-2009), *Por el breve polvo* (1948), *El sonido de tus pasos* (2005); **Edwin Madrid** (born 1961), *Mordiendo el frío* (2004); **Xavier Oquendo** (1972), *Salvados del naufragio* (2005), *Esto fuimos en la felicidad* (2009); **Cristóbal Zapata** (1968), *No hay naves para Lesbos* (2004), *La miel de la higuera* (2012); and **Pedro Gil** (born 1971), *Paren la guerra que yo no juego* (1989), *Diecisiete puñaladas no son nada* (2010).

Many schools and workshops promote poetry in Ecuador, notably the **Centro Internacional de Estudios Poéticos del Ecuador (CIEPE)**, which has published collections like *Poemas de luz y ternura* (Quito 1993). The work of many other poets can be found in collections and articles online.

Fine art and sculpture

The 16th and 17th centuries

Colonial Quito was a flourishing centre of artistic production, exporting works to many other regions of Spanish South America. The origins of this trade date back to the year of the Spanish foundation of Quito, 1534, when the Franciscans established a college to train *indígenas* in European arts and crafts. Two Flemish friars, Jodoco Ricke and Pedro Gosseal, are credited with teaching a generation how to paint the pictures and carve the sculptures and altarpieces that were so urgently needed by the many newly founded churches and monasteries in the region. As well as the initial Flemish bias of the first Franciscans, stylistic influences on the Quito school came from Spain, particularly from the strong Andalucían sculptural tradition.

Colonial painting was as much influenced by Italy as by Spain. An important early figure in this was the Quito-born mestizo Pedro Bedón (1556-1621). Educated in Lima where he probably had contact with the Italian painter Bernardo Bitti, Bedón returned home to combine the duties of Dominican priest with work as a painter. He is best-known for his illuminated manuscripts.

Indigenous influence is not immediately apparent in painting or sculpture despite the fact that so much of it was produced by natives. The features of Christ, the Virgin and saints are European, but in sculpture the proportions of the bodies are often distinctly Andean: broad-chested and short-legged. In both painting and sculpture the taste – so characteristic of colonial art in the Andes – for patterns in gold applied over the surface of garments may perhaps be related to the high value accorded to textiles in pre-conquest times.

The 18th century

Representations of the Virgin are very common, especially that of the Virgin Immaculate, patron of the Franciscans and of the city of Quito. This curious local version of the Immaculate Conception represents the Virgin standing on a serpent and crescent moon as tradition dictates, but unconventionally supplied with wings.

In the later 18th century the sculptor Manuel Chili, known to his contemporaries as *Caspicara* 'the pockmarked', continued the tradition of polychrome images with powerful emotional appeal ranging from the dead Christ to sweet-faced Virgins and chubby infant Christs. Outside Quito the best-known sculptor was Gaspar Sangurima of Cuenca who was still producing vividly realistic polychrome crucifixions in the early 19th century.

Painting in the later 18th century is dominated by the much lighter, brighter palette of Manuel Samaniego (c 1766-1824), author of a treatise on painting which includes instructions on the correct human proportions and Christian iconography, as well as details of technical procedures and recipes for paint.

Independence and after

As elsewhere in Latin America, the struggle for Independence created a demand for subjects of local and national significance and portraits of local heroes. **Antonio Salas** (1795-1860) became the unofficial portrait painter of the Independence movement. His paintings of heroes, military leaders and notable churchmen can be seen in Quito's Museo Jijón y Caamaño. Antonio's son, **Rafael Salas** (1828-1906), was among those to make the Ecuadorean landscape a subject of nationalist pride, as in his famous bird's-eye view of Quito sheltering below its distinctive family of mountain peaks (private collection).

Rafael Salas and other promising young artists of the later 19th century studied in Europe, returning to develop a style of portraiture which brings together both the European rediscovery of 17th-century Dutch and Spanish art and Ecuador's own conservative artistic tradition. They also brought back from their travels a new appreciation of the customs and costumes of their own country. The best-known exponent of this new range of subject matter was **Joaquín Pinto** (1842-1906). Although he did not travel to Europe and received little formal training, his affectionate, often humorous paintings and sketches present an unrivalled panorama of Ecuadorean landscape and peoples.

The 20th century and beyond

Pinto's documentation of the plight of the *indígena*, particularly the urban *indígena*, presaged the 20th-century indigenist tendency in painting whose exponents include **Camilo Egas** (1899-1962), **Eduardo Kingman** (1913-1997) and most famously **Oswaldo Guayasamín** (1919-1999). Their brand of social realism, while influenced by the Mexican muralists, has a peculiarly bitter hopelessness of its own. Their work can be seen in Quito at **Museo Camilo Egas, Museo La Casa de Kingman** and **Posada de las Artes Kingman**, and **Museo Guayasamín** and **Capilla del Hombre** (the Chapel of Man).

The civic authorities in Ecuador, particularly during the middle years of the 20th century, have been energetic in peopling their public spaces with monuments to commemorate local and national heroes and events. Inevitably such sculpture is representational and often conservative in style, but within these constraints there are powerful examples in most major town plazas and public buildings are generously adorned with sculptural friezes, such as in the work of **Jaime Andrade** (1913-1989) on the **Central University** and **Social Security buildings** in Quito. **Estuardo Maldonado** (born 1930) works in an abstract mode using coloured stainless steel to create dramatic works for public and private spaces. **Milton Barragán** (born 1934) sculpts metal in dialogue with wood; he designed el *Templo a la Patria* on Cima de la Libertad in Quito. **Gonzalo Endara Crow's** (1936-1998) mosaic-tiled sculptures adorn plazas in several cities.

In recent years there have been many interesting artistic experiments which can be appreciated in museums and especially the galleries of the **Casa de la Cultura** across the country. Information on some contemporary artists is found in www.latinartmuseum. com. **Cuenca** hosts an important biennial and Ecuador is unusual among the smaller Latin American countries for its lively international art scene. Among prominent contemporary artists are: **Oswaldo Viteri** (born 1931, www.viteri.com.ec), **Nicolás Svistoonoff** (1945-2014), **Marcelo Aguirre** (born 1956, http://marceloaguirrebelgrano.com), **Jaime Zapata** (born 1957), **Luigi Stornaiolo** (born 1956), **Miguel Betancourt** (born 1958), **Jorge Velarde** (born 1960), and **Mario Tapia** (born 1967).

Land & environment

Ecuador, named for its position on the equator, is the smallest country of South America (256,370 sq km) after Uruguay and the Guianas. It is bounded by Colombia in the north, by Peru to the east and south, and by the Pacific Ocean to the west. Its population of 14.5 million (in 2010) is also small, but it has the highest population density of any of the South American republics, at 59 inhabitants per sq km. The border had been a source of conflict with its neighbours and Ecuador lost a significant part of its former territory towards the Amazon to Peru in 1941-1942 (see Ecuador's neighbours, page 355).

The Galápagos Islands became part of Ecuador in 1832. They lie in the Pacific, 970 km west of the mainland, on the equator, and consist of six principal islands and numerous smaller islands and rocks totalling about 8000 sq km and scattered over 60,000 sq km of ocean. They are the most significant island group in the eastern Pacific Ocean.

Geology

Geologically, Ecuador is the creation of the Andean mountain-building process, caused in turn by the South American Plate moving west, meeting the Nazca plate which is moving east and sinking beneath the continent. This process began in the late Cretaceous Period around 80 million years ago and has continued to the present day. Before this, and until as late as perhaps 25 million years ago, the Amazon basin tilted west and the Amazon river drained into the Pacific through what is now southern Ecuador.

The Andes between Peru and Colombia are at their narrowest (apart from their extremities in Venezuela and southern Chile), ranging from 100-200 km in width. Nevertheless, they are comparatively high with one point, Chimborazo, over 6000 m and several others not much lower. Unlike Peru to the south, most of the peaks in Ecuador are volcanoes, and Cotopaxi is one of the highest active volcanoes in the world, at 5897 m. The 55 volcanic craters that dot the landscape of the northern highlands suggest a fractured and unstable area beneath the surface. A dramatic example of volcanic activity was an eruption of Cotopaxi in 1877 which was followed by a pyroclastic flow or *nuée ardente* (literally, a burning cloud) which flowed down the side of the volcano engulfing many settlements. Snow and ice at the summit melted to create another volcanic phenomenon called a *lahar*, or mud flow, which reached Esmeraldas (150 km away) in only 18 hours. The most recently volcanic episodes began in 1999, with eruptions of Guagua Pichincha, Tungurahua, Reventador and Cotopaxi. For detailed information about Ecuador's volcanoes, see the website of the **National Geophysical Institute**, www.igepn.edu.ec.

The eastern third of the country is part of the Amazon basin filled with sedimentary deposits from the mountains to the west. The coastlands rise up to 1000 m and are mainly remnants of Tertiary basalts, similar to the base rocks of the Amazon basin on the other side of the Andes.

The Galápagos are not structurally connected to the mainland and, so far as is known, were never part of the South American Plate. They lie near the boundary between the Nazca Plate and the Cocos Plate to the north. A line of weakness, evidenced by a ridge of undersea lava flows, stretches southwest from the coast of Panama. This meets another undersea ridge running along the equator from Ecuador but separated from the continental shelf by a deep trench. At this conjuncture appear the Galápagos. Volcanic activity here has been particularly intense and the islands are the peaks of structures that rise over 7000 m from the deepest parts of the adjacent ocean floor. The oldest islands are San Cristóbal and Española in the east of the archipelago: three to 3½ million years old. The youngest ones, Fernandina and Isabela, lie to the west, and are between 700,000 and 800,000 years old. In geological terms, therefore, the Galápagos Islands have only recently appeared from the ocean and volcanic activity continues on at least five of them.

The Andes

The Andes form the backbone of the country. In Colombia to the north, three distinct ranges come together near Pasto, with three volcanoes overlooking the border near Tulcán. Although it is essentially one range through Ecuador, there is a trough of between 1800 m and 3000 m above sea level running south for over 400 km with volcanoes, many active, on either side. The snowline is at about 5000 m and rising due to global climate change, with 10 peaks over that height, making for a dramatic landscape.

Overlooking Quito to the west is **Pichincha**, which was climbed by Charles-Marie de La Condamine in 1742 and, in 1802, by Alexander Von Humboldt. Humboldt climbed many other Ecuadorean volcanoes, including Chimborazo. Although he did not make it to the summit, he reached over 6000 m, the first recorded climb to this height. He christened the road through the central Andes the 'Avenue of the Volcanoes'.

Further south, near Riobamba, is **Volcán Sangay**, 5230 m, which today is the most continuously active of Ecuador's volcanoes. There are fewer volcanoes towards in the southern highlands and the scenery is less dramatic. Here, the mountains rarely exceed 4000 m and the passes are as low as 2200 m. Although active volcanoes are concentrated in the northern half of the country, there are many places where there are sulphur baths or hot springs and the whole Andean area is seismically active with severe earthquakes from time to time.

The central trough is crossed by several transverse ranges called *nudos*, made up of extruded volcanic material, creating separate basins or *hoyas*. South of Quito, the basins are lower, the climate hotter and drier with semi-desert stretches. The lack of surface water is aggravated by large quantities of volcanic dust which is easily eroded by wind and water and can produce dry 'badland' topography. Landslides in this unstable and precipitous terrain are common.

The coast

West of the Andes there are 100-200 km of lowlands with some hilly ground up to 1000 m. The greater part is drained by the Daule, Vinces and Babahoyo rivers that run north to south to form the Guayas, the largest river on the Pacific coast of South America, which meets the sea near Guayaquil. There are several shorter rivers in the north including the Esmeraldas, whose headwaters include the Río Machángara which unfortunately is the open sewer of Quito. Another system reaches the ocean at La Tola. All of these rivers have created fertile lowlands which are used for banana, cacao and rice production, and there are good cattle lands in the Guayas basin. This is one of the best agricultural areas of South America.

Mangrove swamps thrived on coastal mudflats in tropical rainforest zones and were typical of parts of Esmeraldas, Manabí and Guayas provinces. Many have been destroyed to make way for shrimp farms.

Amazonia

The eastern foothills of the Andes are mainly older granite (Mesozoic) rocks, more typical of Brazil than the Pacific coast countries. As with most of the western Amazon basin, it has a heavy rainfall coming in from the east and much is covered with tropical forest along a dozen or so significant tributaries of the Amazon.

With good water flow and easy gradients, many of the rivers of this region are navigable at least to small craft. The Napo in particular is a significant potential communications route from Coca to Iquitos in Peru and the Brazilian Amazon beyond.

Climate

In spite of its small size, the range of tropical climates in Ecuador is large. The meeting of the north-flowing Humboldt current with warm Pacific equatorial water takes place normally off Ecuador, giving the contrast between high rainfall to the north and desert conditions further south in Peru. Periodic changes in the balance between these huge bodies of water, known as the El Niño phenomenon, can lead to heavy rains and flooding (see box, page 368).

The coast

The climate along the Pacific coast is a transition area between the heavy tropical rainfall of Colombia and the deserts of Peru. The rainfall is progressively less from north to south, with lush tropical rainforests in Esmeraldas and semi-desert conditions by the Peruvian border.

The Andes and Oriente

Inland, the size of the Andean peaks and volcanoes create many different microclimates, from the permanent snows over about 5000 m to the semi-desert hollows in the central trough. Most of the basins and the adjoining slopes have a moderate climate, though at altitude daily temperature fluctuations can be considerable. In the north, the basins are higher and temperatures are warm by day and cool at night. It rains mostly between October and May; Quito has an average of 1300 mm per year. Near the border with Peru, the mountain climate can be very pleasant. Vilcabamba in Loja province is reputed to have a most favourable climate for a long and healthy life. In the Oriente the climate is indistinguishable from the hot, very humid lands of the western Amazon basin. There is heavy rainfall all year round, particularly May to December.

Galápagos

Although lying on the equator, there is considerable variation in the weather of the Galápagos Islands. The islands are affected by the cool water from the southeast Pacific which turns west near the equator. Surface water temperatures can fall to 20°C in July to September, causing *garúa* (mist) and cool air. Temperatures are highest from January to May and brief tropical downpours occur frequently at this time.

El Niño

Among the early European scientists to visit South America, Alexander von Humboldt observed a cold ocean current flowing from south to north along the coast of Peru; it was later given his name. The Humboldt current follows South America s Pacific coastline northward as far as the equator, causing very low precipitation (because of low evaporation from its cool waters) and creating deserts in northern Chile, Peru and southern Ecuador. At the equator it turns due west, sweeping past the Galápagos Islands into the central Pacific.

North of the equator, a warm countercurrent flows in the opposite direction, eastward towards Panama and then south along the Pacific coast (where it is called the Panama current) until it meets the Humboldt current at the equator. This warm current brings warm moist air and high precipitation to the Pacific coasts of Panama, Colombia and northern Ecuador. The relative strength of these two currents, warm and cold, varies with the time of year. The warm Panama current can be stronger around Christmas and hence was dubbed the *Corriente del Niño*, the current of the (Christ) child. Under certain circumstances, which tend to recur in an irregular two- to seven-year cycle, this warm current can be exceptionally strong and sweep as far south as Chile, causing very heavy rains and associated calamities in these normally desert areas. This is the El Niño phenomenon (referred to scientifically as El Niño-Southern Oscillation, or ENSO).

A more global outlook notes that under normal conditions the trade winds, which blow westward across the tropical Pacific Ocean, pile up warm sea surface water in the west. Consequently, the sea level by Indonesia is normally about 50 cm higher than it is by Ecuador. This movement of warm water to the west causes an up-welling of deeper cold water in the east (the Humboldt current) resulting in a temperature difference of about 8°C at the same latitude, between the water by the coast of South America and that by Southeast Asia. When the westerly movement of both trade winds and warm water becomes excessive, this is called La Niña.

When the trade winds diminish in intensity, there is a gradual eastward-moving warming of surface water in the Pacific. Heavy rainfall follows the warmer water east to the Pacific coast of South America (the El Niño phenomenon) and is accompanied by simultaneous drought in Southeast Asia and Australia. The ocean level rises along the west coast of South America causing *marejadas*, exceptionally high tides which can destroy beaches and seaside property.

Very strong El Niños took place in 1982-1983 and 1997-1998, and both were devastating for the Ecuadorean coast. Since then the phenomenon has been weak to moderate. Most recently 2015-2016 experienced a stronger El Niño than usual, followed by two years of La Niña, 2016 and 2017-2018. For more details, see www.climate.gov/enso.

Wildlife and vegetation

No country in the world has as much biological diversity in as little space as Ecuador. The geologically recent uplift of the Andes has caused this diversity by dividing the country into two parts, west and east, and by creating a complex topography that fosters the evolution of new species. It is an exciting thing to experience this diversity first hand and Ecuador's extensive road system makes it easy. Our brief survey of this diversity, from west to east, gives an idea of the enormous range of Ecuador's life forms. For the Galápagos wildlife, see pages 302-311.

Northwestern lowlands

The westernmost part of mainland Ecuador is a broad rolling plain covered in the north by some of the wettest rainforest in the world. (There are some low coastal mountains but they do not reach significant elevations.) The biological centre of this region is the Chocó forest of neighbouring Colombia, so Ecuador's northwest shares many species with that area. Among the so-called Chocó endemics that reach Ecuador are some very fancy birds like the **long-wattled umbrellabird**, **banded ground-cuckoo** and **scarlet-breasted dacnis**. Many other birds, mammals and plants of this region are found all along the wet Pacific lowlands from northwest Ecuador to Central America. Visitors familiar with Central American wildlife will feel at home here amongst the **mantled howler monkeys**, **chestnut-mandibled toucans** and **red-capped manakins**. Unfortunately this forest is severely endangered by commercial logging, cattle ranching and farming, and good examples of it are now hard to find.

Southwestern lowlands

The cold Humboldt ocean current creates a completely different environment in the southwestern lowlands. Here the forest is deciduous (driest in July and August), and the southernmost parts of this area are desert-like. The birds and plants of this region are very different from those of the wet northwest; they belong to the Tumbesian bioregion and many are restricted to this small corner of Ecuador and adjacent northwest Peru. Some of the Tumbesian endemic birds are the **El Oro parakeet**, **rufous-headed chachalaca** and **elegant crescentchest**. This is a densely populated region, however, and many of the species endemic to it are threatened with extinction.

Western slopes

Rising suddenly from these flat lowlands are the western Andes, very steep and irregular. Here the constant mists keep the forest wet all the way from north to south. In southern Ecuador it is therefore possible to go from desert to cloudforest in the space of a few hundred metres of elevation. This cloudforest is thick, tall and dark and every branch is loaded with bromeliads, orchids and mosses. Orchids reach their maximum diversity in Ecuadorean cloudforests and many spectacular varieties are found in the west, especially the weird Draculas. Many of the birds in these mountains are restricted to western Ecuador and western Colombia, including spectacular species like the gaudy **plate-billed mountain-toucan**. At higher elevations there are more similarities with the eastern slope of the Andes. Among the highlights of these forests are the mixed foraging flocks of colourful **tanagers**, with exotic names like Glistening-green, Beryl-spangled and Flame-faced tanagers. Mammals are scarce; lower elevations have **capuchin**, **spider** and **howler monkeys**, while high elevations have the elusive **spectacled bear**. Insects too diminish as elevation increases and their role as flower pollinators is taken over by the many hummingbirds, including the **violet-tailed sylph**, **velvet-purple coronet** and **gorgeted sunangel**, to name but a few.

Western páramo

The cloudforest becomes low and stunted above about 3300 m, and at higher elevations the forest is replaced by the grassland environment called *páramo*. Here, in contrast to the lower forests, the plants are largely from familiar temperate-zone families like the daisy and blueberry. They take on increasingly bizarre forms as the altitude increases and the species of the highest elevations look like cushions of moss. Mammals are scarce but include **spectacled bear**, which feeds on the terrestrial bromeliads called *puyas* or *achupallas* (which look a lot like pineapple plants); and **rabbits**, which can be so numerous that they make broad trails in the vegetation. Preying on the rabbits are a form of **great horned owl** and the **Andean fox**. The birds and insects of these elevations are mostly drab, and many of the families represented here have their origins in North America or temperate southern South America. Forming islands of high forest in the *páramos* are the polylepis trees, in the rose family; their distinctive flaky reddish bark is the favorite foraging substrate for the **giant conebill**.

Inter-Andean basins

Between the western and eastern Andes lies the Inter-Andean basin, really a series of basins formed by various river valleys. This region is in the rain shadows of both the western and eastern Andes, so it is relatively dry all year. Much of the original vegetation was destroyed centuries ago, replaced with grasses and more recently with introduced pine and eucalyptus trees. Only on high mountains like Chimborazo or Cotopaxi do relatively undisturbed habitats remain. Here a desolate zone of volcanic ash and bare rock marks the upper end of the *páramo*. There is little vegetation beyond, apart from the colonization of lichens, which grow right up to the 5000 m snow line.

Eastern páramo

To the east of the Inter-Andean basins are the high eastern *páramos*, very much like the western ones but wetter. Here **mountain tapirs** are the largest animal, but they survive only in remote regions. **Spectacled bears** are here too, along with **white-tailed deer** and its faithful predator the **mountain lion**. A miniature deer, the **pudu**, also lives here but is rarely seen. **Andean condors**, one of the largest flying birds in the world, can be seen soaring majestically overhead. Condors are scavengers and clean up the larger animals after they die.

Eastern slopes

The eastern slope of the Andes is clothed in cloudforest like the western slope, but this cloudforest is much less seasonal, and has a higher diversity. Many west slope species of plants and birds have east slope sister species; the plate-billed mountain-toucan, for example, is here replaced by the **black-billed mountain-toucan**. The lower elevations have some Amazonian species like **woolly monkey**, and there are a few birds that have no western or Amazonian counterparts, like the strange **white-capped tanager**. Plant diversity is very high here; orchids are especially diverse, even more so than in the west. The eastern cloudforests are much less damaged by man than the western ones, and there are still a few wildernesses that are virtually unknown biologically.

Eastern lowlands

The eastern Amazonian lowland rainforest is the most diverse habitat in Ecuador for birds and mammals, with up to 14 primate species and 550 bird species at a single site. This is as diverse as life gets on this planet. Here is the home of the biggest snake in the world, the semiaquatic **anaconda**, and various species of alligator-like caimans. The birds are very impressive, like the multicoloured **macaws**, the monkey-eating **harpy eagle**, the comical **hoatzin** and the elusive **nocturnal curassow**. Mammals include five species of cats, three anteaters, a couple of sloths, two dolphins and an endless variety of bats – bats that troll for fish, bats that suck nectar, bats that catch sleeping birds by smelling them, bats that eat fruit, bats that catch insects, and even vampire bats that really drink blood. The variety of fish is even greater than the variety of birds and bats, and include piranhas, stingrays, giant catfish and electric eels. There are fewer epiphytes here than in cloudforests, but many more species of trees: 1 ha can have over 300 species of trees! Insect life reflects the diversity of plants; for example, there can be over 700 species of butterflies at a single site, including several species of huge shining **blue morphos**.

National parks

Ecuador has an outstanding array of 50 protected natural areas. National parks and other government reserves cover almost five million hectares of land plus another 14 million hectares of marine reserves. These are distributed throughout the country and include many unique tracts of wilderness. But the term 'protected' may not mean what it does in other parts of the world; native communities, settlements, haciendas, and even oil drilling camps can be found in the heart of some Ecuadorean national parks. Park boundaries are seldom clearly defined, and less often respected. What park facilities exist, along with most park rangers, are concentrated at the access points to a few frequently visited areas. Elsewhere, infrastructure ranges from very basic to nonexistent.

National parks are administered by the **Ministerio del Ambiente** ⓘ *Madrid 1159 y Andalucía, T02-398 7600, www.ambiente.gob.ec*. Entry to all national protected areas is free except for Parque Nacional Galápagos. Some parks can only be visited with authorized guides. For information on specific protected areas, contact park offices in the cities nearest the parks, they have more information than the ministry in Quito. See also http://areasprotegidas.ambiente.gob.ec for descriptions of all parks, how to get to them and contact details.

For further details see the map and table, pages 372 and 374, which list those parks mentioned in the travelling text.

Private reserves

In addition to national parks, there are many private or NGO-run nature reserves throughout Ecuador. Most cater to birdwatchers but are also of interest to hikers or anyone with an interest in nature. In healthy forest where birds abound, chances are that you can also find orchids, frogs, butterflies and many other fascinating plants and animals.

Below, we list some of the best national parks, private reserves, lodges and roads for birding according to their biological region; within each region the sites are listed from north to south. The number of bird species is approximate and usually a lower bound. Both sites and regions are more fully described in the main text.

National parks & reserves

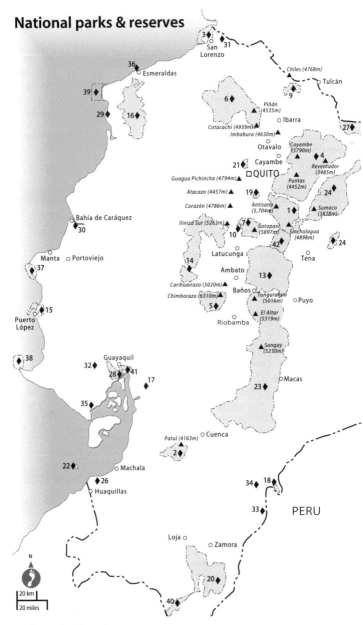

San Lorenzo
Esmeraldas
Chiles (4768m)
Tulcán
Piñán (4535m)
Ibarra
Cotacachi (4939m)
Imbabura (4630m)
Otavalo
Cayambe (5790m)
Cayambe
Reventador (3485m)
QUITO
Guagua Pichincha (4794m)
Puntas (4452m)
Atacazo (4457m)
Antisana (5,704m)
Sumaco (3828m)
Corazón (4786m)
Iliniza Sur (5263m)
Cotopaxi (5897m)
Sincholagua (4898m)
Bahía de Caráquez
Latacunga
Tena
Manta
Portoviejo
Carihuairazo (5020m)
Ambato
Baños
Tungurahua (5016m)
Puyo
Chimborazo (6310m)
El Altar (5319m)
Puerto López
Riobamba
Sangay (5230m)
Guayaquil
Macas
Cuenca
Patul (4163m)
Machala
Huaquillas
PERU
Loja
Zamora

N
20 km
20 miles

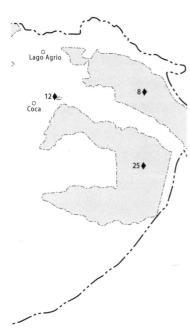

COLOMBIA

Lago Agrio

12◆

Coca

8◆

25◆

Galápagos

Pinta
(Abingdon)

Marchena
(Bindloe)

Santiago
(San Salvador/
James)

Santa Cruz
(Indefatigable)

11◆

San Cristóbal
(Chatham)

Fernandina
(Narborough)

Isabela

Floreana
(Charles,
Santa María)

To Ecuador coast
(1000 km)

N

Not to scale

Birdwatching areas

Western lowlands and lower foothills
Bilsa (400-700 m, 305 species, access from Santo Domingo de los Tsáchilas, see www.jatunsacha.org), a virgin site in Esmeraldas province, contains even the rarest foothill birds (such as banded ground-cuckoo and long-wattled umbrellabird), though access can be an ordeal in the wet season.
Tinalandia (700-900 m, 360 species, temporarily closed 2018, see Tinalandia-Lodge-Ecuador-Suramérica on Facebook), near Alluriquín on the Alóag–Santo Domingo road, is a great introduction to the world of tropical birds. There are lots of colourful species and they are easier to observe here than at most other places, but some of the larger species have been lost from this area.
Río Palenque (200 m, 370 species, access from Santo Domingo de los Tsáchilas, permission to visit must be sought from the Wong Foundation, part of My Favorita fruit company, www.my-favorita.com/responsibility.php) between Santo Domingo and Quevedo is one of the last islands of western lowland forest. It is a very rich birding area although it has lost some species because of its isolation from other forests.
Parque Nacional Machalilla (0-850 m, 115 species, page 235), on the coast near Puerto López, has lightly disturbed dry forest and cloudforest, with many dry-forest specialities. The higher areas are slightly difficult to access.
Ecuasal Ponds (0 m), on the Santa Elena peninsula (page 232), hold a variety of seabirds and shorebirds; famous for their Chilean flamingos and other migratory species.
Cerro Blanco (250-300 m, 190 species, page 213), just outside Guayaquil, is one of the best remaining examples of dry forest. There have on occasion been breeding great green macaws, and even jaguars have been spotted.

BACKGROUND

National parks and reserves

	Map	Name	Created	Size (ha)
Coast	26	Arenillas	2001	17,082
	3	Cayapas-Mataje	1995	51,300
	32	Parque-Lago	2002	2283
	28	Manglares El Salado	2002	5217
	30	Isla Corazón	2002	700
	22	Isla Santa Clara	1999	5
	31	La Chiquita	2002	809
	15	Machalilla	1979	56,184
	16	Mache-Chindul	1996	119,172
	17	Manglares Churute	1979	49,894
	29	Río Muisne	2003	3173
	35	Manglares El Morro	2007	10,030
	36	Estuario Río Esmeraldas	2008	242
	37	Pacoche	2008	13,630
	38	Puntilla Santa Elena	2008	47,455
	39	Galera San Francisco	2008	54,604
	41	Isla Santay	2010	2179
Highlands	1	Antisana	1993	120,000
	2	Cajas	1977	28,808
	5	Chimborazo	1987	58,530
	7	Cotopaxi	1975	33,396
	9	El Angel	1992	15,715
	10	El Boliche	1979	400
	14	Ilinizas	1996	149,900
	19	Pasochoa	1996	500
	21	Pululahua	1966	3383
	40	Yacuri	2009	43,090
Highlands to coast	6	Cotacachi-Cayapas	1968	204,420
Highlands to Oriente	4	Cayambe-Coca	1970	403,103
	13	Llanganates	1996	219,707
	20	Podocarpus	1982	146,280
	23	Sangay	1975	517,765
	42	Colonso Chalupas	2014	93,246
Oriente	27	Cofán Bermeo	2002	55,451
	8	Cuyabeno	1979	603,380
	18	El Cóndor	1999	2440
	12	Limoncocha	1985	4613
	24	Sumaco	1994	205,249
	25	Yasuní	1979	982,000
	33	El Zarza	2006	3643
	34	El Quimi	2006	9071
Galápagos	11	Galápagos	1936	693,700
		Galápagos Marine Reserve	1996	14,110,000

Habitats/features	Access	Page
dry forest, restricted access	Arenillas	372
mangrove	San Lorenzo	256
recreation area	Guayaquil	372
mangrove	Guayaquil	372
mangrove, nesting frigate birds	Bahía de Caráquez	246
island	Puerto Bolívar	372
jungle	San Lorenzo	372
beach, dry forest, Isla de la Plata	Puerto López	235, 373
dry forest	Esmeraldas	254
mangrove, dry forest	Guayaquil	213, 376
mangrove	Muisne	254
mangrove	Guayaquil	231
mangrove	Esmeraldas	255
ocean, seashore	Manta	237
ocean	Salinas	232
ocean	Esmeraldas	254
river estuary, wetland	Guayaquil	213
glacier, *páramo*	Quito	265
páramo	Cuenca	186, 377
glacier, *páramo*, vicuñas	Riobamba	159
glacier, *páramo*	Machachi, Latacunga	130, 377
páramo, frailejones	El Angel	114, 376
planted pine forest, recreation area	Quito	76
glacier, *páramo*	Machachi	130
páramo, cloudforest, recreation area	Quito	130
agricultural, extinct volcanic crater	Quito	85
lakes, cloudforest	Loja	372
páramo to jungle	Cotacachi, Borbón	110
glacier to jungle	Cayambe, Papallacta	83
páramo, cloudforest	Píllaro, Baños	144
páramo to jungle	Loja, Zamora	191, 297
glacier to jungle, active volcanoes	Baños, Riobamba, Macas	160
páramo, cloudforest, rainforest	Tena	372
jungle	Lago Agrio	372
jungle	Lago Agrio	271, 378
jungle, international park	Gualaquiza	372
jungle	Coca	372
jungle to *páramo*	Coca, Baeza, Tena	273
jungle	Coca	272
jungle, river gorge	Zamora	283
jungle	Gualaquiza	372
island	Quito, Guayaquil	294, 344
ocean	Quito, Guayaquil	344

Manglares Churute (50-650 m, 65 species), southeast of Guayaquil, contains a dry-to-moist forest and a mangrove forest. The bird list is short but the area has not been well studied.

Lalo Loor (200-600 m 171 species, access from Pedernales, page 248, see http://ceiba.org) about 20 km southwest of Pedernales, is in the rich and highly endangered transition zone between dry and wet forest in the largely deforested province of Manabí. In addition to birds, it has monkeys and other wildlife.

Puyango (300-400 m, 130 species, access from Loja or Machala, page 190), a pertified forest in the far south, which also has live trees and typical dry forest birds.

Jorupe (500-2000 m, access from Macará, page 193) is a beautiful dry forest reserve with almost all the rare southwestern endemic birds. A lodge is operated here by the **Jocotoco Foundation**, www.fjocotoco.org.

Western Andes

Reserva Ecológica El Angel (2500-4500 m, 160 species, page 114) south of Tulcán, is a spectacular grassland dotted with tall tree-like herbs called *frailejones*.

Intag Cloud Forest Reserve (1800-2800 m), Junín Cloud Forest Reserve (1500-2200 m) and Reserva Alto Chocó are all in the Intag region (page 110), with a full set of cloudforest birds. Access is via Otavalo, page 100.

Los Cedros Reserve (1000-2700 m, page 111), near the Cotacachi-Cayapas Ecological Reserve, has excellent forest over an interesting range of elevations. Populations of many bird species are higher here than in more accessible places.

Yanacocha (3300-4000 m, page 104) is a surprisingly well preserved high-elevation forest on the west side of the Pichincha volcano. Access is from Quito.

Ecoruta (the Nono–Mindo road, 1500-3400 m, page 84) is a famous birding route starting from Quito and passing through a wide variety of forest types. It is somewhat disturbed in its higher sections but quite good in its lower half, where there are several excellent lodges.

Tandayapa Lodge (1700 m, 318 species, page 88) on the Nono–Mindo road is well done, easily accessible and comfortable. Serious birders seeking rarities will benefit from the knowledge-able guides who can show practically any species they are asked to find.

Bellavista (1800-2300 m, page 84) on the Nono–Mindo road is a perfectly situated lodge with colourful easy-to-see birds, and plenty of rarities for hard-core birders.

El Pahuma (1600-2600 m, 139 species, http://ceiba.org) is an easy day trip from Quito (about 1 hr) on the Calicali–La Independencia road. There is a large orchid garden and a visitor centre offering lodging.

Maquipucuna (1200-2800 m, 300 species, page 85) north of the Calacalí–La Independencia road has extensive good forest and cabins for guests.

Mindo (1300-2400 m, 400 species, page 87), has many good lodges. Mindo has repeatedly won the **American Birding Association's** (www.aba.org) Christmas bird count. Even the road into town (easily reached from Quito in 2 hrs) is excellent for good views of beautiful birds like quetzals and tanagers.

Chiriboga road (900-3200 m) from the south of Quito to near Santo Domingo is good for birds in its middle and lower sections, but it can be very muddy; a 4WD vehicle is recommended.

Otonga (800-2300 m, run by Fundación Otonga, http://otonga.org) is a private reserve rising into the mountains south of the Alóag–Santo Domingo road. The birdlife here is known for not being shy, especially the dark-backed wood-quails.

Chilla, Guanazán, Manú and Selva Alegre (2800-3000 m, access from Saraguro, page 190), on the road from Saraguro to the coast, have remnant forests and good birds.
Buenaventura (800-1000 m, 310 species, page 223) 24 km north of the road from Loja to the coast is a **Jocotoco Foundation** bird reserve, particularly important because there are few remaining tracts in the area. Piñas has many rare birds.
Guachanamá Ridge (2000-2800 m, access from Alamor) between Celica and Alamor in extreme southwest Ecuador contains many rare southwestern endemic birds.
Sozoranga–Nueva Fátima road (1300-2600 m, 190 species, access from Sozoranga, page 193) near the Peruvian border in Loja has remnants of a wide variety of mid-elevation forests, and has many southwest endemics.

Inter-Andean forests and páramos
Guandera Reserve (3100-3800 m, page 115), near the Colombian border, has beautiful temperate forest with Espeletia *páramo* and many rare birds.
Pasochoa (2700-4200 m, about 120 species, page 130) provides a very easy cloudforest to visit just south of Quito, with lots of birds.
Parque Nacional Cotopaxi (3700-6000 m, 90 species, page 130), 1½ hrs south of Quito, is a spectacular setting in which to find birds of the high arid *páramo*. There is also a birdy lake and marsh, Limpiopungo.
Parque Nacional Cajas (3000-4500 m, 125 species, page 186) has extensive *páramo* and high-elevation forest, accessible from Cuenca. Birds include condor and the violet-throated metaltail, an endemic hummingbird.

Eastern Andes
Papallacta (3000-4400 m, page 82), 1½ hrs east of Quito, has a dramatic cold wet landscape of grassland and high elevation forest. Condors are regular here, along with many other highland birds.

Guango (2700 m, 95 species, www.guango lodge.com) is a lodge with good birding in temperate forest below Papallacta.
Baeza (1900-2400 m, page 265), about 2 hrs east of Quito, has forest remnants near town which can be surprisingly birdy. The road to the antenna above town is especially rich.
San Isidro (2000 m, 260 species, page 275), 30 mins from Baeza just off the Baeza–Tena road, is a comfortable lodge with bird-rich forests all around, and wonderful hospitality.
San Rafael Falls (1400 m, 200 species, page 265) on the Baeza–Lago Agrio road is a good place to see cock-of-the-rocks and other subtropical birds. Access is an easy walk. A massive hydroelectic project has been built here.
Guacamayos Ridge (1700-2300 m, access from Baeza, page 265) on the Baeza–Tena road has excellent roadside forest rich in birdlife.
Wildsumaco Lodge (1300-1600 m, 432 species, page 273) off the road from Tena to Coca via Loreto, and near Parque Nacional Sumaco. A very comfortable lodge with nice trails. Birds include coppery-chested jacamar and military macaws as well as various other rare species.
Baños–Puyo corridor (900-5000 m) offers an interesting mix of Amazonian and highland birds. The San Antonio area (2400-3300 m) above the Río Ulba is the most accessible place to see high cloudforest birds. Machay (1700-2200 m) is the most accessible good mid-elevation cloudforest, and the Topo–Zuñac area (1300-1600 m) is the most accessible good forest for foothill birds.
Gualaceo–Limón road (1400-3350 m, 200-300 species, page 186) northeast of Cuenca has perhaps the best roadside birding on the east slope, in a spectacular natural setting.
Parque Nacional Podocarpus (950-3700 m, 800 species, page 191), near Loja, is one of the most diverse protected areas in the world. There are several easy access points

at different elevations. The park is very rich in birds, including many rarities.

Loja–Zamora road (1000-2850 m, 375 species, page 284), segments of the old road (parallel to the current one) are good for birds.

Tapichalaca Reserve (1800-3100 m, page 198) south of Loja between Yangana and Valladolid protects the cloudforest home of the Jocotoco Antpitta. A fine lodge has been built here by the **Jocotoco Foundation**.

***

Oriente jungle

Reserva Faunística Cuyabeno (200-300 m, 400 species, page 271) in the northern Oriente has seasonally flooded forests not found elsewhere and lots of wildlife.

Lower Río Napo lodges (200-300 m, 550 species, page 277) in the north and central Oriente provide a wide spectrum of facilities and prices, in forest ranging from moderately disturbed to absolutely pristine. Some of these lodges are among the most bird-rich single-elevation sites in the world.

Upper Río Napo lodges (300-600 m, page 286) in west-central Oriente are much easier and cheaper to reach than other sites, and the lodges are especially comfortable. The forest in this area is somewhat disturbed, however, so larger birds and mammals are scarce or absent. **Gareno Lodge**, further from Tena but still accessible by vehicle, has virgin forest and a full set of wildlife including occasional nesting harpy eagles (www.garenolodge-huao.com).

Kapawi Lodge (200-300 m, page 287) in the southern Oriente has a slightly different set of birds than the other areas, and a different cultural environment.

***

Galápagos

See the Galápagos chapter, page 294.

Hot springs

Ecuador is located on the 'Ring of Fire' and has many volcanoes: active, dormant and non-active (dead). Hot springs are associated with all three, although they are mostly found near the older volcanoes where sufficient time has elapsed since the last eruption for water systems to become established. Below is a selection of Ecuador's best thermal springs. Some are inside protected natural areas, others are in towns or part of private hotels and spas.

Aguas Hediondas About 1½ hrs west of Tulcán (page 115). A complex of indoor and outdoor pools fed by a boiling river. The name comes from the sulphurous fumes emitted by the water.

Baños (Tungurahua) The hot springs of Baños in the province of Tungurahua are the best known in Ecuador. There are several separate bathing complexes here, and the town of Baños is overflowing with accommodation, restaurants and activities. See page 148.

Baños (Cuenca) This is another Baños, near the city of Cuenca, which has the hottest commercial springs in the country. It is only 10 mins by bus from the city centre. See page 185.

Baños de San Vicente These springs are not far from Salinas on the coast. They are not all that attractive but they are famed for the curative properties of the warm mud lake which people slide into before baking themselves dry. See page 232.

Chachimbiro A thermal area with several places to stay and an upmarket resort/spa. Access is from Ibarra. See page 113.

Nangulví These small and simple baths are reached from Otavalo. See page 111.

Oyacachi There are 4 simple but clean hot pools. Also several small places to stay, or you can camp at the springs. See page 99.

Papallacta These are the best-developed hot springs in the country, and can be visited on a day trip from Quito. You can also stay overnight at the luxury hotel and spa on the site, or at one of several more economical places nearby. See page 82.

Books

See also Literature, page 361.

Birdwatching

Canaday, C and Jost, L *Common Birds of Amazonian Ecuador* (Ediciones Libri Mundi, Quito, 1997).

Hilty, S and Hoppe Wolf, M *Birds of Tropical America* (University of Texas Press, 2005).

Hilty, S and Brown, W *A Guide to the Birds of Colombia* (Princeton University Press, USA, 1986).

Moore, J *CDs of Ecuadorean birdsongs.* Available at **Libri Mundi** in Quito.

Restall, R and Freile, J *Birds of Ecuador* (Christopher Helm, 2018).

Ridgely, R and Greenfield, P *The birds of Ecuador* (Cornell University Press, Ithaca, NY, USA, 2001).

Williams, R, Best, B and Heijnen, T *A Guide to Birdwatching in Ecuador and the Galápagos* (Biosphere Publications, UK, 1996).

Climbing

Brain, Y *Ecuador: A Climbing Guide* (The Mountaineers, Seattle, 2000).

Cruz, M *Montañas del Ecuador* (Dinediciones, Quito, 2000) and *Die Schneeberge Ecuador.*

Schmudlach, G *Bergfürer Ecuador* (Panico Alpinverlag, 2nd ed, 2009).

Trekking

Kunstaetter, R and D *Trekking in Ecuador* (The Mountaineers, Seattle, 2002, www.trekkinginecuador.com).

Rachoweicki, R and Thurber, M *Ecuador: Climbing and Hiking Guide* (Viva Travel Guides, 2009).

Galápagos Islands

General

Angermeyer, J *My Father's Island* (Pelican Press, 2007).

Darwin, C *Voyage of the Beagle* (1839; many modern editions).

Latorre, O *The Curse of Giant Tortoise* (National Cultural Fund, 1997).

Melville, H *The Encantadas* (1854; in The Encantadas and Other Stories, Dover Publications, 2005).

Treherne, J *The Galápagos Affair* (Pimlico, 2002).

Weiner, J *The Beak of the Finch* (Vintage, 1995).

Wittmer, M *Floreana* (Moyer Bell, 2013).

Field guides

Castro, I and Phillips, A *A Guide to the Birds of the Galápagos Islands* (Princeton University Press, 1996).

Constant, P *Galápagos: A Natural History Guide* (Odyssey, 7th ed, 2007), and *Marine Life of the Galapagos* (Airphoto International, 2008).

Horwell, D and Oxford, P *Galápagos Wildlife* (Bradt, 2011)

Hickman, J *The Enchanted Isles* (Eland Books, 2009).

Hickman, P and Zimmerman, T *Galapagos Marine Life Series* (Sugar Spring Press, 2000).

Humann, P and DeLoach, N *Reef Fish Identification* (New World Publications, 2003).

Jackson, MH *H, Galápagos: A Natural History Guide* (University of Calgary Press, 2016).

McMullen, C *Flowering Plants of the Galápagos* (Comstock Publishing, 1999).

Merlen, G *A Field Guide to the Fishes of Galápagos* (Libri Mundi, 1988).

Schofield, E *Plants of the Galápagos Islands* (Universe Books, New York, 1984).

Coffee-table books

De Roy, T *Galapagos: Islands Born of Fire* (Princeton University Press, 2010). There are a great many others.

Oriente jungle

Barrett, PM *Law of the Jungle* (Broadway Books, 2014; see also Goldhaber, MD *Crude Awakening*, ebook 2014; both on the legal case concerning Chevron in the Ecuadorean rainforest).

Kane, J *Savages* (Vintage Books, New York, 1996).

Kimerling, J *Amazon Crude* (Natural Resource Defense Council, 1991; Spanish translation, Abya-Yala, 2006).

Perkins, J *Confessions of an Economic Hit Man* (Ebury, 2006; plus *The New Confessions of an Economic Hit Man*, Ebury, 2016, and *The Secret History of the American Empire*, Plume, 2008).

Smith, A *The Lost Lady of the Amazon* (Constable, UK, 2003).

Smith, R *Crisis Under the Canopy* (Abya-Yala, Quito, 1993).

Whitaker, R *The Mapmaker's Wife* (Basic Books, New York, 2004).

Practicalities

Getting there

Air

International flights into Ecuador arrive either at **Quito** (UIO) or **Guayaquil** (GYE); there are frequent domestic flights between the two, as well as ample bus services. International airfares from North America and Europe to Ecuador may vary with low and high season. High season is generally July to September and December. International flights to Ecuador from other South or Central American countries, however, usually have one price year-round. See also Tour operators, page 399.

From Europe
KLM, Air Europa, Iberia and **LATAM** offer direct flights from Europe to Ecuador, the former originating in Amsterdam, the other three in Madrid. Connections on several other carriers can be made in Bogotá. US carriers offer connections from Europe through their respective North American hubs, see below.

From North America
Miami's busy international airport is the most important air transport gateway linking Ecuador with North America. **American** has two daily non-stop flights from Miami to both Quito and Guayaquil. American also flies to Quito from Dallas/Fort Worth. **LATAM** flies daily from Miami to Quito and from New York City (JFK) to Guayaquil. **United** flies daily from Houston to Quito, and **Delta** flies daily from Atlanta to Quito. **Jetblue Airways** flies between Fort Lauderdale and Quito, while Ecuadorean carrier **TAME** has flights from Quito and Guayaquil to Fort Lauderdale and New York.

From Australia and New Zealand
There are three options: 1) To Los Angeles, USA, with **Qantas, Air New Zealand** or **United**, continuing to Ecuador via Houston or Miami (see above); 2) From Auckland to Santiago, Chile, continuing to Ecuador, all with **LATAM**; 3) To Buenos Aires, Argentina, from Sydney with **Aerolíneas Argentinas**, continuing to Ecuador with various South American carriers. These are all expensive long-haul routes. Round-the-World and Circle Pacific fares may be convenient alternatives.

From Latin America
There are flights to Quito and/or Guayaquil from Bogotá, Buenos Aires, Cali, Caracas, Lima, Mexico City, Panama City, San Salvador and Santiago. Connections can easily be made from other South American cities. **Copa** and **Avianca** offer connections between Ecuador and various destinations in Central America, Mexico and the Caribbean.

TRAVEL TIP

Packing for Ecuador

Everybody has their own list, below are a few things which are particularly useful for travelling in Ecuador. Try to think light and compact. All but the most specialized products are available in Quito and Guayaquil, while most basic commodities are readily purchased throughout the country.

A **moneybelt** or **pouch** is absolutely indispensable. Be sure to bring an adequate supply of any **medications** you take on a regular basis, plus two weeks' spare supply, as these may not be available in Ecuador. Sturdy comfortable **footwear** is a must for travels anywhere. **Sun protection** is very important in all regions of the country and for visitors of all complexions. This should include a sun hat, sunglasses and sunscreen for both skin and lips. Take **insect repellent** if you plan to visit the coast or jungle. Also recommended are **flip-flops** for use on the beach, at hot springs and in hotel showers. If you use **contact lenses**, be sure also to bring a pair of glasses. A small lightweight **towel** is an asset, as is a short length of **clothesline**. A compact **torch** (flashlight), **alarm**, **watch** and **pocket knife** may all be useful. Always carry some **toilet paper**, as this is seldom found in public washrooms unless it is sold at the entrance.

A good general principle is to take half the clothes and twice the money you think you will need. You should pack spring **clothing** for the highlands (mornings and evenings are cool), but on the coast tropical or lightweight clothes are needed. In general, clothing is less formal in the lowlands, both on the coast and in Oriente, where men and women wear shorts. In the highlands, people are more conservative; wearing shorts is acceptable for sports and on hiking trails, but long trousers or skirts are needed for churches or cemeteries. Nude bathing is generally unacceptable in Ecuador, so a swimsuit is essential.

Road and river

There are roads and international bus services to Ecuador from neighbouring Colombia and Peru as well as South American countries further afield, but no vehicle road connecting with Central America. The most advisable border crossings are at Tulcán in the north and Macará in the south.

Peru For land borders with Peru, see pages 192, 198 and 223; for river travel to and from Peru, see Coca, page 274. For details of immigration procedures at these borders, see under the relevant sections of respective towns.

Except for the Ecuadorean bus companies with routes from Guayaquil, Cuenca and Loja to cities in northern Peru, it is usually much cheaper to buy bus tickets only as far as the nearest border town, cross on foot or by taxi, and then purchase tickets locally in the country you have just entered. If entering Ecuador by car, customs procedures are given on page 387.

Getting around

Air

Ecuador is a small country and flying times are typically under one hour to all destinations, with the exception of Galápagos. Most flights originate in Quito but Guayaquil also has direct service to Coca, Cuenca, Loja and Galápagos, and there are frequent flights between the Guayaquil and Quito. Domestic airfares (except to Galápagos) are generally less than US$120 one way. Foreigners pay more than Ecuadoreans for flights to Galápagos. Seats are not assigned on domestic flights.

TAME is the most established Ecuadorean carrier and several other airlines also operate domestic routes, see below for details. The routes covered by domestic carries and their itineraries change frequently. For Galápagos flight details see page 342.

Domestic airlines

Avianca, T1-800-003434 or Quito T02-294 3100, www.avianca.com. Serving Quito, Guayaquil, Coca, Manta and Galápagos and international routes to Bogotá and Lima.
LATAM, T1-800-000527, www.latam.com. Quito, Guayaquil, Cuenca and Galápagos and international routes including Miami, New York, Madrid, Lima and Santiago.

TAME, T1-700-500800 or Quito T02-396 6300, www.tame.com.ec. Quito, Guayaquil, Cuenca, Loja, Coca, Lago Agrio, Salinas, Santa Rosa (for Machala), Esmeraldas, Manta and Galápagos and international routes to Bogotá, Cali, Caracas, Lima, New York and Fort Lauderdale.

Rail

A series of mostly short tourist rides (some combining train and bus travel) have replaced regular passenger service along the spectacular Ecuadorean railway system, extensively restored in recent years. Some trains have two classes of service, standard and plus; carriages are fancier in the latter and a snack is included. On some routes, an *autoferro* (a motorized railcar) runs instead of the train. The following routes are on offer: **Alausí to Sibambe** via the Devil's Nose; **Quito to Machachi** and **El Boliche** (Cotopaxi); **Ambato to El Boliche**; **Ambato to Urbina**; **Riobamba to Urbina**; **Otavalo** and **Ibarra to Salinas**; **Durán** (outside Guayaquil) **to Bucay**; and the **Tren Crucero**, an upmarket all-inclusive tour of up to four days along the entire line from Quito to Durán. Details are given under What to do, in the corresponding city listings. Further details area avialable from **Empresa de Ferrocarriles Ecuatorianos** ⓘ *T1-800-873637, www.trenecuador.com.*

River

Few of Ecuador's jungle rivers are navigable by very large craft but a couple of tourist vessels operate on the lower Río Napo out of Coca (see page 279). Large motorized canoes provide local services downstream from Coca to the Peruvian border at Nuevo Rocafuerte and riverside towns en route.

Road

An excellent network of paved roads runs throughout most of the country. Maintenance of major highways is franchised to private firms, who charge tolls of around US$1-1.15. Roads are subject to damage during heavy rainy seasons. Always check road conditions before setting out and always ask directions from local people when on the road: signposting is lamentable. Driving is safer during the daytime, especially on mountain roads, and it is best to stay off the road altogether at the beginning and end of busy national holidays. It is a sad fact that better roads have meant higher speeds and more serious accidents. Bus and truck drivers, in particular, are known for their speed and recklessness. On some main highways, eg north to the Colombian border, the camber has been set wrong so take care when driving at speed.

Highlands to the coast Several important roads, almost all paved, link the highlands and the Pacific coast. These include from north to south: Ibarra to San Lorenzo; Quito to Esmeraldas via Calacalí and La Independencia; Quito to Guayaquil via Alóag and Santo Domingo de los Tsáchilas (the busiest highway in Ecuador); Latacunga to Quevedo via La Maná; Ambato to Babahoyo via Guaranda; Riobamba to Guayaquil via Pallatanga and Bucay; Cuenca to Guayaquil via Zhud and La Troncal; Cuenca to Guayaquil via Molleturo; Cuenca to Machala via Girón and Pasaje; Loja to Machala or Huaquillas.

Coastal roads Santo Domingo de los Tsáchilas is the hub of most roads on the coast of Ecuador. From Guayaquil, the coastal route south to Peru is a major artery, with four lanes from Machala to the border. From Guayaquil north, there are coastal roads all the way to Mataje on the Colombian frontier.

East of the Andes On the eastern side of the Andes, roads from Quito, via Baeza, to Lago Agrio and Coca, Baños to Puyo, and Loja to Zamora are fully paved, as is the entire lowland road from Lago Agrio south to Zamora. Other access roads to Oriente (many are paved or in the process of being paved) include: Tulcán to Lago Agrio via Lumbaqui, Riobamba to Macas, and three different roads from Cuenca to Macas and Gualaquiza. Some roads are narrow and tortuous and subject to landslides in the rainy season, but all have regular bus service and all can be travelled in a 4WD or in an ordinary car with good ground clearance.

Buses, vans and shared taxis

Most destinations in Ecuador have frequent bus service and bus travel is generally convenient except for the location of bus terminals in Quito and some other cities very far from the centre. Many itineraries are listed on **http://andestransit.com** and **www.multipasajes.com**, where tickets for some major routes can be purchased online (for a fee). The fares given in the text are approximate; confirm locally for exact amounts.

Vans and shared taxis operate between major cities and offer a faster, more comfortable and more expensive alternative to buses. Some provide pick-up and drop-off at your hotel.

Bus travel in Ecuador can be a great way to get to know the country and its people. Buses go almost everywhere and if you travel in the day, you will be rewarded with great views. In fact, travelling by day is the best policy for safety reasons as well. As noted elsewhere, there tend to be more traffic accidents at night and there is a risk of hold-ups (some bus lines try to protect against this on their longer routes by not stopping to pick

TRAVEL TIP

Driving in Ecuador

Bringing a vehicle to Ecuador To bring a foreign car or motorcycle into the country, its original registration document (title) in the name of the driver is required. If the driver is not the owner, a notarized letter of authorization is required. All documents must be accompanied by a Spanish translation. A 90-day permit is granted on arrival, extensions are only granted if the vehicle is in the garage for repairs. No security deposit is required and you can enter and leave at different land borders. Procedures are generally straightforward but it can be a matter of luck. Shipping a vehicle requires more paperwork and hiring a customs broker. The port of Guayaquil is prone to theft and particularly officious. Manta and Esmeraldas are smaller and more relaxed, but receive fewer ships. A valid driver's licence from your home country is generally sufficient to drive in Ecuador and rent a car, but an international licence is helpful.

Car hire To rent a car you must be at least 21 and have an international credit card. Surcharges apply to drivers aged 21-25. You will be asked to sign two blank credit card vouchers, one for the rental fee and the other as a security deposit for the vehicle, and authorization for a charge of as much as US$5000 may be requested against your credit card account if you do not purchase full insurance. The uncashed vouchers will be returned to you when you return the vehicle. Make sure the car is parked securely at night. A small car suitable for city driving costs around US$350 per week including unlimited mileage, tax and basic insurance. A 4WD or pick-up truck (recommended for unpaved roads) costs about US$850 a week. Drop-off charges are about US$125.

Fuel There are two grades of petrol, 'Extra' (87 octane, US$1.48 per US gallon) and 'Super' (92 Octane, US$2.26-2.33). Both are unleaded. Extra is being replaced by Ecopaís (same octane, same price), a mixture of 95% gasoline, 5% bio-ethanol. It is available everywhere, but Super may not be available in more remote areas. Diesel fuel (US$1.04) is notoriously dirty and available everywhere.

---

up passengers between towns or by photographing passengers when they first board the bus). Salesmen and women will invariably join the bus to persuade you to buy food and drinks and to lecture the passengers on the benefits of some elixir or other. Take your own snacks and water, but if tempted to buy food and drinks on the road keep an eye out for hygiene and make sure you have small change on hand. Bus drivers usually know the best places for meal stops and some roadside *comedores* can be quite good. Politely refuse any food, drink, sweets or cigarettes offered by strangers on a bus. These may be drugged as a way of robbing you. Some buses have a toilet on board, but avoid the very back seats if you can, as you will be right next to it. Luggage can be checked with the larger bus companies and will be stowed in a locked compartment. On smaller buses it usually rides on the roof, in which case you should make sure it is covered with a tarpaulin to protect against dust and rain. In all cases it is your own responsibility to keep an eye on your gear; never leave it unattended at bus stations. Moreover, never leave items unattended in the cabin either. If you want to hold your seat at a stop, leave a newspaper or other insignificant item on it, not your bag. Keep your daypack on your lap as the overhead rack, or under your seat are not secure places.

Cycling

Given ample time and reasonable energy, a bicycle is one of the best modes of transport for exploring Ecuador. It can be ridden, carried by almost every form of transport from an aeroplane to a jungle canoe, and can even be lifted across one's shoulders over short distances. Also see Mountain biking, page 23.

Tips Strong and waterproof front and back panniers are a must. When packed these are likely to be heavy and should be carried on the strongest racks available. Everything should be packed in plastic bags for protection against dust and rain. Take care to avoid dehydration; drink regularly. In hot, dry areas with limited water, be sure to carry an ample supply.

Security When sightseeing, try to leave your bicycle with someone such as a café owner or shopkeeper. Always see that your bicycle is secure (most hotels will allow bikes to be kept in rooms). A good bike lock is essential equipment. Visit www.warmshowers. org for a hospitality exchange for touring cyclists.

Dogs Dogs are ubiquitous in Ecuadorean towns and the countryside; they love to chase bikes (just as they love to chase anything with wheels) and you may have to fend them off to avoid being bitten.

Traffic Main roads and highways are a nightmare; it is far more rewarding to keep to the smaller country roads. When riding in big cities, Ecuadorean cyclists recommend behaving like a car and occupying the entire lane; this is safer and drivers usually respect you. Quito and Cuenca have bike lanes on some streets. Make yourself conspicuous by wearing bright clothing and always use a helmet. A rearview mirror is indispensable.

Repairs Most towns have a bicycle shop of some description, but it is best to do your own repairs and adjustments whenever possible. Big city bike shops may also have boxes/cartons in which to send bicycles home.

Transporting a bike Check with airlines about their policy regarding bicycles before purchasing tickets. Most Ecuadorean bus lines will carry bicycles on the roof racks for little or no extra charge. It is advisable to supervise the loading and assure that the derailleur is not jammed up against luggage which might damage it. If you can, take some cardboard to protect the bike while it's on the bus. If you take a long bus journey with major altitude changes let a little air out of the tyres especially when going from lower to higher altitudes.

Hitchhiking

Public transport in Ecuador is so abundant that there is seldom any need to hitchhike along the major highways. On small out-of-the-way country roads however, the situation can be quite different, and giving passers-by a ride is common practice and safe. A small fee is usually charged, check in advance. For obvious reasons women should not hitch alone. Besides, you are more likely to get a lift if you are with a partner, be they male or female.

Taxis

In major cities, all taxis must in principle use meters. At especially busy times or at night drivers may nonetheless refuse to so, in which case you should always agree on the fare before you get in. **Cabify** and **Easy Taxi** operate in big cities. **Uber** entered the market in a small way in 2017.

Maps and city guides

Instituto Geográfico Militar (IGM) ⓘ *Senierges y Telmo Paz y Miño, east of Parque El Ejido, Quito, T02-397 5100, www.geoportaligm.gob.ec, Mon-Fri 0730-1630, take ID.* Country and topographic maps are available in a variety of printed and digital formats. Prices range from US$3 to US$7. Maps of border and sensitive areas are 'reservado' (classified) and not available for sale without a permit. It's best to buy all your maps here as they are rarely available outside Quito.

Essentials A-Z

Accident and emergency

For all emergencies nationwide, T911.
Policía Nacional, T101.

Children

Travel with children can bring you into
closer contact with Ecuadorean families
and, generally, presents no special
problems – in fact the path may even be
smoother for family groups. Officials are
sometimes more amenable where children
are concerned and they are pleased if your
child knows a little Spanish.

Bus travel Remember that a lot of time
can be spent waiting for and riding buses.
You should take on-screen entertainment
with you, or reading material as it is difficult
to find and expensive. Also look for the
locally available comic strip *Condorito*, which
is quite popular and a good way for older
children to learn a bit of Spanish. Reading
or looking at a screen on the bus itself,
especially on winding mountain roads,
may not be a good idea because of the risk
of travel sickness. On long-distance buses
you pay for each seat, and there are no
half fares. For shorter trips it is cheaper, if
less comfortable, to seat small children on
your knee. Sometimes there are spare seats
which children can occupy after tickets have
been collected. Make sure that children
accompanying you are fully covered by
your travel insurance policy.

Food This can be a problem if the children
are not adaptable. It is easier to take food
with you on longer journeys than to rely on
meal stops where the food may not be to
taste. Avocados are safe, readily available,
easy to eat and nutritious; they can be fed
to babies as young as 6 months and most
older children like them. Best stick to simple
things like bread, bananas and tangerines
while you are actually on the road. Biscuits,
packaged convenience food and bottled
drinks abound. In restaurants, you can try to
buy a *media porción* (half portion), or divide
a full-sized helping between 2 children.

Customs and duty free

On arrival

Customs inspection is carried out at airports
after you clear immigration. When travelling
by land, customs authorities may also set up
checkpoints along the country's highways.
Tourists seldom encounter any difficulties but
if you are planning to bring any particularly
unusual or valuable items to Ecuador then
you should enquire beforehand with an
Ecuadorean diplomatic representative
(see Embassies and consulates, page 391)
and obtain any necessary permits, or be
prepared to pay the prevailing customs
duties. Reasonable amounts of climbing
gear, personal photo/video equipment and
one laptop are generally not a problem. For
details on bringing a vehicle into Ecuador,
see box, page 387.

Shipping goods to Ecuador

Except for documents, customs duties must
be paid on all goods shipped to Ecuador.
Enforcement is strict, duties are high and
procedures are very slow and complicated.
You are therefore advised to bring anything
you think you will need with you when you
travel, rather than having it sent to you once
you are in the country.

On departure

Your airline baggage will be inspected by
security personnel and sniffed by dogs

looking for drugs. Never transport anything you have not packed yourself, you will be held responsible for the contents.

No export duties are charged on souvenirs you take home from Ecuador, but there are various items for which you require special permits. These include specimens of wild plants and animals, original archaeological artefacts, certain works of art and any objects considered part of the country's national heritage. When in doubt, enquire well in advance.

Disabled travellers

Disabled Ecuadoreans have finally been receiving a little more attention since Lenin Moreno, who is paraplegic, served as vice-president (2007-2013) and became president in 2017. As with most Latin American countries however, facilities for the disabled traveller are still sadly lacking. Wheelchair ramps are a rare luxury in most of the country, but they are present in the resort town of **Baños**, see page 148. Getting a wheelchair into a bathroom or toilet is well nigh impossible, except for some of the more upmarket hotels. Quito's trolley system has wheelchair access in principle, but it is much too crowded to make this practical. Disabled Ecuadoreans obviously have to cope with these problems and mainly rely on the help of others to move around; fortunately most bystanders are very helpful.

Some travel companies specialize in exciting holidays, tailor-made for individuals with a variety of disabilities (**Ecuador for All**, www.ecuadorforall.com, is a tour operator catering to travellers with special needs).

Electricity

110 v AC, 60 cycles, US-type flat-pin plugs.

Embassies and consulates

For all Ecuadorean embassies and consulates abroad and for all foreign embassies and consulates in Ecuador, see http://embassy.goabroad.com and http://cancilleria.gob.ec.

Health

Health care in Ecuador is varied: there are some excellent clinics and hospitals, which usually follow the North American style of medicine (where you are referred straight to a specialist), but as with all medical care, first impressions count. If a facility looks grubby, then be wary of the general standard of medicine and hygiene. The best medical facilities and physicians who speak languages other than Spanish are located in Quito, Guayaquil and Cuenca, and are generally expensive. Your embassy or consulate can usually make recommendations.

Medical services

The following hospitals and clinics are recommended.

Cuenca

Hospital Monte Sinaí, Miguel Cordero 6-111 y Av Solano, near the stadium, T07-288 5595, www.hospitalmontesinai.org, several English-speaking physicians. **Hospital Santa Inés**, Av Toral 2-113, T07-282 7888, Facebook: sisantaines. Dr Jaime Moreno Aguilar speaks English.

Galápagos Islands

Puerto Ayora Hospital, Av Baltra, Puerto Ayora. Hospital, Roldós y Flores, Puerto Baquerizo Moreno.

Guayaquil Kennedy hospital group has 3 facilities: Av del Periodista, Av 11 NO, Barrio Kennedy; C Crotos, off Av Rodolfo Baquerizo Nazur, Barrio Alborada; and in Samborondón, T1-800-536 6339, www.hospikennedy.med.ec. Reliable, with many specialists and a very competent emergency department. **Clínica Alcívar**, Coronel 2301 y Azuay, T04-372 0100, www.hospitalalcivar. com, and **Clínica Guayaquil**, Padre Aguirre 401 y General Córdova, T04-256 3555, www. clinicaguayaquil.com (Dr Roberto Gilbert speaks English and German) are also reliable.

Ibarra
Instituto Médico de Especialidades, Egas 1-83 y Av Teodoro Gómez de La Torre, T06-295 5612, www.ime.amawebs.com.

Latacunga
Clínica Latacunga, Sánchez de Orellana 11-79 y Marqués de Maenza, T03-281 0260, Facebook: ClinicaLatacunga. Open 24 hrs.

Loja
Clínica San Agustín, 18 de Noviembre 10-72 y Azuay, T07-257 3002, www. hospitalclinicasanagustin.com.

Quito
For hospitals, doctors and dentists, contact your consulate or the tourist office for advice. **Clínica Pichincha**, Veintimilla E3-30 y Páez, T02-256 2296, emergencies 02-299 8777, http://hcp.com.ec/website/. Very good, but expensive. **Metropolitano**, Mariana de Jesús y N Arteta, T02-399 8000, http://hospitalmetropolitano.org. Very professional and recommended, but expensive. **Voz Andes**, Villalengua Oe 2-37 y Av 10 de Agosto, T02-397 1000 or 1-700-700700, www.hospitalvozandes.org. Quick and efficient, fee based on ability to pay, a good place to get vaccines.

Before you go
See your GP/practice nurse or travel clinic at least 6 weeks before your departure for general advice on travel risks, malaria prevention and recommended vaccinations. Make sure you have travel insurance, get a dental check (especially if you are going to be away for more than a month), know your own blood group and if you suffer a long-term condition such as diabetes or epilepsy make sure someone knows or that you have a **Medic Alert** (www.medicalert.org.uk) bracelet/necklace with this information on it.

Vaccinations
Vaccinations for yellow fever and rabies (if travelling to jungle and/or remote areas), as well as hepatitis B are commonly recommended for Ecuador. The final decision, however, should be based on a consultation with your GP or travel clinic. You should also confirm your primary courses and boosters are up to date (diphtheria, tetanus, poliomyelitis, hepatitis A, typhoid). A yellow fever certificate is required by visitors over one year old who are entering from an infected area. **Malaria** precautions are important for the Oriente jungle and far northern Pacific coast (below 1500 m) all year round, see below. Specialist advice should be taken on the best anti-malarial to use.

Health risks
Altitude sickness is a common but usually mild affliction for most visitors to Ecuador. Flying into Quito (2840 m) from sea level is likely to leave you feeling a bit lightheaded for the first few days, so give yourself a chance to acclimatize before heading off on trips and treks. Smokers and those with underlying heart or lung disease are often hardest hit. Take it easy for a few days, rest from your trip and drink plenty of water; you will feel better soon. It is essential to get acclimatized before undertaking long treks or arduous activities. No one should attempt to climb over 5000 m until they have spent at least a week at the height of Quito and then a couple of nights around 4000 m. Agencies who offer 2-day climbs without adequate acclimatization are not to be trusted.

Because you are so close to the equator, **sun protection** is a must throughout

Ecuador, especially on the beach and in the highlands regardless of how cool it may feel; always use sun block and a hat. All travellers, especially mountaineers, should use sunglasses that provide 100% UV protection.

The major health risks in lower parts of the country are those **diseases carried by insects** such as mosquitoes and sandflies. These include malaria, dengue fever, chikungunya, and less frequently Chagas disease and leishmaniasis. Cases of zika virus, similarly spread, have also been reported. Because insects bite at different times of day, repellent application and covered limbs are a 24-hr issue. Long trousers, a long-sleeved shirt and insect repellent all offer protection. Mosquito nets dipped in permethrin provide a good physical and chemical barrier at night.

A bout of **stomach upset** is almost inevitable on a longer visit to Ecuador. Consider it part of the travel experience and don't get scared or overreact. The standard advice to avoid diarrhoea is to be careful with water and ice for drinking. If you have any doubts and bottled water is unavailable, then boil it, filter it or treat it. There are many filter/treatment devices available on the market. Food can also transmit disease. Be wary of salads, undercooked meat, reheated foods or food that has been left out in the sun having been previously cooked. There is a simple adage that says wash it, peel it, boil it or forget it. The key treatment with all diarrhoea is rehydration. Try to keep hydrated by taking the right mixture of salt and water. This is available in Ecuadorean pharmacies as an oral rehydration solution (*suero oral*) or can be made up by adding a teaspoon of sugar and a half teaspoon of salt to a litre of clean water. If diarrhoea persists for several days or you develop additional symptoms, then see a physician.

Road accidents are an often overlooked threat to travellers' health.

You can reduce the likelihood of accidents by not travelling at night, avoiding overcrowded buses, not drinking and driving, wearing a seatbelt in cars and a helmet on bicycles and motorbikes (even if some Ecuadoreans do not).

If you go **diving** make sure that you are fit do so. The **British Sub-Aqua Club** (**BSAC**), www.bsac.com, can put you in touch with doctors who do medical examinations. Protect your feet and keep an eye out for secondary infection. Check that the dive company has appropriate certification from **BSAC** or **PADI**, www.padi.com, and that the equipment is well maintained. In case of emergency, there is a hyperbaric chamber in Puerto Ayora. Make sure you allow plenty of time after diving before taking a flight (see box, page 340).

(see box, page 340).

Useful websites

www.cdc.gov Centres for Disease Control and Prevention (USA).

www.nhs.uk/nhsengland/ Healthcareabroad/pages/ Healthcareabroad.aspx Department of Health advice for travellers.

www.fitfortravel.scot.nhs.uk Fit for Travel (UK), a site from Scotland providing a quick A-Z of vaccine and travel health advice requirements for each country.

www.itg.be Institute for Tropical Medicine, Antwerp.

http://nathnac.net National Travel Health Network and Centre (NaTHNaC).

www.who.int World Health Organisation.

Identification

You are required by Ecuadorean law to carry your passport at all times. Whether or not a photocopy is an acceptable substitute is at the discretion of the individual police officer, having it notarized can help.

Insurance

As of May 2018 it is mandatory for foreigners to have purchased health insurance before arriving in Ecuador. Always take out insurance that covers both medical expenses and baggage loss, and read the small print carefully before you set off. Check that all the activities you may end up doing are covered. Mountaineering and scuba diving, for example, as well as 'adrenalin sports' like bridge jumps and canyoning are excluded from many policies. Also check if medical coverage includes air ambulance and emergency flights back home. Be aware of the payment protocol: in Ecuador you are likely to have to pay out-of-pocket and later request reimbursement from the insurance company. Have the receipts for expensive personal effects like cameras and laptops on file, take photos of these items and note the serial numbers.

Internet

Cyber cafés are common in the cities and towns of Ecuador but are gradually being replaced by widespread Wi-Fi access. Wi-Fi is available in most hotels, at many cafés and in some public places.

Language

The official languages of Ecuador are **Spanish** and **Quichua**. English and a few other European languages may be spoken in some establishments catering to tourists in Quito and the most popular tourist destinations. Away from these places, knowledge of Spanish is essential, so it's a good idea to learn some before you go, or begin your travels in Ecuador with a period of language study. Language training opportunities abound; see box, Language schools in Quito, page 72. Schools in Cuenca, Otavalo, Baños, Montañita, Puerto López and Manta can be found in the 'What to do' listings for each town. The following USA-based companies can also organize language training in Ecuador: **AmeriSpan**, T1-800-511 0179, www.amerispan.com and **Spanish Abroad**, T1-888-722 7623, www.spanishabroad.com.

There may be opportunities to learn Quichua at the **Universidad Católica** in Quito (see box, page 72), at the **Universidad de Otavalo**, T06-292 3850, ext 113, and at **CEDEI** in Cuenca (see page 183); enquire well in advance.

LGBT travellers

The Ecuadorean constitution prohibits discrimination on the basis of sexual orientation and attitudes have gradually become more liberal in big cities including Quito, Guayaquil and Cuenca, especially with younger people. In small towns, however, values are still conservative. In order to avoid offending local sensibilities, discretion is advised to same-sex couples travelling in Ecuador.

See www.quitogay.net, www.galapagosgay.com (part of **Zenith Travel**) and international sites such as www.gaytravel.com, or https://nomadicboys.com.

Media

The main national newspapers include *El Comercio* (Quito, **www.elcomercio.com**), *El Mercurio* (Cuenca, **www.elmercurio.com.ec**), *El Universo* (Guayaquil, **www.eluniverso.com**) and *La Hora* (various regional editions, good for local news, **www.lahora.com.ec**). They all offer reasonably accurate reporting without any strong political bias.

Ecuadorean television tends to be more sensationalist than the print media, and radio is best reserved for music. Among the major television broadcasters are **Ecuavisa** (www.ecuavisa.com), **TC Televisión** (www.tctelevision.com) and

Teleamazonas (www.teleamazonas.com). A smaller highly regarded TV station is **Telerama** (www.telerama.ec) from Cuenca. **Ecuador TV** (www.ecuadortv.ec) is public broadcasting; some of their programs feature the tourist attractions of the country.

International satellite or cable television is common even in inexpensive hotels and streaming video from anywhere in the world can be had wherever there is Wi-Fi. Foreign newspapers and magazines are available in luxury hotels and a few speciality shops in Quito and Guayaquil.

Money

The **US dollar** (US$) is the official currency of Ecuador. Only US$ bills circulate. US coins are used alongside the equivalent size and value Ecuadorean coins. Ecuadorean coins have no value outside the country. Many establishments are reluctant to accept bills larger than US$20 because of counterfeit notes or lack of change. There is no substitute for cash-in-hand when travelling in Ecuador; US$ cash in small denominations is by far the simplest and the only universally accepted option. Other currencies are difficult to exchange outside large cities and fetch a poor rate. Some of the US$ banknotes circulating in Ecuador are tattered and grubby. If travelling on to Peru try to exchange these for crisper cleaner bills, as the scruffy ones will not be accepted there.

Credit cards, ATMs and banks

The most commonly accepted **credit cards** are Visa, MasterCard, Diners and, to a lesser extent, American Express. Paying by credit card may incur a surcharge, bargaining and obtaining discounts is easier if you pay cash. Cash advances on credit cards can be obtained through many ATMs (only Banco de Guayaquil for Amex), but daily limits apply. Larger advances on Visa, MasterCard and less frequently Amex are available from several banks. Their fees, procedures and the time required vary considerably and are subject to change, confirm all details locally. Among the more efficient banks for cash advances in Ecuador are: **Banco del Austro** (www.bancodelaustro. com), up to US$2000 a day on Visa or MC, 4% commission; **Banco Bolivariano** (www. bolivariano.com.ec), up to US$1000 a day on Visa or MC, no commission.

Internationally linked **ATMs** are common, although not all machines work with all cards. Credit cards are generally easier to use in Ecuadorean ATMs than debit cards. Withdrawals from ATMs are subject to limits, between US$300-500 per transaction. Check also what charges your own bank will make for using ATMs. Always be vigilant when using cash machines. Funds may be rapidly wired to Ecuador by **Western Union** (www.westernunion.com) or **MoneyGram** (https://secure.moneygram.com), fees and taxes apply, enquire in advance. With very few exceptions, traveller's cheques are of no use in Ecuador.

Cost of living/travelling

A budget of US$65-80 pp a day, including transport, will allow you to travel fairly comfortably. Your budget will be higher if you are staying in big cities, Galápagos and resort areas (especially in high season) and depending on how many internal flights you take. Rooms range from about US$10-15 pp for basic accommodation to about US$40-60 for mid-range places, to more than US$100 for upmarket hotels.

Opening hours

Banks Mon-Fri 0900-1700. **Government offices** Variable hours Mon-Fri, some close for lunch. **Other offices** 0900-1230, 1430-1800. **Shops** 0900-1900; close at midday in smaller towns, open till 2100 on the coast.

Post and courier

The Ecuadorean post office is known as **Correos del Ecuador** (www.correosdelecuador.gob.ec).

Opening hours for post offices may vary from town to town and from branch to branch. In Quito they are generally Mon-Fri 0800-1300, 1400-1700 (branches at Japón and Ulloa – below – also open Sat 0900-1300). Postal branches in small towns may not be familiar with all rates and procedures. Your chances are better at the main branches in provincial capitals, also in Otavalo, and better yet in Quito: at Colón y Reina Victoria in La Mariscal district, at the main sorting centre on Japón N36-153 y Naciones Unidas (behind the CCI shopping centre), or at Ulloa 273 y Ramírez Dávalos for very large parcels.

EMS (Express Mail) is the fastest and most expensive service. Registered mail is a slower and more economical option for important items. Both can be tracked on line.

For international courier service, **DHL** (www.dhl.com.ec) has offices in the larger cities. For courier service within Ecuador, **Servientrega** (www.servientrega.com.ec) has offices throughout the country; a reliable 1- to 2-day service is available to all areas and costs about US$4 for up to 2 kg. There are also other courier companies operating in Ecuador, but quality of service and reliability vary greatly.

Public holidays

The following are national public holidays. Other local holidays are listed under the corresponding cities and towns. There is no hard and fast rule for public holidays which fall on a weekday. They are sometimes moved at the last moment to make a long weekend (*un puente*), ask around in advance.

1 Jan **New Year's Day**.
Feb/Mar **Carnival**, Mon and Tue before Lent.
Mar/Apr **Good Fri**, **Easter Sun**.
1 May **Labour Day**.
24 May **Battle of Pichincha** (Independence Day).
10 Aug **1st attempt at independence**.
9 Oct **Independence of Guayaquil**.
2 Nov **All Souls' Day**.
3 Nov **Independence of Cuenca**.
25 Dec **Christmas Day**.

Punctuality

Ecuadoreans, like most Latin Americans, have a fairly relaxed attitude towards time. They will think nothing of arriving an hour or so late on social occasions. If you expect to meet someone at an exact time, you can tell them that you want to meet at such and such an hour *'en punto'*.

Safety

The majority of Ecuadoreans are helpful and want you to enjoy your stay in their country. There are, however, public safety issues which Ecuadoreans themselves recognize. These include bag snatching and slashing, robbery (sometimes armed) and holdups on the country's highways. Also beware of 'express kidnapping', whereby victims are taken from ATM to ATM and forced to withdraw money; fake taxis are often involved. Radio taxis are usually safer.

It is the larger cities, especially Guayaquil, Quito, Cuenca, Manta, Machala, Esmeraldas and Santo Domingo which call for the greatest care. Small towns and the countryside in the highlands are generally safer than on the coast or in the jungle. Some out of the way areas on the border with Colombia call for precautions. If heading north out of Ecuador, leave the country at Tulcán only. The region west of Tulcán was reported safe in 2017, but anywhere else, double-check the security situation.

Although currently uncommon, sporadic social unrest remains part of life in Ecuador and you should not overreact. Strikes and protests are usually announced days or weeks in advance, and their most significant impact on tourists is the restriction of overland travel. It is usually best to wait it out rather than insisting on keeping to your original itinerary.

Drugs

Almost all foreigners serving long sentences in Ecuador's squalid jails are there on drug charges. The authorities carry out sporadic raids in bars and clubs, anti-narcotics police set up checkpoints along the country's roads, and drug searches may be conducted at international departures areas of airports.

Anyone found carrying even the smallest amount of drugs may be automatically considered a trafficker. If arrested, the wait for trial in prison can take several years. Your foreign passport will not shield you in this situation, indeed you may be dealt with more harshly because of it. If you are unconvinced, then visit an Ecuadorean prison to see for yourself. Your embassy can give you the names of citizens of your country serving sentences who would appreciate a visitor.

Hotel security

The cheapest hotels are usually found near markets and bus stations but these are also the least safe areas of most Ecuadorean towns. Look for something a little better if you can afford it, and if you must stay in a suspect area, try to return to your hotel before dark. If you trust your hotel, then you can leave any valuables you don't need in their safe deposit box, but always keep an inventory of what you have deposited.

An alternative to leaving valuables with the hotel administration is to lock everything in your luggage and secure that in your room; a light bicycle cable and a small padlock will provide at least a psychological deterrent for would-be thieves. Even in the safest hotels, never leave valuables strewn about your room.

Protecting money and valuables

Make copies of important documents and send/give them to your family or travelling companion; this may speed up replacement if documents are lost or stolen and will allow you to have some ID while getting replacements. Keep all documents (including your passport, credit and debit cards) secure and hide your main cash supply in several different places. If one stash is lost or stolen, you will still have the others to fall back on.

The following means of concealing cash and documents have all been recommended: extra pockets sewn inside shirts and trousers, pockets closed with a zip or safety pin, money-belts (best worn below the waist and never within sight) and neck or leg pouches. Never carry valuables in an ordinary pocket, purse or daypack. Keep fancy cameras in bags or daypacks and generally out of sight. Do not wear expensive wrist watches or jewellery. If you are wearing a shoulder bag in a crowd, carry it in front of you. In crowded places wear your daypack on your chest with both straps looped over your shoulders. Whenever visiting an area which is considered unsafe, take the bare minimum of valuables with you.

Street crime and scams

Pickpockets, bag snatchers and slashers operate, especially in crowded areas such as markets. Keep alert and avoid swarms of people. Crowded city buses and the various Quito and Guayaquil mass transit lines are notorious for thieves. Likewise avoid deserted areas, such as parks or plazas after hours. If someone follows you when you're in the street, slip into a nearby shop or hail a cab. If you are the victim of an armed assault, never resist or hold back your valuables; they can always be replaced.

The old scam of smearing tourists with mustard, ketchup, shaving cream and almost anything else, in order to distract and rob them, is alive and well in Ecuador. It happens on the street and in cybercafés. An apparently well-meaning bystander usually helps clean you up, while their accomplice expertly cleans you out. If you are smeared, move along quickly to a secure location or hail a cab.

More sinister but fortunately less frequent is drugging people in order to rob them. The drugs can be added to food, drink or cigarettes. Politely refuse these and keep an eye on your drink in bars. Victims usually awaken hours or days after the fact with a splitting headache and without their belongings.

Volcanoes

Ecuador's active volcanoes are spectacular, but have occasionally threatened nearby communities. The **National Geophysics Institute** provides daily updates at www.igepn.edu.ec.

Smoking

Smoking is not permitted on buses and is not appropriate in restaurants. A few better hotels have non-smoking rooms or are entirely non-smoking.

Student travellers

An **International Student Identity Card (ISIC)** may help you obtain some discounts when travelling in Ecuador. ISIC cards are sold by **Grupo Idiomas**, Circunvalación Sur 501-c y Ebanos, Urdesa Central, Guayaquil, T04-238 0400, www.grupoidiomas.com. They need proof of full-time enrolment in Ecuador or abroad (minimum 20 hrs per week), 2 photos, passport, US$20 and the application form found in www.isic.com.ec.

Tax

Airport tax International and domestic departure tax is included in the ticket price.
VAT/IVA 12%. It may in principle be reclaimed on departure if you keep official invoices with your name and passport number; don't expect a speedy refund or bother with amounts under US$100. High surtaxes applied to various imported items make them expensive to purchase in Ecuador.

Telephone

Country code +593.

There are independent phone offices, *cabinas*, in most cities and towns, but mobile (cellular) phones are by far the most common form of telecommunication. You can purchase a SIM card (*un chip*) for US$5 for either of the 2 main mobile carriers: **Claro** and **Movistar**; in principle an Ecuadorean *cédula* (national ID card) is required but a passport is sometimes accepted or ask an Ecuadorean friend to buy a chip for you. The chips work with many foreign mobile phones, but enquire about your unit before purchasing. Mobile phone shops are everywhere, look for the carrier's logo. You get an Ecuadorean mobile phone number and can purchase credit (*recarga*) anywhere for as much or as little as you like. Calls cost about US$0.20 per min and only the caller pays. Mobile phone numbers have 10 digits starting with 09, landlines (*fijos*) have 7 digits plus an area code (eg 02 for Quito, 04 for Guayaquil). When calling a landline from a mobile, you must include the area code. Skype, WhatsApp and similar services on Wi-Fi-enabled devices are the most economical form of international communication from Ecuador.

Time

GMT-5 on the Ecuadorean mainland, GMT-6 in Galápagos.

In most of the better restaurants a 10% service charge is included in the bill, but you can give a modest additional tip if the service is especially good. Many simpler restaurants, especially those serving set meals, do not include service in the bill and tips are not expected. Taxi drivers are not usually tipped, but you can always round up the fare for particularly good service. Tipping for all other services is entirely discretionary, how much depends on the quality of service received.

Tour operators

For local operators see Quito (page 72), Guayaquil (page 219), Galápagos (page 342), and cities throughout the text.

UK and rest of Europe

For further information on specialist travel firms, contact the **Latin American Travel Association**, www.lata.travel.

Andean Trails, 33 Sandport St, Leith, Edinburgh EH6 6EP, T0131-467 7086, www. andeantrails.co.uk. Small group trekking, mountain biking and jungle tours in the Andes and Amazon.

Audley Travel, New Mill, New Mill Lane, Witney, Oxfordshire OX29 9SX, T01993-838000, www.audleytravel.com. Tailor-made holidays to South America (and elsewhere).

Cox & Kings Travel, 6th floor, 30 Millbank, London SW1P 4EE, T020-3797 8866, www. coxandkings.co.uk. Quality group tours and tailor-made holidays to many of the world's most fascinating regions; from the lavish to the adventurous, planned by experts.

Discover South America, T01273-921655 (UK), www.discoversouthamerica.co.uk. British/Peruvian-owned operator offering tailor-made and classic holidays to Quito, the Amazon and Galápagos and throughout South America (specialists in Peru).

Explore, Nelson House, 55 Victoria Rd, Farnborough, Hampshire GU14 7PA, T01252-883620, www.explore.co.uk. Highly respected operator with offices in Australia, New Zealand, USA and Canada, running 2- to 5-week tours in more than 90 countries worldwide, including Ecuador.

Fairtravel4u, Jan van Gentstraat 35, 1755 PB Petten, The Netherlands, T0031-6152 92565, www.fairtravel4u.org. 1- to 3-week tours including yoga and wellness tours as well as trips to the Galápagos, Amazon and volunteering.

Galapagos Classic Cruises, 6 Keyes Rd, London NW2 3XA, T020-8933 0613, www. galapagoscruises.co.uk. An experienced company providing specialist cruises, diving holidays and adventure tours for individuals and groups.

Geodyssey, 116 Tollington Park, London N4 3RB, T020-7281 7788, www.geodyssey.co.uk.

Fair Travel Tours to Ecuador, Peru and Bolivia
Galapagos| Amazon | Yoga Tours | Trekking | Mountain Climbing |
Machu Picchu | Colca | Huaraz | Uyuni

www.fairtravel4u.org | (0031) (0) 615292565 | info@fairtravel4u.org

In-depth travel service for Ecuador and the Galápagos, with specialist itineraries and tailor-made tours available.

Journey Latin America, 401 King St, London W6 9NJ, T020-3733 4413/8747 3108 (flights only), www.journeylatinamerica.co.uk. Specialist in tailor-made holidays in Latin America; offers a wide range of flight options.

Last Frontiers, The Mill, Quainton Rd, Waddesdon, Bucks HP18 0LP, T01296-653000, www.lastfrontiers.com. South American specialists offering tailor-made itineraries to Ecuador including the Galápagos, plus specialist themed tours.

Llama Travel, 55 Rochester Place, London, NW1 9JU, T020-7263 3000, www.llamatravel.com. Promises high-quality holidays to Latin America at the lowest possible prices.

Pura Aventura, T01273 676712, www.pura-aventura.com. UK/Spanish-owned company with tours throughout Latin America, as well as trips to mainland Ecuador and Galápagos, wildlife and family tours.

Select Latin America based in Central London, contact via website or phone T020-7407 1478, www.selectlatinamerica.co.uk. Tailor-made holidays and small group tours. Specialist in cruises around the Galápagos Islands; many years' experience.

Steppes Travel, 51 Castle St, Cirencester GL7 1QD, T01285-601758, www.steppestravel.co.uk. Ecuador mainland and Galápagos tours. Tailor-made itineraries for destinations throughout Latin America.

Yampu Tours, 6 Bruce Grove, London N17 6RA, T0800-011 2424, www.yampu.com. Personalized tours to suit any special interest from popular attractions to less-visited sights, from the historical to the culinary, spiritual and adventure. Named "South America's Leading Tour Operator" for 5 years running.

North and South America

Amazing Peru and Beyond, Av Petit Thouars 5356, Lima, Peru, T1-800-704 2915, www.amazingperu.com. Adventure, cultural and ecological tours including land-based tour to the Galápagos.

Chimu Adventures, 1321 Blanshard St, Suite 301, Victoria BC, V8W 0B6, Canada, T(718) 473 0815, www.chimuadventures.com. Offers tailor-made itineraries throughout South America.

Condor Travel, Armando Blondet 249, San Isidro, Lima 27, T01-615 3000, www.condortravel.com. In USA T1-855-926 2975. A full range of tours, including custom-made, and services in Argentina, Bolivia, Brazil, Chile, Colombia, Ecuador and Peru (offices in each country), with a strong commitment to social responsibility.

Ecoventura-Galapagos Network, 5805 Blue Lagoon Dr, Suite 160, Miami, FL 33126, T1-800-633 7972, T1-305-262 6264, www.ecoventura.com. Galápagos cruises and mainland tours.

Exito Travel, 108 Rutgers Av, Fort Collins, CO80525, USA, T800-655 4053 (USA), T970-482 3019 (worldwide), www.exitotravel.com. International flight specialists, experts in multi-stop and airpass itineraries.

International Nature & Cultural Adventures (INCA), 1311 63rd St, Emeryville CA94608, T1-510-420 1550, www.inca1.com. Tailor-made itineraries in the Galápagos aboard their 16-passenger luxury yacht *Integrity*.

Ladatco Tours, 3006 Aviation, Suite 3A, Coconut Grove, FL 33133, T1-800-327 6162, www.ladatco.com. South American specialists, operate explorer tours.

Tambo Tours, T1-888-2-GO-PERU (246-7378), www.2GOPERU.com. Long-established adventure and tour specialist with offices in Peru and USA. Customized trips to the Amazon and archaeological sites of Peru and Ecuador.

Tropical Birding, 113 Wind Tree Valley Rd, Parkton, MD 21120, T1-409-515 9110, www.tropicalbirding.com. International tour operator specializing in birding, nature and nature photography tours.

Vaya Adventures, 2120 University Av, Berkeley, CA 94704, USA, T1-800-342 1796, www.vayaadventures.com. Galápagos cruises plus extensions and customized, private itineraries throughout South America.

Australia and New Zealand
Contours Travel, 287 Victoria St, West Melbourne, VIC 3003, T03-9328 8488, www.contourstravel.com.au. Specializes in Latin American destinations.

Tourist information

Tourist information and promotion is handled at the national level by the **Ministerio de Turismo**, Av Gran Colombia y Briceño, Quito, T02-399 9333 www.turismo.gob.ec. Its website www.ecuador.travel is a good general introduction. The *ministerio* has regional offices in the larger provincial capitals and there are **municipal tourist offices** in almost every town; details are given in the text. The quality of service and information provided varies considerably. Some tourist offices are identified by signs marked 'iTur'.

Useful websites
www.ecuador.com; **www.quito adventure.com** and **www.paisturistico. com** General guides with information about services, activities and national parks. **www.ecuadorexplorer.com**; **www. ecuadortravelsite.org** and **www.ecua world.com** Are all travel guides; the latter includes volunteering options. **www.trekkinginecuador.com** for hiking information.

Visas and immigration

All visitors to Ecuador must have a passport valid for at least 6 months and an onward or return ticket, but the latter is seldom asked for. Citizens of Afghanistan, Bangladesh, Cuba, Eritrea, Ethiopia, Kenya, Nepal, Nigeria, North Korea, Pakistan, Senegal and Somalia require a visa to visit Ecuador; other tourists do not require a visa unless they wish to stay more than 90 days. Upon entry all visitors must complete an international embarkation/disembarkation card.

Tourists are granted 90 days upon arrival and there are no extensions except for citizens of the Andean Community of Nations. Visitors are not allowed back in the country if they have already stayed 90 days during the past 12 months. If you want to spend more time studying, volunteering, etc, you may be able to get a purpose-specific visa at the end of your 90 days as a tourist. Purpose-specific visas are issued by the **Ministerio de Relaciones Exteriores** (Foreign Office, http://cancilleria.gob.ec or http://consuladovirtual.gob.ec, where a full list of visa types is given; they cost US$100-400, plus US$50 for paperwork). There is no fine at present for overstaying but if you do so then you must obtain an exit permit form an immigration office 48 hrs before departure and you may be barred from returning to Ecuador.

There are immigration offices in all provincial capitals (see www.ministeriointerior.gob.ec/migracion). If your passport is lost or stolen then, after it has been replaced by your embassy, you will have go to an immigration office to obtain a *movimiento migratorio* (a certificate indicating the date you entered Ecuador) in order to be able to leave the country.

Tourists are not permitted to work under any circumstances. Visas for work, study and longer stays are issued by the Ministerio de Relaciones Exteriores (see above) through Ecuador's diplomatic representatives abroad. All of the foregoing regulations are subject to change.

Volunteering

'Voluntourism' is very popular in Ecuador, attracting many visitors, from students to retirees. It is a good way to become more intimately acquainted with the country and, at the same time, to try and lend a hand to its people. If you are seriously interested in volunteering, you should research both local and international organizations well before you leave home. Try to choose a position that matches your individual skills. Think carefully about the kind of work that you would find most satisfying but remember that you may also be assigned menial tasks. Likewise be realistic about how much you might be able to achieve. The shorter your stay, the more limited should be your expectations in all regards. One month is a reasonable minimum. You must speak at least basic Spanish, and preferably a good deal more, in order to work effectively in a community.

You always have to pay your own airfare, and generally also contribute toward your room and board. There are many different areas where voluntary work is possible, of which we list a few. Many nature reserves in and around Mindo and on the Western slopes of Pichincha currently offer volunteer opportunities, see page 85. Note that the following categories often overlap with each other and with conventional tourism.

Community work
Centro Integral de la Niñez y Adolescencia (CENIT), Huacho E2-63 y José Peralta, Quito, T02-265-2861 ext 4, http://cenitecuador. org. This local organization helps working children. US$100 one-off fee (does not provide accommodation or meals), minimum 2 months.

Environmental conservation

Fundación Jatun Sacha, Teresa de Cepeda N34-260 y República, p2, Urbanización Rumipamba, Quito, T02-331 7163, www.jatunsacha.org. A large Ecuadorean NGO running 5 biological research stations, all in exceptional natural areas. Fees and conditions vary from reserve to reserve.

Fundación Maquipuicuna, Baquerizo Moreno E9-153 y Tamayo, Quito, T02-250 7200, www.maquipucuna.org. This NGO works with ecotourism, reforestation and environmental education at their reserve northwest of Quito. US$25 application, US$360-450 per month depending on length of stay, minimum 1 month.

Los Cedros Research Station, in the Intag region, T06-301 6550, http://reserva loscedros.org. A cloudforest reserve protecting many bird and orchid species. US$300 for 2 weeks, US$500 per month, minimum 2 weeks.

Rumi Wilco, contact Orlando or Alicia Falco, Vilcabamba, rumiwilco@yahoo.com, http://rumiwilco.com. A family-run 40-ha private nature reserve. Volunteers receive a discount on accommodation (see page 201), minimum 1 week.

Santa Lucía, Nanegal, outside Quto, T02-215 7242, www.santaluciaecuador.com. A community-based conservation and ecotourism project which protects a 730-ha tract of cloudforest.

Yunguilla, Calacalí, outside Quito, T09-8021 5476, www.yunguilla.org.ec. This community of 50 local families combines environmental conservation with sustainable agriculture.

Permaculture

Parque Bambú, El Limonal, along the road from Ibarra to San Lorenzo, contact Piet Sabbe, T06-301 6606, http://bospas.org. A small family-run reserve and centre for permaculture and reforestation. US$260 per month, US$18 per day for 2 weeks, additional week US$15 per day; can volunteer up to 3 months.

Río Muchacho Organic Farm, contact Nicola Mears or Darío Proaño, near Canoa, T05-302 0487, www.riomuchacho.com. A small organization working with sustainable agriculture, local education and community development. 1st week US$15 per day; additional weeks US$10 per day; 1st month US$300, additional months US$250-100. Group volunteering and internships also accepted.

Sacred Sueños, contact Yves Zehnder, Vilcabamba, T09-9143 1689, www.sacredsuenos.wordpress.com. A small young 'intentional community' involved with permaculture, 1½ hrs' walk from town. About US$30 per week depending on length of stay, minimum 2 weeks.

Weights and measures

Officially metric, some English measures are used for hardware, some Spanish measures for produce.

Women travellers

See www.journeywoman.com.

Generally women travellers should find visiting Ecuador an enjoyable experience. Gender stereotyping has diminished, however machismo lives on. You should be prepared for this and try not to overreact. When you set out, err on the side of caution until your instincts have adjusted to the customs of a new culture. If, as a single woman, you can befriend an Ecuadorean woman, you will learn more about the country and its current norms.

Note that tampons may be hard to find in smaller towns; sanitary towels are available everywhere.

Footnotes

Basic Spanish for travellers

Learning Spanish is a useful part of the preparation for a trip to Latin America and no volumes of dictionaries, phrase books or word lists will provide the same enjoyment as being able to communicate directly with the people of the country you are visiting. It is a good idea to make an effort to grasp the basics before you go. As you travel you will pick up more of the language and the more you know, the more you will benefit from your stay.

General pronunciation

Whether you have been taught the 'Castilian' pronounciation (*z* and *c* followed by *i* or *e* are pronounced as the *th* in think) or the 'American' pronounciation (they are pronounced as *s*), you will encounter little difficulty in understanding either. Regional accents and usages vary, but the basic language is essentially the same everywhere.

Vowels

a	as in English *cat*
e	as in English *best*
i	as the *ee* in English *feet*
o	as in English *shop*
u	as the *oo* in English *food*
ai	as the *i* in English *ride*
ei	as *ey* in English *they*
oi	as *oy* in English *toy*

Consonants

Most consonants can be pronounced more or less as they are in English.
The exceptions are:

g	before *e* or *i* is the same as *j*
h	is always silent (except in *ch* as in *chair*)
j	as the *ch* in Scottish *loch*
ll	as the *y* in *yellow*
ñ	as the *ni* in English *onion*
rr	trilled much more than in English
x	depending on its location, pronounced *x*, *s*, *sh* or *j*

Spanish words and phrases

Greetings, courtesies

hello	*hola*	I speak Spanish	*hablo español*
good morning	*buenos días*	I don't speak Spanish	*no hablo español*
good afternoon/ evening/night	*buenas tardes/ noches*	do you speak English?	*¿habla inglés?*
		I don't understand	*no entiendo/*
goodbye	*adiós/chao*		*no comprendo*
pleased to meet you	*mucho gusto*	please speak slowly	*hable despacio*
see you later	*hasta luego*		*por favor*
how are you?	*¿cómo está?/ ¿cómo estás?*	I am very sorry	*lo siento mucho/ disculpe*
I'm fine, thanks	*estoy muy bien, gracias*	what do you want?	*¿qué quiere? ¿qué quieres?*
I'm called...	*me llamo...*	I want	*quiero*
what is your name?	*¿cómo se llama? ¿cómo te llamas?*	I don't want it	*no lo quiero*
		leave me alone	*déjeme en paz/ no me moleste*
yes/no	*sí/no*		
please	*por favor*	good/bad	*bueno/malo*
thank you (very much)	*(muchas) gracias*		

Questions and requests

Have you got a room for two people?
¿Tiene una habitación para dos personas?
How do I get to_? *¿Cómo llego a_?*
How much does it cost?
¿Cuánto cuesta? ¿Cuánto es?
I'd like tomake a long-distance phone call
Quisiera hacer una llamada de larga distancia
Is service included? *¿Está incluido el servicio?*
Is tax included?
¿Están incluidos los impuestos?

When does the bus leave (arrive)?
¿A qué hora sale (llega) el bus?
When? *¿Cuándo?*
Where is_? *¿Dónde está_?*
Where can I buy tickets?
¿Dónde puedo comprar boletos?
Where is the nearest petrol station?
¿Dónde está la gasolinera más cercana?
Why? *¿Por qué?*

Basics

bank	*el banco*	market	*el mercado*
bathroom/toilet	*el baño*	mobile phone	*el celular*
bill	*la factura/la cuenta*	note/coin	*le billete/la moneda*
cash	*el efectivo*	police (policeman)	*la policía (el policía)*
cheap	*barato/a*	post office	*el correo*
credit card	*la tarjeta de crédito*	public telephone	*el teléfono público*
exchange house	*la casa de cambio*	SIM card	*el chip*
exchange rate	*el tipo de cambio*	supermarket	*el supermercado*
expensive	*caro/a*	ticket office	*la taquilla*

Getting around

aeroplane	*el avión*	to insure yourself against	*asegurarse contra*
airport	*el aeropuerto*		
arrival/departure	*la llegada/salida*	luggage	*el equipaje*
avenue	*la avenida*	motorway, freeway	*la autopista/ la carretera*
block	*la cuadra*		
border	*la frontera*	north, south,	*norte, sur,*
bus station	*la terminal de buses/ la terminal terrestre*	west, east	*oeste (occidente), este (oriente)*
bus	*el bus/el autobús*	oil	*el aceite*
shared taxi	*el colectivo*	to park	*estacionarse*
corner	*la esquina*	passport	*el pasaporte*
customs	*la aduana*	petrol/gasoline	*la gasolina*
first/second class	*primera/segunda clase*	puncture	*el pinchazo*
left/right	*izquierda/derecha*	street	*la calle*
ticket	*el boleto*	that way	*por allí/por allá*
empty/full	*vacío/lleno*	this way	*por aquí/por acá*
highway, main road	*la carretera*	tourist card/visa	*la tarjeta de turista*
immigration	*la inmigración/ migración*	tyre	*la llanta*
		unleaded	*sin plomo*
insurance	*el seguro*	to walk	*caminar/andar*
insured person	*el/la asegurado/a*		

Accommodation

air conditioning	el aire acondicionado	power cut	el apagón/corte
all-inclusive	todo incluido	restaurant	el restaurante
bathroom, private	el baño privado	room/bedroom	el cuarto/ la habitación
bed, double/	la cama matrimonial/	sheets	las sábanas
single	sencilla	shower	la ducha/regadera
blankets	las cobijas/mantas	soap	el jabón
to clean	limpiar	toilet	el sanitario/excusado
dining room	el comedor	toilet paper	el papel higiénico
guesthouse	la casa de huéspedes	towels, clean/dirty	las toallas limpias/
hotel	el hotel		sucias
noisy	ruidoso	water, hot/cold	el agua caliente/fría
pillows	las almohadas		

Health

aspirin	la aspirina	diarrhoea	la diarrea
blood	la sangre	doctor	el médico
chemist	la farmacia	fever/sweat	la fiebre/el sudor
condoms	los preservativos,	pain	el dolor
	los condones	head	la cabeza
contact lenses	los lentes de contacto	period/	la regla/
contraceptives	los anticonceptivos	sanitary towels	las toallas sanitarias
contraceptive pill	la píldora	stomach	el estómago
	anticonceptiva	altitude sickness	el soroche

Family

family	la familia	husband/wife	el esposo (marido)/
brother/sister	el hermano/		la esposa
	la hermana	boyfriend/girlfriend	el novio/la novia
daughter/son	la hija/el hijo	friend	el amigo/la amiga
father/mother	el padre/la madre	married	casado/a
		single/unmarried	soltero/a

Months, days and time

January	enero	Monday	lunes
February	febrero	Tuesday	martes
March	marzo	Wednesday	miércoles
April	abril	Thursday	jueves
May	mayo	Friday	viernes
June	junio	Saturday	sábado
July	julio	Sunday	domingo
August	agosto		
September	septiembre	at one o'clock	a launa
October	octubre	at half past two	a las dos y media
November	noviembre	at a quarter to three	a cuartopara las tres/
December	diciembre		a las tres menos quince

it's one o'clock	es la una	it's five to nine	son las nueve menos cinco
it's seven o'clock	son las siete		
it's six twenty	son las seis y veinte	in ten minutes	en diez minutos
		five hours	cinco horas
		does it take long?	¿tarda mucho?

Numbers

one	uno/una	sixteen	dieciséis
two	dos	seventeen	diecisiete
three	tres	eighteen	dieciocho
four	cuatro	nineteen	diecinueve
five	cinco	twenty	veinte
six	seis	twenty-one	veintiuno
seven	siete	thirty	treinta
eight	ocho	forty	cuarenta
nine	nueve	fifty	cincuenta
ten	diez	sixty	sesenta
eleven	once	seventy	setenta
twelve	doce	eighty	ochenta
thirteen	trece	ninety	noventa
fourteen	catorce	hundred	cien/ciento
fifteen	quince	thousand	mil

Food

avocado	el aguacate	fried	frito
baked	al horno	garlic	el ajo
bakery	la panadería	goat	el chivo
banana	el plátano	grapefruit	la toronja
beans	los fréjoles/ los porotos	grill	la parrilla
		grilled/griddled	a la plancha
beef	la carne de res	guava	la guayaba
beef steak or pork fillet	el bistec	ham	el jamón
boiled rice	el arroz blanco	hamburger	la hamburguesa
bread	el pan	hot, spicy	picante
breakfast	el desayuno	ice cream	el helado
butter	la mantequilla	jam	la mermelada
cake	el pastel	knife	el cuchillo
chewing gum	el chicle	lime	el limón
chicken	el pollo	lobster	la langosta
chilli or green pepper	el ají/pimiento	lunch	el almuerzo/ la comida
clear soup, stock	el caldo		
cooked	cocido	meal	la comida
dining room	el comedor	meat	la carne
egg	el huevo	minced meat	la carne molida
fish	el pescado	onion	la cebolla
fork	el tenedor	orange	la naranja

pepper (ground)	*la pimienta*	seafood	*los mariscos*
pasty, turnover	*la empanada/*	soup	*la sopa*
	el pastelito	spoon	*la cuchara*
pork	*el cerdo*	squash	*la calabaza*
potato	*la papa*	squid	*los calamares*
prawns	*los camarones*	supper	*la cena*
raw	*crudo*	sweet	*dulce*
restaurant	*el restaurante*	to eat	*comer*
salad	*la ensalada*	toasted	*tostado*
salt	*la sal*	turkey	*el pavo*
sandwich	*el sánduche*	vegetables	*las legumbres/*
sauce	*la salsa*		*los vegetales*
sausage	*la longaniza/el chorizo*	without meat	*sin carne*
scrambled eggs	*los huevos revueltos*	yam	*el camote*

Drink

beer	*la cerveza*	juice	*el jugo*
boiled	*hervido/a*	lemonade	*la limonada*
bottled	*en botella*	milk	*la leche*
camomile tea	*la manzanilla*	mint	*la menta*
canned	*en lata*	rum	*el ron*
coffee	*el café*	soft drink	*la cola*
coffee, white	*el café con leche*	sugar	*el azúcar*
cold	*frío*	tea	*el té*
cup	*la taza*	to drink	*beber/tomar*
drink	*la bebida*	water	*el agua*
drunk	*borracho/a*	water, carbonated	*el agua mineral*
firewater	*el aguardiente*		*con gas*
fruit milkshake	*el batido/licuado*	water, still	*el agua*
glass	*el vaso*		*mineral sin gas*
hot	*caliente*	wine, red	*el vino tinto*
ice/without ice	*el hielo/sin hielo*	wine, white	*el vino blanco*

Key verbs

to go	**ir**	**to have** (possess)	**tener**
I go	*voy*	I have	*tengo*
you go (familiar)	*vas*	you (familiar) have	*tienes*
he, she, it goes,		he, she, it,	
you (formal) go	*va*	you (formal) have	*tiene*
we go	*vamos*	we have	*tenemos*
they, you (plural) go	*van*	they, you (plural) have	*tienen*
		there is/are	*hay*
		there isn't/aren't	*no hay*

Index

Entries in bold refer to maps

FOOTPRINT

Features

Advertisers' index

About the authors

Ben Box and Sarah Cameron

Ben Box and Sarah Cameron have been working on the *South American Handbook* since the late 1970s. Together they produced the first editions of Footprint's *Caribbean Islands Handbook* and *Mexico and Central American Handbook*. Ben then took over editorship of the *South American Handbook* in 1989 while Sarah concentrated on the Caribbean. They have both travelled extensively throughout the region and have produced many titles for Footprint, both individually and together. Their family base is an old cottage in Suffolk (UK) which is surrounded by animals and a rather unruly country garden. Other distractions include village cricket for Ben and exploring the network of local footpaths with their dog.

Acknowledgements

This edition of the *Ecuador and Galápagos Handbook* is based on the work that Robert and Daisy Kunstaetter devoted to the project through many previous editions. We, Ben Box and Sarah Cameron, the present authors, wish to express, first and foremost, our gratitude to Robert and Daisy for such an excellent base on which to research our own version.

A number of other people have helped in the preparation of this book. We are extremely grateful to José Navarrete and Caroline Frey of Pushaq, and to José's father, also José, for organizing and transporting us on a journey from Quito to Tulcán, back to Ibarra and then along the Pacific coast from Esmeraldas to Guayaquil. Without their help, enthusiasm and guidance, the trip would have been a lot less thorough and enjoyable.

Also on the Pacific Coast we should like to thank Darío Proaño and Nicola Mears for welcoming us at Río Muchacho where we had an enlightening time, despite the rain. In Puerto López, we are most grateful to Werner Grunagel and the staff at La Terraza, also to Ross C Bright in Canoa, while in Guayaquil we wish to thank Francisco Baca and staff at the Hotel del Parque and Fanny Paltán at Hostal Macaw. Also in Guayaquil, thanks again to the team at William H Coleman and all those involved in the running of Travel Mart Latin America.

In Quito we are most grateful to Verónica Sevilla (Gerente General), Carla Cárdenas (Jefe de Promoción), Oscar López (Coordinador de Promoción Internacional) and Rubén Lara (Especialista de Promoción y Operación Turística) of Quito Turismo, www.quito.com. ec, who arranged a tour of new developments in tourism in the city, in the care of our guide Gustavo Pfeil.

Also in Quito our warmest thanks are due to Jean Brown, Emma Morgan of Original Ecuador and Jorge the driver, Lorraine Caputo, and especially to László Károlyi and Joan Pérez of Cultura Manor for their hospitality and help before and during our visit to the city.

For this edition Robert and Daisy Kunstaetter updated the Cuenca to the Peruvian border section and they would like to thank the following for their help: Jean Brown in Quito, Michael Resch in Baños, Carmen Mora, Emil Stenzig and Beatriz Yaguachi in Loja. The current and former authors travelled together to Bellavista and Mindo in September 2017 and can verify that four pairs of eyes are even better than two. For his hospitality and guiding at Bellavista Cloud Forest Reserve, we are all very grateful to Richard Parsons.

In Northern Ecuador we should like to thank everyone at Polylepis Lodge, Tunas y Cabras and Hacienda Cusín, and Angie Arias and Alejandro Naranjo in Tulcán.

In the Cotopaxi area we received much help and a great welcome from Gabriel Espinosa and family at Hacienda La Alegría; Raúl Guarderas at Sierra Alisos; Cristina Coronel and Jascivan Carvalho at Chilcabamba, plus the hotel staff and Fabián the guide; Alvaro Reinoso the chef; and Sebastián Cornejo of Cotopaxi Pungo (also Juan Carlos Ríos). Our warmest thanks to all.

In Riobamba Popkje van der Ploeg welcomed us to the city, arranged a trip up Chimborazo and updated the Riobamba/Guaranda text, for which we are most grateful. In the city we'd also like to thank Ben and Jenny Cox of Mansión Santa Isabella.

In Cuenca we should like to thank Jeaneth Barrionuevo for meeting us and giving us a guided tour.

We were guests at Sacha Lodge thanks to Guillermo Zaldumbide and we should also like to thank the management, Fausto Cornejo and Michael Sauer, and guides Oscar and Shanshu.

Finally, in Ecuador, we'd like to say thank you to the following: Dominic Hamilton, Jorge Vinueza and Carla Novoa of Ñan magazine and Bram van Leeuwen of Andean Travel Company.

Last but by no means least our thanks go to Felicity Laughton (editorial), Emma Bryers (layout), Debbie Wylde (advertising), Kevin Feeney (maps) and John Hendry (colour section) who pulled all the different strands of the project together.

Picture credits: Galápagos Islands

Page 293: biasifab/Shutterstock.com. **Page 294**: farbled/Shutterstock.com. **Page 298**: Alan Brookstone / Shutterstock.com. **Page 300**: Fotos593/Shutterstock.com. **Page 302**: Jess Kraft/Shutterstock.com. **Page 303**: roroto12p/Shutterstock.com; Shaun Jeffers/Shutterstock.com. **Page 304**: Longjourneys/Shutterstock.com. **Page 305**: Roland Spiegler/Shutterstock.com; DigitalMagus/Shutterstock.com. **Page 306**: Watchtheworld/Shutterstock.com; Thomas O'Neil/Shutterstock.com. **Page 307**: Gail Johnson/Shutterstock.com. **Page 308**: Frank Wasserfuehrer/Shutterstock.com; photoiconix/Shutterstock.com. **Page 309**: Anna Azimi/Shutterstock.com. **Page 310**: Anastasia Koro/Shutterstock.com; Mr. Tobin/Shutterstock.com. **Page 311**: Amanda Nicholls/Shutterstock.com; Stephen Frink/SuperStock.com; Minden Pictures /SuperStock.com; National Geographic/SuperStock.com. **Page 312**: Steve Allen/Shutterstock.com. **Page 313**: Minden Pictures/Superstock.com. **Page 314**: RPBaiao/Shutterstock.com. **Page 315**: Minden Pictures/Superstock.com. **Page 316**: Marisa Estivill/Shutterstock.com. **Page 317**: foxie/Shutterstock.com; RHIMAGE/Shutterstock.com. **Page 318**: Stacy Funderburke/Shutterstock.com; Marisa Estivill/Shutterstock.com. **Page 319**: Fotos593/Shutterstock.com; Jess Kraft/Shutterstock.com. **Page 320**: Mint Image/SuperStock.com. **Page 321**: Ecuadorpostales/Shutterstock.com; sunsinger/Shutterstock.com; Guido Vermeulen-Perdaen/Shutterstock.com. **Page 322**: Fotos593/Shutterstock.com. **Page 323**: Ingram Publishing/SuperStock.com; Steve Allen/Shutterstock.com; Alberto Loyo/Shutterstock.com. **Page 324**: David Thyberg/Shutterstock.com; farbled/Shutterstock.com. **Page 325**: Ammit Jack/Shutterstock.com. **Page 326**: Erkki & Hanna/Shutterstock.com; Alfie Photography/Shutterstock.com. **Page 331**: Terence Mendoza/Shutterstock.com. **Page 332**: Fotos593/Shutterstock.com.

Duotones Page Pages 38 and 94: Anton_Ivanov/Shutterstock.com. **Page 126**: Ecuadorpostales/Shutterstock.com. **Page 170**: onairda/Shutterstock.com. **Page 204**: Fotos593/Shutterstock.com. **Page 228**: Fotos593/Shutterstock.com. **Page 262**: Ksenia Ragozina/Shutterstock.com.

Credits

Footprint credits
Project editor: Felicity Laughton
Production and layout: Emma Bryers
Maps: Kevin Feeney
Colour section: John Hendry

Publisher: John Sadler
Marketing: Kirsty Holmes
Advertising and Partnerships:
Debbie Wylde

Photography credits
Front cover: Carlos Ojeda/Shutterstock.com
Back cover top: Emiliano Barbieri/
Shutterstock.com
Back cover bottom: Alejo Miranda/
Shutterstock.com

Colour section
Inside front cover: MindStorm/
Shutterstock.com; Fotos593/Shutterstock.
com; Lenorko/Shutterstock.com. **Page 1**:
Barna Tanko/Shutterstock.com. **Page 2**:
GARY GRANJA/Shutterstock.com.
Page 4: Fotos593/Shutterstock.com.
Page 5: Ecuadorpostales/Shutterstock.
com; sunsinger/Shutterstock.com; DFLC
Prints/Shutterstock.com; Alejo Miranda/
Shutterstock.com. **Page 6**: Barna
Tanko/Shutterstock.com; Diana Zuleta/
Shutterstock.com; Angela N Perryman/
Shutterstock.com. **Page 7**: Marisa Estivill/
Shutterstock.com; Fotos593/Shutterstock.
com; David M. Roberts/Shutterstock.com.
Page 10: Fotos593/Shutterstock.com.
Page 11: Matyas Rehak/Shutterstock.com.
Page 12: mundosemfim/Shutterstock.
com; Fotos593/Shutterstock.com. **Page 13**:
Alberto Loyo/Shutterstock.com. **Page 14**:
NadyaRa/Shutterstock.com; Fotos593/
Shutterstock.com. **Page 15**: Hemis.fr/
Superstock.com; Andreea Dragomir/
Shutterstock.com; FotoLibre Studio/
Shutterstock.com. **Page 16**: Barna Tanko/
Shutterstock.com.

Publishing information
Footprint Ecuador and Galápagos
9th edition
© Compass Maps Ltd
July 2018

ISBN: 978 1 911 082 56 9

CIP DATA: A catalogue record for this book
is available from the British Library

® Footprint Handbooks and the Footprint
mark are a registered trademark of
Compass Maps Ltd

Published by Footprint
5 Riverside Court
Lower Bristol Road
Bath BA2 3DZ, UK
T +44 (0)1225 469141
footprinttravelguides.com

Every effort has been made to ensure that
the facts in this guidebook are accurate.
However, travellers should still obtain
advice from consulates, airlines, etc about
travel and visa requirements before
travelling. The authors and publishers
cannot accept responsibility for any loss,
injury or inconvenience however caused.

Printed in the UK
Print and production managed by
Jellyfish Solutions

Colour map index

Ambato

40	**Baños**																	
306	309	**Cuenca**																
390	430	667	**Esmeraldas**															
288	288	250	472	**Guayaquil**														
251	291	557	433	535	**Ibarra**													
397	388	700	579	674	365	**Lago Agrio**												
47	87	353	343	335	204	350	**Latacunga**											
511	514	205	832	415	764	904	558	**Loja**										
230	190	231	620	432	479	456	277	436	**Macas**									
382	383	188	608	191	633	766	429	235	419	**Machala**								
404	444	446	442	196	505	649	355	611	628	387	**Manta**							
231	271	537	413	515	20	345	184	742	459	613	485	**Otavalo**						
101	61	370	491	349	350	327	148	519	129	444	505	330	**Puyo**					
136	176	442	318	420	115	259	89	647	366	518	390	95	237	**Quito**				
52	55	254	442	233	303	440	99	459	245	328	456	283	116	188	**Riobamba**			
451	451	413	622	163	685	803	498	578	595	354	225	665	512	570	396	**Salinas**		
205	245	482	185	287	248	394	158	647	435	423	257	228	306	133	257	437	**Santo Domingo**	
185	140	449	497	428	271	248	227	598	208	523	584	251	79	186	195	591	312	**Tena**

Distances in kilometres 1 kilometre = 0.62 miles

Footprint Mini Atlas
Ecuador &
Galápagos

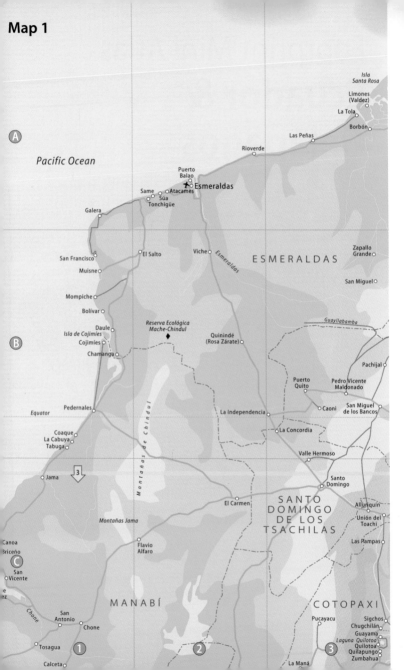

Map 2

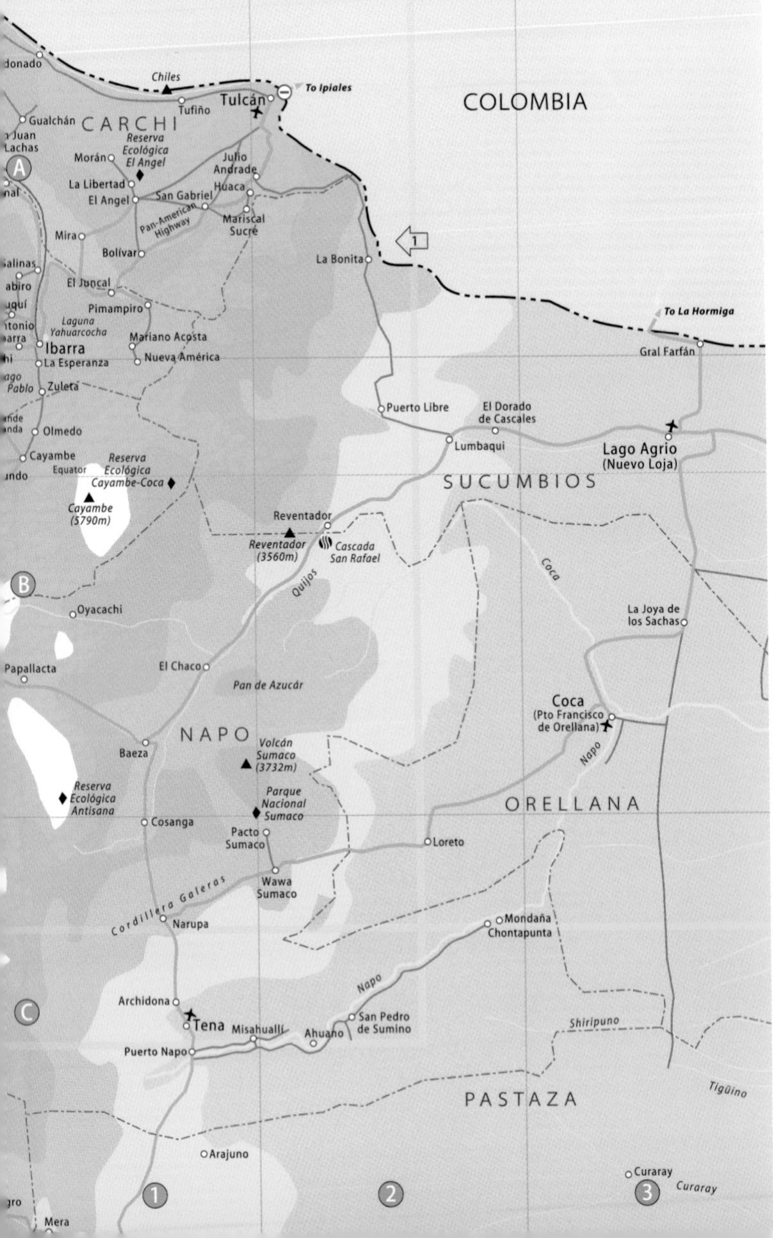

COLOMBIA

Chiles
Tufiño
Tulcán
To Ipiales

CARCHI
Gualchán
Reserva Ecológica El Angel
Morán
Julio Andrade
La Libertad
Huaca
El Angel
San Gabriel
Pan-American Highway
Mira
Mariscal Sucré
Bolívar
La Bonita
To La Hormiga
El Juncal
Pimampiro
Laguna Yahuarcocha
Mariano Acosta
Ibarra
Nueva América
La Esperanza
Gral Farfán
Zuleta
Olmedo
Cayambe
Puerto Libre
El Dorado de Cascales
Reserva Ecológica Cayambe-Coca
Equator
Lumbaqui
Lago Agrio (Nuevo Loja)
Cayambe (5790m)
SUCUMBÍOS
Oyacachi
Reventador
Reventador (3560m)
Cascada San Rafael
Quijos
Coca
La Joya de los Sachas
Papallacta
El Chaco
Pan de Azúcar
Coca (Pto Francisco de Orellana)
Baeza
NAPO
Volcán Sumaco (3732m)
Napo
Reserva Ecológica Antisana
Parque Nacional Sumaco
ORELLANA
Cosanga
Pacto Sumaco
Loreto
Wawa Sumaco
Cordillera Galeras
Narupa
Mondaña
Chontapunta
Napo
Archidona
Tena
Shiripuno
Misahualli
San Pedro de Sumino
Ahuano
Puerto Napo
PASTAZA
Tigüino
Arajuno
Curaray
Curaray
Mera

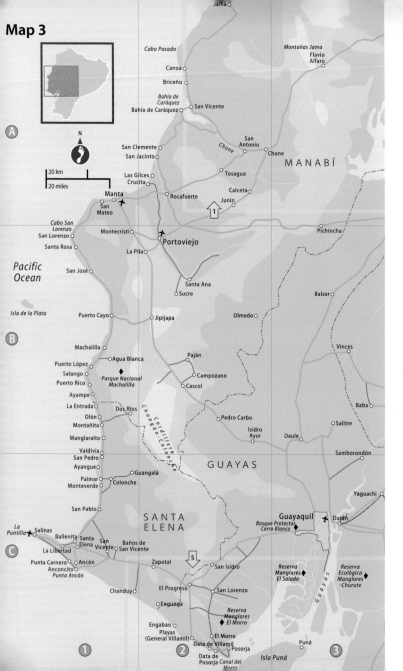

Map 3

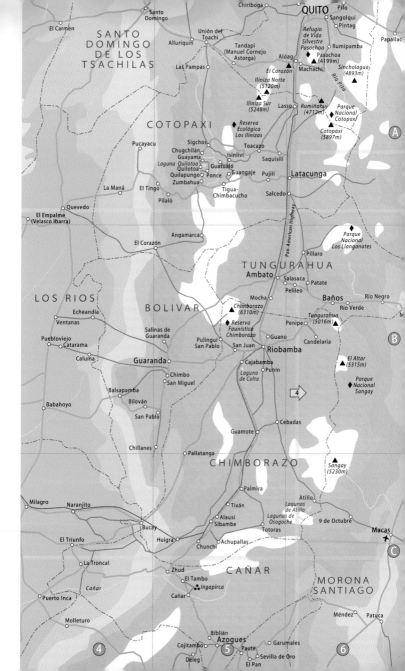

Map 4

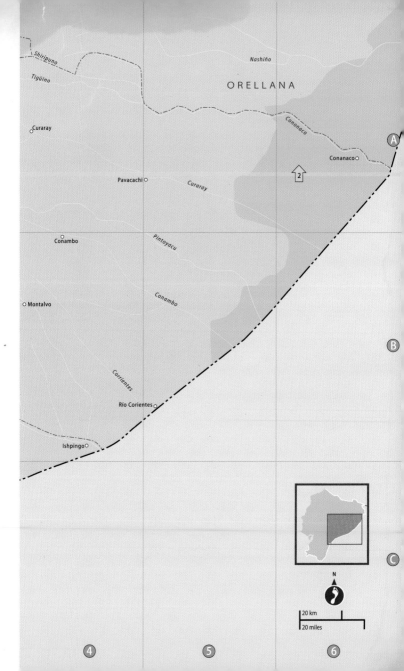

Shiripuno
Tigüino
ORELLANA
Nashiño
Cononaco
Curaray
A
Conanaco○
Pavacachi ○
Curaray
2
Conambo ○
Pintoyacu
Conambo
○ Montalvo
B
Corrientes
Río Corrientes ○
Ishpingo○
C
N

20 km
20 miles

④ ⑤ ⑥

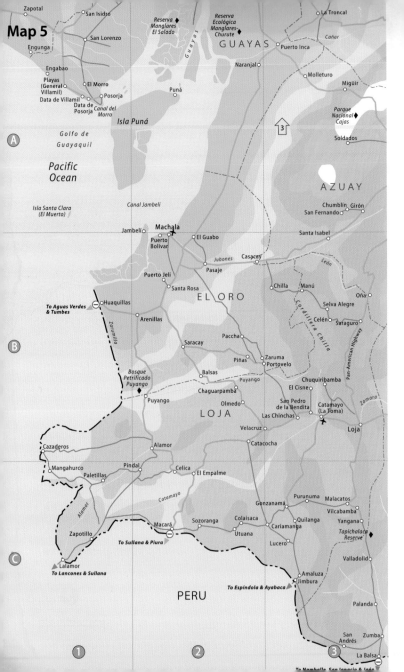